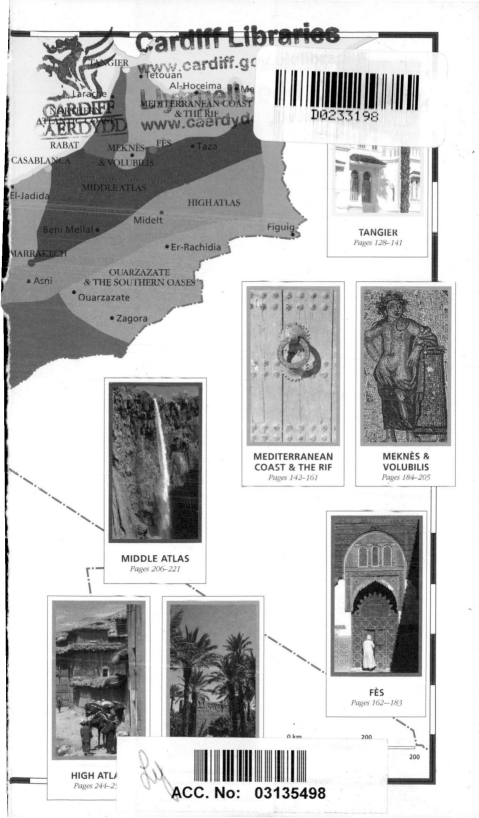

Cardiff Libraries
www.cardiff.gov
Llyfrgelloedd
www.caerdy

D0233198

TANGIER
Pages 128–141

MEDITERRANEAN COAST & THE RIF
Pages 142–161

MEKNÈS & VOLUBILIS
Pages 184–205

MIDDLE ATLAS
Pages 206–221

FÈS
Pages 162–183

HIGH ATL
Pages 244–2

TANGIER
Tetouan
Al-Hoceima   Me
Larache   MEDITERRANEAN COAST & THE RIF

RABAT   MEKNÈS   FÈS   Taza
CASABLANCA   & VOLUBILIS

El-Jadida   MIDDLE ATLAS
HIGH ATLAS
Midelt
Beni Mellal   Figuig
MARRAKECH   Er-Rachidia
Asni   OUARZAZATE & THE SOUTHERN OASES
Ouarzazate
Zagora

0 km   200
200

EYEWITNESS TRAVEL

MOROCCO

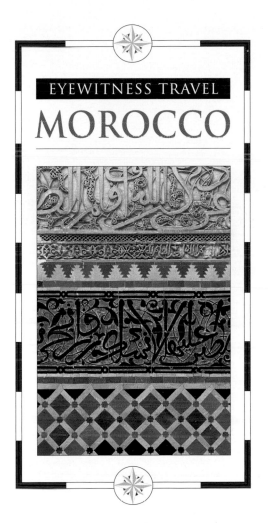

EYEWITNESS TRAVEL
MOROCCO

DK

LONDON, NEW YORK,
MELBOURNE, MUNICH AND DELHI
www.dk.com

Produced by Hachette Tourisme, Paris, France

EDITORIAL DIRECTOR Catherine Marquet
PROJECT EDITORS Hélène Gédouin-Hines,
Catherine Laussucq, Paulina Nourissier
ART DIRECTOR Guylaine Moi
DESIGNERS Maogani
CARTOGRAPHY Fabrice Le Goff

CONTRIBUTORS
Rachida Alaoui, Jean Brignon, Nathalie Campodonico,
Fabien Cazenave, Gaëtan du Chatenet, Alain Chenal,
Carole French, Emmanuelle Honorin, Maati Kabbal,
Mohamed Métalsi, Marie-Pascale Rauzier, Richard Williams

Dorling Kindersley Limited
PUBLISHING MANAGER Jane Ewart
MANAGING EDITOR Anna Streiffert
ENGLISH TRANSLATION & EDITOR Lucilla Watson
CONSULTANT Christine Osborne
DTP Jason Little, Conrad van Dyk
PRODUCTION Sarah Dodd

Printed in China by L. Rex Printing Co. Ltd.

First published in the UK in 2002
by Dorling Kindersley Limited
80 Strand, London WC2R 0RL

12 13 14 15 10 9 8 7 6 5 4 3 2 1

Reprinted with revisions 2003, 2004, 2006, 2008, 2010, 2012

Copyright © 2002, 2012 Dorling Kindersley Limited, London
A Penguin Company

A CIP CATALOGUE RECORD IS AVAILABLE FROM THE BRITISH LIBRARY.

ISBN 978-1-40537-085-1

Front cover main image: Decorated arched door, Marrakech

MIX
Paper from
responsible sources
FSC™ C018179

◁ **The kasbah at Aït Benhaddou, near Ouarzazate**

The Dadès valley *(see pp272–3)*

CONTENTS

HOW TO USE
THIS GUIDE **6**

INTRODUCING
MOROCCO

DISCOVERING
MOROCCO **10**

PUTTING MOROCCO
ON THE MAP **14**

A PORTRAIT OF
MOROCCO **16**

MOROCCO THROUGH
THE YEAR **38**

THE HISTORY
OF MOROCCO **44**

**Detail of the mosque
at Tin Mal** *(see p252)*

MARRAKECH **222**

HIGH ATLAS **244**

OUARZAZATE &
THE SOUTHERN OASES
260

SOUTHERN MOROCCO
& WESTERN SAHARA
282

Rose petals gathered for making rosewater

MOROCCO REGION BY REGION

MOROCCO
AT A GLANCE **62**

RABAT **64**

NORTHERN
ATLANTIC COAST **82**

CASABLANCA **94**

An illuminated manuscript

SOUTHERN
ATLANTIC COAST **108**

TANGIER **128**

MEDITERRANEAN
COAST & THE RIF **142**

FÈS **162**

MEKNÈS & VOLUBILIS
184

MIDDLE ATLAS **206**

Olives from the Dadès valley

TRAVELLERS' NEEDS

WHERE TO STAY
298

WHERE TO EAT
322

SHOPPING IN
MOROCCO **344**

ENTERTAINMENT IN
MOROCCO **350**

SPORTS & OUTDOOR
ACTIVITIES **354**

SURVIVAL GUIDE

PRACTICAL
INFORMATION **360**

TRAVEL INFORMATION
370

INDEX **378**

ACKNOWLEDGMENTS
400

FURTHER READING **404**

GLOSSARY **405**

Dish from the Fès region

The Mausoleum of
Moulay Ismaïl at Meknès *(pp194–5)*

HOW TO USE THIS GUIDE

This guide helps you get the most from your visit to Morocco, providing expert recommendations and detailed practical information. *Introducing Morocco* maps the country and sets it in its historical and cultural context. The 13 sections comprising *Morocco Region by Region*, six of which focus on the country's major towns, describe important sights, using photographs, maps and illustrations. Restaurants and hotel recommendations, and information about hiking, trekking and other outdoor activities, can be found in *Travellers' Needs*. The *Survival Guide* contains practical tips on everything from visiting mosques to transport around the country.

MAJOR CITIES

In this guide, Morocco is described in 13 sections, three of which concentrate on Morocco's historic imperial cities – Fès, Meknès and Marrakech – and three on the country's major modern cities – Rabat, the capital, Casablanca and Tangier. A section is devoted to each city, except for Meknès. Each city's major sights are described in detail.

A country map shows the city's location in Morocco.

Coloured thumb tabs indentify the various towns and regions of Morocco.

1 Introduction
Each town's geographical setting and economic life are described, as well as its historical development and features of interest to the visitor.

2 City Map
For easy reference, the sights are numbered and located on a map. The main streets, bus stations and railway stations, parking areas and tourist offices are also shown.

Sights at a Glance lists the chapter's sights by category: mosques and churches, historic buildings, museums, parks and historic districts.

A locator map shows the central area of each city.

3 Detailed Information
All the sights in each city are described individually. Addresses, telephone numbers, opening hours, admission charges and information on how to get there are given for each sight. The key to symbols is shown on the back flap.

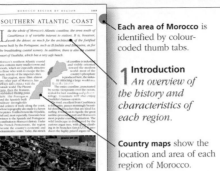

Each area of Morocco is identified by colour-coded thumb tabs.

1 Introduction
An overview of the history and characteristics of each region.

Country maps show the location and area of each region of Morocco.

MOROCCO REGION BY REGION

In this book, the country is described in 13 chapters, six of which concentrate on Morocco's major cities and seven on the country's main regions. The map on the inside front cover shows this regional division. The most interesting places to visit are given on the *Regional Map* at the beginning of each chapter.

2 Regional Map
This shows the main road network and gives an illustrated overview of the whole region. All interesting places to visit are numbered and there are useful tips on getting around.

Story boxes explore some of the region's historical and cultural subjects in detail.

3 Detailed Information
All the important towns and other places to visit are dealt with individually. They are listed in order, following the numbering given on the Regional Map. Each entry also contains practical information such as map references, addresses, telephone numbers and opening times.

Practical information at the beginning of each entry includes a map reference relating to the road map on the inside back cover.

The Visitors' Checklist provides a summary of the practical information you need to plan your visit.

4 Morocco's Top Sights
These are given two or more full pages. Buildings are dissected to show their interiors.

Stars indicate the best sights and important features.

INTRODUCING
MOROCCO

DISCOVERING MOROCCO 10–13
PUTTING MOROCCO ON THE MAP 14–15
A PORTRAIT OF MOROCCO 16–37
MOROCCO THROUGH THE YEAR 38–43
THE HISTORY OF MOROCCO 44–59

DISCOVERING MOROCCO

Morocco's varied geography, multicultural atmosphere and rich history make it a fascinating country. Its towns offer a striking contrast of ancient kasbahs, mosques and souks and modern architecture, with a mix of Berber, Arab and African peoples. Most major cities are on

Moroccan water-seller

or near the coast in the north; the Atlas mountains run like a spine from southwest to northeast, separating the urban centres from the desert. The landscape includes beaches, mountains, lakes, forests and desert. These pages offer a brief overview to help you plan your visit.

Rabat's imposing 14th-century Chellah Necropolis

RABAT

- Oudaïa Kasbah fortress
- The majestic Mausoleum of Mohammed V
- Impressive Chellah Necropolis
- Ancient artifacts at the Musée Archéologique

Morocco's administrative and political capital, Rabat is the country's second-largest city after Casablanca. It has a relaxed, though cosmopolitan, ambience. With its ancient ramparts, palace, mosque and gardens, the 12th-century **Oudaïa Kasbah** (see pp68–9) is the main attraction, followed by the 17th-century medina to the south, with its colourful souks. Other must-sees are the splendid **Mausoleum of Mohammed V** (see pp74–5), the **Chellah Necropolis** (see pp80–81) and the impressive collections in the **Musée Archéologique** (see pp78–9).

NORTHERN ATLANTIC COAST

- Sandy beaches and forests
- Birdwatching at Moulay Bousselham
- Lixus's Phoenician ruins
- Neolithic and Roman sites

The coastline between Rabat and Tangier boasts some of the finest unspoilt beaches in the country, as well as lush forests and lagoons. The motorway follows the coastline, offering tempting glimpses of the sea. You can see cork-oak trees in the **Forest of Mamora** (see p87) and, in December and January, migratory birds at the Merja Zerga lagoon near **Moulay Bousselham** (see p90).

Morocco was shaped by waves of invaders, including the Phoenicians, Romans, Spanish, Portuguese and Dutch. The Roman ruins at **Thamusida** (see p87), the ancient Phoenician city of **Lixus** (see pp90–91) and the Portuguese town of **Asilah** (see p91) are all worth a visit.

This area also features some fascinating structures from a much earlier time, such as the Neolithic stone circle at **M'Soura** (see p91).

CASABLANCA

- Splendid Art Deco heritage
- The second-largest mosque in the world
- Bustling Old Medina
- Strolling around the Quartier Habous

Expanded by the French from the 1920s onwards, Casablanca is now the financial capital of Morocco and its biggest city. Architecturally, the city offers an interesting combination of Art Deco and the more restrained Moorish styles. Some of the city's most impressive Art Deco buildings can be found in and around the **Place des Nations Unies** and the **Boulevard Mohammed V** (see pp98–9) in the heart of the new town.

The colossal **Mosque of Hassan II** (see pp102–3), on the seafront, is the second biggest in the world, after

The vast interior of the Mosque of Hassan II, in Casablanca

◁ *Moroccan Festival*, a painting by André Suréda (1872–1930)

The white city of Essaouira, on the Southern Atlantic coast

the mosque in Mecca, while the **Old Medina** *(see p100)*, still surrounded by ramparts, gives an idea of the city's humble origins as a tiny port. A colourful market is held here daily. There is also a fishing harbour and a large modern **port** *(see p100)* with excellent fish restaurants.

With its flower-lined streets and souks, the **Quartier Habous** *(see p106)*, also known as the New Medina, is a pleasant place for a stroll.

SOUTHERN ATLANTIC COAST

- **Portuguese history at El-Jadida**
- **Surfing at Oualidia**
- **Beautiful Essaouira**
- **Hiking around Imouzzer des Ida Outanane**

This coastline has some beautiful deserted beaches interspersed with fortified towns dating back to the era of the Portuguese occupation. The region is undergoing a period of revitalization. Several new resorts have opened and more hotels and apartments are planned.

El-Jadida *(see pp114–15)* is a small town with a fort and a fascinating Portuguese-built cistern. Just to the east is the impressive 18th-century **Kasbah Boulaouane** *(see pp112–13)*, located in the heart of a region famous for falconry and wine-making.

Oualidia *(see p115)* has made a name for itself thanks to the quality of its oysters. It is also a famous surfing centre, as is the pretty town of **Essaouira** *(see pp120–21)*. Visitors to the city should not miss its labyrinthine medina, harbour and ramparts.

In the foothills of the High Atlas, the **Imouzzer des Ida Outanane** *(see pp126–7)* offers good hiking among waterfalls and argan trees.

A waiter and relaxed customers at a streetside café in Tangier

TANGIER

- **Tangier's literary heritage and the Café de Paris**
- **The Dar el-Makhzen palace in the Kasbah**
- **Shopping at the colourful Fondouk Chejra**

As the main port linking Europe and Africa, Tangier has a bustling cosmopolitan atmosphere. The writers and artists who have visited over the centuries – from Samuel Pepys to William Burroughs, from Eugène Delacroix to Henri Matisse – have helped establish the city's liberal and bohemian credentials.

The **Place de France** and **Place de Faro** *(see p139)* are adjacent squares. Famous artists and writers would gather here, at places like the **Café de Paris**, to sip drinks and enjoy the views over

the medina and the harbour. The medina is located to the northeast of the city, and the **Kasbah** *(see p132)* is at its northern end, along with the **Dar el-Makhzen palace-museum** and the **Kasbah Mosque**. The **Grand Socco (Place du 9 Avril 1947)** *(see p138)* provides the link between the medina and the Ville Nouvelle; it hosts a busy street market at night.

The bustling **Fondouk Chejra** *(see p138)* is like an Oriental bazaar packed with weavers' workshops.

MEDITERRANEAN COAST AND THE RIF

- **Riffian towns and villages**
- **Ceuta and Melilla's Spanish connection**
- **Holy Chefchaouen**
- **Birdwatching around the Moulouya Estuary**

This coast has some beautiful beaches around Ceuta, developing into rocky cliffs further towards Melilla. Inland, the **Rif mountains** *(see pp154–5)* run from west to east; myriad villages nestle among their low hills, with higher summits to the east.

The area has a strong Spanish feel, with **Ceuta** *(see p147)* and **Melilla** *(see pp158–9)* being Spanish territories. More interesting are the cities of **Tetouan** *(see pp148–9)*, with its successive settlements by the Jews, Moors and Spaniards, and the holy town of **Chefchaouen** *(see pp150–51)*, with its steep, narrow streets and limewashed buildings.

Nature lovers should head to the **Moulouya Estuary** *(see p159)*, where a reserve plays host to a great variety of birds.

The typical white-and-indigo buildings of Chefchaouen

Meknès's Bab Mansour el-Aleuj, one of the finest city gates in Morocco

FÈS

- **World Heritage Site status**
- **Mosques and medersas**
- **Workshops and tanneries around Place el-Saffarine**
- **Shopping in the souks**

The oldest city in Morocco, Fès is also the country's religious and cultural capital. Its old town, Fès el-Bali, is a UNESCO World Heritage Site. It features a rich architectural tapestry of fortresses, city gates and ramparts; mosques and medersas (theological schools); palaces and gardens; and souks and workshops.

Visitors should not miss the intricately decorated 14th-century **Bou Inania Medersa** *(see pp172–3)* and **El-Attarine Medersa** *(see p171)*, considered pinnacles of Moorish architecture; the **Karaouiyine Mosque** *(see pp176–7)*; the **Tanners' Quarter** *(see p175)* and the souks *(see p167)*; and the **Fondouk el-Nejjarine** *(see p167)*, a former caravanserai.

Museums include the **Musée Dar el-Batha** *(see*

Aerial view of the colourful Tanners' Quarter in Fès

pp168–9), of interest as much for its building and its fine Andalusian garden as for its collections of local crafts.

MEKNÈS AND VOLUBILIS

- **The monumental Bab Mansour el-Aleuj arch**
- **The splendid Mausoleum of Moulay Ismaïl**
- **Moroccan arts at the Musée Dar Jamaï**
- **Ancient ruins at Volubilis**

Moulay Ismaïl is to be credited for the lavish architecture of **Meknès** *(see pp186–201)*, which he built as his imperial capital in the 17th century. The fabulous gate of **Bab Mansour el-Aleuj** *(see p189)* leads to the kasbah, which contains the finest buildings in the city, such as the **Mausoleum of Moulay Ismaïl** *(see pp194–5)* and the **Dar el-Makhzen** royal complex *(see pp192–3)*.

The medina features many fascinating souks, with cloth merchants, metalworkers, cobblers and a Berber carpet bazaar. Other sights include the **Grand Mosque** *(see p188)* and the **Musée Dar Jamaï** *(see pp190–91)*, a museum of Moroccan arts with a fine Andalusian garden.

Dating from the 3rd century BC, **Volubilis** *(see pp202–5)* is worth visiting for its extensive Roman ruins, including the Arch of Caracalla, the Basilica and the Capitol, as well as the remains of Roman houses and mosaics.

MIDDLE ATLAS

- **Mountains, forests and lakes**
- **Trekking in Jbel Tazzeka National Park**
- **The spectacular Cascades d'Ouzoud**

This region occupies the central area of Morocco and features several fortified ancient towns. Most visitors, however, will be drawn to its unspoilt landscape of peaks, valleys, lakes and lush forests.

Good bases from which to explore the area include **Taza** *(see p210)*, one of the oldest towns in Morocco; **Imouzzer du Kandar** *(see p211)*, with its troglodytic dwellings; **Ifrane** *(see p212)*, with its distinctly French feel; and Berber-style **Azrou** *(see p212)*.

With its caverns and gorges, **Jbel Tazzeka National Park** *(see p210)*, on the east side of the range, offers some spectacular scenery. At the south-west end of the Middle Atlas, the **Cascades d'Ouzoud** *(see p221)* are worth visiting – not just for the waterfall, but also for the macaque monkeys that have made their home in the surrounding fig trees.

A group of musicians performing at Place Jemaa el-Fna in Marrakech

MARRAKECH

- **Bustling Place Jemaa el-Fna**
- **The vast Koutoubia Mosque**
- **Peaceful city gardens**
- **Grand palaces and museums**

Marrakech, the red-walled city that gave Morocco its name, is set on a plain between the Atlas mountains and the Sahara. Its origins were as a staging post on the spice route, and the bustle of its souks reflects the commercial soul of the city.

On the central square, **Place Jemaa el-Fna** *(see p234)*, food-sellers vie for your attention, along with snake-charmers, jugglers, performing monkeys, henna-painters and professional storytellers. The minaret of the huge **Koutoubia Mosque** *(see pp236–7)*, built in 1147, watches over all.

Beautiful green spaces on the outskirts of the city – such as the **Menara**, **Aguedal** and **Majorelle** gardens and **La Palmeraie** *(see pp242–3)* – provide a tranquil counterpoint to the general bustle, while the **Palais Bahia** *(see pp234–5)* and the **Dar Si Saïd Museum** *(see pp240–41)* offer a fascinating insight into the architecture, culture and crafts of this imperial city.

HIGH ATLAS

- **Hiking in the Jebel Toubkal Massif**
- **Berber dwellings**
- **Skiing and mountain-biking**

The highest mountain range in North Africa runs west–east from **Jebel Toubkal** *(see p249)* – the highest peak at 4,167 m (13,676 ft) – to Jbel Ayachi, towering above the Ziz gorges. There are few roads here, and the terrain is harsh, though every possible patch of land is irrigated and given over to growing crops and grazing livestock.

This region is the mountain stronghold of the Berbers, and here it is possible to observe their subsistence lifestyle. The 28 villages of the remote **Aït Bouguemez valley** *(see pp254–7)* consist of pisé houses made from sunbaked earth and straw and fortified *tighremts*, larger dwellings usually occupied by the village chief.

Oukaïmeden *(see p248)* is a small ski resort that also acts as a good base for summer mountain-biking and hiking.

Trekking through the Erg Chebbi dunes, near Merzouga

OUARZAZATE AND THE SOUTHERN OASES

- **Ancient towns and *ksour***
- **Camel-riding over the dunes**
- **Film studios at Ouarzazate**
- **Scenic kasbahs at Skoura**

This region is sandwiched between the High Atlas mountains to the north and the Sahara to the south. Ancient towns and *ksour* (fortified villages) are scattered along the main roads that follow the Draa, Dadès and Tafilalt valleys, usually featuring crumbling kasbahs, markets and workshops. Because of its trading history, this region has been occupied by Berber, Arabs and black Moroccans, who still remain.

You will need several days with a guide and a four-wheel-drive vehicle to explore the region's gorges, including the impressive **Todra gorge** *(see p274)*, and longer if you want to get to

the Sahara and ride a camel over the **Erg Chebbi dunes** near **Merzouga** *(see p281)*. Trekkers and rock-climbers will also find plenty to keep them entertained.

Less energetic travellers may wish to visit the film studios at **Ouarzazate** *(see p264)*, or the palm groves and beautiful kasbahs at **Skoura** *(see p272)*.

SOUTHERN MOROCCO AND WESTERN SAHARA

- **Activities on Agadir beach**
- **Boundless expanses of sand dunes**
- **Birdwatching at Souss Massa National Park**
- **Guelmim's camel souk**

The town of **Agadir** *(see pp286–7)* was destroyed by an earthquake in 1960 and has since been rebuilt as the main package-holiday resort of Morocco. It has modern architecture, big hotels, a wide range of activities and a large sandy bay.

Agadir is a good base for trips to the Souss plains to the east, the Anti-Atlas mountains to the southeast and the disputed territory of the Western Sahara to the south. The most popular excursions are to **Taroudannt** *(see p288)*, with its great ramparts and lively souks; **Tafraoute** *(see p293)* in the Ameln Valley, with its lunar landscape; **Souss Massa National Park** *(see p292)*, for birdwatching; and **Guelmim** *(see p294)*, renowned for its camel souk and the mysterious "blue men" of the desert.

The long, sandy beach of Agadir, Morocco's premier holiday resort

Putting Morocco on the Map

Morocco has many faces. It is situated on the African continent and has traces of African heritage. But its climate and varied topography, its historical association with Andalusian Spain, and its wish to join the European Union give it a European facet. In the distant past it belonged to the indigenous Berbers. To the Arabs and Muslims who have held Morocco since the 7th century, it is known as Maghreb el-Aqsa – the westernmost country of the Muslim world. Morocco has 33,750,000 inhabitants, almost 40 per cent of whom are under 15 years old. The population is unevenly distributed over the country's 710,850 sq km (274,388 sq miles), being concentrated along the Atlantic coast and in the Rif and the High Atlas mountains.

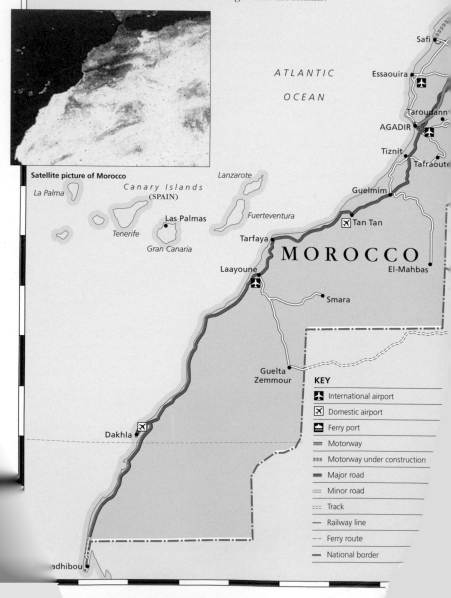

Satellite picture of Morocco

ATLANTIC
OCEAN

Safi

Essaouira

Taroudann

AGADIR

Tiznit

Tafraoute

Guelmim

Lanzarote

Canary Islands
(SPAIN)

La Palma

Fuerteventura

Las Palmas

Tenerife

Gran Canaria

Tarfaya

Tan Tan

MOROCCO

Laayoune

El-Mahbas

Smara

Guelta
Zemmour

Dakhla

adhibou

KEY

✈	International airport
☒	Domestic airport
⛴	Ferry port
▬	Motorway
▦	Motorway under construction
▬	Major road
═	Minor road
⋯	Track
—	Railway line
--	Ferry route
—	National border

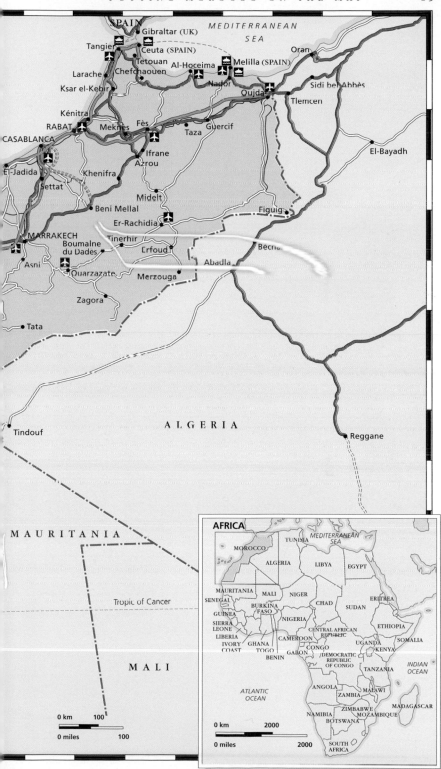

A PORTRAIT OF MOROCCO

Morocco is like a tree whose roots lie in Africa but whose leaves breathe in European air. This is the metaphor that King Hassan II (1929–99) used to describe a country that is both profoundly traditional and strongly drawn to the modern world. It is this double-sided, seemingly contradictory disposition that gives Morocco its cultural richness.

Morocco is a country that is unique in the Muslim world. Its richly diverse culture has been shaped by 3,000 years of history, by ethnic groups whose roots go far back in time, and also by its geographical location, with the Atlantic Ocean to the west, sub-Saharan Africa to the south, Europe to the north and the Mediterranean countries to the east.

Moroccan girl in the traditional costume of the Atlas

The Moroccan people are torn between the lure of modernity on the one hand and a profound desire for Islamic reform on the other. With events such as the death in 1999 of Morocco's king, Hassan II, and the enthronement of his son, Mohammed VI, as well as the establishment of a left-wing coalition government and the problems that the government faces regarding the economy and the proposal of a new constitution by Mohammed VI, Morocco today stands on the threshold of a challenging new phase in its history.

Au Petit Poucet, an historic bar in Casablanca

◁ A woman from Essaouira, dressed in the traditional white *haik*

Members of a Gnaoua brotherhood

AN EVOLVING SOCIETY

Since the 1950s, Morocco has undergone profound social change. Traditional tribal cohesion has been replaced by the European-style nuclear family, polygamy has become distinctly rare, a money-based economy is now the norm, and the notion of individuality has emerged. These changes have been accompanied by a growth in the urban population and by the rise of a bi-cultural elite, with a traditional background and a European outlook. With an unusually large percentage of young people, Moroccan society is unmistakably breaking away from the

Water-seller
in Marrakech

past. However, Morocco still faces the challenge of resolving the difficulties that sharp contradictions in its social, political and economic life present.

Since gaining independence from France in 1956, Morocco has made attempts to tackle three major scourges: illiteracy, unemployment and poverty. The government has increased spending on education at all levels and education is compulsory, but many children – particularly girls in rural areas – do not attend school. Country-wide literacy rates are estimated at 39 per cent among women and 64 per cent among men, but the female literacy rate in rural areas is only 10 per cent.

BERBER CULTURE

With its mixed Berber and Arab population, Morocco has, however, successfully maintained ethnic and cultural stability and equality between the Berber and Arabic languages. Although Tamazight, the Berber language, is not spoken or taught in schools, it is one of the languages heard on Moroccan radio and television. The movement to promote Berber language and culture through

Filming at the Atlas Studios at Ouarzazate

Traditional agricultural labour in the Ourika valley

the medium of newspapers, concerts and other cultural events is dynamic, as are efforts to encourage the wider use of the language and to nurture respect for the rich Berber culture.

Pilot projects, such as the construction of mosques, wells, roads and schools, have been undertaken in the southern Souss region, funded by money sent back by Berbers of southern Morocco working abroad.

THE STATUS OF WOMEN

Women today work in all sectors – as political delegates and ambassadors, airline pilots, company directors and royal advisers; they are also Olympic champions, writers, publishers, active militants and journalists. Thus they have a secure place in Moroccan society.

In the space of 30 years, the status and position of women has radically changed. The constitution of 10 March 1972, which granted women the right to vote and to be elected, was the first of these changes. In 1994, 77 women were elected to the Chamber of Representatives. However, the highly militant feminist associations were still not entirely satisfied. They demanded the abolition

of the *mudawwana* – a statute of 1957 that dominates the lives of Moroccans and prevented women from being treated as fully fledged adults. Moves to raise the status of women made in March 1999 were met by opposition and incited the wrath of the Minister of Religious Affairs, the *ulemas* (councils) and Parliament's Islamic deputies. In 2005, following years of resistance from religious bodies, Morocco's king introduced a new *mudawwana*, which has improved the status of women.

POLITICAL CHANGE

Until the death of Hassan II in 1999, Morocco was ruled by a distant and autocratic king. The

Westernized young girls in Casablanca

effect of the attempted coups d'état of 1971 and 1972 was to encourage the Moroccan authorities to control the wheels of government even more tightly. Driss Basri, then Minister of the Interior, was responsible for this clamp-down.

Berber women in the traditional costume of the Rif

The Rose Festival in El-Kelaa M'Gouna

At the end of his reign, Hassan II began to relax his authoritarian grip on power by involving the left wing in the country's government. In February 1998, a government of national unity, led by the Socialist leader Abderrahmane Youssoufi, was formed, although in the years since, its success is deemed to have been limited.

Since 1999, Mohammed VI has ushered in a different style of government. Underlying his political approach are a willingness to listen more closely to his people and a commitment to countering Islamic radicals. He also won popular support for sacking Driss Basri, Minister of the Interior. Brushing aside protocol, he publicly presented his wife and ordered the setting-up of royal commissions to look into economic development, the problem of the Western Sahara, employment and education.

Berber cameraman

For the September 2002 parliamentary election, Morocco had more than 20 parties, many of which had been specially formed. This led to the success of the Islamic Party of Justice and Development (PJD), the third political party in the country after the Socialist Party (USFP) and the Istiqual Party, the principal opposition party to the coalition government. The terrorist bombs of May 2003 in Casablanca, which killed 43 people, brought instability to the country, halting the progress of democratization started by Mohammed VI. However, parliamentary elections were again held in 2007.

A VARIED ECONOMY

Morocco's geographical location, at the nexus between Africa and Europe, brings it considerable economic advantage, especially in the fields of tourism, agriculture and the textile industry. The discovery of extensive oil-fields has also been a boost for the country's economy. Fishing and hydroelectric power are Morocco's other two natural resources. The economy also benefits from the influx of funds sent back by Moroccans

Schoolchildren in the Dadès valley

working abroad. Some US $2,000 million are sent back to Morocco each year.

The arrival of multinational companies has transformed telecommunications and has led to an explosion in the use of mobile phones. The number of computers has also risen.

Nevertheless, the Moroccan economy is handicapped in several ways: agriculture is dependent on rainfall, the education system is inadequate, energy costs are prohibitively high, and sparse investment is made in the population. In 1999, the number of people living in poverty stood at 5 million. Every year, almost 460,000 rural emigrants swell the poor ghettos in the towns and cities. For a number of reasons, the economic reforms introduced by the government of national unity have not had the anticipated effect. Morocco is being encouraged by the World Bank to liberalize its economy, boost exports and devalue its currency.

The country has a positive image in Europe, and relations are being consolidated. Free trade between Morocco and the EU is projected for 2012. The

A spice and medicinal plant seller in one of the souks of Marrakech

arrangement depends on Morocco putting in place a solid financial and technological infrastructure.

The country is in need of modernization, although the evolution of true democracy is likely to be slow. This is a key policy since the slow progress of reforms is encouraging young people to emigrate. Under Mohammed VI there has been economic liberalization but time will tell whether he will succeed in significantly reducing poverty and unemployment, controlling Islamic radicals and abolishing illiteracy.

The picturesque Place Jemaa el-Fna in Marrakech

The Landscape and Wildlife of Morocco

With a mountain range exceeding a height of 4,000 m (13,130 ft) and a coastline stretching from the Mediterranean to the Atlantic, Morocco has a varied topography. In environments ranging from arid scrublands to cedar forests and high mountains, plant life comprises over 4,000 species adapted to extreme conditions. The coast is visited by migratory birds while the mountains are the habitat of Barbary sheep and birds of prey, including the lammergeier *(see p219)*.

Eleonora's falcon

The argan, a tree growing only in southwestern Morocco *(see p127)*

MOUNTAIN FORESTS & HIGH STEPPES

Forests grow in the Rif, the Middle Atlas and the western High Atlas, at altitudes of 1,400–2,500 m (4,600–8,200 ft), where annual rainfall is 650 mm–2,000 mm (25–78 in). The varied vegetation here includes Atlas cedar, maritime pine and holm-oak. The high steppes, covered with low, thorny vegetation, are found at altitudes over 2,700 m (8,860 ft) in the High Atlas *(see p218–19)*.

The golden eagle *is seen mostly in the mountains, where it preys on jackals, bustards and small mammals.*

The lammergeier *builds its nest on rocky outcrops. It is a scavenger but sometimes also kills its prey by knocking it off high rocks with a strong flap of its wing.*

ARID COASTAL REGIONS & DESERT

The rocky coastal lowlands between Safi and Agadir has an annual rainfall ranging from 40 to 150 mm (1.5 to 6 in). Vegetation, which is adapted to saline conditions, consists of sparse shrubs, mostly acacia. Further south is the desert with *ergs* (sand dunes) and the stony *hammada*.

The bald ibis, *almost extinct, is found in the Souss Massa National Park* (see p292), *a fertile exception to the arid littoral.*

The Barbary squirrel, *whose favourite food is argan nuts, inhabits the arid lowlands of southwestern Morocco.*

The great cormorant *nests on sea cliffs between Agadir, in the north, and the Arguin sand banks of Mauritania.*

THE MACAQUE OR BARBARY APE

The macaque is North Africa's only monkey. Three-quarters of the population lives in the cedar forests of the Middle Atlas, up to an altitude of 2,000 m (6,565 ft). Macaques are also found in the Rif, the High Atlas and on the Rock of Gibraltar. The animals live in colonies of 10 to 30 individuals, consisting of adults and young monkeys of both sexes. In summer, they feed on caterpillars, acorns, mushrooms and asphodel bulbs. In winter, their diet consists of grasses, cedar leaves and sometimes bark.

The macaque, a tail-less monkey of North Africa

SCRUB & STEPPE

Southeastern Morocco consists of steppes covered in esparto grass and artemisia. On the high plateaux, on the southern slopes of the High Atlas and on part of the Anti-Atlas annual rainfall ranges from 100 mm to 300 mm (4 in to 12 in) and snow is rare. Trees include Atlas pistachio, juniper and ash.

The Houbara bustard *lives in the semi-desert plains of the south.*

The Numidian crane *nests on Morocco's high plateaux in summer.*

The golden jackal *is found throughout North Africa and in the Sahara. It can survive for long periods without water.*

DRY WOODLAND

Almost all the low-lying and middle-altitude regions on the northern side of the Atlas are covered by dry woodland. Annual rainfall here ranges from 350 mm to 800 mm (14 in to 31 in) and snowfall is occasional. Trees include holm-oak, cork oak (pictured above) and kermes oak, olive, Barbary thuya, and Aleppo and maritime pine.

Dorca's gazelle *inhabits the semi-desert regions of the south and east. It feeds on grasses and acacia shoots.*

The booted eagle *lives in the forests of the north and the Atlas Mountains. It makes its nests in tall trees.*

The Urban Architecture of Morocco

The history of urban architecture in Morocco goes back more than 1,000 years. The Karaouiyine Mosque in Fès was built in 857 by the first Idrissid rulers of Morocco *(see p46)*, who founded the city. From the age of the Idrissids until the 20th century, a succession of many different architectural styles has produced a rich architectural heritage. The artistic conventions and styles of each period shed light on the secular and religious life of the rulers and people who lived in those times.

Karaouiyine Mosque *(see pp176–7)*, the earliest Idrissid building

THE ALMORAVIDS (11TH–12TH C.)
It was under the Almoravids that the Moorish style developed in Morocco, which was then the centre of an Ibero-Maghrebian empire. Andalusian elements included the horseshoe arch and the lobed arch, Kufic script, which was often used in conjunction with floral decoration, the scrolling acanthus-leaf motif and the use of decorative plasterwork.

The exterior of the 12th-century Koubba Ba'Adiyn dome

The interior of the Koubba Ba'Adiyn (see p231) *is made up of interlaced pointed arches and radiating rosettes.*

THE ALMOHADS (12TH–13TH C.)
The Almohads, under whom the Ibero-Maghrebian empire reached its apogee, established an architectural style that later dynasties were to emulate. The Koutoubia Mosque in Marrakech, the Hassan II Mosque in Casablanca and grand monumental gateways each exemplify this style.

The Koutoubia minaret

The carved decoration *of the Koutoubia minaret (see pp236–7) consists of an interlacing geometric pattern.*

THE MERINIDS (13TH–15TH C.)
The Merinids used the same building techniques and mostly the same architectural forms as those of the preceding period. They were, however, the greatest builders of *medersas (see pp172–3)*, those peculiarly Moroccan masterpieces of architecture. They also displayed a remarkable aptitude for exquisite architectural ornamentation.

The inner façade of the Bou Inania Medersa *displays a wide range of techniques, ornamental styles and materials.*

Pyramidal roof of green tiles

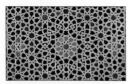

***Zellij* tilework** *of coloured terracotta squares in the Bou Inania Medersa in Fès depicts complex geometric patterns.*

Carved wooden corbels

Carved or incised plaster

Carved wooden double doors

THE SAADIANS (16TH–17TH C.)

Morocco's Saadian rulers gave the country two master-pieces: the Palais el-Badi *(see p235)* and the Saadian Tombs, both in Marrakech *(see p238)*. These embody the Andalusian traditions that had taken root in Morocco.

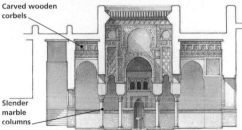

Carved wooden corbels

Slender marble columns

Decorative plasterwork, *with a lattice of floral and geometric motifs, covers the upper walls of the mausoleum.*

The royal mausoleum, *in Marrakech, is a magnificent building. It was completed in the 16th century by the sultan Ahmed el-Mansour.*

THE ALAOUITES (17TH C.–PRESENT DAY)

The two great builders of the Alaouite period were Moulay Ismaïl, who made Meknès the royal city, and Sidi Mohammed ben Abdellah, who founded Essaouira *(see pp120–25)*.

The Mausoleum of Moulay Ismaïl (see pp194–5) *is designed in a style similar to that of the Saadian Tombs.*

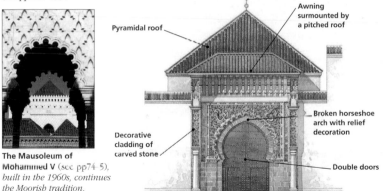

Pyramidal roof

Awning surmounted by a pitched roof

Decorative cladding of carved stone

Broken horseshoe arch with relief decoration

Double doors

The Mausoleum of Mohammed V *(see pp74–5), built in the 1960s, continues the Moorish tradition.*

THE MODERN ERA

During the French Protectorate, in the early 20th century, Nouvelles Villes (modern towns) were built outside the medinas, whose traditional layout *(see pp26–7)* thus was spared from development. A Neo-Moorish style evolved in many towns, while Art Deco was predominant in the city of Casablanca *(see p101)*.

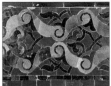

The Casablanca Post Office *(1918–20) has a loggia decorated with zellij tilework. The interior is in Art Deco style.*

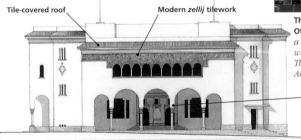

Tile-covered roof

Modern *zellij* tilework

Arched entrance in the Moorish style

Medinas

Almost all Morocco's medinas have the same layout. The typical medina (meaning "town" in Arabic) consists of a densely packed urban conglomeration enclosed within defensive walls set with lookout towers. The tangle of narrow winding streets and countless alleyways turns the layout of a medina into a labyrinth. The centre of the medina is cut through by wide avenues running between the main gateways and by other main streets, which, as a defensive measure, are either angled or closed off by houses or projecting walls.

Minaret in the medina

Hundreds of narrow streets *wind through the medina. Some are no more than 50 cm (20 in) wide.*

The monumental gateway, *a fortified entrance flanked by projecting crenellated towers, leads into the medina. Bab el-Chorfa in Fès is a particularly splendid example.*

Roof-terrace

THE LAYOUT OF A MEDINA

Despite their apparent chaos, medinas are laid out according to certain set considerations. The mosque is always located at the heart. Other features include the separation of different religious and ethnic groups, the distinction between home and the workplace, and the location of activities according to a social and commercial hierarchy. Every medina is laid out according to these factors.

Street partly blocked by a house

Lookout tower

Open-air souks, *like the basket souk in Marrakech, are markets where specialist crafts and other products are sold. Souks are also the regular meeting places of city people and visiting country-dwellers.*

QUARTERS

The quarters of a medina are no more than loosely defined areas. A quarter, or *hawma*, is really just a communal space consisting of several small streets and alleyways, and it is the focus of the inhabitants' material and spiritual life. Each quarter has a communal oven, a hammam (steam bath), a Koranic school, and a grocer's shop, which is always located in one of the smaller streets. The shop sells such basic necessities as vegetables, fruit, oil, coal, sugar, spices and other foods. There are no shops selling luxury goods in quarters like these.

A grocer's shop in a quarter of Fès

The grand mosque is the central point of the city.

The patio, *or* riad, *like this one in Essaouira, is the focal point of a building. The rooms are arranged around the courtyard, which often contains a fountain.*

Sturdy defensive walls protect the medina.

The souk for valuable items is located next to the mosque.

Craftsmen, *like the tanners of Fès, work together in parts of the medina known as* souk, kissaria *or* fondouk. *Their location, from the centre to the periphery, depends on the craft's rarity and its pollution level.*

Workshops in the souks, *like the dyers' souk in Marrakech, shown here, are often tiny. The craftsman has only just enough space to make and sell his products.*

Moroccan Crafts

Chichaoua
carpet detail

The custom of producing utilitarian objects that are visually pleasing and enlivened with decoration is a deeply rooted tradition among Moroccan craftsmen. They inject beauty into the humblest of materials, from leather, wood and clay, to copper and wool. The importance given to decoration is often so great that it sometimes takes precedence over the object to which it is applied. The endless interplay of arabesques, interlacing patterns, beguiling floral motifs and intricate inscriptions are an integral part of traditional Moroccan life.

Perfume bottle

LEATHERWORK

Leatherworking has always been a major industry in Morocco, particularly in Fès, Meknès, Rabat, Salé and Marrakech. The leather-workers and tanners of Marrakech and Fès, whose numerous workshops fill the picturesque quarters of the medina, are those with the most illustrious reputation. Tanners first clean the hide – either sheepskin or goatskin – and then dye it red, yellow or orange. Gold-leaf decoration may also be applied. The leatherworkers then fashion the material into utilitarian or decorative objects such as pouffes, handbags, *babouches* (slippers) and desk sets.

Sheepskin binding for the Koran, with geometric decoration

Sheepskin binding for the Koran with gold-leaf decoration

WOODWORK

The traditional craft of woodworking is centred mostly in Essaouira, Fès, Meknès, Salé, Marrakech and Tetouan. The many different kinds of wood used by Moroccan wood-workers and cabinet-makers come from the forests of the Atlas and the Rif. Cedar and walnut are used mostly by cabinet-makers, who are highly skilled makers of carved or studded doors, and also in the construction of wooden ceilings. Ebony and citrus wood are used for marquetry and veneering. Thuya, with its beautiful rosewood hue, can be made into elegant furniture and decorative objects.

Painted wooden bread box from Meknès (early 19th century)

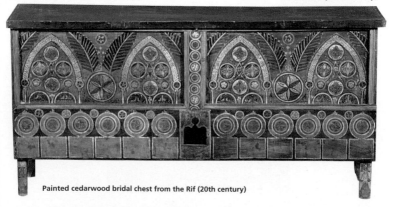

Painted cedarwood bridal chest from the Rif (20th century)

CARPETS

Carpets are a ubiquitous part of the furnishings of the Moroccan home *(see p348)*. City-made carpets, woven mostly in Rabat and Médiouna, are characterized by bright colours and a pattern consisting of a rectangular field on a red background, framed by bands of edging and with geometric motifs. Symmetry is a central feature of carpets made in Rabat. Village carpets, which are

either woven or knotted, are produced in the Middle and High Atlas, in Marrakech and in Haouz. They have more imaginative patterns, such as animal, plant and architectural motifs, which the weavers (mostly women) themselves devise. Weaving and knotting techniques vary according to region, and the various types of village carpets are referred to by their place of origin, such as Middle Atlas, High Atlas, Haouz or Marrakech.

Sahraoui woman weaving a carpet

A knotted carpet from Rabat

POTTERY

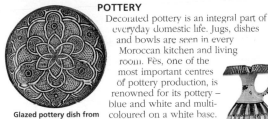

Decorated pottery is an integral part of everyday domestic life. Jugs, dishes and bowls are seen in every Moroccan kitchen and living room. Fès, one of the most important centres of pottery production, is renowned for its pottery – blue and white and multi-coloured on a white base. Safi, whose potting industry is more recent,

Glazed pottery dish from Fès (19th century)

produces pieces characterized by shimmering colours. Local tradition dictates shape, colour, glaze and type of decoration. Meknès and Salé are two other important centres of pottery manufacture.

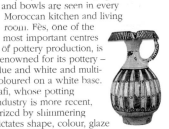

Pottery oil jar

Ceramic honey jar with floral decoration

COPPER AND BRASS

Copper and brass are metals that lend themselves to being cut, hammered, embossed, inlaid and engraved. The repertoire of the Moroccan coppersmith ranges from the humblest domestic objects to the most ostentatious, such as inlaid or panelled doors, trays and chandeliers. This craft reveals a highly developed skill and a love of intricate detail, and follows an ancient tradition.

Brass door with geometric and other decorative motifs

Copper jug from Meknès (19th century)

The Islamic Faith in Morocco

Morocco's official religion is the orthodox, or Sunni, sect of Islam. It is based on the Koran and the Sunna, in which the words and deeds of the Prophet Mohammed are recorded. It is this religion, which was introduced to Morocco in the 7th century, that underpins both the country's law and its faith. Islam is also the unifying force in the daily life of every Moroccan, whose duty it is to respect the Five Pillars of Islam. These are *chabada* (profession of faith), *salat* (prayer), *zakat* (ritual almsgiving), Ramadan (fasting) and *hadj* (the pilgrimage to Mecca). The king of Morocco is both the country's secular and spiritual leader. On his accession to the throne in 1999, Mohammed VI strongly reaffirmed this double prerogative.

Mohammed VI, *King of Morocco, at prayer. For 1,000 years, each Moroccan sovereign has borne the title "leader of the faithful".*

Ritual ablutions *must be performed before prayers. The courtyards of mosques always contain fountains and basins, with hammams (steam-baths) nearby. The Islamic faith places great importance on personal cleanliness.*

Maghrebi calligraphy, characteristic of North Africa, is derived from the more austere Kufic script.

Ceramic tiles *painted with religious motifs, carved plaster and carved wood are the three main elements in the decoration not only of mosques and medersas but also of traditional Muslim homes.*

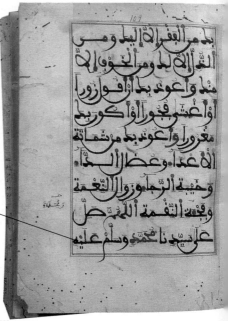

KORAN IN MAGHREBI SCRIPT

The Koran, the holy pronouncements of Allah dictated to the Prophet Mohammed, is central to Islamic faith. Islamic calligraphy, a major art form in the Muslim world, is highly stylized and combines perfect legibility with visual harmony and colourful illumination.

Dish with three mihrabs (niches)
Calligraphy and religious symbols are two prominent themes in the traditional decorative arts of the Muslim world.

FRIDAY PRAYERS

The five daily prayers *(salat)* form part of the five obligations, or "pillars", of Islam that are incumbent on Muslims. The faithful are required to come to the mosque for the midday prayers that are said every Friday. On this day devoted to Allah they also hear a sermon delivered by the *khotba*, or preacher. The gathering at Friday prayers also reinforces the sense of belonging that Muslims have in their community.

Muslims leaving a mosque

Muslim prayer beads *consist of a string of 33 or 99 beads separated by markers. Muslims use the beads to recite the 99 names or attributes of Allah.*

The chapters, or suras, of the Koran are separated by illuminations.

Daily prayer *consists of a series of recitations and prostrations. Kneeling in rows, on a strictly egalitarian basis, the faithful face the direction of Mecca. This direction is called* qibla, *and it is symbolized by the mihrab, a niche in the wall of the mosque. The imam, who leads the prayers, kneels in front.*

ISLAMIC FESTIVALS

The Muslim calendar is based on the lunar year, which is a little shorter than the solar year *(see p41)*. The ninth month, Ramadan, is a time of fasting. Aïd el-Fitr, or Aïd es-Seghir, marks the end of Ramadan, and at Aïd el-Adha, or Aïd el-Kebir, a sheep is sacrificed in memory of the sacrifice of Abraham. Mouloud commemorates the birth of the Prophet Mohammed.

Cakes baked for Ramadan

Sacrificial sheep

The Berbers

Terracotta vessel

Two out of every three Moroccans are, in cultural and linguistic terms, Berber. Thought to be the descendants of people of mixed origins – including Oriental, Saharan and European – the Berbers settled in Morocco at different times, and they do not make up a homogeneous race. By finding refuge in mountainous regions, they survived several successive invasions – those of the civilizations of the Mediterranean basin, of the Arabs, then, much later, those of the French and the Spaniards. The Berbers still speak several dialects and maintain distinct cultural traditions. They are renowned for their trading activities and for the strength of their tribal and family ties.

The fouta *is a rectangular piece of fabric with red and white stripes. It is worn with a conical straw hat by women of the Rif.*

Young Berber girls *dress in bright colours and from an early age wear a headscarf knotted at the top of the head, as their mothers do.*

Veils of many colours cover the women of the Tiznit region.

Henna patterns, *which Berber women paint on themselves, give protection against supernatural forces. Besides keeping evil spirits away, they are supposed to purify and beautify the wearer. On feast days, women decorate their hands and their feet.*

Young girls do not wear veils. Only when they reach adulthood do girls cover their face.

The hendira, *a striped cape woven on a simple loom, is the typical overgarment worn by Berber women.*

The grand souk at the *moussem* **of Imilchil** *is both a social and a commercial gathering. It is an opportunity for Berbers from all over the Atlas Mountains to buy all that they need for the year ahead.*

The *jellaba, an ankle-length robe with long sleeves and a hood, is worn over a wide-sleeved shirt by Berber men of the Atlas mountains. The turban is also part of Berber men's traditional attire.*

RELIGIOUS *MOUSSEMS*

For Berber women, religious *moussems (see pp38–41)* are occasions when they sometimes travel far from home. This is an opportunity for them to meet other women, to sing and dance, and to get away from their everyday chores.

Berber woman in feast-day dress

BERBER TRIBES

Although Berber tribal structure is complex, three groups, each with their own histories, can be identified. The Sanhaja, nomadic herdsmen originating from the south, inhabit the central and eastern High Atlas, the Middle Atlas and the Rif. They speak the dialects of the Tamazight group. The Masmouda, settled farmers, live mostly in the western High Atlas and the Anti-Atlas, and they speak the Chleuh dialect. It was a Masmoudian tribe that founded the Almohad empire in the 12th century.

The Zenets are hunters and herdsmen who came from the East and settled in eastern Morocco. They speak the dialect of the Znatiya group. They founded the Merinid dynasty in the 13th century.

The *situla, a copper vessel of distinctive shape, is used by the women of the Igherm region in the Anti-Atlas to fetch water.*

A mule *is a prized possession among the Berbers. It is used as a beast of burden, to carry such heavy loads as fodder, sacks of grain and containers of water.*

This amber and silver necklace, *from the Taliouine region of the Anti-Atlas, is part of the attire traditionally worn on feast days.*

Horses of Morocco

Two thousand years ago, at the time of the Phoenician, Carthaginian and Roman invasions, the first horses to be used in Morocco were cross-bred with Mongolian stock. The Arab horse was introduced to Morocco by the Arab conquest in the 7th century and, used in war, it played an important part in the establishment of Islam here. Today, owning horses is considered to be a sign of wealth in rural areas. Horses are shown off at festivals, especially in the performance of fantasias (displays of horsemanship), and are also used in daily life.

Detail from an ancient manuscript

Mokahlas, long ceremonial guns, have engraved butts inlaid with mother-of-pearl and ivory.

Tall embroidered leather boots *and loose white short breeches are worn by riders in a fantasia.*

Horse harness, *brightly coloured and made of sumptuous materials, is made by skilled and specialized craftsmen. The severe bit allows the rider to stop abruptly and steer his mount deftly. The blinkers protect the horses' eyes from sand and smoke.*

STUDS

There are national studs in Meknès, El-Jadida, Marrakech, Oujda and Bouznika. Their purpose is to promote the breeding of horses and to produce horses for racing, for equestrian sports and for fantasias. In Morocco today there are 180,000 horses, 550,000 mules and 1 million donkeys. To encourage horse-breeding, stallions are made available to breeders free of charge to cover their mares. On average, 15,000 mares are put to a stallion and 5,000 foals are registered every year.

Thoroughbreds *are used for racing. The racing season runs from September to May.*

The Barb, *a type of horse used by the Berbers before the arrival of the Arabs, is strong, compact and capable of covering long distances.*

The fantasia saddle, *with typically elaborate decoration, consists of a wooden framework sheathed in goatskin. It is covered in embroidered silk and rests on several layers of woven saddle-cloths decorated with pompoms. The high pommel and back restraint keep the rider securely in place.*

Large stirrups *made of sheet metal or leather are attached to the saddle by stirrup-leathers.*

FANTASIAS

Fantasias are displays of horsemanship that are performed according to precise rules. Galloping at full speed down a course 200 m (650 ft) long, the riders whirl their guns in the air and, at a signal from their leader, fire them in unison.

The mule, *a robust beast of burden, is more widely used than the horse. Here, its owner perches on a pack-saddle made out of thick blankets.*

Fantasia horses, which are at least four years old, are Barb or Arabian Barb stallions.

At the *moussem* of Sidi Abdallah Amghar, *in El Jadida, horses are bathed in the sea at dawn. Later in the day, in the fierce August heat, they will perform the galloping charges of the fantasia.*

The Arabian Barb, *an agile and robust horse, was produced by crossbreeding Arabs and Barbs in the 7th century. It is a saddle horse particularly well suited to the fantasia.*

The pure-bred Arab *was introduced to Morocco in the 7th century. Its elegance and beauty, as well as its capacity for endurance, make it one of the world's best-loved horses.*

Moroccan Dress and Jewellery

Traditional dress indicates the wearer's geographical origin and social status. Berber women wrap themselves in rectangular pieces of fabric, secured by a brooch and a belt, while the men wear a *jellaba* and a burnous against the cold. In towns, the elegant kaftan, a long garment with buttons down the front, has become standard formal wear for women, who increasingly often dress in the Western style. Jewellery has long been made by Jewish craftsmen. Berber jewellery is made of silver, sometimes with the addition of coral and amber; necklaces, bracelets and brooches may simply be decorative, or may be a status symbol or an heirloom. Gold, sometimes inlaid with precious stones, is the material of city-made jewellery.

Brooch

Zemmour women *of the Middle Atlas wear a belt in the form of a long plaited and twisted cord decorated with pompoms.*

In oases *bordering the Sahara, women cover their head with a large black or white cotton shawl. On feast days, they bedeck themselves with all their jewellery.*

Hoodless collar

The shape of the sleeves and of the neck-opening varies from one kaftan to the next.

Berber women, *on feast days, don more elaborate headwear. The shape often indicates the wearer's status, either as a married woman or as an unmarried girl.*

Silk brocade kaftan *made in Fès in the 18th–19th century.*

This golden diadem from Fès *consists of hinged plates that are decoratively pierced and set with many precious stones.*

In the High Atlas, *capes worn by women identify their belonging to a particular tribe. Aït Haddiddou women are recognizable by their hendira, a cloak made of woollen cloth with blue, white, black and red stripes.*

Cherbils, *velvet slippers embroidered with gold thread, elegantly curved and with pointed toes, are an essential part of a woman's feast-day dress.*

In rural areas, *older men still wear a voluminous* jellaba *with pointed hood The garment is made of handwoven woollen cloth, which is either of one colour or with patterned stripes.*

For special occasions, *women may wear a gold or silver belt. Silver is most usually worked by being liquefied and poured into a mould, but it may also be beaten into sheets, cut to shape, and then incised or engraved.*

Gold lace

These musicians and dancers *from the Rif are wearing their festival costume. On their head they wear the traditional orange and white* rezza,

KAFTANS

The women's kaftan, an ankle-length, tunic-like garment, collarless and with wide sleeves, is always made of such fine fabric as silk, satin, velvet or brocade. It is often worn with a *mansourya*, a light, transparent overgarment made of silk that sets off the kaftan. The garments are secured at the waist by a wide belt embroidered with silk and gold thread.

Cotton, silk and velvet kaftan, *made in Salé in the 19th century.*

Tiny buttons made of silk or gold thread are sewn down the front of the kaftan.

This young bride *wears a kaftan and, over it, a luxuriant veil, which is traditional in Fès.*

Embroidery, *decorating kaftans, belts and jellabas, is an integral part of women's clothing. The patterns, such as geometric, floral and animal motifs, the colours and the materials used are different in every city.*

Coral, amber and shells, *combined with silver, are strung together to make attractive necklaces, which are worn proudly by Berber women.*

MOROCCO THROUGH THE YEAR

Muslim feast days, agricultural festivals and *moussems* (pilgrimage-festivals) punctuate the Moroccan year. Because the Muslim calendar is lunar, the dates of religious festivals are never fixed. After the harvests of early summer and during the autumn, lively festivals at which the local produce is fêted are held in every region of the country.

Young girl dressed for the Feast of the Throne

More than 600 *moussems* take place each year in Morocco; besides the pilgrimage to the tomb of a saint, there is large regional souk, singing and dancing, and sometimes a fantasia. The month of Ramadan is a major religious occasion; then, the inactivity of the daylight hours, when fasting is required, is followed by joyful night-time festivities.

SPRING

If rainfall is not scarce, spring in Morocco is a remarkable season. In the space of a few days, the dry ochre earth becomes carpeted in flowers of every hue and the mountainsides are flushed with the pale green of new barley. The high peaks, however, are still covered in snow. In the Saharan south, spring is much like summer. It is already warm enough to swim in the Mediterranean and off the southern Atlantic coast.

MARCH

Amateur Theatre Festival, Casablanca.
Cotton Festival, Beni Mellal *(after the harvest)*.
Classic Car Rally *(10 days)*. The itinerary of this international rally for cars

dating from 1939 crosses part of Morocco.
***Moussem* of Moulay Aissa ben Driss**, Aït-Attab (in the Beni Mellal region). Pilgrimage to the holy man's tomb.

APRIL

Candle Festival, Salé. At Achoura, 10 days after the Muslim New Year, boatmen come to place candelabras full of flaming candles at the the Marabout of Sidi Abdallah ben Hassoun.
Marathon des Sables *(8 days)*. Foot race run over 200 km (124 miles) in the Saharan south of Morocco.
***Moussem* of the Regraga** *(40 days)*. Pilgrimage that takes place in 44 stages, passing through the provinces of Essaouira and Safi, in honour of the Regraga – descendants of the Seven Holy Men of Berber history.

The Candle Festival at Salé, which takes place at Achoura

Rose Festival at El-Kelaa M'Gouna, near Ouarzazate

MAY

Rose Festival *(after the rose harvest)*, El-Kelaa M'Gouna (near Ouarzazate). Held in the town that is the capital of rose cultivation *(see p272)*, this festival features folk music and dance.
International Festival of Sacred Music *(1 week)*, Fès. Concerts every day. Jewish, Christian and Sufi religious music, gospel singing, Senegalese songs, and so on.
Aïcha Gazelles' Trophy *(1 week)*. An international event for women rally drivers, along tracks in the desert regions.
Harley-Davidson Raid *(15 days)*. Harley-Davidson motorbike rally through Spain and Morocco.
Crafts Festival, Ouarzazate.
***Moussem* of Moulay Abdallah ben Brahim**, Ouezzane. Pilgrimage held in honour of the holy man

Cherry Festival in Sefrou, at the foot of the Middle Atlas

who came to the town in 1727 and then made it a religious centre.
***Moussem* of Sidi Mohammed Ma al-Aïnin**, Tan Tan. This commercial and religious festival is held in honour of the founder of the town of Smara, who was a great hero of the French Resistance. Events include a performance of the *guedra*, the famous dance of the Guelmim region.
Oudaïa Jazz Festival *(4 days)*, Rabat. This jazz festival is named after the loyal Oudaïa, a well-known tribe that is descended from an Arab tribe, and that Moulay Ismaïl entrusted with watching over the town *(see p68)*.

SUMMER

In summer the only parts of the country that are spared high temperatures are the coasts, which are cooled by sea breezes, and the Atlas mountains. This is not the best time to tour the inner countryside or visit inland towns and cities. In the Saharan south, the sky becomes leaden with the heat, and elsewhere the medinas are stifling. Despite this, the start of summer is marked by many festivals.

JUNE

National Folklore Festival *(10 days)*, Marrakech. At this festival, in the Palais El-Badia, troupes of dancers and musicians from Morocco and elsewhere bring Moroccan folk traditions to life.

Gnaoua Festival *(4 days)*, Essaouira. Gnaoua musicians perform their distinctive music at this event. There is also other traditional Moroccan music, as well as visiting American and European jazz groups.
Cherry Festival *(2 days, after the cherry harvest)*, Sefrou. Folk performers take part in this festival, which is held in honour of Sefrou's famous cherries.
Fig Festival *(after the fig harvest)*, Bouhouda, near Taounate.
***Moussem* of Sidi el-Ghazi** *(last Wednesday in June)*, Guelmim. Sahraouis gather to attend a major camel market. A fantasia is also performed.
Sahraoui Festival, Agadir. Camel races, dancing and music.
***Moussem* of Moulay Bousselham**. Religious festival, with music and festivities.

JULY

***Moussem* of Moulay Abdessalam ben Mchich**, Tetouan. Thousands of people, most of them from local tribes, take part in this great pilgrimage to the holy man's tomb.
Throne Day *(30 July)*. Major celebrations marking the anniversary of the accession to power of Mohammed VI in 1999 take place throughout the country.
Music Festival, Tangier.
***Moussem* of Sidi Mohammed Laghdal**, Tan Tan. Religious pilgrimage.

Camel race at the Sahraoui Festival in Agadir

AUGUST

Honey Festival *(between 15 and 20 August)*, Imouzzer des Ida Outanane (north of Agadir). Celebrations marking the end of the honey harvest, with folk performances and an exhibition showcasing different kinds of honey, one of the region's major products.
***Moussem* of Moulay Abdallah Amghar** *(1 week)*, El-Jadida. Major pilgrimage with renowned fantasias and other entertainments.
International Cultural Festival, Asilah *(2 weeks)*. Music, poetry and painting competitions, discussions with artists, and other events, including street performances.
Festival of Folk Music, Al-Hoceima.

Performer at the Gnaoua Festival

***Moussem* of Setti Fatma**. Pilgrimage and souk in the Ourika valley, southeast of Marrakech.
***Moussem* of Dar Zhiroun**, Rabat. Religious festival.
***Moussem* of Sidi Ahmed (or Sidi Moussa)**, east of Tiznit. Religious festival in honour of the holy man and Acrobats' Festival.
Apple Festival, Imouzzer du Kandar, 38 km (24 miles) south of Fès.
***Moussem* of Sidi Daoud**, Ouarzazate. Religious pilgrimage.
***Moussem* of Sidi Lahcen ben Ahmed**, Sefrou. Festival in honour of the town's patron saint, who lived during the 18th century.
***Moussem* of Sidi Yahya ben Younes**, Oujda. Religious festival in honour of St John the Baptist, the town's principal saint, to whom Muslims, Jews and Christians all pray.

Moussem of Moulay Idriss II in Fès

AUTUMN

September and October are very pleasant months in which to explore the Atlas mountains, visit the imperial cities, or experience the vastness of the Moroccan desert, where the heat is then bearable. In November, heavy rains can sometimes make the *wadis* burst their banks and render tracks impassable.

SEPTEMBER

Festival of Fantasia *(early September, 4 days)*, Meknès. Thousands of horsemen gather to demonstrate their skills in fantasias. Traditional dances are also performed.
Marriage Fair *(towards end*

of September, 3 days), Imilchil. Tribal gathering of the Aït Haddidou at which betrothals are made. Performances of folk song and dancing take place at this colourful event.
Moussem of Moulay Idriss Zerhoun. Pilgrimage to the tomb of Moulay Idriss, founder of the first dynasty, marked by major festivities.
Moussem of Moulay Idriss II *(1 week)*, Fès. Processions of craftsmen's guilds and of brotherhoods to the mausoleum of the city's founder.
Moussem of Sidi Alla el-Hadj, Chefchaouen. Religious festival held in the hills around the city.
Festival of Volubilis *(1 week)*, Meknès. Performances by musicians and dancers from Morocco and the Arab world, but also from Europe and the United States.
Moussem of Sidi Ahmed ben Mansour, Moulay Bousselham. Religious festival.
Moussem of Dar Zhira, Tangier. Religious festival.
Jazz Festival, Tangier.

OCTOBER

Date Festival *(3 days after the date harvest in the groves of the Tafilalt)*,

Erfoud. Many tribes from the Tafilalt gather, and several varieties of dates are sold in the souks. Folk dancers and musicians perform in the streets of Erfoud.
Apple Festival *(after the harvest)*, Midelt.
Horse Festival *(1 week)*, Tissa. Various breeds of horses compete and take part in shows, and many fantasias are performed.
Walnut Festival, Al Haouz.
Festival of Andalusian Music, Rabat.

Date Festival in Erfoud, taking place after the harvest

NOVEMBER

Moussem of Mohammed Bou Nasri, Tamegroute. This religious festival is held in memory of the great saint *(see p269)*.
International Music Festival, Ouarzazate.

Charging horsemen at a fantasia performed at the Horse Festival in Tissa

Almond trees in blossom in the Tafraoute region

FEBRUARY

Almond Blossom Festival, Tafraoute *(south of Agadir)*. Agricultural festival marking the short-lived but spectacular pink and white almond blossom.

PUBLIC HOLIDAYS

Year's Day
(1 January)

Manifesto of Independence Day
(11 January)

Labour Day (1 May)

Throne Day
(30 July)

Allegiance Day
(14 August)

King Mohammed VI's Birthday and **Youth Day**
(21 August)

Day of the Green March
(6 November)

Independence Day, return from exile of King Mohammed V
(18 November)

WINTER

The best time to explore Morocco's Saharan region is in the winter. The days are sunny and the sky is a deep blue but the nights are cold. On the coasts, the temperature remains mild. By contrast, the valleys of the High Atlas can receive heavy snowfalls and may be inaccessible. In February, the almond trees of the Tafraoute valley are covered in blossom. Few festivals take place in winter.

DECEMBER

Olive Tree Festival, Rhafsaï *(north of Fès)*. Agricultural festival.

JANUARY

Go-Kart 24-Hour Race, Marrakech.

RELIGIOUS FESTIVALS

The dates of Muslim festivals are set according to the lunar calendar of the Hegira (the beginning of the Muslim era in 622). The Muslim year is 10 or 11 days shorter than that of the Gregorian calendar. Religious festivals also take place 11 days earlier each year in relation to the Western calendar. Guided by the phases of the moon, the religious authorities wait until the last moment before deciding on the exact date of each festival

Moharem: Muslim New Year.

Achoura: traditional almsgiving *(zakat)* to the poor; presents are also given to children.

Mouloud (aïd al-wawlid): anniversary of the birth of the Prophet Mohammed. Many *moussems* also take place at the same time as Mouloud, and their dates are therefore different each year. Among the most important are the *moussem* of Moulay Brahim, near Marrakech, that of Moulay Abdessalam ben Mchich, in the north, the *moussem* of Sidi Mohammed ben Aïssa, of Sidi Ali ben Hamdouch, the Candle Festival in Salé and the *moussem* of Moulay Abdelkader Jilali.

Ramadan: practising Muslims fast for a month, eating only after sunset.

Aïd es-Seghir ("the small festival"), also known as Aïd el-Fitr: festival marking the end of the 30-day fast of Ramadan.

Aïd el-Kebir ("the grand festival"), also known as Aïd el-Adha: this festival, taking place 68 days after Aïd es-Seghir, commemorates the day when, by divine order, Abraham prepared to sacrifice his son Isaac, when Allah interceded by providing a ram in place of the child. Every household sacrifices a sheep and shares the meat at a family meal.

Souk in the High Atlas with sheep for sale just before **Aïd el-Kebir**

The Climate of Morocco

Bordered by the Atlantic and the Mediterranean, joined to the African continent by the Sahara, and diagonally bisected by the long mountain chain of the High and Middle Atlas, Morocco does not have a uniform climate. It is cooled by moist northwesterly winds and seared by hot, dry southeasterlies such as the *chergui*. In summer, conditions are those of a hot arid zone. In winter, which is very mild except in the mountains, conditions switch to those of a temperate coastal zone. Water is in relatively short supply everywhere and agriculture, involving about 40 per cent of the economically active population, is acutely dependent on adequate rainfall.

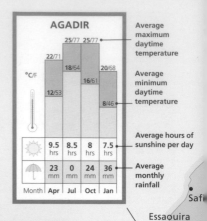

AGADIR

	Apr	Jul	Oct	Jan
Average maximum daytime temperature	22/71	25/77	25/77	20/68
Average minimum daytime temperature	12/53	18/64	16/61	8/46
Average hours of sunshine per day	9.5 hrs	8.5 hrs	8 hrs	7.5 hrs
Average monthly rainfall	23 mm	0 mm	24 mm	36 mm

°C/F

Month

Landscape in the arid, mountainous Anti-Atlas region

Saf

Essaouira

● Agadir

Tiznit ●

Tafraoute

● Guelmim

● Tan Tan

● Laayoune

CLIMATE ZONES

Moist mountainous region: the Rif has the highest precipitation; rainfall is heaviest in the north and lightest in the south.

Atlantic region: mild winters and temperate summers; the dry season lengthens towards the south.

Eastern region: very light rainfall here, protected by the high mountains; hot, dry summer conditions.

Pre-Saharan and Saharan regions: rainfall becomes increasingly light and irregular; contrasts in temperature are more marked, with relatively cool winters and scorching summers.

Moist northwesterly winds.

Dry, hot southwesterly winds.

0 km   100

0 miles   100

Nouadhibou ●

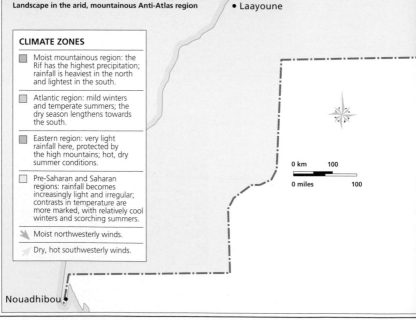

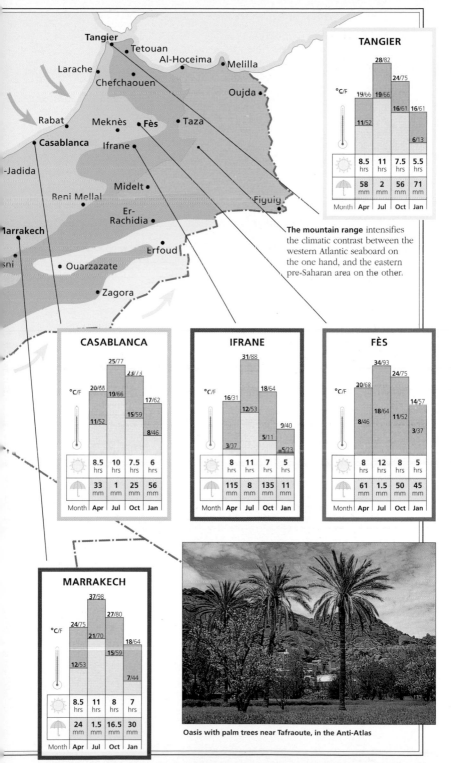

TANGIER

	°C/F	28/82		
	19/66	19/66	24/75	
	11/52		16/61	16/61
				6/13

☀	8.5 hrs	11 hrs	7.5 hrs	5.5 hrs
☂	58 mm	2 mm	56 mm	71 mm
Month	Apr	Jul	Oct	Jan

The mountain range intensifies the climatic contrast between the western Atlantic seaboard on the one hand, and the eastern pre-Saharan area on the other.

Tangier
Tetouan
Larache
Chefchaouen
Al-Hoceima
Melilla
Oujda
Rabat
Meknès
Fès
Taza
Casablanca
Ifrane
-Jadida
Midelt
Beni Mellal
Figuiy
Er-Rachidia
Marrakech
Erfoud
sni
Ouarzazate
Zagora

CASABLANCA

	°C/F	25/77	23/73	
	20/68	19/66		17/62
	11/52		15/59	8/46

☀	8.5 hrs	10 hrs	7.5 hrs	6 hrs
☂	33 mm	1 mm	25 mm	56 mm
Month	Apr	Jul	Oct	Jan

IFRANE

	°C/F	31/88		
	16/31	12/53	18/64	
	3/37		5/11	9/40
				5/23

☀	8 hrs	11 hrs	7 hrs	5 hrs
☂	115 mm	8 mm	135 mm	11 mm
Month	Apr	Jul	Oct	Jan

FÈS

	°C/F	34/93		
	20/68		24/75	
	8/46	18/64	11/52	14/57
				3/37

☀	8 hrs	12 hrs	8 hrs	5 hrs
☂	61 mm	1.5 mm	50 mm	45 mm
Month	Apr	Jul	Oct	Jan

MARRAKECH

	°C/F	37/98		
	24/75	27/80		
	12/53	21/70	15/59	18/64
				7/44

☀	8.5 hrs	11 hrs	8 hrs	7 hrs
☂	24 mm	1.5 mm	16.5 mm	30 mm
Month	Apr	Jul	Oct	Jan

Oasis with palm trees near Tafraoute, in the Anti-Atlas

THE HISTORY OF MOROCCO

Morocco is an ancient kingdom. It came under the influence of Carthage and Rome, but its origins are Berber, Arab and African. Since the arrival of Islam in the 7th century, the country has been an independent power, and at times an empire. The only Arab country not to have fallen to the Ottomans, it entered the modern era under the Alaouite dynasty at the end of the colonial period.

For 40,000 years Morocco has been a bridge between the East, Africa and Europe. Archaeological finds and rock engravings prove that it was settled in the remote past, but little is known of the first Berbers, who may have come from the east.

The Phoenicians, fearless navigators, established trading posts – such as Russaddir (Melilla) and Lixus (Larache) – along the Moroccan coast. They also introduced iron-working and the cultivation of vines.

In the 5th century BC, Hanno, a naval commander from Carthage (in modern Tunisia), set out to explore the Atlantic coast westwards, and soon the trading posts were taken over and developed by Carthage. Under their influence, the Berber tribes eventually joined forces and established the kingdom of Mauretania.

In 146 BC, having destroyed Carthage, the Romans extended their control westwards over the northern half of Morocco. Emperor Augustus made Tingis (Tangier) a Roman city. In 25 BC, the kingdom of Mauretania was entrusted to Juba II, king of Numidia. A Berber ruler who had been Romanized and educated, he married the daughter of Antony and Cleopatra. Ptolemy, Juba's son and heir, was murdered in AD 40 on the orders of Emperor Caligula. Emperor Claudius later annexed the kingdom, dividing it into Mauretania Caesariensis (west Algeria) and Mauretania Tingitana (Morocco). The Romans established few new towns here, but developed the existing ones, among them Tangier, Volubilis, Lixus, Banasa, Sala and Thamusida. The southern frontier lay at the level of Rabat. In the 3rd century, however, Christianity began to spread and Roman domination was severely diminished.

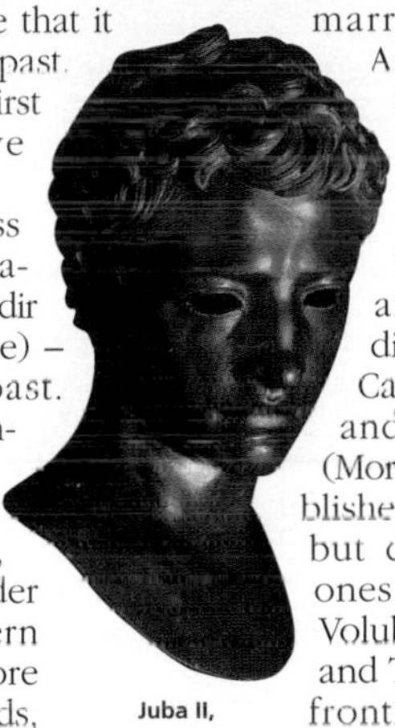

The Vandals, whose king Genseric (428–77) conquered North Africa, followed by the Byzantines, maintained a lasting presence only at a few points along the Mediterranean coast. Religious unrest and local uprisings gradually extinguished the hold of all the ancient civilizations.

Juba II, the Romanized Berber ruler

TIMELINE

8000 BC		4000 BC			AD 1	
			c.400 BC Berber tribes unite to establish the kingdom of Mauretania	**46 BC** Numidia becomes a Roman province	**430–533** Vandals conquer North Africa	**6th century** Byzantine domination
		c.1000 BC Arrival of the Phoenicians				
8000–7000 BC Ancestors of the Berbers arrive from the east. They domesticate the horse and use iron			**c.800 BC** Foundation of Carthage	**201 BC** End of the Second Punic War. Rome destroys Carthage in 146 BC		

A Moor and a Christian in combat

◁ **The Sultan Moulay Abderrahman Leaving Meknès**, by Eugène Delacroix

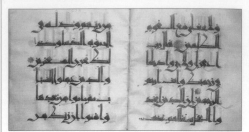

Pages from the Koran in the Maghrebi Kufic script of North Africa

ARRIVAL OF ISLAM

From the end of the 7th century, a new set of invaders, and with them a new religion, began to make its mark on Morocco. The Arabs had started to expand their rule westwards, and in 681 there was a first attempt into Morocco. But the true conqueror of Morocco was Moussa ibn Nosaïr, who, active from 705, brought the territory from Tangier to the Draa valley under the control of the Ummayyad caliph in Damascus. With some resistance, Islam was introduced to the Berber population. Quickly rallying a mainly Berber army, Moussa then turned his attention to Europe, initiating the conquest of Spain in 711.

Reacting against their haughty Arab overlords, the Berbers of the Maghreb rebelled against them and, usually but not always, against Islam. Battles with troops sent from the East continued for more than 30 years, from 739 to 772. Petty kingdoms were formed and the western Maghreb kept the power of the caliphs at bay.

THE IDRISSID DYNASTY (789–926)

Meanwhile, Islam divided itself into two main sects: Sunni and Shia. In 786, the Sunnite Ummayad caliph crushed the Shi'ite Muslims. One of them, Idriss ibn Abdallah, escaped the massacre and was received in Morocco as a prestigious religious leader. In 789, the Aouraba, a Berber tribe in Volubilis, made him their leader. Idriss I carved out a small kingdom, and set about building a new city, Fès. He died soon afterwards, probably poisoned by an envoy of the caliph. His son, Idriss II (793–828), succeeded him and made Fès the Idrissid capital. The Idrissids are considered to be the founding dynasty and the first of Morocco's seven ruling dynasties.

Fès soon became densely populated and a prestigious religious centre. At the death of Idriss II, the kingdom was divided between his two sons, then between their descendants. They were unable to prevent the simultaneous attacks of the two powerful rivals of the Abbassid caliph, the Shi'ites of Tunisia and Egypt, and the Ummayyad caliphs of Córdoba in Andalusia – Sunnis who for long fought over Fès and the allegiance of the Berber tribes.

THE ALMORAVIDS (1062–1147)

An unexpected push came from the south. A tribe of nomadic Sanhadja Berbers, based in present-day Mauritania and converts to Islam in the 9th century, were to give rise to a powerful new empire. The tribe's headman, Yahia ibn Ibrahim, invited a holy man to preach the Islamic faith to his people. A fortified camp, or *ribat*, was built on the

Fountain in the 9th-century
Karaouiyine Mosque in Fès

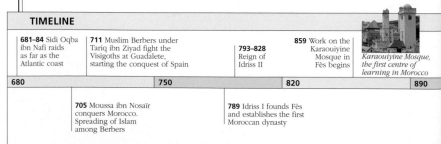

TIMELINE

680		750		820		890
681–84 Sidi Oqba ibn Nafi raids as far as the Atlantic coast	**711** Muslim Berbers under Tariq ibn Ziyad fight the Visigoths at Guadalete, starting the conquest of Spain			**793–828** Reign of Idriss II	**859** Work on the Karaouiyine Mosque in Fès begins	*Karaouiyine Mosque, the first centre of learning in Morocco*
	705 Moussa ibn Nosaïr conquers Morocco. Spreading of Islam among Berbers		**789** Idriss I founds Fès and establishes the first Moroccan dynasty			

Remains of the Koubba Ba'Adiyn in Marrakech, built in 1106 *(see p231)*

the Faithful. Having founded Marrakech, which became Morocco's second capital, in 1062, he conquered the country as far north as Tangier and in 1082 as far east as Algiers.

In Al-Andalus (Andalusia), the fall of the Umayyad caliphate of Córdoba in 1031 led to the creation of *taifas,* small Muslim principalities. Alfonso VI, King of Castile and León, led the Christian Reconquest, taking Toledo in 1085. In response to a call for aid from the *taifas,* Youssef ibn Tachfin crossed the strait and routed Alfonso VI's forces at the Battle of Badajoz in 1086. He soon extended his empire as far north as Barcelona. In the south, Almoravid influence stretched to the Senegal and the Niger (1076).

The empire was unified by the orthodox, Sunni branch of Islam. On the death of Youssef ben Tachfine, his son Ali, whose mother was an Andalusian Christian, succeeded him. During his long reign (1107–43) the refined culture of Andalusia took hold in Morocco, although the empire itself was in decline. More Andalusian than Moroccan, the last Almoravids fled to Spain to escape a new rebellion from the south, that of the Almohads.

estuary of the Senegal river. In 1054, "the people of the *ribat*" (the al Mourabitoun, or Almoravids), fighters for a pure Islamic state, launched a holy war northward as far as the Atlas. The founder of the Almoravid empire was Youssef ibn Tachfin (1061–1107), who proclaimed himself Leader of

Carved wooden lintel from a mosque in Marrakech, dating from the 9th century

929 Abderrahman III establishes an independent caliphate in Córdoba	1062 Youssef ibn Tachfin founds Marrakech and starts to expand his Almoravid empire	1086 Spanish king Alfonso VI is defeated at Badajoz. The Reconquest is temporarily halted
960	1030	1100
1010 Berbers sack Abderrahman's palace at Medina Azahara, Córdoba	Zellij *tilework in the Palais du Glaoui, Marrakech*	1107–43 Andalusian culture takes root during the reign of Ali ben Youssef

Morocco and Al-Andalus

The philosopher Maïmonides

For almost eight centuries – from 711, when Tariq ibn Ziyad and his Berber forces crossed the Straits of Gibraltar to reach Spain, to the fall of the Nasrid kingdom of Granada in 1492 – the Iberian peninsula was partly under Muslim control. Muslim territory, known as Al-Andalus (the Land of the Vandals), was at times a melting pot of Muslims, Jews and Mozarabs (Christians adopting an Islamic lifestyle), philosophers, traders, scientists and poets. This gave birth to the most illustrious civilization of the late Middle Ages.

A love of gardens was one aspect of the cultured civilization of Al-Andalus

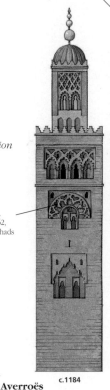

The Giralda, the clocktower of Seville Cathedral, added in the 16th century.

The minaret of the Great Mosque in Seville, transformed after the Christian Reconquest into the famous Giralda.

Irrigation

Under the Umayyad caliphs and their Berber successors, irrigation in Andalusia underwent a dramatic advance. The introduction of the noria, *a waterwheel for the mechanical extraction of water – shown here in a 13th-century manuscript – was to change, permanently, the method of water distribution in Spain.*

The minaret of the Koutoubia Mosque, in Marrakech, which was begun in 1162, was the model for those that the Almohads built later in Andalusia.

c.1184   1172–1198

Averroës

One of the greatest Islamic thinkers, and a protégé of the Almohad rulers, Averroës was born in Córdoba in 1126 and died in Marrakech in 1198 (see p231).

JUDAISM IN MOROCCO

Inscriptions in Hebrew dating from the Roman period show that there has been a Jewish community in Morocco since antiquity. It was involved chiefly in agriculture, stock-farming and trade. Judaism flourished thanks to the conversion of the Berber tribes and to the immigration of Jews fleeing from the east and from Spain. When Fès was founded, a Jewish community settled there, and scholars and rabbis travelled throughout the country. Although strictures imposed by the Almoravids and Almohads caused some Jews to emigrate, they flourished once again under the Merinids and Wattasids, who welcomed thousands of Jews expelled from Spain after 1492. The Alaouite sultans also protected them. Although their numbers are reduced, Jews hold certain influential positions in Morocco today.

Bronze Hanukkah lamp, 19th century

MINARETS

After the end of the independant Cordoban caliphate, Almoravids and Almohads directly controlled Al-Andalus, where their monumental architecture flourished. The architectural heritage of Al-Andalus, above all of religious architecture, is a clear expression of Andalusian culture. The striking similarity between the minarets of the three mosques built by the Almohads in Marrakech, Rabat and Seville demonstrates the unity of the Almohad architectural style.

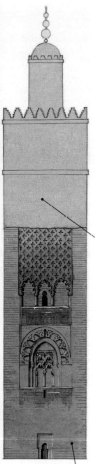

Reconstruction of the unfinished part of the Hassan Tower.

c. 1195

The Hassan Tower in Rabat, a colossal project and an over-ambitious undertaking, was never completed.

The Battle of Higueruela
This 15th-century fresco depicts an episode in the Reconquest, a centuries-long struggle between Muslim rulers and Christians for control of Spain.

King Boabdil's Farewell
Painted by the Orientalist Alfred Dehodencq (1822–82), this famous scene from Spanish history is redolent with nostalgia but is probably spurious. It depicts the fall of the last Moorish kingdom in Andalusia, that of the Nasrids of Granada, in 1492. Al-Andalus was to acquire a mythical aura in the minds of the Moorish communities who fled the Iberian peninsula during the Reconquest. In architecture, daily life, cuisine, music and vocabulary, Andalusian culture lives on in Moroccan towns cities to this day.

THE ALMOHADS AND THE APOGEE OF THE WESTERN MUSLIM EMPIRE

In 1125, after a life devoted to study and to travelling in the Muslim world, Ibn Toumart, a Berber man of letters, settled in Tin Mal, a narrow valley in the High Atlas. A religious puritan driven by the doctrine of unity, he declared himself the *mahdi* (messiah) and, in opposition to the increasingly decadent Almoravids, began preaching moral reform. On his death, his successor Abd el-Moumen assumed the title of Leader of the Faithful. In 1146–7 he took control of the main cities of the Almoravid empire, including Marrakech, Fès and the great cities of Al-Andalus. Now the leader of the greatest empire that ever existed in the Muslim west, he went about centralizing it and reorganizing its army, administration and economy. He imposed taxes and land surveys, created a navy, founded universities and

Mihrab of the mosque at Tin Mal, birthplace of the Almohads

enlisted the support of the great Arab dynasties. With such thinkers as Ibn Tufaïl and Averroës *(see p231)*, intellectual life flourished. In 1162, Abd el-Moumen, founder of the Almohad dynasty, proclaimed himself caliph. The dynasty was at its peak during his reign, and that of his grandson Yacoub el-Mansour ("the Victorious", 1184–99).

But over the following decades the dynasty declined. The combined forces of the Spanish Christian princes inflicted a heavy defeat on Mohammed el-Nasser at the Battle of Las Navas de Tolosa. With the fall of Córdoba in 1236 and of Seville in 1248, the Muslims lost Spain, with only the small Nasrid kingdom of Granada surviving until 1492. The last Almohad sultans, who were reduced to the Maghreb, were challenged by dissidents: the Hafsids – Almohads who established their own dynasty (1228–1574) in Tunisia and western Algeria – and the Abdelwadid Berbers in Tlemcen in 1236.

In the south, the Almohads lost control of Saharan trade routes, while at the very heart of the kingdom, the Meri-

Carved wooden Merinid chest

nids, the Almohads' Berber allies of the high plateaux, defied their authority. The cycle described by the great Maghrebi historian Ibn Khaldoun *(see p181)*, in which over the centuries simple nomads wrench power from corrupt city-dwellers, and who are themselves overthrown, began again.

The age of the Almohads, a period of unequalled splendour, has left a lasting impression on Morocco: a form of Islam that is both spiritual and precisely defined, a *makhzen* (central

Tiled panel depicting the Battle of Las Navas de Tolosa of 1212, at which the Almohads were defeated

---

TIMELINE

1130–63 Abd el-Moumen, the first Almohad caliph, conquers the Maghreb as far as Tripoli	**1212** Alfonso VIII of Castile defeats Mohammed el-Nasser at Las Navas de Tolosa		**1248–86** Abou Yahia, followed by Abou Youssef Yacoub, establishes the Merinid dynasty
1120	**1180**	**1240**	**1300**
1125 The *mahdi* Ibn Toumart settles in Tin Mal	**1195** Yacoub el-Mansour defeats the Castilians at Alarcos	**1212–69** Decline of the Almohad dynasty; gradual loss of territories in Al-Andalus	*Standard captured from the Muslims at the Battle of Las Navas de Tolosa*

power) to control tribal self-determination, and a great urban Moorish civilization that is still in evidence.

THE MERINIDS (1248–1465)

Under the Merinids, Morocco was gradually reduced to the territory that it covers today. Unsuccessful on the battlefield, the Merinids were, however, inspired builders, and during their rule a brilliant urban civilization came into being. Led by Abou Yahia, these Zenet Berber nomads took control of the major cities and fertile plains from 1248, although it was not until 1269 that they conquered Marrakech, thus putting an end to the Almohad dynasty. Fès, which had been made capital by Abou Yacoub Youssef, experienced a new phase of expansion.

Despite some minor victories, the Merinids were unsuccessful in their attempts to reconquer territory on the Iberian peninsula. In 1415, the Portuguese, led by Henry the Navigator, took Ceuta. However, Abou el-Hassan (the "Black Sultan") managed to re-establish temporary order and unity in the Maghreb. He and his successor, Abou Inan, were great rulers and great builders. But crises of succession grad-

GEOGRAPHY

Geography was a favourite discipline with Arabs in the early Middle Ages. Ibn Battuta (c.1300–c.1370), who was born in Tangier and studied in Damascus, took the art of the *rihla* – encyclopedic travel writing – to its height. Towards the end of his life he dictated an entertaining account of his travels over almost 30 years. He visited the holy cities of Arabia, was a minister in the Maldives, a merchant in India and China, and explored Indonesia and the Persian Gulf. Having returned to the Maghreb, he travelled through the kingdoms of sub-Saharan Africa.

Map by the cartographer Al Idrissi (1099–1166), born in Ceuta, who put together one of the first geographic accounts of the known world

ually undermined their authority, and the Wattasids, another Zenet Berber dynasty, started taking over power from 1420 and ruled solely 1465–1549. With the 15th century began the slow decline of Moroccan power: fortune now favoured the Europeans.

Tapestry depicting the fall of Ceuta to the Portuguese in 1415

1331–49 The Merinid period reaches its peak under Abou el-Hassan

1415 Henry the Navigator wins Ceuta for Portugal

Tiled panel depicting the conquest of Ceuta

1360	1420	1480

1349–58 Reign of Abou Inan, a great builder

1420 The Merinids come under the control of the Wattasids

1465 The Wattasids oust the Merinids permanently

1497–1508 After the fall of Granada to the Christians, the Spanish move into northern Morocco

THE TWO SHORFA DYNASTIES

Since the time of Idriss I, the *shorfa* (the plural form of sherif) – Arabs of high social standing who are descendants of the Prophet Mohammed – have always played an important part in the social and political life of Morocco. Putting an end to Berber rule, they emerged from the south and governed Morocco from the 16th century to the present day. Because of their social origins, these two final dynasties, the Saadians and the Alaouites, are known as the Shorfa dynasties.

A gold dinar, proof of Saadian prosperity

SAADIAN PROSPERITY (1525–1659)

At the beginning of the 16th century, the encroachment of Christian armies on Moroccan soil stimulated a vigorous renewal of religious fervour. From 1509, supporters of the movement of resistance against the Europeans found a leader in El-Kaïm, sherif of the Beni Saad, an Arab tribe from the Draa valley. Boldly leading the campaign for the reconquest of the Portuguese enclaves and for the seizure of power, they took control of the Souss, of Marrakech (1525), which was to become their capital, and of Fès (1548), ousting the last Wattasid sultans.

Dom Sebastião, the young king killed in battle in Morocco in 1578

The Saadians stepped onto the stage of international relations; in 1577, France even appointed a Moroccan consul. To help counter the threat of the Turks, who had settled in Algiers, Mohammed ech-Cheikh requested the support of Madrid, whose attention was then focused on the Americas rather than the Maghreb. The Ottomans had Mohammed assassinated in 1557, but did not conquer Morocco.

The Saadians traded with Europe and drew up treaties with England and the Netherlands. From the Moriscos, the last Spanish Muslims, they received the final heritage of Al-Andalus.

Once the Saadians had retaken Agadir (1541), only Mazagan (El-Jadida), Tangier and Ceuta remained in Portuguese hands. Portugal's "Moroccan dream" was extinguished at the Battle of the Three Kings in 1578, when two rival Saadian sultans and Dom Sebastião, the young king of Portugal, all died at Ksar el-Kebir *(see p92)*. His uncle, Philip II of Spain, swiftly annexed the Portuguese kingdom.

Saadian prosperity culminated with Ahmed el-Mansour, (1578–1603) whose conquests secured control of Saharan trade, and who set up the *makhzen* (a central administration). Gold from Mali and slaves reached Marrakech. Political and religious links with western Africa, and the presence of African folk culture brought here by slaves, made a mark on Morocco that can still be seen today.

Like their preceding dynasties, the Saadians declined as the result of ambition and disputed succession. In the distant Tafilalt, the ascetic *shorfa*, descendants of Ali, cousin of the Prophet, revolted against the decadence of Saadian rule under Moulay Sherif, and seized control of the region, which they held until 1664.

TIMELINE

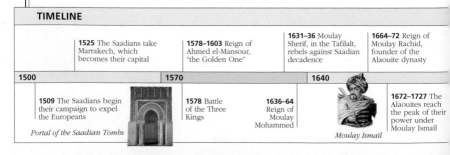

1525 The Saadians take Marrakech, which becomes their capital

1578–1603 Reign of Ahmed el-Mansour, "the Golden One"

1631–36 Moulay Sherif, in the Tafilalt, rebels against Saadian decadence

1664–72 Reign of Moulay Rachid, founder of the Alaouite dynasty

1500

1570

1640

1509 The Saadians begin their campaign to expel the Europeans

Portal of the Saadian Tombs

1578 Battle of the Three Kings

1636–64 Reign of Moulay Mohammed

Moulay Ismaïl

1672–1727 The Alaouites reach the peak of their power under Moulay Ismaïl

ALAOUITE GREATNESS AND EXTERNAL THREATS

The Alaouite dynasty, the seventh and present ruling dynasty, has given the country some rulers of great stature. During its long reign, each ruler concentrated on bringing stability to the country and on countering the threat of imperialist powers. It took ten years for Moulay Rachid (1664–72), founder of the dynasty, to bring the country under his control. The long and glorious reign of his younger brother, Moulay Ismaïl (1672–1727), marked Morocco's final apogee *(see pp54–5)*. He transferred the capital from Fès to Meknès, imposed central authority in the remotest corners of the country, recaptured Mehdya, Tangier and Larache from the Europeans, and maintained relations with the courts of Europe.

After a period of instability, his grandson, Sidi Mohammed ben Abdallah, restored order, expelled the

Trade agreement of 1767. During his reign Sidi Mohammed signed treaties with France, Denmark, Sweden, England, Venice, Spain and the newly created United States

Portuguese from Mazagan and founded Mogador (Essaouira) to facilitate trade with Europe. Under Moulay Yazid and Moulay Sliman, epidemics, uprisings and diplomatic isolation caused the country to withdraw into itself. Moulay Abderrahman, another great ruler, attempted to modernize the country, but was frustrated by European colonial expansion. He was defeated by the French at Isly in 1844.

Moulay Abderrahman and his successors, Mohammed IV and Hassan I, were forced to concede commercial and consular privileges to Britain, France and Spain. In 1860, Spain took control of Tetouan. Hassan I, a dynamic ruler, attempted to balance the influence of these rivals, but the Conference of Madrid of 1880 sanctioned the intervention of foreign powers in Morocco. On his death, the country was stable and the dynasty's prestige intact, but Morocco was weakened.

French victory at the Battle of Isly, near Oujda, in 1844, depicted by the French painter Horace Vernet

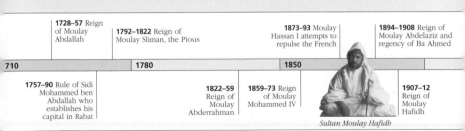

1728–57 Reign of Moulay Abdallah

1792–1822 Reign of Moulay Sliman, the Pious

1873–93 Moulay Hassan I attempts to repulse the French

1894–1908 Reign of Moulay Abdelaziz and regency of Ba Ahmed

710

1780

1850

1757–90 Rule of Sidi Mohammed ben Abdallah who establishes his capital in Rabat

1822–59 Reign of Moulay Abderrahman

1859–73 Reign of Moulay Mohammed IV

1907–12 Reign of Moulay Hafidh

Sultan Moulay Hafidh

The Great Age of Moulay Ismaïl

Moulay Ismaïl, of partial Saharan parentage and a man of phenomenal vitality, stamped his authority on Morocco during a long and brilliant reign. Ruling for 55 years (1672–1727), he was a contemporary of Louis XIV. He made Meknès his capital and maintained a powerful army, recruited tens of thousands of men for the Black Guard, and modernized the artillery. With these forces, he was able to overcome rebellious tribes and bring temporary peace to the country. He wrenched from European control several fortresses, including Tangier and Larache. He also exchanged ambassadors with the French court.

The capital of Moulay Ismaïl in 1693.

Sultan Moulay Ismaïl
He was the greatest, most ruthless ruler of the Alaouite dynasty.

Morocco's Ambassador in Paris (1682)
In conflict with Spain, Moulay Ismaïl sought an alliance with France in order to vanquish the fortresses that Spain held in Morocco. Once in France, the sultan's ambassador, Hadj Tenim, concluded a treaty of Franco-Moroccan friendship in 1682. Morocco then became an important trading partner for European countries.

Moulay Ismaïl's retinue

Black Guard
Moulay Ismaïl greatly expanded the army, which consisted of three contingents: units provided by the tribes, Christian renegades and abid, black slaves and mercenaries, whose exclusive duty was to protect the sultan. This latter regiment led to the formation of the famous Black Guard, which still exists.

Anne Marie de Bourbon

So as to strengthen his links with Europe, Moulay Ismaïl sent a request to Louis XIV for the hand of the princess, the French king's cousin, in marriage. His request was not granted.

THE ARCHITECTURAL HERITAGE OF MOULAY ISMAÏL

Moulay Ismaïl's achievements as a builder are most clearly seen in Meknès. This was formerly a small town overshadowed by the prestigious city of Fès, but the sultan transformed it into Morocco's fourth imperial city. It was enclosed by a double line of defensive walls and was described by some as the Versailles of Morocco. Next to the medina, the sultan built a kasbah, an extensive architectural complex enclosed within its own walls. This was the seat of power and of administration, consisting of several palaces, mosques, garrisons and studs, cisterns and stores for water. It was the ideal imperial city.

Chevalier de Saint-Olon

AUDIENCE GIVEN BY MOULAY ISMAÏL

As depicted in this painting in the Palace of Versailles by M. P. Denis (1663–1742), Louis XIV, the Sun King, sent an ambassador to Meknès in 1689. The ambassador, the Chevalier François Pidou de Saint-Olon, was received with full honours. For 20 years, Louis XIV and Moulay Ismaïl exchanged embassies, but relations between them soured when France declined to engage in conflict with Spain.

Large-scale building projects *undertaken by Moulay Ismaïl, such as the Dar el-Ma, shown here (see p193), called for an army of crafts-men. These were recruited from* other tribes, Christian prisoners and slaves. Contemporary writers record that the cruel sultan supervised the work himself, passing a death sentence on the slowest workers.

Bab el-Berdaïne, *the Gate of the Pack-Saddle Makers (see p188), takes its name from the pack-saddle market held nearby. In the 17th century, Meknès was enclosed by triple walls with imposing gates.*

The Sultan's Mausoleum *(see pp194–5), which was built in the 17th century, was completely restored by Mohammed V in 1959. The clocks in the burial chamber were presented as gifts by Louis XIV.*

Marshal Lyautey, Morocco's first resident-general, shown here in 1925 with Moulay Youssef

EUROPEAN DOMINATION

When Moulay Abdel Aziz, a weak ruler, ascended the throne in 1894, France already had an imperial presence in Algeria and Tunisia. The French now aimed to secure a free hand in Morocco, parallel with Britain's designs in Egypt and those of Italy in Libya. After controversial fiscal reform, Moulay Abdel Aziz entered into heavy debt with France. Meanwhile, the French military administration in Algeria gradually pushed back the frontier with Morocco, which was to lead to a long-drawn-out conflict. When Kaiser Wilhelm II of Germany arrived in Tangier in March 1905 to claim his share, the "Moroccan question" took on another dimension. The Conference of Algeciras of 1906, in which all the interested powers took part, forcibly opened Morocco to international trade, and assigned France and Spain as administrators.

In 1907, various incidents provided the French forces with the pretext to move into Oujda and Casablanca. In the same year, Abdel

Aziz was deposed by his brother Moulay Hafidh, who attempted to resist but was forced to yield. Numerous uprisings led the French to impose a protectorate, through the Treaty of Fès in 1912. Moulay Hafidh was then replaced by his half-brother, Moulay Youssef.

What was called "pacification" at the time continued until 1934: it took French forces 22 years to bring the whole country under control. In the Rif, a state of war persisted up until 1926. Abd el-Krim Khattabi, a brilliant strategist and organizer, defeated the Spanish at Anoual in 1921, proclaimed a republic in 1922, and long held out against the forces of the Spanish and French colonial powers, led by Francisco Franco and Philippe Pétain respectively. He left the country and died in exile in Cairo in 1963.

Marshal Hubert Lyautey, an exceptional man who was made France's first resident-general in Morocco in 1912, played a decisive role in the imposition of French rule. He installed the capital in Rabat, and worked to promote the country's economic development, but firmly refused to consider assimilation, a process by which colonies were modelled on the mother country. The country's traditional infrastructure was left intact and town planners safeguarded the imperial cities.

On the death of Moulay Youssef in 1927, his third son, Sidi Mohammed ben

Abd el-Krim Khattabi, heroic leader of an ephemeral Rifian republic

TIMELINE

1912 Protectorate agreement is signed at the Treaty of Fès

Sultan Moulay Youssef

1921–26 Revolt in the Rif

1930 France imposes the Berber *dahir*

1910

1920

1930

1911 French troops enter Fès

1912–27 Reign of Moulay Youssef, who deposed his half-brother

Marshal Pétain received by Marshal Lyautey in Rabat in 1925

1927 Start of the reign of the sultan Mohammed ben Youssef, the future Mohammed V

Youssef, who was then 18, succeeded him, taking the name Mohammed V. He was to restore the country's independence.

THE FIGHT FOR ISTIQLAL

Morocco was divided into two zones: a French zone, covering the largest part of the country, and a Spanish zone, in the north and south. Tangier was an international free city

1930s building, Casablanca, dating from the Protectorate

The French Protectorate was both beneficial and detrimental to Morocco. The country's infrastructure was modernized, its mineral resources were exploited and the most fertile land turned over to agriculture. The population of Casablanca, the economic capital, doubled every ten years, and the city became a major port.

The administration of Lyautey's 13 successors, however, was increasingly direct, so that the role of the local *makhzen* became redundant. Colonial ideology triumphed in the 1930s. When France imposed a Berber *dahir*, giving Berber areas a separate legal system, the effect was to divide the country.

World War II justified the Moroccan people's desire for freedom. In 1942, the Allies arrived in Morocco and President Roosevelt pledged the sultan his support. Showing a progressively higher profile, Mohammed V drew a following of young nationalists, who set up the Istiqlal (Independence) Party. The Manifesto of Independence called on the sultan to head a movement for independence, a challenge that he formally accepted in a speech in Tangier in 1947. The power struggle with Paris lasted almost a decade. In 1951, the French authorities supported the rebellion of El-Glaoui, the pasha of Marrakech *(see p253)*. The sultan refused to abdicate but the French deposed him in 1953, replacing him with the elderly Ben Arafa. The royal family were forced into exile but the fight for independence gained momentum.

International opinion no longer supported the colonial powers, and the United Nations took over the Moroccan question. After negotiations with France, the deposed sultan made his triumphant return from exile as King Mohammed V, with Hassan, the heir apparent, at his side. The Protectorate ended in 1956, and in 1958 Tangier and the Spanish enclave of Tarfaya were restored to the kingdom. Independence had been won, although national unity was still to be achieved.

Mohammed V and his son, the future king, Hassan II, on their return from exile in 1955

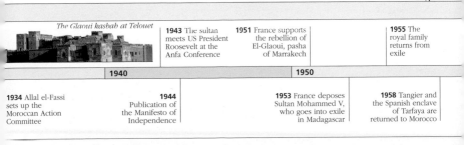

The Glaoui kasbah at Telouet

	1943 The sultan meets US President Roosevelt at the Anfa Conference	1951 France supports the rebellion of El-Glaoui, pasha of Marrakech		1955 The royal family returns from exile
1940			**1950**	
1934 Allal el-Fassi sets up the Moroccan Action Committee	1944 Publication of the Manifesto of Independence		1953 France deposes Sultan Mohammed V, who goes into exile in Madagascar	1958 Tangier and the Spanish enclave of Tarfaya are returned to Morocco

The future Hassan II, in 1957, with Allal el-Fassi, the founder of Istiqlal, on his right and Medhi Ben Barka, leader of UNFP, on his left

POLITICAL AND SOCIAL CHANGE IN CONTEMPORARY MOROCCO

In the rest of the Arab world monarchies were replaced by authoritarian republican regimes (as in Iraq, Egypt, Yemen and Tunisia). In Morocco, however, Mohammed V's patriotic sentiment united the country behind a monarchy that has long-established roots and that ensures its unity and stability. A pious and outward-looking Muslim, the king encouraged the emancipation of women, the education of his people, and agrarian reform. During this period, Morocco, unlike neighbouring countries, embraced political pluralism (albeit in a tightly controlled form) and relative economic liberalism, choices that were decisive for its future. In 1958, having broken away from Istiqlal, the progressive wing of the nationalist movement founded a left-wing party – the Union Nationale des Forces Populaires, the future USFP – with Abderrahim Bouabid and Mehdi Ben Barka.

The king also had to contend with the impatience of nationalist sentiment, which believed that the country should engage in armed conflict to regain all Saharan territory and that it should give military aid to Algeria, which was still fighting its war for independence.

Mohammed V died suddenly, after an operation, in 1961. His eldest son, Moulay Hassan, who had been closely associated with power for many years, succeeded him as Hassan II. A skilled politician, he was to witness political as well as social change in his country, in the course of a reign lasting 38 years. It was, however, often marked by unrest and mixed success.

THE NATIONAL QUESTION

The question of the reintegration of Moroccan territory is a long-standing theme in contemporary Moroccan politics. At issue is the western Sahara, an area of 266,000 sq km (102,700 sq miles), from which Spain withdrew in 1975. In November that year Hassan II launched a Green March to win back this mineral-rich territory. The Polisario Front, an armed movement supported by Algeria, meanwhile fought for the territory's independence. Open conflict raged until 1988, when both sides accepted a plan drawn up by the United Nations, with consideration for the area's Sahraoui population. Since 1991, a referendum on the issue has been continually postponed because of lack of agreement on voters' lists.

Green March, keeping the national question at the top of Morocco's political agenda

TIMELINE

1956 The Protectorate formally ends

1963 Outbreak of war with Algeria

1965 Mehdi Ben Barka is murdered in Paris, where he lived in exile after being accused of plotting against the king

1975 Start of the Green March

1981 (Jun) Unrest in Casablanca

1950   1960   1970   1980

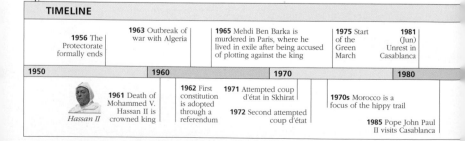

Hassan II

1961 Death of Mohammed V. Hassan II is crowned king

1962 First constitution is adopted through a referendum

1971 Attempted coup d'état in Skhirat

1972 Second attempted coup d'état

1970s Morocco is a focus of the hippy trail

1985 Pope John Paul II visits Casablanca

The ceremony marking Throne Day in Marrakech, during the reign of Hassan II

On the international front, Hassan II steered Morocco in the direction of the Western world and even spoke of the country joining the European Union. He pursued policies that were distinctive in the Muslim world, leading the Al Qods Committee in Jerusalem and encouraging reconciliation between Israel and the Palestinians. By contrast, deep-seated caution marked his relations with neighbouring Algeria, which had gained independence in 1962. Disputes over the border between the two countries led to war in 1963. Algiers also supported the Polisario Front, and the border was closed on several occasions.

On the domestic front, supported by General Oufkir, Dlimi then Driss Basri, Hassan II alternated liberalizing policies with repression. The first constitution, drawn up in 1962 and followed by parliamentary elections in 1963, failed to unify the country. A new constitution was drawn up in 1970. Social unrest caused by poverty marked the following years, as public life returned to normal. When a new constitution was drawn up in 1996, the time had come for a less autocratic style of government.

After parliamentary elections in 1997, Hassan II opened the doors to political change. Abderrahmane Youssoufi, a political opponent, was instructed to form a broad coalition government around the Socialist Union, and wisely brought in thoroughgoing reforms to modernize the country.

The king died in 1999, and was succeeded by his eldest son, Mohammed VI. He has addressed human rights issues, has allowed remaining exiles to return and takes a close interest in the northern provinces that were neglected by his father. Fundamental problems such as underdevelopment, illiteracy and poverty still remain. After the terrorist bombs of 2003, the king proclaimed "the end of the era of indulgence", and limited human rights and freedom of the press. In 2011 young Moroccans began demonstrating for democracy and social change; this became known as the 20th February Movement. The king and his government created a new constitution and held a referendum on 1 July 2011. Ninety-eight per cent of voters agreed to the new constitution.

Mohammed VI, who came to the throne in 1999, is seen as being close to his people

	Hassan II attends the first Maghrebi Union Treaty		**2003** Birth of Prince Moulay Hassan	**2007** Birth of Princess Lalla Khadija	**2011** Months of demonstrations begin on 20th February in Rabat, with thousands of Moroccans calling for constitutional reform
	1994 (Feb) Islamic riots on the campus in Fès				
1990		**2000**		**2010**	**2020**
1988 First Maghrebi Union Treaty in Algiers	**1991** (6 Sep) Ceasefire agreed with the Polisario Front	**1999** Death of King Hassan II. His son Mohammed VI is enthroned	**2004** Morocco's parliament approves a free-trade agreement with the US	**2011** (1 Jul) A referendum is held for constitutional reforms. Parlimentary elections held in November	
	1998 Abderrahmane Youssoufi forms a new government				

MOROCCO REGION BY REGION

MOROCCO AT A GLANCE 62–63

RABAT 64–81

NORTHERN ATLANTIC COAST 82–93

CASABLANCA 94–107

SOUTHERN ATLANTIC COAST 108–127

TANGIER 128–141

MEDITERRANEAN COAST & THE RIF 142–161

FÈS 162–183

MEKNÈS & VOLUBILIS 184–205

MIDDLE ATLAS 206–221

MARRAKECH 222–243

HIGH ATLAS 244–259

OUARZAZATE & THE SOUTHERN OASES 260–281

SOUTHERN MOROCCO & WESTERN SAHARA 282–295

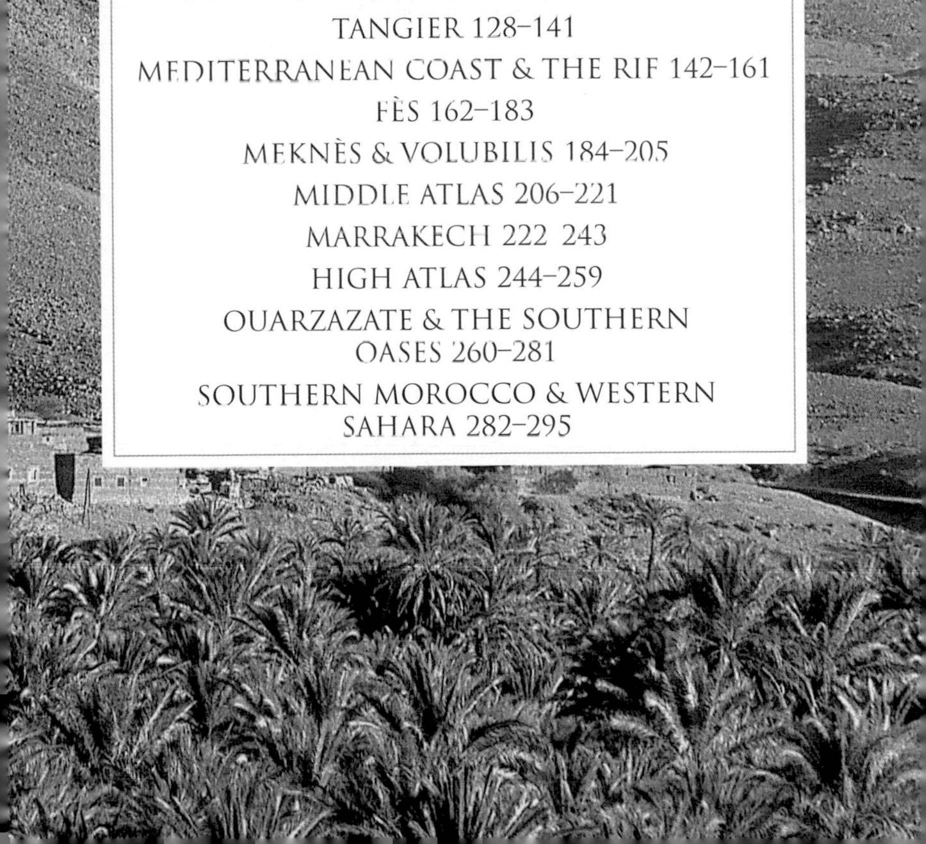

Morocco at a Glance

From the Mediterranean coast to the High Atlas, beyond which the country stretches out into the boundless expanses of the Sahara Desert, Morocco forms a gigantic semicircle facing onto the Atlantic. Its major towns and cities, the focus of the country's economic and political activity, are located along the Atlantic seaboard from Tangier to Agadir and from Fès to Rabat. Topography, climate and history have together created a multifaceted country which offers everything from beaches, high mountain valleys and fertile agricultural land with almond and peach trees to majestic mountains and an extensive desert dotted with oases and palm groves. In secret medinas, in labyrinthine souks, or at the foot of Almohad and Merinid minarets, traders and craftsmen can be seen continuing ancient artistic traditions.

Casablanca *is renowned for its Art Deco architecture. It also boasts the richly decorated Hassan II Mosque (see pp102–3).*

Essaouira, *a strikingly white town that appears to rise up out of the water, is also a surfer's dream location (see pp120–25).*

SOUTHERN ATLANTIC COAST

SOUTHERN MOROCCO & WESTERN SAHARA

Agadir *is the place to go for sun, sand and relaxation. An attractive medina has been built in the south of the town (see pp286–7).*

The South *is a varied region of deserts, oases, mountains and coastline. The architecture and the colours of the houses in Tafraoute, in the Anti-Atlas, are highly distinctive (see p293).*

◁ **Landscape of the Draa Valley**

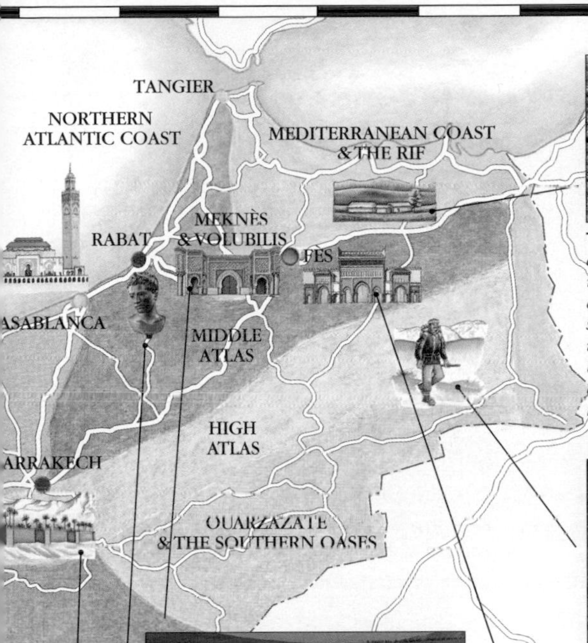

TANGIER

NORTHERN
ATLANTIC COAST

MEDITERRANEAN COAST
& THE RIF

MEKNÈS
& VOLUBILIS

RABAT

FÈS

ASABLANCA

MIDDLE
ATLAS

HIGH
ATLAS

ARRAKECH

OUARZAZATE
& THE SOUTHERN OASES

The Rif, *between Chefchaouen
and Oujda, is a region that
invites exploration. Berbers
dressed in striped foutas,
stunningly beautiful beaches,
valleys carpeted with almond
blossom in spring (as above)
are among the attractions of
this region* (see pp142–61).

**The breathtaking landscape
of the High Atlas**, *here near
Wadi Goum, is home to Berber
tribespeople, and is ideal for
hiking* (see p259).

Volubilis, *the Roman city* (see pp202–5),
*lies a short distance from Meknès, one
of Morocco's imperial cities.*

Rabat *is known for
the picturesque
Oudaïa Kasbah
and the Mausoleum
of Mohammed V,
whose mihrab and
minbar are seen
here* (see pp74–5).

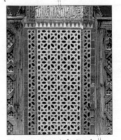

Fès, *an imperial city, has
many splendid sights,
including the zellij tilework
of the Karaouiyine Mosque*
(see pp176–7).

Marrakech, *a
city enclosed
within its ochre
ramparts, stands
in the shadow of
the snowy Atlas*
(see p227).

| 0 km | 100 |
| 0 miles | 100 |

RABAT

acing onto the Atlantic Ocean, Rabat is an attractive city of domes and minarets, sweeping terraces, wide avenues and green spaces. It is markedly more pleasant than some other Moroccan cities and is also undergoing fundamental change. Facing Salé, its ancient rival, across Wadi Bou Regreg, Rabat is the political, administrative and financial capital of Morocco, the country's main university town and its second-largest metropolis after Casablanca.

Archaeological excavations of the Merinid necropolis at Chellah *(see pp80–81)* have shown that this area was occupied by the Romans, and even earlier too. Much later, around 1150, Abd el-Moumen, the first ruler of the Almohad dynasty, chose to establish a permanent camp here and ordered a small imperial residence to be built on the site of a for-mer *ribat* (fortified monastery).

The caliph Yacoub el-Mansour then embarked on the construction of a great and splendid city that was to be known as Ribat el-Fath (Camp of Victory), in celebration of his victory over Alfonso VIII of Castile at the Battle of Alarcos in 1195. On the death of the caliph in 1199, work on this ambitious project ceased: although the city gates and walls had been completed, the Hassan Mosque and its minaret *(see p49)* were unfinished. The Almohads' defeat at the Battle of Las Navas de Tolosa in 1212 weakened their power and led to the city's decline.

In 1610, Philip III of Spain expelled from his kingdom the remaining Moors, who fled to the cities of the Maghreb. Among them were a large colony of emigrants from Andalusia who settled in Rabat.

Rabat became the capital of a minor and relatively autonomous coastal republic. Funds brought by the Andalusian refugees were put to equipping a flotilla of privateers that preyed on European shipping. The "Republic of Bou Regreg", as it was known, was then annexed to the she rif's kingdom in 1666, although piracy was not brought to an end until the mid-19th century.

In 1912 Marshal Lyautey *(see p56)* made Rabat the political and administrative capital of Morocco. Its population now exceeds 1.5 million.

The majestic Mausoleum of Mohammed V

◁ The Gate of the Ambassadors at the Dar el-Makhzen (Royal Palace) in Rabat

Exploring Rabat

Rabat has four main areas of interest. In the north is the picturesque Oudaïa Kasbah, which is partly enclosed by ramparts dating from the Almohad period. The medina, which contains the city's souks, is bounded to the west by Almohad ramparts and to the south by the 17th-century Andalusian Wall, which runs parallel to Boulevard Hassan II. Avenue Mohammed V is the new town's busy central north–south axis, with residential blocks dating from the Protectorate (1912–56). In the northeast stands the Hassan Tower and Mausoleum of Mohammed V. In the Merinid necropolis at Chellah, to the south, are vestiges of the Roman town of Sala.

The Sliman Mosque and the medina in Rabat

SIGHTS AT A GLANCE

Districts, Streets & Squares
City Walls ❶
Place Souk el-Ghezel and Rue Hadj Daoui ❹
Rue des Consuls ❺
Rue Souïka ❼
Rue Souk es-Sebat ❻
Ville Nouvelle ⓫

Museums
Musée Archéologique pp78–9 ⓬
Musée des Oudaïa (Museum of Moroccan Crafts) ❸

Historic Buildings
Andalusian Wall ❽
Bab er-Rouah ⓭
Bab Oudaïa ❷
Chellah Necropolis ⓯
Dar el-Makhzen ⓮
Hassan Tower ❾
Mausoleum of Mohammed V pp74–5 ❿

The Andalusian Wall surrounding the medina

SEE ALSO

- **Where to Stay** pp302–3

- **Where to Eat** pp328–9

GETTING AROUND

The main sights of Rabat are easily reachable on foot. The city's many one-way streets, however, make driving difficult. It is best to park on Boulevard Hassan II, since parking spaces are hard to find in the city centre. Although Rabat is served by a bus and tram network, it is often more practical to travel around the city in a *petit taxi*, which is only a little more expensive.

KEY

■	Street-by-Street map *pp68–9*
	Medina
—	City walls
🚇	Railway station
🚌	Bus station
⛴	Port
P	Parking
i	Tourist information
⊠	Post office
✝	Church
✡	Synagogue
C	Mosque
🕌	Muslim cemetery

0 m	400
0 yards	400

Street-by-Street: the Oudaïa Kasbah

Bab Oudaïa

The kasbah takes its name from the Oudaïas, an Arab tribe with a warrior past that was settled here by Moulay Ismaïl (1672–1727) to protect the city from the threat of rebel tribes. Part of the city walls that surround this "fortress", built on the top of a cliff, and Bab Oudaïa, the gate that pierces it, date from the Almohad period (1147–1248). On Rue Jamaa, the main thoroughfare of this picturesque district, stands the El-Atika Mosque, built in the 12th century and the oldest mosque in Rabat.

★ **Bab Oudaïa**
An archetypal example of Almohad military architecture, this monumental gate was built by Yacoub el-Mansour in the 12th century. ❷

City Walls
The western ramparts were built by Yacoub el-Mansour in 1195, after his victory over Alfonso III. ❶

El-Alou cemetery

★ **Musée des Oudaïa**
Since 1915 the historic palace of Moulay Ismaïl (see pp54–5) has housed a museum with a rich collection of Moroccan folk art and crafts. ❸

RUE

RUE

RUE — BAZZO

★ **Andalusian Garden**
This pleasant garden, laid out in the Moorish style at the beginning of the 20th century, features a traditional Arabic noria (waterwheel for irrigation).

Café Maure
This is where Rabatis come to relax and pass the time. From here there are views of Salé's medina, of the Bou Regreg and of the Atlantic Ocean. A doorway leads through to the Andalusian Garden.

For hotels and restaurants in this region see pp302–3 and pp328–9

Narrow Kasbah Street
Although some elements date back to the 12th century, the houses in the kasbah, lime-washed in blue or white, were built in the late 17th to early 18th centuries, at the time of the first Alaouite rulers.

VISITORS' CHECKLIST

Northern district. *Accessible via Place du Souk el-Ghezel and Bab Oudaïa or Place de l'Ancien-Sémaphore.*
Andalusian Garden
accessible from the Café Maure. The narrow streets of the kasbah are best explored on foot.

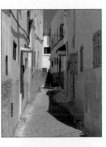

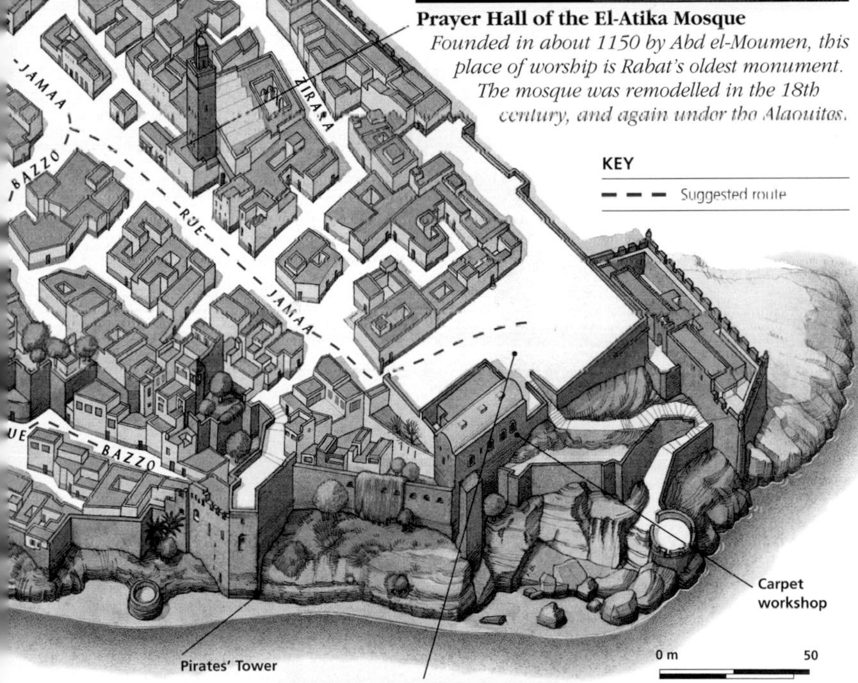

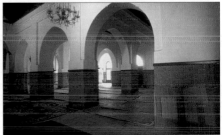

Prayer Hall of the El-Atika Mosque
Founded in about 1150 by Abd el-Moumen, this place of worship is Rabat's oldest monument. The mosque was remodelled in the 18th century, and again under the Alaouites.

Fountain
Almohad walls
RUE
ZIRARA
JAMAA
BAZZO
RUE
JAMAA
RUE
BAZZO
Carpet workshop
Pirates' Tower
0 m
50
0 yards
50

KEY

- - - Suggested route

Platform of the Former Oudaïa Signal Station
Built in the 18th century by Sultan Sidi Mohammed ben Abdallah, this signal station defended the Bou Regreg estuary. The warehouse to its right contains a carpet workshop.

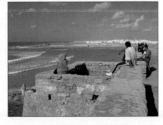

STAR SIGHTS

★ Andalusian Garden

★ Bab Oudaïa

★ Musée des Oudaïa

Walls of the Andalusian Garden, built in the reign of Moulay Rachid

City Walls ❶

In the north of the city. *Accessible via Place du Souk el-Ghezel and Place de l'Ancien Sémaphore.*

Separated from the medina by the Place du Souk el-Ghezel, the Oudaïa Kasbah is defended by thick ramparts. These were built mostly by the Almohads in the 12th century, and were restored and remodelled in the 17th and 18th centuries by the Moriscos *(see p68)* and the Alaouite kings.

Most of the Almohad walls facing onto the sea and running inland survive. The walls surrounding the Andalusian Garden date from the reign of Moulay Rachid (founder of the Alaouite dynasty). The Hornacheros (Andalusian emigrants) who occupied the kasbah and rebuffed attacks from both sea and land rebuilt the curtain wall in several places and constructed the Pirates' Tower, whose inner stairway leads down to the river. They also pierced the walls of the old Almohad towers with embrasures to hold cannons. A complex system of underground passages leading from within the kasbah to the exterior beyond the walls was also dug.

The city walls are built of rough-hewn stone covered with a thick coating of ochre plaster. They are set with imposing towers and bastions, which are more numerous along the stretch of the walls facing the sea and the river. Standing 8 to 10 m (26 to 33 ft) high, and having an average thickness of 2.50 m (8 ft), the walls are surmounted by a rampart walk bordered by a low parapet; part of the rampart walk survives.

This sturdy building and sophisticated military construction defended the pirates' nest and withstood almost all attacks from European forces.

Bab Oudaïa ❷

Oudaïa Kasbah. *The gate leads to the kasbah from Place du Souk el-Ghezel.*

Towering above the cliffs that line the Bou Regreg, and dominating Rabat's medina is Bab Oudaïa, which is the main entrance into the kasbah. This monumental city gate, built in dressed stone of red ochre, is considered to be one of the finest examples of Almohad architecture. But the particular design and conception of this gateway, built by Yacoub el-Mansour in 1195, make it more of a decorative feature than a piece of military defence work.

Stylized seashell on Bab Oudaïa

Flanked by two towers, it is crowned by a horseshoe arch. The inner and outer façades are decorated with rich ornamentation carved in relief into the stone, starting at the opening of the arch and continuing in several tiers as far up as the base of the parapet. Above the arch, two bands with interlacing lozenges are outlined with floral decoration. Both sides of the gate are crowned by a band of calligraphy.

As in all Moorish palaces, the gatehouse of the former Oudaïa Palace was also a defensive feature and a tribunal. Today, the gatehouse serves as an exhibition hall.

Musée des Oudaïa ❸

Oudaïa Kasbah. *Accessible via a gateway in the southwestern walls.* **Tel** *(0537) 73 15 37.* ☐ *9:30am–4:30pm Wed–Mon.* ⬤ *Tue and public holidays.*

In the 17th century, Moulay Ismaïl built a small palace within the kasbah. This became the residence of the first Alaouite sultans while they were based in Rabat, as an inscription on the wooden lintels of the central patio indicates: "Unfailing fortune and brilliant victory to our lord Smaïl, leader of the faithful." The palace was completely restored and slightly altered in 1917, during the Protectorate, and has undergone further phases of restoration, as well as a renovation since then.

The palace as it is today consists of a main building arranged around an arcaded courtyard. The four sides of the courtyard lead off into large rectangular rooms with marble floors and geometrically coffered ceilings. The surrounding buildings include a prayer room for private worship, a hammam (steam bath) and a tower. A beautiful garden laid out in the Andalusian style gives the palace the status of a princely residence.

The Musée des Oudaïa, laid out in a 17th-century palace

Since 1915, the palace has housed the Musée des Oudaïa. On display here are carpets and copperwork, astrolabes (for measuring the altitude of stars) dating from the 14th and 17th centuries, and collections of ceramics and of musical instruments. One room in the museum is laid out as a traditional Moroccan interior, with sofas covered in sumptuous gold-embroidered silk fabrics made in Fès. Another room is devoted to the traditional dress of the region between the Rif and the Sahara.

The museum also contains collections of jewellery, including Berber jewellery, antique pottery, and fine collections of woodcarving and of funerary art.

A small shop in the Souk el-Ghezel district of Rabat

Place Souk el-Ghezel and Rue Hadj Daoui ④

A convenient place to start exploring Rabat's medina is the Place Souk el-Ghezel, (Wool Market Square), so named because of the market that once took place here. This was also the place where Christian prisoners were once sold as slaves. Today, it is the fine carpets made in the city that are auctioned here every Thursday morning.

Rue Hadj Daoui, just southwest of Place Souk el-Ghezel, leads into the residential area of the medina, where the streets are quieter and where houses built by the Moriscos are still visible.

The unmistakable mark that the Moriscos made on the architecture of Rabat can be seen in certain styles of building: for example, those involving the use of

semicircular arches and ornamental motifs such as the pilasters consisting of vertically arranged mouldings that decorate the upper parts of doors. The smaller houses are of simple design, most of them built of stone rendered with limewashed plaster. Most of the richer houses tucked away in the different quarters of Rabat are built around a central courtyard, like those in other Moroccan medinas, and have a refined elegance.

Walking west along Rue Hadj Daoui leads to Dar el-Mrini, a fine private house built in 1920 and today has been transformed into an exhibition and conference centre.

Rue des Consuls ⑤

Eastern part of the medina.

Running through the medina, Rue des Consuls begins at the Wool Market in the north and leads down towards the Andalusian Wall in the south. Up to the time of the Protectorate, this street was where all foreign consuls in Rabat were obliged to live. Covered with rushes and a

Shops selling leather goods, in the eastern part of the medina

glass roof, the street is lined with the shops of craftsmen and traders, making it the most lively quarter in the medina. The two former *fondouks* at No. 109 and No. 137 are now the work-shops of leatherworkers and woodworkers.

South of Rue Souk es-Sebat *(see p 76)* the street changes name to Rue Ouqqasa, which borders the mellah (Jewish quarter). In Rue Tariq el-Marsa is the Ensemble Artisanal, selling Moroccan crafts, and, a little further on, is a restored 18th-century naval depot.

Rue des Consuls, one of the lively thoroughfares in the medina

▷ **Courtyard of the mosque of the Mausoleum of Mohammed V**

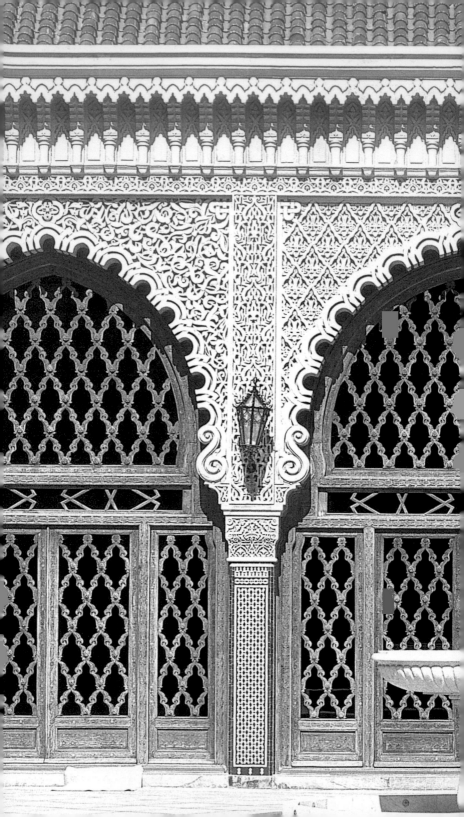

Mausoleum of Mohammed V ⑩

Copper censer

Raised in memory of Mohammed V, the father of Moroccan independence, this majestic building was commissioned by his son, Hassan II. It was designed by the Vietnamese architect Vo Toan and built with the help of 400 Moroccan craftsmen. The group of buildings that make up the mausoleum of Mohammed V include a mosque and a museum devoted to the history of the Alaouite dynasty. The mausoleum itself, in white Italian marble, stands on a platform 3.5 m (11.5 ft) high. Entry is through a wrought-iron door that opens onto a stairway leading to the dome, beneath which lies the sarcophagus of Mohammed V.

★ **Dome with *Muqarnas***
This twelve-sided dome, with painted mahogany muqarnas *(stalactites), crowns the burial chamber.*

★ **Sarcophagus**
Carved from a single block of marble, the sarcophagus rests on a slab of granite, facing a qibla (symbolizing Mecca).

Guard
The traditional attire of the royal guard is white in summer and red in winter (see p75).

Fountain
Embellished with polychrome zellij *tilework and framed by a horseshoe arch of Salé sandstone, this fountain is in the Moorish style.*

Burial vault
containing the body
of Mohammed V.

Stained-Glass Windows
The stained-glass windows in the dome were made in France, in the workshops of the factory at St-Gobain.

VISITORS' CHECKLIST

Boulevard El-Alaouiyine.
⬜ 8:30am–6pm daily
(also to non-Muslims).

Brass spheres symbolize a holy or religious building.

Calligraphy
This marble frieze features a song of holy praise carved in Maghrebi script.

Polychrome *zellij* tilework

Doorways lead to the balcony from which the sarcophagus can be seen from above.

Esplanade

Doorways
The doorways on the four sides of the mausoleum are fronted by slender columns of Carrara marble.

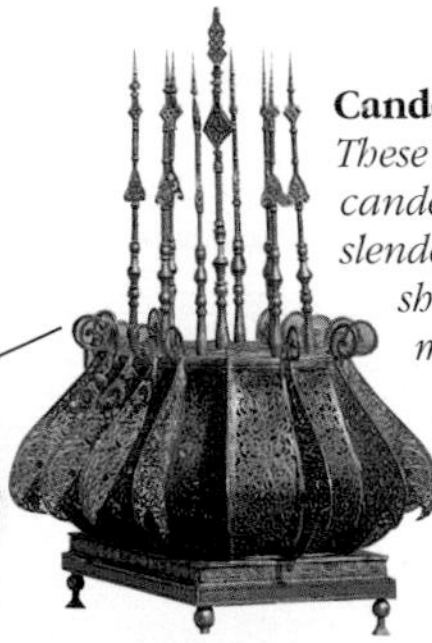

Candelabra
These large candelabra, with slender vertical shafts, are made of pierced and engraved copper.

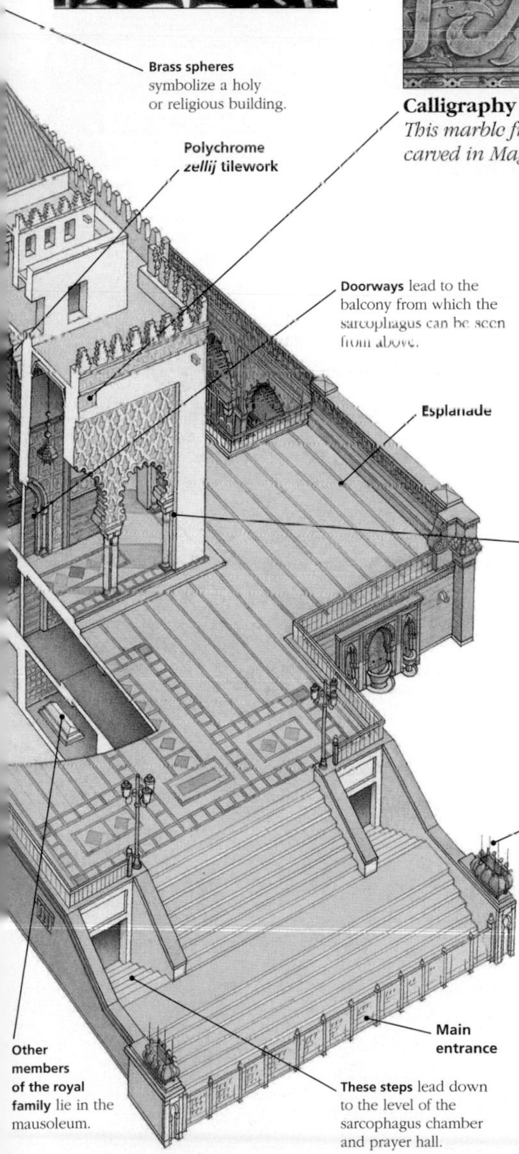

Other members of the royal family lie in the mausoleum.

Main entrance

These steps lead down to the level of the sarcophagus chamber and prayer hall.

STAR FEATURES

★ Dome with *Muqarnas*

★ Sarcophagus

Merinid fountain in the Great Mosque district

Rue Souk es-Sebat
6

In the medina.

This thoroughfare, which begins at the Great Mosque and ends at Bab el-Bhar (Gate of the Sea) crosses the Rue des Consuls. Covered by a rush trellis, this lively street is filled with the shops of leatherworkers, jewellers and fabric merchants and of traders in all sorts of other goods.

Rue Souïka **7**

In the medina.
Great Mosque ⬤ to non-Muslims.

Running southwest from Rue du Souk es-Sebat, Rue Souïka (Little Souk Street) is the main artery through the medina and also its most lively thoroughfare. Lined with all manner of small shops selling clothes, shoes, food, radios and cassettes, with restaurants and with spice merchants, the street throngs with people several times a day.

At the intersection with Rue de Bab Chellah stands the Great Mosque, built probably

between the 13th and the 16th centuries and remodelled and restored on several occasions during the Alaouite period. The mosque's most prominent feature is the minaret, rising to a height of 33 m (109 ft) and completed in 1939. It is built of ashlars (blocks of hewn stone), decorated with dressed stone, and pierced with openings in the shape of lobed or intersecting arches.

Opposite the mosque is a fountain with a pediment of intersecting arches, built in the 14th century, during the reign of the Merinid sultan Abou Fares Abdelaziz. Further along the street, on the corner of Rue Sidi Fatah, is the Moulay Sliman Mosque, or Jamaa el-Souika. It was built in about 1812 on the orders of Moulay Sliman, on the site of an earlier place of worship.

Andalusian Wall **8**

Between Bab el-Had and Place Sidi Makhlouf.

In the 17th century, the Moriscos – Muslim refugees from Andalusia – found the medina undefended and so encircled it with a defensive wall. Named after its builders, the Andalusian Wall stands about 5 m (16 ft) high and runs in a straight line for more than 1,400 m (4,595 ft) from Bab el-Had (Sunday Gate) in the west to the *borj* (small fort) of Sidi Makhlouf in the east. Boulevard Hassan II runs parallel to it. During the Protectorate, a stretch of the walls about 100 m (328 ft) long, and including Bab

el-Tben, was destroyed to allow easier access to a market.

The walls are set with towers placed at intervals of some 35 m (115 ft) and are topped by a rampart walk. This is protected by a parapet that the Andalusians pierced with numerous narrow slits known as loopholes.

To the east of the walls they built the Bastion Sidi Makhlouf, a small, irregular fort which consists of a platform resting on solid foundations, with a tower close by. They also built embrasures over two of the Almohad gates, Bab el-Alou and Bab el-Had.

Bab el-Had was once the main gateway into the medina. Dating from the Almohad period (1147–1248), it was rebuilt by Moulay Sliman in 1814. On the side facing Boulevard Misr, one of gate's two pentagonal towers stands close to the Almohad walls, which probably date from 1197.

Moulay Sliman Mosque

Bab el-Had contains several small chambers which were intended to accommodate the soldiers who were in charge of the guard, the armouries and the billetting of the troops.

Hassan Tower **9**

Rue de la Tour Hassan.
⬤ to the public.

For more than eight centuries, the Hassan Tower has stood on the hill overlooking Wadi Bou Regreg. Best seen as one approaches Rabat by the bridge from Salé, it is one of the city's most prestigious monuments and a great emblem of Rabat.

It is the unfinished minaret of the Hassan Mosque, built by Yacoub el-Mansour in about 1196. The construction of this gigantic mosque, of dimensions quite out of proportion to the population of Rabat at the time, suggests that the Almohad ruler intended to make Rabat

Bab el-Had, the "Sunday Gate", built in the 17th century

For hotels and restaurants in this region see pp302–3 and pp328–9

The Hassan Tower and remains of the Hassan Mosque's prayer hall

his new imperial capital. An alternative interpretation is that the Almohads were attempting to rival the magnificent Great Mosque of Córdoba, the former capital of the Islamic kingdom in the West *(see pp48–9)*. Either way, after the death of Yacoub el-Mansour in 1199, the unfinished mosque fell into disrepair. All but the mosque's minaret was destroyed by an earthquake in 1755.

The Hassan Mosque was built to a huge rectangular plan 183 m (600 ft) by 139 m (456 ft); the Great Mosque of Córdoba was just 175 m (574 ft) by 128 m (420 ft). It was the largest religious building in the Muslim West, in size inferior only to the mosque of Samarra in Iraq. A great courtyard lay at the foot of the tower, while the huge columned prayer hall was divided into 21 avenues separated by lines of gigantic columns crowned with capitals. Remains of these imposing stone columns survive and still convey an impression of infinite grandeur.

The minaret, a square-sided tower about 16 m (52 ft) wide and 44 m (144 ft) high, was to have surpassed the height of the Koutoubia Mosque *(see pp236–7)* and the Giralda in Seville *(see pp48–9)*, but it was never completed. According to Almohad custom, it would have reached 80 m (262 ft), including the lantern. Even unfinished it seems huge. Each of its four sides is decorated with blind lobed

arches. On the topmost level of the minaret extended interlacing arches form a *sebkha* motif (lozenge-shaped blind fretwork) as on the Giralda of Seville. The interior is divided into six levels, each of which consists of a domed room. The levels are linked and accessed by a continuous ramp.

It was from the Hassan Tower that Mohammed V conducted the first Friday prayers after independence was declared.

Mausoleum of Mohammed V ⑩

See pp74–5

Ville Nouvelle ⑪

During the 44 years of the Protectorate, Marshal Lyautey and the architects Prost and Ecochard built a new town in the empty part of the extensive area enclosed by the Almohad walls.

Laying out wide boulevards and green spaces, they created a relatively pleasant town. Avenue Mohammed V, the main avenue, runs from the medina to the El-Souna Mosque, or Great Mosque, which was built by Sidi Mohammed in the 18th century. The avenue is lined with residential blocks in the Hispano-Maghrebi style. They were built by the administration of the Protectorate, as were the Bank of Morocco, the post office, the parliament building and the railway station. The Bank of Morocco also houses the **Musée de la Monnaie** (Coin Museum).

Rue Abou Inan leads to the **Cathédrale Saint-Pierre**, a pure white building dating from the 1930s.

🏛 **Musée de la Monnaie**
Bank of Morocco, Rue du Caire.
Tel (0537) 26 90 96. ⬜ 9am–5:30pm Tue–Fri, 9am–noon Sat, 9am–1pm Sun. ⬤ Mon.

🔒 **Cathédrale Saint-Pierre**
Place du Golan. *Tel* (0537) 72 23 01. ⬜ 3–6pm Sat, 9am–1pm Sun.

The dazzling white Cathédrale Saint-Pierre, built in the 1930s

Musée Archéologique ⑫

The most extensive collection of archaeological artifacts in the country is housed in the Musée Archéologique. The museum building was constructed in the 1930s, to house the Antiquities Services. The initial prehistoric and pre-Islamic collections, consisting of objects discovered by archaeologists working in Volubilis, Banasa and Thamusida, were put on public display for the first time in 1930–32. The addition of further material from Volubilis in 1957 considerably enlarged the museum's collections, raising it to the status of a national museum. The displays present the collections according to theme. These range from the prehistoric period up to the findings of recent archaeological excavations.

Roman pitcher of the 1st to 2nd centuries, with strainer and spout

The House of the Ephebe, Volubilis *(see pp204–5)*

Acheulian culture, known at sites in Sidi Abderrahmane and Daya el-Hamra; the Mousterian culture; and, finally, the Aterian culture of around 40,000–20,000 BC. The latter, specific to North Africa, is illustrated by the only human remains to have been discovered at Dar al-Soltane and el-Harhoura.

SALA-CHELLAH AND ISLAMIC ARCHAEOLOGY

The site of **Sala-Chellah** *(see pp80–81)* is that of a Mauretanian and Roman town which flourished up to the 4th century AD and which in the 13th century became a royal necropolis under the Merinids.

Head of a Berber youth

The collection of implements and other objects (including pottery and oil lamps) displayed on the upper floor of the museum traces the history of the site. Particularly striking exhibits include the bronze bust of Juba II (52 BC–AD 23) which was discovered in Volubilis and probably came from Egypt. An Early Christian altar, a Byzantine censer and an ivory figure of the Good Shepherd show the presence of Christianity in Morocco from the 3rd to the 8th centuries.

The section on Islamic archaeology highlights the principal sites that have been

TEMPORARY EXHIBITIONS

The space on the ground floor reserved for temporary exhibitions illustrates the results of archaeological investigations in Morocco, using photographs, graphics, models, sculpture and various other objects.

A map of Morocco in the lobby shows the various archaeological sites that have been discovered to date, and the methods used to excavate them are explained. The reconstruction of a mosaic from Volubilis is laid out on the floor of the room opposite. The marble statue in the centre of the room, dating from AD 25–40, is that of **Ptolemy**, king of Mauretania Tingitana and the son and successor of Juba

Roman bone and ivory carving

II and Cleopatra Selene, who was assassinated by the Roman emperor Caligula.

PREHISTORIC CULTURES

Also on the ground floor is a collection of stone artifacts relating to the earliest cultures and civilizations. Exhibits include altars and stelae carved with inscriptions, sarcophagi, stone arrowheads, pebble tools, pottery, polished stones, axes and swords, fragments of tombs and mouldings, as well as rock carvings.

Among the cultures highlighted here are the Pebble Culture, known from sites at Arbaoua, Douar Doum and Casablanca; the excavated. The displays of objects that have been unearthed include coins, pottery made in Sijilmassa and other ceramics, notably a 14th-century dish from Belyouneck, as well as fragments of carved plaster and sugar-loaf moulds from Chichaoua.

PRE-ISLAMIC CIVILIZATIONS

Artifacts uncovered during excavations at Volubilis, Banasa, Thamusida, Sala and Mogador are arranged by theme, illustrating in an informative fashion the most salient aspects of both pre-Roman Morocco (Mauretanian civilization) and Roman Morocco (Mauretania Tingitana). A range of objects show the extent of trade relations between Morocco and the Mediterranean world, particularly Carthage; and public and private life is illustrated through everyday objects, including the taps that were used in public baths, fragments of terracotta piping, and cooking utensils such as plates, dishes, glasses and knives. A section on the Roman army includes a military diploma from Banasa, certificates of good conduct

Head of Oceanus (1st century BC)

engraved on bronze plaques and military decorations.

The collection of white marble sculpture includes the *Head of a Berber Youth* from Volubilis carved during the reign of Augustus, a *Sphinx* from a votive throne, and a *Sleeping Silenus* from Volubilis. There are also figures of Roman gods such as Venus, Bacchus and Mars, and of Egyptian deities such as Isis and Anubis.

A particularly impressive part of the museum's displays is the collection of antique bronzes which come mainly from Volubilis and which demonstrate the wealth enjoyed by Morocco's Roman towns. A well-preserved bust of *Cato the Younger*, this 1st-century sculpture discovered in the House of Venus was imported into Morocco.

Ephebe Crowned with Ivy is, without a doubt, the star piece in the collection. The naked *ephebe* (young soldier in training) wears a crown of delicate ivy and is depicted in a standing position. The stance suggests that in his left hand he held a torch; this type of representation, known as a "lampadophore", together with the classicism of the statue, are typical of sculpture of the 1st century. The *Dog of Volubilis*, found on the site in 1916 in the

VISITORS' CHECKLIST

23 Rue el-Brihi (behind the Grand Mosque, opposite the Chellah hotel). **Tel** *(0537) 70 19 19.* ☐ *9am–5pm Wed–Mon (last admission 45 mins before closing).* ● *Tue, public hols.* ▨

vicinity of the triumphal arch, dates from the reign of Hadrian (early 2nd century) and was also made outside Morocco. The position of the dog, which is clearly designed to be accompanied by a human figure (undoubtedly Diana), suggests that it was made to decorate a fountain in public baths. The *Lustral Ephebe*, also discovered in Volubilis in 1929, brings to mind the *Lustral Dionysus* of Praxiteles, preserved in a museum in Dresden, in Germany, and known through numerous copies. Finally, the bust of Juba II which dates from 25 BC was probably imported from Egypt.

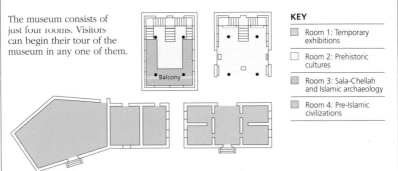

Roman votive stele from Volubilis, 1st–2nd century AD

GALLERY GUIDE

The museum consists of just four rooms. Visitors can begin their tour of the museum in any one of them.

Balcony

KEY

▧ Room 1: Temporary exhibitions

☐ Room 2: Prehistoric cultures

▨ Room 3: Sala-Chellah and Islamic archaeology

▥ Room 4: Pre-Islamic civilizations

Bab er-Rouah ⓭

Place an-Nasr. **Gallery** ☐ *daily during exhibitions.*

A sturdy and imposing Almohad gateway, Bab el-Rouah, the Gate of the Winds, dates from the same period as Bab Oudaïa *(see p68)*.

The entrance is decorated with the outline of two horseshoe arches carved into the stone and surrounded by a band of Kufic calligraphy.

The interior of the gate contains four rooms with elegant domes. These rooms are now used for exhibitions.

Bab el-Rouah, a fine Almohad gate with arches set into the stonework

Dar el-Makhzen ⓮

In the northwest of the city. ☐ *to the public. The exterior of the palace complex is of interest in its own right. The méchouar (assembly place) and the gardens are open to the public.*

An extensive complex enclosed within its own walls, the Dar el-Makhzen (royal palace) is inhabited by about 2,000 people. Built on the site of an 18th-century royal residence, the current palace was completed in 1864, but was constantly enlarged thereafter; today, it even includes a racecourse.

The palace now houses the offices of the Moroccan government, the Supreme Court, the prime minister's offices, the ministry of the Habous (responsible for religious organizations), and the El-Fas Mosque. The *méchouar*, a place of public assembly, is the venue for major gatherings, including the *bayaa*, a ceremony at which senior government ministers swear

Rabat's Dar el-Makhzen (royal palace), where 2,000 people live and work

their allegiance to the king. Traditionally, the king would reside in the former harem though Mohammed VI stays in his own private residence.

Besides private buildings, the palace also includes an extensive garden, immaculately kept and planted with various species of trees and with flowers in formal beds.

Chellah Necropolis ⓯

In the southeast of the city.
☐ *8:30am–6pm daily. Access via Bab Zaer but best reached by taxi.* 🖼

Access to the Chellah Necropolis is via Bab Zaer. This gate, named after a local tribe, was the only one on the southern side of the ramparts built by Yacoub el-Mansour. The necropolis is nearby.

Detail of the Gate of Ambassadors at the Royal Palace

The entrance to the necropolis itself is marked by an imposing Almohad gate with a horseshoe arch flanked by two towers. Above the arch is a band of Kufic calligraphy with the name of its builder, Abou el-Hassan, and the date 1339. On the left, inside a former guardhouse, there is a café. Through the gate, a stepped walkway leads to a terrace offering spectacular views of the Bou Regreg valley, the Merinid necropolis and the remains of the Roman town of Sala Colonia, which are surrounded by lush vegetation.

It was Abou Yacoub Youssef, the first Merinid caliph, who chose this as the site of a mosque and the burial place of his wife, Oum el-Izz, in 1284. Abou Yacoub Youssef died in Algeciras in 1286, and his body was brought back to the necropolis. His two successors, Abou Yacoub, who died in 1307, and Abou Thabit, who died in 1308, were also laid to rest here. The burial complex was completed by the sultan Abou Saïd (1310–31) and his son Abou el-Hassan (1331–51), and was later embellished by Abou Inan. The walls around the necropolis, which have the ochre tones typical of the earth stone of Rabat, were built by Abou el-Hassan, who probably reconstructed the existing Roman walls. In 1500, Leo Africanus recorded the existence of 30 Merinid tombs.

Situated within the walls of the necropolis are the ruins of the mosque built by Abou

Storks nesting on the minaret of the former *zaouia* at Chellah

Youssef and of the buildings that surrounded it. To the right behind the mihrab is the *koubba* (shrine) of Abou Yacoub Youssef.

Opposite the *koubba*, the Mausoleum of Abou el-Hassan, the Black Sultan and the last Merinid ruler to be buried here, in 1351, lies alongside the walls. His funerary stele is still in place. Also to be seen here is the *koubba* of his wife, who died in 1349. Named Chams el-Doha (which can be translated as "light of the dawn"), she was a Christian who converted to Islam. She was the mother of Abou Inan *(see p51)*, one of the most illustrious Merinid rulers.

Her accomplishments include the building of the Bou Inania Medersa in Fès *(see pp172–3)*.

Also within the walls of the necropolis was a *zaouia*, a religious institution that functioned simultaneously as a mosque, a centre of learning and a hostel for pilgrims and students (some of the cells can still be made out). Built by Abou el-Hassan, the *zaouia* is designed and decorated like the medersas in Fès, and it is thought that it may have been even more luxuriously appointed. Abou el-Hassan covered the upper part of the minaret with a decorative design of white, black, green and blue *zellij* tilework, which is still visible today.

The necropolis at Chellah was abandoned at the end of the Merinid dynasty, and in the course of the following centuries was ransacked several times. It was largely destroyed by the earthquake of 1755. Vegetation invaded the stonework and colonies of storks built their nests in the trees and on the minarets, giving the place a supernatural atmosphere, particularly at sunset.

The necropolis has become the subject of much folklore and many legends, as can be seen from the large number

of *marabouts* (shrines) of holy men that are scattered about the garden. The sacred eels in the fountain (once the ablutions fountain for the mosque) are also believed to bring good fortune to barren women. These supplicants feed them eggs, symbols of fertility, which are offered for sale by young boys in the square.

Environs

Archaeological excavations at Chellah have uncovered the remains of the major buildings of **Sala Colonia**. Once a prosperous Roman city, Sala Colonia later declined and by the 10th century had fallen

The interior of the mosque built by Abou Youssef

into ruin. Still visible today is the *decumanus maximus*, the main thoroughfare that crossed all Roman cities from east to west. It led out from Sala Colonia to the port, built in the 1st century BC and now buried in sand.

From the forum, a road to the right leads towards the Merinid necropolis.

The walls around the Chellah Necropolis, raised by Abou el-Hassan in the 14th century

NORTHERN ATLANTIC COAST

Morocco's Northern Atlantic coast offers extensive beaches of soft fine sand, lagoons, winter havens for migratory birds, and forests that are highly prized by hunters. But to explore it is also to travel back in time, since the heritage of the Phoenicians and the Romans, the corsairs, the Portuguese and the Spanish, as well as of the colonial epoch is present alongside the modern prosperity brought by agriculture, port activity, trade and tourism.

Although it attracts far fewer tourists than the interior or the imperial cities, the Moroccan coastline from Rabat to Tangier has much to offer visitors. It has not undergone the high level of development that has transformed the coastal area from Rabat to Casablanca and the south. Nevertheless, this region is no less characteristic of the modern, vibrant and outward-looking country that Morocco has become. For 250 km (155 miles), the ocean seems omnipresent, as roads and motorways often skirt the coastline and the beaches. For motorists following the coastal roads, the ocean may suddenly come into sight at an estuary or over a dune. The road follows roughly the course of a Roman road linking Sala Colonia (known today as Chellah, see pp80–81) and Banasa, Lixus and Tangier. This is the heart of one of earliest regions of Morocco in which towns and cities were established.

The ocean has shaped the history of the coastal towns: occupied from Phoenician times and into the Roman period, they have attracted pirates, invaders and Andalusian, Spanish and French occupiers, each of whom left their mark. It is also the ocean that gives the region its gentle, moist climate (strawberries, bananas and tomatoes are grown in greenhouses) and that drives industry and port activity from Kenitra to Tangier, where a port has been built to handle cargo bound for Europe.

Asilah, a small Andalusian-style town (see p91), facing the Atlantic from behind coastal defences

◁ Ruins at the ancient site of Thamusida (see p87), once inhabited by the Romans

Exploring the Northern Atlantic Coast

Travelling along Morocco's Atlantic coast between Salé and Tangier reveals a natural paradise of sea, forests, lagoons, hunting and fishing within sight of beaches that appear to stretch to infinity. The coast is punctuated by ancient sites: Thamusida, nestling in a bend of Wadi Sebou; Banasa, set a little way back from the sea, in the fertile plain of the Rharb; and Lixus, standing on a promontory opposite Larache, on the estuary of the Loukkos. From Salé to Tangier, a succession of small walled towns with interesting monuments bears testament to a rich history: Mehdya, whose kasbah dominates the final meanders of Wadi Sebou; Moulay Bousselham, with its attractive lagoon and beach protected by the tomb of the eponymous saint, which draws numerous pilgrims; Asilah, where walls pierced by mysteriously screened windows enclose narrow, secretive streets; Larache, a charmingly Andalusian town; and Tangier, which looks over the Straits of Gibraltar towards Spain and Europe.

Agriculture in the region of Kenitra

0 km   10

0 miles   10

SIGHTS AT A GLANCE

Asilah ⑩

Banasa ⑭

Forest of Mamora ④

Kenitra ⑤

Ksar el-Kebir ⑫

Larache ⑧

Lixus ⑨

Mehdya ③

Moulay Bousselham ⑦

M'Soura Stone Circle ⑪

RABAT pp64–81

Salé ①

Sidi Bouknadel ②

Souk el-Arba du Rharb ⑬

Thamusida ⑥

MOULAY BOUSSELHAM ⑦

ATLANTIC OCEAN

Sidi-el-Hachemi

Sidi-Allal-Tazi

Morrhane

THAMUSIDA ⑥

Sidi Yahya du-Rharb

MEHDYA ③   ⑤ KENITRA

FOREST OF ④

SIDI BOUKNADEL ②

Aïn-Johra

SALÉ ①

RABAT

Sidi-Allal-el-Bahraoui

Casablanca

Tiflèt

Wadi Bou Regreg

Migratory birds in the lagoon at Moulay Bousselham

SEE ALSO

- *Where to Stay* pp303–4

- *Where to Eat* p329

GETTING AROUND

A motorway (with toll) provides a direct link between Rabat and Tangier. Even when driving on a motorway, care should be taken: animals or people may try to cross unexpectedly. The N1 goes further inland, reaching the coast at Asilah. A bus service running from Rabat and Tangier provides transport to and from most places.

KEY

▬▬▬	Motorway
▬▬▬	Major road
═══	Minor road
- - -	Track
▬▬▬	Railway

Colourfully painted doors in the medina at Asilah

The tropical gardens in Sidi Bouknadel

Salé ❶

Road map C2. West of Rabat, on the right bank of Wadi Bou Regreg. 🏔 *710,000.* 🛬 *Rabat-Salé, 10 km (6 miles) on the Meknès road.* 🚌 *Route de Casablanca.* ℹ️ *Rabat; (0537) 66 06 63.* 🎭 *Festival and night-time Candle Procession (on the eve of Mouloud).* 🏬 *Thu.*

Founded in about the 11th century, Salé was fortified and embellished at the end of the 13th century by the Merinids. They built a medersa, a mosque, a medical school and a magnificent aqueduct, which can still be seen from the road to Kenitra. During the Middle Ages, Salé was a busy port, used by traders from the northern Mediterranean, and in 1609 it provided sanctuary for refugees from Andalusia. Salé shared the lucrative business of privateering with its neighbour and rival Rabat *(see pp64–81)*, with which it came into conflict. When piracy was brought to an end in the 18th century, the town went into decline.

In the 20th century, however, Salé found prosperity once more, as a major centre of the crafts industry.

At the entrance to the town (from the direction of Rabat) stands the 13th-century **Bab el-Mrisa** (Gate of the Sea). This was the entrance to the maritime arsenal built by Yacoub el-Mansour, and a canal linking Wadi Bou Regreg to the harbour passed through it.

Within the town, near Rue Bab el-Khebbaz, the main street through the medina, are the Kissaria and souks, both filled with craftsmen and traders. Nearby are the **Grand Mosque** and the medersa. A doorway framed by a horseshoe arch and covered with a carved wooden porch leads into the medersa. Built during the reign of the Merinid ruler Abou el-Hassan, it is notable for its central tower surrounded by a colonnaded gallery covered in *zellij* tilework and carved plaster and wood. The mihrab has a decorated wooden ceiling.

The **Seamen's Cemetery**, in the northeast of the town, is dotted with the *marabouts* (shrines) of such holy men as Sidi ben Achir. In the 16th century, he was credited with the power to calm the waves so as allow vessels to

Chest, Musée Dar Belghazi

enter the harbour safely. The *marabout* of Sidi Abdallah ben Hassoun (patron of Salé, of boatmen and of travellers) has an unusual dome that abuts the Grand Mosque. Further north along the coast the *marabout* of Sidi Moussa overlooks the sea.

Sidi Bouknadel ❷

Road map C2. 10 km (6 miles) north of Salé on the N1 to Kenitra. 🏔 *6,900.* 🚌 *Rabat.* 🏬 *Sun.*

The tropical gardens (**Jardins Exotiques**) just outside Sidi Bouknadel were laid out in 1951 by the horticulturist Marcel François and are today owned by the State. Some 1,500 species native to the Antilles, South America and Asia grow in the garden.

🌿 **Jardins Exotiques**
⏰ *9am–6:30pm daily.* 🎫

Environs
Two kilometres (1.25 miles) to the north is the **Musée Dar Belghazi**, with its collection of fine objects, including jewellery, kaftans, marriage belts, carved wooden doors, minbars, pottery and musical instruments. This privately run museum was established by a master woodcarver, with bequests from artists and collectors.

🏛️ **Musée Dar Belghazi**
Km 47, Route de Kenitra. **Tel** *(0537) 82 21 78.* ⏰ *10am–6pm daily.* 🎫

Mehdya ❸

Road map C2. 39 km (24 miles) from Salé on the N1 to Kenitra, at km 29 turning onto the Mehdya-Plage road. 🏔 *5,800.* 🚌 *Kenitra, then by taxi.*

This small coastal resort is much frequented by the inhabitants of Rabat and Kenitra. On the estuary of Wadi Sebou, it stands on the

The walls of Salé, near Bab el-Mrisa

site of what may have been a Carthagenian trading post in the 5th century BC, and then an Almohad naval base, which was known at the time as El Mamora ("the populous one"). Later, the town was occupied by the Portuguese, the Spanish and the Dutch, and was finally captured by Moulay Ismaïl *(see p53)* at the end of the 17th century.

The kasbah which stands on the plateau, dominating the estuary, still has its original walls, which were built by the Spanish, and its moated bastions. The monumental gate, built by Moulay Ismaïl, leads to the governor's palace, which has a central courtyard, rooms, outbuildings, hammam and mosque.

Environs

The **Sidi Bourhaba Lake**, 27 km (17 miles) along the Mehdya-Plage road, is a large bird sanctuary: thousands of birds, such as teal and coot, rest here during their migration between Europe and sub-Saharan Africa.

Sidi Bourhaba Lake
Tel (0537) 74 72 09. **Exhibition centre and marked walks**
noon–4pm Sat, Sun and public holidays.

Forest of Mamora ❹

Road map C2. East of Rabat on the N1 to Kenitra or the N6 to Meknès.

The Forest of Mamora, between Wadi Sebou and Wadi Bou Regreg, covers an area 60 km (37 miles) long and 30 km (19 miles) wide. Although the forest is now planted mostly with eucalyptus, which grows

Pieces of bark stripped from the cork-oak

much faster than other species, large tracts of it are still covered with cork-oak, which is grown for its bark. At a factory in Sidi Yahia eucalyptus wood is turned into a pulp that is used in paper-making and the manufacture of artificial silk.

Being intensively exploited and degraded by the grazing of cattle, sheep and goats, the forest is becoming increasingly bare. However, enough cover remains to allow a refreshingly cool walk in summer, when wood pigeons, kites, rollers and spotted flycatchers can be seen.

Kenitra ❺

Road map C2. 300,000.
Rabat. Mon & Sat.

Established in 1913 in the early days of the French Protectorate, from 1933 to 1955 this town was known as Port-Lyautey. Nowadays, Kenitra consists of distinct districts: residential areas with villas, a European-style town centre and poorer suburbs.

In the harbour, on the right bank of Wadi Sebou, regional produce from the Rharb (such as citrus fruit, cork, cotton, cereals and pulp for papermaking) are unloaded for use in local industries. Once a marshy area where malaria was rife (but still used for extensive stock-farming), the alluvial plain of the Rharb has been transformed by irrigation. It is

now one of Morocco's major agricultural areas, specializing in rice, sugar beet, cotton and citrus fruits.

The Roman baths at Thamusida, on the banks of Wadi Sebou

Thamusida ❻

Road map D2. 55 km (34 miles) northeast of Rabat, 17 km (10.5 miles) northeast of Kenitra. Motorway exit: Kenitra N.

On the N1, at the milestone reading "Kenitra 14 km, Sidi Allal Tazi 28 km", a track heading westwards leads to this ancient site on Wadi Sebou. It was inhabited by the Romans from the 2nd century BC to the 3rd century AD.

Part of the walls can still be seen, along with the outline of the Roman army camp (with streets intersecting at right angles) and the site's major feature, the *praetorium* (headquarters), with columns and pilasters. To the northeast the remains of baths and a temple with three chambers, or *cellae*, can be made out. North of Wadi Sebou are vestiges of the harbour docks.

Fishing harbour at Mehdya, on Wadi Sebou

Cork-oaks in the Forest of Mamora ▷

Moulay Bousselham ❼

Road map D2. 48 km (30 miles) south of Larache. 🏠 900. 🚌
Boat trips *available from Café Milano.* 🐎 *Moussem (early summer).*

The small town of Moulay Bousselham is a coastal resort that is very popular with Moroccans. The mosque and the tomb of Moulay Bousselham tower above the ocean and the Merja Zerga lagoon. As the burial place of Moulay Bousselham, the 10th-century holy man, it is also a major place of pilgrimage, attracting many followers in late June and early July.

The life of the holy man is wreathed in legends associated with the ocean and its perils. The Moulay Bousselham sandbar is, indeed, highly dangerous: the waves come crashing in over the reefs and onto the beach. The waters of the lagoon are calmer; boat trips are organized to see the thousands of birds – herons, pink flamingoes, gannets and sheldrake – that come to the lagoon on their migrations in December and January. Boat trips around the lagoon depart from the small fishing harbour.

The town of Moulay Bousselham and the Merja Zerga lagoon

Larache ❽

Road map D1. 🏠 95,000. 🚌 *from Tangier, Rabat.* 🛥 *Sun.*

Set a little way back from major roads, Larache is both an Andalusian and an Arab town. The modern part bears obvious signs of the Spanish Protectorate.

Established in the 7th century by Arab conquerors, by the 11th century Larache was an important centre of trade on the left bank of Wadi

Andalusian-style fountain on Place de la Libération, Larache

Loukkos. In the 16th century it was used as a base by corsairs from Algiers and Turkey, and was subject to reprisals by Portuguese forces from Asilah. The town passed to Spain in 1610, and was then taken by Moulay Ismaïl at the end of the 17th century. During the Spanish Protectorate (1911–56) Larache was held by Spain.

The medina is reached from Place de la Libération, a very Spanish plaza, and through Bab el-Khemis, a brick-built gate roofed with glazed tiles. In the fabrics souk – the *kissaria (socco de la alcaicería)* – a market offers a wide range of goods. Narrow streets lined with houses with floral decoration lead down towards the harbour. Bab el-Kasba separates the southern edge of the fabrics souk from Rue Moulay el-Mehdi, a street covered with overhead arches that leads to an octagonal minaret and a terrace overlooking the meandering Wadi Loukkos, salt-marshes and the Lixus promontory.

Not far from Lixus is the Château de la Cigogne (Stork's Castle), a fortress that was built in 1578 by the Saadian rulers and then remodelled by the Spanish in the 17th century. It is closed to the public.

It is pleasant to stroll along the seafront – the "balcony of the Atlantic". Nearby is the Moorish market. Finally, in the **Catholic Cemetery**, the tomb of the French writer Jean Genet (1910–86) can be found, lying facing the ocean.

Lixus ❾

Road map D1. 5 km (3 miles) northeast of Larache on the N1. 🚌 *from Larache.*

This ancient site, which commands a view of the ocean, of Wadi Loukkos and of Larache, is to become one of UNESCO's World Heritage Sites. According to legend, this is where one of the Labours of Hercules – picking the golden apples in the Garden of the Hesperides – took place. The ancient Roman writer Plinius, writing in the 7th century BC, described Lixus as the most ancient Phoenician colony in the western Mediterranean.

In the 7th century BC the Phoenicians established a trading post here, serving as a stage on the Gold Route. After it had been taken by the Romans between 40 and 45 AD, Lixus became a colony and a centre of the manufacture of *garum*, sauce made with scraps of fish marinaded in brine from

The Roman ruins of Lixus, set on a magnificent promontory

salting vats. The Romans
abandoned Lixus at the end
of the 3rd century AD. The
wall built around the city at
that time reduced its inhabited
area by half.

The vats in which meat and
fish were salted and *garum*
made – Morocco's major
industry in Roman times –
can be seen around the edges
of the site. In the amphitheatre, with its circular arena,
public games took place.

The **Acropolis** above the
town has its own walls; only
on the western side, where
there is a sheer drop, do they
coincide with the town walls.
An apsidal building, preceded
by an atrium with a cistern,
has been excavated. The
Great Temple (1st century
BC–1st century AD), to the
south, features an arcaded
area (courtyard). The *cella,*
where the god dwelt, on the
axis of the peristyle, backs
onto an apsidal wall; opposite
is a large semicircular apse
with a mosaic floor.

Asilah ⑩

Road map D1. 🏘 *25,000.*
🚉 *2 km (1.5 miles) north of
town.* 🚌 *from Tangier or Rabat.*
🎭 *Cultural Festival (Aug).* 🛒 *Thu.*

Established by the
Phoenicians, Asilah was an
important town in Maure-
tania's pre-Roman period
(when coins were minted
here), and also under the
Romans. It was captured by
the Portuguese in 1471 and
became a centre of trade
with connections to the
Mediterranean countries. The
town came under Moroccan
control in 1691, during the
reign of Moulay Ismaïl.

At the end of the 19th
century, Raissouli, a pretender
to power and a brigand,
extortioner and kidnapper,
made Asilah his base. In
1906, taking advantage of the
intrigues that surrounded the
sovereign, Abdul Aziz, he
assumed the mantle of pasha
then that of governor of the
Jebala. He built himself a
palace facing the sea, from
which he was expelled by
the Spanish in 1924.

Colourful display of fruit on a stall in the market at Asilah

This small Andalusian-style
town is enclosed within
ramparts. The narrow streets
are paved or limed, and lined
with houses fronted by
balconies with restrained
mashrabiyya, and with blue-
or green-painted woodwork.

The Criquia jetty, northwest
of the town, overlooks a tiny
cemetery with tombstones
covered in glazed tiles. At the
foot of the square tower on
Place Ibn Khaldoun stands
Bab el-Bahr (Gate of the Sea).
On the opposite side of the
square, Bab Homar (Gate
of the Land), with the Portuguese royal coat of arms,
leads out from the ramparts
and into the new town.

In summer, the **Centre
Hassan II des Rencontres
Internationales**, in Rue de
la Kasbah, within the walls,
hosts cultural events and
exhibitions. Asilah is also
frequented by painters, who
are fond of marking the walls
with signs of their passing.

M'Soura Stone Circle ⑪

Road map D1. El-Utad to Chouahed.
27 km (17 miles) southeast of Asilah
on the N1, then R417 towards
Tetouan.

This Neolithic site is reached
via a 7-km (4-mile) track
running from Sidi el-Yamani
towards Souk et-Tnine.

Perhaps the burial place of an
important local ruler, it consists
of 200 monolithic standing
stones ranging in height from
50 cm (20 inches) to 5 m (16
ft) and surrounding a burial
area about 55 m (180 ft) in
circumference. Unique in the
Maghreb and the Sahara, by
its sheer size this monument
is reminiscent of those seen
in Spain. The type of pottery
decorated with impressions
of *cardium* shells and bronze
weapons, which excavations
have brought to light, are also
identical to Spanish examples.

**One of the 200 standing stones at
the M'Soura Neolithic stone circle**

Sugarcane plantation in the fertile region around Ksar el-Kebir

Ksar el-Kebir ⑫

Road map D1. 👥 *107,000.*
🚉 *Moulay el-Mehdi (approx. 3 km/
2 miles).* 🚌 *from Tangier.* 🅿 *Sun.*

The town takes its name from
a great fortress which, during
the Almoravid and Almohad
periods, controlled the road
leading to the ports along the
Straits of Gibraltar.

It was at Wadi el-Makhazin
nearby that the Battle of the
Three Kings took place in
1578. The conflict has been
described as the "last crusade
undertaken by the Christians
of the Mediterranean". It was
instigated by the Saadian
sultan El-Mutawakkil, who,
having been driven from
Morocco, was zealous for
a crusade. In alliance with
Sebastião I, king of Portugal,
he made a bid to win back
his kingdom. Sebastião,
El-Mutawakkil and their
opponent, the Saadian sultan
Abd el-Malik (who was
victorious over the invaders),
all died in the battle. Moulay
Ahmed, brother of Abd
el-Malik, succeeded him,
becoming known not only
as Ahmed el-Mansour ("the
Victorious") but also as
Ahmed el-Dhebi ("the
Golden"), because of the
ransom that he exacted.

Ksar el-Kebir is, today,
a sizeable country town. A
particularly large souk is held
here on Sundays: goods on
offer include the produce of
local market gardens, as well
as that of the area's olive
plantations and citrus groves.

Souk el-Arba du Rharb ⑬

Road map D2. 👥 *38,000.*
🚉 🚌 *Rabat, Tangier.* 🅿 *Wed.*

A major agricultural centre
on the northwest border of
the Rharb, Souk el-Arba du
Rharb is especially busy on
Wednesdays, when the souk
is held. The town's position
on the intersection of roads
leading to Tangier, Rabat,
Meknès and the coastal town
of Moulay Bousselham has
made it a key staging post.

Banasa ⑭

Road map D2. 103 km (64 miles)
northeast of Rabat on the N1 or
Rabat-Tangier freeway (Kenitra
North exit).

This ancient town, an inland
port on Wadi Sebou and the
most developed in
Mauretania Tingitana, was a
centre of ceramic production
from the 3rd century and
during the 1st century BC.
A Roman colony from 33
to 25 BC, Banasa was a
prosperous and bustling
commercial town until the
end of the 3rd century AD.

The entrance to the town,
through a vaulted gateway,
leads to the basilica and the
paved and arcaded forum.
South of the forum rises the
capitol, where several altars
stand before the temple's five
cellae (chambers). In the
public baths to the west, the

various rooms for the Roman
ritual of bathing – robing
rooms, a *caldarium* and *tepi-
darium* (hot and warm rooms)
with underfloor heating, and
frigidarium (cold room) can
be distinguished. Wall paintings and a brick floor paved
in a herringbone pattern can
be made out in another bath-
house at a lower level.

A famous document
engraved on bronze was
discovered at Banasa. Known
as the *Banasa Table*, it was
an edict by which Caracalla
granted the province relief
from taxes in return for lions,
elephants and other animals
that the emperor desired for
public spectacles in Rome.

From the N1 or freeway,
Banasa is reached by taking
the R413, then, 3 km (2 miles)
before Souk Tleta du Rharb,
by turning off onto the P4234.
As it approaches the site, the
road is reduced to a track.

**Stele with an inscription in Latin,
standing in the ruins of Banasa**

For hotels and restaurants in this region see pp303–4 and p329

Roman Towns in Morocco

During the reigns of Juba II and Ptolemy, kings of Mauretania who ruled under the aegis of Rome, towns were established in Morocco. Under Roman control, they developed either into *coloniae* (colonies such as Lixus and Banasa) or *municipiae* (free towns such as Sala and Volubilis).

Head of Hercules

to the Roman way of life, they built houses with columned courtyards and mosaic floors in the Roman style, and imported bronze sculptures from Egypt and Italy and pottery from Etruria. Public and private baths fulfilled the desire for personal cleanliness and also acted as places in which to socialize. The arcades along the

The inhabitants, who grew prosperous through the cultivation of the land, endowed their towns with such civic features as forums, basilicas, capitols and triumphal arches. Adapting

decumanus maximus (main thoroughfare) were filled with shops, while cottage industries were established around the edges of the town.

Juba II *(52 BC–AD 23), who married the daughter of Cleopatra and Mark Antony, turned Mauretania into a highly prosperous country.*

Ptolemy, *who succeeded Juba II, was murdered in Rome in AD 40. Under him, Mauritania became completely romanized.*

ROMAN RULE

Juba II was made king of Mauretania by Augustus. After Ptolemy's death, the province was administered by Rome under Claudius. Triumphal arches were built during the reigns of Commodius and Caracalla. In the late 3rd century, under Diocletian, the country was administered with the province of Spain.

Mauretania's cities *were centres of trade and administration, as well as garrison towns. As in Rome, the focal point was the forum (a market place and public area) and the basilica, simultaneously a monetary exchange, law court and meeting place. The capitol was the city's religious centre.*

The basilica and the columns of the capitol at Volubilis

ART

As Rome imposed political unity, so Roman artistic influence spread throughout the Maghreb.

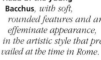

Head of the young Bacchus, *with soft, rounded features and an effeminate appearance, in the artistic style that prevailed at the time in Rome.*

Roman funerary art *can be seen in Morocco. Many stelae (free-standing stone columns) take the shape of a pointed rectangle carved with a figure dressed in a full-length tunic.*

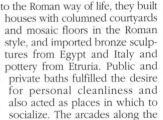

Mosaic depicting Aeolus, *Roman god of wind, whose breath restores nature to life. It comes from the floor of the house in Volubilis.*

CASABLANCA

*S*traddling east and west, Casablanca, the commercial and financial capital of Morocco, is a baffling metropolis where tradition and modernity co-exist. A city where skyscrapers stand in stark contrast to the small shops of the medina, with its narrow, winding streets, this is where the prosperous rub shoulders with paupers.

In the 7th century, Casablanca was no more than a small Berber settlement clinging to the slopes of the Anfa hills. However, for strategic and commercial reasons, it was already attracting the attention of foreign powers. In 1468, the town was sacked by the Portuguese, who wrought wholesale destruction on the city's privateer ships. Then, in the 18th century, with the sultanate of Sidi Mohammed ben Abdallah, Dar el-Beïda (meaning "White House" – "Casa Blanca" in Spanish) acquired a new significance. This was thanks to its harbour, which played a pivotal role in the sugar, tea, wool and corn markets of the Western world. But it was in the 20th century, under the French Protectorate *(see pp56–7)*, that Casablanca underwent the most profound change. Against expert advice, Marshal Lyautey, the first resident-governor, proceeded with plans to make Casablanca the country's economic hub. To realize this vision, he hired the services of town planners and modernized the port. For almost 40 years, the most innovative architects worked on this huge building project. Casablanca continued to expand even after independence. Futuristic high-rise buildings and a colossal mosque sending its laser beams towards Mecca once again expressed the city's forward-looking spirit. With about 4 million inhabitants, Casablanca is, today, one of the four largest metropolises on the African continent, and its port is the busiest in Morocco.

Moroccans relaxing on the terrace of a café in the Parc de la Ligue Arabe

◁ Casablanca's Hassan II Mosque, seen from the sea

Exploring Casablanca

The centre of the new town (Ville Nouvelle) revolves around two focal points: the Place des Nations Unies and the Place Mohammed V, squares that are lined with fine 1930s buildings. To the north, the old medina is still enclosed within ramparts, while the Parc de la Ligue Arabe, Casablanca's green lung, extends to the southeast. Further out, towards the west, is the residential district of Anfa and the coastal resort of Aïn Diab. The Boulevard de la Corniche leads to the monumental Hassan II Mosque. The Quartier Habous, a modern medina built in the 1920s, also features some interesting architecture.

SIGHTS AT A GLANCE

Avenues and Boulevards
Avenue des Forces
   Armées Royales ❷
Boulevard Mohammed V ❸

Squares
Place Mohammed V ❹
Place des Nations Unies ❶

Districts
Anfa ⓬
Corniche d'Aïn Diab ⓭
Old Medina ❻
Port ❼
Quartier Habous
   (New Medina) ❾

Park
Parc de la Ligue Arabe ❺

Building
Casablanca Twin Center ❿

Mosque
Hassan II Mosque
   pp102–3 ❽

Museum
Musée du Judaïsme
   Marocain ⓫

Environs
Mohammedia ⓮

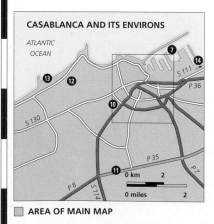

CASABLANCA AND ITS ENVIRONS

ATLANTIC OCEAN

0 km   2

0 miles   2

☐ AREA OF MAIN MAP

Detail of a 1930s façade in Casablanca

GETTING AROUND

Allow at least one day to explore
Casablanca. The old medina and the new
town, with their fine architectural heritage, are best seen on foot. By contrast,
the Quartier Habous and the Hassan II
Mosque can be reached only by motorized transport. Parking is not a problem
as there are many car parks. It is also
possible to travel around Casablanca
by bus or *petit taxi*. Bus and
tram routes serve both
the city centre and
outlying districts.

Stained-glass window in the
Church of Notre-Dame-de-Lourdes

KEY

⬜	Old Medina
—	Ramparts
🚇	Railway station
🚌	Bus station
🅿	Parking
ℹ	Tourist information
⊠	Post office
✝	Church
☪	Mosque
•	Jewish cemetery

SEE ALSO

- *Where to Stay* pp305–6
- *Where to Eat* pp330–32

0 m   400

0 yards   400

The Moretti Milone apartment block, one of the highest in 1934

Place des Nations Unies ❶

South of the old medina.

At the beginning of the 20th century, this was still no more than a market square, a place which, by evening, would become the haunt of storytellers and snake charmers. Today, it is the heart of the new town, a hub where major thoroughfares converge.

Window of the Excelsior hotel

When the square was laid out in 1920, it was known as Place de France, but was later renamed. Beneath the arcades of 1930s apartment blocks are rows of brasserie terraces and souvenir shops. In the northeast corner of the square, the **clocktower**, which dates from 1910, was demolished in 1940 and then rebuilt to an identical design. At the time that it was built, the clock symbolized colonial rule, indicating to the population that it should now keep in time with an industrial society.

At the **Hyatt Regency Hotel** memories of Humphrey Bogart and Ingrid Bergman, stars of the famous film *Casablanca*, made in 1943 by Michael Curtiz, hang on the walls. In the southeast corner of the square is the **Excelsior Hotel** (1914–16), with Moorish friezes and

balconies, which was the first of Morocco's Art Deco hotels and is one of the square's finest buildings. In 1934, the 11-storey **Moretti Milone** apartment block, at the corner of Boulevard Houphouët Boigny, was the first high-rise building in central Casablanca. **Boulevard Houphouët Boigny**, lined with shops and restaurants, runs from the square to the port. At the end, on the right, the *marabout* of Sidi Belyout, patron saint and protector of Casablanca, stands in stark contrast to the neighbouring residential buildings.

Avenue des Forces Armées Royales ❷

South of the old medina, running between Place Oued el-Makhazine and Place Zellaga.

Lined with high-rise buildings, major hotels such as the **Sheraton** and **Royal Mansour**, with airline offices and travel agents and the towering, futuristic glass building of **Omnium Nord Africain** (ONA), this avenue marks the boundary of the commercial district. Further development is planned for its continuation towards the Mosque of Hassan II.

Boulevard Mohammed V ❸

Running from Place des Nations Unies to Boulevard Hassan Seghir.

Running through the city like a spine, this boulevard links Place des Nations Unies with the railway station in the east of the city. When it was built in 1915, it was intended to be the major artery through the

No. 208 Boulevard Mohammed V, faced with friezes and balconies

commercial heart of Casablanca. On both sides, covered arcades house shops and restaurants.

A raised strip sections off traffic and widens into a square level with the **Central Market**. The high-rise buildings here are notable for their façades, which feature loggias, columns, *zellij* tilework and

The Glaoui residential block, built in 1922 by M. Boyer

The Palais de Justice, built in the Moorish style in 1922

geometric carvings. Peculiar to the buildings of this period is the mixture of styles – Art Deco, on the one hand, seen in white façades of simple design, and the typically Moroccan, more decorative style on the other. Among the finest of these buildings are three residential blocks: the **Glaoui** (designed by M. Boyer, 1922), on the corner of Rue El-Amraoui Brahim; the **Bessonneau** (H. Bride, 1917), opposite the market; and the **Asayag** (M. Boyer, 1932), at the corner of Boulevard Hassan Seghir. The latter, very innovatory at the time it was built, is five storeys high and has three towers set around a central hub. From the fourth storey upwards, terraces extend the studio apartments. Buildings at numbers 47, 67 and 73 are also fine examples, with overhanging loggias and rounded balconies.

Another particular feature of Boulevard Mohammed V is its covered arcades, which are similar to the shopping arcades built during the same period (the 1920s) along the Champs-Élysées in Paris. Among the most interesting of these arcades is the **Passage du Glaoui**, which links Boulevard Mohammed V to Rue Allal ben-Abdallah. Lit by prismatic lamps, the arcade is punctuated by glass rotundas. **Passage Sumica**, opposite Passage du Glaoui, is closer to the Art Deco style. This runs through to **Rue du Prince Moulay Abdallah**, which

also contains some notable 1930s apartment blocks. This pedestrianized street is very popular with shoppers.

In Rue Mohammed el-Quori, off Boulevard Mohammed V, stands the **Rialto**. This renovated cinema is renowned for its fine ornamentation, stained-glass windows and Art Deco lighting.

Central Market
Boulevard Mohammed V.
7am–2pm daily.

Place Mohammed V ❹

North of the Parc de la Ligue Arabe.

Exemplifying the architecture of the Protectorate, this square, the administrative heart of Casablanca, combines the monumentality of French architecture with Moorish sobriety. This is the location of the Préfecture, the law courts, the central post office, banks and cultural organizations.

The **Préfecture** (by M. Boyer, 1937), over which towers a Tuscan-style campanile 50 m (164 ft) high, stands on the southeastern side of the square. Its buildings are set around three courtyards, each with a tropical garden. The central stairway is framed by two huge paintings by Jacques Majorelle *(see p243)* depicting the festivities of a *moussem*

Zellij decoration on the façade of the Post Office

and the performance of the *ahwach*, a Berber dance.

Behind stands the **Palais de Justice** (law courts, designed by J. Marrast and completed in 1922). The strong verticality of the Moorish doorway, with its awning of green tiles, contrasts with the horizontal lines of the arcaded gallery, which are emphasized by a carved frieze running the length of the building.

Two buildings set slightly back abut the façade of the law courts on either side. On the right is the **Consulat de France** (French Consulate, by A. Laprade, 1916), whose gardens contain an equestrian statue of Marshal Lyautey, by Cogné (1938), which stood in the centre of the square until Moroccan independence. On the left, in the northeastern corner, is the **Cercle Militaire** (by M. Boyer). To the north is the **Post Office** (A. Laforgue, 1920), fronted by an open arcade decorated with *zellij* tilework and semi-circular arches, which leads through to an Art Deco central hall within.

Opposite, along Rue de Paris, a small area of greenery where people like to stroll gives a more picturesque feel to the square, in the centre of which is a monumental **fountain** dating from 1976. At certain times of day, the fountain plays music and gives light displays.

A long, straight walkway in the Parc de la Ligue Arabe

Parc de la Ligue Arabe ❺

South of Place Mohammed V (between Boulevard Rachidi and Boulevard Mohammed Zerktouni).

Laid out by the architect A. Laprade in 1919, this huge garden incorporates café terraces and is a popular place for a stroll. Avenues lined with impressively tall palm trees, ficus, arcades and pergolas frame some stunning formal flowerbeds. The streets surrounding the park, including Rue d'Alger, Rue du Parc and Boulevard Moulay-Youssef, contain Art Nouveau and Art Deco houses.

Northwest of the park stands the **Église du Sacré-Cœur**, built in 1930–52 by Paul Tournon. A white concrete twin-towered building with an Art Deco flavour to its façade, it is now de-consecrated and used for cultural events.

To the southeast stands the **Église Notre-Dame-de-Lourdes** (1956). Its stained-glass windows depict scenes from the life of the Virgin against motifs taken from Moroccan carpets. They are the work of G. Loire, a master-craftsman from Chartres.

A cannon in the *sqala*, facing the port and onto the ocean

To the southwest is the **Villa des Arts** displaying contemporary Moroccan paintings.

🔒 **Église du Sacré-Cœur**
Rond-point de l'Europe. ☐ only for concerts and other events.

🏛 **Villa des Arts**
30 Bd Brahim Roudani. *Tel* (0522) 29 50 87. ☐ 9am–7pm Tue–Sun.

Old Medina ❻

Between Boulevard des Almohades and Place des Nations Unies.

At the beginning of the 20th century, Casablanca consisted only of the old medina, which itself comprised no more than a few thousand inhabitants. The walls around the old town were originally pierced by four gates, two of which survive today. **Bab Marra-kech** and **Bab el-Jedid**, on the western side, face onto Boulevard Tahar el-Alaoui. A daily **market**, with jewellers, barbers, public letter-writers and so on, stretches out along the length of the walls.

Opposite the fishing harbour is the *sqala*, a fortified bastion built in the 18th century, during the reign of Sidi Mohammed ben Abdallah. Behind the bastion, the *marabout* (shrine) with a double crown of merlons contains the **Tomb of Sidi Allal el-Kairouani**, who became Casablanca's first patron saint in 1350. **Bab el-Marsa** (Gate of the Sea), which opens onto Boulevard des Almohades, also dates from the 18th century. It was at this spot that the French disembarked in July 1907.

Port ❼

East of the old medina.

Casablanca is Morocco's principal port. Covering an area of 1.8 sq km (0.70 sq miles), the port was built during the Protectorate and

A fish auction on the quay, where fishing boats land their catch

is one of the largest artificial ports in the world. A groyne protects it from the pounding of the ocean that destroyed several earlier constructions. The port is equipped with ultra-modern commercial, fishing and leisure facilities.

Access to the port complex is via the fishing harbour. On the seafront in the port itself, as well as along the avenue leading down to it, some excellent fish restaurants are to be found (*see pp331–2*).

The building of a marina covering a wide area and in-corporating hotels, restaurants, shops and offices is underway. The first phase is due to be completed at the end of 2012.

For hotels and restaurants in this region see pp305–6 and pp330–32

Architecture of the 1920s and 1930s

In 1907, when innovative architects set to work to create buildings in a range of contemporary styles, Casablanca began to look like a huge building site. In the early 1920s, numerous teams of architects were working in the city. Whatever the style, avant-garde tendencies were often counterbalanced by the traditional Moroccan style.

Thus, as the architects drew on the repertoire of Neo-Classicism, Art Nouveau and Art Deco, which were fashionable at the time, they also took inspiration from the Moorish style that Europeans found so fascinating. Towards the end of the 1920s and into the early 1930s, a new taste for simplicity became apparent. Emphasizing shape and outline at the expense of decoration, this gave prominence to the interplay of convex and concave shapes, and to balconies and bow windows. Another significant factor was the expectations of the colonial population and of European speculators: lifts, bathrooms, kitchens and parking areas appeared.

Architectural detail, 1930

FAÇADES

The façades of residential blocks were encrusted with putti, fruit, flowers and pilasters and featured roofs covered in green tiles, stucco and *zellij* tilework. Colonial houses, in the suburbs, were built in a style that was a cross between a grand Parisian town house and a Moroccan-style seaside residence.

The dome is an example of the Western use of a Moorish architectural element.

Balconies are an adaptation to the sunny climate and bright light.

Mosaic decoration

Wrought-iron balconies, *like this one from the Darius Boyer House, are typical of the Art Nouveau ironwork that often graced French windows and balconies.*

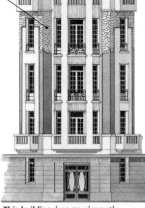

Mosaic decoration on the law courts *consists of multi-coloured* zellij *tilework in geometric shapes overlying a frieze of stucco carved with inscriptions.*

1930s architecture *features traditional Moorish elements, including semicircular arches and decoration in the form of carved stucco.*

This building *has an elegantly classical appearance, with decoration consisting of columns, belvederes and a dome with Art Nouveau motifs.*

Casablanca's main post office *has a loggia of semicircular arches and* zellij *tilework.*

Hassan II Mosque ⑧

Mosque door, interior view

With a prayer hall that can accommodate 25,000, the Hassan II Mosque is the second-largest religious building in the world after the mosque in Mecca. The complex covers 9 hectares (968,774 sq ft), two-thirds of it being built over the sea. The minaret, the lighthouse of Islam, is 200 m (656 ft) high, and two laser beams reaching over a distance of 30 km (18.5 miles) shine in the direction of Mecca. The building was designed by Michel Pinseau, 35,000 craftsmen worked on it, and it opened in 1993. With carved stucco, *zellij* tilework, a painted cedar ceiling and marble, onyx and travertine cladding, it is a monument to Moroccan architectural virtuosity and craftsmanship.

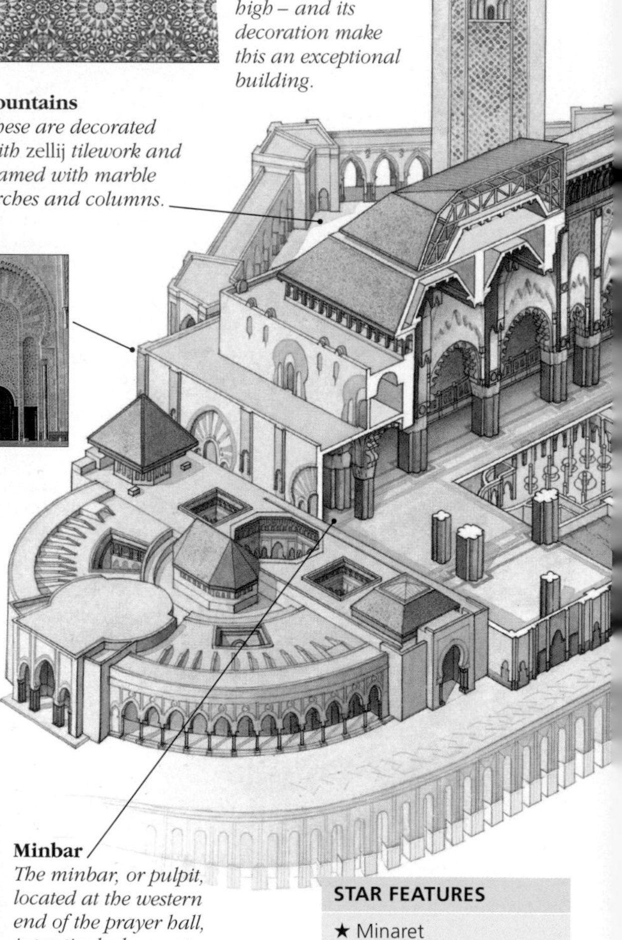

★ The Minaret
Its size – 25 m (82 ft) wide and 200 m (656 ft) high – and its decoration make this an exceptional building.

Fountains
These are decorated with zellij *tilework and framed with marble arches and columns.*

Marble
Covering the columns of the prayer hall and seen on doorways, fountains and stairs, marble is ubiquitous, sometimes used in combination with granite and onyx.

Minbar
The minbar, or pulpit, located at the western end of the prayer hall, is particularly ornate. It is decorated with verses from the Koran.

STAR FEATURES

★ Minaret

★ Prayer Hall

For hotels and restaurants in this region see pp304–6 and pp330–32

Women's Gallery
Above two mezzanines and hidden from view, this gallery extends over 5,300 sq m (57,000 sq ft) and can hold up to 5,000 women.

Dome
The cedar-panelled interior of the dome over the prayer hall glistens with carved and painted decoration.

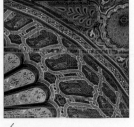

Royal Door
This is decorated with traditional motifs engraved on brass and titanium.

Columns

Doors
Seen from the exterior, these are double doors in the shape of pointed arches framed by columns. Many are clad in incised bronze.

Mashrabiyya screenwork at the windows protects those within from prying eyes.

Hammam

★ Prayer Hall
Able to hold 25,000 faithful, the prayer hall measures 200 m (656 ft) by 100 m (328 ft). The central part of the roof can be opened to the sky.

Stairway to the Women's Gallery
The stairway features decorative woodcarving, multiple arches and marble, granite and onyx columns, arranged in a harmonious ensemble.

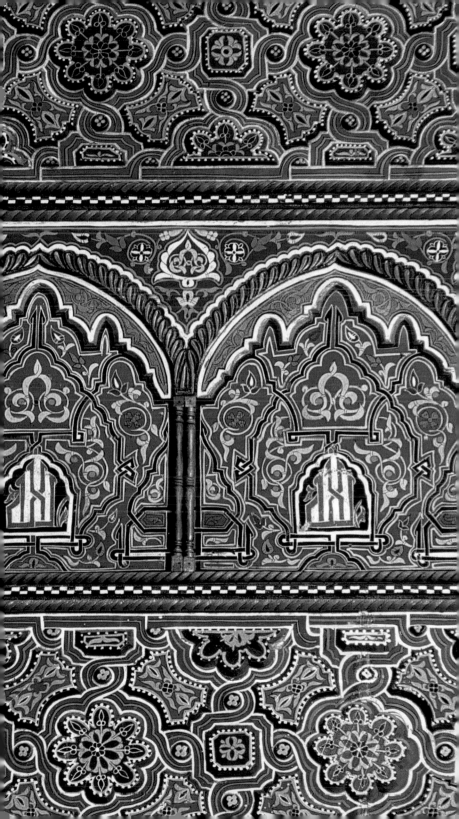

The copper and brass souk in the Quartier Habous

Quartier Habous (New Medina) 9

In the southeast of the city centre, near Boulevard Victor Hugo.

In the 1930s, in order to address the problem of an expanding urban population and to prevent Casablanca's underprivileged citizens from being forced to settle in insalubrious quarters, French town planners laid out a new medina (Nouvelle Medina). Land to the south of the existing city centre earmarked for this development was given over to the Habous, the administration of religious foundations, hence the new town's name.

This new town – which did not, however, forestall the later development of shanty towns – was built in the traditional Arab style at the same time as obeying modern town planning and public health regulations. It contains public areas, such as a market, shops, mosques, a *kissaria* and baths, as well as private dwellings (arranged around a courtyard separated from the street by a solid wall).

The new medina is another facet of colonial town planning during the Protectorate, and its flower-filled, arcaded streets offer the opportunity for a stroll in a scenic quarter of the city. While the most modest houses are located around the market, the finest are set around the mosque.

Northeast of the medina are the copper and brass Souk and **Chez Bennis**, Casablanca's

most famous patisserie, which sells pastries known as *cornes de gazelle* (gazelles' horns), fritters and *pastilla*. There are also shops specializing in curios and collectors' items, and they can be good places to find Art Deco objects. A wide range of Moroccan rugs and carpets is also on sale at the weekly auction in the carpet souk.

Northwest of the Quartier Habous is the **Mahakma du Pacha**, a formal tribunal and today one of the city's eight *préfectures* (administrative headquarters). The building (by A. Cadet, 1952), which centres around a tall tower and two courtyards, is a fine example of the adaptation of traditional Arab architecture to modern needs. The traditional Arabic decoration of its 64 rooms is the work of Moroccan craftsmen: it consists of carved stucco and *zellij* tilework on the walls, carved cedarwood panels on the ceiling and wrought iron on the doors.

The **Royal Palace**, on the fringes of the Quartier des Habous and set in extensive Mediterranean gardens, was built in the 1920s by the Pertuzio brothers, whose aim was to create a luxuriously appointed yet modern dwelling.

🏛 **Mahakma du Pacha**
Boulevard Victor Hugo.

⚜ **Royal Palace**
Between Boulevard Victor Hugo and Rue Ahmed el-Figuigui.
⬤ *to the public.*

Carpets displayed for sale in the Quartier Habous

The Twin Center, shaped like the hull of a ship, and its two towers

Casablanca Twin Center 10

At the intersection of Boulevard Zerktouni and Boulevard El-Massira.

Dominated by its two towers, which rise to a height of 100 m (328 ft), this extensive complex is proof and symbol of the city's economic importance. Built by Ricardo Bofill and Elie Mouyal, it comprises offices, shopping malls and a hotel. By its outward appearance no less than in its infrastructure, the building signals the economic role that Casablanca plays on both the national and international stage.

Musée du Judaïsme Marocain 11

81 Rue Chasseur Jules Gros, Quartier de l'Oasis. **Tel** *(0522) 99 49 40.*
⬤ *10am–5pm Mon–Fri.*

The modernized Museum of Moroccan Judaism contains displays of scarves, kaftans, prayer shawls and other religious objects, and a reconstructed synagogue.

From Roman times up to independence in 1956, Morocco had a sizeable Jewish community. Today numbering some 5,000, Morocco's Jews occupy prominent positions in the spheres of politics, economics and culture.

◁ **Painted plasterwork in the prayer hall of Hassan II Mosque**

The Anfa quarter occupies a hill overlooking the city

Anfa ⓬

Northwest of the city.

Occupying a hill that overlooks Casablanca from the northwest, Anfa is a residential quarter with wide flower-lined avenues where luxurious homes with terraces, swimming pools and lush gardens bring to mind Beverly Hills. Since the 1930s, villas in a great variety of styles have been built here, and they constitute a catalogue of successive architectural styles and fashions.

It was at the Hôtel d'Anfa, now demolished, that the historic meeting between US president Franklin D. Roosevelt and British prime minister Winston Churchill took place in January 1943, during World War II, at which the date of the Allied landings in Normandy was decided. Although they got wind of the meeting, the Germans were misled by the literal translation of "Casablanca".

Under the impression that the location was to be the White House in Washington, they failed to prevent it from going ahead.

During the meeting, President Roosevelt also formally pledged his support to Sultan Mohammed V in his aim to obtain independence from France, thus opening new avenues for Morocco in the postwar period.

Corniche d'Aïn Diab ⓭

West of the Mosque of Hassan II.

The Corniche d'Aïn Diab has been an upmarket part of Casablanca since the 1920s. Running from the **El-Hank Lighthouse** (built in 1916) in the east, to the *marabout* of Sidi Abderrahman in the west, this coastal avenue is lined with a succession of tidal swimming pools, hotels,

restaurants, fashionable night-clubs and an institute of thalassotherapy.

The earliest establishments to be built here – with the needs of a wealthy clientèle in mind – opened in the 1930s. A string of public beach clubs, each one rivalling its neighbour, lines the Corniche, offering a variety of pools and restaurants. The most modern and fashionable is the **Tahiti Beach Club**.

At the foot of the hill of Anfa, near the **Palais Ibn Séoud**, the foundation of the same name houses a mosque and one of the most comprehensive libraries on the African continent. At the western end of the Corniche, 3 km (2 miles) further on, the **Marabout of Sidi Abderrahman**, perched on a rock, is accessible only at low tide. It attracts Muslim pilgrims suffering from nervous disorders and those who have had evil spells cast on them.

Mohammedia ⓮

28 km (17 miles) northeast of Casablanca. 🚉 🚌

At the beginning of the 20th century, Mohammedia (formerly called Fedala) was nothing more than a kasbah. This changed in the 1930s, when its port began to receive oil tankers. Today, petroleum accounts for 16 per cent of all Moroccan port traffic. Although the flaming chimneys of the refineries blight the landscape, this town of over 300,000 inhabitants, now part of greater Casablanca, is still residential. It has a golf course and a yacht club. Its fine beaches and friendly atmosphere have helped to turn Mohammedia also into an upmarket coastal resort for wealthy Moroccans.

A visit to the kasbah and the fish market can be followed by a stroll along the seafront. From the port, the clifftop walk offers fine views of the sea and Mohammedia.

El-Hank lighthouse

SOUTHERN ATLANTIC COAST

L*ike the whole of Morocco's Atlantic coastline, the area south of Casablanca is of variable interest to visitors. It is, however, worth the detour, as much for the architecture of the fortified towns built by the Portuguese, such as El-Jadida and Essaouira, as for the breathtaking coastal scenery. In addition, there is also the coastal resort of Oualidia, which has a very safe beach.*

Morocco's southern Atlantic coastal area contains many smaller towns and resorts, which are especially attractive to those who wish to escape the frenetic activity of the imperial cities.

This region, more than almost any other part of Morocco, has always had contact with the outside world. The Phoenicians, then the Romans, established trading posts here. The Portuguese and the Spanish built military strongholds and centres of trade along the coast, whose topography also made it a haven for pirates. Fortified towns like El-Jadida, Safi and, most especially, Essaouira bear witness to the Spanish and Portuguese contribution to Morocco's history. Under the French Protectorate, the region became the country's economic and administrative centre. Today, this stretch of coastline is industrial and visibly oriented toward the modern world: most of the country's phosphate is produced here, the industry attracting a large workforce from the interior.

The entire coastline, punctuated by scenic viewpoints over the ocean, is ideal for bird-watching and palaeontology. Gourmets will also enjoy Oualidia's famous oysters.

The road, excellent from Casablanca to Essaouira, passes stunningly beautiful deserted beaches that are ideal for surfing. It winds on to Agadir, the great sardine-processing port and Morocco's most popular coastal destination. The wild landscape is dominated by the curious argan tree, with goats climbing in its branches *(see p127)*. It produces the highly prized argan oil

Fishing boats in the harbour at Imessouane, south of Cap Tafelney

◁ The caretaker of the kasbah at Boulaouane *(see p112)*

Exploring the Southern Atlantic Coast

This part of Morocco's Atlantic coastline is punctuated by the fortified towns of Azemmour, El-Jadida, Safi and Essaouira, which were established by the Portuguese in the 15th and 16th centuries. The road running inland from Settat to Boulaouane crosses a stunningly beautiful plateau, carved out of the landscape by Wadi Oum er-Rbia (Mother of Spring), where all the colours of the splendid Doukkala region can be seen. Further south, the road leading to Agadir offers interesting tours up into the lower foothills of the High Atlas. In the 1970s, the most accessible part of the foothills was given the name Paradise Valley. The well-marked road that winds between luxuriant cascades provides points of departure for hikes in the mountains, and it eventually leads to Imouzzer des Ida Outanane, a quiet summer resort.

GETTING AROUND

A motorway runs between Casablanca and El-Jadida, which is a distance of 99 km (62 miles). From here, the N1 goes to Agadir. This major road goes inland from El-Jadida as far as Essaouira, 360 km (224 miles) from Casablanca, and runs near or actually on the coast for the 165 km (103 miles) between Essaouira and Agadir. However, the quickest route to Agadir is by motorway via Marrakech. A dual carriage-way runs between Marrakech and Essaouira. The R301 is a minor road that follows the coast between El-Jadida and Essaouira, passing through Oualidia and Safi, 241 km (150 miles) from Casablanca. A motorway and the N9 run inland from Casablanca towards Settat (and Marrakech). From Settat, the R316 leads to Kasbah Boulaouane, from where it is easy to rejoin the coast road.

Azemmour, on Wadi Oum er-Rbia

SEE ALSO

- **Where to Stay** pp306–7
- **Where to Eat** pp332–3

SIGHTS AT A GLANCE

AGADIR pp286–7
Azemmour ③
CASABLANCA pp94–107
Chiadma Region ⑨
El-Jadida ④
Essaouira pp120–25 ⑩
Kasbah Boulaouane ②
Kasbah Hamidouch ⑧
MARRAKECH pp222–43
Moulay Abdallah ⑤
Oualidia ⑥
Safi ⑦
Settat ⑰
Tamanar ⑪
Tamri ⑫

Tour
Imouzzer des Ida
  Outanane ⑬

The *sqala* (bastion) in the harbour at Essaouira

The Portuguese Cistern at El-Jadida

KEY

▬▬	Motorway
▪▪▪	Motorway under construction
▬	Major road
══	Minor road
---	Track
⊶⊶	Railway
△	Summit

0 km   20

0 miles   20

A village near Settat, on the fertile coastal plain of Chaouia

Settat ❶

Road map C3. 100,000.
Avenue Hassan II,
El-Haram building; (0523) 40 58 05.
Moussem of the Chaouia (first
week in July or in Sept), Chaouia Folk
Art Festival (final week in Nov).
daily; livestock market Sat.

A crossroads between north
and south, Settat is the capital
of a province with some
850,000 inhabitants. It is the
economic hub of the Chaouia,
a coastal plain that is known as
Morocco's grainstore. While the
north of the region is famous
for its fertile agricultural land,
the southern part is given
over to livestock (*chaoui*
means "breeder of sheep").

When Moulay Ismaïl built
the Kasbah Ismaïla, at the
end of the 17th century, the
security and stability of the
region – which was traversed
by major caravan routes –
was strengthened. The sultan
would stay in the kasbah on
his travels between Fès and
Marrakech. Vestiges of the
building can still be seen
in the modern town.

Today, Settat offers little of
interest to tourists. However,
under the aegis of Driss Basri,
a native of the region and
Minister of the Interior for
almost 20 years, it stood as a
model of urban development
in the 1990s. The merits of this
distinction can be seen from
Place Hassan II, in the town
centre, in the arrangement of
open spaces and of pedestrian
and shopping areas, and in
buildings combining Art Deco
and Moorish styles.

Environs
The tiny village of
Boulaouane can be reached
by road from Settat. The journey there gives a foretaste
of the semi-arid southern
landscapes. The roads are
lined with Barbary fig trees,
and donkeys can be seen
carrying barrels of the local
rosé wine.

Kasbah Boulaouane ❷

Road map C3.

Located in a meander of
Wadi Oum er-Rbia, this
stunning kasbah stands on a
promontory in the heart of a
forested area covering 3,000
hectares (7,400 acres). It
was apparently built by the
Almohads, who made it an
imperial stopping place on
the road running along the
coast and inland to Fès. At
the beginning of the 16th

century, it was the scene of a
battle that halted the advance
of the Portuguese towards the
interior. Moulay Ismaïl revitalized the village by choosing
to build a kasbah here in
1710 – in an attempt to pacify
and control the region.

The stone-built fortress is
encircled by a crenellated
wall set with bastions and
pierced by an angled gate
with three pointed arches.
Above the gate is an
inscription with the name of
Moulay Ismaïl and the date
of the kasbah's foundation.
This gate, which accom-
modated sentries, is the
only point of entry into the
fortress. It leads through to
the sultan's palace, which
is built around a central
courtyard with elaborate
mosaic decoration. Beside
the palace, a square tower
about 10 m (33 ft) high,
and now disfigured by
cracks, afforded a vantage
point over the surrounding
territory. Disused vaulted
armouries were used for
storing food supplies. The
mosque, with five aisles,
is in a very bad state of
preservation. Next to it is
the tomb of a saint named
Sidi Mancar, whom the
region's inhabitants still
revere today, since he
is believed to have the
power to cure paralysis
and sterility.

Ceaselessly battered by
the elements, the kasbah
has suffered a great deal
of deterioration over the
centuries. It was declared a
historic monument in 1922.

Kasbah Boulaouane, built in the 18th century

BOULAOUANE WINE

Connoisseurs consider that the wine known as Gris de Boulaouane, a rosé with an orange tint, is one of the best Moroccan wines. Although the Romans successfully exploited the soil and climate of Mauretania Tingitana to grow vines, the establishment of Islam in the Maghreb did not further the upkeep of the vineyards. Under the French Protectorate, the vineyards were revived, and in 1956 wine production passed into state control. The state-

Extensive vineyards near Boulaouane

owned company that marketed Gris de Boulaouane collapsed, however, and the quality of the wine deteriorated. The French company Castel retook control of Moroccan wine production in the 1990s: the old vines were dug up and new stock planted, this time Cabernet-Sauvignon, Merlot, Cinsault, Syrah and Grenache gris. Today, Moroccan vineyards cover 350 hectares (865 acres) in the district of Boulaouane, the Doukkala region, the foothills of the Atlas and along the Atlantic coast. The vines are planted in sand, the heat of which prevents the development of phylloxera. The grapes are hand-harvested at the end of August and the wine, bottled in France, is exported mostly to Europe.

A bottle of Gris de Boulaouane

The Mosque and city walls are undergoing restoration work.

The region is also famous for its tradition of falconry, a sport still practised today by falconers from several important local families.

Azemmour ❸

Road map B2. 🏠 *32,800.* 🚍
🚩 *Avenue Mohammed V.*
📅 *Moussem (Aug).* 📅 *Tue.*

An ancient Almohad town located on the left bank of the Wadi Oum er-Rbia estuary, Azemmour is also known by the name of Moulay Bouchaïb – the town's patron saint, who, in the 12th century, was also patron saint of the trade that then flourished between the town and Málaga, in Spain.

In 1513, the Portuguese took control of the town. The fort that they built became the kasbah that can be seen

A door in the medina, Azemmour

today. They abandoned the town when Agadir fell in 1541.

Despite its year-round gentle climate and coastal location, Azemmour has few hotels and not many tourists come here. The narrow white streets of the medina are peppered with architectural

features recalling the former Portuguese presence – the style of the doors being particularly prominent in this respect. The town also has a tradition of Portuguese-style embroidery, which features dragons and lions depicted face to face, an exclusively Moroccan motif. The mellah (Jewish quarter), once within walls, is now derelict. The synagogue, however, has a notable pediment with an inscription in Hebrew.

Environs

Eight kilometres (5 miles) north on the coast road, the **Sidi Boubeker lighthouse** offers a view of the town's Portuguese defences. **Haouzia** beach, starting 2 km (1.5 miles) southeast of Azemmour, stretches for 15 km (9 miles) from the Oum er-Rbia estuary to El-Jadida. Along the way it passes a forest of eucalyptus, pine and mimosa with flowering cacti.

Embroidery with dragon motifs, of Portuguese inspiration and typical of Azemmour

El-Jadida ❹

The Portuguese settled here in 1502 and built a fort that they named Mazagan. In time, the town became a major centre of trade, and ships from Europe and the East anchored here to take on provisions. In 1769, the sultan Sidi Mohammed expelled the Portuguese, who dynamited it as they fled. It was resettled by local Arab tribes and a large Jewish community from Azemmour at the beginning of the 19th century. The town was then known as El-Jadida (The New One), but temporarily reassumed its original name – Mazagan – under the French Protectorate.

⚓ Ramparts

Entry into the old town is through a gateway that leads to Place Mohammed ben-Abdallah. The walls were originally fortified with five bastions but only four of these were rebuilt after the Portuguese had destroyed the town as they escaped Sidi Mohammed in 1769. The rampart walk leads to the Bastion de l'Ange, which commands a panoramic view over the old town. The Bastion de St Sébastien was once the seat of the Inquisition's tribunal and the prison.

Bastion de l'Ange, commanding a fine view of El-Jadida's harbour

⚓ Medina

The main street leads to the sea gate (Porta do Mar), from where there is access to the rampart walk. This gate, now blocked in, once linked the town to the seashore. Halfway along the main street is the entrance to the Citerne Portugaise, originally an underground arsenal, which is one of El-Jadida's most interesting sights and should not be missed.

The mellah has a deserted air: most of the Jewish community emigrated to Israel in the early 1950s.

The old town of El-Jadida, built by the Portuguese

CITERNE PORTUGAISE (PORTUGUESE CISTERN)

The Portuguese built this underground "cistern" in 1514. First an arsenal, then an armoury, it came to be used as a cistern only in 1541. The reflection of the columns and the vaulting on the water is an unreal and mysterious sight.

A well, 3.5 m (11.5 ft) across, was sunk through the central span, allowing daylight to enter.

The vaults rest on five lines of columns.

The cistern takes the form of a square 34 m by 33 m (111 ft by 108 ft).

The 25 pillars are reflected in the stagnant water.

OUALIDIA OYSTERS

Lovers of seafood hold Oualidia oysters in especially high esteem. The species of edible oyster that is raised in the local oyster farms is related to those from the Marennes-Oléron region of France, which were imported in the 1950s. Oyster Farm No. 7, which was set up in 1992 in the lagoon here, is one of the most modern in Morocco. The oysters and other shellfish that are farmed here are raised according to stringent European health and hygiene regulations.

Oualidia oysters

VISITORS' CHECKLIST

Road map B2. 🏛 *150,000.* 🚌 📇 ℹ️ *20 bis, Ave Maukawama & Place Mohammed V; (0523) 34 47 88.* 🎪 *Moussem of Moulay Abdallah (Aug).* 🔵 *Sun.*

🏺 Citerne Portugaise

🔵 *9am–1pm & 3–6pm daily.* 🎟

This former armoury, in the Manueline Gothic style, was converted into a cistern after the citadel was enlarged in 1541. It was then constantly fed by fresh water so as to guarantee the town's water supply in the event of a prolonged siege. Rediscovered by chance in 1916 when a shopkeeper was knocking down a wall to enlarge his shop, it has fascinated many artists as well as visitors. Orson Welles used it as a location for certain scenes of his film *Othello*, released in 1952.

Environs

El-Jadida is a short bus ride away from the very popular **Sidi Bouzid** beach, which is about 5 km (3 miles) further south.

Moulay Abdallah ❺

Road map B3. 11 km (7 miles) south of El-Jadida and 82 km (51 miles) north of Oualidia. 🎪 *Moussem (Aug).*

The origins of this fishing village lie in a 12th-century Almohad settlement which was then known as Tit. The old site's impressive ruins can still be seen today, together with a minaret dating from the same period as that of the Koutoubia Mosque in Marrakech *(see pp236–7)*. The settlement was, at that time, a *ribat*, or fortified monastery, built around the cult of the saint Moulay Abdallah, whose purpose was to guard the coast. It became a busy port, but was destroyed in the early 16th century to prevent the Portuguese, who were at Azemmour, from

taking it. The fishing industry revived the village, which then assumed the name of the saint in whose honour it was established. The *moussem* held here in August is renowned for its fantasias *(see p35)*.

Environs

From the coast road leading south from Moulay Abdallah you can see the huge installations of the mineral **Port de Jorf Lasfar**, the largest port in Africa. Built in the 1980s, it has a chemical complex and petrol refinery.

Oualidia ❻

Road map B3. 🏛 *3,000.* 🚌 🔵 *Sat.*

This small coastal resort takes its name from the sultan El-Oualid, who built a kasbah here in 1634. The rather unattractive town centre leads through to a stunningly beautiful beach on the edge of a lagoon. Swimming is safe here but on either side, the sea is rough and foaming. This is one of the beaches on the Atlantic coast that is good for surfing, particularly for beginners. Among the summer villas here is the residence built for Mohammed V.

The town is an important centre of the oyster industry. A visit to the oyster farms *(parcs à huitres)*, particularly **Oyster Farm N° 7** – including the opportunity to sample some oysters – is a pleasant way to pass some time. The **Ostrea** restaurant and hotel is also located here.

Oyster Farm N° 7 (and Ostrea)
On the El-Jadida road. **Tel** *(0523) 36 64 51/ (0664) 49 12 76.*

Environs

The coast road running southwards along the clifftop leads to **Cap Beddouza**, and on to Safi.

Heaps of phosphate in the mineral port of Jorf Lasfar

Safi

Road map B3. 260,000.
tourist office, Rue Imam-Malek &
main market, Ave de la Liberté;
(0524) 62 24 96. Moussem of the
Seven Saints (mid-Aug), Moussem of
Lalla Fatna (mid-Nov). Mon.

An important Moroccan port
since the 16th century, the
town of Safi is today an
industrial centre and a major
sardine-processing port. It
owes its importance to the
growth of the fishing industry
and to the processing and
export of phosphates, as well
as to its pottery. A rapidly
expanding town, Safi has an
interesting medina as well as
traces of its Portuguese history.

Medina
The area covered by the
medina takes the form of a
triangle whose widest side
faces onto the coast. Rue du
Souk, lined with shops and
workshops, leads to Bab
Chaaba (Gate of the Valley).
Near the Grand Mosque,
south of the medina, is
the **Portuguese Chapel**,
originally the choir of
Safi's cathedral, built by
the Portuguese in 1519.

Dar el-Bahr
8:30am–noon & 2:30–
5:30pm Wed–Mon.
This small fortress, also
known as the Château
de la Mer, overlooks
the sea. It was built by the
Portuguese at the beginning
of the 16th century, and
served as a residence for the
governor, then for the sultans
in the 17th century. On the
esplanade are cannons cast in
Spain, Portugal and Holland.

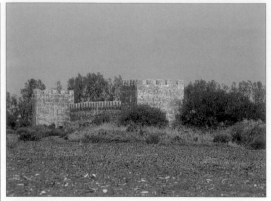
Kasbah Hamidouch, built by Moulay Ismaïl

Musée National de la Céramique
Kechla. 8:30am–noon & 2–6pm
Wed–Mon.
Built by the Portuguese in
the 16th century, the citadel,
known as the Kechla, encloses
a mosque and garden dating
from the 18th and 19th centuries. Since 1990 the Kechla
has housed the Musée
National de la Céramique,
which contains displays
of traditional and modern
ceramics, including blue-
on-white wares made in
Safi, pottery from Fès and
Meknès, and pieces by
Boujmaa Lamali
(1890–1971).

**Safi candlestick,
20th century**

Colline des Potiers
In the Bab Chaaba
district, craftsmen can
be seen making the ceramic
wares that have made Safi
famous. Finished pieces are
displayed and offered for sale
in commercial showrooms and
visitors can follow the various
stages of pottery production
at the training school.

Kasbah Hamidouch

Road map B3. 29 km (18 miles)
south of Safi on the coast road.

This kasbah forms part of a
system of fortified outposts
that Moulay Ismaïl (see
pp54–5) established along the
main routes of communication
so as to control the region
and accommodate travellers.
The kasbah is encircled by
an outer wall, within which
stand a mosque and various
buildings, now in ruins. An
inner wall, set with square
towers and reinforced by a
dry moat, surrounds a courtyard that is lined with shops,
various houses and a chapel.

Chiadma Region

Road map B3–4.

The territory of the Chiadma,
in the provinces of Safi and
Essaouira, is inhabited by
Regraga Berbers. They are
descended from seven saint
apostles of Islam, who, during
a journey to Mecca, were
directed by the Prophet
Mohammed to convert the
Maghreb to Islam. In spring,
a commemorative pilgrimage
is made, ending at the small
village of **Ha Dra**.
A souk, one of the most
authentic markets in the
area, takes place in Ha
Dra on Sunday mornings.
Grain, spices, animals and a
wide range of goods, mostly
food, are offered for sale.

A potter at work in Safi, where a particularly high-quality clay is used

Fishing boats on the shore below Essaouira's ramparts

Sea Fishing in Morocco

The Moroccan coastline, which is more than 3,500 km (2,175 miles) long, faces both the Atlantic Ocean and the Mediterranean Sea, and gives the country access to some of the richest fishing grounds in the world – with some 240 species of fish. Morocco brings in the largest catches of fish in the whole of Africa. Its pre-eminence is due especially to sardines, of which Morocco is the largest processor and exporter in the world. Coastal fishing has created a major canning industry, too. The Moroccan sea fishing industry employs some 200,000 people and exports bring in US $600 million per year. Modern fishing methods, however, have not completely replaced traditional ways.

Small trawlers, *many of them made of wood, as well as motorized dinghies, ply the coastal waters as far out to sea as the edge of the Continental Shelf. Their catches consist of many different species of fish.*

Sardine fishing *in Essaouira uses swivel nets. In spite of their expert knowledge of the sea bed, the fishermen often have to repair damaged nets when they return to harbour every day.*

The eateries *in Essaouira's harbour invite customers to select a plateful of fish and eat it on the spot. Many such establishments are to be found in the port, at the exit from the sqala.*

The fish market at Agadir *is one of the largest sardine ports in the world. An auction, which sells almost 250 different kinds of fish, takes place here every day.*

Crates of fish *are packed ready for sale. Sardines are the most important catch, but other fish, including hake and grey mullet, are also on offer.*

Conservor, *the canning company, is one of Safi's major industries. It revitalized the local economy in the 1920s.*

Essaouira ⑩

Burnous

With the brilliant whiteness of its lime-washed walls and the sight of women enveloped in voluminous *haiks*, Essaouira, formerly Mogador, is a quintessentially Moroccan town and one of the most enchanting places in the country. By virtue of its location on this stretch of the Atlantic coast, where trade winds prevail almost all year-round, the town enjoys a particularly pleasant climate. It is a prime location for surfing, but has managed to escape mass tourism. A mecca for hippies during the 1970s, it is still an artists' town and is very fashionable with independent travellers.

The Porte de la Marine, built by Sidi Mohammed ben Abdallah

Women in Essaouira wearing the characteristic *haik*

Exploring Essaouira

In the 7th century BC, the Phoenicians founded a base on the site where Essaouira now stands, and in the 1st century BC Juba II made it a centre of the manufacture of purple dye. The Portuguese established a trading and military bridgehead here in the 15th century, and named it Mogador. The town itself, however, was not built until around 1760, by the Alaouite sultan Sidi Mohammed ben Abdallah (Mohammed III), who had decided to set up a naval base here. The town, the harbour and the fortifications, in the style of European fortresses, were designed and built by Théodore Cornut, a renowned French architect who had worked for Louis XV.

🏛 Ramparts

On the side facing the sea, the outer walls, which have bevelled crenellations, were designed to give protection from naval attack and are thus typical of European fortifications. By contrast, the inner walls, which have square crenellations and are similar to the fortifications around Marrakech, are Islamic in style. These are built in stone and roughcast with a facing of earth. The walls are pierced by gates – Bab Sebaa on the southern side, Bab Marrakech on the eastern side and Bab Doukkala on the northeastern side – that lead into the medina.

🏛 Sqalas

Two *sqalas* (sea bastions) were built to protect the town: the **Sqala de la Ville**, in the northwest, and the **Sqala du Port**, in the south.

The Sqala de la Ville consists of a crenellated platform featuring a row of Spanish cannons and defended at its northern end by the North Bastion. This was built by Théodore Cornut on the site of the Castello Real, a citadel constructed by the Portuguese in about 1505. The esplanade (where scenes from Orson Welles' film *Othello* were shot in 1949) commands a view of the ocean and the Îles Purpuraires. A covered passage leads from the bastion to the former munitions stores, which now house marquetry workshops.

Port

Sqala du Port. ⬜ *daily.* 📷

The Porte de la Marine, leading to the docks, is crowned by a classical triangular pediment and dominated by two imposing towers flanked by four turrets. The rectangular Sqala du Port is surmounted by battlements.

From the 18th century, 40 per cent of Atlantic sea traffic passed through Essaouira. It became known as the Port of Timbuctu, being the destination of caravans from sub-Saharan Africa bringing goods for export to Europe. Once one of Morocco's largest

Sqala de la Ville, a favourite place for strolls at sunset

View of the Sqala du Port, at the southern entrance to the town

sardine ports, Essaouira now provides a living for no more than 500 to 600 families. But it still has its traditional shipyard, where vessels are made out of wood. Visitors can also watch the fish auction and sample freshly grilled sardines.

Medina

The layout of Essaouira is unusual because it was planned before the town was developed. It was laid out by the French architect Cornut, who, between 1760 and 1764, built the Sqala de la Ville and the Sqala du Port, endowing them with fortifications and outer and inner walls.

As elsewhere in Morocco, the medina in Essaouira is a labyrinth of narrow streets; the town itself, by contrast, has straight, wide streets laid out at right angles to one another and cut by gateways. The **Grand Mosque** is situated in the heart of the medina. Further north, the market, **Souk Jdid**, is divided into four by the intersection of two thoroughfares: there is a daily souk for fish, spices and grains, and a souk for second-hand and collectable items, known as *joutia*.

VISITORS' CHECKLIST

Road map B4. 70,000. 1 km (0.5 mile) northeast of the medina. Link to Marrakech coach station (departure opposite the Hôtel des Îles). Rue du Caire, (0524) 78 35 32. Festival of Gnaoua music (Jun). Regraga Pilgrimage (Beginning of Apr). Festival des Alizés (Apr/May).

The daily spice souk, laid out next to the fish souk

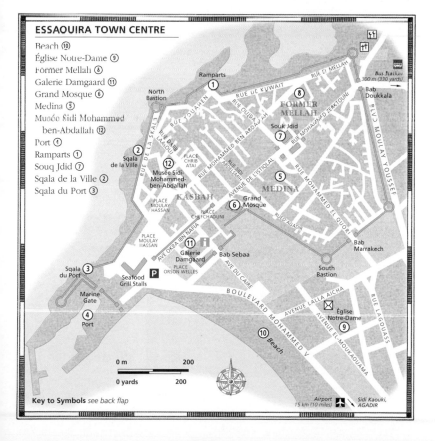

ESSAOUIRA TOWN CENTRE

Beach ⑩
Église Notre-Dame ⑨
Former Mellah ⑧
Galerie Damgaard ⑪
Grand Mosque ⑥
Medina ⑤
Musée Sidi Mohammed ben-Abdallah ⑫
Port ④
Ramparts ①
Souq Jdid ⑦
Sqala de la Ville ②
Sqala du Port ③

Key to Symbols see back flap

Working with Thuya

Thuya, a highly prized wood with a delicious perfume, grows abundantly in the region of Agadir and Essaouira, and has been the source of that latter's prosperity. Thuya is a very dense hardwood, and almost every part of the tree apart from the branches can be used: the trunk, with its relatively light-coloured wood; the stump, used for making small objects; and the gnarl, a rare excrescence streaked with brown and pink. The gnarl is polished, inlaid with decorative motifs in citron wood, mother-of-pearl or ebony and sometimes with threads of silver or copper, or slivers of camel bone. It is used to make such items as coffee tables, caskets, small statues, boxes in all shapes and sizes, trays and jewellery. The country's best marquetry craftsmen can be seen working at this traditional craft in the former munitions stores beneath Essaouira's ramparts.

MARQUETRY

Essaouira's cabinet-makers were already renowned in antiquity, and the town has remained the capital of marquetry ever since. Tradition dictates that the artistically skilled part of the work (from the construction of a piece to its decoration) be done by men. Women and children are given the task of polishing the finished items.

The high sheen *of this bread box is produced by polishing the surface with methylated spirit and gum arabic. Linseed oil feeds the wood and prevents it from developing cracks.*

The decoration *of this dish is based on a geometric scheme. The border pattern consists of an inlay of alternating pieces of ebony and citron wood.*

THE THUYA GNARL

This excrescence, which grows on certain trees, particularly the thuya, is very sought after by cabinet-makers for its veined and speckled appearance.

Craftsmen *apply all their ingenuity and imagination to produce novel shapes.*

The thuya gnarl *is separated from the trunk.*

The old part of the Jewish cemetery at Essaouira

🏛 Former Mellah

From Bab Doukkala, accessible via
Rue Mohammed Zerktouni.
Controlled access

Having risen to prominence
and prosperity in the 18th
and 19th centuries, the Jewish
community in Essaouira came
to hold an important
economic position in the
town, and Jewish jewellers
acquired wide renown.

The town's former Jewish
quarter is no longer inhabited
by Jews, but on Rue Darb
Laalouj the former houses
of Jewish businessmen can
still be seen; they are now
converted into shops. In
contrast to Muslim houses,
they are fronted by balconies
opening onto the street and
some have lintels with
inscriptions in Hebrew.

Rue Mohammed Zerktouni,
the main street in the quarter,
has a very lively market.
Leaving by Bab Doukkala,
you will pass the austere
Jewish cemetery, which is
worth a visit. (The keys are
available on request from
the caretaker.)

🕍 Église Notre-Dame

Avenue El-Moukaouama, south of
the post office. 🕐 8:30am Mon–Sat,
10am Sun. *Tel* (0524) 47 58 95.

This Catholic church stands
outside the walls of the
medina, on the road leading
to the beach. It is the only
church in the country where
the bells are rung on Sundays
to summon the faithful to
mass at 11am.

Most of the church furnishings are made of thuya wood.
On an alternating basis, the
services here are said in one
of four languages: French,
English, Dutch or German.

🏖 Beach

Essaouira's beach, to the
south of the town centre, is
known as one of the finest
in Morocco. All through the
summer, the trade winds
keep this part of the coast
surprisingly cool. At times,
however, the gusty winds
are so strong that they
drive people to seek
shelter in the medina.

At the estuary of
Wadi Qsob, on the
far side of the beach,
vestiges of the system
of defences built on
a rocky promontory
by the sultan Sidi
Mohammed are
visible. Although
they have
crumbled, thick
walls can still be made out.

By following the *wadi*
upstream, after a tumbled-
down bridge, you reach the
village of Diabet. It is also
accessible via the road to
Agadir, turning off to the
right after 7 km (4 miles). An
interesting sight here are the

Surfer

ruins of **Dar Soltane
Mahdounia**, a palace built by
Sidi Mohammed ben Abdallah
in the 18th century and now
almost completely engulfed in
sand. It inspired Jimi Hendrix
(who lived in Diabet for
several years) to write the
song *Castles in the Sand*.

Surfers will particularly
enjoy the many beaches each
side of Essaouira. Thanks to
the enterprise of dynamic
local associations, Morocco is
about to become one of the
top destinations for surfers
and windsurfers. (The Océan
Vagabond café is a good
place to hire surfing
equipment.) The windiest
time of year in the Essaouira
area, and therefore the best
time for surfing and
windsurfing here, is from
April to September.

However, while the air,
at 20–30 °C
(68–86 °F),
is always
pleasantly warm, the
water is always a very cool
16–18 °C (61–64 °F).

South of Essaouira, at
Cap Sim (beyond Diabet)
and at **Sidi Kaouki**, and
to the north, at **Moulay
Bouzerktoun**, the waves are
very strong, and safe only
for experienced surfers.

Also to the south, at
Tafelney (beyond the village
of Smimou), there is a
magnificent bay where the
water is warmer. In spite of
the constant gusty wind, it is
easier to get into the water on
the beach at Essaouira, as the
waves are much gentler.

Essaouira beach, swept by strong gusts of wind all year round

For hotels and restaurants in this region see pp306–7 and pp332–3

🏛 Galerie Damgaard

Avenue Oqba Ibn Nafia.
Tel (0524) 78 44 46. **Fax** *(0524) 47 58 57.* ☐ *9am–1pm & 3–7pm daily.*

For about a quarter of a century, a generation of painters and sculptors has made Essaouira an important centre of artistic activity. Many talented artists have been brought to public attention by the Dane Frederic Damgaard.

Formerly an antique dealer in Nice, since 1988, Damgaard devoted his energies to the art produced in Essaouira, opening his own art gallery in the medina until he retired in 2006. On display is the work of artists from the humblest walks of life. Among the best known are Mohammed Tabal, a Gnaoua painter who has become known as "the trance painter", Zouzaf, Ali Maïmoune, Rachid Amarlouch and Fatima Ettalbi. Others to be discovered include the expressionist Ali, whose style is midway between naive and Brutalist. All of them draw their inspiration from Essaouira's cultural variety, and reflect the traditions of different schools. Many exhibitions and other projects, in Morocco and throughout the world, have been devoted to the painters of Essaouira.

🏛 Musée Sidi-Mohammed-ben-Abdallah

Rue Darb Laalouj. ☐ *9am–6pm Wed–Mon.* 🖼

This small ethnographic museum is laid out in a

Art gallery of Frederic Damgaard, the great discoverer of artistic talent

19th-century house that was a former pasha's residence and the town hall during the Protectorate. It contains fine displays of ancient crafts and of weapons and jewellery. There are also instruments and accessories used by religious brotherhoods, Moorish musical instruments and some stunning examples of Berber and Jewish costumes in silk, velvet and flannel. Carpets illustrating the traditional weaving of local tribes are also exhibited.

Rbab, in the Musée Sidi-Mohammed

Environs

On the **Îles Purpuraires**, visible across the bay from Essaouira, is a bird sanctuary where gulls and the rare Eleonora's falcon, a threatened species, and other birds can be seen.

Phoenician, Attic and Ionian amphorae discovered on the Île de Mogador, the main island, and now in the Musée Archéologique in

Rabat *(see pp78–9),* prove that trade was taking place here from the 7th century BC. In the 1st century BC, Juba II *(see p45),* founder of Volubilis, set up a centre for the production of purple dye, from which the islands take their name. Purple dye, highly prized by the Romans, was obtained from the murex, a mollusc. The ruins of a prison, built in the 19th century by the sultan Moulay el-Hassan, are also visible.

Some 12 km (7.5 miles) south of Essaouira, the splendid beach at **Sidi Kaouki** is very popular with surfers. A mausoleum, which appears to rise up out of the water, contains the tomb of a *marabout* (holy man) who, according to legend, had the power to cure barren women. An annual pilgrimage, with many devotees, takes place here in mid-August.

🏃 Îles Purpuraires

Controlled access (information available from the tourist office).

Mausoleum of Sidi Kaouki, at the far end of a spectacularly extensive beach south of Essaouira

For hotels and restaurants in this region see pp306–7 and pp332–3

The Painters of Essaouira

Essaouira, a town imbued with art and culture, is home to a group of painters known as "free artists", each of whom has his or her own unique style. Their talents have won recognition abroad and their work has been shown in many European art galleries. Using bright colours, their naive or "tribal" art is inspired by the myths,

Detail of a
work by Tabal

Arab-Berber history and African origins of Moroccan popular culture. These self-taught painters are also woodcarvers, sailors and builders, and they have in common an unconditional love of their town. Arabesques, geometric designs, dots, stippling and a swarm of objects, animals and human figures populate their poetic world.

MOHAMMED TABAL

A leading figure in Essaouira's artistic circles, Mohammed Tabal draws inspiration from his Gnaoui ancestry – from the ritual of spiritual possession and from the trances that form part of the rites of this popular brotherhood of African origin. His paintings are splashed with bright, contrasting colours and feature a multitude of tiny details, such as naive motifs rich in symbolism.

Mohammed Tabal's paintings *are imbued with mysticism.*

Abdallah Elatrach *is inspired by scenes of daily life in the souks and by the traditions of various brotherhoods whose rituals involve trance.*

Ali Maïmoune *paints tree-filled worlds that are populated by terrifying monsters, animals and fantastic warriors.*

Imouzzer des Ida Outanane ⑬

This tour follows a very scenic river valley with many natural swimming pools surrounded by palm trees. From Agadir, a winding road leads to the village of Imouzzer, set on a hilltop in the foothills of the High Atlas. It is the heart of the territory of the Ida Outanane, a confederation of Berbers whose traditional speciality is gathering honey. Despite the exodus from the country into the towns, many women – dressed in brightly coloured robes – can still be seen at work on the hillsides.

Win t'mdoum Caves ①
Located 35 km (22 miles) from Imouzzer, these caves are the most extensive in North Africa. Work is under way to make them accessible to the public.

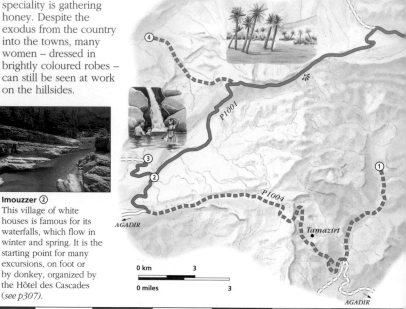

Imouzzer ②
This village of white houses is famous for its waterfalls, which flow in winter and spring. It is the starting point for many excursions, on foot or by donkey, organized by the Hôtel des Cascades (*see p307*).

0 km   3
0 miles   3

Tamanar ⑪

Road map B4. 🚌 *Thu in Tamanar, Fri in Arba des Ida Outrhouma, 10 km (6 km) south of Tamanar.*

The small town of Tamanar, which extends along its one main street, is a regional administrative centre and, effectively, the capital of the argan industry. It is at the heart of Haha territory, home to a sedentary yet dynamic Berber population which was self-governing in the 15th century.

On the way out of the village, near Café Argane, is a store selling locally produced argan oil. The highly organized women who run it show the fruits of their labour in a friendly atmosphere and sell their products in a cooperative.

Landscape near Tamanar

Environs
Between Smimou (where there is a picturesque souk on Sundays) and Tamanar, a small sign saying "Tafadna" indicates the route to **Tafelney**. Two-thirds along this road, the

landscape takes on a majestic beauty. The road comes to a sudden stop at a magnificent bay, where fishermen can often be seen mending their nets on the beach.

To the left, a huddle of identical shanty houses are home to thousands of birds. To those with a taste for remote spots, the strange beauty of this place will have a strong appeal.

Tamri ⑫

Road map B4. 🎣

This village is located on the estuary of a river that in winter is fed partly by the waterfall at Imouzzer (*see above*). There is an extensive

Tamaroute ③
The waterfalls in this attractive village are known as "The Bridal Veil". They are the southernmost waterfalls above the Sahara. Flowing from several levels, the waters are abundant when the snow begins to melt in spring.

Assif el-Had ④
The natural bridge at Assif el-Had was created by water flowing down from the mountains.

Imi Irhzer ⑤
In February, the red-ochre houses of the villages almost disappear in a sea of almond blossom. A sheepfold has been converted into a gîte.

ARGANA, MARRAKECH

P1001

Biramane •
Tasguint •

Bigoudine ⑥
The road to Bigoudine offers a succession of panoramic views. This is where the argan forests begin. When it is completed, a new road crossing the N8 and passing through Bigoudine will provide a link to Imouzzer.

AGADIR

KEY
- **▬** Itinerary (road)
- **▬ ▬** Itinerary (track)
- **═** Other roads
- **═ ═** Other tracks
- **⚡** View point

TIPS FOR TRAVELLERS

Departure : Imouzzer des Ida Outanane, at l'Hôtel des Cascades.
How to get there: From Agadir, northwards on the N1 turning off after 12 km (7.5 miles) onto a track. From the north, turn left onto the road 20 km (12 miles) after Cap Rhir. From Agadir, a bus departs from next door to the bus station at about 12:30pm daily (allow three and a half hours), returning from Imouzzer at 8am the next day.
Stopping-off point: Hôtel des Cascades at Imouzzer has relaxing gardens and a restaurant.

banana plantation. On the left, as you approach Tamri from the north, an inland road leads to a major bird-watching area, where Audouin's gulls, Barbary falcons, Lamier's falcons, sparrows and various other species can be seen.

Environs
About 19 km (12 miles) north of Agadir is **Taghazoute**, a fishing village that is popular with surfers. It was also colonized by the hippie movement, and, on the way out of Taghazoute, you can see curious signs saying "Banana Village" and "Paradise Valley" – names that were originally given by those who followed in the footsteps of Jimi Hendrix in the 1970s.

THE ARGAN TREE

Bottle of argan oil

The argan *(Argania sideroxylon)* is North Africa's weirdest tree. It is interesting not only in its own right, but is also important ecologically and economically. This tenacious, twisted tree, which never grows higher than 6 m (19.5 ft), has a multitude of uses. Being a very hard wood, it is ideal for making charcoal. It is also used to feed animals (camels and goats find the leaves and fruit delectable), and to make argan oil, which is extracted from the kernel. The vitamin-rich oil has a wide range of applications, according to the degree to which it is refined. It is used in cosmetics for what are thought to be its hydrating and anti-ageing properties, and in medicine to combat arteriosclerosis, chicken pox and rheumatism. Argan oil also has culinary uses – a few drops are enough to bring out the flavour of salads and *tajines* – and is used as fuel for lamps.

Goat perched in an argan tree, feeding on its fruit

TANGIER

*O*nce *an international city, Tangier has a special character that sets it apart from other Moroccan cities. It has drawn artists and writers, from Henri Matisse to Paul Bowles and writers of the Beat generation. Tangier's port, dominated by the medina, is the main link between Africa and Europe. With a road now linking Tangier to Rabat and the construction of a port, the city continues to expand.*

The history of Tangier has been shaped by the sea and by its strategic location on the Straits of Gibraltar. The Phoenicians established a port here in the 8th century, and it was later settled by the Carthaginians. In 146 BC, Tangier, known as Tingis, became a Roman town and the capital of Mauretania, to which it gave the name Tingitana. In 711, Arab and Berber forces gathered here to conquer Spain. By the 14th century, the town was trading with Marseilles, Genoa, Venice and Barcelona. Tangier was captured by the Portuguese in 1471, by the Spanish (1570–1640) and then the English, who were expelled from the city by Moulay Ismaïl in 1684. In the 19th century, Morocco was the object of dispute between European nations. When, in 1905, Kaiser Wilhelm II denounced the *entente cordiale* between France and Britain, the stage was set for Tangier's transformation into an international city. This was sealed by the Treaty of Algeciras (1906), after which the diplomatic corps in Tangier took over Morocco's political, financial and fiscal affairs. When colonial rule was established in 1912, Spain took control of the northern part of the country. Tangier, however, remained under international administration. This was the city's heyday. Its image as a romantic and sensuously exotic place was made in literature and on the big screen.

After independence in 1956, Tangier was returned to Morocco, but suffered political ostracism. However, the city became industrialized, and new districts sprang up. Mohammed VI now includes it in his royal visits, and this has given a boost to the city.

Locals relaxing in the Café du Grand Socco in the Ville Nouvelle district of Tangier

◁ The elegant whitewashed façade of Tangier's Ancien Palais du Mendoub, built in 1929

Exploring Tangier

The best overview of the city is from the vantage point of the
Colline du Charf or Colline de Bella-Vista, to the southeast.
While the historic heart of Tangier is the medina, the soul
of the city is the kasbah, which has a palace-museum,
narrow streets, gateways and a seafront
promenade. In the evening, when it is
wise not to linger in the medina, visitors
who explore Ville Nouvelle (New Town),
along Avenue Pasteur and Avenue
Mohammed V, will come across the
Spanish custom of the *paseo* (evening
promenade). Alternatively, the cafés
on Place de France and Place de Faro
offer relaxing views of the port and
the Straits of Gibraltar, and, in clear
conditions, a sight of the lights
along the coast of Spain.

SIGHTS AT A GLANCE

Avenues, Streets and Squares
Avenue Pasteur ⑭
Place de France & Place de Faro ⑬
Rue de la Liberté ⑫
Rue Es-Siaghine ⑥

Quarters and Promenades
Bay of Tangier ⑲
Colline du Charf ⑱
Grand Socco
  (Place du 9 Avril 1947) ⑧
Kasbah ①
Petit Socco ④
Quartier du Marshan ⑰
Ramparts ③

Mosque and Church
Anglican Church of
  St Andrew ⑨
Grand Mosque ⑤

Historic Buildings
Ancien Palais
  du Mendoub ⑮
Café Hafa ⑯
Fondouk Chejra ⑪

Museums
American Legation ⑦
Galerie d'Art
  Contemporain
  Mohammed Drissi ⑩
Musée Archéologique ②

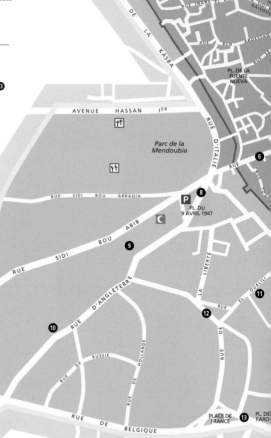

0 m   200

0 yards   200

SEE ALSO

- *Where to Stay* pp308–9
- *Where to Eat* pp333–4

GETTING AROUND

Parking is available in Ville Nouvelle, on Place du 9 Avril 1947 (Grand Socco) or on the Plateau du Marshan. The medina and kasbah must be explored on foot. The only practical use for cars and taxis is for reaching the Colline du Charf and Colline de Bella-Vista, the Plateau du Marshan and La Montagne, or for a trip along the bay, from the port to the edge of the wooded hills before Cap Malabata.

ENVIRONS OF TANGIER

0 km   1 km
0 yards 1000

S 704

P 2

P 36

▢ AREA OF MAIN MAP

KEY

▮	Medina
▮	Former sultan's palace
—	Ramparts
🚌	Bus station
P	Parking
i	Tourist information
✝	Church
✡	Synagogue
☪	Mosque
⚰	Christian cemetery
⚰	Jewish cemetery
⚰	Muslim cemetery

PL. DE L'ARSENAL

RUE MOUL...

R. RAHMOUNI

EDINA

RUE M. TORRES

RUE DES CHRETIENS

RUE MSA EL KEIR

INE

RUE MOKHTAR AHARDAN

5

4

BAB EL BAHAR

PLACE DE LA TANNERIE

PL DU PROGRES

RUE EDOUK

RUE DU PORTUGAL

Bus Station 🚌

1

AVENUE

RUE SALAH EDDINE EL AYOUBI

RUE ANOUAL

R. MANUEL PENA

KHALID BEN OUALID

R. OMAR IBN AL KHASS

R. DU PRINCE MOULAY ABDALLAH

OULEVARD PASTEUR

14

D'ESPAGNE

RUE EL JABHA EL OUATANIA

RUE IBN JOUBAYI

Port

3

Bab el-Assa, leading through to Place de la Kasbah

The fountain at Bab el-Assa, a gateway in the Kasbah, with mosaic decoration and ornamental stuccowork and woodcarving

Kasbah ❶

From the Marshan, accessible via Bab el-Kasbah; from the medina, via Rue Ben Raissouli and Bab el-Assa; from the Grand Socco, via Rue d'Italie and Rue de la Kasbah.

The kasbah was built on the site of the Roman settlement. Its present appearance dates from the Portuguese period and that of Moulay Ismaïl *(see pp54–5)*. With its quiet streets and friendly inhabitants, it has a special character, and its walls and gates command stunning views over the strait, the bay and the city.

Place de la Kasbah was once the *méchouar* where the sultan or his pashas held public audiences. It is also the location of the Dar El-Makhzen, the former palace that is now a museum *(see below)* and of the **Kasbah Mosque**, whose octagonal minaret is clad in coloured tiles. Its present form dates from the 19th century; the

mendoub led Friday prayers here. Also on the square is the Dar ech-Chera, the former tribunal, fronted by an arcade of three white marble columns. The large fig tree growing against the wall of an elegant house is supposed to be the place where Samuel Pepys wrote about Tangier in his diary in the 17th century.

Bab el-Assa (Gate of Basti-nado) leads from the square to the medina. It was set at an angle so as to make it more difficult to attack. The gate gets its name from the basti-nado (caning the soles of the feet) that was once the punishment of criminals. In the lobby, between the two porches, stands a fountain decorated with mosaics, stuccowork and woodcarving. Gnaouas, distantly related to those of Marrakech and Essaouira, regularly perform music and dance here. In the evening, audiences can talk with them about their musical traditions and their repertoire.

From the lobby, a narrow passage allows sight of a small *derb* (alleyway) lined with very fine houses, while beyond the gate is a view over the city. The **Musée d'Art Contemporain**, located in the former British Consu-late building, which dates from 1890, houses collections of modern Moroccan art and temporary exhibitions featur-ing the works of foreign artists.

🏛 **Musée d'Art Contemporain**
52 Rue d'Angleterre, Tanger.
ℹ *(0539) 94 99 72.* ⬤ *9am–noon, 2:30–6:30pm daily.* ⬤ *Tue.*

Central courtyard, Musée Archéologique

Musée Archéologique ❷

Place de la Kasbah. ℹ *(0539) 93 20 97.* ⬤ *9am–4pm Wed–Mon.* 🖼

The Museum of Archaeology is laid out in the Dar el Makhzen, a former sultans' palace built in the 17th century by Ahmed ben Ali, whose father Ali ben Abdellah al Hamani Errifi liberated Tangier from the British settlers in 1664. The palace was remodelled and enlarged several times in the 17th and 19th centuries. Bit el-Mal, the treasury – a separate room with a magnificent painted cedar ceiling – contains large 18th-century coffers with a complex sys-tem of locks.

A gallery leads to the pal-ace itself. It is built around a

The octagonal minaret on the Kasbah Mosque

central courtyard paved with *zellij* tilework and surrounded by a gallery supported by white marble columns with Corinthian capitals. The seven exhibition rooms opening onto the patio display artifacts evoking the material history of Tangier from prehistoric times to the 19th century. These include sets of bone and stone tools, ceramics, terracotta figurines and Phoenician silver jewellery.

The Voyage of Venus, a Roman mosaic from Volubilis *(see pp202–5),* is displayed in the museum's courtyard. Reproductions of several famous bronzes from the Musée Archéologique in Rabat *(see pp78–9)* are also on display. One room is devoted to Morocco's major archaeological sites. On the upper floor, the prehistory and history of Tangier and its environs, from the Neolithic period to its occupation by foreign powers, are presented through displays of grave goods, pottery and coins.

Adjacent to the palace is the Andalusian Garden.

Ramparts ❸

Place de la Kasbah. *Accessible via Bab el-Bahar.*

On the side of the square facing the sea, opposite Bab el-Assa, stands Bab el Bahar (Gate of the Sea), which was built in the walls in 1920. From the terrace there is a breathtaking view of the port, the straits and, in clear conditions, the Spanish coast.

The walkway, which starts on the left, follows the outside of the ramparts and leads to the impressive **Borj en Naam**, a fort. Continuing along the seafront and through residential districts, the route leads to Hafa.

🏨 **Borj en Naam.**
◑ *to the public.*

The Petit Socco, or Souk Dakhli, a pale reflection of its lively past

Petit Socco ❹

Accessible via Rue Es-Siaghine or Rue Jma el-Kbir.

Known today as the Souk Dakhli, the Petit Socco probably corresponds to the area on which the forum of Roman Tingis once stood. It was a country souk, where people would come to buy food, and with the arrival of Europeans at the end of the 19th century it became the pulsing heart of the medina. This was where business was done: diplomats, businessmen and bankers, whose offices were located around the square or in the close vicinity, could be seen in the cafés, hotels, casinos and cabarets of the Petit Socco. The Fuentes, a café restaurant and hotel, now gives but a faint impression of these halcyon days. From the 1950s, the hub of city life shifted to Ville Nouvelle, leaving the Petit Socco to a few writers, and to idlers, smokers of kif and shady traffickers.

Doorway of the Grand Mosque

Grand Mosque ❺

Rue Jma el-Kbir. ◑ *to non-Muslims.*

The Grand Mosque, built on the site of a Portuguese cathedral, probably also overlies a former Roman temple dedicated to Hercules. Dating from the reign of Moulay Ismaïl, it was enlarged in 1815 by Moulay Sliman. Mohammed V led Friday prayers here on 11 April 1947, during a visit to Tangier, when he also made a historic speech in the Mendoubia Gardens *(see p138).* Opposite the mosque, the state primary school (established by nationalists during the French Protectorate) is a former Merinid medersa that was remodelled in the 18th century.

Nearby, the Borj el Hadjoui commands a view of the port and a pair of Armstrong cannons, each weighing 20 tonnes. They were purchased from the British in Gibraltar, but were never used.

From the *borj,* Rue Dar el Baroud leads to the **Hôtel Continental**, located opposite the port and one of Tangier's oldest hotels. The building's architectural style, its Andalusian-style lounges and its open terraces give this establishment great appeal. Its patrons have included writers and painters – among them Edgar Degas – and film producers.

🏨 **Hôtel Continental**
36 Rue Dar el-Baroud.
Tel (0539) 93 10 24. ◑ *daily.*

The Hôtel Continental, one of the oldest hotels in Tangier

A jeweller's shop near Rue Es-Siaghine

Rue Es-Siaghine 6

Running from the Petit Socco to the Grand Socco.

This street was once the *decumanus maximus*, the main axis and busiest thoroughfare of the Roman town. It led from the harbour out through the southern gate, marked today by Bab Fahs. Lined with cafés and bazaars, the street is as lively now as it must have been in antiquity.

The small administrative building at No. 47, with a courtyard planted with orange trees, was from 1860 to 1923 the residence of the *naib*, the Moroccan high official who served as intermediary between the sultan and foreign ambassadors. The Spanish **Church of the Immaculate Conception** (La Purísima),

at No. 51, was built by the Spanish government, work beginning in 1880. It was used by the whole city's Christian community, as well as by foreign diplomats. It is now used for social activities.

Further up the street, on the left, is Rue Touahine, which is lined with jewellers' shops and which leads to the **Fondation Lorin**, an arts centre in a disused synagogue. On display here are newspapers, photographs, posters and plans relating to the political, sporting, musical and social history of Tangier since the 1930s. Temporary exhibitions of paintings also take place here.

🏛 Fondation Lorin
44 Rue Touahine. 🛈 (0539) 93 91 03. 🕐 11am–1pm & 4–7pm Sun–Fri. ⬤ Sat.

American Legation 7

8 Rue d'Amérique. **Tel** (0539) 93 53 17. 🕐 10am–1pm & 3–5pm Mon–Fri. ⬤ Sat & Sun.

The American Legation consists of a suite of rooms that originally formed part of the residence that Moulay Sliman presented to the United States in 1821, and which served as the US Consulate for the next 140 years. Another suite, on several floors looking out onto a garden, was presented by a Jewish family: the doors, windows and ceilings were decorated by craftsmen from Fès.

The rooms contain engravings of Gibraltar and Tangier, old maps, and paintings (by Brayer, Mohammed ben Ali Rbati, James McBey, Claudio Bravo and others), which were given to the legation by Margarite McBey, wife of James McBey and a resident of Tangier. Through photographs, early editions and recordings, a room devoted to Paul Bowles gives an overview of the writer's life and work during the years that he lived in Tangier. A reference library is also available for the use of scholars and specialists on North Africa.

The elegant interior courtyard of the American Legation

For hotels and restaurants in this region see pp308–9 and pp333–4

Artists and Writers in Tangier

At the beginning of the 20th century, many writers from Europe and the United States came to Tangier, most of them settling here more or less permanently. Drawn not only by the climate, they also came in search of stimulation and spiritual wellbeing, and in particular sought the atmosphere, freedom and sense of adventure that the city seemed to project. Tangier's exotic reputation as a den of traffickers and spies, and of drugs, sex and dissipation was also a powerful draw.

PAINTERS

The light, architecture and inhabitants of Tangier have inspired many European and American painters. Discovered by Eugène Delacroix at the end of the 19th century, the city later became the subject of paintings by Georges Clairin, Jacques Majorelle, James Wilson Morrice, Kees Van Dongen, Claudio Bravo and the Expressionist painter Henri Matisse.

Henri Matisse *(1869–1954) was one of the greatest Fauvist painters. His* Odalisque à la Culotte Grise *is typical of his work.*

Eugène Delacroix *(1798–1863) discovered Morocco in 1832. The experience of visiting the country marked a turning point in his career. Orientalism was then to inspire his work for the rest of his life.*

WRITERS

In the wake of Paul Bowles came writers and musicians of the Beat, Rock and Hippie generations. Tennessee Williams arrived in 1949, followed by Truman Capote, who came to Tangier "to escape from himself". William Burroughs lived here for longer than all other foreign writers, finding Tangier a city where "throbbed the heartbeat of the world".

Paul Bowles, *who came to Tangier for the first time in 1931 on the advice of Gertrude Stein, settled there permanently in 1947. He died in 1999.*

Mohammed Choukri, *born in the Rif in 1935, was a friend of Jean Genet and Tennessee Williams. Discovered by Paul Bowles, he came to fame in the 1980s with* For Bread Alone.

Paul Morand **Hécate et ses chiens**

Paul Morand, *a diplomat and writer, and also a great traveller, wrote* Hécate et ses chiens *in Tangier in 1955. A unique atmosphere pervades this short novel on the subject of couples: "In Africa, the first thing you learn is to live life as it comes."*

Grand Socco (Place du 9 Avril 1947) ⑧

The link between the medina and Ville Nouvelle, Place du Grand Socco was renamed Place du 9 Avril 1947 in memory of the speech that Mohammed V made in support of independence. The square comes to life in the evenings, when vendors spread out their wares – extensive displays of a huge variety of second-hand goods – on the ground. A colourful market, where peasant women in striped *foutas* and wide-brimmed straw hats come to sell fruit and fowl, takes place above the square, near the Anglican Church of St Andrew, at the far end of Rue d'Angleterre.

The minaret of the **Mosque of Sidi Bou Abib** (1917), decorated with polychrome tiles, overlooks the square from the southwest. Near Bab Fahs, a double gateway leading into the medina, are the grounds of the Mendoubia. This was the residence of the *mendoub* when Tangier was under international administration (1923–56).

Anglican Church of St Andrew ⑨

Rue d'Angleterre. ◯ 9:30am–12:30pm & 2:30–6pm. Keys obtainable from the caretaker. 🕇 11am Sun.

Built on land that Moulay Hassan donated to fulfil the needs of an increasingly large

Church of St Andrew, with a bell-tower in the shape of a minaret

British population in Tangier, the church of St Andrew was completed in 1894. The interior is a curious mixture of styles, in which the Moorish style predominates.

The lobed arch at the entrance to the choir, and the ceiling above the altar, which is decorated with a quotation from the Gospel in Arabic, are of particular interest. The belltower, in the shape of a minaret, overlooks the cemetery. Among those buried here are Walter Harris, a journalist and correspondent for *The Times,* and Sir Harry McLean, a military adviser to the sultans.

A plaque at the west end of the church commemorates Emily Kean: she came to Tangier in the 19th century, married the Cherif of Ouezzane and devoted her life to the welfare of the people of northern Morocco.

Galerie d'Art Contemporain Mohammed Drissi ⑩

Rue d'Angleterre. 🕇 (0539) 93 60 73. ◯ 9am–1pm & 2–6pm Tue–Sun. 🖼

This contemporary art gallery, named in homage to the Moroccan artist Mohammed Drissi (1946–2003), hosts regular exhibitions by Moroccan and international artists.

Fondouk Chejra ⑪

Rue de la Liberté. Accessible via the steps below the level of the Hôtel el-Menzah. 🕇 (0539) 94 80 50.

The buzzing atmosphere in Fondouk Chejra, known as the Poor People's Souk or Weavers' Souk, is that of an Oriental bazaar. Above the shops on the ground floor, the rooms that were once used by travellers and passing tradesmen have been converted into weavers' workshops, where the white and red fabric that is typical of the Rif is produced. The original layout of the former *fondouk*, or caravanserai, is difficult to make out, the central courtyard having been much altered.

Rue de la Liberté ⑫

This street runs from Place du 9 Avril 1947 (or Grand Socco) to Ville Nouvelle. It was formerly known as Rue de Fès, then as Rue du Statut, its current name dating from the beginning of Moroccan independence. The French Consulate, which is set in the centre of a pleasant and attractive park, dates from 1929; the classical arcade of the façade is offset by decoration in the Moorish style.

In the **Galerie Delacroix**, housed in the French Cultural Institute next door, temporary exhibitions are organized by the Institut Français. The Hôtel el-Minzah, dating from 1930, is one of the most illustrious hotels in Morocco, with

The Grand Socco, also known as Place du 9 Avril 1947

an Andalusian-style courtyard and gardens, comfortable lounges and bars. Winston Churchill, Paul and Jane Bowles, Jean Genet and Hollywood stars from Rita Hayworth to Errol Flynn stayed in this magical place.

🏛 **Galerie Delacroix**
86 Rue de la Liberté. *Tel (0539)* 93 21 34. ◯ *11am–1pm, 4–8:30pm Tue–Sun.*

Place de France & Place de Faro ⓭

Place de France is a major meeting place for the inhabitants of Tangier. The **Café de Paris**, which opened in 1920, was the first establishment to open outside the medina. Among its regular customers were Paul Bowles, Tennessee Williams and Jean Genet, as well as foreign

The **Café de Paris**, once one of the most fashionable cafés in Tangier

diplomats. The café has remained a hub of city life.
    Very near Place de France, on Avenue Pasteur, is Place de Faro (named after the Portuguese town twinned with Tangier in 1984), complete with cannons. It is one of the few places to have escaped the attentions of the developers. It offers a view of the medina and of ferry traffic in the harbour and the strait.

Avenue Pasteur ⓮

Together with Avenue Mohammed V, which extends eastwards from it, Avenue Pasteur is Ville Nouvelle's main artery and its economic centre. In the evening, the avenue is given over to the

The dilapidated Art Deco façade of the Gran Teatro Cervantes

Spanish custom of the *paseo*, a leisurely evening stroll. The Moroccan tourist office, at No. 29, occupies the first building to be constructed on the avenue, while the villa at No. 27 houses the **Great Synagogue**. The **Librairie des Colonnes**, the bookshop at No. 54, has lost some of its former prestige and importance. All the writers in Tangier, whether visitors or residents, regularly patronized this bookshop, which stocks most available books on Tangier. Lectures and signing sessions are still held here.
    The **Gran Teatro Cervantes** (accessible from Avenue Pasteur, which is reached along Rue du Prince Moulay Abdallah and via steps continuing from it) opened in 1913. One of North Africa's major theatres, it was here that the greatest singers and dancers of the age performed. The building, with an Art Deco façade, is in a bad state of repair. Restoration has been delayed by disputes between the city and the Spanish state, which had undertaken to finance its upkeep.

✡ **Great Synagogue**
27 Avenue Pasteur.

📚 **Librairie des Colonnes**
54 Avenue Pasteur.

Ancien Palais du Mendoub ⓯

Avenue Mohammed Tazi *(in the northwest of Ville Nouvelle).* ◯ *to the public.*

The Mendoub was the sultan's representative during the international administration of Tangier. While his main residence was the Mendoubia, near the Grand Socco, this palace, built in 1929, was used mostly for receptions. It was acquired in 1970 by Malcolm Forbes (1919–90), the American multimillionaire who founded *Fortune* magazine. It became a luxury residence where

The elegant Ancien Palais du Mendoub

Forbes threw lavish parties and where such international stars as Elizabeth Taylor were guests. The house also contained a display of Forbes' 120,000 piece collection of toy soldiers. The Palace is now state-owned and will be used as a residence for important visitors from abroad.

For hotels and restaurants in this region see pp308–9 and pp333–4

Café Hafa ⑯

Rue Mohammed Tazi *(in a narrow street opposite the football stadium, leading towards the sea).*

The café opened in 1921, and neither the furniture nor the décor seem to have changed since then. Assorted tables and rush matting are laid out on terraces rising in tiers from the edge of the cliff, offering a breathtaking view of the strait. Writers and singers, from Paul Bowles to William Burroughs and from the Beatles to the Rolling Stones, have come here, seeking out Tangier's young generation or the company of local fishermen. People come here to smoke and drink mint tea, which is probably brewed exactly as it was in 1921.

Quartier du Marshan ⑰

Rue Mohammed Tazi, Rue Assad Ibn Farrat, Avenue Hassan II *(western part of the kasbah).*

Located west of the kasbah, the Quartier du Marshan was developed from the late 19th to the early 20th century. Being removed from the bustle of the medina and of Ville Nouvelle, it was an attractive residential location, and high officals and the *shorfa* of Ouezzane built their palaces and grand villas here in the late 19th century. The Italian Consulate (Rue Assad Ibn Farrat), rebuilt in 1916 and with walls covered in *zellij* tilework, housed Garibaldi in 1849–50. The former palace of the sultan Moulay Hafid, in Moorish style, became the Palais des Institutions Italiennes in 1926. On the edge of the strait, the

An elegant villa in the Quartier du Marshan

Beaches around Tangier

The Bay of Tangier, a grand crescent that is some-times likened to the Baie des Anges in Nice or to Copacabana in Rio de Janeiro, stretches for almost 4 km (2.5 miles) from the edge of the port round to the residential districts and resort areas and to the first spurs of land that mark its eastern extremity. The proximity of the city and the rivers that flow into it unfortunately make this the most polluted beach in Morocco. For swimming and sunbathing, it is better to make for the beaches between Cap Spartel and the Grottes d'Hercule and beyond, or for the coves of Cap Malabata, or, further east, the beaches at Sidi Khankroucht and Ksar es-Seghir.

③ **The Bay of Tangier** *forms a splendid and extensive sweep, but is unfortunately very polluted.*

② **Between Tangier** *and Cap Spartel, small coves are reachable on foot from the Perdicaris Belvedere. The walk down passes through mimosa and woods of umbrella pine.*

① **Between Cap Spartel** *and the Grottes d'Hercule are many attractive little bays separated by rocky outcrops.*

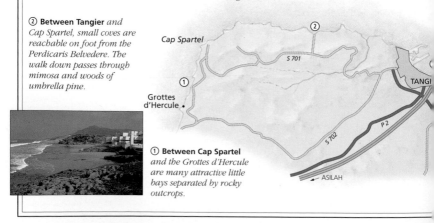

Cap Spartel

Grottes d'Hercule •

S 701

② ①

TANGI

P 2

S 702

← ASILAH

Marshan ends at the limits of Hafa, a poorer residential district with a great deal of local colour, up on the sea cliff.

Colline du Charf ⑱

In the southeast of the city.

A hill rising to a height of about 100 m (328 ft), the Colline du Charf commands the most impressive and most complete view of Tangier.

The panorama stretches from Cap Malabata in the east to La Montagne, which rises over the old town to the west. From here the beach appears as a strip lining the bay, and the white, densely packed medina seems to cling to the hillside as it slopes down towards the port, while the high-rise blocks of Ville Nouvelle stand along its wide avenues. Poorer residential districts stretch out southwards: in among them, at the foot of the hill, can be seen Plaza Toro, whose bullrings are now used for public functions. Further north is the Syrian Mosque, with a style of minaret rarely seen in the Maghreb.

The mosque-like building on the hill was a café during Tangier's international period. A favourite form of relaxation for the inhabitants of Tangier is to stroll on the hill or sit and gaze out over the strait.

Bay of Tangier ⑲

Between the port and Cap Malabata, the bay forms a beach-lined semicircle. Avenue d'Espagne, which runs along the bay, is lined with hotels, from small guesthouses to large modern establishments. Dotted with the blues, reds and whites of

Tangier's fishing harbour, at the foot of the medina

the boats and the ochre, green and orange of the nets, the small fishing harbour is a colourful sight, and the freshly caught fish that is offered makes a delicious meal.

It was on Avenue d'Espagne that Bernardo Bertolucci shot scenes for his 1990 film *The Sheltering Sky*. Many literary works, by William Burroughs and others, took shape in the small guesthouses here. The French philosopher Michel Foucault would stay at the Hôtel Cecil, while Samuel Beckett preferred the Solazur.

④ **The beach at Mrissa**, *beneath Cap Malabata, has fine, soft sand and is well sheltered by stands of pine.*

⑤ **Plage des Amiraux** *has developed in front of the elegant houses of a small village.*

⑥ **The double beach at Sidi Khankroucht**, *at Km 18, beneath shaded hills, is clean and pleasant. Chez Hassan is a small, friendly restaurant here.*

⑦ **Wadi Aliane** *is an attractive sandy beach with a small resort complex that is still in the process of being built.*

Ksar es-Seghir ⑧

CEUTA

⑥

⑤

Malabata

⑦ S 704

S 601

④

8912

8302

S 704

TÉTOUAN

⑧ **At Ksar es-Seghir**, *33 km (20 miles) along a road with beautiful scenery, a splendid beach stretches out in front of woods and groves from which emerge the ruins of Almohad, Merinid and Portuguese buildings.*

KEY

▬ Motorway

▬ Major road

▬ Minor road

0 km   2

0 miles   2

MEDITERRANEAN COAST & THE RIF

The great mountainous crescent of the Rif forms a natural barrier across northern Morocco. Its proud Berber-speaking inhabitants haughtily guard their traditions and independence, and historically the Rif has always resisted conquest. The Rif, today, is friendly and welcoming, with sandy Mediterranean coves and beaches, many of them with a backdrop of majestic cliffs.

Inaccessible and intricately partitioned, the Rif reaches a height of 2,452 m (8,047 ft) at Jbel Tidirhin, in the central part of the mountain range, then tails away eastwards towards the Moulouya estuary and the Algerian border. The northwestern Rif is a region of low mountains and hills dotted with villages, while the central part consists of lofty summits and enclosed valleys. To the east, what is regarded as the real Rif gently slopes away.

All Riffians fiercely defend their cultural identity. The Spanish, to whom the region fell when Morocco was divided under the French Protectorate, came face to face with this intransigence during the uprisings of 1921–6 and were soundly defeated at Anoual in 1921 (see p56). The history of the Rif and its coastline is closely linked to that of Spain. For Morocco, the Mediterranean became a bridgehead for the conquest of Spain. From the 15th century, the Portuguese occupation, followed by that of the Spanish, cut Morocco off from the Mediterranean and accelerated its decline. Spain still maintains a foothold in Ceuta and Melilla, and on a few rocky islets. Morocco has worked for closer cooperation with Spain and Europe to tackle problems of illegal trafficking and emigration here. The increase of tourism in Tangier and Ceuta has resulted in dramatic changes to the area, including a modern port and airport.

The fishing harbour at Al-Hoceima

◁ A brightly painted wooden door in Chefchaouen

Exploring the Mediterranean Coast & the Rif

Stretching from the land of the Jebala in the west to Morocco's eastern frontier, the Rif presents a great variety of landscapes. Here are high, steep valleys where almond trees blossom and oleanders flower, mountain roads that command wild and magnificent vistas, forests of cedar, fir and oak, and villages and isolated houses with pitched tin roofs. Between Ceuta and Cabo Negro, the coast is punctuated by sweeping beaches of golden sand and, from Wadi Laou to Al-Hoceima and Saïdia, by more secluded bays beneath rocky cliffs. The medinas of Tetouan and Chefchaouen are among the most picturesque in Morocco.

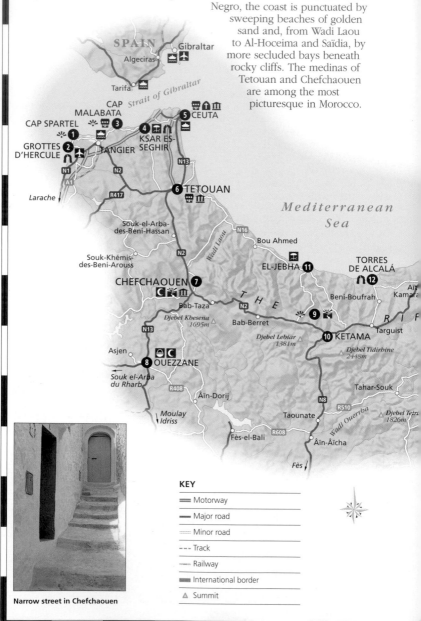

KEY

▭	Motorway
▬	Major road
▭	Minor road
---	Track
⌁	Railway
▬	International border
△	Summit

Narrow street in Chefchaouen

SIGHTS AT A GLANCE

Al-Hoceima ⑬
Cap des Trois Fourches ⑯
Cap Malabata ③
Cap Spartel ①
Ceuta ⑤
Chefchaouen pp150–51 ⑦
El-Jebha ⑪
Figuig ㉑
Grottes d'Hercule ②
Ketama ⑩
Ksar es-Seghir ④
Melilla ⑮
Moulouya Estuary ⑰

Nador ⑭
Ouezzane ⑧
Oujda ⑳
The Rif pp154–5 ⑨
Saïdia ⑲
TANGIER pp128–41
Tetouan pp148–9 ⑥
Torres de Alcalá ⑫

Tour
Zegzel Gorge ⑱

LOCATOR MAP

GETTING AROUND

Air links to the region arrive in Tangier, Al-Hoceima, Melilla and Oujda. Once there, it is better to hire a car rather than use *grands taxis*. Having your own means of transport gives you the freedom to stop off at secluded beaches and seek out the high valleys. In this mountainous environment, the roads are sometimes in a bad state of repair, and there are often roadworks, particularly along the arterial routes.

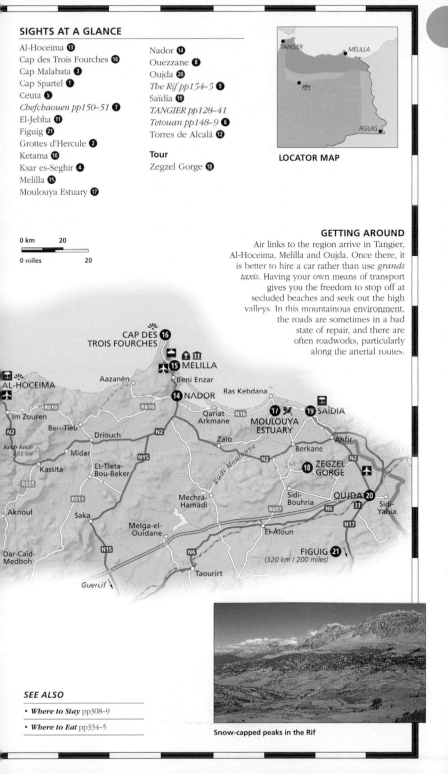

Snow-capped peaks in the Rif

SEE ALSO

• **Where to Stay** pp308–9

• **Where to Eat** pp334–5

Cap Spartel ❶

Road map D1. 14 km (9 miles) west of Tangier.

From Tangier, the road leading to Cap Spartel runs through La Montagne, the city's western suburb, which is bathed in the perfume of eucalyptus and mimosa. Long walls surround the residences of Moroccan, Kuwaiti and Saudi kings and princes and the luxury villas dating from the golden age of Tangier's international period. Beyond stretch forests of holm-oak, cork oak, umbrella pine, mastic-tree, broom and heather, which all flourish here, watered by the highest rainfall in Morocco.

At the cape, the most northwesterly point of Africa, is the promontory known in antiquity as Cape Ampelusium or Cape of the Vines, and a lighthouse dating from 1865.

The lighthouse at Cap Spartel, where sea and ocean meet

From beneath the lighthouse, there is a breathtaking view of the ocean where the Mediterranean and Atlantic meet, and on clear days you can see the strait and coast of Spain from Cape Trafalgar to the Rock of Gibraltar.

Grottes d'Hercule ❷

Road map D1. 5 km (3 miles) southwest of Cap Spartel.

At the place known as Achakar, the sea has carved impressive caves out of the cliff. The people who, from prehistoric times, came to

these caves knapped stones here and quarried millstones for use in oil presses. The opening to the caves, facing onto the sea, is a cleft shaped like a reversed map of Africa.

According to legend, Hercules slept here before performing one of his 12 labours – picking the golden apples in the Garden of the Hesperides. The location of the legendary garden belonging to these nymphs of darkness and guarded by the dragon with 100 heads is said to be further south, near Lixus.

The best time to visit the caves is in the late afternoon, after which the light of the setting sun can be enjoyed from the cafés nearby. Further south, beneath the level of the caves, are the **Ruins of Cotta** (1st century BC to 3rd century AD). With vats for salting fish, making *garum* and producing purple dye, this was one of the largest industrial centres of the Punic-Mauretanian period.

The Grottes d'Hercule, like a reversed map of Africa

The unfinished medieval "castle" at Cap Malabata

Cap Malabata ❸

Road map D1. 12 km (7.5 miles) east of Tangier.

The route out of Tangier skirts an area of large tourist hotels and continues eastwards round the curve of the bay. Soon after a tiny estuary, at the edge of the road, are the remains of a 16th-century fortress, from which Moroccan soldiers could watch and attack the Portuguese, Spanish and English occupiers of Tangier. Nearby, white crenellated walls surround the lush and extensive grounds of the **Villa Harris**. It was once the residence of Walter Harris (1866–1953), a flamboyant journalist and diplomatic correspondent for *The Times*. He chronicled life in Tangier for many years from 1892.

The road ascending the hills passes through magnificent pine forests and by many small coves where there are cafés which, like Café Ryad, have an old-world charm. Just before the cape, a strange building appears. Conceived in the medieval style, it was the work of a whimsical Italian, who left it unfinished in the 1930s.

The view from Cap Malabata is stunning, especially in the morning, looking westwards over the city and suburbs of Tangier and across to the Straits of Gibraltar, and eastwards to Jbel Moussa, which rises over Ceuta.

For hotels and restaurants in this region see pp309–10 and pp334–5

Ksar es-Seghir ❹

Road map D1. 33 km (20 miles) east of Tangier. 🏘 *8,800.* 🚌 *Sat.*

A town with a small fishing harbour and a fine beach, Ksar es-Seghir faces the Spanish town of Tarifa across the Straits of Gibraltar. The souk that takes place here on Saturdays is filled with women of the Rif, conspicuous in their white, red-striped *foutas*.

Since the 17th century, forts have stood on this well sheltered spot on an estuary, and it was from here that Moroccan troops set sail for Spain. The Almohads made it an important centre of shipbuilding and skilled crafts. The remains of buildings in a large forest are those of a town built by the Merinids in the 14th century. The circular walls that surround it are unusual, but were obviously preferred to the customary square plan by the town's Muslim builders; the gateway facing the sea is the best-preserved. The Portuguese, who held the town from 1458 to 1549, strengthened it with new fortifications that reached to the sea.

Ksar es-Seghir, an attractive coastal town

Ceuta ❺

Road map D1. 63 km (39 miles) east of Tangier. 🏘 *75,000.* 🛈 *Calle Edrissis, Edif Baluarte de los Mallorquines; 00 34 856 20 05 60.*

Standing on a narrow isthmus between Monte Hacho and the mainland, Ceuta occupies a favourable location opposite Gibraltar. The Rock of Gibraltar and Monte Hacho are the two legendary Pillars of Hercules.

From the 12th century onwards, the town was visited by traders from Genoa,

Ceuta, like an amphitheatre on the isthmus linking it to the mainland

Pisa, Marseilles and Catalonia. In 1415, Ceuta became a Portuguese enclave, then passed to Spain in 1578. Today, it is an important garrison town. Its livelihood depends mainly on the tax-free trade that its status as a free port allows. Ceuta (like Melilla) is a self-governing town within the Spanish state. Morocco views the Spanish presence as anachronistic and claims sovereignty.

The 12-km (7.5-mile) circuit of Monte Hacho (part of it accessible by road) affords views over the town, the mountains and coast of the Rif and Gibraltar, especially from the lighthouse at Punto Almina. The Castillo del Desnarigado, a fortress that is now a military museum, encloses the Ermita de San Antonio. This chapel draws a large pilgrimage on 13 June each year.

The **Plaza de Africa** is, in architectural terms, the centre of the town, where the main public buildings are concentrated. The cathedral, whose present appearance dates from the 18th century, stands on the site of a Grand Mosque. Religious paintings and objects are displayed in its museum. **Nuestra Señora de Africa** (the Church of Our Lady of Africa) was built in the early

18th century, also on the site of a mosque, in an arresting Baroque style. On the high altar stands a statue of the Virgin, patroness of Ceuta, who is believed to have saved the town from an epidemic of plague in the 16th century. The cathedral treasury contains some fine paintings, banners and 17th-century illuminated books.

The **Ayuntamiento** (town hall), built in 1929, is of interest to visitors for the paintings that it contains by Mariano Bertuchi, an artist active during the colonial period.

The **Museo Municipal** (Archaeological Museum) is laid out above underground passages dug in the 16th and 17th centuries to supply the town with water. The displays include Neolithic, Carthaginian and Roman pottery, including amphorae, as well as coins and armour.

Through maps, photographs and visual displays, the **Museo de la legión** documents the activities of the Spanish Foreign Legion and its efforts in 1921–6 to subdue the Rif uprising and the rebel leader Abdel Krim. The legion, formed in 1920, suffered serious losses during this war.

🏛 **Museo Municipal**
On the corner of Paseo de Revellín and Calle Ingenieros. **Tel** *00 34 856 51 73 98.* 🕘 *9am–2pm Mon–Fri.* 🈂

🏛 **Museo de la Legión**
Paseo de Colón. ⬤ *Sun.* 🈂

Tetouan

In the words of Arab poets, Tetouan is a white dove, "the sister of Fès", "the little Jerusalem" or "the daughter of Granada". The town, built partly on the slopes of Jbel Dersa, was inhabited by Jewish refugees from Granada in the 15th century, then by Moors from Andalusia in the 17th century. The town's Andalusian heritage can be seen in its medina, and also in its culinary traditions, as well as in its music and in the craft of embroidery. From the 15th to the 18th centuries, Tetouan was a lively centre of privateering, then of thriving trade with Europe, becoming a sort of city-state comparable to Florence or to Venice at the time of the doges. In the 18th century, the town was the diplomatic capital of Morocco. The Spanish, who held it from 1860 to 1862, made it their capital during the Protectorate, building a new town on the west side of the old Andalusian medina.

The church on Place Moulay el-Mehdi, built in 1926

Place Hassan II, a link between Ville Nouvelle and the medina

⛩ Ville Nouvelle

Place Moulay el-Mehdi and Boulevard Mohammed V.

It is on Place Moulay el-Mehdi – which is sometimes still referred to by the town's inhabitants as Place Primo (after the Spanish politician José Primo de Rivera) – that the Spanish colonial architecture of Ville Nouvelle (New Town) is at its most eloquent. With a main post office, bank and church (1926), the square looks like any other central town square in Spain. Elegant homes with doors, windows and balconies with Moorish-style ornamentation can be seen on Boulevard Mohammed V, the town's principal thoroughfare.

Place Hassan II links Ville Nouvelle and the medina. Modern tiling has replaced the old mosaic decoration of

the royal palace that stands on the side of the square nearest the medina. Both the boulevard and the square come to life in the evenings with the *paseo* (promenade), a Spanish custom that is more deeply ingrained in Tetouan than elsewhere.

🏛 Musée Archéologique

Boulevard El-Jazaïr, near Place El-Jala.
◯ Mon–Fri pm only.

The rooms of the Archaeological Museum contain objects dating from the Roman period that were discovered at Volubilis, Lixus and Thamuda, a Roman site on the outskirts of present-day Tetouan (on the road to Chefchaouen). Mosaics, including a

depiction of the Three Graces of classical mythology, as well as pottery, coins, bronzes and other pieces, are displayed. The most interesting exhibits – such as ancient inscriptions, mosaic floors and Muslim funerary stelae with the Star of David – are laid out in the garden.

⛩ Medina

Entry through Place Hassan II, then via Rue Ahmed Torres to the southeast.

Tetouan's medina, now a World Heritage Site, is the most strongly Andalusian of all Moroccan medinas. Emigrants from Spain who arrived in the 15th and 17th centuries implanted their architectural traditions here, including a taste for wrought-iron decoration and a liking for doors with elaborate metal fittings.

The aroma of spices, freshly sawn wood and *kesra* (bread) fills the medina's narrow streets, squares and souks, which bustle with carpenters, slipper-makers, drapers, tanners and sellers of secondhand goods. Rue El-Mokadem (between Place Souk el-Fouqui and Place Gharsa el-Kebira) is the street most densely packed with shops, but also one of

Kesra (bread) on sale in the El-Fouqui Souk

The medina, on the slopes of Jbel Dersa

the most noteworthy for its impressive white buildings and its paving. Sellers of fabrics and pottery fill the small shady square where the El-Houts Souk takes place. It leads to the former mellah, Tetouan's Jewish quarter, where the balconied houses have large windows, wrought-iron gates and arcaded façades.

Musée d'Art Marocain

Avenue Hassan Ier and Rue Sqala, near Bab Oqla. ***Tel*** *(0539) 97 27 21.* *9am–noon & 2–6pm Wed–Mon.*

Occupying a bastion built in 1828, the museum is laid out in an Andalusian palace with a garden, a fountain clad in *zellij* tilework, and red-tiled awnings, typical of buildings in Tetouan. The furniture, the craftsman-made pieces, the costumes and musical instruments illustrate the town's traditions. Tetouani rooms, with marriage scenes (such as putting together the trousseau and presenting the bride), have also been convincingly re-created.

The Craft School, near the museum, opposite Bab Oqla, occupies a residence built in 1928 in Moorish style.

VISITORS' CHECKLIST

Road map D1. *310,000.* *5 km (3 miles).* *Tnine-Sidi-Lyamani.* *30 Bld Mohammed V; (0539) 96 19 15.* *Wed, Fri, Sun by Place Moulay-el-Medhi.*

Specializing in local traditions, the school teaches leatherwork, pottery, mosaic-making, carpet-weaving and decorative plasterwork. The students' work is displayed in a domed exhibition hall.

Detail of a façade on Boulevard Mohammed V

TETOUAN'S JEWS

A large Jewish community, expelled from Spain at the end of the Christian Reconquest, settled in Tetouan, thrived here and reached its height in the 16th century. Like the many Muslims who had also arrived from Spain, these Jews cherished the memory of Andalusia as a lost paradise. On feast days, they would listen to Andalusian music and don Andalusian costume and jewellery.

Exploiting their contacts in Gibraltar, Antwerp, Amsterdam and London, Tetouan's Jews played a central role in the economic life of the town and through them it became an important trade link with the West. At the beginning of the 19th century, subjected to violence and heavily taxed, the Jews repaired to a quarter of their own, the *judería*. Marginalized in professional and social life, many Jews left to settle in Melilla, Gibraltar or Iran, and also in Latin America. Despite an improvement in their situation under Spanish rule, the Jewish community – which still counted some 3,000 people in 1960 – continued to shrink progressively after independence, many leaving for Israel. By the early 1990s, there were no more than 200 Jews remaining in Tetouan.

Jewish Feast Day in Tetouan**, painting by Alfred Dehodencq (1822–82)**

Chefchaouen ❼

The white town of Chefchaouen nestles in the hollow of the two mountains – ech-Chaoua (The Horns) – from which it takes its name. Steep narrow streets with white and indigo limewashed buildings, small squares, ornate fountains and houses with elaborately decorated doorways and red tile roofs make this a delightful town. It was founded in 1471 by Idrissid *shorfa*, descendants of the Prophet Mohammed, as a stronghold in the fight against the Portuguese. Chefchaouen, esteemed as a holy town, has eight mosques and several *zaouias* and *marabouts*.

Courtyard of the kasbah, around which the museum is laid out

A café on Place Uta el-Hammam, in the heart of the town

🕌 Place Uta el-Hammam

The square is the heart of the old town and the focal point on which all the streets of the medina converge. It is lined with trees, and paved with stones and pebbles, and in the centre stands a four-sided fountain decorated with arches and crowned by a pavilion of green tiles. With shops and cafés, this is an ideal place for a relaxed stroll.

🕌 Grand Mosque

Place Uta el-Hammam.
🚫 to non-Muslims.
The Grand Mosque was founded probably in the 16th century and has been re-modelled several times since.

The *fondouk*, with rooms round the courtyard

The later minaret, which dates from the 17th century, is distinctive in being octagonal. It is decorated with three tiers of plain and lobed arches on a painted ochre background. The uppermost tier is decorated with *zellij* tilework.

🕌 Fondouk

Corner of Place Uta el-Hammam and Rue Al-Andalus.
The *fondouk* still serves the purpose for which it was originally built. About 50 rooms, arranged around the courtyard, still accommodate travellers and passing traders.
It is a building of strikingly simple design, with a gallery of semicircular arches lining the pebble-paved courtyard. The only contrast to this simplicity is provided by the main entrance; the doorway is surmounted by an awning and framed by a broken horseshoe arch surrounded by interlacing arches.

🕌 Kasbah and Museum

West corner of Place Uta el-Hammam.
🔲 *Wed–Mon.* ⬤ *Tue & Fri pm.* 📷
The kasbah, with crenellated walls of red beaten earth and ten bastions, is the essential heart of the town. The fortress was begun in the 15th century by Moulay Ali ben Rachid, and was completed by Moulay Ismaïl in the 17th century, as was the residence within. The kasbah's plan and architectural style show Andalusian influence. A pleasant garden with fountains is laid out within, from where there is a good view of the walls and the rampart walk. The **Musée Ethnographique** (Ethnographic Museum) occupies the residence built in the garden. This is a traditional Moroccan house with a courtyard and gallery on the first floor. The museum contains displays of pottery, armour, embroidery, costume, musical instruments, palanquins and painted wooden chests.

🕌 Medina

A small street running between the kasbah and the Grand Mosque leads to the Souïka district. This is the oldest district of Chefchaouen, and the town's finest houses, with carved and decorated doors, are found here. The name *souïka*, meaning "little market", comes from the district's *kissaria,* where there are many small shops along its narrow streets.
The medina contains more than 100 weavers' workshops.

For hotels and restaurants in this region see pp309–10 and pp334–5

Narrow street with houses painted white and blue

Indeed, Chefchaouen is famous for the woollen *jellabas* that are woven here, as well as for the red and white striped fabrics worn by the women of the Jebala, a tribe of the mountainous western Rif. One such weaver's workshop is located in Rue Ben Dibane, identifiable by an exterior stairway.

One of the most distinctive fountains in Chefchaouen is Aïn Souika, set in a recess in the district's main street. Covered by a porch, it has a semicircular basin and interlaced lobed arches.

🏚 Quartier Al-Andalus

This district is reached from the northwestern corner of Place Uta el-Hammam, leaving the *fondouk* on the left. The Quartier Al-Andalus received the second wave of immigrants – Muslims and Jews expelled from Spain – who arrived in 1492, after the fall of Granada.

Here, the houses, painted white, green or blue, have decorated doors and wrought-iron railings at some of their windows. They follow the steep gradient of the terrain, which makes for many exterior stairways and entrances at various levels.

🏔 Ras el-Ma and the Mills

The steep streets of Al-Andalus leading up towards the mountain pass through Bab Onsar, the town's

VISITORS' CHECKLIST

Road map D1. 🏘 *45,000.*
🚌 🛈 *(0539) 96 19 15/16.*
🎪 *Moussem of Sidi Allal el-Hadj (9 Aug).* 🛍 *Mon & Thu.*

northeast gateway, which has been restored and renovated.

Beyond is the spring of Ras el-Ma, which is now enclosed by a building. The presence of this underground spring was the reason why the town was established here. It accounts for the town's lush gardens, and the water also powers the mills. Steps leading towards the metalled road run alongside the wash-houses, then the mills, whose origins go back to the arrival of the Andalusian refugees.

The route then leads to the bridge across Wadi Laou, which is built in the form of a semicircular arch with bevelled buttresses. With its cascades, wash-houses and cafés, this is one of the most pleasant quarters of Chefchaouen.

CHEFCHAOUEN TOWN CENTRE

Fondouk ③
Grand Mosque ②
Kasbah and Museum ④
Medina ⑤
Place Uta el-Hammam ①
Quartier Al-Andalus ⑥

0 m   200
0 yards   200

Key to Symbols *see back flap*

A mantle of olive trees covering the hills near Ouezzane

Ouezzane ⓼

Road map D2. 60 km (37 miles) south of Chefchaouen. 🚶 70,000. 🚌 🏠 Thu.

A large market town, Ouezzane spreads out over the slopes of Jbel Bou Hillal, in a landscape of extensive olive groves and plantations of fig trees fed by abundant springs. It is important for its textiles (*jellabas* and carpets) and olive oil.

In the 15th century, the town, which was populated by Andalusians, also counted many Jews among its inhabitants. It began to prosper in the 18th and 19th centuries under the influence of the Idrissid *shorfa*. In 1727, a descendant of Idriss II established the religious brotherhood of the Taïbia, whose influence spread throughout Morocco, Algeria and Tunisia.

The medina at Ouezzane

In the 19th century, the *shorfa* played a prominent religious and political role in Morocco. The sherif of Ouezzane's policy of openness also assisted trade relations with France. The Zaouia (or Green Mosque) and, with its *zellij*-covered minaret, the Mosque of Moulay Abdallah Cherif, founder of the Taïbia brotherhood, attract many pilgrims.

Jews also come to **Asjen**, 8 km (5 miles) west of the town, to venerate the tomb of Rabbi Abraham ben Diouanne, who died in about 1780. The pilgrimage that takes place 33 days after Easter is an occasion when Morocco's Jewish community acknowledges its allegiance to the king.

The Rif ⓽

See pp154–5.

Ketama ⓾

Road map D-E1. 107 km (66 miles) east of Chefchaouen on the N2, the "Route des Crêtes" (Mountain Crests Road). 🏠 Wed.

Located in the heart of a forest, Ketama used to be a popular summer and winter resort but the presence and perseverance of illegal kif and hashish salesmen will make most visitors move on.

Leaving the town, the road leading eastward reveals the slopes of Jbel Tidirhin (or Tidiquin), at 2,448 m (8,034 ft) the highest peak in the Rif. In the valleys, the houses have

pitched roofs, with a covering of planks and corrugated metal, the modern substitute for thatch. In some villages, such as Taghzoute, the craft of leather embroidery is very much alive.

El-Jebha ⓫

Road map D1. 137 km (85 miles) east of Tetouan along the coast road N16; 73 km (45 miles) from Ketama on the N2 then the P4115. 🏠 Tue.

The small fishing town of El-Jebha nestles at the end of Fishermen's Point. Its one-storey, cube-like houses, covered in white roughcast, give it a typically Mediterranean air. On the right of the harbour, where *lamparo* boats are moored, is Crayfish Cove, which is ideal for underwater fishing. On the left, a soft sandy beach stretches away towards the west.

Torres de Alcalá ⓬

Road map E1. 144 km (89 miles) from Chefchaouen and 72 km (45 miles) from Ketama on the N2 then the P5205.

Located on the estuary of Wadi Bou Frah, the fishing village of Torres de Alcalá lies at the foot of a peak crowned by the ruins of a Spanish fortress. About 5 km (3 miles) further east is **Peñon de Velez de la Gomera**, a tiny island attached to the mainland by a narrow spit of sand. Held by the Spanish from 1508 to

1522, it later became a hide-out for pirates and privateers. A convict station under the Protectorate, it is still under Spanish sovereignty.

Some 4 km (2.5 miles) west of Velez is **Kalah Iris**, a cove that is an oasis of calm outside the summer season.

Al-Hoceima ⑬

Road map E1. ⛰ *65,000.*
✈ *17 km (10 miles).* 🚌 ℹ *Zankat Al Bahia; (0539) 98 11 85.*
🎪 *Festival late Jul–early Aug.* 🛒 *Tue.*

Peñon de Velez de la Gomera, still under Spanish sovereignty

This ancient fishing and trading port, seat of the emirate of Nokour during the Middle Ages, was long the object of dispute between European traders. The modern town was founded by General Sanjurjo in 1926, at the place where the Spanish garrison landed, and was known initially as Villa Sanjurjo.

Peñon de Alhucemas, a small island held by Spain

The town's location is one of the most beautiful along Morocco's Mediterranean coast. Whitewashed houses line the bay – an almost perfect semicircle between two hilly promontories. The coastline to the east, opposite the **Peñon de Alhucemas**, a small island held by Spain, commands the most impressive view of the bay.

A few dozen trawlers are usually moored in the harbour; in the evenings their *lamparos* are lit up ready for a night's fishing.

Plage Quemado stretches out in front of the town. This beach is better than others near Al-Hoceima, such as that at **Asfiha**, in the direction of Ajdir, opposite the small island known locally as Nokour's Rock.

The souk at **Im Zouren**, 17 km (10 miles) east on the road to Nador, is unusual: for the first few hours in the day, only women may go there. Both **Im Zouren** and **Beni Bou Ayach**, large market towns on the road out of Al-Hoceima, have a slightly unreal appearance, created by residential blocks painted in ochres, blues, greens and pinks. The towns come to life for only a few weeks of the year, when emigrant workers based in Germany and Holland return.

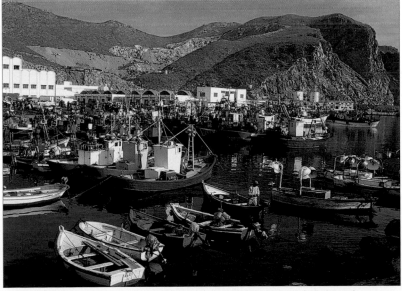

Trawlers and fishing boats moored in the harbour at Al-Hoceima, with warehouses in the background

The Rif ⓿

This region is well known for its atmospheric and beautiful medinas but, covering an area of some 30,000 sq km (11,580 sq miles), it offers much else besides. Among its natural wonders are high mountains, capes, gorges and rock formations. The country souks held weekly in Riffian towns and villages provide the opportunity to come into contact with local people as they go about their daily business. In July, the *moussem* of Jbel Alam, one of Morocco's best-known pilgrimages, takes place: the object is the tomb of Moulay Abdesselam ben Mchich, a highly venerated Sufi mystic who died in 1228. In the environs of Chefchaouen, ramblers and those with four-wheel-drive vehicles can visit one of the rare collective granaries of the western Rif at Akrar d'El-Kelaa, and the nature reserve at Talassemtane, where the fir forests are protected.

Souk at Wadi Laou
The Saturday souk, where women in foutas sell their hand-made pottery goods, is the largest and most colourful in the Rif.

The Jebala District
In a landscape of hills and middle-altitude mountains, the villages of the Jebala tribe have taken root where springs cascade from the hillside, surrounded by olive groves and smaller cereal plantations.

Gorge of Wadi Laou
Running between sheer high cliffs and below precariously perched villages, the gorge offers stunningly beautiful sights.

Mountain Crests Road
This road commands breathtaking views of the mountains, villages and isolated houses of the Rif, as well as of the cultivated terraces, olive groves and forests of holm-oak that typify the region.

Riffian Coastline
East of the small village of Torres de Alcalá there are some attractive and unspoilt coves and bays, including Kalah Iris, a haven of calm and solitude.

VISITORS' CHECKLIST

Road map: use a 1/100,000-scale map of Chefchaouen, Ouezzane and Al-Hoceima. *Information on treks in the Chefchaouen region is available from the Casa Hassan hotel in Chefchaouen: contact details from the Association Culture et Randonnée.* **Tel** *(0539) 98 61 53.* **Fax** *(0539) 98 81 96.* **www**.casahassan. com *Guides, guesthouse accommodation and mules are provided.*

Al-Hoceima
The coastal town of Al-Hoceima, which nestles around the bay, is a modest resort that is quiet outside the tourist season. The busy harbour has many restaurants.

Al-Hoceima Bay, into which flow the Wadi Nekor and Wadi Rhis, is lined by a pleasant, peaceful beach.

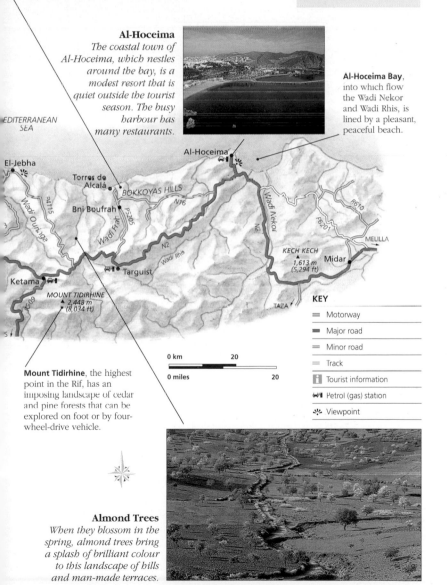

EDITERRANEAN SEA

El-Jebha

Torres de Alcalá

BOKKOYAS HILLS

Bni Boufrah

Wadi Ouringa

Wadi Rhis

Wadi Frah

Ketama

Targuist

MOUNT TIDIRHINE
▲ 2,448 m
(8,034 ft)

Al-Hoceima

Wadi Nekor

KECH KECH
▲ 1,613 m
(5,294 ft)

Midar

MELILLA

TAZA

Mount Tidirhine, the highest point in the Rif, has an imposing landscape of cedar and pine forests that can be explored on foot or by four-wheel-drive vehicle.

0 km   20
0 miles   20

KEY

▬	Motorway
▬	Major road
▬	Minor road
▬	Track
🛈	Tourist information
⛽	Petrol (gas) station
☆	Viewpoint

Almond Trees
When they blossom in the spring, almond trees bring a splash of brilliant colour to this landscape of hills and man-made terraces.

Nador ⓮

Road map E1. 154 km (96 miles) east of El-Hoceima and 13 km (8 miles) south of Melilla. 🚶 *200,000.* 🚌 🚢 🏨 *Sun & Mon.*

With wide avenues, shops, a multitude of cafés, restaurants and hotels, banks and residential blocks, Nador, somewhat unexpectedly, has all the trappings of a major town. It is, indeed, enjoying great prosperity.

Nador's dramatic economic growth has been fuelled both by its traditional industries, such as metallurgy (its metal-processing complex is supplied with iron ore from the Rif and anthracite from Jerada) and by modern ones, namely textiles, chemicals and electrics. The waves of emigration that have affected the whole of the eastern Rif have also contributed significantly to Nador's development. While immigrants here are key investors and consumers, funds sent home by workers from abroad have swelled the town's economy.

Nador's location, 13 km (8 miles) from the Spanish enclave of Melilla, also accounts for the town's prosperity, through illegal trafficking. Through well-oiled channels, goods cross the border at many points, including **Beni Enzar**, the border post nearest Melilla. Here, small consignments are transported across the border several times a day, packed in

The mountainous Mediterranean coastline near Melilla

small trucks or loaded onto the backs of women and children. The goods are then disposed of in broad daylight in two huge markets in Nador.

Beni Enzar, on the edge of Nador, is the foremost fishing port on the Mediterranean coast, and it also has modern naval dockyards.

Melilla ⓯

Sovereign Spanish town.
Road map E1. 167 km (104 miles) east of El-Hoceima and 153 km (95 miles) northwest of Oujda. 🚶 *70,000.* 🚌 ℹ️ *Tourist and information office near Plaza de Toros; (952) 67 54 44.* 🎎 *Easter Week; Festival of Spain (early Jul); Our Lady of Victory (early Sep).*

Although about 40 per cent of the population of the Spanish town of Melilla is Moroccan, the way of life here is still very Andalusian.

It was once a Carthaginian, then a Roman, trading post. Located on the road from Fès and being the destination of caravans from Sijilmassa and the Sahara, Melilla became a busy port during the Middle Ages. The town has been in Spanish hands since 1497.

Under the Protectorate, Melilla underwent rapid development thanks to its status as a free zone. However, Moroccan independence and the closure of the border with Algeria cut it off from the hinterland. The town is now experiencing a difficult period. Consumer demand in this Spanish town means that tax-free goods find a ready

market. This has contributed to a thriving illegal trade, which in turn creates the appearance of prosperity.

Set on a rocky peninsula and enclosed within 16th- and 17th-century walls, the fortress-like Medina Sidonia district constitutes the upper town. The Puerta de la Marina leads through to a tracery of alleys, vaulted passages, steps and several small squares, some with a chapel or church. The Puerta de Santiago leads through to Plaza de Armas, west of the old town.

The church of **La Purísima Concepción**, in the northwest

General view of Melilla

of the old town, contains some fine Baroque altarpieces; on the high altar stands an 18th-century statue of Our Lady of Victory, patron saint of Melilla. Passing behind the church and following the ramparts, you will come to the **Musée Municipal** (Town Museum). Here, Melilla's Phoenician, Carthaginian and Roman periods are represented by ceramics, coins and bracelets that were discovered in the vicinity of the town.

Mediterranean cactus

◁ **Blossoming almond trees in the Nekkor valley**

Kif plantation in the Rif

KIF

The cultivation of kif (cannabis) was once the preserve of a few tribes around Ketama. Kif plantations have multiplied and are now found in several provinces between Chefchaouen and Al-Hoceima. Once grown only in the high valleys of the central Rif, the plant is today also cultivated on the slopes of low-lying valleys. Growing *Cannabis sativa*, "the curative herb", as well as Indian hemp, is highly lucrative and underpins the entire economy of the Rif. Although growing and smoking it (which are traditional in the region) are tolerated on a localized basis, its commercial exploitation is illegal. This has given rise to a major smuggling trade, which the Moroccan authorities are fighting with financial assistance from the European Union. The proposed solution is to introduce alternative crops and to open up the Rif by building a coastal road from Tangier to Saïdia, passing through Ceuta and Al-Hoceima.

Various stone implements from the western Sahara are also exhibited.

The circular Plaza de España links the old town with the new, which was begun at the end of the 19th century. Avenida del Rey Juan Carlos is the new town's busiest street.

🏛 **Musée Municipal**
◯ *Tue–Sun.* 📷

Cap des Trois Fourches ⓰

Road map E1. 30 km (18 miles) from Melilla by road then track.

The road from Beni Enzar to the Cap des Trois Fourches offers some stunning views of Melilla and the Mediterranean Sea. The part of the cape beyond the Charrana lighthouse is one of the most beautiful promontories in Morocco.

The cape is lined with bays and beaches nestling against the rocky coast. However, the coast road is narrow and difficult to drive, so care should be taken.

Moulouya Estuary ⓱

Road map E1. From Nador to Ras Kebdana, then on to Saïdia, road N16.

The whole area between the Bou Areg lagoon and the estuary of Wadi Moulouya is a rich and fascinating nature reserve. A great variety of birds – dunlin, plover, oystercatcher, little egret, redshank, black-tailed godwit and flamingoes, terns, and different species of gulls –

Peasant woman, Moulouya valley

come to spend the winter in this marshy area. The dunes are home to woodcock, plovers, herons and storks.

The vegetation in this area is equally diverse: spurge and sea holly grow on the dunes, while glasswort, reeds and rushes cover the marshes, which are the habitat of dragonflies, grasshoppers and sand spiders.

The Cap des Trois Fourches, offering some breathtaking views and stunning coastal landscapes

Zegzel Gorge ⑱

One of the most scenic routes in Morocco is road P6012 from Berkane to Taforalt. It follows the course of Wadi Zegzel as the river winds through deep gorges and along valleys and hillsides. Many of the caves that have been hollowed out of the cliffs by the action of water, such as the Grotte du Chameau and Grotte de Tghasrout, contain impressive stalactites and stalagmites. Continuing along this road offers breathtaking views of the mountains and the Angad plain, and of almond groves, villages and isolated *marabouts*. Road P6017 then road N2 lead back to Oujda, or Berkane via Ahfir, a town established by the French in 1910.

Grotte du Chameau ②
Dug into the mountainside by a hot underground stream, Grotte du Chameau (Camel Cave) contains several great halls with stalactites and stalagmites.

Wadi Zegzel Gorge ①
With the reddish cliffs of the mountainside towering above, the river valley traverses a lush green landscape, sometimes widening in places where it cuts through terraces planted with olive and fruit trees.

Beni-Snassen Mountains ③
In several places, the road offers spectacular views of the mountains, which bear the marks of erosion. Here also are hamlets with pisé houses and terraces with vines and olive trees.

Saïdia ⑲

Road map F1. 50 km (31 miles) northwest of Oujda. 🏠 2,800. 🚌 🎭 Folk Arts Festival (Aug). 🕐 Sun.

At the northern extremity of the fertile Triffa plain, an agricultural and wine-growing area, is the little town of Saïdia, located on the Wadi Kiss estuary. For the last 20 km (12 miles) before it reaches the sea, this river constitutes the border between Morocco and Algeria.

Saïdia is a coastal resort with a fine beach edged with mimosa and eucalyptus, the reason behind the town's name "Blue Pearl". In summer the beach is crowded with

Moroccan tourists. A folk arts festival is held at the Palais du Festival on Boulevard Mohammed V in August.

Saïdia is also home to a modern resort that overlooks a marina and accommodates more than 1,000 guests.

Oujda ⑳

Road map F2. 🏠 800,000. ✈ 15 km (9 miles). 🚌 🚉 🅸 Place du 16 Août 1953; (0536) 68 56 31, and railway station. 🎭 Moussem of Sidi Yahia (Sep). 🕐 Wed & Sun.

The history of Oujda has been shaped by its geographical location on a crossroads. In the Ville

Nouvelle, the main shops and the banks, and several large brasseries with spacious terraces, are concentrated on Avenue Mohammed V and around Place du 16 Août 1953.

The medina, still partly enclosed by ramparts, is easy to explore, being small enough to wander about in without becoming disoriented. Rue el-Mazouzi, a major axis, crosses the medina from west to east, ending at Bab Sidi Abdel Ouahab. Various souks are located on this main street. The *kissaria*, which is lined with arcades, has shops selling various types of textiles, kaftans and velvets as well as looms and skeins of wool. The small squares where the

View of Jbel Fourhal ④
The highest point of the Beni Snassen mountains, Jbel Fourhal (1,532 m/5,025 ft) is partly covered with forests of holm-oak and scarred by areas of limestone scree.

KEY

■ Suggested route

= Other roads

☼ Viewpoint

0 km   3

0 miles   3

SAÏDIA P6024 *Abfir*

P6024

N2

N2

Col de Guerbouss
539 m
(1,769 ft)

OUNTAINS

OUJDA

P6017

in Almou

④ ⑤
⑥
⑦

TIPS FOR DRIVERS

Departure point: Berkane, 60 km (37 miles) from Oujda on the N2.
Length: 134 km (83 miles). Follow the P6012 for 20 km (12 miles) along the Zegzel Gorge. The Route de Corniche, skirts the Beni Snassen Mountains but is in a bad state of repair. Road P6017 leads back to the N2, for the return trip to Oujda.
Stopping-off points: Although it is possible to find a meal in Ahfir, it is best to take a picnic. Berkane (Hotel Laetizia) offers basic accommodation. For this trip it is more convenient to stay at Oujda (Hotel Ibis Moussafir, Blvd Abdellah). Tel (0536) 68 82 02.

Oulad Jabeur Fouaga ⑤
In this small village the houses that cluster around the mosque have roofs of earth and thatch, which is typical of the region. Some have a central courtyard.

Almond Trees ⑥
Almond trees, grown on terraces, are widely cultivated in the region. Their blossom adds a splash of colour to this often harsh, high limestone environment.

Beni-Snassen Mountain Road ⑦
This mountain road winds up the hillsides and threads its way above dramatic precipices. On certain days there is a view of the Angad plain, where the town of Oujda was built.

El-Ma Souk (Water Market) and the Attarine Souk take place contain trees and fountains, and are the living centre of the medina.

The **Musée Ethnographique**, outside the ramparts, contains local costumes and items relating to daily life.

⋔ Musée Ethnographique
Parc Lalla Meriem.
Tel (0536) 68 56 31.
◻ daily. 📷

Environs
Sidi Yahia, 6 km (4 miles) east of Oujda, is an oasis with abundant springs. Nearby is the tomb of Sidi

Doorway in the medina at Oujda

Yahia ben Younes, patron saint of Oujda. Venerated by Muslims, Jews and Christians alike, he is sometimes equated with St John the Baptist.

Figuig ㉑

Road map F3. 368 km (229 miles) south of Oujda. 🏠 14,600. 🚌 from Oujda. 🚹 Oujda; (0536) 68 56 31. 🛒 Tue & Sun.

An oasis located at an altitude of 900 m (2,955 ft), Figuig consists of seven villages, or *ksour*, spread out in a vast palm plantation that

covers almost 20 sq km (8 sq miles). The water provided by the artesian springs irrigates a large number of gardens, which lie behind clay walls.

Zenaga, a typical *ksar*, is the largest of the villages, while El-Oudaghir is the administrative centre. The top of its minaret offers a view of the palm grove.

Figuig, at the crossroads of major caravan routes, was a busy caravanserai in the Middle Ages but lost its importance later. More recently, the closure of the border with Algeria deprived it of its role as a border post, which it once shared with Oujda.

FÈS

*L*ocated between the fertile lands of the Saïs and the forests of the Middle Atlas, Fès is the oldest of Morocco's imperial cities. It is the embodiment of the country's history and its spiritual and religious capital, and has been declared a World Heritage Site by UNESCO. Morocco's third-largest city, it consists of Fès el-Bali, the historic centre; Fès el-Jedid, the imperial city of the Merinids; and, located further south, the modern districts created under the Protectorate.

Idriss I founded Madinat Fas, on the right bank of the River Fès, in 789. In 808, his son, Idriss II, built another town on the left bank, which was known as El-Alya (High Town). In 818, these two cities, each within its own walls, received hundreds of Muslim families who had been expelled from Córdoba. Soon afterwards, some 300 refugee families from Kairouan, in Tunisia, found asylum in El-Alya, which then became known as Karaouiyine, after them. Within a few years, thanks to these two communities, the two towns became the centre of the Arabization and Islamization of Morocco.

In the mid-11th century, the Almoravids united the two towns, building a wall around them. The Almohads took the city in 1145, after a long siege. Fès then became the country's foremost cultural and economic metropolis, thanks in large part to the founding of its university. In 1250, the Merinids raised Fès to the status of imperial capital and endowed it with prestigious buildings. To the west of the old town they established a new royal city, Fès el-Jedid (New Fès). Conquered by the Alaouites in 1666, Fès was spurned by Moulay Ismaïl, who chose Meknès as his capital. The city's decline continued until the early 20th century.

When the Protectorate was established in 1912, a Ville Nouvelle (New Town) was built. After independence this was filled by the prosperous citizens of the old medina, while the country people, rootless and poor, crowded into the old town. However, UNESCO's ongoing restoration programme has saved the historic city of Fès el-Bali.

The rooftops of the Karaouiyine Quarter, Fès el-Bali

◁ The entrance to the Bou Inania Medersa in the Karaouiyine Quarter, Fès el-Bali

Exploring Fès

Seen from the summit of the hill of the Merinid
tombs, Fès appears as a compact and tightly woven
urban fabric. Enclosed within its defensive walls,
Fès el-Bali, the historic medina, is a sea of rooftops
from which emerge minarets and domes. Wadi Fès
separates the two historic entities: the Andalusian
Quarter to the east, and the Karaouiyine Quarter
to the west. Fès el-Jedid (see pp180–83) is built on
a height south of the medina. Notable features here
include the royal palace and the former Jewish
quarter. The Ville Nouvelle (New Town), dating
from the Protectorate, lies further south.

Rue Talaa Kebira, Fès el-Bali

KEY

- Medina
- Historic building
- — Ramparts
- Bus station
- P Parking
- ⊠ Post office
- ✚ Hospital
- C Mosque
- ✴ Synagogue
- ¶¶ Muslim cemetery
- ⬝•⬝ Jewish cemetery

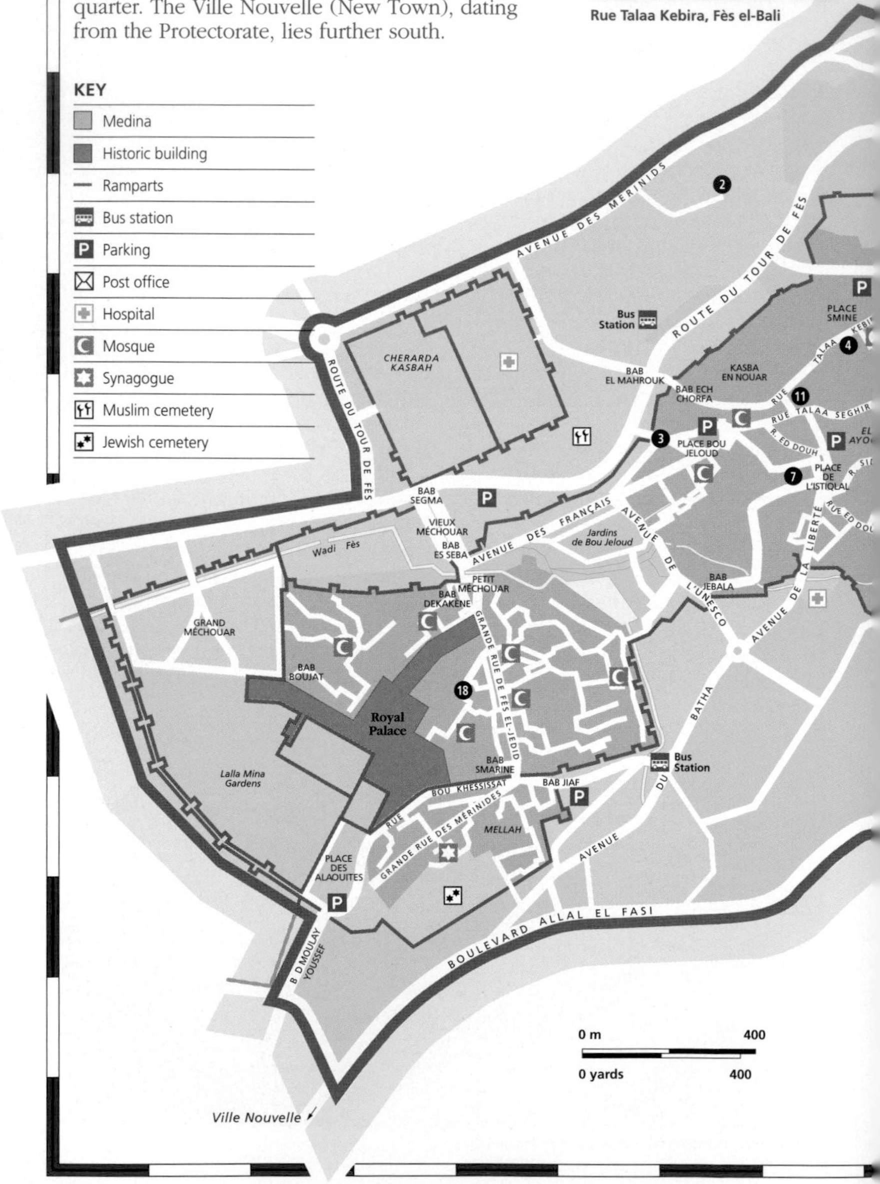

CHERARDA KASBAH

ROUTE DES MERINIDS

AVENUE DES MERINIDS

ROUTE DU TOUR DE FÈS

PLACE SMINE

Bus Station

BAB EL MAHROUK

KASBA EN NOUAR

BAB ECH CHORFA

PLACE BOU JELOUD

BAB SEGMA

VIEUX MÉCHOUAR

BAB ES SEBA

AVENUE DES FRANÇAIS

Jardins de Bou Jeloud

PETIT MÉCHOUAR

BAB DEKAKENE

GRAND MÉCHOUAR

Wadi Fès

GRANDE RUE DE FÈS EL-JEDID

BAB BOUJAT

BAB JEBALA

Royal Palace

AVENUE DE L'UNESCO

AVENUE DE LA LIBERTÉ

Lalla Mina Gardens

BAB SMARINE

BAB JIAF

Bus Station

BOU KHESSISSAT

MELLAH

PLACE DES ALAOUITES

GRANDE RUE DES MERINIDES

B D MOULAY YOUSEF

BOULEVARD ALLAL EL FASI

PLACE DE L'ISTIQLAL

BATHA

| 0 m | 400 |

| 0 yards | 400 |

Ville Nouvelle

GETTING AROUND
Both Fès el-Bali and Fès el-Jedid can be explored only
on foot since the labyrinthine layout of these quarters is
unsuitable for motorized traffic. Parking is available near
Bab Boujeloud or Bab el-Ftouh, or on Place des Alaouites.
Buses (often very crowded) run between Ville Nouvelle
and both Fès el-Bali and Fès el-Jedid. It is best to take
a *petit taxi (see p374)*. *Petits taxis* can be found near
the post office, at Bab Boujeloud and in the vicinity
of the large hotels.

**Carpets spread out on a terrace
in the medina**

SEE ALSO

- *Where to Stay* pp310–12
- *Where to Eat* pp335–6

SIGHTS AT A GLANCE

Historic Buildings
Fondouk el-Nejjarine ❻
Merinid Tombs ❶
Zaouia of Moulay Idriss II ❽

**Streets, Squares and
Historic Quarters**
Andalusian Quarter ❶❺
Fès el-Jedid pp180–83 ❶❽
Place el-Seffarine ❶❸
Rue Talaa Kebira ❹
The Souks ❺
Tanners' Quarter ❶❷

Mosques
Andalusian Mosque ❶❹
*Karaouiyine Mosque
pp176–7* ❶❼

Medersas
*Bou Inania Medersa
pp172 3* ❶❶
El-Attarine Medersa ❾
El-Cherratine Medersa ❶⓪

Museums
Musée des Armes ❷
*Musée Dar el-Batha
pp168–9* ❼

Gates
Bab Boujeloud ❸
Bab el-Ftouh ❶❻

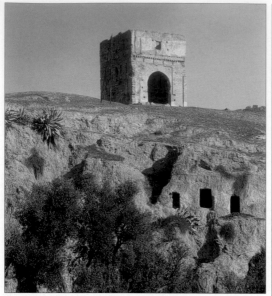

The Merinid tombs, overlooking the medina of Fès

Merinid Tombs ❶

North of the medina, on the hill of the Merinid tombs.

Standing among olive trees, cacti and blue agaves, the 16th-century ruins that overlook Fès el-Bali are those of a Merinid palace and necropolis. Ancient chroniclers recorded that these tombs elicited wonderment because of their magnificent marble and the splendour of their coloured epitaphs. Today, the tombs are very dilapidated, and the area is popular with petty thieves, but it offers an impressive view of the city. The view from the terrace of the Hôtel Les Mérinides *(see p310)* is equally fine.

The stretch of wall immediately beneath the hill is the oldest part of the medina's defences. Parts of the curtain wall date from the Almohad period (12th century), notably Borj Kaoukeb, near which the lepers' quarter was once located. The tombs overlook a tiered cemetery which stretches as far as Bab Guissa, an Almohad gateway dating from the 13th century.

Silver dagger, Musée des Armes

Musée des Armes ❷

Borj Nord. **Tel** *(0535) 64 75 66.* ⬜ *9am–4:30pm Tue–Sun.* 📷

Borj Nord was built in 1582, on the orders of the Saadian sultan Ahmed el-Mansour (1578–1603). From its vantage point over the city, the fortress both defended and controlled Fès el-Bali. In 1963 the collection of weapons from the Musée Dar el-Batha *(see pp168–9)* was transferred here to create the Museum of Arms. Much of the collection, comprising more than 8,000 pieces, comes from the Makina, the arsenal built by Moulay Hassan I at the end of the 19th century, although it was enriched by donations from various Alaouite sultans.

Some 1,000 pieces of weaponry are exhibited in 16 rooms, in a chronological display running from prehistory to the first half of the 20th century. Moroccan weapons are well represented and demonstrate the technical knowledge of Moroccan craftsmen. There is also an interesting collection of weapons from all over the world.

Bab Boujeloud ❸

Place du Pacha el-Baghdadi.

Enclosed within high walls, the large Place Pacha el-Baghdadi links the medina and Fès el-Jedid. On one side of the square stands Bab Boujeloud. Built in 1913, this fine monumental gate is the principal entrance into Fès el-Bali.

With the development of heavy artillery, the fortified gates of Fès lost their effectiveness as defences and came to be seen as decorative buildings, contributing to the city's prestige and helping to justify the levy of city taxes.

Bab Boujeloud, built in the Moorish style, consists of three perfectly symmetrical horseshoe arches. A rich decorative scheme consisting of geometric patterns, calligraphy, interlaced floral motifs and glazed tilework of many colours, with blue predominating, graces the façade. From this entranceway the silhouette of the minaret of the Bou Inania Medersa can be glimpsed on the left.

The Musée des Armes, housed in a 16th-century fortress

Rue Talaa Kebira ❹

Reached via Bab Boujeloud.

This thoroughfare, whose name means "Great Climb" and which is partly covered by a cane canopy, is lined with small shops along almost its entire length. It is continued by the Ras Tiyalin and Aïn Allou souks and by spice markets. The street passes the *kissaria* and

Rue Talaa Kebira, the main thoroughfare in the medina of Fès

ends at the Karaouiyine Mosque *(see pp176–7)*. Running parallel to it at its southern end is another important street, Rue Talaa Seghira ("Short Climb"), which joins up with Rue Talaa Kebira at Aïn Allou. These streets are the two principal cultural and economic thoroughfares of Fès el-Bali. The city's most important buildings are located here.

Opposite the Bou Inania Medersa *(see pp172–3)* stands **Dar el-Magana** (House of the Clock), built by the ruler Abou Inan in 1357. It contains a water-clock built by Fassi craftsmen during the Merinid period.

Not far from here, level with a covered passage in the Blida Quarter, is the **Zaouia el-Tijaniya**, containing the tomb of Ahmed el-Tijani, master of *Tariqa el-Tijaniya* (The Way), a doctrine that spread widely throughout the Maghreb and sub-Saharan Africa. Further on are three musical instrument workshops. Makers of stringed instruments have almost completely disappeared from Fès; the only remaining practitioner is a craftsman in Rue Talaa Seghira, opposite Dar Mnebhi, who still makes *ouds* (lutes) by traditional methods. Beyond is the skin-dressers' *fondouk*, which contains leather workshops.

Across the Bou Rous bridge stands the **Ech Cherabliyine Mosque** (Mosque of the Slipper-Makers). Built by the Merinid sultan Abou el-Hassan, it is distinguished by its elegant minaret.

The Souks ❺

The souks of Fès el-Bali spread out beyond the Ech Cherabliyine Mosque.

The location of each souk reflects a hierarchy dictated by the value placed on the various goods on offer in each of them. Makers and sellers are grouped together according to the products that they offer. Every type of craft has its own street, or part of a street, around the Karaouiyine Mosque, which has resulted in a logical but relatively complex layout. While the **El-Attarine Souk** sells spices, there is also a **Slipper Souk** and a **Henna Souk**, which is laid out in an attractive shaded square planted with arbuses. A plaque records that the Sidi Frijthe *maristan*, which was the largest mental asylum in the Merinid empire, once stood on this square. Built by Abou Yacoub Youssef (1286–1307), it also functioned as a hospital for storks. It was still in existence

Skin-dressing workshops, unchanged since the Middle Ages

in 1944. In the 16th century, Leo Africanus, known today for his accounts of his travels, worked there as a clerk for two years.

The *kissaria*, near the Zaouia of Moulay Idriss, marks the exact centre of the souks. This is a gridwork of covered streets where shops selling luxury goods are especially conspicuous. Some of the fine silks and brocades, high-quality kaftans and jewellery on offer here supply the international market.

Fondouk el-Nejjarine, a UNESCO World Heritage Site

Fondouk el-Nejjarine ❻

Place el-Nejjarine. **Tel** *(0535) 74 05 80*. **Musée du Bois** ☐ *10am–5pm daily.* 🖼

Not far from the Henna Souk, the impressive Fondouk el-Nejjarine, with an elegant fountain, is one of the most renowned buildings in Fès. Built by the *amine* (provost) Adeyel in the 18th century, this former caravanserai provided food, rest and shelter to the traders in luxury goods arriving from the interior. Classed as a historic monument in 1916, it is now one of UNESCO's World Heritage Sites. Its restoration formed part of the preservation programme carried out on the whole medina. The *fondouk's* three floors house the privately run **Musée du Bois** (Museum of Wood). The displays include carved doors from the magnificent Bou Inania Medersa *(see pp172–3)*.

Musée Dar el-Batha ❼

Dish with calligraphy, 14th century

The palace of Dar el-Batha was begun between 1873 and 1875 by Moulay el-Hassan, and was completed by Moulay Abdel Aziz in 1897. The location of the palace was an area of neglected gardens, which had been irrigated by a river. The sultan, who wanted to make the palace a residence worthy of being used for official receptions, added an imposing courtyard covered with coloured tiles and featuring a large fountain. He also laid out a large and very fine Andalusian garden. Despite many later alterations, the traditional Moorish features of this building have survived.

EXPLORING THE COLLECTIONS OF THE MUSÉE DAR EL-BATHA

In 1914, the Orientalist Alfred Bel made the first bequest to the future ethnographic musem which, by royal decree, became the museum of local crafts (Musée des Arts et des Traditions) in 1915.

Today, the permanent exhibition, which fills 12 rooms, consists of more than 500 objects selected from the 5,000 that the museum has acquired. They are shown in two large sections. The ethnographic section, featuring the arts and crafts of Fès and the rural crafts of neighbouring areas, fills the first eight rooms. The archaeological section is laid out in the four remaining rooms. Particularly notable is the display tracing the development of architecture in Fès, from the Idrissid period to that of the Alaouites.

A soup tureen with blue and white decoration

BOOKS AND MANUSCRIPTS

Room 1 contains some extremely fine leather-bound books dating from the 11th century. Their embossed and gold-painted decoration is a tradition peculiar to Fès that stayed alive until the 17th century. Also on display are manuscript copies of the Koran made on parchment in the 16th to 18th centuries; prayer books by the Sufi scholar El-Jazouli; and important manuscripts written in the Andalusian cursive style of calligraphy, which was widely used in Morocco in the 8th and 9th centuries. Examples of illuminated calligraphy with geometric decorative motifs, as well as other exhibits, highlight the role that Fès played in the development and diffusion of learning.

CERAMICS

The original location of the potters' souk, next to the Karaouiyine Mosque, is proof of the respect and repute in which the makers of the famous Fès blue and white ware were held. As well as this pottery, Room 2 contains dishes and *jebbana* (traditional earthenware vessels) with polychrome decoration in blue, green, yellow and brown over a white tin glaze, or with *shoula* (herringbone) or *chebka* (scale) motifs. Some of the dishes with green motifs displayed in Case 11 are examples of the famous *zarghmil*, the famous "centipede" style of decoration characteristic of Fès.

LEATHERWORK

The exhibits in Room 3 include a fragment of a 13th-century candelabra from the Karaouiyine Mosque, alms measures made in Fès in the 14th to 18th centuries, some fine astrolabes and a number of instruments for determining the times of day at which prayers are to be said, for indicating the direction of Mecca and for tracking the lunar calendar.

Alms measure (18th century)

There are also lamps, writing tables and a medicine bowl decorated with verses from the Koran and formulae; various equipment for use in the hammam and for brewing and drinking tea; and a fine 18th-century tray embellished with a complex geometric pattern. Each of these pieces demonstrates the consummate skill and exceptional creativity of the craftsmen of Fès, who in making them fulfilled the religious, scientific and symbolic needs of their time.

WOOD, EMBROIDERY AND WEAVING

The furniture in Room 4, including chests and sets of shelves, shows both the range of woods used (cedar, thuya, almond, walnut, ebony, citron and mahogany) and a range

Lintel from the Andalusian Mosque, carved in 980

Detail of 19th-century embroidery from Fès

of cabinet-making skills. Shown here are carved and painted or leather-covered furniture, and furniture with iron fittings, marquetry decoration and mother-of-pearl and ivory inlay. There is also a fine 14th-century Moorish chest, made to hold the most valuable pieces of a bride's trousseau as they were carried to her new home. The exhibits in Room 5 consist of examples of the different types of Fassi embroidery. These include exquisite examples of *terz sqalli*, lamé embroidery in which gold thread and gold dust are used; *al-aleuj* embroidery, a technique very similar to Persian stitch; and *erz alghorza*, counted-thread embroidery, the most famous type of Fassi embroidery, usually in red, blue, purple and green silk. Women's

Double pitcher from the Rif (19th century)

costumes, headdresses and accessories in embroidered silk decorated with trimmings demonstrate the high degree of refinement in traditional Fassi dress.

RURAL CRAFTS

Objects of everyday life from various regions of Morocco are exhibited in Room 6: pottery made by the women of the Rif, carpets from the Middle Atlas, and fine Berber jewellery, such as brooches, pectorals, necklaces, finger rings and bracelets. All these show the skills and inventiveness of Moroccan craftsmen and craftswomen.

DOORS

A display of doors fills Room 7. Doors from ordinary houses and large palace doors carved and decorated with patterns of nails are shown with a selection of door locks from houses in Fès.

THE ART OF ZELLIJ

Room 9 is devoted to *zellij* tilework made in Fès from the 14th to the 18th centuries and among the finest of its kind.

One of the exhibits, a remarkable panel from the Bou Inania Medersa, perfectly exemplifies this brilliant tradition of architectural decoration in Morocco. The rich aesthetic vocabulary of this art form brings to life plain surfaces with a lively play of patterns and colours.

MONUMENTAL WOODCARVING

The displays in Rooms 10 and 11 trace the evolution of monumental woodcarving in Fès from the 9th century to the present day. Among the most interesting pieces are a lintel from the Karaouiyine Mosque (877) and the monumental door from the El-Attarine Medersa (1325). The splendid lintel from the Andalusian

Minbar dating from 1350, from the Bou Inania Medersa

Mosque, made in 980, is a masterpiece of religious art of the early years of Islam in Morocco. The museum's collection also includes the minbar from the Andalusian Mosque, which is exhibited alternately with that from the Bou Inania Medersa (1350).

FUNERARY ARCHITECTURE

Various pieces of Muslim funerary architecture and a selection of tombstones from Volubilis end the museum's displays.

GALLERY GUIDE

The collections are divided into two large sections. The ethnographic section occupies eight rooms: Room 1 contains exhibits relating to the art of the book; Room 2 contains ceramics and paintings; Room 3 is devoted to leatherwork; Room 4 to marquetry, embroidery and weaving; Rooms 5 and 6 to carpets, Berber jewellery and objects from everyday life; Room 7 to wooden doors, and Room 8 to genealogy. The archaeological section begins in Room 9 with zellij and ceramics, Rooms 10 and 11 contain displays of wood used in architecture; Room 12 is devoted to archaeology relating to Islam and funerary stelae. There is also a workshop which offers visitors the chance to watch the woodcarvers at work.

Arabic Calligraphy

Islam traditionally forbids all figurative representation, and since the 8th century this prohibition has encouraged the use of calligraphy in Arabic civilization. Decorative writing became an art form that was used not only for manuscripts but also to decorate buildings. Islamic calligraphy is closely connected to the revelation of the Koran: the word of God is to be transcribed in a beautiful script far finer than secular writing. Writing out not only the Koran, but also the 99 names of Allah is considered to be a very pious

Calligraphic manuscript

undertaking. The importance of this art form in Islamic civilization is shown by the carved, painted or tiled friezes that decorate the walls and domes of mosques and medersas, as well as by the thousands of scientific, literary and religious calligraphic manuscripts preserved in public and private libraries. Maghrebi script, used in the Maghreb, in Andalusia and in the Sudan, is derived from Kufic script, which is named after the town of Kufa, in Iraq, where this style of writing originated.

MANUSCRIPTS AND FRIEZES

Quotations from the Koran are omnipresent in manuscripts and calligraphic friezes. Calligraphy appears in all dimensions and on a great variety of surfaces. Maghrebi script is characterized by rounded letters combined with slender descenders and ascenders.

This detail from an illuminated manuscript *in Maghrebi script, produced in Rabat in the 8th century, features plant motifs.*

This illuminated manuscript *of a* hadih, *recording the words and deeds of the Prophet Mohammed, is in Maghrebi script. With gold and bright colours, illumination enriches both religious and secular manuscripts. The finest illuminated manuscripts are preserved in the Royal Library in Rabat.*

Cursive script, *like this example from the Bou Inania Medersa, may appear in the form of carved zellij work. Calligraphic friezes, often with a religious content, were made both for public buildings and private houses.*

Decorative details, *like this one from an anonymous manuscript of a musical score, shows that calligraphy was sometimes more ornamental than purely functional.*

Calligraphy on marble, *Hassan II Mosque.*

INKWELLS

Used for calligraphy and for illumination, inkwells were made in the shape of a *koubba*, the shrine of a Muslim saint.

The compartments *in these* mejma *inkwells were designed to hold the inks of different colours that were used for illumination.*

Fountain for ablutions at the Zaouia of Moulay Idriss II

Zaouia of Moulay Idriss II ❽

🚫 to non-Muslims. Glimpses possible through the open doors.

The Zaouia of Moulay Idriss II, containing the tomb of the second Idrissid ruler (considered to be the founder of Fès) is the most venerated shrine in Morocco. Built in the centre of the city at the beginning of the 18th century, during the reign of Moulay Ismaïl, the building was restored in the mid-19th century. The pyramidal dome that covers the saint's tomb and its polychrome minaret give it a majestic silhouette. The courtyard of the mosque contains a fountain which consists of a white marble basin on a shaft, richly decorated with *zellij* tilework.

The *horm*, the perimeter wall around the *zaouia*, is also holy. The narrow streets leading to the shrine are barred at mid-height by a wooden beam that is supposed to prevent the passage of beasts of burden. The *horm* also made the shrine an inviolable place, so that in the past outlaws would find sanctuary here.

At the end of each summer, during a *moussem* lasting two to three days, this place of pilgrimage attracts not only the inhabitants of Fès but also people from the surrounding countryside and mountain-dwellers from distant tribes. They all come to receive a blessing and *baraka* ("beneficient force"). The motley crowd of the faithful is made up of pilgrims and beggars, as well as nougat, candle and incense sellers whose goods are used as tomb offerings.

Decorative column in the El-Attarine Medersa

El-Attarine Medersa ❾

Opposite the Karaouiyine Mosque. **Tel** (0535) 62 34 60. ☐ 9am–4pm daily. 🚫 Fri. 🖼

The El-Attarine Medersa (Medersa of the Spice Sellers) stands in the neighbourhood of the Karaouiyine Mosque and the El-Attarine Souk. With the Bou Inania Medersa (*see pp172–3*), it is considered to be one of the wonders of Moorish architecture. It was built between 1323 and 1325 by the Merinid sultan Abou Saïd Othman, and has all the elements specific to a medieval Muslim school.

The highly decorated entrance leads through to a courtyard paved with *zellij* tilework in a two-colour pattern of brown and white, and enclosing an ablutions fountain. A cladding of polychrome tiles covers the base of the courtyard's four interior walls and its columns. A door with fine decoration and exquisite fittings leads from the courtyard to the prayer hall, which contains a mihrab. The prayer hall has a highly decorated ceiling, walls featuring luxuriant stuccowork and *zellij* work, and lintels with epigraphic decoration.

The students' rooms, looking onto the courtyard from the upper floor, have windows fronted by turned wooden railings. The terrace offers a view of the rooftops of Fès el-Bali and the courtyard of the Karaouiyine Mosque.

El-Cherratine Medersa ❿

Rue El-Cherratine. 🖼

Located southeast of the Karaouiyine Mosque, in Rue el-Cherratine (Street of the Ropemakers), this medersa was built by Moulay Rachid, the first Alaouite sultan, in 1670. Although it is structurally similar to the Merinid medersas, it is less elaborately decorated. Adding to the building's austerity are the high, narrow residential units known as *douiras*, which stand in three corners of the courtyard. The tiny cells inside were for the use of students.

Entry into the medersa is through beautiful double doors cased in engraved bronze. The doors open onto a passageway with a fine carved and painted wooden ceiling, which in turn leads to the Moorish courtyard.

The El-Cherratine Souk, where rope-makers sell their wares

Bou Inania Medersa ⑪

Glazed tiles on the medersa's roof

This is the largest and most sumptuously decorated medersa ever built by the Merinids. Constructed between 1350 and 1355 by the sultan Abou Inan, it is the only medersa in Morocco that has a minbar (pulpit) and a minaret. A mosque, cathedral, students' residence and school combined, its functions have determined its architectural complexity. The one-storey building, on a rectangular plan, is arranged around a square Moorish courtyard paved with marble and onyx, and surrounded on three sides by a cloister. It is one of the few Islamic religious buildings that is open to non-Muslims.

Stained-glass Windows
The windows of the prayer hall feature old stained-glass panels.

Capitals
The carved motifs on the capitals in the medersa show Moorish influence.

Pitched roofs over the mosque

★ Prayer Hall
The mihrab (above) is surmounted by stained-glass windows. The minbar (1350) is now in the Musée Dar el-Batha (see pp168–9).

Zellij Tilework
In the medersa, the three decorative bands always appear in the same order: geometric tilework below, cursive script carved into tiles in the centre, and stuccowork above.

STAR FEATURES

★ Façade
★ Prayer Hall

Student at a medersa

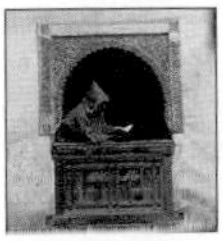

THE MOROCCAN MEDERSA

The medersa was both a cultural and a religious establishment. It was primarily a residential college, designed for local students from the town or city and especially for those from the immediate or more distant rural areas, but also for anyone who came in search of learning. It was an extension of the great university-mosque, an institution once restricted to the study of religion, law, science and even the arts. It was finally a place of prayer and reflection. The medersas of Fès, home to the greatest scholars in the country, were the most highly esteemed in Morocco.

VISITORS' CHECKLIST

Rue Talaa Kebira. *(to non-Muslims) 8:30am–6:30pm Wed–Mon.*

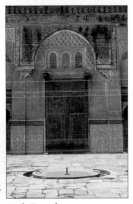

Windows
The ornate windows of the students' rooms on the upper floor are framed by stuccowork surmounted by muqarnas.

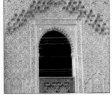

★ Façade
Richly decorated with zellij *tilework, stuccowork and sculpted wood, the façade runs the gamut of the Moorish decorative repertoire.*

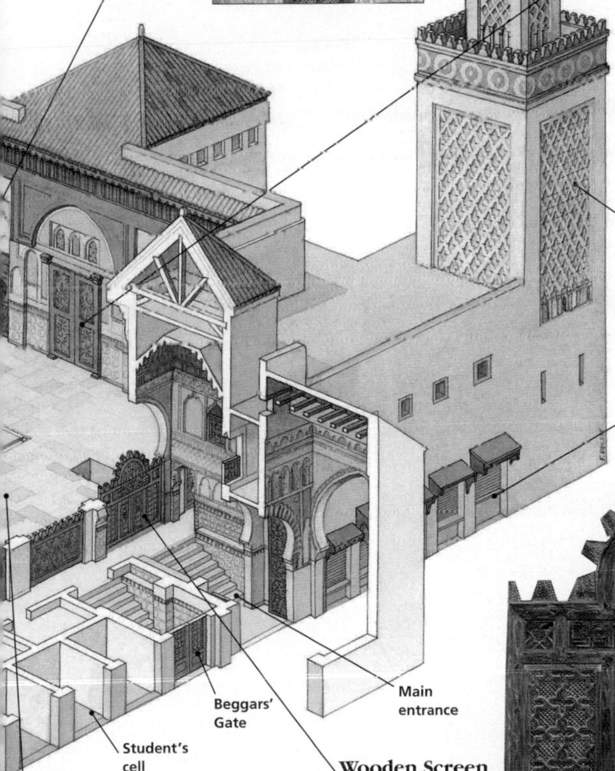

The minaret, one of the finest in Fès, is decorated with a frieze featuring merlons. The lantern is topped by a similar frieze.

Shops

Main entrance

Beggars' Gate

Student's cell

Courtyard paved with marble and onyx

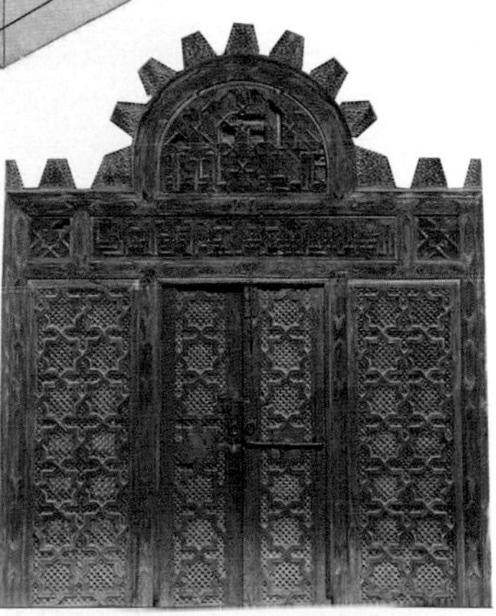

Wooden Screen
The magnificent carved wooden screen of the main entrance is framed by sturdy pillars. The adjoining door, of much plainer design, was known as Beggars' Gate.

The Tanneries of Fès

Often located near watercourses, and usually some distance from residential quarters because of the unpleasant odours that they produced, tanneries made a substantial contribution to a city's

Blue leather bag

economy. Tanning is a craft with traditions that go back thousands of years. The process turns animal hides into soft, rot-proof leather. Once tanned, the hides are passed on to leatherworkers.

Vats, *some of which have been in use for centuries, are used for soaking skins after the hair and flesh have been removed. The tanning solution that turns them into leather is obtained from the bark of pomegranate or mimosa.*

The tanned hides *are hung out to dry on the terraces of the medina, as here, or in other parts of Fès, such as the Bab el-Guissa cemetery. The roofs of houses and the hillsides around the city may also be used as drying areas.*

STAGES IN THE TANNING PROCESS

In Fès, the tanneries *(chouaras)* are located near Wadi Fès. The hides of sheep, goats, cows and camels undergo several processes – including the removal of hair and flesh, followed by soaking in vats, then by drying and rinsing – before they are ready to be dyed and handed over to leatherworkers.

The dried hides are rinsed *in generous quantities of water. They are then softened by being steeped in baths of fatty solutions.*

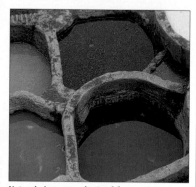

Natural pigments, *obtained from certain plants and minerals, are still used by Moroccan craftsmen to colour the hides. However, chemical dyes are also used today.*

Dyed leather *is used to make many types of useful and decorative objects, such as embroidered bags, babouches, pouffes and clothing. These goods are offered for sale in the numerous souks in the medina of Fès.*

Tanners' Quarter ⑫

North of Place el-Seffarine.

The Chouara, or Tanners' Quarter, has been located near Wadi Fès since the Middle Ages. Its dyeing vats, in the midst of houses in the Blida quarter, are best seen from neighbouring terraces. Although pervaded by an unpleasantly strong smell, this is the most lively and picturesque of all the souks in Fès.

Place el-Seffarine ⑬

Fès is the most important centre for the production of brassware and silverware in Morocco. The workshops of brass-workers and coppersmiths that line Place el-Seffarine have been here for centuries. The pretty fountain with fleur-de-lis decoration is worth a look. It was probably built by French convicts in the 16th century.

North of the square is the 14th-century **Karaouiyine Library**, which was set up on the orders of the sultan Abou Inan. It was used by the greatest Moorish men of learning, including the philosopher and doctor Ibn Rushd, known as Averroës *(see p231)*, the philosopher Ibn Tufayl, the historian Ibn Khaldoun and the 16th-century traveller Leo Africanus. The manuscripts that once formed part of the library's collection have been transferred to the Royal Library in Rabat.

Brassworker making trays in Place el-Seffarine

The **El-Seffarine Medersa**, opposite the Karaouiyine Library, was built in 1280 and is the oldest medersa in Morocco that is still in use. The **El-Mesbahiya Medersa**, also north of the square, was built by the Merinid sultan Abou el Hassan in 1346. Further on, on the right, is the 16th-century **Tetouani Fondouk**, which accommodated traders and students from Tetouan.

Place el-Seffarine leads to **Rue des Teinturiers** (Dyers' Street), which runs parallel to the *wadi* and where skeins are hung out to dry.

Karaouiyine Library
Place el-Seffarine. *Tel (0535) 62 34 60.* ☐ *8am–noon & 2–5pm Mon–Thu, 8am–noon Fri (times may vary).*

The north entrance of the Andalusian Mosque

Andalusian Mosque ⑭

Accessible via Rue el-Nekhaline or Bab Ftouh and Rue Sidi Bou Ghaleb. ● *to non-Muslims.*

According to legend, this mosque was established by a religious woman, Mariam el Fihri, sister of the founder of the Karaouiyine Mosque, and by the Andalusians who lived in the Karaouiyine Quarter. Its present appearance dates from the reign of the Almohad ruler Mohammed el-Nasser (13th century). The Merinids added a fountain in 1306 and funded the establishment of a library here in 1416. Non-Muslims can only admire the building from the exterior; notable are the great north entrance, with a carved cedar awning, and the domed Zenet minaret.

Andalusian Quarter ⑮

The Andalusian Quarter did not undergo the same development as the Kairaouiyine Quarter, located on the opposite bank of Wadi Fès and better provided with water. Nevertheless, this part of the city, which is quieter and more residential, has monuments that are worth a visit.

The **El-Sahrij Medersa**, built in 1321 takes its name from the large water basin in one of the courtyards. This is considered to be the third-finest medersa in Fès after the Bou Inania and the El-Attarine medersas. The **Mausoleum of Sidi Bou Ghaleb**, in the street of that name, is that of a holy man from Andalusia who lived and taught in Fès in the 12th century.

El-Sahrij Medersa
Rue Sidi Bou Ghaled. *Tel (0535) 62 34 60 (information).* ☐ *Closed for restoration.* 🖉

Bab el-Ftouh ⑯

Southeast of the medina.

Literally meaning "Gate of the Aperture", the huge Bab el-Ftouh is also known as the Gate of Victory. It leads through to the Andalusian Quarter. The gate was built in the 10th century by a Zenet emir, and was altered in the 18th century, during the reign of the Alaouite ruler Sidi Mohammed ben Abdallah. Outside the ramparts, on a hill opposite the city, is the Bab el-Ftouh cemetery, where some of the most illustrious inhabitants of Fès are buried.

Bab el-Ftouh cemetery, resting place of some renowned teachers

For hotels and restaurants in this region see pp310–12 and pp335–6

Karaouiyine Mosque ⑰

Established in 859, the Karaouiyine Mosque is one of the oldest and most illustrious mosques in the western Muslim world. The first university to be established in Morocco, it was frequented by such learned men as Ibn Khaldoun *(see p181)*, Ibn el-Khatib, Averroës *(see p231)* and even Pope Sylvester II (909–1003). Named after the quarter in which it was built – that of refugees from Kairouan, in Tunisia – it was founded by Fatima bint Mohammed el-Fihri, a religious woman from Kairouan, who donated her worldly riches for its construction. It is still considered to be one of the main spiritual and intellectual centres of Islam and remains the seat of the Muslim university of Fès.

Pitched Roof
The roof of the mosque is covered in emerald-green tiles.

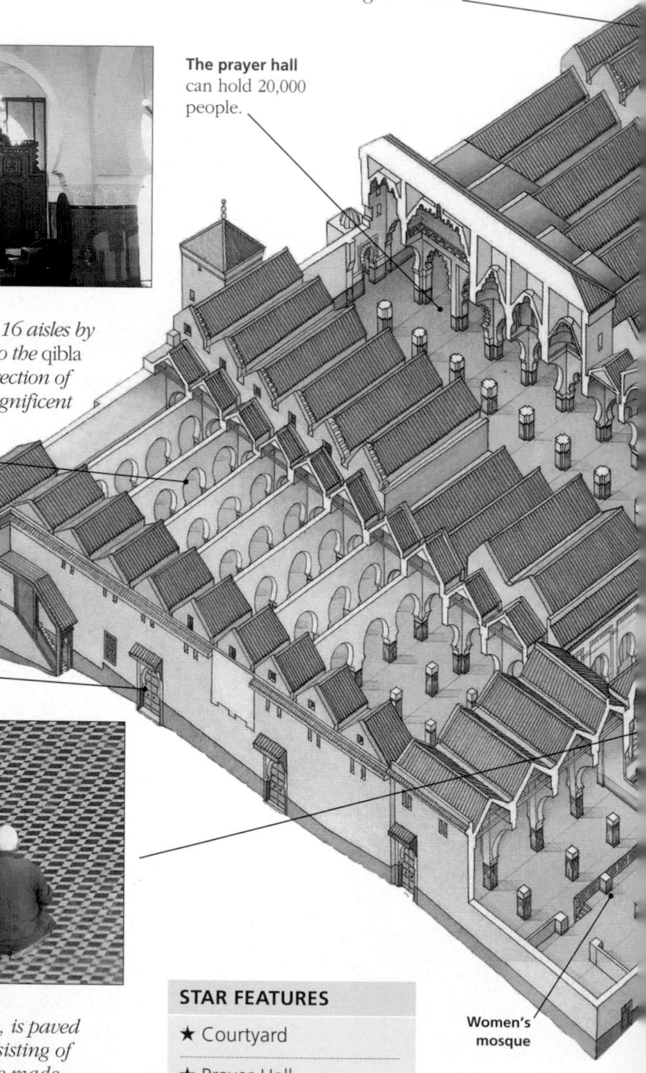

The prayer hall can hold 20,000 people.

★ **The Prayer Hall**
The hall is divided into 16 aisles by 270 columns, parallel to the qibla wall (indicating the direction of Mecca). It is lit by a magnificent 12th-century Almohad candelabra.

This door is one of 14 entrances to the mosque.

★ **The Courtyard**
The courtyard, or sahn, is paved with zellij tilework consisting of 50,000 pieces that were made especially for the floor of the mosque.

STAR FEATURES

★ Courtyard

★ Prayer Hall

Women's mosque

Ablutions Basin
This basin, in the centre of the courtyard, is carved from a single block of marble. It rests on a marble fountain to which the faithful come to carry out their ablutions, an essential preparation for prayer.

The minaret, in an early Almoravid style, is very similar in shape to a lookout tower.

VISITORS' CHECKLIST

Rue Bou Touil (which continues from Rue Talaa Kebira) runs parallel to the Karaouiyine Mosque. *to non-Muslims. Glimpses can sometimes be had through an open door, but be respectful.*

THE ROLE OF THE MOSQUE

Each quarter of Fès has one or more mosques and other places of worship. Friday prayers take place in both large and small mosques. *Msids*, small oratories without a minaret, are designed for prayer and for teaching the Koran. *Zaouias* are sanctuaries where religious brotherhoods gather. The mosque, which stands both as a civic and a social symbol, is simultaneously a place of worship, a university, a tribunal, an inviolable place of asylum and a friendly meeting place. The call to prayer is given by the muezzin five times a day.

Saadian pavilion

Mashrabiyya
The main doorway has a mashrabiyya screen to protect worshippers from prying eyes.

Dome Over the Entrance
The main entrance into the courtyard of the mosque faces Rue Bou Touil. The monumental doorway is surmounted by a small striated dome.

Fès el-Jedid ⑱

Fès el-Jedid, meaning New Fès or White Fès, was built in 1276 by Merinid princes as a stronghold against the permanent threat of the rebellious Fassis, and as a vantage point from which to survey their activities in the old town. Surrounded by ramparts, Fès el-Jedid was primarily a kasbah, and its political and military role predominated over the civic functions of a true Islamic town. It was the administrative centre of Morocco up to 1912.

Fès el-Jedid consists of several distinct units. In the west is the royal palace, and other buildings associated with it, and the Moulay Abdallah Quarter. In the south is the mellah, or Jewish quarter, a maze of dark, narrow streets. In the east are the Muslim quarters.

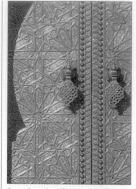

Brass doors into the Dar el-Makhzen engraved with a geometric pattern

Dar el-Makhzen, the royal palace in Fès

🏛 Dar el-Makhzen

🚫 to the public.

This palatial complex in the centre of Fès el-Jedid is surrounded by high walls and covers more than 80 ha (195 acres). It was the main residence of the sultan, together with his guard and his retinue of servants. It was also where dignitaries of the *makhzen* (central government) came to carry out their duties. Part of the palace is still used by the king of Morocco when he comes to stay in Fès.

The main entrance to the complex, on the huge Place des Alaouites, is particularly imposing. Its magnificent Moorish gateway, which is permanently closed, is richly ornamented. The exquisitely engraved bronze doors are fitted with fine bronze knockers.

The walls enclose a disparate ensemble of buildings: palaces arranged around courtyards or large patios, as well as official buildings, notably the Dar el-Bahia, where Arab summit meetings are held; the Dar Ayad el-Kebira, built in the 18th century by Sidi Mohammed ben Abdallah; administrative and military buildings; and gardens, including the enclosed **Lalla Mina Gardens**.

The complex also includes a mosque and a medersa, which was built in 1320 by the Merinid prince Abou Saïd Othman. There is also a menagerie.

🏛 Moulay Abdallah Quarter

Accessible via Bab Boujat or Bab Dekaken.

Completely closed off on its western side by the palace walls and the ramparts of Fès el-Jedid, this

quarter has two gateways linked by a central thoroughfare with a latticework of narrow streets leading off it. **Bab Dekaken**, the east gate, leads to the former *méchouar* (parade ground) and **Bab Boujat**, the west gate, pierces the city's walls. Nearby, in the main street, stands the **Grand Mosque**, a Merinid building dating from the 13th century that houses the necropolis of the sultan Abou Inan. Also on this street, in the direction of Bab Boujat, stands the **Mosque of Moulay Abdallah**, which was built in the mid-18th century.

🏛 Grande Rue de Fès el-Jedid and the Muslim Quarters

Accessible via Bab el-Semarine to the south and Bab Dekaken to the north.

The Muslim quarters – Lalla Btatha, Lalla Ghriba, Zebbala, Sidi Bounafaa, Boutouil and Blaghma – are the principal components of the urban agglomeration that Fassis know as Fès el-Jedid. The quarters are enclosed by the walls of Dar el-Makhzen to the west, and by a double line of walls to the east.

Two gateways lead into the Muslim quarters; that on the northern side is Bab Dekaken, a simple opening in the fortifications

A tower set in the walls of the *méchouar*

◁ Courtyard of the Es Sahrij Medersa, in the Andalusian Quarter

IBN KHALDOUN

Abderrahman Ibn Khaldoun was born in Tunis in 1332 into a family of great scholars. In about 1350 he came to Fès, which at the time was the leading intellectual centre in the Maghreb, and became diplomatic secretary to the sultan Abou Inan. He taught in Cairo, where he died in 1406. His extensive writings include *Discourse on Universal History*. He is considered to be the founder of sociology, and is without a doubt one of the greatest historians of all time.

Modern-day portrait of Ibn Khaldoun

that once led to the former *méchouar*. On the southern side is the monumental **Bab el-Semarine** (Gate of the Farriers). This is a monumental vaulted gateway, beneath which a souk for all sorts of food takes place; the stalls are laid out in the old Merinid grain stores.

The two gates are connected by **Grande Rue de Fès el-Jedid**, the main north–south artery through the city. The street, covered by a cane canopy at its northern extremity, is lined with an almost continuous succession of shops. This congested thoroughfare is the economic centre of the royal city. At intervals it is flanked by quiet residential quarters with a maze-like layout like that of all Muslim towns.

On the western side of the street, a small quarter huddles around the Lalla el-Azhar Mosque (Mosque of

Detail of Bab Segma, north of the old *méchouar*

the Lady Flower), which was built by the Merinid sultan Abou Inan in 1357. On the eastern side are the humble quarters inhabited by the families of old warrior tribes. There are two important mosques here: Jama el-Hamra (Red Mosque) with a 14th-century minaret, and Jama el-Beïda (White Mosque).

FÈS EL-JEDID CITY CENTRE

Danan Synagogue ⑥
Dar el-Makhzen ①
Grand Méchouar ⑦
Grande Rue de Fès el-Jedid and Muslim Quarters ③
Grande Rue des Mérinides and Rue Boukhessissat ⑤
Kasbah Cherarda ⑩
Mellah ④
Moulay Abdallah Quarter ②
Petit Méchouar ⑨
Vieux Méchouar ⑧

0 m   200
0 yards   200

Key to Symbols *see back flap*

Richly ornamented door to a house in the mellah

🏛 Mellah

Accessible via Place des Alaouites or Bab el-Mellah.

Bab el-Semarine, then Bab el-Mellah leads into the mellah, the Jewish quarter of Fès. The name *mellah* probably comes from the Arabic word for "salt", the terrain on which the quarter grew up.

This quarter, thought to be the first Jewish enclave to be established in Morocco, was originally located in the northern part of Fès el-Bali, in the El-Yahoudi Quarter next to the Karaouiyine district. In the early 13th century the Merinid rulers moved it near the palace, to the site of a former kasbah that was once occupied by the sultan's Syrian archers. The rulers of Fès had undertaken to protect the Jewish community, in return for an annual levy collected by the state treasury. The Jewish quarter's new location afforded the inhabitants greater security.

With its souks, workshops, schools, synagogues and a cemetery, the quarter flourished, providing the Jewish community with strong social cohesion and unrivalled opportunities for social advancement. Like the Muslims elsewhere, most of the Jews in the district were grouped according to their craft speciality. Thus Leo Africanus mentioned metal-working, recording that only the Jews worked with gold and silver. Today, the Jews of Fès have left to settle in Casablanca or have emigrated abroad, to Israel in particular.

Exploring the mellah reveals a striking contrast with the Muslim quarters. In architectural terms it is another world, the buildings being higher, narrower and more closely spaced. The present boundaries of the Jewish quarter were established only at the end of the 18th century, during the time of the Alaouite sultan Moulay Yazid, and the space available was small. As a result, the inhabitants were forced to build two-storey houses around tiny court-yards, and space to move around in is very restricted.

🏛 Rue des Mérinides and Rue Boukhessissat

Accessible via Bab el-Semarine or Place des Alaouites. **Jewellery Souk** 🕐 from 9am Sat–Thu.

A central rectilinear axis, lined with various workshops and a *kissaria*, divides the mellah into two. All the commercial activity in the quarter takes place in this street, which was once the economic and spiritual centre of the mellah.

Rue des Mérinides cuts through the jewellery souk, where Jewish goldsmiths could once be seen at work.

Rue Boukhessissat separates the mellah from the Dar el-Makhzen. With some luxury residences, this was once the aristocratic area. The design of the houses here is the most unified and harmonious in the mellah. The rows of houses open onto the street, each house having a workshop on the ground floor. The upper storeys are fronted by the generously proportioned, finely carved wooden balconies that are characteristic of the Jewish architecture of Fès.

The Danan Synagogue, nestling between houses in the mellah

✡ Danan Synagogue

Rue Der el-Feran Teati. 🕐 9am–5pm daily. No entrance fee but a small contribution is requested.
Jewish Cemetery ◼ Sat.

The 17th-century synagogue, the property of a family of rabbis from Andalusia, looks as if it has been squeezed in between the houses in the mellah. The interior is divided into four aisles. A trap door in the aisle on the far right opens onto a stairway that leads down to a *mikve* – a bath for ritual purification where the faithful were cleansed of their sins. Above this fourth aisle is the *azara*, the women's gallery, which

Tombs in the Jewish cemetery

The Vieux Méchouar, accessible via Bab el-Seba

offers an overall view of the synagogue. It is worth going out onto the terrace for a sweeping view of the mellah, and of the white tombs of the Jewish cemetery below.

The Méchouars

Méchouars are wide, walled parade grounds used on ceremonial military occasions. Processions and ceremonies, such as acts of allegiance and the acknowledgment of the royal right to rule, are also performed here. There are three such esplanades in Fès. The **Grand Méchouar**, in the northwest, also known as the Méchouar de Bab Boujat, is an extensive parade ground. The **Méchouar de Bab Dekaken** (Gate of the Benches), or **Vieux Méchouar**, in the northeast, is a rectangular esplanade with the high ramparts of the Makina on one side. It links

Bab Segma, the Merinid gate, and Bab el-Seba. It is here that the population gathered at sunset to watch dancers, musicians and storytellers. The **Petit Méchouar**, the smallest of the three, links the Méchouar de Bab Dekaken and Dar el-Makhzen. It can be reached through **Bab el-Seba** (Gate of the Lion), which once defended the entrance to the palace.

On Avenue des Français, just south of Bab el-Seba, a narrow street on the right, reachable through an opening in the wall, leads, after about 150 m (165 yards), to a large *noria* (waterwheel) built in 1287 by the Andalusians. The **Makina** was an arsenal, established by Moulay el-Hassan in 1855 with the help of Italian officers. It was built on the west side of the Méchouar de Bab Dekaken. Having fallen into disuse, the Makina

was restored. It is now used as a concert hall and conference venue.

Kasbah Cherarda

North of the town, accessible via Bab Segma.

Once known as the Kasbah el-Khmis (Thursday Fort), after the El-Khmis Souk which took place along the northern and eastern walls, this kasbah was built by Moulay Rachid in the 17th century. Its present name is derived from a former kasbah built nearby by a Cherarda *caid* (chief) to defend his tribe's grain stores. With Bab Segma and Bab Dekaken, the kasbah formed a system of fortifications that controlled the road to Meknès and Tangier, and protected Fès el-Jedid and the inter-section with Fès el-Bali.

Enclosed within crenellated walls set with sturdy square towers, the kasbah has two monumental gateways, one on the western and the other on the eastern side. The kasbah now contains a hospital and an annexe of the Karaouiyine university. Beneath the walls on the southern and western sides, in an area where Almoravid and Almohad grain stores once stood, are the tombs of the Bab el-Mahrouk cemetery. Among them the small Mausoleum of Sidi Boubker el-Arabi can be seen.

Walls of the Kasbah Cherarda, built by Moulay Rachid in the 17th century

MEKNÈS & VOLUBILIS

Located between the fertile plain of the Rarb and the Middle Atlas, Meknès and Volubilis lie at the heart of an agricultural area that has been Morocco's grain store since ancient times. The historical importance of the two cities can be clearly seen in the ruins of Volubilis, capital of Mauretania Tingitana and the most important archaeological site in Morocco, as well as in the grandeur of the Moorish buildings in Meknès.

From the time of its foundation in the tenth century to the arrival of the Alaouites in the 17th century, Meknès was no more than a small town overshadowed by Fès, its neighbour and rival. It was not until the reign of Moulay Ismaïl *(see pp54–5)*, which began in 1672, that Meknès first rose to the rank of imperial city. With tireless energy, the sultan set about building gates, ramparts, mosques and palaces.

This ambitious building programme continued throughout his reign and involved robbing the ruins of Volubilis *(see pp 202–5)* and the Palais el-Badi in Marrakech *(see p235)*. After 50 years, work was still not completed. Although the sultan's impatience was often a hindrance, he reinvigorated palace architecture.

Today, Meknès is the fifth-largest city in Morocco, with a population of 550,000. It is a dynamic economic centre, renowned for its olives, wine and mint tea. The imperial city stands alongside the new town, on the banks of Wadi Boufekrane.

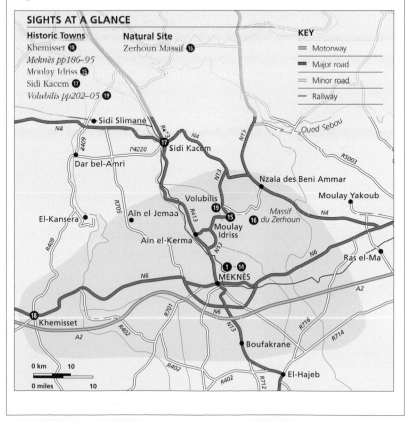

SIGHTS AT A GLANCE

Historic Towns
Khemisset ⑱
Meknès pp186–95
Moulay Idriss ⑮
Sidi Kacem ⑰
Volubilis pp202–05 ⑲

Natural Site
Zerhoun Massif ⑯

KEY

═ Motorway
▬ Major road
═ Minor road
— Railway

Sidi Slimane
N4
R409
N4220
Sidi Kacem ⑰
Dar bel-Amri
Oued Sebou
N13
N15
R5003
Nzala des Beni Ammar
Moulay Yakoub
Volubilis ⑲
El-Kansera
R705
Aïn el Jemaa
R413
Moulay Idriss ⑮ ⑯
Massif du Zerhoun
N4
R409
Aïn el-Kerma
N13
N6
Ras el-Ma
MEKNÈS ① ⑭
N6
A2
⑱ Khemisset
R701
A2
R402
N6
N13
R716
R714
Boufakrane
0 km 10
0 miles 10
R402
R402
R712
El-Hajeb

◁ **Mosaic of Bacchus, from the House of Dionysus and the Four Seasons in Volubilis**

Exploring Meknès

Three well-defined quarters –
the medina, the imperial city
and Ville Nouvelle (the
New Town) – make up the
city of Meknès. The medina
is a densely packed quarter.
The kasbah, or imperial
city, contains the finest
of the lavish buildings
constructed by Moulay
Ismaïl. Ville Nouvelle is
located on the east bank
of Wadi Boufekrane.

A Moroccan in Place el-Hedime,
"Square of Ruins"

SEE ALSO

- **Where to Stay** pp312–13
- **Where to Eat** pp336–7

GETTING AROUND

Place el-Hedime is a good starting point for exploring the medina and the imperial city. Parking is available not far from this square. From here, it is an easy walk to the area around Bab Mansour and to the Mausoleum of Moulay Ismaïl. To see the rest of the imperial city, particularly Dar el-Ma, a car is needed.

VISITORS' CHECKLIST

990,000. 🚉 🚌
Place Administrative
(0535) 52 55 38.

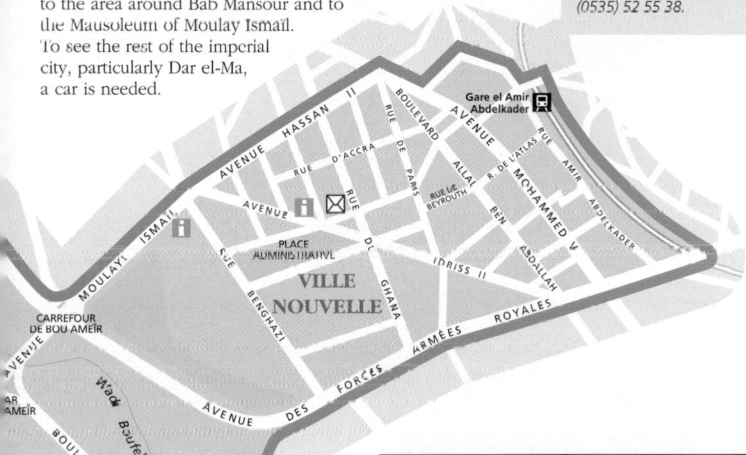

View over the rooftops of the medina in Meknès

SIGHTS AT A GLANCE

Historic Sites and Quarters
Bassin de l'Aguedal ⑫
Haras de Meknès ⑭
Souks and Kissaria ②

Buildings and Monuments
Bab Mansour el-Aleuj
  and Place el-Hedime ⑥
Bou Inania Medersa ④
Dar el-Kebira Quarter ⑦
Dar el-Ma and Heri es-Souani ⑬
Dar el-Makhzen ⑪
Grand Mosque ③
Koubba el-Khayatine
  and Habs Qara ⑨
Lalla Aouda Mosque ⑧
Mausoleum of Moulay Ismaïl
  pp194–5 ⑩
Ramparts ①

Museum
Musée Dar Jamaï pp190–91 ⑤

GETTING AROUND area map (labels):

AVENUE HASSAN II
BOULEVARD
RUE D'ACCRA
RUE DE PARIS
AVENUE ALLAL
AVENUE MOHAMMED V
R. DE L'ATLAS
RUE AMIR ABDELKADER
Gare el Amir Abdelkader 🚉
RUE BEYROUTH
RUE BEN ABDALLAH
AVENUE MOULAY ISMAIL
RUE BENGHAZI
PLACE ADMINISTRATIVE
VILLE NOUVELLE
DU GHANA
IDRISS II
AVENUE DES FORCES ARMÉES ROYALES
CARREFOUR DE BOU AMEIR
AR AMEIR
Wad Boufekrane
BOULEVARD ABDERRAHMANE
BEN ZIDANE
MECHOUAR
BAB EN NOUARA
⑪

KEY

	Medina
	Historic building
—	Ramparts
🚉	Railway station
ℹ️	Tourist information
✉️	Post office
☪	Mosque
⚰	Muslim cemetery

0 m — 400
0 yards — 400

Bab el-Berdaïne, one of the gates into the medina of Meknès

Ramparts ❶

Encircling the medina, Meknès.

Protected by three stretches of wall that together amount to about 40 km (25 miles), the medina has the appearance of a sturdy fortress set with elegant gates. **Bab el-Berdaïne** (Gate of the Pack-Saddle-Makers), on the northern side, was built by Moulay Ismaïl. It is flanked by protruding square towers crowned by merlons, and stylized flowers in *zellij* tilework decorate its exterior façade. West of the gate, the walled cemetery contains one of the most highly venerated mausoleums in Morocco – that of Sidi Mohammed ben Aïssa, founder of the brotherhood of the Aïssaoua *(see p198).*

On the southern side of the cemetery stands **Bab el-Siba** (Gate of Anarchy) and **Bab el-Jedid** (New Gate, although in fact it is one of the oldest in Meknès). Further south is **Bab Berrima**, which leads into the medina's principal souks. To the west stands **Bab el-Khemis** (Thursday Gate), which once led into the mellah, now non-existent. The remarkable decoration of the gate's façade is on a par with that of Bab el-Berdaïne.

The layout of the medina, a medieval labyrinth, is identical to that of the other imperial cities. There are a few main thoroughfares. Rue Karmouni, which runs through the quarter from north to south links Bab el-Berdaïne with the spiritual and economic heart of the medina. Rue des Souks runs from Bab Berrima, in the west, also to the heart of the medina. Several smaller streets radiate from this centre, which is marked by the Grand Mosque and the Bou Inania Medersa.

Souks and Kissaria ❷

Rue des Souks, Meknès. ☐ *daily.*

A network of small covered or open streets lined with shops and workshops, the souks are a fascinating en-capsulation of the 17th- and 18th-century Moroccan urban environment. Rue des Souks, near Bab Berrima, is filled with hardware merchants *(akarir),* corn chandlers *(bezzazine),* and fabric sellers *(serrayriya),* while metalsmiths *(haddadin)* are to be found in the old Rue des Armuriers.

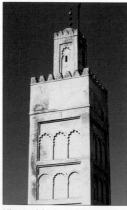

Minaret of the En-Nejjarine Mosque, the Mosque of the Carpenters

Bab Berrima leads through to Souk En-Nejjarine, the Carpenters' Souk, which is next to that of the brass and coppersmiths, and to the Cobblers' Souk *(sebbat).*

The **En-Nejjarine Mosque**, built by the Almohads in the 12th century, was restored by Mohammed ben Abdallah in about 1756, when it was given a new minaret. Set back from the En-Nejjarine Souk, in the **Ed-Dlala Kissaria**, is the location of a Berber souk. Every day from 3pm to 4pm, the mountain-dwellers of the Middle Atlas come to sell carpets and blankets here at auction.

Ablutions fountain in the Grand Mosque in Meknès

Grand Mosque ❸

Rue des Souk es Sebbat, Meknès. ☐ *daily.* ◑ *to non-Muslims.*

The Grand Mosque, which stands near the souks and the Bou Inania Medersa, was established in the 12th century during the reign of the Almoravids. It was remodel-led in the 14th century. The main façade is pierced by an imposing doorway with a carved awning. The green-glazed terracotta tiles of the roof and of the 18th-century minaret are particularly striking, the bright sunlight giving them an almost translucent appearance.

The **Palais el-Mansour**, a sumptuous 19th-century residence in Rue Karmouni, has been converted into a carpet and souvenir bazaar.

Bou Inania Medersa ❹

Rue des Souks es Sebbat, Meknès.
⬜ 8am–noon, 3–6pm daily. 📷

This Koranic school opposite the Grand Mosque was established by the Merinid sultans in the 14th century. The building is divided into two unequal parts with a long corridor between them. On the eastern side is the medersa proper, while on the western side is an annexe for ablutions (now no longer in use). The main entrance is crowned by a flat-sided dome and faced with horseshoe arches with delicate stucco work decoration.

A corridor leads to a beautiful courtyard in the centre of which is a pool. While three sides of the courtyard are lined with a gallery, the fourth opens onto the prayer hall. The green-tiled awnings, the sophisticated decoration of carved wood, stuccowork and colourful *zellij* tilework, as well as the mosaic-like tiled floor make the whole courtyard an entrancing sight.

The prayer hall, with carved stucco decoration and an elegant mihrab within a horseshoe arch, remains unaltered. Students' cells fill the rest of the ground floor and the upper floor. The terrace offers a fine view of the medina and the Grand Mosque next to the medersa.

Zellij tilework
in the Bou Inania
Medersa

Place el-Hedime, once the grand entrance to the imperial city of Meknès

it pierces the walls of the kasbah and leads through to Place Lalla Aouda and the Dar el-Kebira Quarter (*see p192*).

Of monumental proportions and distinguished for its decoration, Bab Mansour el-Aleuj is held to be the finest gate in Meknès, or even in Morocco. It was begun by the sultan Moulay Ismaïl in about 1672, when the building of the kasbah, his first project, was under way. The gate was completed during the reign of his son, Moulay Abdallah, in 1732. The gate stands about 16 m (52 ft) high, while the arch has a span of 8 m (26 ft) wide and is surmounted by a pointed horseshoe arch. An intricate pattern of interlacing motifs is carved in relief on a background of predominantly green mosaics and tiles. The cornerpieces are filled with sgraffito floral decoration incised into dark-glazed terracotta. The gate is framed by protruding towers built in the style of loggias. Temporary exhibitions are sometimes held here.

Place el-Hedime (Square of Ruins) links the medina and the kasbah. It was laid out on the ruins of the Merinid kasbah that Moulay Ismaïl razed to make space for the palaces, water tanks, gardens, stables, arsenals and forts with which he planned to surround himself. The square has been restored and is now lined with modern residential buildings that are not in keeping with its historic character. Nearby, to the left of the square, is a covered food market.

Musée Dar Jamaï ❺

See pp190–91.

Bab Mansour el-Aleuj and Place el-Hedime ❻

South of the medina, Meknès.

Bab Mansour el-Aleuj (Gate of the Victorius Renegade) is named after the Christian who designed and built it. Standing like a triumphal arch before the imperial city,

SACRED SNAKES

Expelled from Meknès by the sultan in the 16th century, Sidi Mohammed ben Aïssa, founder of the Aïssaoua brotherhood (*see p198*), and his disciples fled to the desert. Famished, they ate whatever they could find – snakes, scorpions and cactus leaves. Ever since, the cobra has been the Aïssaoua's mascot, and no member ever kills one. Being immune to their venom, the Aïssaoua are often called upon to rid villages of the dangerous reptiles. Cobras also feature in the Aïssaouas' religious rituals, in which participants fall into a trance-like state.

An Aïssaoua in a trance

Musée Dar Jamaï ❺

Painted wood, museum door

This museum, in which Moroccan arts are displayed, is laid out in a delightful residence built in about 1882 by Mohammed Belarbi el-Jamaï, who was a grand vizier of Moulay el-Hassan in 1873–4. The sophisticated architecture of the palace includes painted wooden cornices. a greentiled roof and a courtyard with two pools and *zellij* tilework. There is also an Andalusian garden planted with tall cypresses. Covering 2,845 sq m (30,600 sq ft), the palace also has several annexes and outbuildings.

The Museum of Moroccan Arts, occupying a large and elegant 19th-century palace

EXPLORING THE MUSEUM OF MOROCCAN ARTS

Before it was converted into a regional ethnographic museum, this palace incorporated a mosque, a garden, a *menzah* (pavilion), a courtyard, a small house, a kitchen and a hammam. Of the 2,000-plus objects in the museum's collection, some 670 are on display.

WOODWORK

Room 1, on the ground floor, contains examples of architectural features in wood – pieces of carved and painted wood that were used in the building or decoration of the palaces and town houses of Meknès.

The exhibits also include a 17th-century minbar (pulpit) that originally stood in the Grand Mosque in Meknès.

CERAMICS

Ceramics from Fès and Meknès are displayed in Room 2. Fassi potters attained unprecedented renown for their famous blue and white ware. Two kinds of blue pigment were used: a pale blueish-grey, which was in use up until the mid-19th century, and a clear blue with a violet tinge that was obtained by more modern industrial means.

The Fassi potting industry probably goes back to the 10th or 11th century. That of Meknès, by contrast, is much more recent, having been imported from Fès in about the 18th century. Three colours – brown, green and yellow – were used.

Perfume bottle from Tamegroute (late 18th century)

Before the pottery was decorated, it was fired in a kiln and was then covered in white glaze. The potter would decorate this surface with elegant motifs of Moorish inspiration.

Painted wooden door from a house in Meknès

CARPETS

The museum's richest section is that devoted to carpets, which fill Room 4. Most of the carpets and kilims on display come from the High and Middle Atlas. Among the latter, the most noteworthy pieces are those made by two Berber tribes, the Zemmour and the Beni M'Guild. Traditions of craftsmanship are still alive among these tribes today – a relatively rare phenomenon in Morocco – and carpets similar to those on display here are still being made.

Meknès carpets are characterized by a mixture of bright colours forming geometric patterns. This section of the museum also includes a fine collection of beautiful gold-thread embroidery, another craft speciality that has brought Meknès renown.

Brass and painted wood coffer from Fès (19th century)

GALLERY GUIDE

The eight exhibition rooms on the ground floor are arranged around the garden. Room 1 contains a display of carved and painted wood; Rooms 2 and 3 are devoted to ceramics; Room 4 to carpets and embroidery; Room 5 to kaftans and belts; Room 6 to jewellery; and Rooms 7 and 8 to the art of damascening (see p191). On the upper floor, the reconstruction of a traditional Moroccan room can be seen. The museum has undergone renovation and its collections are now effectively displayed.

COSTUMES

The costumes of town and city-dwellers, especially the kaftan (see pp36–7), is the theme of Room 5. The brightly coloured kaftan, a long robe worn by women on special occasions, is the quintessential garment of city-dwellers. Kaftans were often embroidered with silk, silver or gold thread, as was the belt (mdamma) worn with the kaftan. Wealthy women might even wear a belt made of silver or solid gold. The mdamma now forms part of a young townswoman's dowry.

JEWELLERY

Jewellery from several regions of Morocco is displayed in Room 6. Particular prominence is given to Berber jewellery.

Metalworking is a traditional craft that was once widespread throughout the country, and was particularly associated with Jewish craftsmen. Moroccan jewellery, which is typically made of gold or silver and sometimes set with precious or semi-precious stones, is made by age-old techniques. It forms an integral part of different types of dress (see pp36–7) and the way that it is worn

Vase in damascened metal

is highly significant. Jewellery also once indicated the wearer's geographical origin or tribal identity. Modern copies of Berber jewellery can be seen today on offer in the souks.

METALWORK

While ceramics reached their apogee in Fès, the craftsmen of Meknès were distinguished masters of the art of damascening. The technique consists of covering a metallic surface with a patterned filigree of gold, silver or copper. There are some particularly fine damascened vases in Rooms 7 and 8. The craft is still very much alive in Meknès today, and some exquisite damascened pieces can be found in the souks of the old town.

VISITORS' CHECKLIST

Place el-Hedime.
Tel (0535) 53 08 63.
☐ 9am–5pm
Wed–Mon. 🖼

This section of the museum also includes an interesting collection of keys decorated with the stylized names of their former owners.

THE MOROCCAN ROOM

As in other ethnographic museums in the country, this museum features a reconstruction of a traditional Moroccan room. On the upper floor, it has walls covered with zellij tilework and a carved wooden domed ceiling. It is furnished with pieces from various houses and palaces in Meknès.

Reconstruction of a traditional Moroccan room, sumptuously decorated

EMBROIDERY

Cotton and silk embroidery from Rabat (19th century)

Embroidery is a time-honoured craft practised by the townswomen of Morocco. Young girls start to learn embroidery from childhood, being taught either in their homes or in a workshop, and always under the supervision of a teacher (maalma). Fès, Meknès, Marrakech, Rabat, Salé, Tetouan, Chefchaouen and Azemmour are the main centres of embroidery. Each town has its own characteristic colours, stitches and repertoire of motifs. Fès embroidery is characterized by tree-like motifs, often depicted in a single colour. That of Salé alternates cross stitch and satin stitch. In Meknès embroidery (terz el-meknassi), motifs are peppered over the fabric, and bright colours are used to decorate tablecloths and scarves.

Chefchaouen gold-thread embroidery

Place Lalla Aouda and the minaret of the Lalla Aouda Mosque

Dar el-Kebira Quarter **7**

Behind Place Lalla Aouda *(between Bab Moulay and the Lalla Aouda Mosque)*, Meknès.

This quarter forms part of what is known as the **Imperial City**, or the Kasbah of Moulay Ismaïl. Covering an area four times as large as that of the medina, the whole quarter is in keeping with the grand ambitions of this enterprising sultan. Protected by a double line of walls and monumental angled gates, the Imperial City has the appearance of an impregnable *ksar* (fortified village). It contains wide avenues and large squares, palaces with attractive pools and extensive gardens, as well as administrative buildings enclosed within their own ramparts.

The Imperial City comprises three palatial complexes: Dar el-Kebira, Dar el-Medrasa and Ksar el-Mhanncha. Dar el-Kebira, the Quarter of the Large House, is located southeast of the medina. It was the first palatial complex of the Imperial City that Moulay Ismaïl ordered to be built, in about 1672. It stands near Place Lalla Aouda, probably on the site of the former Almohad kasbah. The complex was cut off from the urban bustle by a double wall and by Place el-Hedime *(see p189)*.

Each palace in Dar el-Kebira contained a harem, reception rooms, hammams, kitchens, armouries, ovens and mosques. They were interlinked by a somewhat haphazard network of open or partially covered alleys. Today, the ancient heart of the Imperial City, which is partly in ruins, has become a poor district that has been filled with shanty dwellings.

The Mausoleum of Moulay Ismaïl, the Lalla Aouda Mosque and a monumental gate near Bab Bou Ameïr are the last surviving vestiges of the ostentatiously grand complex that the sultan had envisaged.

The second complex, which is now in complete ruins, was the Dar el-Medrasa. The palace comprised suites of residential rooms, some of which were used exclusively by the sultan and his harem.

Lalla Aouda Mosque **8**

Place Lalla Aouda, Meknès. ☐ *daily.* ☻ *to non-Muslims.*

The first major place of worship to be built by Moulay Ismaïl, in 1680, this mosque is one of the few of the sultan's projects to have survived intact. The building has three doorways. Two on the northwestern side open onto the former *méchouar* (parade ground) and a smaller one, on the side of the mosque where the mihrab is located, leads to a corridor running behind the mosque. It was probably the sultan's private entrance. The pitched roof is covered with green tiles.

Koubba el-Khayatine and Habs Qara **9**

Place Habs Qara. ☐ *9am–noon, 3–6pm daily.* ☻ *public holidays.* 📷

This imperial pavilion, also known as the Pavilion of the Ambassadors, was used originally to receive diplomats who came to negotiate, among other things, the ransom of Christian prisoners. Later, the building was used by tailors *(khiyatine)*, who made military uniforms here. The building is crowned by a conical dome decorated with geometric and floral motifs.

Behind the pavilion are the former underground storage areas that were converted into the **Christian Prison**, or Habs Qara. The prisoners – probably Europeans captured by the corsairs of Rabat – were made to work on the sultan's herculean building projects. Chroniclers recorded that thousands of convicts were incarcerated in these underground galleries, which were later partly destroyed by an earthquake.

Mausoleum of Moulay Ismaïl **10**

See pp194–5.

Dar el-Makhzen **11**

Place Bab el-Mechouar, Meknès. ☻ *to the public.*

This royal complex was formerly known as the Palace of the Labyrinth, after a white marble pool fashioned as a labyrinth. In contrast to Dar el-Kebira and Koubbet el-Khiriyatine, the complex has a neat and compact layout. It is divided into eight parts and is surrounded by walls set with bastions. In the centre stands a monumental gate,

Gate of the Kasbah Hedrach, Dar el-Makhzen

The Bassin de l'Aguedal, a water tank created by Moulay Ismaïl

the fulsomely decorated **Bab el-Makhzen** (Gate of the Warehouse), built by Moulay el-Hassan in 1888. A second gate, **Bab el-Jedid** (New Gate), was made on the northwestern side. Features of the complex include a *méchouar* and **Kasbah Hadrach**, the former barracks of the sultan's army of black slaves.

Bassin de l'Aguedal ⑫

Aguedal Quarter, Meknès.

This water tank (*sahrij*) was built within the kasbah by Moulay Ismaïl. It has a surface area of 40,000 sq m (430,000 sq ft) and its purpose was to supply water to the palace and the Imperial City, including its mosques, hammams, gardens and orchards. The women of the harem, so it is said, would sail on it in their pleasure boats. Only a few stretches of its crenellated walls survive.

The spot has suffered some unfortunate alterations carried out in an effort to create a place where the people of Meknès could come to walk.

Dar el-Ma and Heri es-Souani ⑬

L'Agdal Quarter, Meknès.
🔲 9am–noon, 3–6pm daily.

Dar el-Ma, the Water House, held the town's water reserves and was another of Moulay Ismaïl's grandiose projects. The huge barrel-vaulted building

contains 15 rooms, each with a *noria* (water wheel) once worked by horses to draw underground water by means of scoops. The terraces offer a fine view of the city.

Dar el-Ma gives access to **Heri es-Souani**, the so-called

Horsemen in Heri es-Souani

Grainstore Stables, which are considered to be one of the sultan's finest creations. This monumental building, with 29 aisles, was designed for storing grain. The thick walls, as well as a network of underground passages, maintained the temperature inside the grainstore at a low and constant level. The ceilings collapsed during the earthquake of 1755.

Haras de Meknès ⑭

Zitoune Quarter of Meknès, southwest of the town. *From Dar el-Ma, 1 km (0.6 mile) towards Dar el-Beïda, turning right 400 m (440 yds) beyond Dar el-Beïda and continuing for 2 km (1 mile) to the south.* 🔲 9am–noon, 2–5pm Mon–Fri 🖼

Although it cannot rival the modern studs in Rabat and Marrakech, the Haras de Meknès is well known in Morocco. The stud was established in 1912 with the aim of improving blood lines and promoting various Moroccan breeds of horse for use in racing, competitive riding and fantasias *(see p.35)*.

The stud can accommodate 231 horses, ranging from pure-bred Arabs and Barbs to English thoroughbreds and Anglo-Arabs. A visit here may include seeing horses being put through their paces

THE ROYAL CITIES

The creation of royal cities in the Islamic world dates from the late 8th century. The Almohads, the Merinids and the Alaouites under Moulay Ismaïl continued this tradition, and it spread throughout the Maghreb, where it survived until recently. The royal city is an architectural complex built to protect the king and his courtiers. Several palaces and other buildings were needed to accommodate all the members of the royal household. Water tanks were built to irrigate the many gardens and to supply the baths and hammams of the harem. Designed both for royal receptions and for the king's private life, the royal city was architecturally the most sophisticated and most sumptuous component of a great urban centre.

Bab el-Makhzen, gateway of Dar el-Makhzen, Meknès

Mausoleum of Moulay Ismaïl ⓾

Featuring a suite of three rooms, 12 columns and a central sanctuary where the great sultan *(see pp54–5)* lies, the Mausoleum of Moulay Ismaïl is in some aspects reminiscent of the Saadian Tombs in Marrakech *(see pp238–9)*. The mausoleum was built in the 17th century and was remodelled in the 18th and 20th centuries. The wife of Moulay Ismaïl and his son, Moulay Ahmed al-Dahbi, as well as the sultan Moulay Abderrahman (1822–59), are laid to rest in the burial chamber, which is decorated with stuccowork and mosaics.

View of Meknès and the mausoleum

Mihrab
The mausoleum's mihrab is located in the open courtyard. This unusual position differs from the arrangement at the Saadian Tombs in Marrakech (see pp238–9).

Finials
The roof of the mausoleum is topped with five brass spheres indentifying the building as a shrine or sacred place.

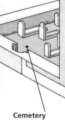

Cemetery

Prayer Hall
The floor of the prayer hall is covered with mats on which worshippers kneel to pray or to reflect before going into the burial chamber.

Clock presented by Louis XIV
(see pp54–5)

Tomb of Moulay Ismaïl

Decorated Door
This carved and painted wooden door between the ablutions room and the second room of the burial chamber is similar to those of the palaces and fine town houses of Meknès.

★ **Burial Chamber**
This consists of a suite of three rooms, including the ablutions room with central fountain (above) and the room containing the tomb of Moulay Ismaïl, and those of his wife and sons.

For hotels and restaurants in this region see pp312–13 and pp336–7

Entrance to Mausoleum
*This imposing carved stone
doorway, surmounted by an
awning and a pyramidal roof,
indicates the importance of
the royal building to which
it gives access.*

Small Courtyards
*En route to the burial
chamber you pass
through several empty
courtyards, which are
decorated in a sober
style. This allows
visitors to leave
behind them the
noise and bustle of
the city.*

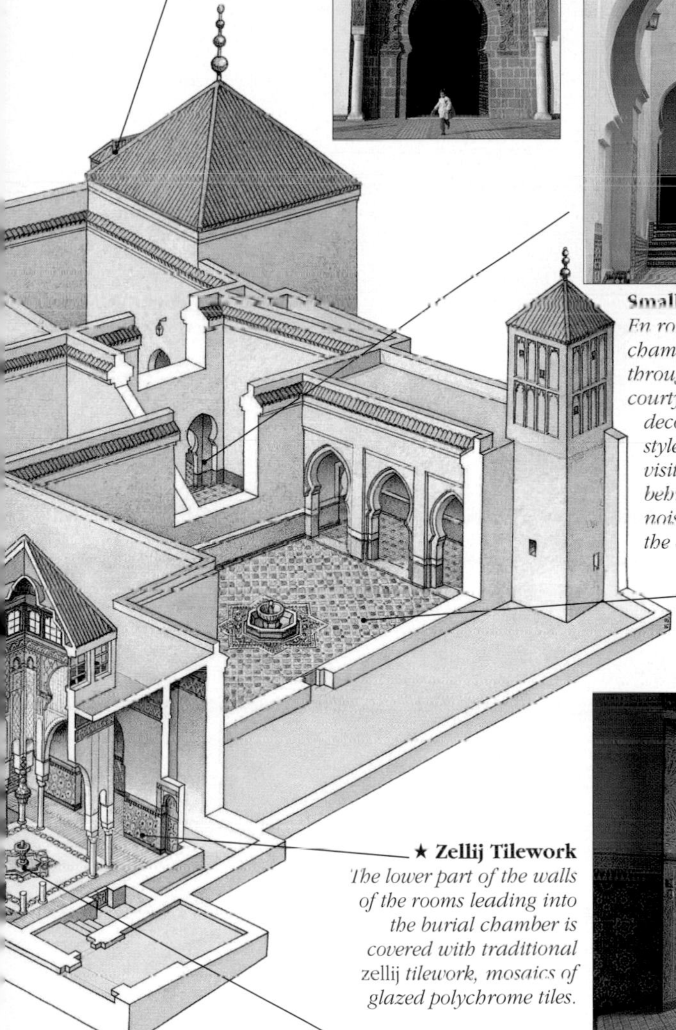

Open
courtyard

★ Zellij Tilework
*The lower part of the walls
of the rooms leading into
the burial chamber is
covered with traditional
zellij tilework, mosaics of
glazed polychrome tiles.*

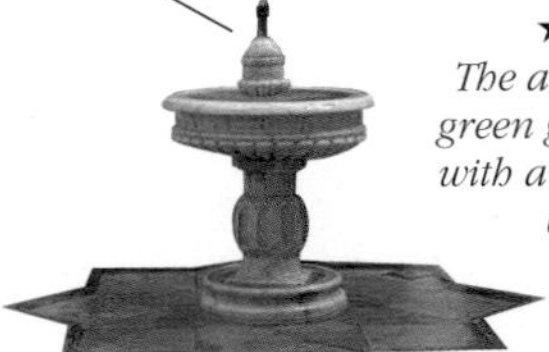

STAR FEATURES

★ Burial Chamber

★ Courtyard & Fountain

★ Zellij Tilework

★ Courtyard & Fountain
*The ablutions room, paved with
green glazed tiles, is a courtyard
with a star-shaped fountain and
bowl. Its 12 columns come
from the el-Badi Palace
in Marrakech.*

The ruins of Volubilis, seen from the triumphal arch ▷

Holy Men and Mystics

In Morocco, the Islamic faith of law-makers *(fkihs)* and learned men *(ulema)* coexists with popular forms of religion, in which the cult of saints and the role of brotherhoods (known as *tariqas*, meaning "ways") are prominent. Many followers of these religions are craftsmen and traders, who gather to perform spiritualist rites *(zikrs)*, involving singing, dancing and music, according to the teaching of their respective founder. These religions are connected to those of Eastern mystics, and they have spread well beyond the boundaries of Morocco. This spiritualist branch of Islam is widely known as Sufism, after the rough woollen garment *(suf)* worn by certain ascetics.

The pilgrimage to Sidi Ahmed Ou Mghanni *takes place near Imilchil, in the territory of the Aït Haddidou. It is known as the Marriage Fair, as many betrothals are made on this occasion.*

THE AÏSSAOUA

This brotherhood came into being in the 16th century. Its beliefs are based on the teachings of Sidi Mohammed ben Aïssa, a mystic who was born in the 15th century. Through El-Jazouli, the holy man of Marrakech, it is connected to Chadhiliya, the great Sufi "way" that spread throughout the Muslim world. The Aïssaoua brotherhood exists in Meknès *(see p189)* and Fès, and also in Algeria.

The Mausoleum of Sidi Mohammed ben Aïssa, *in Meknès, contains the tomb of the holy man who founded the Aïssaoua "way".*

The spectacular ceremonies of the Aïssaoua, involving banners, drums and incense, have always made a deep impression on foreigners in Morocco. This scene, entitled *Les Aïssaouas,* was painted by Georges Clairin (1843–1919).

The Aïssaoua are always dressed in white. They have a fear of black.

Like the Hamadcha, the Aïssaoua *are a popular brotherhood because of some of their practices. During their* moussem *(festival) they perform long-drawn-out and impressive rituals, called* hadras, *which are accompanied by singing, dancing and drumming. These rituals may send them into a trance or lead followers to perform orgies of self-mutilation.*

The *moussem* of Moulay Abdallah, *near El-Jadida, can draw up to 150,000 visitors and a huge tent city springs up on the site.*

The *moussem* in Guelmim, *a town on the caravan route on the edge of the Sahara (see p294), takes place each June in honour of the holy man Sidi el-Ghazi. Attended by the Reguibat, nomads known as the "blue men", this is also when a major camel fair takes place.*

During the *moussem* of Moulay Idriss II *in Fès, the various guilds of craftsmen, such as tanners, shoemakers, blacksmiths, brass-founders and coppersmiths, as here, process through the medina, bringing gifts and sacrifices to the zaouia (shrine) of this highly venerated holy man.*

TOMBS OF HOLY MEN

Followers gather eagerly in order to make pilgrimages to the many tombs of holy men *(marabouts)* so as to seek a blessing *(baraka)*. These small mausoleums, which are often covered with a white dome known as a *koubba*, can be seen throughout the country. Some of the more important shrines – or *zaouias* – are the seat of a religious brotherhood and, besides the tomb of the holy man, consist of buildings in which pilgrims are accommodated and religious instruction given. Once a year, certain pilgrimages take the form of *moussems*, great gatherings that are simultaneously joyous occasions, festivals for the performance of traditional shows and commercial fairs.

Marabout of Sidi Ahmad Ou Mghanni

Moussem in Guelmim

Moulay Idriss ⑮

Road map D2. 27 km (38 miles)
north of Meknès. 🏠 12,600. 🚌 from
Meknès. 🅿 Sat. 🗓 last Thu in Aug.

The most spectacular sight of
Moulay Idriss is from the scenic
route from Volubilis to Nzala
des Beni Ammar, which runs
above the more frequently
used N13. In a superb setting,
the bright white town clings
to two rocky outcrops between which rises the **Tomb
of Idriss I**, conspicuous with
its green-tiled roof.

Fleeing the persecution
of the Abbassid caliphs of
Baghdad, Idriss found a
haven in Oualili (Volubilis). A
descendant of Ali, son-in-law
of the Prophet Mohammed,
he founded the first Arab-
Muslim dynasty in Morocco.
He died in 791 and was
buried in the town that now
bears his name. It was not
until the 16th century that the
town began to prosper, and it
was still in the process of developing in the 17th century,
during the reign of Moulay
Ismaïl *(see pp54–5)*. The latter

The grand entrance to the Tomb of Idriss I in Moulay Idriss

endowed it with defensive
walls and a monumental gate,
as well as Koranic schools,
fountains and a new dome
for the mausoleum.

The Tomb of Idriss I is closed
to non-Muslims, and a wooden
beam across the entrance
marks this as sacred ground,
or *horm*. However, from the
terrace, near the Mosque of
Sidi Abdallah el-Hajjam,
which perches above the
town, there is a splendid view

of the town and the mausoleum. The minaret (1939),
whose cylindrical shape is
unusual in the Maghreb, is
covered with green tiles with
verses from the Koran.

Zerhoun Massif ⑯

Road map D2. About 50 km
(31 miles) northwest of Meknès.

Culminating in Jbel Zerhoun,
which rises to a height of
1,118 m (3,670 ft), the massif
forms part of an extensive
range of hills bordering the
southern side of the Rif and
running from the region of
Meknès to the environs of
Taza in the east.

This pre-Riffian terrain,
consisting mostly of clay
and marl, is very susceptible
to fluvial erosion. As a result,
a few outcrops of harder
limestone and sandstone
have emerged, one of which
is Jbel Zerhoun, whose
gorges, peaks and cliffs have
all been created by erosion.

Water is abundant here, and
the Romans tapped the springs
to supply Volubilis. Large
villages grew up on the hillsides, along the line of springs
and at the foot of the massif.
While fig trees, orange trees
and olive trees grow on the
higher slopes, corn and
barley thrive in the valleys
and on the lower hillsides.
Enclosures *(zriba)* made
of loose stones or thorny
branches, for small herds of
cattle, sheep and goats, can
be seen near the villages.

Moulay Idriss, clinging to an outcrop of rock

For Moroccans, Zerhoun is a holy mountain, the home of many religious men, and the setting of numerous stories and legends.

The verdant Zerhoun Massif, where water is plentiful

Sidi Kacem ⑰

Road map D2. 46 km (29 miles) northwest of Meknès. 70,000. from Meknès. Thu.

Sidi Kacem grew out of a military outpost that was set up in 1915 near a *zaouia* and the souk of the local Cherarda tribe. It is now an important agricultural and industrial centre on the plain of the eastern Rharb.

The three building complexes that dominate the town bear witness to the history and economic activity of Sidi Kacem. One is the railway station, at the intersection of lines running between Rabat and Fès and between Tangier and Fès. The second is the oil refinery (initially for local, then for imported fuel). Thirdly, there are the grain silos, at the heart of a well-watered and productive region.

Sidi Kacem is a major centre of agricultural food production and of brick-making. These industries have made the town an important banking and commercial hub.

Khemisset ⑱

Road map D2. 90,000. from Meknès. Tue.

This town was founded in 1924, on the site of a military outpost on the road from Rabat to Fès. Now a provincial capital, Khemisset is also the

Carpet made by the Zemmour, with graphic geometric motifs

"capital" of the confederation of the Berber-speaking Zemmour tribes.

This is a good place to stop, since there are many cafés and restaurants. The town also has a crafts cooperative where you can buy regional specialities, such as carpets and mats woven in palm fibre or wool. Every Tuesday, Khemisset is the venue for one of the most important country souks in Morocco, with almost 1,900 stalls.

COUNTRY SOUKS

At daybreak, hundreds of country people travelling on foot, on donkeys or in heavily laden trucks make their way to a site where tents and stalls are being set up. Around 850 country souks – named after the day on which they take place – are held every week in Morocco, drawing people from up to 10 km (6 miles) around. On an area of open ground, alleys between the stalls form according to a well-defined plan. The pattern on which the goods are laid out is similar to that of the economic layout of a medina. In the centre are such prized goods as fabric and clothing, followed by basketwork, carpets and blankets; on the periphery are second-hand items, scrap metal, humble traders such as cobblers and hair-dressers, and also food stalls. Beyond, various livestock markets are laid out in separate areas.

Returning from the souk

Souks allow townspeople to buy agricultural produce and craft items brought in by country people, who in turn stock up with groceries, sugar, tea and fruit. They provide services, entertainment and food, but also attract charlatans and storytellers. The civic authorities also use souks to set up temporary registry offices, post offices and health centres. Permanent shops that may appear on the site of a weekly souk sometimes lead to the establishment of a new town.

A country souk, with tents set up for a day

Volubilis ⑲

The ancient town of Volubilis backs on to a triangular spur jutting out from the Zerhoun Massif. The site was settled and began to prosper under the Mauretanian kings, from the 3rd century BC to AD 40. Temples from this period, as well as a strange tumulus, have been uncovered. When Mauretania was annexed by the Roman emperor Claudius in AD 45, Volubilis was raised to the status of *municipia* (free town), becoming one of the most important cities in Tingitana. The public buildings in the northeastern quarter date from the 1st century, and those around the forum from the 2nd century. After Rome withdrew from Mauretania in the 3rd century, the city declined. It was inhabited by Christians but had been Islamicized when Idriss I arrived in 788.

Mosaic from the House of Dionysus and the Four Seasons

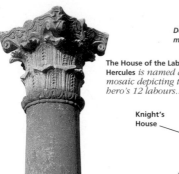

Gordian Palace

House of the Bathing Nymphs

House of Dionysus and the Four Seasons

Decumanus maximus

The House of the Labours of Hercules *is named after a mosaic depicting the Greek hero's 12 labours.*

Knight's House

House of the Columns
This house is arranged around a huge peristyle courtyard with a circular pool. Columns with twisted fluting and composite capitals front the grand reception room.

House of the Dog

House of the Athlete

Macellum (market)

★ **Triumphal Arch**
Bestriding the decumanus maximus, *the triumphal arch overlooks plantations of cereals and olive trees. The fertile plain to the west of Volubilis has provided the area with grain and oil since antiquity.*

STAR FEATURES

★ Basilica

★ Diana and the Bathing Nymphs

★ Triumphal Arch

THE SITE OF VOLUBILIS TODAY

The forum, basilica and capitol were built in the 2nd century, under the Severi dynasty. Richly appointed residences paved with mosaics also graced the city. These buildings are still easily identifiable today. Excavations have shown that the site was still inhabited during the Almoravid period (see pp46–7).

Tangier Gate

House of the Golden Coins

Aqueduct

★ **Diana and the Bathing Nymphs**
In this mosaic in the House of the Cortège of Venus, the nymphs admire Diana as she receives water from Pegasus, the winged horse. A similar scene is depicted in a mosaic in the House of the Bathing Nymphs.

Artisans' quarters

★ **Basilica**
Apart from the triumphal arch, this was the only building whose ruins were still impressive when excavations began. The interior is divided into three aisles and two apses.

Visitors' entrance

The Capitol
Of the original building (dating from the early 3rd century) only the foundations remain. The sacrificial altar, identifiable by its moulded base, stood in front of the steps.

House of Orpheus

Exploring Volubilis

The ancient site of Volubilis was known from the 18th century, but it was not until the late 19th century that it was first investigated. Excavations resumed in 1915, and have continued almost uninterrupted since, although extensive areas still remain to be investigated. Although Volubilis is not as large as some other Roman towns, it shows how thoroughly romanized Mauretania Tingitana had become. This is seen in the public buildings and sophisticated town houses within the 2nd-century walls, which enclose an area of more than 400,000 sq m (4300,000 sq ft). The site, a pre-existing settlement on which the Romans imposed their way of life, features baths, oil presses, bakeries, aqueducts, drains and shops that evoke the inhabitants' daily lives. Well signposted, Volubilis is easy to explore.

Reconstruction of an oil press, showing the baskets used for pressing the olives

The House of Orpheus

Located in the southern quarter of the city, the House of Orpheus is remarkable not only for its size but for the rooms that it contains. Opposite the entrance is a large peristyle courtyard, with a slightly sunken square pool that is decorated with a mosaic of tritons, cuttlefish, dolphins and other sea creatures. The *tablinum*, looking onto the courtyard, is the main reception room; the centre is paved with the Orpheus Mosaic, the largest of the circular mosaics that have been discovered in Volubilis. A richly dressed Orpheus is depicted charming a lion, an elephant and other animals with his lyre. The house also has an oil press with purification tanks, as well as private areas. These have further rooms paved with mosaics in geometric patterns and bath suites with hypocausts (underfloor heating).

Oil Press

The reconstruction of an oil press near the House of Orpheus shows how this device worked in Roman times. The olives were crushed in a cylindrical vat by the action of a millstone fixed to a vertical axis. The resulting pulp was emptied into rush or esparto baskets laid beneath planks of wood on which pressure was exerted by means of a beam that acted as a lever. The oil ran out along channels and into purification tanks set up outside. Water poured into the tanks forced the

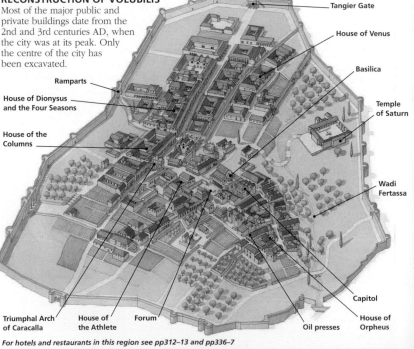

RECONSTRUCTION OF VOLUBILIS

Most of the major public and private buildings date from the 2nd and 3rd centuries AD, when the city was at its peak. Only the centre of the city has been excavated.

Tangier Gate

House of Venus

Basilica

Ramparts

House of Dionysus and the Four Seasons

Temple of Saturn

House of the Columns

Wadi Fertassa

Triumphal Arch of Caracalla

House of the Athlete

Forum

Capitol

Oil presses

House of Orpheus

For hotels and restaurants in this region see pp312–13 and pp336–7

better-quality oil to float to the surface. It was then poured off into large earthenware jars for local use or for export.

The Forum, Basilica and Capitol

Like the other major public buildings in the heart of the city, the unusually small forum dates from the early 3rd century. It was the focal point of public life and administration, as well as a meeting place where business was done. It is continued on its western side by the *macellum*, a market that was originally covered.

On the left of the entrance, from the direction of the oil press, stands the stele of Marcus Valerius Servus, which lists the territory that the citizens of Volubilis possessed in the hinterland.

The *decumanus*, linking Tangier Gate and the triumphal arch

On the eastern side of the forum, a short flight of steps and three semicircular arches leads into the basilica. This was the meeting place of the curia (senate), as well as the commercial exchange and tribunal, and somewhere to take a stroll. On the capitol, south of the basilica, public rites in honour of Jupiter, Juno and Minerva were performed.

House of the Athlete

The athlete that gives this house its name is the *desultor*, or chariot jumper, who took part in the Olympic Games. He would leap from his horse or his chariot in the

The Chariot Jumper, parodied in this mosaic

middle of a race and remount or get back in immediately.

The mosaic here depicts the *desultor* as a parody. The naked athlete is shown bestriding a donkey backwards, and holding a *cantharus*, a drinking vessel given as a prize. The scarf, another emblem of victory, flutters in the background, behind the horseman.

House of the Dog and House of the Ephebe

The House of the Dog, behind the triumphal arch on the western side, is laid out to a typical Roman plan. A double doorway opens onto a lobby leading through to the atrium. This room, which is lined on three sides by a colonnade, contains a pool and leads in turn to a large dining room, or *triclinium*. In 1916, a bronze statue of a dog (see p79) was discovered in one of the rooms off the *triclinium*.

Opposite the House of the Dog stands the House of the Ephebe, where a beautiful statue of an ivy-wreathed ephebe (youth in military training) was found in 1932. It is now in the Musée Archéologique in Rabat (see pp78–9).

Triumphal Arch and Decumanus Maximus

According to the inscription that it bears, the triumphal arch was erected in AD 217 by the governor Marcus Aurelius Sebastenus in honour of Caracalla and his mother Julia Domna. The statues that originally filled the niches in the arch were surmounted by busts of Caracalla and his mother within medallions. Above the inscription, at the

top of the monument, ran a frieze and a band, and the whole was crowned by a chariot drawn by six horses.

The arch, which stands over 8 m (26 ft) high, was reconstructed in 1933. It faces west onto the plain and east onto the *decumanus maximus*. This main axis through the city, 400 m (1,312 ft) long and 12 m (39 ft) wide, leads from the triumphal arch in the southwest to the gateway known as Tangier Gate in the northeast.

Parallel with the *decumanus maximus*, and a few metres away on its southern side, ran an aqueduct, substantial parts of which survive. This brought water from the Aïn Ferhana, a spring 1 km (0.6 mile) east-southeast of Volubilis, on Jbel Zerhoun, to the city's baths and fountains. The largest of these fountains can be seen between the basilica and the triumphal arch.

Aristocratic Quarter

Fine houses, such as the elegant House of the Columns, House of the Knight and House of the Labours of Hercules, constituted the aristocratic quarter. The House of Dionysus and the Four Seasons, and the House of the Bathing Nymphs, have high-quality mosaics. The Gordian Palace, named after Emperor Gordian III (238–44) and probably the residence of the Roman governor, is notable for the 12 columns that front it and the horseshoe-shaped pool with almost perfectly semicircular outlines.

Autumn, from the Four Seasons

Cortège of Venus

Busts of Cato the Younger (see p79) and Juba II were found south of the *decumanus*. The mosaic depicting the Cortège of Venus, which paved the *triclinium*, is displayed in the Museum of Moroccan Crafts and Antiquities in Tangier (see pp132–3). Some of the mosaics have motifs very similar to those seen in Berber carpets today.

MIDDLE ATLAS

A wild region of rare beauty, the Middle Atlas is surprisingly little visited. The great cedar forests that cover the mountain sides between deep valleys stretch as far as the eye can see. Bordered by the fertile plain of the Saïs and the cities of Fès and Meknès, the mountainous heights of the Middle Atlas are the territory of Berber tribes, whose population is thinly scattered in the area.

The mountains of the Middle Atlas are traversed by one of the main routes through to southern Morocco, running from Fès to the Tafilalt. Unless they take their time, travellers on this road will remain sadly ignorant of the beauty and serenity of the region's landscapes.

This mountain chain northeast of the Atlas is 350 km (217 miles) long, and is delimited on its eastern side by Tazzeka National Park, whose terrain is scarred with caves and gorges. South of Sefrou, forests of cedar, holm-oak and cork oak form a patchwork with the bare volcanic plateaux and small lakes brimming with fish.

The Oum er-Rbia rises in the heart of the mountains. The longest river in Morocco, it runs for 600 km (375 miles) before reaching the Atlantic.

To the west, the Middle Atlas abuts the foothills of the High Atlas. Here, the Cascades d' Ouzoud crash down 100 m (328 ft) to the bottom of a natural chasm wreathed in luxuriant vegetation. Nicknamed the Switzerland of Morocco, the Middle Atlas also features some exquisitely scenic small towns at mid-altitude. Ifrane, which has stone-built chalets with red-tiled roofs, Azrou, a resort on the slopes of a cedar plantation, and Imouzzer du Kandar are among the most attractive; they also serve as bases for hikes and tours in the mountains. A tour of the lakes takes in the wild and arid mountain landscape, which is populated only by Berbers. Forest roads darkened by towering stands of cedar are patrolled by peaceable macaques.

Berber shepherd with his flock of sheep in the lakes region of the Middle Atlas

◁ The Cascades d'Ouzoud, a spectacular waterfall in the Middle Atlas

Exploring the Middle Atlas

A varied landscape characterizes the Middle Atlas. The eastern part receives scant rainfall and is thus only sparsely covered with vegetation, but above the deep valleys rise Jbel Bou Naceur and Jbel Bou Iblane: reaching a height of 3,340 m (10,962 ft) and 3,190 m (10,470 ft) respectively, these are the highest peaks of the Middle Atlas. In the thinly populated central high plateaux between Azrou and Timhadit, lakes (known as *dayet* or *aguelmame*) fill the craters of extinct volcanoes and are surrounded by forests. The western part receives the highest rainfall and arable areas have attracted denser populations. Here, plateaux and valleys are covered in forests of cedar, cork oak and maritime pine. From December, peaks over 2,000 m (6,564 ft) are covered with snow. The Middle Atlas is the territory of the semi-nomadic Beni M'Gild and Zaïana.

SEE ALSO

- *Where to Stay* pp313–14
- *Where to Eat* pp337–8

The desert-like shores of Sidi Ali Lake

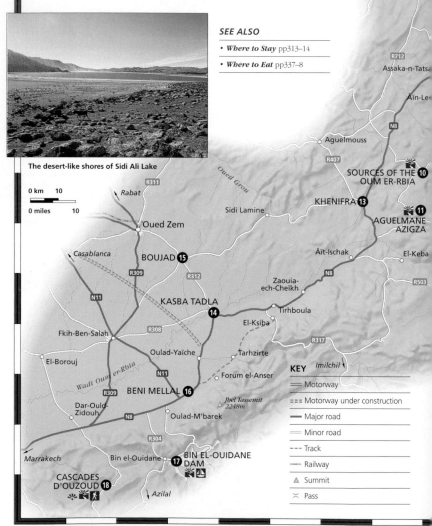

0 km   10

0 miles   10

KEY

- ═══ Motorway
- ≡≡≡ Motorway under construction
- ━━ Major road
- ═══ Minor road
- --- Track
- ⵯⵯ Railway
- △ Summit
- ✕ Pass

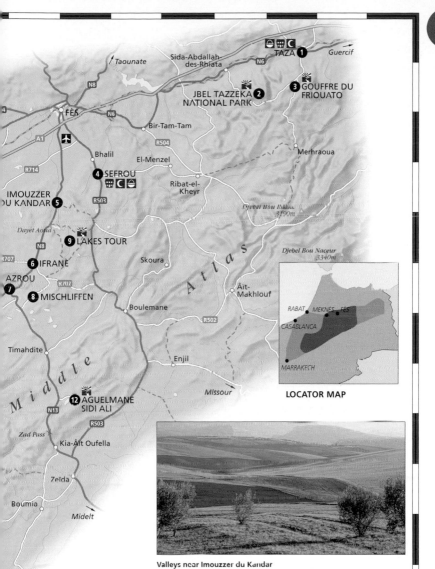

Valleys near Imouzzer du Kandar

SIGHTS AT A GLANCE

Aguelmane Azigza **11**
Aguelmane Sidi Ali **12**
Azrou **7**
Beni Mellal **16**
Bin el-Ouidane Dam **17**
Boujad **15**
Cascades d'Ouzoud **18**
FÈS pp162–83
Gouffre du Friouato **3**
Ifrane **6**
Imouzzer du Kandar **5**
Jbel Tazzeka National Park **2**

Kasba Tadla **14**
Khenifra **13**
MEKNÈS pp184–95
Mischliffen **8**
Sefrou **4**
Sources of the
　Oum er-Rbia **10**
Taza **1**

Tour
Lakes Tour **9**

GETTING AROUND

The major roads between Fès
and Khenifra and between Fès
and Midelt are in a reasonably
good state of repair. By
contrast, the minor roads are
narrow and the distances that
they cover are long because
the terrain is hilly; they can be
impassable in winter. These
minor roads are, however, the
only means of exploring the
Middle Atlas. In the eastern part
of the mountains, many tracks
lead to small isolated lakes.

Taza, between the Rif and the Middle Atlas, on the route towards eastern Morocco

Taza ❶

Road map E2. 👥 *120,000.* 🚉 *from Oujda, Fès and Meknès.* 🚌 *from Nador, El-Hoceima, Fès and Oujda.* ℹ️ *56 Avenue Mohammed V.* 🎪 *Moussem of Sidi Zerrouk (Sep).*

Located on the route between Fès and Oujda, in the lower foothills of the Rif and the Middle Atlas, the town of Taza is a stopping-place that seldom figures on the tourist route. It is, however, one of the oldest towns in Morocco.

Taza was founded in the 8th century by the Meknassa, a Berber tribe, and was regularly seized by sultans who wished to establish their authority before going on to take Fès. The old town, built on a rocky hill, overlooks the new town, 3 km (2 miles) below, which the French began to build in 1920. The 3-km (2-mile) walls surrounding the medina date mostly from the 12th century, the Almohad period, and were restored on several occasions, notably by the Merinids in the 14th century. Moulay Ismaïl, of the Alaouite dynasty, embellished the town and heightened its role as a military stronghold on the eastern frontier.

The Andalusian Mosque, with a 12th-century minaret, stands at the entrance of the medina, from where the main street runs through to the **Grand Mosque.** Founded by the Almohad sultan Abd el-Moumen in 1135, this is one of the oldest mosques in

Morocco. It is closed to non-Muslims, who are therefore unable to see the interior of the magnificent pierced dome or the fine bronze candelabrum.

There is a lively souk in the medina, as well as an unusual minaret whose summit is wider than the base of Djemma Es Souk, the Market Mosque. Bab er-Rih, in the north of the town, offers a splendid view of the orchards and olive trees below, the hills of the Rif and the slopes of Jbel Tazzeka.

Jbel Tazzeka National Park ❷

Road map E2. 🚶 *76-km (47-mile) tour starting from Taza.* 🛍️ *Sun, at Es-Sebt.*

Established in 1950 to protect the cedar forests of Jbel Tazzeka, this national park offers a spectacular tour southwest of Taza.

In the middle of a valley of almond, cherry and fig trees are the **Cascades de Ras el-Oued** (falls which only flow between November and April). The winding road crosses the fertile plateau of the **Chiker**, a punch-bowl which at certain times of year becomes a small lake (*dayet*) fed by underground water.

Beyond Bab Taka, a mountain pass at an altitude of 1,540 m (5,054 ft), a narrow track leads over 9 km (5.5 miles) to the summit of Jbel Tazzeka. The peak, at an altitude of 1,980 m (6,498 ft), supports a television mast. There is a fine view north over the mountains of the Rif, west over the plain of Fès and south to the higher foothills of the Middle Atlas and the snow peaks of the Jbel Boulblanc. The road then winds through the Wadi Zireg gorge. Caves in the cliffs here are used by local shepherds.

A single-storey house in the foothills of Jbel Tazzeka

Gouffre du Friouato ❸

Road map E2. 22 km (13.5 miles) southwest of Taza.

This natural chasm, which was first explored in 1934, is open to visitors, although sturdy walking boots are necessary. A flight of 500 slippery steps leads down to the cave. It is 180 m (590 ft) deep and contains galleries and halls filled with fascinating stalactites, stalagmites and other curious formations. The adjacent **Chiker Caves** are open only to speleologists.

The canyons of the Sebou gorge

Sefrou ❹

Road map D2. 🏠 230,000. 🚌 from Fès and Midelt. 🏠 Thu. 🎪 Cherry Festival (Jun); Moussem of Sidi Lahcen Lyoussi (Aug).

This ancient town has always stood in the shadow of Fès, the imperial capital. It takes its name from the Ahel Sefrou, a Berber tribe that was converted to Judaism 2,000 years ago, and that was then Islamicized by Idriss I in the 8th century. In the 12th century, trade with the Sahara brought Sefrou prosperity. A century later, it became home to a large colony of Jews who had fled from the Tafilalt and southern Algeria. In 1950, a third of Sefrou's population was Jewish. The majority of Jews emigrated to Israel in 1967, and the town's population is now mostly Muslim.

Sefrou is surrounded by crenellated ramparts pierced by nine gates. These ochre pisé walls have been restored on several occasions.

The town is bisected by Wadi Aggaï, which irrigates the surrounding fertile plain. Four bridges link the two parts of the town. South of the *wadi* is the mellah, the former Jewish quarter, a district of narrow winding streets. North of the *wadi* is the old medina, with its souks centred around the Grand Mosque and the *zaouia* of Sidi Lahcen Lyoussi, who became patron saint of Sefrou in the 18th century. On the north side of the town, outside the ramparts, is a crafts centre where leather goods, pottery and wrought-iron items are made.

The Cherry Festival, marking the end of the cherry harvest in June, is a major event in the town, which is surrounded by cherry orchards. The festival goes on for several days, and the major event is a grand procession marked by the coronation of the Cherry Queen. Folk dancers and musicians from the Middle Atlas, Fès and the Rif perform and there are sometimes fantasias.

The road following the river upstream for 1 km (0.6 mile) west of Sefrou leads to the **Kef el-Moumen Caves**, natural caves in the cliff face containing tombs that are venerated by Muslims and Jews. One of them is said to be that of the prophet Daniel. The **Wadi Aggaï Falls** here bring a welcome freshness to the surrounding hills.

The green-roofed **Koubba of Sidi bou Ali Serghine**, 2 km (1 mile) west of Sefrou, offers a scenic view over Sefrou and the Kandar hills. Nearby is the miraculous spring of **Lalla Rekia**, which is reputed to cure madness.

The village of **Bhalil**, 7 km (4 miles) north of Sefrou, has troglodytic dwellings. Its population, Christian during the Roman period, was converted to Islam by Idriss II.

A minor road east of Sefrou leads to the small town of El-Menzel. The kasbah here overlooks the **Sebou Gorge**, which has impressively sheer cliffs.

Fortified gateway into the mellah in Sefrou

Imouzzer du Kandar ❺

Road map D2. 🏠 12,000. 🏠 Mon. 🎪 Apple Festival (Jul).

Built by the French, the small hillside town of Imouzzer du Kandar overlooks the Saïss plain, which abuts the plateaux of the Middle Atlas. At an altitude of 1,345 m (4,414 ft), the town is pleasantly cool in summer, providing a welcome respite from the heat of Fès and Meknès. Many Moroccans come here for the weekend.

The dilapidated kasbah of the Aït Serchouchène, where the souk takes place, contains troglodytic dwellings, of which there are many in the region. The caves were dug into the hillside and, in times gone by, protected Berbers from attacks by their enemies. Some are still inhabited. Steps or just a slope lead up to the entrance. The openings – no more than a small door and a few ventilation holes – are small so as to keep out the cold, and the spartan interiors have neither water nor electricity.

Troglodytic dwelling in the kasbah of Imouzzer du Kandar

The King's summer residence at Ifrane, set in a dense cedar forest

Ifrane ⑥

63 km (39 miles) south of Fès on road N8. 👥 10,000. 🚍 from Fès and Azrou. 🛈 Avenue Mohammed V; (0535) 56 68 21.

Established in 1929 during the Protectorate, Ifrane is a small, noticeably clean town with a European rather than a Moroccan character. Located at an altitude of 1,650 m (5,415 ft), it is cool in summer and may be snow-bound from December to March. On the descent into the valley, a green-roofed palace, the King's summer residence, comes into view. Al-Akhawaya University, inaugurated by Hassan II in 1995, has contributed considerably to the town's development.

Ifrane serves as the departure point for many tours, including a trip to the waterfalls known as the **Cascades des Vierges**, 3 km (2 miles) west (follow the signs to Source Vittel), and north to the **zaouia** of Ifrane, which is surrounded by caves and *koubbas*.

Wooden chalet in Ifrane

Holm-oak in the forests surrounding Azrou

Environs
Road R707 out of Ifrane, going up to the Tizi-n-Tretten Pass, leads to the **Forêt de Cèdres**. After running along the Mischliffen and Jbel Hebri, it reaches a legendary 900-year-old cedar, the Cèdre Gouraud.

Azrou ⑦

48 km (30 miles) south of Ifrane on road N8. 👥 45,000. 🚍 from Meknès, Fès, Marrakech and Er-Rachidia; Grands taxis. 🛈 Ifrane; (0535) 566821. 🗓 Tue.

A large outcrop of volcanic rock at the entrance to the town gave Azrou (meaning "rock" in Berber) its name. At an altitude of 1,250 m (4102 ft), it is located at the crossroads of routes linking Meknès and Erfoud, and Fès and Marrakech.

The town nestles in the centre of a geological basin, with Jbel Hebri to the southeast. It is circled by a dense belt of cedar and holm-oak, where the Beni M'Gild, the most prominent Berber tribe in the region, once came to spend their summers. These nomadic pastoralists from the Sahara gradually adopted a sedentary lifestyle and founded the town.

Azrou is still a regional market town, with a large weekly souk. At the **crafts centre** (opposite the police station) items made of cedar, thuya, walnut and juniper are on sale, as are wrought-iron objects and the renowned carpets, with geometric motifs on a red background, made by the Beni M'Gild.

During the Protectorate the town became a health resort, and highly reputed treatment centres are still found here. It is also the departure point for tours of the cedar forests and plateaux. The lakes in the vicinity offer fishing for trout, pike and roach (a permit is compulsory).

Environs
North of Azrou, the road to El-Hajeb runs along the edge of the **Balcon d'Ito** plateau, offering good views of the lunar landscape. The Berber hill village of **Aïn Leuh**, 32 km (20 miles) south of Azrou, hosts the Middle Atlas Arts Festival in July. There is a souk here on Mondays and Thursdays.

The ski resort on the Mischliffen, located in a volcanic crater

Mischliffen ⑧

Road map D2.

A shallow bowl surrounded by cedar forests, the Mischliffen is the crater of an extinct volcano. The villages here are outnumbered by the tents of the shepherds who bring their flocks for summer grazing. A small winter sports resort (also called Mischliffen) has also been set up, at an altitude of 2,000 m (6,564 ft), among the trees. The resort's facilites, which consist of just two ski-lifts, are, however, relatively basic.

Lakes Tour ➒

Three attractive lakes – Dayet Aoua, Dayet Ifrah and Dayet Hachlaf – lie 9 km (6.5 miles) south of Imouzzer du Kandar. A turning off road N8 leads to Dayet Aoua, which formed in a natural depression. The narrow road running along it leads to Dayet Ifrah, surrounded by a cirque of mountains, and on to Dayet Hachlaf. Beyond a forestry hut, a track on the right leads to the Vallée des Roches (Valley of the Rocks). Ducks, grey herons, cranes, egrets, birds of prey and dragonflies populate these arid expanses.

Bird sanctuary ➁
When the lakes are full, the area becomes a nature reserve for many species of birds. It attracts waders – such as avocets, cattle egrets, grey herons and crested coots – wildfowl, birds of prey – such as red kites and kestrels – and swallows.

Dayet Aoua ➀
This lake sits in a natural depression surrounded by hills. It sometimes remains dry for several years in a row and this is due to persistent drought and the fact that the water table has been tapped to irrigate orchards in the area.

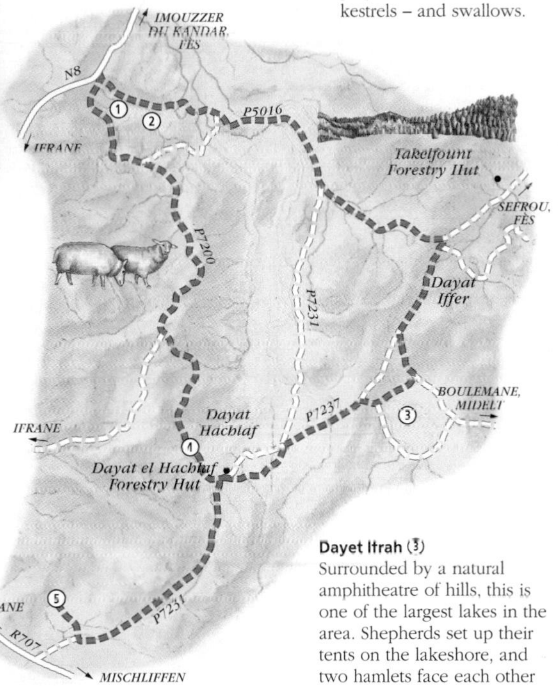

Map labels:
- IMOUZZER DU KANDAR, FES
- N8
- IFRANE
- P5016
- Takelfount Forestry Hut
- SEFROU, FES
- P7200
- P7231
- Dayat Iffer
- BOULEMANE, MIDELT
- IFRANE
- Dayat Hachlaf ➀
- P7237
- ➂
- Dayat el Hachlaf Forestry Hut
- IFRANE
- ➄
- P7231
- R707
- MISCHLIFFEN

Dayet Itrah ➂
Surrounded by a natural amphitheatre of hills, this is one of the largest lakes in the area. Shepherds set up their tents on the lakeshore, and two hamlets face each other across the water, their white minarets rising up into the sky.

Vallée des Roches ➃
A track on the right, beyond the forestry hut, leads to these outcrops of limestone, strangely shaped by erosion, and to caves inhabited by bats.

```
0 km                    5
0 miles                 5
```

Rock formations ➄
Continuing along track P7231 in the direction of the Ifrane-Mischliffen road, a rough track branching off to the right leads to this circle of rocks which, shaped by natural forces, have the appearance of ruins.

KEY

■■ Tour route (track)

= Road

== Track

TIPS FOR DRIVERS

Tour length: about 60 km (37 miles).
Departure point: 16 km (10 miles) north of Ifrane on the N8, forking left to Dayet Aoua.
Duration: one day.
Stopping place: Chalet du Lac, on the shores of Dayet Aoua.

The sources of the Oum er-Rbia, the "Mother of Spring"

Sources of the Oum er-Rbia ⑩

160 km (99 miles) from Fès and from Beni Mellal. Please note: there are no hotels or petrol stations on road N8 between Azrou and Khenifra.

A winding road runs above the valley of the Oum er-Rbia, then leads down to the *wadi*. The river's sources – more than 40 springs – form cascades that crash down the limestone cliffs, joining to form the Oum er-Rbia, the longest river in Morocco. The springs can be explored via a footpath.

Aguelmane Azigza, a lake in a verdant setting

Aguelmane Azigza ⑪

12 km (7.5 miles) south of the sources of the Oum er-Rbia.

The rivers whose sources lie in the heart of the Middle Atlas have formed lakes in the craters of extinct volcanoes. One such is Aguelmane Azigza. It is enclosed by cliffs and forests of cedar and holm-oak and contains plenty of fish.

Aguelmane Sidi Ali ⑫

Junction with road N13.

A right turn off road N13 from Azrou to Midelt leads to Aguelmane Sidi Ali, a deep, fish-filled lake that is 3 km (2 miles) long and lies at an altitude of 2,000 m (6,564 ft). With Jbel Hayane rising above, it is surrounded by rugged hills and desolate pasture where the Beni M'Gild's flocks are brought for summer grazing.

Continuing towards Midelt, this very scenic road climbs up to the Zad Pass, which at 2,178 m (7,148 ft), is the highest in the Middle Atlas.

Khenifra ⑬

160 km (99 miles) from Fès; 130 km (81 miles) from Beni Mellal. 🏠 15,000. 🚌 from Fès and Marrakech. 🌙 Sun & Wed.

In the folds of the arid hills and on the banks of the Oum er-Rbia stand houses painted in the carmine red that is typical of Khenifra. Until the 17th century, the town was the rallying point of the Zaïane tribe, which resisted attempts by the French to pacify the region. In the 18th century Moulay Ismaïl asserted his authority by building imposing kasbahs in which armies were garrisoned. The livestock market here is one of the few interesting aspects of the town.

An elegant gate in Khenifra

THE LIONS OF THE ATLAS

Before World War I, the roaring of lions in the Moroccan Atlas could be heard at dusk and during the night. The last Atlas lion was killed in 1922. During the Roman period, lions were plentiful in North Africa. They flourished in Tunisia until the 17th century, although by 1891 not one remained. In Algeria, the last lion was killed in 1893, about 100 km (60 miles) south of Constantine. The lions of the Atlas were large, with a thick mane, which was very dark or almost black. Because the genetic make-up of the Atlas lion is known, it should be possible to bring this extinct sub-species back to life. With this end in view, a breeding programme is under way, using lions bred in circuses and in zoos, most particularly the zoo in Rabat.

The Atlas lion, portrayed by Eugène Delacroix (Musée Bonnat, Bayonne)

◁ A beautiful olive grove in the Taza area *(see p210)*

OLIVES AND OLIVE OIL

Olive groves are a common sight around Meknès and Beni Mellal and in the Rif. The gnarled and knotty olive tree survives in poor soil, taking root in rough and uneven ground. Olive oil is extracted by time-honoured methods. In the autumn, the green, black and violet-tinged olives are harvested, the mixture of all three determining the flavour and aroma of the oil. A heavy grindstone turned by donkeys grinds the olives, crushing both the flesh and the kernel. The resulting dark-hued pulp is emptied into large, shallow, circular porous containers placed beneath the oil press. The oil seeps out

Piles of olives set out for sale in the souk

and runs into vats, where, mixed with water, it floats to the surface, free of debris. A whole 5 kg (11 lb) of olives makes just 1 litre (1.76 pints) of oil. On the colourful stalls in the souks, the different kinds of olives are piled up into pyramids; there are green olives with herbs, violet-hued olives with a sharp taste, piquant olives spiced with red peppers, olives with bitter orange, crushed black olives that have been sun-dried and steeped in oil, and olives for making *tajine*.

Grindstones, carved from a single block

Environs
The village of **El-Kebab** clings to a hillside southeast of Khenifra. Here craftsmen make pottery and carpets. Above the village is the hermitage where Father Albert Peyriguère, a doctor and companion to the French ascetic Charles de Foucauld, lived from 1928 to 1959. A souk is held on Mondays.

Kasba Tadla ⑭

82 km (51 miles) southwest of Khenifra on road N8. 🏠 36,000. 🚌 from Beni Mellal and Khenifra. 🛈 Beni Mellal. 🅰 Mon.

The focal point of this former garrison town is, predictably, the kasbah, which was built by Moulay Ismaïl in the 1600s. So as to subdue rebellious tribes, Moulay Ismaïl made his son governor of the province. The latter built a second kasbah, contiguous with the one that his father had built. A double line of walls thus surrounds the town, enclosing two dilapidated mosques, the former governor's palace and grain stores. Below the town, a ten-span bridge crosses Wadi Oum er-Rbia.

Environs
Plantations of olive trees cover the Tadla plain between Kasba Tadla and Khenifra, and many traditional olive mills line the road at **Tirhboula**, about 10 km (6 miles) from Khenifra. In the autumn, visitors can see the various stages in the oil-producing process and buy

olive oil here. **El-Ksiba** is an attractive village on the edge of the forest 22 km (13.5 miles) east of Kasba Tadla. It has a souk, which is very busy on Sundays. Beyond El-Ksiba, the road becomes a track that crosses the High Atlas via Imilchil, descending to Tinerhir, in the southern foothills.

The ten-span bridge over the Oum er-Rbia at Kasba Tadla

The Mountains of Morocco

Lammergeier

From the high peaks down to altitudes above 600 m (1,970 ft), the climate is permanently moist. Annual precipitation ranges from 650 mm (25 in) in the eastern Grand Atlas to over 2 m (80 in) in the Rif, and snowfall is often heavy. The vegetation in this band is particularly luxuriant, and many forests thrive in this well-watered environment. These consist mostly of cedar, cork oak, deciduous oak, evergreen holm-oak and, in the Rif, Moroccan pine.

Holm-oak *grows at altitudes of 600 to 2,700 m (1,970 to 8,860 ft) and makes up a quarter of all Morocco's forested areas.*

Aleppo pine, *which grows naturally in the mountains, is planted almost everywhere since its timber is used for a wide range of purposes.*

Forests of Atlas cedar *are impressive for their sheer size, and the trees for their beauty, their majestic appearance and their height, which can exceed 50 m (164 ft).*

Atlas cedar

Barbary thuya

Holm-oak

Aleppo pine can grow to a height of 25 m (82 ft).

The carob produces sugar-rich pods that are a nutritious food for both humans and animals.

Argan

Kermes oak

Wild olive can be used as grafting stock. Its timber is suitable for carpentry and is also used as firewood.

The argan (see p127) *is a small tree that grows exclusively in southwestern Morocco. Argan nuts are a favourite food of goats, which climb up into the branches to reach them. Oil extracted from the kernels is used in foods, in cosmetics and as a tonic.*

HIGH-ALTITUDE VEGETATION

At altitudes above 2,700 m (8,860 ft), the mountains consist of cold and arid steppe, which is often covered in snow. No trees grow here but there are abundant streams. The low-growing vegetation, including some endemic species, is varied and forms a covering of spiny, cushion-like clumps.

Juniper

The Tizi-n-Test Pass *commands a view of the snowy heights of the Atlas and the Souss valley, 2,000 m (6,564 ft) below.*

MOUNTAIN FAUNA

The Barbary sheep, Africa's only wild sheep, inhabits the High and Middle Atlas. It can also be seen in Jbel Toubkal National Park *(see p249)*, which was created especially to ensure its survival. Three-quarters of the country's population of macaques live in the cedar forests of the Middle Atlas. Wild boar is found in all mountainous areas and the Barbary stag was reintroduced in 1990. Birds are plentiful at altitudes between 2,200 and 3,600 m (7,220 and 11,815 ft) They include the golden eagle, Bonelli's eagle, booted eagle, the huge lammergeier, Egyptian vulture, partridge, Moussier's redstart and the rare crimson-winged finch, which nests only at altitudes above 2,800 m (9,190 ft).

Barbary sheep

Adult booted eagle, feeding chicks in the nest

Female macaque carrying her newborn on her back

M'Goun, *which rises to a height of more than 4,000 m (13,128 ft), is the second-highest peak in the High Atlas.*

The Aïn-Asserdoun springs, "Springs of the Mule"

Boujad ⑮

24 km (15 miles) north of Kasba Tadla on road R312. 🏚 15,000. ⛴ Thu.

The holy town of Boujad, which is filled with *koubbas* (tombs) and shrines, is set in the Tadla plain, on the caravan route that once ran between Marrakech and Fès. It was established in the 16th century by Sidi Mohammed ech-Cherki, patron saint of Tadla, who built an important *zaouia* here. The saint and his descendants, bearers of *baraka* (blessing, luck or good fortune) from one generation to the next, have always been highly venerated by the Beni Meskin and Seguibat, local Berber tribespeople. In 1785, sultan Sidi Mohammed ben Abdallah, who was resentful of this power, razed the town, including the *zaouia*. The latter was rebuilt in the 19th century and is still inhabited by the saint's descendants.

The tombs of the saintly dynasty can be seen around the market square in the north of the town. The largest, the **Koubba of Sidi Othman**, is open to visitors. There are many other mausoleums here, most notably that of the sheik Mohammed ech-Cherki, which is closed to non-Muslims. On a promontory outside Boujad, in the direction of Oued Zem on the northern side of the town, stand five white *koubbas*, to which crowds of pilgrims come for annual gatherings.

Beni Mellal ⑯

30 km (18.5 miles) southwest of Kasba Tadla on road N8. 🏚 140,000. ⛴ from Khenifra, Marrakech and Demnate. 🚹 Avenue Hassan II; (0523) 48 78 29. ⛴ Tue; Sun in Sebt-Oulad-Nemaa 35 km (22 miles) to the west.

The modern town of Beni Mellal lies at the foot of the Middle Atlas, on the edge of the great Tadla plain, where cereals are extensively cultivated. Although it is devoid of any obvious appeal, it is still a convenient stopping-place.

Inhabited by Berbers and Jews well before the arrival of Islam, the town was known successively as Day, Kasba Belkouche and Beni Mellal. In the 13th century, it stood on the border between the kingdoms of Fès and Marrakech, which were the object of bitter dispute between the Merinid and Almohad dynasties. In 1680 Moulay Ismaïl built a kasbah here, which was restored on several occasions.

The town is surrounded by orange groves (oranges from Beni Mellal are renowned), and olive groves stretch to the horizon. Beetroot and sugarcane have replaced bananas as cultivated crops. All are unusually well watered thanks to the Bin el-Ouidane dam.

South of the town, in the lower foothills of the Middle

Cedar-dwelling macaque

Atlas, a road marked "Circuit touristique" leads to the **Aïn Asserdoun springs**, which run between trees and small gardens. It is worth making the short detour to **Ras el-Aïn**, a little further up. This stone and pisé *borj* (tower) offers a picturesque view of Beni Mellal and its orchards.

Environs

The area around Beni Mellal has many waterfalls, springs, caves and wooded gorges populated by monkeys. About 10 km (6 miles) east, a road leads to **Foum el-Anser**, where a waterfall crashes into a gorge. The rockface here is marked by artificial caves, access to which is difficult. South of Beni Mellal, a hillside track leads up to **Jbel Tassemit** (2,248 m/7,378 ft), which is the departure point for scenic mountain hikes. Hikers can also reach the **Tarhzirte Gorge** and the Wadi Derna valley, 20 km (12 miles) northeast of Beni Mellal.

Bin el-Ouidane Dam ⑰

43 km (27 miles) southwest of Beni Mellal on road N8, branching left on road R304. 🚹 Beni Mellal.

From Beni Mellal the road climbs through wooded hills to reach the grandiose site of an artificial lake, the Bin el-Ouidane reservoir. The dam

The *borj* of Ras el-Aïn, offering a spectacular view over the Tadla plain

The Bin el-Ouidane reservoir, at the foot of the High Atlas

here is 285 m (935 ft) long and 133 m (436 ft) high and the reservoir, with a surface area of 380,000 sq m (94 acres), is the largest lake in Morocco. Fed by Wadi el-Abid and Wadi Ahansalt, it irrigates the intensively cultivated Tadla plain, while the hydroelectric generator provides a quarter of Morocco's electricity. The turquoise waters of the lake, which are broken by spits of land and small islands, are surrounded by red hills, and the lakeshore is dotted with a few isolated houses.

Watersports and fishing are permitted on the lake and Wadi el-Abid is suitable for kayaking and rafting in spring, when the water level is sufficiently high. A track leading from the lake ends at a rock formation known as La Cathédrale. This rock, with a covering of red soil and a setting among Aleppo pines, is well known to abseilers.

From the dam, Azilal and the Aït Bouguemez valley (see pp254–7) can be reached on road R304.

Cascades d'Ouzoud ⓲

65 km (40 miles) southwest of Bin el-Ouidane on road R304, or 156 km (97 miles) from Marrakech via Demnate. 🚌 for Beni Mellal-Azilal then grand taxi.

One of the most spectacular sights in Morocco, the Cascades d'Ouzoud attract large numbers of visitors. The waterfall is particularly impressive in spring, when the waters pour down from the top of reddish cliffs, crashing off a succession of rocky ledges to fall into the canyon of Wadi el-Abid 100 m (328 ft) below.

The road to the site leads to a spot above the waterfall, which can be reached along a footpath with steps cut into the earth. From platforms set at intervals on the path, visitors can marvel at the majestic succession of cascades and admire the permanent rainbow created by the mist thrown up by the water. Mills, whose only vestiges are small rectangular recesses, once worked a grindstone on which corn and barley were ground to make flour. The fig trees and carobs that grow beside the path are often full of monkeys – the beige-coated macaques with eyes outlined in black. Bathing is permitted in the natural pools.

Starting from the bottom of the waterfall, energetic visitors wearing strong walking boots can hike to the Wadi el-Abid gorge.

Environs

Six kilometres (4 miles) southwest of Demnate, on road R304, is **Imi-n-Ifri**, a natural bridge that has been partly carved out by the *wadi*. A track leads down to the bottom of the chasm.

The Cascades d'Ouzoud in spring, at their most spectacular

MARRAKECH

*S*uch is the importance of Marrakech that it gave its name to Morocco. For more than two centuries, this Berber city at the point of interchange between the Sahara, the Atlas and the Anti-Atlas was the hub of a great empire, and the achievements of illustrious builders can be seen within the city's walls. It is the capital of the great South and, although it is now only Morocco's third city after Casablanca and Rabat, its fabulous palaces and luxuriant palm grove continue to hold a powerful fascination for visitors.

Marrakech was founded in 1062 by Almoravids from the Sahara. These warrior monks soon carved out an empire that stretched from Algiers to Spain. In 1106, Ali ben Youssef hired craftsmen from Andalusia to build a palace and a mosque in the capital. He also raised ramparts around the city and installed *khettaras* (underground canals), an ingenious irrigation system that brought water to its great palm grove.

The Almohads took the city in 1147. Abd el-Moumen built the Koutoubia, a masterpiece of Moorish architecture, and his successor was responsible for building the kasbah. But the Almohad dynasty collapsed, to the benefit of the Merinids of Fès, and for over 200 years Marrakech stagnated. It was not until the 16th century that the city was reinvigorated by the arrival of the Saadians, most notably by the wealthy Ahmed el-Mansour. The Saadian Tombs, the Ben Youssef Medersa and the remains of the Palais el-Badi mark this golden age. In 1668, Marrakech fell to the Alaouites, who made Fès, then Meknès, their capital. In the 20th century, Marrakech embraced the modern age with the creation of the Quartier Guéliz, built during the Protectorate. Visitors continue to flock to this magical city, and tourism is central to its economy today.

A woman leaving the *zaouia* of Sidi bel Abbès

◁ The garden of the Villa Majorelle

Exploring Marrakech

The rich history of Marrakech is reflected in
its various quarters. The medina, above which
rises the minaret of the Koutoubia Mosque, the
emblem of the city, corresponds to the old town.
Place Jemaa el-Fna, the hub of all activity, is
its heart. Within the ramparts are the souks
(north of Place Jemaa el-Fna), the kasbah
and the mellah (the Jewish quarter). Guéliz,
in the northwest, is the new town
laid out by Marshal Lyautey under
the Protectorate. It is filled with
Western-style offices, businesses and a
residential area. Avenue Mohammed V
is the district's main thoroughfare.
Extending Guéliz in the southwest
is Hivernage, a verdant quarter with
many hotels that also dates from the
Protectorate. The district is bordered
on its western side by the Menara
Gardens, and on its eastern side
by the walls of the medina.

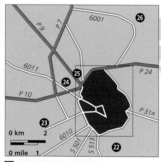

AREA OF MAIN MAP

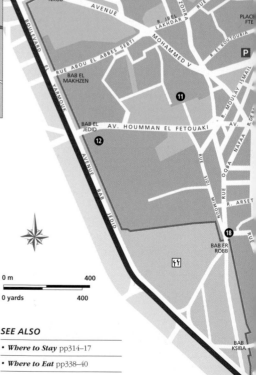

Railway Station
1km (0.6 miles)

KEY

▨	Medina
▨	Historic building
—	Ramparts
🚌	Bus station
P	Parking
⊠	Post office
✚	Hospital
◖	Mosque
▪	Jewish cemetery
⑂⑂	Muslim cemetery

0 m   400

0 yards   400

SEE ALSO

• **Where to Stay** pp314–17

• **Where to Eat** pp338–40

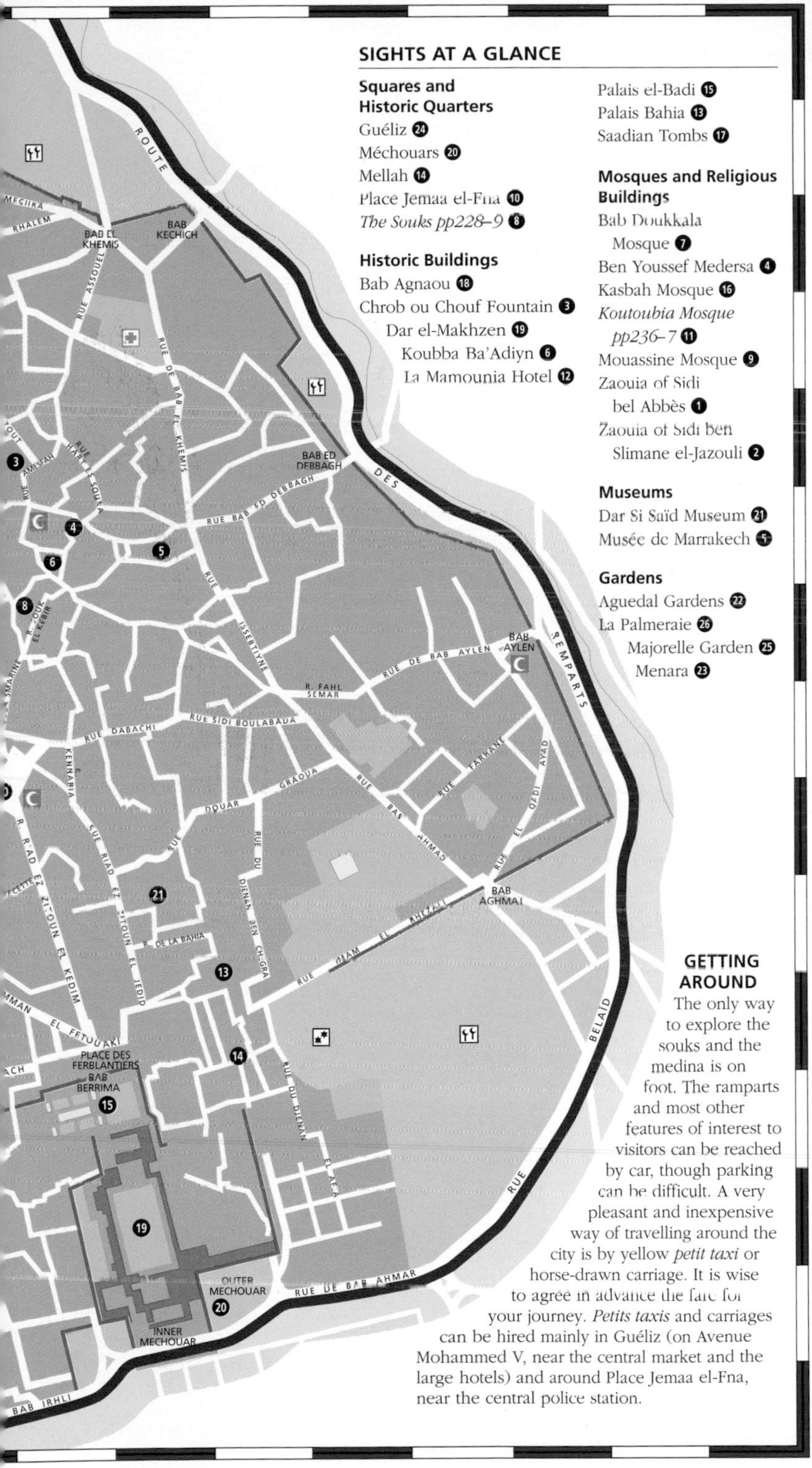

SIGHTS AT A GLANCE

Squares and Historic Quarters
Guéliz ㉔
Méchouars ⑳
Mellah ⑭
Place Jemaa el-Fna ⑩
The Souks pp228–9 ⑧

Historic Buildings
Bab Agnaou ⑱
Chrob ou Chouf Fountain ③
Dar el-Makhzen ⑲
Koubba Ba'Adiyn ⑥
La Mamounia Hotel ⑫

Palais el-Badi ⑮
Palais Bahia ⑬
Saadian Tombs ⑰

Mosques and Religious Buildings
Bab Doukkala Mosque ⑦
Ben Youssef Medersa ④
Kasbah Mosque ⑯
Koutoubia Mosque pp236–7 ⑪
Mouassine Mosque ⑨
Zaouia of Sidi bel Abbès ①
Zaouia of Sidi ben Slimane el-Jazouli ②

Museums
Dar Si Saïd Museum ㉑
Musée de Marrakech ⑤

Gardens
Aguedal Gardens ㉒
La Palmeraie ㉖
Majorelle Garden ㉕
Menara ㉓

GETTING AROUND

The only way to explore the souks and the medina is on foot. The ramparts and most other features of interest to visitors can be reached by car, though parking can be difficult. A very pleasant and inexpensive way of travelling around the city is by yellow *petit taxi* or horse-drawn carriage. It is wise to agree in advance the fare for your journey. *Petits taxis* and carriages can be hired mainly in Guéliz (on Avenue Mohammed V, near the central market and the large hotels) and around Place Jemaa el-Fna, near the central police station.

Zaouia of Sidi bel Abbès ❶

Sidi bel Abbès quarter (north of the medina). ◐ to non-Muslims. Pilgrimage on Thu.

From Bab el-Khemis, Rue Sidi Rhalem leads to the Zaouia of Sidi bel Abbès. The sanctuary is a focal point for the pilgrimage of the Regraga (the Seven Saints), which was instituted by Moulay Ismaïl so as to obtain forgiveness for his depredations in Marrakech.

Sidi bel Abbès (1130–1205) is the city's most highly venerated patron saint. A disciple of the famous Cadi Ayad, he devoted his life to preaching and to caring for

The monumental entrance to the Zaouia of Sidi bel Abbès

and defending the weak and the blind. Because of him, it was said throughout Morocco that Marrakech was the only city where a blind man could eat his fill. To this day, the gifts of pilgrims are distributed to the poor and the blind.

In 1605, the Saadian sultan Abou Faris raised a mausoleum for the saint in the hope of curing his epilepsy. Moulay Ismaïl added a dome in the 18th century and the mausoleum was given its present appearance by Sidi Mohammed ben Abdallah a few years later.

The *zaouia* also includes a mosque, a hammam, a home for the blind, a small market, an abattoir and a cemetery.

South of the *zaouia* is the **El-Mjadlia Souk**, the Passe-menterie Souk, built in a covered alley during the reign of Sidi Mohammed ben Abderrahman, at the end of the 19th century. Going from here towards the centre of the medina, you will pass **Bab Taghzout**, an Almoravid gate that has been integrated into the surrounding architecture.

Zaouia of Sidi ben Slimane el-Jazouli ❷

North of the medina (near Rue Dar el-Glaoui). ◐ to non-Muslims. Pilgrimage on Fri.

After Bab Taghzout, if you follow Rue de Bab Taghzout, then take the first right, and then go right again, you will reach this *zaouia*, which also features in the Regraga pilgrimage (*see p38*). The mausoleum dates from the Saadian period and was remodelled in the late 18th century during the reign of Sidi Mohammed ben Abdallah.

Sidi Mohammed ben Slimane el-Jazouli, another venerated mystic, founded Moroccan Sufism in the 15th century. Under the Wattasids, this religion spread to every level of the population. A champion of the holy war against the Portuguese and a politically influential figure, this holy man attracted thousands of followers; his reputedly occult powers even worried the sultan.

Interior of the Zaouia of Sidi ben Slimane

Chrob ou Chouf Fountain ❸

Rue Amesfah, near the Mosque of Ben Youssef.

As its name – meaning "Drink and Admire" – suggests, this Saadian fountain is one of the most beautiful in the medina. It was built during the reign of Ahmed el-Mansour (1578–1603), and it is shaded by a carved cedar awning with coloured *zellij* tilework and inscriptions in cursive and Kufic script engraved into the wood.

In a town like Marrakech, located at the head of pre-Saharan valleys, water was a very precious commodity. An underground network of channels supplied the mosques and the houses and fed the fountains. Obeying the precepts of the Koran, according to which water must be given to the thirsty, many of the leading citizens of Marrakech financed the building of fountains.

Detail of the cedar awning over the Chrob ou Chouf Fountain

The Ramparts of Marrakech

Skirting the Guéliz and Hivernage quarters on their eastern side, the ramparts completely encircle the medina. From the time of its foundation, Marrakech was defended by sturdy walls set with forts. Although their outline has hardly altered from the time of the Almoravids, they were extended to the south by the Almohads and to the north by the Saadians in the 16th century. These pisé walls are 19 km (12 miles) long, up to 2 m (6 ft) thick and up to 9 m (30 ft) high. Some of the monumental gates that pierce them are very fine examples of Moorish architecture. The best time to walk around the ramparts is in the early morning or just before sunset. Their warm ochre colour changes according to the time of day and the intensity of the light. In the evening, they take on an almost rust-coloured hue.

Bab el-Khemis *was remodelled after the Almoravid period (1147–1269). An open-air market is held outside the gate on Thursdays. The tomb of the Seven Saints is a small dome-topped building dedicated to a* marabout.

Bab Agnaou (see p239), *whose name is derived from the Berber for "hornless black ram", is one of the finest gates in Marrakech. It is carved in an ochre stone with tinges of pink. It once led into the Almohad palace.*

THE GATES
Bab Aghmat and Bab Aylen, on the eastern side of the ramparts, date from the 12th century, and are relatively plain. Bab ed-Debbagh, dating from the same period, opens onto the tanners' quarter. On the northern side stands Bab el-Khemis and on the southern, Bab el-Robb (1308). The latter takes its name from a grape liqueur in which the city once did a brisk trade. Bab el-Jedid, on the western side, leads to La Mamounia hotel *(see p234).*

These lower pisé walls, *which are just high enough to close a harem off from a house or a garden, or to shield a sanctuary from prying eyes, were not built for defensive purposes.*

The ramparts of Marrakech, *which date from the 12th century, are the most impressive city walls in Morocco. The well-preserved defences encircle the old town, with its palaces and gardens.*

The Souks

Olives

The souks of Marrakech are among the most fascinating in the Maghreb. Arranged according to the individual nature of the goods on offer, they are laid out in the narrow streets north and east of Place Jemaa el-Fna. On the map shown here, the area marked in orange denotes the historic heart of the souks, which stretches from the Ben Youssef Mosque in the north to the Souk Smarine in the south. Many of the souks are known by the name of whatever is sold here. Today a very wide range of goods, from fabric to jewellery and slippers, is on offer. Leatherwork is particularly prominent. Around this commercial hub are the crafts traditionally associated with country people, such as blacksmithing, saddle-making and basketry. Because of rank odours, the tanneries are banished to the edge of the city.

KEY

■ Historic souk

■ Historic monument

0 m — 100

0 yards — 100

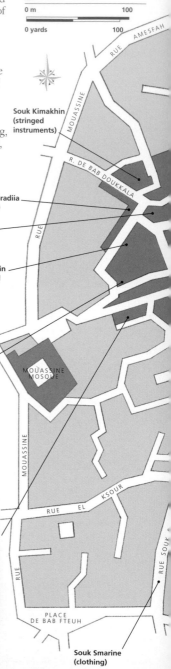

Souk Kimakhin (stringed instruments)

Souk El-Bradiia (pitchers)

Souk Atarin (brass and copper)

RUE AMESFAH

MOUASSINE

R. DE BAB DOUKKALA

RUE

MOUASSINE MOSQUE

MOUASSINE

RUE EL KSOUR

RUE SOUK

PLACE DE BAB FTEUH

Souk Addadine (metalwork)

Amid a deafening clatter, brass and copper workers tirelessly hammer hot metal, shaping it into a range of everyday items such as trays, ashtrays, lanterns, wrought-iron grilles, locks and keys.

Souk Chouari (basketry and woodturning)

The chouari is the double pannier that is put on the backs of donkeys. These baskets are woven from palm fibre.

Dyers' Souk

Skeins of wool or silk, freshly dyed and still wet, are hung out to dry in the sun and warm air.

Souk Smarine (clothing)

Souk Smata (slippers and belts)
The craftsmen of Marrakech are master-leatherworkers. The craft of leatherworking is said to have originated in the city.

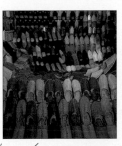

VISITORS' CHECKLIST

Place Jemaa el-Fna (via Rue du Souk Smarine or Bab Doukkala). *A petit taxi or horse-drawn carriage can be taken as far as the entrance to the souks, which must be explored on foot.*
9am–7pm daily.
noon–4pm Fri.

BEN YOUSSEF MOSQUE
BEN YOUSSEF MEDERSA
MUSÉE DE MARRAKECH
KOUBBA BA'ADIYN
RUE SOUK EL KEBIR
RAHBA KEDIMA
Souk Siyyaghin (jewellery)
Souk Fakharin
Souk El-Kebir (leatherwork)
Souk Zarbia (the Criée Berbère, the main carpet market)
Souk El-Maazi (goatskin)
Former slave market

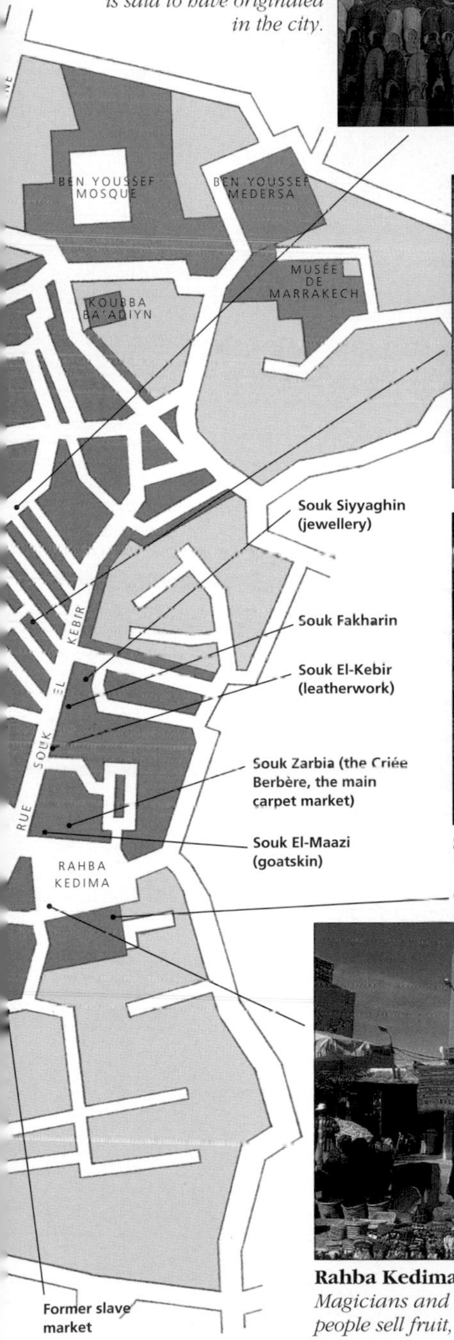

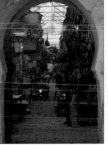

Kissarias
Clothing, fabric, leather goods and passementerie are on sale in these lit and covered galleries. This was once where the most highly prized goods, some of them imported, were sold.

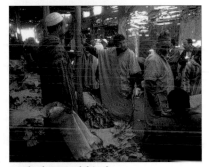

Souk el-Btana (skins)
Thousands of skins for use in leatherwork are sold in the skinners' souk.

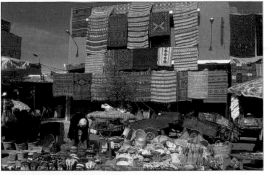

Rahba Kedima, "Old Square"
Magicians and healers buy their supplies here, and country people sell fruit, vegetables and live chickens.

Zellij tilework in the Ben Youssef Medersa

Ben Youssef Medersa ❹

Place ben Youssef *(in the medina)*. **Tel** *(0524) 44 18 93.* ☐ *9am–6pm daily.* 🖼

This Koranic school is not only one of the finest but also one of the largest in the Maghreb, with a capacity for up to 900 students.

It was founded by the Merinid sultan Abou el-Hassan in the mid-14th century, and was rebuilt by the Saadian sultan Moulay Abdallah in the 16th century. This fact is recorded by the inscriptions carved into the lintel above the entrance, together with the date, 1564.

Bronze door of the Ben Youssef Medersa

The medersa takes its name from the Almoravid mosque of Ali ben Youssef to which it was once attached. For four centuries this mosque was the focal point of worship in the medina, and with the medersa it constituted an important centre of religion.

Architecturally, and with its sumptous decoration, it is on a par with the Merinid medersas, particularly the Bou Inania Medersa of Fès *(see pp172–3)*. By building it, Moulay Abdallah was expressing his desire to restore to Marrakech the prestige of an imperial capital and simultaneously to affirm his devotion to Allah.

Covering an area of some 1,720 sq m (18,514 sq ft), this harmoniously proportioned medersa appears as it was originally designed, with no later alteration. The dome, decorated with exquisite stalactites within, can be seen from the street. The main entrance, a bronze door topped by a carved cedar lintel, opens onto a mosaic-paved corridor, which in turn leads to the courtyard. This masterpiece of Moorish design is paved with white marble and has an ablutions pool in the centre. The walls are decorated with *zellij* tilework below and carved plaster above. A double tier of galleries supported on thick columns lines both sides of the courtyard. The students' cells on the ground and upper floors opened onto the courtyard. Those that are shielded from daylight are arranged around seven smaller interior courtyards.

A magnificently ornate doorway leads through to the large prayer hall. The room is crowned by a pyramidal cedar dome and divided into three by marble columns with capitals with calligraphy praising Moulay Abdallah. The mihrab is decorated with verses from the Koran in calligraphic script and is lit by 24 windows decorated with a tracery of plasterwork.

Musée de Marrakech ❺

Place ben Youssef. **Tel** *(0524) 44 18 93.* ☐ *9am–6pm daily.* 🖼

This museum is laid out in the Dar Menebhi, a palace built at the end of the 19th century by the grand vizier of Sultan Moulay Mehdi Hassan. The building is in the style of a traditional Moorish house.

The decorated door – which, as in many Moorish houses, is the only opening in the otherwise featureless external walls – leads through to an open courtyard with *zellij* tilework and three marble basins in the centre. The courtyard gives access to the rooms on the ground and upper floors.

The museum's collection is displayed in two wings. One contains contemporary art, Orientalist paintings and a series of original engravings of Moroccan subjects.

The second wing contains a rather haphazard display of objects: coins from the Idrissid period of the 9th century to that of the Alaouites in the present day; illuminated copies of the Koran, including a 12th-century Chinese example and a 19th-century book of Sufi prayers; southern Moroccan jewellery; Tibetan dress, 17th- and 18th-century ceramics; and some fine decorated Berber doors.

Zellij tilework in the courtyard of the Musée de Marrakech

The Koubba Ba'Adiyn, the only vestige of the Almoravid mosque

Koubba Ba'Adiyn ❻

Place ben Youssef. *Tel (0524) 44 18 93.* ☐ *9am–6pm daily.* ▨

This brick-built dome is the only example of Almoravid architecture in Marrakech. Built by Ali ben Youssef in 1106, originally it formed part of a richly decorated mosque that was demolished by the Almohads. Miraculously spared, the rectangular pavilion was rediscovered in 1948. It contained an ablutions pool fed by three reservoirs. While the exterior is decorated with chevrons and pointed arches in relief, the interior is graced by scalloped and horseshoe arches and floral ornamentation. These elements anticipate the full-blown artistic creativity of Islamic architecture.

Bab Doukkala Mosque ❼

Rue de Bab Doukkala. ◕ to non-Muslims. **Dar el-Glaoui** ◕ to visitors.

This place of worship was built in the mid-16th century by the mother of the Saadian ruler Ahmed el-Mansour. Its slender minaret, crowned by four golden orbs, and its refined decoration are reminiscent of the Kasbah Mosque *(see p238).* Next to the building stands an ornate fountain with a bowl surmounted by three domes.

From here, Rue de Bab Doukkala, going towards the centre of the medina, leads to **Dar el-Glaoui**,

---

AVERROËS

Born in Córdoba in 1126, Averroës (Ibn Rushd) was one of the most renowned Muslim scholars of his day. Like other men of learning at the time, his knowledge encompassed medicine, law, philosophy, astronomy and theology. Born into an important Cordoban family, he was the grandson of an imam at the Great Mosque in Granada. Under the patronage of Abou Yacoub Youssef, Averroës divided his time between Seville, Córdoba and Marrakech. He took the place of his friend and teacher, the famous physician Abubacer (Ibn Tufayl). Basing his approach on his own reading of Aristotle, he promoted a rationalist, rather than an esoteric, interpretation of the Koran. This brought him condemnation from Córdoba. However, he was soon rehabilitated by the Almohad ruler Yacoub el-Mansour, who gave him asylum in Marrakech until his death in December 1198.

Averroës, the great 12th-century philosopher

---

the palace built by El-Glaoui, the famous pasha of Marrakech *(see p57),* at the beginning of the 20th century. While one part of the building contains a library, another is used to receive heads of state during official visits.

The palace has several beautifully decorated courtyards lined with *zellij* tilework, stuccowork, painted wood and *muqarnas* (stalactites). It also features a fine Andalusian garden planted with fruit trees. The palace is reputed to have been the venue for some wild and extravagant parties.

The Souks ❽

See pp228–9.

Mouassine Mosque ❾

Mouassine Quarter. ◕ to non-Muslims.

The Saadian sultan Moulay Abdallah established this place of worship, which was built between 1562 and 1573 on what is thought to be a former Jewish quarter. Its design as well as its decoration

bear certain similarities to the Koutoubia Mosque *(see pp236–7)* and the Kasbah Mosque *(see p238).*

The minaret, which is crowned by a gallery with merlons, is of strikingly simple design. The adjacent Mouassine Fountain consists of three large drinking troughs for animals and a fourth for people. The fountain is enclosed within a portico with decorative stuccowork and carved wooden lintels.

Dar el-Glaoui, palace of the extravagantly hospitable pasha of Marrakech

Small open-air restaurants on Place Jemaa el-Fna

Place Jemaa el-Fna ⑩

East of Gueliz *(off the southern extremity of Avenue Mohammed V).*

For centuries, this unique and extraordinary square has been the nerve centre of Marrakech and the symbol of the city. Although it is in fact no more than an irregular space devoid of a harmonious ensemble of buildings, it is of interest to visitors mainly because it is a show-case of traditional Morocco. UNESCO has declared it a World Heritage Site.

It has a gruesome past: until the 19th century, criminals on whom the death sentence had been passed were beheaded here. Sometimes up to 45 people were executed on a single day, their heads being pickled and suspended from the city gates.

A monkey-handler on Place Jemaa el-Fna

No traces are left of this today. A large market is held in the mornings, and medicinal plants, freshly squeezed orange juice as well as all kinds of nuts and confectionery are sold.

From sunset, the life and bustle on the square reaches its peak. It becomes the arena of a gigantic, multifaceted open-air show. As the air fills with smoke from grilling meat and the aroma of spices, the square fills with musicians, dancers, storytellers, show-men, tooth-pullers, fortune-tellers and snake-charmers, who each draw a crowd of astonished onlookers.

Koutoubia Mosque ⑪

See pp236–7.

La Mamounia Hotel ⑫

Avenue Bab el-Jedid. *Tel (0524) 38 86 00.* See also p316.

Opened in 1923, the legendary hotel La Mamounia stands on the site of a residence that, in the 18th century, belonged to the son of the Alaouite sultan Sidi Mohammed. All that remains of that residence is the magnificent 130,000-sq-m (32-acre) garden, planted with olive and orange trees and containing a pavilion that was probably built by a Saadian ruler in the 16th century.

The original hotel was designed by Henri Prost and Antoine Marchisio, who achieved a pleasing mix of Art Deco and Moorish styles. Many famous people, including Winston Churchill and Richard Nixon, have stayed here. The Mamounia reopened in 2009 following renovations.

Palais Bahia ⑬

Riad Zitoun Jedid *(medina).* *Tel (0524) 38 91 79.* ☐ 9am–4:30pm daily.

This palace, whose name means "Palace of the Favourite", was built by two powerful grand viziers – Si Moussa, vizier of Sultan Sidi Mohammed ben Abderrahman, and his son Ba Ahmed, vizier of Moulay Abdelaziz – at the end of the 19th century.

The palace complex consists of two parts, each built at different times. The older part, built by Si Moussa, contains apartments arranged around a marble-paved court-yard. It also has an open courtyard with cypresses, orange trees and jasmine, with two star-shaped pools.

The newer part, built by Ba Ahmed, is a huge palace without a unified plan. It consists of luxurious apartments looking onto courtyards planted with trees. So as to make it easier for the obese master of the house to move around, almost all the apartments were located on the ground floor. The main

The entrance to the hotel La Mamounia *(see p316)*

◁ La Palmeraie, the famous palm grove in Marrakech, with the High Atlas in the background

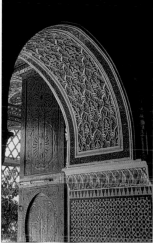

Intricately decorated arch leading to the main courtyard in Palais Bahia

courtyard is paved with marble and *zellij* tilework. It is surrounded by a gallery of finely fluted columns, while three fountains with bowls stand in the centre. This courtyard, once used by the viziers' concubines, faces the main reception room. It has a cedar ceiling painted with arabesques. The decoration of the palace apartments and of the council chamber is equally splendid.

Ba Ahmed hired the best craftsmen in the kingdom to build and decorate this palace. It is decked out with highly prized materials, such as marble from Meknès, cedar from the Middle Atlas and tiles from Tetouan. Not surprisingly, Marshal Lyautey chose to live here during the Protectorate.

Maison Tiskiwin, at No. 8 Rue de la Bahia, houses the **Bert Flint Museum**. This charming residence with a courtyard is an example of a traditional 19th-century Marrakech house. Here, Bert Flint, a Dutch anthropologist who fell in love with Morocco and settled here in the 1950s, amassed a collection of folk art and artifacts from the Souss valley and the Saharan region (*see pp283–96*). Exhibits include jewellery and daggers from the Anti-Atlas, pottery from the Rif and carpets from

the Middle Atlas. The museum is close to another museum, the Dar Si Saïd (*see pp240–41*).

🏛 Bert Flint Museum
8 Rue de la Bahia, Riad Zitoun Jedid. **Tel** *(0524)* 38 91 92. ⬜ *9am–12:30pm & 2:30–6pm.* 📷

Mellah ⑭

East of Palais el-Badi and south of Palais Bahia.

Once accommodating some 16,000 inhabitants, the former Jewish quarter of Marrakech was the largest mellah in Morocco until the country's independence. Previously located on what became the site of the Mouassine Mosque, the mellah was established in the mid-16th century by the Saadian sultan Moulay Abdallah, and it was almost identical to the mellah in Fès (*see p182*). Until 1936, it was surrounded by a wall pierced by two gates, one opening east onto the cemetery and the other leading into the city. The jewellers' souk that is held opposite the Palais Bahia.

Palais el-Badi ⑮

Hay Salam, Rue Berrima. ⬜ *8:45–11:45am & 2:30–5:45pm daily.* 📷

Five months after acceding to the throne, Ahmed el-Mansour decided to consolidate his rule and banish the memory of earlier dynasties. Having emerged victorious

over the Portuguese at the Battle of the Three Kings on 4 August 1578 (*see p52*), Ahmed el-Mansour, "the Golden", ordered a luxurious palace to be built near his private apartments. It was to be used for receptions and audiences with foreign embassies. Its construction was financed by the Portuguese whom he had defeated in battle, and work continued until his death in 1603.

El-Badi, "the Incomparable", is one of the 99 names of Allah. For a time, the palace was indeed considered to be one of the wonders of the Muslim world. Italian marble,

Door opening onto a narrow street in the mellah of Marrakech

Irish granite, Indian onyx and coverings of gold leaf decorated the walls and the ceilings of the 360 rooms.

In 1683, Moulay Ismaïl demolished the Palais el-Badi and salvaged the materials to embellish his own imperial city of Meknès (*see p192*). Today, all that remains of the palace are empty rooms.

The remains of the Palais el-Badi, built in the 16th century

Koutoubia Mosque ⑪

In about 1147, to mark his victory over the Almoravids, the Almohad sultan Abd el-Moumen set about building one of the largest mosques in the Western Muslim world. The minaret, a masterpiece of Islamic architecture, was completed during the reign of Yacoub el-Mansour, grandson of Abd el-Moumen. It later served as the model for the Giralda in Seville, as well as for the Hassan Tower in Rabat *(see p76)*. The "Booksellers' Mosque" takes its name from the manuscripts souk that once took place around it. The interior of the minaret contains a ramp used to carry building materials up to the summit. The mosque has been restored to reveal the original pink colour of the brickwork.

Four gilt-bronze spheres surmount the lantern.

Denticulate merlons

★ Minaret
This splendid tower in pink Gueliz stone stands like a sentinel above the city. It is 70 m (230 ft) high and its proportions obey the canons of Almohad archi-tecture: its height equals five times its width.

The interior of the minaret contains six superimposed rooms.

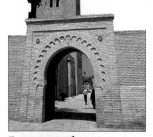

Entrance to the Koutoubia Courtyard
This restrained and simple entrance follows the design of most gateways to important Moroccan buildings: a horseshoe arch with moulded arcature.

Detail of the East Side of the Minaret
Each side of the minaret has a different decorative scheme. Common to all, with variations, are floral motifs, inscriptions, bands of moulded terracotta and, as here, windows with festooned arches.

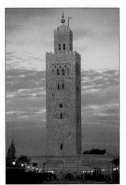

West View of the Minaret
The minaret is the highest building in the city and it stands as a landmark for many miles around. Only Muslims may enjoy the unforgettable view from the top of the building.

VISITORS' CHECKLIST

Place de la Koutoubia.
(0524) 43 61 31/79.
to non-Muslims.

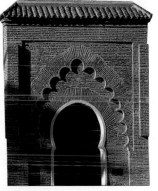

Eastern Entrance to the Prayer Hall
This is the main entrance for the faithful. The design of the doorway is relatively plain, with minimal ornamentation.

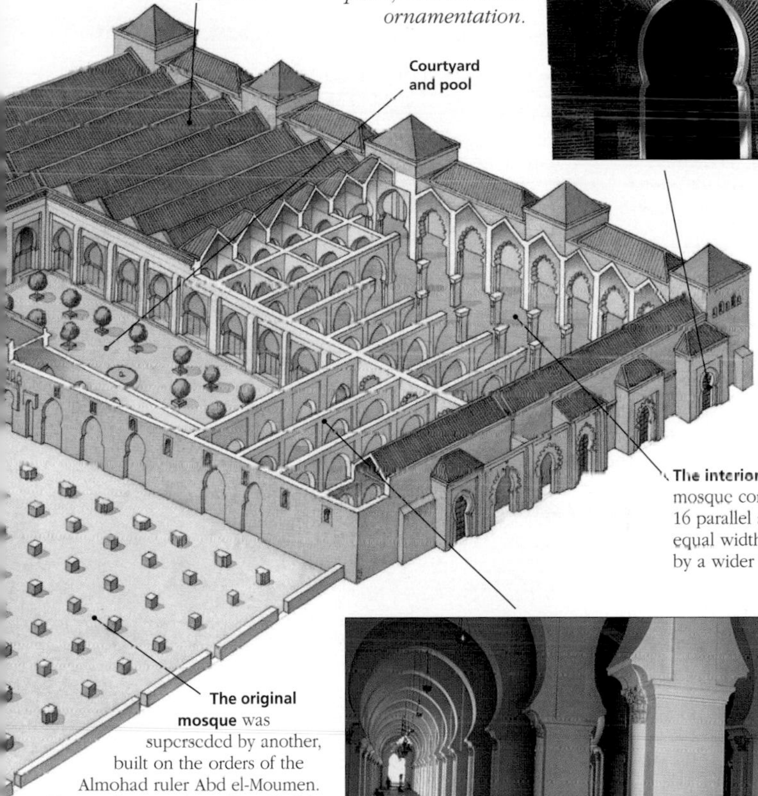

Roof of green tiles
Courtyard and pool

The interior of the mosque consists of 16 parallel aisles of equal width bisected by a wider nave.

The original mosque was superseded by another, built on the orders of the Almohad ruler Abd el-Moumen. This was because the *qibla* wall of the earlier mosque was not accurately oriented towards Mecca. Its foundations can still be seen today.

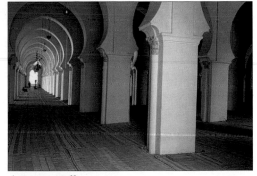

★ Prayer Hall
This can accommodate some 20,000 faithful. The white columns supporting horseshoe arches and the braided pattern of the floor create a striking perspective.

STAR FEATURES

- ★ Minaret
- ★ Prayer Hall

Detail of the minaret of the Kasbah Mosque

Kasbah Mosque ⑯

Rue de la Kasbah, near Bab Agnaou.
⬤ *to non-Muslims.*

Built by Yacoub el-Mansour
(1184–99), the Kasbah
Mosque is the only other
Almohad building besides
Bab Agnaou to survive in
Marrakech. Its distinctive
minaret, a beautiful stone
and brick construction in
shades of ochre, was used
as a model by later builders.
Successive remodelling in the
16th and 17th centuries has
robbed the mosque of its
original appearance. Even
so, it is not without interest.

Built to a rectangular plan,
77m (253 ft) long by 71 m
(233 ft) wide, the mosque
consists of a prayer hall and
five interior courtyards separated by arcades. The 80-m
(263-ft) long façade is topped
by crenellations and denticulate merlons. According to
Almohad custom, the minaret
is devoid of ornamentation
up to the height of the walls.
Above this, it has restrained
decoration and is crowned
by an attractive terracotta
frieze. Turquoise tiles
moulded with a magnificent
pattern of interlaced lozenges
almost completely cover the
four faces of the minaret.

Two-fifths of the tower
are taken up by the lantern,
which is crowned by three
spheres. These are made of
brass, but legend has it that
they are made of gold, hence
their popular name, the
Golden Apples.

Saadian Tombs ⑰

Rue de la Kasbah. ℹ (0524) 43 61
31. ◯ 9am–noon & 2–6pm
Wed–Mon. 📷

Although they were neglected
for more than two centuries,
the tombs of the Saadian
dynasty constitute some of
the finest examples of Islamic
architecture in Morocco. Their
style is in complete contrast
to the simplicity of Almohad
architecture, as the Saadian
princes lavished on funerary
architecture the same ostenta-
tion and magnificence that
they gave to other buildings.

A necropolis existed here
during the Almohad period
(1145–1248), continuing in
use during the reign of the
Merinid sultan Abou el-Hassan
(1331–51). The Saadian Tombs
themselves date from the late
16th to the 18th centuries. Out
of respect for the dead, and
even though he had been at
pains to erase all traces of his
predecessors, the Alaouite
sultan Moulay Ismaïl raised a
wall round the main entrance.

It was not until 1917 that
the tombs were made accessible to the public. They

Mausoleum of Ahmed el-Mansour, with marble-columned mihrab

consist of two mausoleums
which are set in a garden
planted with flowers
symbolizing Allah's paradise.

The central mausoleum is
that of Ahmed el-Mansour
(1578–1603). It consists of
three funerary rooms laid out
to a plan reminiscent of that
of the Rawda in Granada. The
first room is a prayer hall
divided into three aisles by
white marble columns. The
mihrab is decorated with
stalactites and framed by
a pointed horseshoe arch
supported by grey marble

Ornate capitals on the columns in the Saadian Tombs

pilasters. The prayer hall is lit by the three windows of the lantern, which rests on a cedar base decorated with inscriptions.

The central room, a great masterpiece of Moorish architecture, is crowned by a remarkable dome with stalactites. Of carved cedar with gold-leaf decoration, it is supported by 12 columns of Carrara marble. The walls are completely covered – the lower part by a graceful interlacing pattern of glazed tiles, and the upper part by a profusion of stuccowork.

In the centre of the room lie Ahmed el-Mansour and his successors. The ivory-coloured marble tombstones are covered with arabesques and inscriptions arranged on two levels: above are verses from the Koran, and below a framed epitaph in verse. The third room, known as the Hall of the Three Niches, has an equally sumptuous decorative scheme. It contains the tombs of young princes.

The second mausoleum, a green-roofed building, has more modest proportions. It consists of a room and a prayer hall. A cedar lintel carved with inscriptions links the columns of the loggias. In the prayer hall, the dome hung with stalactites is a splendid sight.

In the burial chamber the tomb of Lalla Messaouda, mother of Ahmed "the Golden", who died in 1591, fills a honeycombed niche.

Bab Agnaou ⑱

Rue de la Kasba, opposite the Kasbah Mosque.

Like its twin, Bab Oudaïa in Rabat (see pp68–9), this monumental gate was built by Yacoub el-Mansour. Its name means "hornless black ram" in Berber.

Protected by Bab el-Robb (see p227), the outer defensive gate, Bab Agnaou marked the main entrance to the Almohad palace, and its function was thus primarily decorative.

Although the gate no longer has its two towers, the façade

Bab Agnaou, the royal entrance to the old Almohad palace

still makes for an impressive sight. In the carved sandstone tinges of red meld with tones of greyish-blue.

The sculpted façade consists of alternating layers of stone and brick surrounding a horseshoe arch. The floral motifs in the cornerpieces and the frieze with Kufic script framing the arch are unusually delicate.

This is another example of the sober, monochrome style of decoration that is typical of Almohad architecture and that gives the gate a dignified and majestic appearance.

Dar el-Makhzen ⑲

Southeast of the Saadian Tombs. ⬤ to the public.

When Sidi Mohammed ben Abdallah arrived in Marrakech in the 18th century, he found the Almohad and Saadian palaces in a state of ruin. On an extensive area within the kasbah that he enclosed within bastioned walls, he ordered a royal palace, Dar el Makhzen, to be built, next to the ruins of the Palais el-Badi.

Sidi Mohammed's building project is notable because, unlike the design of other palaces in Marrakech, it took into account the perspective and dimensions of the terrain.

Restored countless times, Dar el-Makhzen consists of several groups of buildings: the Green Palace (el-Qasr el-Akhdar), the Nile Garden (Gharsat el-Nil) and the main

house (el-Dar el-Kubra), as well as outbuildings and several pavilions (menzah) set in the park. The palace is still a royal residence today.

Méchouars ⑳

Near Dar el-Makhzen.

Dar el-Makhzen has three large parade grounds, known as méchouars, where royal ceremonies are held.

The inner méchouar, located south of the palace, is connected to it by Bab el-Akhdar and is linked to the Aguedal Gardens. The outer méchouar, east of the palace, is connected to the Berrima quarter by Bab el-Harri. The large méchouar south of the inner méchouar is outlined by a wall set with merlons.

Procession gathering on one of the méchouars at Dar el-Makhzen

Dar Si Saïd Museum ㉑

A stone's throw from the Palais Bahia *(see pp234–5)* is the contemporary Dar Si Saïd. This delightful palace, now a museum, was built in the late 19th century by Si Saïd ben Moussa, brother of Ba Ahmed and a vizier of Moulay Abdel Aziz. Consisting of *zellij* tilework, intricate plasterwork and carved or painted wooden domes, the decoration alone is worth the visit.

Detail of the door of the reception room

THE PALACE

Following Islamic tradition, the palace is enclosed within solid walls and consists of a two-storey central building arranged around courtyards with graceful arcades. It also has an Andalusian garden, with a pavilion and fountain in the centre.

The sumptuous **Reception Room** on the upper floor is a jewel of Moorish design. The cedar dome and the walls, with *zellij* tilework and a stuccowork frieze, are a mesmerizing sight.

The room contains a wooden candelabrum, a cedar sofa and benches covered with colourful fabric. From the topmost floor there is a view over the medina and towards the High Atlas.

THE COLLECTIONS

Converted into a museum in 1932, Dar Si Saïd houses a fine collection of carpets, doors, chests, weapons, ceramics, costume and jewellery illustrating the skill of the craftsmen of southern Morocco, particularly of the High Atlas, the Tafilalt, the Anti-Atlas, the Souss and the Tensift.

Also on display are a few archaeological pieces and architectural fragments from Fès. The museum's collections are laid out thematically on three levels.

DOORS AND CARRIAGES

Entry to the museum is through an imposing door studded with nails and fitted with locks. A map at the entrance shows the geographical location of the main centres of craft production in southern Morocco.

Marble basin for ritual ablutions

Arranged along the walls are a cedar chest and some interesting old doors from the region's kasbahs and *ksour* (fortified villages). These unusual and finely worked doors consist of a single panel of oak, almond wood, poplar or walnut. Some of them are decorated with applied relief patterns of wood cut to geometrical shapes. Others are decorated with engraved or painted motifs. As these doors were made by craftsmen working in isolation in a rural environment, they are unique pieces, each one different from the next.

At the end of the corridor a splendid basin for ritual ablutions is on display. The basin was carved from a single block of marble in Andalusia in the late 10th or early 11th century. The decoration features three tiers of ornament: floral motifs, four-legged creatures and heraldic eagles.

The next room contains a display of antique children's carriages and swings.

JEWELLERY

Located to the left of the entrance, the room in which jewellery is displayed holds a collection of headdresses typical of southern Morocco as well as earrings, diadems, finger rings, necklaces, fibulas (pin-like brooches), bracelets and anklets.

These pieces are engraved, inlaid with niello (a black

The pavilion and fountain of the *riad* (Andalusian garden)

compound) or enamelled, and are set with polished gems, shells, coral, amber or coins.

Geometric shapes such as rectangles, triangles, lozenges, circles, crosses and zigzags are the principal Berber motifs. Some have a symbolic meaning: for example, motifs arranged in sets of five refer to the fingers of one hand, symbolizing life, creativity and representing a lucky charm. Arabesques and floral motifs, by contrast, belong to the Moorish canon of decorative motifs.

Mastered by Jewish metal-workers, these various styles led to the creation of jewellery inspired both by city and rural traditions.

and various dishes. These pieces, most of which are made of terracotta, have incised, relief or painted decoration.

Two major regional types of pottery can be seen in this room. One is from Safi (see p118), a continuation of the Fassi tradition and characterized by restrained polychrome decoration, often on a white ground. The other is from Tamegroute (see p269), south of Zagora, typified by glazed monochrome ware in which green predominates.

Silver pendant from the Tafilalt

VISITORS' CHECKLIST

Riad Zitoune Jedid.
Tel (0524) 38 95 64.
⬛ 9am–4pm
Wed–Mon. 🖼

objects such as teapots and combs. Certain motifs are based on tribal tattoos.

The more unusual figure of a horseman was brought from the Sudan by slaves who worked in local plantations.

WOODWORK

The interesting collection of woodwork displayed in the second courtyard includes house doors, house frontages and delicate *mashrabiyya* (screenwork), some of it painted in bright colours. These architectural elements, most of them carved in cedar, originate from old houses and shops in Marrakech. The beautiful pieces in wood and marble dating from the Saadian period (16th century) are not to be missed.

Cedar dome on the ceiling of the reception room

POTTERY

The room on the right of the entrance contains a display of everyday objects consisting mostly of pottery from Amizmiz, stone oil lamps from Taroudannt, amphorae, pitchers, storage jars, churns, cooking pots

CARPETS

The upper floor is devoted to village carpets, most notably those from the Tensift and Boujad. The display includes antique carpets and thick woollen blankets (*banbel*) in which madder-red predominates. The latter are loosely woven so as to retain more warmth.

The display continues in the second courtyard with carpets from the High Atlas. These include Glaoui and Ouaouzguite carpets, which are both embroidered, woven and knotted and which feature bright colours. Carpets from Chichaoua, with a red or rosewood background, display a variety of motifs: geometric patterns including zigzags, chevrons and squares; animal motifs depicting snakes, scorpions and camels; and motifs derived from everyday

A room in the richly decorated former palace

COSTUME

The corridor leading to the exit contains a display of boots and burnouses worn by the shepherds of the Siroua mountains. Made of black wool, they are decorated with motifs worked in cotton or in silk. Such garments are still worn today, although the workmanship is less refined.

GALLERY GUIDE

The building has three storeys. The exhibition rooms on the ground floor open onto the riad. Beyond the entrance, large-scale pieces such as wooden doors and chests are displayed. To the left of the entrance is the jewellery room, and on the right of it are displays of everyday objects. Next comes the pottery room. The room at the far end of the garden contains objects made of brass and copper, and in the second courtyard is a display of woodwork. The reception room is on the first floor while village carpets can be seen on the second floor. The corridor leading to the exit displays the traditional costume of the Ouzguita tribe.

The pool and pavilion in the Menara imperial garden

Aguedal Gardens ㉒

Rue Bab Ahmar. Reached via the outer méchouar near Bab Ighli. ◯ *daily.*

This vast enclosed space, 3 km (2 miles) long and 1.5 km (1 mile) wide, contains an orchard planted with lemon, orange, apricot and olive trees.

The historic gardens were laid out in the second half of the 12th century by the Almoravids, who also installed two large irrigation pools connected by *khettaras*, or underground channels *(see pp276–7)*. Enlarged and embellished by the Almohads, and later by the Saadians, the gardens were then completely neglected until the 19th century. At that time the

One of the many orange trees in the Aguedal Gardens

Alaouite sultans Moulay Abderrahman and Sidi Mohammed ben Abdallah restored the gardens and the pavilions. So as to provide irrigation, they also diverted the course of Wadi Ourika. Gates were also built into the surrounding wall.

While the public have free access to the gardens, the pavilions, on the northern side, are for the exclusive use of the king's guests. Dar el-Hana, the largest pool, located south of the garden, dates from the Almohad period. The terrace of the small Saadian pavilion that stands next to it commands stunning views in two opposite directions: northwards across olive groves and the city rising in tiers to the hill of Jbilet, and south-wards to the serene and distant snow-capped peaks of the High Atlas.

Pavilion window in Aguedal Gardens

Menara ㉓

Avenue de la Ménara (west of Hivernage). ◯ *8am–noon & 2–6pm daily.*

A welcome haven of coolness and shade, this imperial garden, covering almost 90 ha (220 acres) and enclosed within pisé walls, is filled mostly with olive and fruit trees. In the 12th century, an enormous pool was dug in the centre of the garden to serve as a reservoir for the Almohad sultans. In the 19th century, Moulay Abderrahman refurbished the garden and built the pavilion with a green-tiled pyramidal roof. This attractive building was used by the sultans for their romantic meetings. It is said that every morning one of them would toss into the water the concubine that he had chosen the night before. The ground floor is fronted by three arches opening onto the pool. The upper floor has a large balustered balcony on its north side. Although the interior decoration is plain, the building's overall conception and location are remarkable, and the view from any point within, with the peaks of the Atlas as a back-drop, is quite unforgettable.

Guéliz ㉔

Northwest of the medina.

Established during the Protectorate, Guéliz is the Ville Nouvelle (New Town). Taking its name from the hill that rises above it, this commercial district was designed by Henri Prost. It has a spacious layout in line with the principles of modern town planning.

The wide avenues, municipal gardens, large hotels and cafés with shady terraces make Guéliz a pleasant quarter to visit. Avenue Mohammed V, which runs between Guéliz and the medina, is lined with offices, banks, restaurants, bars, pavement cafés and chic shops.

Despite the number of modern buildings, a few vestiges of the European architecture introduced by the French remain. A notable example of this style, known as "Mauresque", is the **Renaissance Café**, on Place Abdel Moumen ben Ali. It is decorated in typical 1950s style and has a dining area on the top floor with panoramic views.

A large municipal market takes place daily in Place du 16 Novembre. It is worth a visit to take in the atmosphere as local shoppers purchase their fresh fruit, vegetables, herbs and spices.

An apartment block in Guéliz, Marrakech's Ville Nouvelle

Majorelle Garden ㉕

Avenue Yacoub el-Mansour (near the bus station). ◯ 8am–noon & 2–6pm daily.

This wonderful garden is like a small paradise in the heart of Ville Nouvelle (the new town). In 1923, Jacques Majorelle (see above) fell in love with Morocco and built himself a splendid Moorish villa, which he called Bou Safsaf, in Marrakech. He designed the patterns of the zellij tilework, painted the front door, and decorated the interior in tones of deep blue, green and dark red. Around the house he laid out a

Villa Majorelle, the painter's residence in Marrakech

JACQUES MAJORELLE

The painter Jacques Majorelle was born in Nancy, in northeastern France, in 1886. The son of the renowned cabinet-maker Louis Majorelle, one of the leading figures of the École de Nancy, he was raised in the artistic milieu of Art Nouveau. He seemed destined to follow in his father's footsteps. However, after studying at the École des Beaux-Arts in Paris, Majorelle decided to devote himself to painting. He travelled to Spain, Italy and Egypt. Recovering from health problems, he went to Morocco in 1919 and fell in love with its intense light. Aided by Marshal Lyautey, he settled in Marrakech, in his now-famous villa. Finding fascination in the souks, kasbahs and villages of the High Atlas, he stayed in Morocco until his death in 1962.

luxuriant garden. In 1931, at Majorelle's request, the architect Sinoir built an Art Deco studio with pergolas and bright blue walls. The garden, which is separate from the house, opened to the public in 1947.

The house was later bought by Yves Saint-Laurent, the famous couturier, and Pierre Bergé. Skilfully restored, the garden is divided by four walkways that cross each other to create parterres of brightly coloured tropical flowers. Besides yucca, bougainvillea, bamboo, laurel, geraniums, hibiscus and cypresses, the garden has over 400 varieties of palm tree and 1,800 species of cactus. Water lilies grow in a pool bordered by papyrus.

The studio was later converted into a small museum that contains a selection of Moroccan crafts such as antique carpets, Fassi ceramics and Berber doors, and some 40 engravings of the villages and kasbahs of the Atlas executed by Jacques Majorelle.

La Palmeraie ㉖

On the road to Casablanca, 22 km (14 miles) north of Marrakech. This interesting tour, 22.5 km (14 miles) long, can be made by car or horse-drawn carriage.

Legend has it that, after eating dates brought back from the Sahara, the soldiers of the 11th-century Almoravid sultan Youssef ben Tachfine spat out the stones around their encampment. The stones are supposed to have germinated and led to the creation of La Palmeraie (Palm Grove) in Marrakech.

Covering an area of some 120 sq km (46 sq miles), the grove consists of fields, gardens and orchards irrigated by ditches and wells supplied by khettaras. Although it contains 150,000 trees, the agricultural function of the grove is being pared away by the advance of buildings and the greed of developers who are making inroads into it by building desirable residences here.

La Palmeraie (Palm Grove) in Marrakech, with 150,000 trees

HIGH ATLAS

*L**ittle-known because of its relative inaccessibility, the High Atlas makes up the largest massif in the Atlas chain. It is also the highest mountain range in North Africa. In this geographical isolation Berber culture and identity prospered. Over the centuries, the tribes established their own economic and social framework, and a unique collective way of life, based on blood ties and solidarity.*

Extending from the plains of the Atlantic seaboard to Morocco's border with Algeria, the High Atlas forms an impregnable barrier some 800 km (500 miles) long and, in certain places, 100 km (60 miles) wide. Consisting of great massifs rising to heights of 3,000–4,000 m (10,000–13,000 ft), and steep valleys, desolate rocky plains and deep narrow canyons, the High Atlas has played a decisive role in the history of Morocco.

From earliest times these mountains have been a place of refuge for populations fleeing from invaders. For centuries, nomads forced northwards by the desertification of the Sahara have come into conflict with the sedentary mountain-dwelling tribes, disputing possession of prized pasture. This tumultuous feudal past led to the development of a strikingly beautiful form of fortified architecture. Today, although the Berbers no longer need to guard their safety, they still live in *tighremts*, old patriarchal houses with thick walls. Hamlets built of pisé still cling to mountainsides, while every last plot of land is used to grow barley, corn, maize, turnips, lucerne and potatoes – crops that can be cultivated at high altitudes. The Berbers channel river water to irrigate small squares of land and graze their flocks of sheep and goats, which they raise for milk, butter and wool.

Sometimes isolated by snowfall in winter, the Berbers of the High Atlas live and work by the seasons, the constant round of labour punctuated by various festivals.

The kasbah in Telouet, abandoned in 1956

◁ Muleteer with heavily laden beast in a village in the High Atlas

Exploring the High Atlas

Crowned with high peaks, the chain of the High Atlas culminates in the west in Jbel Toubkal. At 4,167 m (13,676 ft), this is the highest peak in North Africa, with pisé villages nestling on its lower slopes. In the centre, Jbel M'Goun, at 4,068 m (13,351 ft), rises over the Tessaout, Aït Bouguemez and Aït Bou Oulli valleys. The only channels of communication between these valleys are mule trails and high passes. On the banks of the *wadi* that snakes along the valley bottoms, villages cluster around fortified houses, punctuating expanses of cultivated land. The eastern end of the High Atlas is marked by the imposing outline of Jbel Ayachi, 3,737 m (12,265 ft) high. Here high desert plateaus stretch to the horizon. From late spring to early autumn they are filled with flocks of grazing sheep.

LOCATOR MAP

KEY

▬▬	Motorway
▬	Major road
═══	Minor road
- - -	Track
▬●▬	Railway
△	Summit
✕	Pass

SEE ALSO

• *Where to Stay* pp317–18

• *Where to Eat* p340

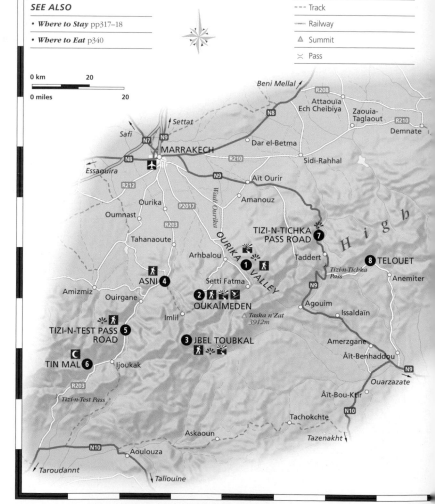

0 km   20

0 miles   20

Beni Mellal
R208
Attaouïa
Ech Cheibiya
Zaouia-
Taglaout
R210
Demnate
Settat
N8
Safi
N7 N9
Dar el-Betma
N8
MARRAKECH
R210
Sidi-Rahhal
Essaouira
R212
N9
Aït Ourir
Ourika
P2017
Amanouz
Oumnast
R203
TIZI-N-TICHKA
PASS ROAD 7
Tahanaoute
OURIKA VALLEY
High
Arhbalou
Taddert
8 TELOUET
ASNI 4
Setti Fatma 1
Tizi-n-Tichka
Pass
Anemiter
Amizmiz
Ouirgane
2 OUKAÏMEDEN
N9
Agouim
Issaldaïn
Imlil
Taska n'Zat
3912m
TIZI-N-TEST PASS
ROAD 5
3 JBEL TOUBKAL
Amerzgane
Aït-Benhaddou
TIN MAL 6
Ijoukak
N9
R203
Ouarzazate
Tizi-n-Test Pass
Aït-Bou-Kti̇r
N10
Tachokchte
Askaoun
Tazenakht
R203
N10
Aoulouza
Taroudannt
Tal:ouine

For additional map symbols see back flap

SIGHTS
AT A GLANCE

Aït Bouguemez Valley
 pp254–7 **9**
Asni **4**
Imilchil **10**
MARRAKECH pp222–43
Oukaïmeden **2**
Ourika Valley **1**
Telouet **8**
Tin Mal **6**
Tizi-n-Test Pass Road **5**
Tizi-n-Tichka Pass Road **7**

Tour

The Jbel Toubkal Massif **3**

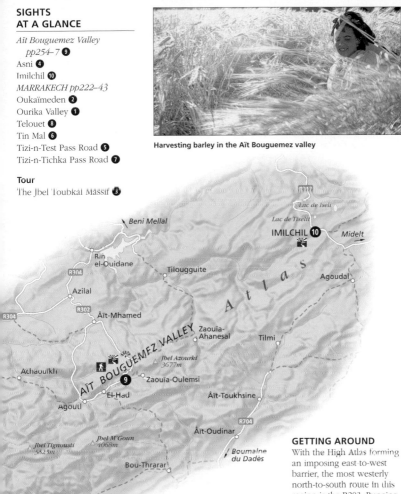

Harvesting barley in the Aït Bouguemez valley

GETTING AROUND

With the High Atlas forming an imposing east-to-west barrier, the most westerly north-to-south route in this region is the R203. Running from Marrakech, it crosses the Tizi-n-Test Pass and leads to Taroudannt and Agadir. South-east of Marrakech, another road, the N9, via the Tizi-n-Tichka Pass, leads to Ouarzazate. In the central stretch of the mountain chain, there is no road over the High Atlas for 200 km (124 miles). Only a track, which is often impassable in winter, crosses the lake-filled plateau to reach the Dadès valley. On the eastern side, a road from Fès runs along the Middle and High Atlas, leading via Midelt to the Tafilalt valley.

The village of Dar Caïd Ouriki, at the entrance to the Ourika valley

Wadi Ourika, irrigating a valley of fruit tree plantations

Ourika Valley ❶

Road map C4. 68 km (42 miles) from Marrakech on road P2017. 🚌 *from Marrakech; alternatively, by taxi.* 🛈 *Marrakech; (0524) 43 61 31.* 🎪 *Moussem of Setti Fatma (mid-Aug).*

The trip to the Ourika valley, 68 km (42 miles) southeast of Marrakech, offers a pleasant tour of the lower foothills of the Atlas. Beyond the village of **Tnine-de-l'Ourika**, the valley, through which flows the Ourika, becomes verdant. The largest souk in the valley takes place in the village on Mondays.

All along the road that follows the course of the *wadi*, small houses, cafés, grocery shops and small hotels cling to the hillside. Gardens and plots of cultivated land shaded by many fruit trees are laid out along the valley bottom. The Ourika river is occasionally subject to

sudden and devastating flooding, such as in August 1995, when many houses were swept away.

Beyond Arhbalou, at an altitude of 1,500 m (4,923 ft), the valley narrows and gently rises. The road comes to an end at **Setti Fatma**, a good starting point for hikes. Seven waterfalls flow down the rocky scree above the village. The first of these is easy to reach by walking up the course of the *wadi*. The walk up to the others is over more uneven ground, and some climbing is involved, so that you will need strong walking boots. From that vantage point there is a superb view over Setti Fatma.

The village may also be used as the starting point for longer hikes to Jbel Toubkal and Yagour Plateau, whose peak is well known for the hundreds of rock engravings that can be seen here.

The tomb of Setti Fatma is the focus of a *moussem* that takes place in the village in mid-August. This religious pilgrimage is also an occasion when Berbers from a wide area can gather together.

Oukaïmeden ❷

Road map C4. 74 km (46 miles) from Marrakech on road P2017. 🚌 *from Marrakech, then taxi.* 🛈 *Marrakech; (0524) 43 61 31.*

A ski resort in winter and base for mountain hikes in summer, Oukaïmeden is a haven of fresh air, just over one hour from Marrakech.

The resort is easily reached on a road that forks off to the right at the village of Arhbalou, with the Ourika valley on the left. Shaded by olive, oak and walnut trees, the road then winds upwards in a series of hairpin bends through a stony landscape.

The chalets and winter sports facilities are in the village itself, encircled by mountain peaks: Jbel Oukaïmeden, rising to a height of 3,273 m (10,742 ft), Jbel Ouhattar, at 3,258 m (10,693 ft), and Jbel Angour, at 3,614 m (11,861 ft). The great Oukaïmeden plateau is carpeted in pasture, the grazing of which is controlled by tradition.

From November to April, if the snow is sufficiently deep, a chair lift – the highest in North Africa – runs up to the summit of Jbel Oukaïmeden, while several ski lifts allow beginners to practise on the lower slopes. The resort also offers long-distance and cross-country skiing.

Rock engravings can be seen in the village and on the plateau. Dating from the Bronze Age, they depict mainly daggers, halbards, shields and humans.

About 2 km (1 mile) from the resort, the site of a transmission mast at an altitude of 2,740 m (8,993 ft) commands a magnificent view of the Atlas and the plain where Marrakech is located. In summer, Oukaïmeden is also the starting point for mountain hikes, particularly up to the Tizi-n-Ouaddi Pass, the beautiful village of Tacheddirt, and to Imlil and the Tizi-n-Test.

The ski resort at Oukaïmeden, built in 1950

Tour of the Jbel Toubkal Massif ❸

As well as the opportunity to climb to the top of Jbel Toubkal, at 4,167 m (13,676 ft) the highest peak in the Atlas, the Jbel Toubkal massif offers great scope for hikes lasting several days. Climbing Toubkal is not particularly difficult, but the fact that it is a high-altitude hike over rough terrain should be taken into account. From the Toubkal Refuge, the summit of Jbel Toubkal can be reached in about four hours. For the finest view over the High Atlas, it is best to reach the summit in the late morning.

Tacheddirt ⑦
This pretty village, at 2314 m (7,595 ft) and set amid mountains, is reached via the Tizi-n-Tamatert Pass, east of Imlil.

Lepiney Hut ⑧
Located at the start of the hike up the Azzaden valley and across the Tazarhart plateau, at 3,000 m (9,846 ft), the hut is used by seasoned hikers and rock climbers.

Imlil ①
Surrounded by walnut and fruit trees, this mountain village is the starting point for the climb up Jbel Toubkal and also for many other mountain hikes.

Aremd ②
The village, in the Mizane valley, lies at 1,900 m (6,236 ft). Its stone houses cling to the rocky mountainside, surrounded by cultivated terraces.

Sidi Chamharouch ③
At the end of a deep gorge, the *koubba* of Sidi Chamharouch, king of the *djnoun* (genies), attracts pilgrims all year-round.

Toubkal Refuge ④
This is the last stopping place before the summit of Jbel Toubkal. The refuge, at 3,200 m (10,502 ft), is open all year-round.

Jbel Angour
3,616 m (11,868 ft) ⑦

Aksoual ▲ 3,842 m (12,609)

Tichki ▲ 3,753 m (12,317 ft)

Tazarhart ▲ 3,843 m (12,615 ft)

Tizi-n-Ouanoums

Ouanoukrim ▲ 4,088 m (13,417 ft)

Tizi Oussem

Azib Tamsoult

Ouaneskra

Tamatert

ASNI

P2015

Lake Ifni ⑥
The lake, five hours' walk from Toubkal Refuge, lies in a mineral-rich environment. Shepherds' huts stand on the lakeshore.

Jbel Toubkal ⑤
You can climb to the top at the end of winter: it offers breathtaking views over the whole of the High Atlas.

KEY

- `-- -` Tour route (footpath)
- `== =` Track
- ⚡ Viewpoint

0 km 5

0 miles 5

TIPS FOR HIKERS

Reasonably fit hikers can climb to the summit of Jbel Toubkal without a guide.
Starting point: *Imlil, 17 km (10.5 miles) from Asni on road P2015, or 1 hour and 30 minutes from Marrakech.*
When to go: *April to October offers the best conditions.*
Huts: *Toubkal (5 hours from Imlil), Lépiney (two days' walk from the Tazarhart plateau) and Tacheddirt (2 hours and 30 minutes from Imlil).*
Information: *Detailed maps of the area can be obtained from the guides' office at Imlil. Mules can also be hired for walks lasting several days.*

The village of Asni, encircled by the Tamaroute mountains

Asni ❹

Road map C4. 42 km (26 miles) from Marrakech on road R203. *from Marrakech, then by taxi.* *Sat.*

With an interesting red-walled kasbah, Asni is the first large village on the road from Marrakech to the Tizi-n-Test Pass. Attractive orchards surround the village and there are many mule tracks leading up to the plateaux in its vicinity.

From this small settlement, a metalled road leads to the village of Imlil, which is the starting point for hikes to Jbel Toubkal *(see p249)*.

Environs

The very popular *moussem* at **Moulay Brahim**, 5 km (3 miles) from Asni, takes place one to two weeks after the festival of Mouloud *(see p41)*. Moroccans ascribe to the saint Moulay Brahim the power to cure barren women. Pilgrims come to lay their gifts before his tomb and to hang small pieces of fabric from the shrubs here. When one of these fragments falls from the shrub, the woman who hung it may expect a child.

Tizi-n-Test Pass Road ❺

Road map B-C4. Accessible from Marrakech on road R203. *from Marrakech or Taroudannt.* *Thu in Ouirgane; Wed in Ijoukak.*

Beyond Asni, the road crosses the High Atlas, then runs down into the Souss plain. This road, in a good state of repair although narrow and tortuous in

places, was built by the French in the 1930s.

Just before Ouirgane, a small road to the right leads to **Amizmiz**, a pretty village with a ruined kasbah, set in the midst of olive trees. The souk here is renowned for Berber pottery made in the village itself. **Ouirgane** is a resort whose coolness in summer makes it popular with the inhabitants of Marrakech. A few salt mines are still worked here.

As the road climbs further up to the Tizi-n-Test Pass, snaking through red, almost purple terrain, the landscape becomes more wild. Starting from **Ijoukak**, keen hikers can reach the Agoundis valley, walking in the direction of Taghbart and El-Maghzen, or make for the Jbel Toubkal massif. Beyond Ijoukak, the massive Tin Mal mosque is visible on the right.

Below the Tizi-n-Test Pass, imposing deserted kasbahs perch on arid out-crops. They all date from the end of the 19th century and belonged to the Goundafa, a powerful Berber tribe that controlled access to the pass. From November to April, the pass, at an altitude of 2,093 m (6,869 ft) is sometimes

Tizi-n-Test pottery

blocked by snow. The descent offers a beautiful view of the Souss plain and of hills covered with argan trees, 2,000 m (6,564 ft) below.

Tin Mal ❻

Road map B4. About 25 km (15.5 miles) south of Asni on road R203. **Mosque** *daily, except Friday for non-Muslims. To visit the mosque, ask the caretaker in the village of Tin Mal.*

In an isolated setting at the foot of the Atlas, 10 km (6 miles) beyond Ijoukak on the Tizi-n-Test Pass road, the **Mosque of Tin Mal** situated uphill from the village, is the last remaining sign of the Almohad conquest in the 12th century.

Tin Mal, once a fortified holy town, was founded by the theologian Ibn Toumart in 1125. From here, he fomented a holy war against the Almoravids and was recognized as a religious leader by the Berber tribes of the High Atlas.

In 1276, the town was sacked and pillaged by the Merinids. Only the sumptuous mosque was left standing. It was built in 1153 by Abd el-Moumen, Ibn Toumart's successor and the first Almohad ruler.

The tortuous road winding up to the Tizi-n-Test Pass

◁ The village of Magdaz, built on an outcrop of rock

The mosque at Tin Mal, with pink brickwork and plaster stalactites

The mosque has been restored and as a UNESCO World Heritage Site, it is one of the few religious buildings in Morocco that is open to non-Muslims. Its high walls and sturdy towers give it a fortress-like look.

Tizi-n-Tichka Pass Road ❼

Road map C4. From Marrakech or Ouarzazate on road N9.
🚌 Marrakech or Ouarzazate.
🕐 Tue in Aït Ourir.

Built by the French in the 1920s, this winding road runs through a landscape that is, by turn, arid, mineral-rich environments and fertile valleys. Pisé villages, in tones of red or grey, huddle at the foot of hillsides.

The first pass, **Tizi-n-Aït Imger**, at an altitude of 1,470 m (4,825 ft), offers a panoramic view of the Atlas chain. Here, the road is lined with stalls selling pottery, mineral rocks and stones whose colours are a little too bright to be natural.

From here up to the **Tizi-n-Tichka Pass** – which, at an altitude of 2,260 m (7,417 ft), is the highest road pass in Morocco – crops gradually give way to a landscape of bare red soil. The mountains become more rounded and the houses are built higher, with more decoration, anticipating those of the Moroccan south. The impressive fortified grainstore on the way out of **Igherm-n-Ougdal** is open to visitors.

Beyond Agouim, on the other side of the *wadi*, stands the restored kasbah at **El-Mdint**, its towers decorated with relief patterns. Palm trees come into view, and a wide stony desert plain with tones of pink and beige leads to Ouarzazate.

Interior of the fortified grainstore at Igherm-n-Ougdal

Telouet ❽

Road map C4. Accessible from road N9. 🕐 daily; caretaker on the premises.

About 5 km (3 miles) along the road running down from the Tizi-n-Tichka Pass, towards Ouarzazate, a narrow metalled minor road leads off to the left. It drops down into a steep valley, and 20 km (12 miles) further on reaches the kasbah of Telouet.

This was one of the principal residences of Al-Thami el-Glaoui, pasha of Marrakech, whose fiefdom covered a large part of the High Atlas. El-Glaoui served the sultan, then switched to the French in 1912. His opposition to Sultan Mohammed V cost

him dear, for on his death his family was exiled and his possessions dispersed.

Thus it was that Telouet, a town with an illustrious past, has been the victim of neglect since 1956. The glazed tiles are disintegrating, the lookout towers crumbling, the walls cracking and the windows shattered. Most of the rooms are inaccessible since the roof has fallen in.

However, low-ceilinged, bare-walled corridors lead to two reception rooms that have miraculously survived the passage of time. They are vestiges of the opulence treasured by El-Glaoui. The Andalusian-style rooms have engraved stuccowork, painted cedar ceilings and doors, and colourful *zellij* tilework. Daylight entering through a glass-covered dome and a small window framed with decorative wrought iron lights the rooms from dawn to sunset.

Environs

From Telouet, a narrow, winding metalled road offers a picturesque route to the village of **Aït Benhaddou** (*see p265*). In this fertile valley, planted with palm, fig and olive trees, and irrigated by Wadi Ounila, kasbahs signal the past importance of El-Glaoui's fiefdom. The attractive village of **Anemiter**, standing at the head of the Ounila valley some 11 km (9 miles) from Telouet, is unusually well preserved.

Painted wooden ceiling in the kasbah of Telouet

For hotels and restaurants in this region see pp317–18 and p340

Aït Bouguemez Valley 9

Wooden door from the valley

The wide, flat Aït Bouguemez valley is flanked by a landscape of high, arid hilltops. This is the domain of the Aït Bouguemez tribe, who are settled farmers. The tribe is thought to be the oldest-established in the region. The valley is covered in meticulously tilled plots of land surrounded by ditches, and walnut trees grow in undulating fields of barley and corn. On the dry slopes, pisé hamlets cluster around *tighremts*, old fortified houses. The valley is the starting point for hikes through spectacular scenery up to the massif of Jbel M'Goun. There are 28 villages scattered along the valley between Agouti and Zaouïa Oulemsi.

Threshing the Corn
Mules attached to a post in the centre of the threshing ground circle slowly, trampling the corn. This separates the grain from the husks and straw.

★ **Painted Ceilings**
In the tamsriyt, *a room set aside for overnight guests, the ceilings – particularly in Agouti – are decorated with geometric motifs and thin coloured lines skilfully drawn freehand or with a compass.*

KEY

▬	Major road
▭	Minor road
⩵	Track
--	Path
☀	Viewpoint
ℹ	Tourist information
P	Parking

The direct route to Aït Mohammed is best avoided. Instead take the easier road from Agouti.

Tizi-n-Tirrhist 2,629 m (8,625 ft)

Zaouïa Oulemsi

Ifrane

Assif-n-Aït Hkim

Aït Wanougdal

Iskattafene

Imelghas · Ikhf-n-Ighir

JBEL TIZAL ▲ 3,041 m (9,977 ft) · Sidi Moussa · Ibaqalliwn · Rbat

Timit · El-Had · Akourbi

Aït Ziri · Aguerd-n-Ouzrou · Aït Imi

AÏT MHAMED · Tabant

P Agouti

Zaouïa Oulemsi is the departure point for hikes to Lake Izourar.

0 km 3
0 miles 3

The restored circular granary in Sidi Moussa is famous in the region.

Tabant is the valley's administrative centre. The souk at El-Had takes place on Sundays.

For hotels and restaurants in this region see pp317–18 and p340

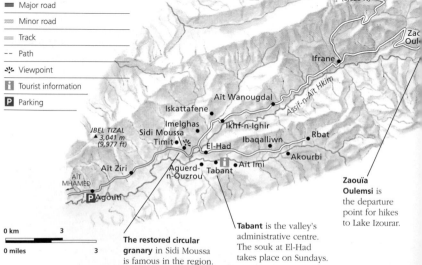

Maize Drying on the Rooftops
In the autumn, maize is laid out carefully on the tiered rooftops. When it has dried, the grain is separated from the cob on a concrete floor by hand.

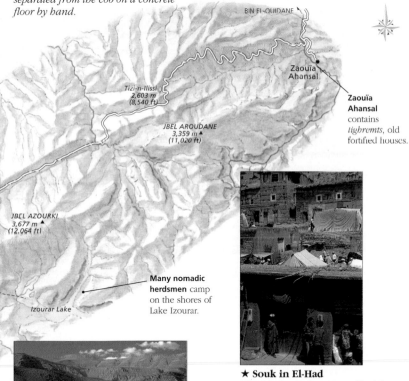

BIN EL-OUIDANE

Zaouïa Ahansal

Zaouïa Ahansal contains *tighremts*, old fortified houses.

Tizi-n-Ilissi 2,603 m (8,540 ft)

JBEL AROUDANE 3,359 m (11,020 ft)

JBEL AZOURKI 3,677 m (12,064 ft)

Izourar Lake

Many nomadic herdsmen camp on the shores of Lake Izourar.

★ Souk in El-Had
The Sunday souk, with weekly deliveries arriving by truck, provides the local inhabitants with necessities, such as tea, coffee, sugar, matches, oil and utensils, that they cannot otherwise obtain.

Valley Landscape
Drawn to the pastures in the region, the industrious Berbers have irrigated the land so as to extract the most from it, and built fortified villages to ensure their safety.

STAR SIGHTS

★ Painted Ceilings

★ Souk in El-Had

Exploring the Aït Bouguemez Valley

Clinging to the mountainside, the hamlets of the Aït Bouguemez valley blend into their setting, being almost the same colour as the landscape. The houses are stacked together like building blocks, the flat roof of the house serving as a terrace for the inhabitants of the house above. Looking down onto the river and the village's communal land, these cube-like houses catch the warmth of the rising sun and are adapted to the rigours of the climate. Houses in the valley bottom are built of pisé, raw earth dug at the spot where the house is to be built, mixed with water and sometimes straw. In villages at altitudes above 2,200 m (7,220 ft), dry stone is used, since pisé is unsuited to cold and wet conditions.

Detail of a painted ceiling, typical of the houses of the Aït Bouguemez

Setting off for the souk in a village below Jbel Ghat

Agouti
At the western extremity of the Aït Bouguemez valley.
The first of the villages that line the valley, Agoutí is located at 1,800 m (5,908 ft). As an outpost of the Aït Bouguemez tribe, it once defended access to the high valley against rival tribes.

A ruined *igherm* (fortified communal granary), set on a sheer rocky promontory, towers above the village. The villagers once kept their possessions and their crops here. In the valley, many houses have electricity, as well as some form of running water.

In Agouti, as in some of the other villages in the valley, visitors can see some beautiful

Mules in the Aït Bou Oulli valley

wood ceilings in the houses of wealthier families. The painted decoration is executed by craftsmen of renown and features an infinite variety of geometric patterns.

Aït Bou Oulli Valley
West of Agouti.
From Agouti, a day trip can be made to the Aït Bou Oulli valley on mule-back or by four-wheel-drive vehicle. A sheer-sided track leads down into the valley, whose name means "the people who raise ewes". The narrow wooded valley, thickly covered with walnut trees, winds the length of the *wadi*, which irrigates small fields.
Jbel Ghat, rising above the valley, is

a peak with mythical associations to which the Berbers come on a pilgrimage in years of drought. **Abachkou**, an interesting, high-set village at the far end of the valley, is renowned for the beautiful white capes produced by the villagers and found nowhere else in Morocco.

Sidi Moussa
East of Agouti.
Perched on the summit of a pointed hill, in the centre of the Aït Bouguemez valley, Sidi Moussa **granary** has benefited from a complete restoration and is on UNESCO's World Heritage list. It is reached by a steep path from the village of Timit.

This collective granary, one of three in the region, is a sturdy circular building with incorporated watch towers.

In the interior, which is lit by sparse loop-hole windows, a spiral staircase leads to the two upper floors. In the half-light, compartments arranged along the walls can be made out. This was where the inhabitants kept their possessions.

Sidi Moussa, the holy man renowned for his good deeds and his powers as a healer, is buried here. Sterile women of the Aït Bouguemez valley and from more distant valleys visit the shrine, where they spend the night and sacrifice a chicken as an offering to him.

From the granary, it is possible to look over the rest of the valley, with the outlines of nearby villages dotting the surrounding hillsides.

Aït Ziri, Timit, Imelghas and Iskattafène

East of Agouti. 🚍 *at El-Had on Sun.*
Walking around these villages, visitors will observe such details as decorated doors (either carved or painted in bright colours) and windows with interlacing wrought iron or *mashrabiyya* screens. Some very fine *tighremts* (fortified houses) dating from the early 20th century are still inhabited by village chiefs and their large families.

Close to Tabant, the administrative centre of the valley, **El-Had** is well known for its Sunday souk. This is the only place in the valley where supplies can be purchased. The village is also the starting point for mountain hikes to the M'Goun or in the footsteps of dinosaurs.

Zaouïa Oulemsi

On the way from Agouti, on a narrow track.
Zaouïa Oulemsi is the last village in the Aït Bouguemez valley, which it overlooks from an altitude of 2,150 m (7,056 ft). It consists of low, red-hued dry-stone houses. Here, the snowfall comes early and tends to be heavy.

The village is the starting point for hikes to **Lake Izourar**, which lies in the heart of the mountains at an altitude of 2,500 m (8,205 ft). Many nomadic shepherds camp beside the lake, which is often dry in summer, when it

Cultivated fields in the Aït Bouguemez valley

turns into pasture, the use of which is carefully controlled to prevent over-grazing.

The shepherds include the Aït Bouguemez, who come for the summer, living in the stone-built sheepfolds, and the Aït Atta, with their sheep, goats and camels, who in summer come up to the High Atlas from Jbel Sarhro.
Seeking good pasture, they settle on the slopes of M'Goun, around Lake Izourar or on the Imilchil plateau, moving south again at the first frosts.

Fortified granary, Aït Bouguemez valley

Zaouïa Ahansal

On the track towards Bin el-Ouidane. 🚗 *Mon.*
A track running along the continuation of the Aït Bouguemez valley goes up to the Tizi-n-Tirhist Pass, at 2,629 m (8,628 ft). The mountains are very bare here. The track passes a "fossilized forest" of juniper, with gnarled, dying trunks; the species faces extinction.

Zaouïa Ahansal, consisting of some old *tighremts* and the tomb of its founder, Saïd Ahansal, dates from the 14th century, when the *marabout* movement loomed large in the history of this mountain region. *Zaouias* (sanctuaries set up around the tombs of *marabouts*, holy figures and the leaders of brotherhoods) were then protected holy places, where pilgrims and the needy found refuge. In exchange for the protection given by the *marabout*, the Berbers maintained the land around the *zaouia*, were taught Arabic and received Koranic instruction.

Heedless of the power of the sultans, the leaders of some *zaouias* controlled the lives of the mountain people, settling disputes over land ownership and imposing their will. Zaouïa Ahansal was a major influence on the local Berber populations, but the descendants of Saïd Ahansal came into conflict with the fiefs of the *caids* of the High Atlas. They held out against the French until 1934.

The track continues for 40 km (25 miles) before reaching **La Cathédrale**, an impressive rock formation, then Lake Bin el-Ouidane.

Animals grazing around Lake Izourar, in summer

Lake Tiselit, on the Plateau des Lacs, near Imilchil

Imilchil ⑩

Road map D3. Accessible via Kasba Tadla (on road N8) and El-Ksiba (on road R317). 🛥 Sat.

On its eastern end, the chain of the High Atlas descends as if it had been crushed, forming a desert plateau surrounded by rolling mountains. Imilchil is at the heart of this sparsely populated region – the territory of the Aït Haddidou.

This group of semi-nomadic shepherds came originally from Boumalne du Dadès, located in the high Dadès valley, where some of them still live. They arrived in Morocco during the centuries immediately after the introduction of Islam, and there is evidence of their presence in the Boumalne du Dadès region durng the 11th century. For several years they were in conflict with the powerful Aït Atta tribe in disputes over pasture, then settled in the Assif Melloul valley in the 17th century.

The village of Imilchil is dominated by a sumptuously decorated kasbah. Its towers have a curious feature: the angles of the crenellation are set with finials resembling inverted cooking pots. This decorative device is also related to superstitious belief, as it gives protection against lightning and the "evil eye" and is a symbol of prosperity.

Chimney with "cooking pot" finial, Imilchil

Although Imilchil is remote, its claim to fame is the annual **Marriage Fair**, a *moussem* at which women may choose a fiancé and many pilgrims and traders from the mountains gather. It takes place at the end of September at a spot known as Aït Haddou Ameur, some 20 km (13 miles) from Imilchil. Arriving on foot, by truck or by mule, all the tribes of the area flock to this great yearly commercial, social and religious gathering. The pilgrims throng around the pisé walls of the shrine of Sidi Ahmed ou Mghanni, a venerated holy man, to present their offerings.

The origin of the Marriage Fair goes back to the story of two lovers, Hadda and Moha, members of rival tribes who were kept apart by their parents. Their tears created two lakes, Iseli, "the fiancé", and Tiselit, "the fiancée", on the Plateau des Lacs (see below). Ever since, young girls who come to the *moussem* with their family may converse freely with men from other tribes, although they must be accompanied by a sister or a female friend.

Young couples who wish to can visit the tent of the *adouls* (lawyers) and sign a betrothal agreement. These unions are often engineered by the respective families ahead of the *moussem*.

The event, which for some years has attracted crowds of tourists, has lost some of its authenticity. The presentation and parade of the couples and the evenings of folk dance and song are but a superficial aspect of what is a great commercial and religious gathering.

The colourful tents of the great souk spread out across the wide plateau. Traders sell basketry, cooking utensils, blankets and handwoven carpets, metalware, clothing, basic foodstuffs, and other items. On the hillside, herds of cows and camels and flocks of sheep await buyers.

The Plateau des Lacs can be reached either by following a long track that runs from El-Ksiba, crossing narrow gorges and undulating passes, or on a surfaced road via Rich, further east. This mineral-rich environment, at an altitude of 2,000–3,500 m (6,500–11,500 ft), is dotted with isolated *tighremts*, and a splash of colour is provided by the emerald waters of lakes Tiselit and Iseli. In summer, sheep are brought to the lush pasture here.

A couple at the Imilchil Marriage Fair

Berbers of the High Atlas

The Berbers of the High Atlas are non-nomadic peasants. Many of them have a completely self-sufficient lifestyle, and in certain valleys mule tracks are the only channel of communication with the outside world. The inhabitants of these remote valleys live by the pattern of the seasons and the round of work in the fields. In the autumn, the men till the soil with a wooden plough and buy and sell goods and produce at the weekly souk. In winter, the women collect water from the river, gather wood and weave thick woollen blankets. In spring, the men dig and maintain vital irrigation channels. In summer, the women harvest and thresh the grain, while the men winnow barley on threshing floors.

Hand painted with henna

FAMILY FESTIVALS
The daily life of the Berber women of the High Atlas is enlivened by family festivals. The women, dressed in dazzling clothes, dance the *ahwach* or the *ahidous*, according to the region, while the men intone chants as they beat out a regular rhythm on their *bendir*.

At the Marriage Fair in Imilchil, *the* raïs, *the dance leader of this folk troupe, beats out the rhythm on his* bendir, *a kind of tambourine, with his right hand.*

Woman carrying barley *on her back. The unripe barley will be deposited on the threshing ground.*

Berber women *from the Aït Haddidou tribe, whose differently striped cloaks signal their belonging to a certain clan.*

This weaver *from Abachkou, in the Aït Bou Oulli valley, washes, cards and spins sheep's wool. She weaves the yarn into cloth to make white capes, which are then decorated with pieces of metal.*

Men come to the souk *at Imilchil to buy and sell livestock and to stock up with vital supplies for the winter.*

OUARZAZATE & THE SOUTHERN OASES

This fascinating region begins at the southern edge of the High Atlas, where desert and mountains meet. The stony desert is broken by green oases where shade-giving date palms grow in profusion. Cut by steep canyons and studded with arid hills, it is criss-crossed by wadis right up to the edge of the Sahara. Here, the light is intensely bright and the colours sumptuously rich.

The history of Morocco is closely linked to this region bordering the Sahara desert, the birthplace of the great Moroccan dynasties. In the 11th century, Almoravid warriors, who came from the Sahara, set out from the south to extend their empire from Senegal to Spain. In the 16th century, the Saadians, who came from Arabia, left the Draa valley to conquer Morocco. Lastly, the Alaouites, the dynasty that holds power in Morocco today, settled in the Tafilalt region in the 13th century.

Trade in gold, salt and slaves between black Africa and Morocco melded the local populations, so that Arabs, Berbers and Haratines, descendants of ancient black populations, lived side by side.

Life here centres on three great *wadis*, the Draa, the Dadès and the Ziz. These rivers have created stunning landscapes, carving gorges and canyons out of the sides of the High Atlas and Anti-Atlas. The date palm that brings welcome shade to small plots of corn and barley accounts for the region's wealth. The palm groves are punctuated by hundreds of kasbahs and *ksour*. These fortified villages and houses protected the sedentary populations against attack from nomadic tribes. Many of them are still inhabited today, although they are slowly crumbling. The desert begins south of the oases. Every year, aided by drought, it encroaches further on arable land.

The central patio of the kasbah at Oulad Driss, in the southern Draa valley

◁ A *marabout*, or tomb of a religious leader, with pisé walls, in the Draa valley

Exploring Ouarzazate and the Southern Oases

The Draa Valley, south of Ouarzazate, and the Tafilalt valley, south of Er-Rachidia, are the two great routes to the Sahara. The valleys are interconnected by the Dadès valley, which covers 120 km (75 miles) between Ouarzazate and Boumalne du Dadès. It cuts through a desert plateau at an average altitude of 1,000 to 1,500 m (3,282 to 4,923 ft), set between the High Atlas on its northern side and the foothills of Jbel Sarhro on its southern side. Other valleys, irrigated by *wadis* flowing down from the Atlas, impinge on the Dadès valley. Negotiable on foot or by four-wheel-drive vehicle, they give access to the interior of the High Atlas. Exploring this region, experiencing the scenic oases and visiting the most interesting *ksour*, takes at least a week.

GETTING AROUND

Roads in a good state of repair run between Ouarzazate and Zagora, Er-Rachidia and Erfoud. However, distances are great, and the mountainous terrain and passes to be negotiated must be taken into account. Although certain tracks can be followed only in a four-wheel-drive vehicle, an ordinary car is sufficient to drive major roads. Buses and *grands taxis* from Ouarzazate cover the whole region.

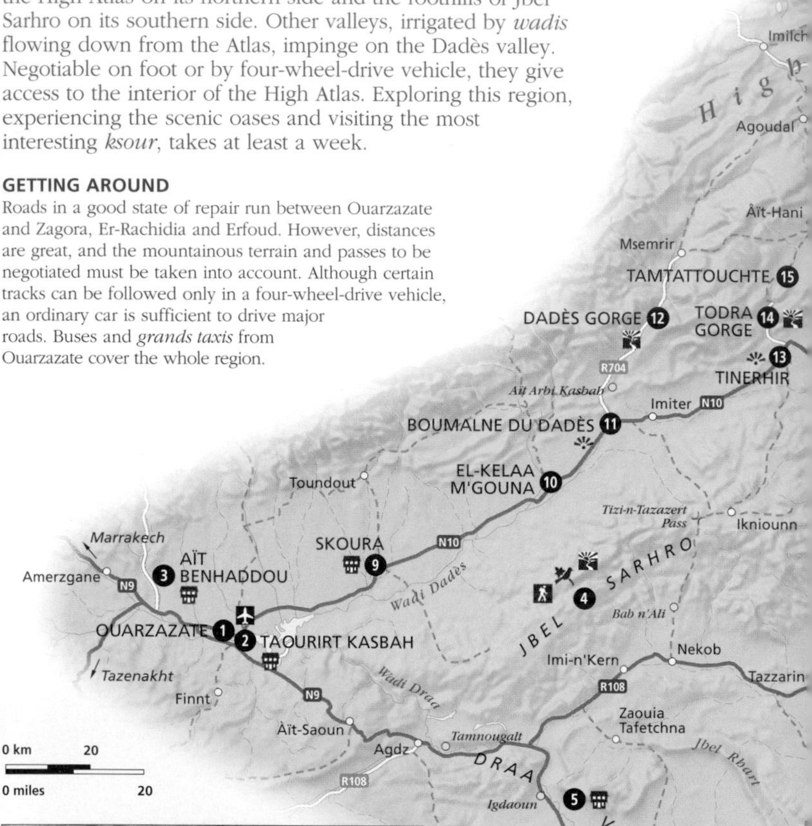

Imilchil

High

Agoudal

Aït-Hani

Msemrir

TAMTATTOUCHTE **15**

DADÈS GORGE **12**   TODRA **14**
GORGE

Aït Arbi Kasbah   TINERHIR **13**

Imiter N10

BOUMALNE DU DADÈS **11**

Toundout   EL-KELAA **10**
M'GOUNA

Tizi-n-Tazazert
Pass   Ikniounn

Marrakech   SKOURA   N10   J B E L   S A R H R O

Amerzgane   N9   AÏT **3**   **9**   **4**   Bab n'Ali
BENHADDOU

Wadi Dadès

OUARZAZATE **1** **2** TAOURIRT KASBAH   Imi-n'Kern   Nekob

Tazenakht   N9   Wadi Draa   R108   Tazzarin

Finnt   Zaouia
Tafetchna   Jbel Rbart

Aït-Saoun   N9   Tamnougalt

| 0 km | 20 |
| 0 miles | 20 |

Agdz   D R A A

Igdaoun   **5** **+++**

R108   V
A
Azlag Gorge   L
L
E
Y   Jbel Tadra

ZAGORA **6**   **7**

Amazraou   TAMEGROUT

Zaouia-el-Barrahnia

Jbel Beni   Anagame

Nesrate Dunes

Tagounite

N9

Msemrir, a village at the foot of the High Atlas *(see p273)*

MHAMID **8**

LOCATOR MAP

Door of the *zaouia* in Tamegroute

SIGHTS AT A GLANCE

Aït Benhaddou ③
Boumalne du Dadès ⑪
Dadès Gorge ⑫
Draa Valley ⑤
El-Kelaa M'Gouna ⑩
Erfoud ㉑
Er-Rachidia ⑲
Goulmima ⑯
Jbel Sarhro ④
Merzouga ㉔
Mhamid ⑧
Midelt ⑰
Ouarzazate ①
Rissani ㉓
Skoura ⑨
Source Bleue de Meski ⑳
Tafilalt Palm Grove ㉒
Tamegroute ⑦
Tamtattouchte ⑮
Taourirt Kasbah ②
Tinerhir ⑬
Todra Gorge ⑭
Zagora ⑥
Ziz Gorge ⑱

SEE ALSO

• *Where to Stay* pp318–19

• *Where to Eat* pp341–2

KEY

— Major road

--- Minor road

-- - Track

△ Summit

✕ Pass

An austere kasbah in the Dadès Gorge

A shop in the crafts centre opposite the Taourirt Kasbah

Ouarzazate ❶

Road map C4. 🏚 *70,000.*
🚌 *Avenue Mohammed V (to Marrakech, Tinerhir, Taroudannt and Zagora) and grands taxis (Tue, Fri, Sat, Sun).* ℹ️ *Avenue Mohammed V; (0524) 88 24 85. Grands taxis, Land Rovers and 4x4 vehicles for hire.* 🎪 *Crafts Festival (May); Moussem of Sidi Daoud (Aug).*

A former garrison town of the French Foreign Legion, Ouarzazate was founded in 1928, having been chosen by the French as a strategic base from which to pacify the South. Located at an altitude of 1,160 m (3,807 ft) at the intersection of the Draa and Dadès valleys, with the Agadir region to the west, it is on the main route between the mountains and the desert. It is also a good base from which to visit Aït Benhaddou and the Skoura palm grove.

Ouarzazate is a peaceful provincial town with wide streets, many hotels and municipal gardens. Avenue Mohammed V, the only main street, crosses the town and leads to the Dadès valley.

About 6 km (4 miles) outside Ouarzazate, off the road to Marrakech, are the **Atlas Film Studios**, surrounded by high pisé walls that look as if they are defended by giant Hollywood-style, pseudo-Egyptian figures. The studios, which cover 30,000 sq m (322,920 sq ft) of desert, provide the livelihood of a considerable portion of the population of Ouarzazate. For a century, hundreds of films have been shot in this region, including Bertolucci's *The Sheltering Sky* (1990) and Scorsese's *Kundun* (1997). On the other side of the town, opposite the Taourirt Kasbah, are the Andromeda Italian film studios.

Detail of a window in the Taourirt Kasbah

Atlas Film Studios
On road N9, 6 km (4 miles) north-west of Ouarzazate. 🕙 *8:30–11:30am & 2:15–6pm daily, except when filming is going on.*

Environs
About 10 km (6 miles) to the south is the **Finnt Oasis**, with fine pisé *ksour*. A little further on is the **El-Mansour Eddahbi Dam**, fed by the Dadès and Ouarzazate rivers, which join to form the Draa. The dam provides water for the golf course, the Draa's palm groves and electricity for the valley. About 7 km (4 miles) north-west of Ouarzazate is the majestic **Tiffoultoute Kasbah**, offering fine views from its terrace. It was converted into a hotel in the 1960s to provide rooms during the shooting of David Lean's *Lawrence of Arabia*. It is now a restaurant.

Taourirt Kasbah ❷

Road map C4. Opposite the crafts centre on the road out of Ouarzazate leading to the Dadès valley. 📷

Ouarzazate's only historic building, the Taourirt Kasbah stands as a monument to Glaoui expansionism. At the beginning of the 20th century, the Glaoui family were the lords of the South and controlled access to the High Atlas. They were the first to collaborate with the French in the expansion of the latter's rule in the South.

Begun in the 18th century and renovated in the 19th, the kasbah has been undergoing restoration from time to time since 1994. It once housed the large Glaoui family, together with their servants.

The façade, consisting of high smooth earth walls, is pitted and decorated with geometric patterns in negative relief.

Inside, a maze of staircases at every level of the building leads to rooms of various sizes lit by low windows. The larger rooms have plasterwork decoration featuring floral and geometric motifs, and colourfully painted wooden ceilings. There are also some tiny rooms with low rush-matted ceilings, doorless arches, red-tiled floors and white walls.

Aït Benhaddou, which has often been chosen as a film location

Next to the kasbah is a former Berber village, which probably predates the kasbah. It is inhabited by a busy population. In the narrow winding streets of the *ksar* (fortified village), you will find an Internet café, a former synagogue that now serves as a carpet shop, and a herbalist. The crafts centre opposite the Taourirt kasbah offers carpets, stone carving, jewellery and pottery, all at relatively high prices.

Aït Benhaddou ❸

Road map C4. 30 km (19 miles) northwest of Ouarzazate, off road N9. ❶ *Ouarzazate; (0524) 88 24 85.*

Backing onto a pinkish sandstone hill, the *ksar* of Aït Benhaddou stands on the left bank of Wadi Mellah. It is reached on foot from the village on the opposite bank. The *wadi* is usually dry, except in winter and spring.

The picturesque village of Aït Benhaddou, which has often been used as a film location, can be explored without a guide. It was once fortified and has a now-ruined *igherm* (communal granary). Built near water and arable land, in a place safe from foreign attack, it contains an impressive group of ochre pisé kasbahs.

Since the village was made a UNESCO World Heritage Site, some of its kasbahs have undergone restoration to their upper sections. The kasbahs' crenellated towers are decorated with blind arches and

geometric designs in negative relief, creating a play of light and shadow. Behind the kasbahs stand plain earth houses. Today, the *ksar* is inhabited by fewer than ten families.

Beyond Aït Benhaddou, a minor road leads to the ruined fortress of **Tamdaght**, once a kasbah inhabited by the Glaoui. Its towers are now inhabited by nesting storks. The road continues to Telouet, 32 km (20 miles) away.

Jbel Sarhro ❹

Road map D4. 98 km (61 miles) south of Ouarzazate. *From Tansikht to Nekob on road R108, or from Boulmane du Dadès.* ❷ *Sun in Nekob, Mon in Iknioun.*

Stretching for over 100 km (60 miles), Jbel Sarhro is a wild and inhospitable region that is still off the tourist track. It is separated from the main Anti-Atlas chain by the Draa valley to the west and from the High Atlas by Wadi Dadès to the north.

Jbel Sarhro is the territory of the Aït Atta, who, from the

17th and 19th centuries, were the most important tribe in southern Morocco. This semi-nomadic people never bowed to the power of the sultans, and they were the last to resist the French at the Battle of Bou Gafer in 1933. They live in *ksour*, but take to tents for part of the year, when they drive livestock to seasonal pastures.

Jbel Sarhro is a region of sheer rockfaces, plateaus and blackish rocky escarpments. The rugged territory is crossed from north to south by tracks, which are best driven in a four-wheel-drive vehicle (routes are seldom signposted).

The Baha Kasbah in Nekob, at the foot of Jbel Sarhro

At the Baha Kasbah in Nekob guides can be hired for hikes and tours in four-wheel-drive vehicles. The route from Nekob to the Tizi n'Tazazert Pass, at 2,200 m (7,220 ft), is difficult, but the spot known as Bab N'Ali is worth the visit for some striking needle-like volcanic rock formations. The track to Boulmane du Dadès crosses the **Vallée des Oiseaux** (Valley of Birds), which is home to over 150 species of birds.

Camels grazing in the rocky landscape of Jbel Sarhro

The Kasbah

Kasbahs (*tighremt* in Berber) have long fulfilled the role of fortified castles, being places of refuge from attack for people and animals, and affording protection from the cold and other threats to safety. A lordly residence or family dwelling, the kasbah is an imposing edifice built to a square plan. While kasbahs in the mountain valleys are thick-set, those in the southern oases have a taller, more slender outline. At the four corners are towers crowned with merlons rising above the height of the walls.

Fortified Citadels
High walls set at a slightly oblique angle give the kasbah a perfectly proportioned outline.

Bricks
Bricks are made from earth mixed with water, sometimes with chopped straw added. They are pressed into wooden moulds and dried in the sun.

A TYPICAL KASBAH

Their dimensions being dictated by the size of the horizontally placed beams, the rooms are often longer than they are wide. The largest room is the reception hall, which often has a painted ceiling and which is reserved for men. The stable and sheepfold are located on the ground floor.

Stepped merlons

Water Jar
Ancient pieces of pottery like this one can be seen in restored kasbahs.

Windows
Mashrabiyya *screens and wrought-iron grilles, made with no soldering, allow the inhabitants to look out without being seen.*

Defensive Walls
The upper parts of the walls are decorated with geometric patterns, incised motifs and blind arches cut into the pisé.

Fortified Granary
The interior of the igherm or agadir is divided into compartments where maize, barley, sugar and cooking vessels are stored.

The Kitchen
Circular loaves of bread, made by the women, are baked in a small igloo-like earth oven. The kitchen is often dark and badly ventilated, and cooking is done on the earth floor.

Maize drying on the roof

Painted Ceilings
Ceilings are painted with volutes, rosettes and interlacing patterns, executed freehand or with a compass. They are a feature of reception rooms of kasbahs and of wealthy houses.

Wooden Doors
They can be opened only from within.

Detail of the interior of the *ksar* at Tamnougalt, in the Draa valley

Draa Valley ❺

Road map C-D4. 200 km (124 miles) between Ouarzazate and Zagora on road N9. 🚌 *Thu in Agdz.*

Rock engravings discovered near Tinzouline show that the Draa valley was inhabited by warriors from prehistoric times. The valley, where buildings are in a good state of preservation, contains a wealth of *ksour* and kasbahs.

The road between Ouarzazate and **Agdz** crosses the desert plateaux of Jbel Tifernine. Beyond Aït Saoun, hills of black rock give way to steep canyons as the road climbs towards the Tizi-n-Tinififft Pass, at 1,660 m (5,448 ft). To the north appear the foothills of the High Atlas and to the east, Jbel Sarhro.

Agdz, an unassuming town on the edge of a palm grove, is convenient for a short stop.

Between Agdz and Zagora, the road follows a string of oases. Villages have grown up around the old kasbahs, on the edge of the road and in the palm grove.

About 6 km (4 miles) from Agdz, a track branching off to the left leads to the majestic *ksar* of **Tamnougalt**, which once controlled access to the trade routes of the Draa valley. The interior reveals some striking frescoes, which were painted in pale colours for the shooting of a film.

Continuing along the left bank of the Draa, the track leads to the pisé village of Tamnougalt, with narrow, partly covered streets. Visitors wishing to see the old kasbah may like to bring a torch, which is useful for viewing its superb painted ceilings. Tamnougalt, which is currently undergoing restoration, also has a former mellah (Jewish quarter) with a synagogue.

Back on the Draa valley road, the elegant **Timiderte Kasbah** comes into view on the left bank of the *wadi*, backing onto Jbel Sarhro. Villages and *ksour* here are rarely signposted. In Tansikht, a narrow road turns off to the left towards Nekob, Jbel Sarhro and Rissani, 233 km (145 miles) away. The bridge over the *wadi* joins a sandy track that passes through villages in the palm grove. To rejoin the road, the river can be forded in several places. Still leading in the direction of Zagora, the road passes the **Igdaoun Kasbah**, with towers

in the shape of truncated pyramids. At Tinezouline, a track to the right leads to a site with rock engravings, 7 km (4 miles) away.

The valley narrows in the approaches to the Azlag gorge, to the right of which is a high, smooth cliff. Soon after, a signpost indicating "Circuit Touristique de Binzouli" leads to the palm grove, which reaches Zagora on the other side of the river. Ochre pisé *koubbas* line the valley, while cemeteries are filled with the vertical flat stones that are typical of Muslim graveyards. Between Tissergate and Zagora, the palm grove stretches away to the distant foothills of Jbel Rhart.

Zagora ❻

Road map D4. 🏘 30,000.
🚌 *Ouarzazate or grands taxis.*
ℹ (0524) 88 24 85.
🛒 *Wed & Sun.*
🎎 Moussem of *Moulay Abdelkader Jilali at Mouloud.*

Established by the French authorities during the Protectorate, Zagora is the most convenient base for exploring the region. The sign saying "Timbuctu, 52 Days by Camel" evokes the great age of the trans-Saharan caravans, although the illusion is spoiled by the presence of the large concrete *Préfecture* behind it.

The village of **Amazraou**, set amid lemon, almond and olive trees and gardens on the

A camel trek through the peaceful palm grove in Zagora

For hotels and restaurants in this region see pp318–19 and pp341–2

Green-glazed pottery vessels characteristic of Tamegroute

southern side of the town, is a haven of peace on the edge of the desert. In the former mellah, the mosque stands next to the abandoned synagogue. Amazraou is inhabited by Arabs, Haratines and Berbers, who continue the Jewish tradition of making silver jewellery. By following a footpath from the La Fibule hotel, the summit of Jbel Zagora can be reached in one hour. It is crowned by a military post and commands a breathtaking view of the valley. The remains of walls indicate the presence of the Almoravids in the 11th century.

Several hotels offer tours in four-wheel-drive vehicles or on camels, lasting from a day to two weeks, the tours take in the Chigaga dunes south of Mhamid, and Foum-Zguid, west of Zagora.

Tamegroute **7**

Road map D4. 🚗 Sat. 🎭 Moussem of Sidi Ahmed ben Nasser (Nov).

Surrounded by ramparts, the *ksar* at Tamegroute contains a *zaouia* and a library. This great centre of Islamic learning was founded in the 17th century by Mohammed Bou Nasri, and its influence extended throughout southern Morocco.

Beneath the arcades of the courtyard, near the entrance to the tomb of Mohammed Bou Nasri, invalids and handicapped people gather, hoping to be cured.

The holy man's works laid the foundations of the **Koranic Library**. A collection of priceless manuscripts is displayed in one of the rooms. It includes an 11th-century gazelle-skin Koran, books of calligraphy with gold dust and saffron illuminations, and treatises on algebra, astronomy and Arabic literature. Exposed to heat and light, these works are, unfortunately, not in the best condition.

Mule in the Draa valley

In the potters' workshop outside, members of seven families produce traditional functional pots with a green glaze typical of Tamegroute ceramics.

Environs

About 5 km (2 miles) south of Tamegroute, and off to the left, are the **Tinfou Dunes**, an isolated ridge of sand rising up abruptly in the middle of the stony desert. From Tagounite, a difficult track leads to the foot of Jbel Tadrart and the beautiful **Nesrate Dunes**.

Mhamid **8**

Road map D4. 🚗 2,000. 🚌 Mon.

This border post and small administrative centre is the last oasis before the great expanse of the Sahara. To the south stretches a stony desert, the Hammada du Draa. From Mhamid, Wadi Draa sinks beneath the sand to reappear on the Atlantic coast 540 km (338 miles) to the west.

The ruins of a *ksar* indicate the former existence of a great caravan centre, from which Ahmed el-Mansour's army set out in the 16th century to take Timbuctu.

Environs

Coming from Zagora, the Tizi-Beni-Selmane Pass, at an altitude of 747 m (2,451 ft), offers a stunning view of Jbel Bani and the desert, which looks black since it is covered with volcanic stone. A little further on, a track to the left leads to **Foum-Rjam**, one of the largest prehistoric necropolises in the Maghreb. Tumuli mark thousands of graves. About 45 km (28 miles) south of Mhamid, the **Chigaga dunes**, which can be reached only by four-wheel-drive vehicle, stretch to the horizon.

Camel and rider on the Tinfou Dunes, south of Tamegroute

The palm grove at Skoura

Skoura ⑨

Road map C4. 🚗 *from Ouarzazate and Tinerhir.* 🗓 *Mon.*

The small sleepy town of Skoura is surrounded by an impressive palm grove, which was laid out in the 12th century by the Almohad sultan Yacoub el-Mansour. The most beautiful kasbahs in southern Morocco are to be found here. Some of these are still partially inhabited, and some are attached to private houses. Many of Skoura's inhabitants, however, have moved into the breeze-block villages that line the road.

The **Ben Morro Kasbah** stands on the left of the road above Skoura. It was built in the 17th century and, now completely restored, has been converted into a guesthouse. The entrance to the palm grove is on the other side of Wadi Amerhidil. The grove can be explored only on foot, by bicycle or on mule-back. The grove is irrigated by *khettaras* (underground channels) and wells dug at regular intervals. Ruined kasbahs stand among palm trees, fig trees, birch and tamarisk – whose tannin-rich flowers are used in the processing of skins. The most imposing is **Amerhidil Kasbah**, which was once owned by the Glaoui family and which dominates the *wadi*. The restored interior is now open to visitors. The kasbahs of Aït Sidi el-Mati, Aït Souss, El-Kebbaba and Dar Aïchil are also worth a visit.

Further east, **Aït Abou**, built in 1863 and the oldest kasbah in the palm grove, has six storeys and walls 25 m (82 ft) high. Its out-buildings have been turned into a small short-stay gîte. An orchard with pomegranate, apple, pear, fig, quince and olive trees provides the necessary shade for growing crops.

Twenty-five kilometres (15 miles) northeast of Skoura is the village of **Toundout**, where there are some highly decorated kasbahs. The **Marabout of Sidi M'Barek** served as a stronghold where the semi-nomadic people stored their crops, under the protection of the saint.

A little way beyond Skoura, towards El-Kelaa M'Gouna, unexpected plantations of grasses imported from Australia in the 1990s help to preserve a little moisture in the arid ground.

El-Kelaa M'Gouna ⑩

Road map D4. ℹ️ *guides office; (0524) 88 24 85 (Ouarzazate).* 🗓 *Wed.* 🌹 *Rose Festival (May).*

This town, whose name means "fortress", is located at an altitude of 1,450 m (4,759 ft), in the heart of rose country. In the 10th century, pilgrims returning from Mecca brought *Rosa damascena* back with them to Morocco. These peppery-scented flowers have developed a resistance to the cold and dry conditions in which they are now grown.

Spectacular landscape at the approach to the M'Goun valley

Each spring, rose-picking produces 3,000 to 4,000 tonnes of petals. The harvest is taken to two local distillation factories. One of them, in El-Kelaa M'Gouna, is laid out in a kasbah, and it is open to visitors in April and May. While a proportion of the roses is used to make rosewater for local distribution, the rest is processed and exported for use in the perfume industry.

The Rose Festival takes place after the harvest and is attended by all the inhabitants of the valleys of the Dadès. Accompanied by a *bendir* (a tambourine), young girls from El-Kelaa M'Gouna perform a sinuous dance, their long hair braided with coloured wool.

On the road out of the town is a craft cooperative with about 30 workshops. Daggers are made here, the craftsmen continuing a Jewish tradition of making sheaths and dagger handles out of cedar or camel bone. The steel blades are made in the mountain village of Azlague, not far from El-Kelaa M'Gouna.

The Amerhidil Kasbah, in the palm grove at Skoura

◁ The Aït Benhaddou *ksar*, ar sunrise

The Rose Festival in El-Kelaa M'Gouna

surrounded by fig, almond and walnut trees and poplars.

About 2 km (1 mile) from Boumalne, in a bend in the road, stands the **Aït Mouted Kasbah**, which once belonged to the Glaoui. Here and there, large constructions in brown breeze-block, built by emigrants who have returned to Morocco, stand out as unfortunate blots on the landscape.

As it rises, the road passes some dramatic geological limestone folds which have been shaped by erosion. At the foot of these natural formations stand the ruins of the **Aït Arbi Kasbah**. Further on are the stone and pisé **Tamnalt Kasbahs**, whose slender towers rise up against a backdrop of rocks that seem to be pressed together sideways like the fingers of a human hand.

Beyond Aït Oudinar, the road crosses Wadi Dadès,

Environs

Between Skoura and El-Kelaa M'Gouna, kasbahs are set among greenery throughout the Dadès valley. The modern concrete houses that line the roads here are an artless imitation of these fine traditional buildings. Ruined kasbahs are now part of the local landscape. From offices on the way out of El-Kelaa M'Gouna, many hikes and tours by four-wheel-drive vehicle are organized, particularly to the **Vallée des Roses** and to the *ksar* at **Bou Thrarar**, a breathtaking mountain tour.

Further into the interior of the High Atlas some impressive gorges lead to the remote M'Goun valley. It is best to hire a guide because the tracks are not signposted.

Boumalne du Dadès ⓫

Road map D4. 🏚 *13,000.*
ℹ️ *Iizzarouine kasbah; (0524) 88 24 85 (Ouarzazate).* 🗓️ *Wed.*

This pleasant stopping place at the beginning of the Dadès gorge is a regional administrative centre. From the edge of the plateau above the

town, the view stretches over the fertile Dadès Oasis. At Tizzarouine Kasbah, from where there are fine views, guides offer tours and camping trips in the High Atlas and Jbel Sarhro.

Dadès Gorge ⓬

Road map D3. Grand taxi *from Boumalne du Dadès.* 🚌 *Sat in Msemrir.*

Bordered by greenery, the course of Wadi Dadès stands out against the rocky landscape. Cultivated land on the banks of the *wadi* is

The Aït Mouted Kasbah, in the Dadès gorge

Tamnalt Kasbah in the Dadès gorge with a dramatic rocky backdrop

following the bottom of the gorge between sheer cliffs. It then runs along the edge of deep canyons, home to royal eagles and vultures. On the plateau, the valley widens again, and attractive stone and pisé villages overlook the opposite riverbank.

The road running up the gorge from Boumalne du Dadès is metalled as far as Msemrir, 60 km (37 miles) to the north. The final stretch before Msemrir passes through much wilder country than in the lower part of the gorge. Beyond Msemrir, a track that is passable only by four-wheel-drive vehicle leads east to the Todra Gorge and north to the High Atlas and Imilchil.

The Tinerhir oasis, stretching out along the banks of Wadi Todra

Tinerhir ⓭

Road map D3-4. 🏔 40,000. 🚌 from Er-Rachidia and Ouarzazate, and grands taxis. ℹ Hôtel Tombouctou; (0524) 88 24 85 (Ouarzazate). 🛍 Mon.

This lively town, the region's administrative centre, lies midway between the Draa valley and the Tafilalt. Built on a rocky outcrop, it has an elongated layout. On its northern and southern sides it is bordered by a lush palm grove laid out at the foot of arid hills and containing dozens of *ksour* and kasbahs.

With several silver mines in the vicinity, Tinerhir is a wealthy town known for its silver jewellery. To the west stands a kasbah once owned by the Glaoui and now in a state of disrepair. To the southeast is Aït el-Haj Ali, the former mellah (Jewish quarter), whose houses make an interesting architectural ensemble. North of the town stretches a palm grove irrigated by Wadi Todra.

Detail of the walls of Tinerhir Kasbah

About 2 km (1 mile) from the bridge across the *wadi*, on the road to the **Todra Gorge**, a viewing platform commands a stunning view. Here, guides with camels offer their services. However, visitors need no assistance to walk down into the palm grove and follow the network of shady paths that lead through orchards and run along irrigation ditches. This is a wonderful walk, as the Todra palm grove stretches for 12 km (7.5 miles).

On the other side of the *wadi* are many semi-ruined *ksour*, where 50 to 100 families once lived. The most interesting and most easily reached are the **Aït Boujane Ksar** and **Asfalou Ksar**.

Further north, about 5 km (3 miles) before the start of the gorge, there is an alternative route to the palm grove; this is via the Imarighen spring, the "Spring of the Sacred Fish".

Environs
At **El-Hart-n-Igouramene**, south of Tinerhir, craftsmen produce a bronze-coloured local pottery that is sold in the souk. The sweep of road taking in El-Hart, Tadafalt and Agoudim offers the opportunity to see many *ksour*, some of which are still inhabited.

Todra Gorge ⓮

Road map D3.

Sheer cliffs 300 m (985 ft) high rise up dramatically each side of the narrow corridor that forms the Todra gorge. These are the most impressive cliffs in southern Morocco, and they are well known to experienced mountaineers.

Wadi Todra flows through this great geological fault and on into the Tinerhir palm grove *(see above)*. Two hotels make possible an overnight stop in the Todra gorge. The best time of day to view the gorge is in the morning, when the rays of the sun break through between the high cliffs on either side.

The cliffs soon widen and a stony track leads to the village of Tamtattouchte, 22 km (14 miles) further on.

The Todra gorge, sandwiched between sheer cliffs

Tamtattouchte ⓯

Road map D3. 36 km (22 miles) north of Tinerhir.

The picturesque village of Tamtattouchte is located at the other extremity of the Todra gorge, its earth houses blending into the red-ochre tones of the mountains. Here, small plots of land that stand out from their arid, rocky surroundings are irrigated by Wadi Todra.

Tamtattouchte is the starting point of tracks to the Dadès gorge to the west and Imilchil to the north, leading over passes, through gorges, across plateaux and over mountains. Ask a local for information about the state of tracks

The village of Tamtattouchte, at the northern end of the Todra gorge, with several fine *ksour*

negotiable by four-wheel-drive vehicles, particularly after periods of rainfall. Visitors should also be aware that no destinations are signposted.

Goulmima ⑯

Road map D3. 🚌 *from Er-Rachidia and Tinejdad.* 🏠 *Mon & Thu.*

Although it is set in the heart of the Rheris oasis, where about 20 *ksour* stand on the banks of Wadi Rheris, the modern village of Goulmima is of no great interest to visitors. The inhabitants of neighbouring *ksour* come to the village to buy supplies.

The sturdiness of their fortifications make the *ksour* here unusual. Their towers are remarkably high and, when tribal feuds were rife, they protected the inhabitants against the incursions of the

The *ksar* at Goulmima, a labyrinth of narrow streets and alleys

Aït Atta, who came to pillage their harvests.

The old fortified village of Goulmima, 2 km (1 mile) east on the road to Erfoud, is worth the detour. Still inhabited, the **Goulmima *ksar***, which exemplifies southern Moroccan defensive architecture, is surrounded by walls set with two massive towers. Cows and

sheep are enclosed within small corrals outside. A gate set at an angle opens onto a second gate. On a small square within the walls stand a mosque and the well that provides the *ksar* with water. The upper floors of some of the houses span the narrow streets, providing a strange contrast of light and shadow.

MOROCCO'S ARCHITECTURAL HERITAGE

The vestiges of a past age and of unique ways of life, kasbahs, *ksour* and granaries – all of them built of earth – are the victims of neglect. The kasbahs are crumbling, the ruins of once-luxurious residences are abandoned and clay walls slowly disappear into the ground. The Moroccan government seems indifferent to the unique value and interest of these buildings. Aside from sparse and sporadic activity, action to protect Morocco's architectural heritage goes little further than listing its

Detail of the Taourirt kasbah in Ouarzazate

monuments and drawing up conservation programmes that produce no concrete results. The only active conservation in Morocco is that resulting from European initiatives. Besides the uncompleted restoration of the *ksar* at Aït Benhaddou, funded by UNESCO, that of the granary at Igherm-n-Ougdal, on the road to the Tizi-n-Tichka Pass, and of the Taourirt kasbah in Ouarzazate, the small number of kasbahs in the Dadès valley that have been restored were saved by private funding. Private initiative is also responsible for the skilful restoration of the Ben Morro kasbah and Aït Abou kasbah in Skoura and the Hôtel Tombouctou in Tinerhir. Unfortunately, most of the Glaoui fortresses in the valleys of the Atlas are being left to their fate.

The Southern and Eastern Oases

Jerboa, or desert rat

Southern and eastern Morocco have many oases. Their existence depends on the presence of water, which is either supplied by rivers flowing down from the mountains or provided by an underground water table. Underground water rises naturally at the foot of dunes or is pumped by artesian wells or along underground channels known as *khettaras*, some of them covering considerable distances. This accounts for the fact that the oases are strung out in a line along the Dadès, Draa and Ziz valleys.

Seguias *are man-made channels that criss-cross the oasis, bringing water to the crops and trees. Clay plugs are sometimes used to divert the water along particular routes.*

IRRIGATION IN THE OASES

Set in particularly hostile surroundings, oases are a very fragile ecological environment that survives thanks only to ceaseless human intervention. Many dams are built to control the flow of water in the *wadis*, which, when they are in flood, can devastate the plantations in the oases in a few hours. *Khettaras* and *seguias* must be regularly cleared.

Clay plugs are used to direct the flow of water to other parts of the oasis.

Date palms, *of which there are many varieties, produce abundant fruit. A single tree can provide 30 to 100 kg (66 to 220 lb) of dates a year. They are harvested in autumn.*

Animai-ski container

Barley

Crops *such as tomatoes, carrots and lettuce, as well as fruit trees such as fig and apricot, thrive in the shade provided by the palm trees.*

Irrigation *is produced by khettaras, underground channels that bring water to the oasis. Here, the water is either drawn from a well or is simply forced to the surface by gravity. The exact amount of water needed for each crop is provided by seguias.*

Work in the fields *is done by women, who carry out all stages in the cultivation of cereals and various kinds of vegetables.*

The tops of the shafts *that are sunk to dig and then maintain the* khettara *are visible on the surface.*

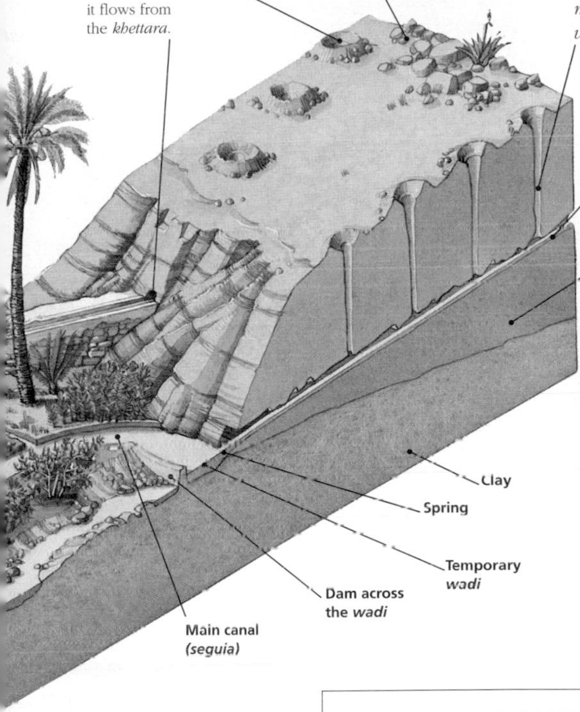

Water is channelled as it flows from the *khettara.*

Well

Arid zone

Underground water gently flows into the oasis.

Impervious layer

Clay

Spring

Temporary *wadi*

Dam across the *wadi*

Main canal **(seguia)**

Temporary wadis, *across which dams are built, feed water to the various* seguias *in the oasis.*

ANIMALS OF THE OASIS

The common bulbul, rufous bush robin, house bunting and doves are some of the more familiar birds seen in the oases. Toads frequent the banks of the water-courses, geckos and lizards cling to stone walls and the trunks of trees, and scorpions hide under stones. During the night, jackals occasionally approach places of human habitation. The fennec, horned viper and herbivorous lizard rarely venture beyond the dunes and rocks where they were born.

At Tinerhir, *many* seguias *channel water from Wadi Todra, bringing it to the beautiful palm grove nearby.*

Herbivorous lizard

Horned viper

Fennec

Majestic Jbel Ayachi, rising over extensive and sparsely populated desert plateaux

Midelt ⑰

Road map D3. 🕌 20,000. 🚌 from Meknès, Rabat, Erfoud, Er-Rachidia and Azrou. 🏛 Timnaï Cultural Centre, 20 km (12 miles) north of Midelt; (0535) 36 01 88. 🛒 Wed & Sun. 🎪 Apple Festival (Oct).

On the border between the High and Middle Atlas, Midelt is considered to be part of southern Morocco. The small villages on each side of the road leading out of the town consist of traditional buildings that are very similar to those typical of southern Morocco. While, at the beginning of the 20th century, Midelt was no more than a modest *ksar*, under the Protectorate it became a French garrison town.

Located at the foot of **Jbel Ayachi**, which rises to a height of 3,737 m (12,264 ft), Midelt is the starting point for tours. At an altitude of 1,500 m (4,923 ft), the town enjoys a continental climate – very cold in winter and very hot in summer.

Beautiful Middle Atlas carpets, as well as fossils and mineral stones, are on sale in Souk Jedid. There is also a workshop in Kasbah Myriem, on the road to Tattiouine, where carpets, blankets and high-quality embroidery are produced. It used to be run by Franciscan nuns who taught the local Berber women these handicrafts, thus ensuring an income for many families.

Environs

The **Cirque de Jaffar**, a limestone gorge on the way out of Midelt, makes for the most interesting tour here. However, the tracks that go there and back, covering 79 km (49 miles), are tough going, being passable only from May to October and only by four-wheel-drive vehicle.

The track along the hillside is overshadowed by the imposing outline of Jbel Ayachi, which can be climbed without much difficulty. The Cirque de Jaffar is set in a wild landscape of cedar, oak and juniper growing in stony ground. The winding track passes through remote Berber hamlets. A turning off to the left, at the Mit Kane forestry hut, leads back to Midelt. The track that continues west leads eventually to Imilchil.

Disused lead and silver mines in the impressive **Aouli Gorge**, 25 km (15 miles) northeast of Midelt, are sunk into the mountainside. They were abandoned in the 1980s, but the machinery is still in place.

Ziz Gorge ⑱

Road map D-E3. 88 km (55 miles) south of Midelt on road N13.

Wadi Ziz, which springs near Agoudal, in the heart of the High Atlas, runs in an easterly direction, then obliquely south, level with the village of Rich. It then carves a gorge in the mountains, irrigates the Tafilalt then disappears into the Saharan sands.

South of Midelt, beyond the Tizi-n-Talrhemt Pass, at an altitude of 1,907 m (6,259 ft), forests give way to arid plains. The fortified villages of the Aït Idzerg tribe, as well as a few old forts of the French Foreign Legion, line the road.

The **Tunnel de Foum-Zabel**, or Tunnel du Légionnaire, was driven through the limestone rock here by the French Foreign Legion in 1927, thus opening a route to the south. The tunnel

Berber women used to learn embroidery with the Franciscan sisters of Midelt

Dates drying after the autumn harvest in the Ziz gorge

opens on to the Ziz gorge, whose impressive red cliffs jut into the Atlas. Two fine *ksour*, Ifri and Amzrouf, both surrounded by palm trees, stand here.

The Hassan-Addakhil dam, contained by a thick dyke of red earth, demarcates the lower foothills of the Atlas. Built in 1970, it irrigates the Tafilalt and Ziz valleys and provides electricity for Er-Rachidia.

Er-Rachidia ⑲

Road map D3. 62,000. *from Erfoud, Midelt, Ouarzazate and Figuig.* Tourist office; (0535) 57 09 44. Tue, Thu & Sun.

As a result of its strategic location between northern and southern Morocco, and between the Atlantic seaboard and Figuig and the Algerian border, Er-Rachidia became

---

KSOUR IN THE OASES

The Ziz valley is *ksar* country. The *ksar* (plural *ksour*) was developed originally as a communal stronghold for sedentary populations, to protect them against the incursions of bandits and nomadic tribes that raided the oases when the harvests had been brought in. The defensive design of these fortified villages is connected to this warlike past. The *ksar* usually overlooks the oasis. Originally, the *ksar* consisted of no more than a central alley with family houses on each side. Over time, it expanded to become a village, with a mosque, a medersa and granaries. Built of pisé and earth bricks in its upper part, every *ksar* bears the individual stamp of its builders, who devised elaborate incised geometric patterns.

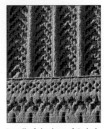

Detail of the *ksar* of Oulad Abdelhalim in Rissani

---

the main town in the province. Here the palm groves of the Ziz and Tafilalt begin, and the town also stands at the start of the road to the south. Er-Rachidia, also an administrative and military centre, was built by the French in the early 20th century, when it was known as Ksar es-Souk. Its present name was bestowed in 1979 in memory of Moulay Rachid, the first of the Alaouites to overthrow Saadian rule in 1666. Many *ksour* here were abandoned after 1960, when the Ziz broke its banks, causing serious floods and washing land away.

Although they are busy, the town's perfectly straight, grid-like streets hold scant appeal. A craft centre offers locally made pottery, carved wooden objects and rush baskets.

Source Bleue de Meski ⑳

Road map E3. 23 km (14 miles) south of Er-Rachidia on road N13.

The spring, located 1 km (0.6 mile) off the main road, is a reappearance of Wadi Ziz, which runs underground for part of its course. The blue spring waters flow from a cave at the foot of a cliff into a pool built by the Foreign Legion. The water provides a natural swimming pool for the campsite in the palm grove.

The clifftop offers a view of the oasis and the ruined *ksar* of Meski. The road to Erfoud (*see p280*) also offers fine views of the Ziz valley and the oases of Oulad Chaker and Aourfous.

Er-Rachidia, a town at the junction of roads leading south

Shop in Erfoud, selling fossils – a local speciality – and a range of craft items

Erfoud 21

Road map E4. 🏛 10,000. 🚌 from
*Fès, Er-Rachidia, Midelt, Rissani and
Tinejdad, and grands taxis.* 🏛 *daily.*
🎪 *Date Festival (Oct).*

Before the development of
the town began in 1930, the
French had set up a military
post here to watch over the
Tafilalt valley. The Berber
tribes put up a long-drawn-
out resistance to the
establishment of French rule,
and the valley was one of
the last parts of southern
Morocco to surrender.

Erfoud's checkerboard layout is a vestige of this military
past. This peaceful town, with
an extensive palm grove, is
the base for tours of the dunes
of the Erg Chebbi. From the
top of the eastern *borj*, a
small bastion 3 km (2 miles)
southeast of Erfoud, the view
takes in a wide swathe of
desert and palm groves.

In October, the souk at
Erfoud overflows with dates
of every variety. This is also
when the three-day Date
Festival, at the end of the date
harvest, takes place. Both a
religious and a secular event,
the festival attracts local
tribes. It begins with prayers
at the mausoleum of Moulay
Ali Cherif in Rissani, 17 km
(11 miles) to the south, and
continues with processions of
people dressed in traditional
costume and with folk dances.

Polished marble containing
fossils is Erfoud's other main
source of income. The cutting
workshops, the **Usine de
Marmar**, is open to visitors.

The road is also bordered with
many small craters – the tops
of shafts down to *khettaras*.

Usine de Marmar
On road R702 to Tinejdad.
🔓 *8am–noon & 2–4pm Mon–Sat.*

Tafilalt
Palm Grove 22

Road map E4. South of Erfoud on
road N13.

Stretching out along the
bends of Wadi Rheris and
Wadi Ziz, which run from
Erfoud, the Tafilalt oasis
nestles in a stretch of greenery,
extending beyond Rissani.
The oasis was once a welcome
stopping-place for caravans,
as they arrived exhausted
after weeks in the desert.

Today, the inhabitants of
the Tafilalt rely on it for their
livelihood: the 800,000 date
palms that grow here are

Date harvest in the Tafilalt
Palm Grove

renowned for their fruit.
Unfortunately, and despite
care, for a century the trees
have suffered from Bayoud
palm sickness – caused by a
microscopic fungus – and the
effects of excessive drought,
both of which can kill them.

The October date harvest in
the palm grove is a spectacular
sight. Each owner climbs to
the top of his tree and, as the
grove resonates to the sound
of machetes, bunches of dates
crash to the ground, falling in
large orange heaps (they turn
brown as they ripen).

Symbols of happiness and
prosperity, dates figure in many
rituals, and in birth, wedding
and burial ceremonies.

Rissani 23

Road map E4. 🏛 15,000. 🚌 from
*Meknès, Erfoud and Er-Rachidia, and
grands taxis.* 🏛 *Tue, Thu & Sun.*

This small town on the edge
of the Sahara marks the end
of the metalled road and the
start of tracks into the desert.
To the east is the Hammada
du Guir, a stony desert
notorious for its violent
sandstorms.

Rissani, built close to the
ruins of Sijilmassa, was once
the capital of the Tafilalt.
Sijilmassa is said to have been
founded in 757–8 as an
independent kingdom,
becoming a major stopping
place on the trans-Saharan
caravan routes. Over the
centuries, it became prosperous from trade in gold, slaves,
salt, weapons, ivory and

spices, reaching its peak in the 13th and 14th centuries. However, religious dissent and the instability of the rival tribes that regularly launched raids on the city led to its destruction. The first town had a pisé wall on stone foundations pierced by eight gates, and contained a palace, fine houses, public baths and many gardens. A few vestiges of these emerge from the sand just west of Rissani.

The **Rissani Souk** is one of the most famous in the area. Donkeys, mules, sheep and goats are enclosed in corrals. Stalls are piled with shining pyramids of dates, as well as with vegetables and spices. Beneath roofs made of palm-matting and narrow pisé alleyways, jewellery, daggers, carpets, woven palm fibre baskets, pottery and fine local leather items, made from goat skins tanned with tamarisk bark, are laid out for sale.

South of Rissani, a 20 km (13 mile) route marked by many *ksour* crosses the palm grove. After 2.5 km (1.5 miles) stands the **Mausoleum of Moulay Ali Cherif**, where the father of Moulay er-Rachid, founder of the Alaouite dynasty, is laid to rest. The mausoleum was rebuilt in 1955, after it was damaged by a serious flooding of Wadi Ziz. A courtyard leads to the burial chamber, to which non-Muslims are not admitted. Behind the mausoleum are the ruins of the 19th-century **Abbar Ksar**. This former residence once housed

Well in the Oulad-Abdelhalim *ksar*

exiled Alaouite princes, the widows of sultans and, protected by a double earth wall, part of the royal treasury.

About 2 km (1 mile) from the mausoleum stands the **Oulad Abdelhalim Ksar**. It was built in 1900 for the elder brother of Sultan Moulay Hassan, who was made governor of the Tafilalt. The monumental entrance, with elaborate decoration in its upper part, opens onto a labyrinth of dilapidated rooms. Two rooms still have their painted ceilings.

The route takes in many other *ksour*, including those of Assererhine, Zaouïa el-Maati, Irara, Gaouz, Tabassamt and Ouirhlane. The *ksar* of Tinrheras, set on a promontory, also comes into view.

The road leading to the Draa valley via Tazzarine and Tansikht starts from Rissani.

Erg Chebbi and the small rain-filled lake Dayet Srji

Merzouga ㉔

Road map E4. 53 km (33 miles) southeast of Erfoud. ⬚ *Sat.*

The small Saharan oasis of Merzouga, much damaged by floods in 2006, is famous for its location at the foot of the **Erg Chebbi Dunes**. These photogenic dunes, which rise up out of the stony, sandy desert, extend for 30 km (19 miles), and reach a maximum height of 250 m (820 ft). At sunrise or dusk, the half-light gives the sand a fascinating range of colours.

Although they are nearer to Rissani, Merzouga and the Erg Chebbi dunes are easier to reach from Erfoud. The services of a guide are not necessary, except when high winds whip up the sand. From Erfoud, going in the direction of Taouz, the metalled road degenerates into a track after 16 km (10 miles). Beyond the Auberge Derkaoua, visitors should follow the line of telegraph poles. The dunes come into view on the left. At Merzouga, camel drivers offer one-hour to two-day tours of the dunes.

Dayet Srji, a small lake west of the village, sometimes fills with water during the winter, after sudden rainfall. It attracts hundreds of pink flamingoes, storks and other migratory birds.

Procession at the foot of the Erg Chebbi dunes, during the Date Festival

SOUTHERN MOROCCO & WESTERN SAHARA

The vast southwestern region of Morocco embraces a variety of spectacular landscapes. The fertile Souss plain, an area dotted with oases and extensive stony deserts, is bordered by the rugged mountains of the Anti-Atlas. On the southern Atlantic coast, sheer cliffs give way to large areas of dunes linking Morocco to the Sahara and the republic of Mauritania.

Six thousand years ago, hunters forced northwards by the desertification of the Sahara moved into southwestern Morocco, as shown by the thousands of rock engravings that have been discovered in the Anti-Atlas. The Arab conquest in the 7th century inaugurated the age of the independent kingdoms. An important point for trans-Saharan trade between Morocco and Timbuctu, the Atlantic coast was coveted from the 15th century by the Portuguese and the Spaniards, who eventually colonized it in the late 19th century, re-naming it Río de Oro (Golden River).

When Spain withdrew from western Sahara in 1975, King Hassan II initiated the Green March during which 350,000 civilians reasserted Morocco's claim to the region *(see p58)*.

The great Souss plain, east of Agadir, lies at the heart of this isolated region. The commercially grown fruit and vegetables here are irrigated by the underground waters of Wadi Souss, and the surrounding argan trees provide food for herds of black goats. To the south, the Anti-Atlas is the final mountainous barrier before the Sahara. Its almost surreal geological folds, shaped by erosion, alternate with verdant oases. Stone-built villages, often with an *agadir* (fortified granary), cluster along *wadis* or at the foot of mountains. Further south, the wide deserted beaches are sometimes cut off by lagoons that attract thousands of migratory birds.

Camel in the Sahara desert, southern Morocco

◁ Spectacular cacti in the gardens of the Musée Municipal du Patrimoine Amazighe in Agadir

Exploring Southern Morocco and Western Sahara

All roads heading into the deep South begin at Agadir, Morocco's foremost coastal resort. To the east lies the great Souss plain, which stretches north as far as the High Atlas and south as far as the Anti-Atlas. This mountain chain of rocky peaks and stony plateaux culminates on its eastern side in Jbel Siroua, a remarkable volcanic massif that reaches a height of 3,304 m (10,844 ft), and whose western side, pitted with isolated valleys, slopes down towards the Atlantic. The resort of Agadir is linked to Tafraoute to the southeast, and to the numerous oases on the Saharan slopes of the Anti-Atlas. The road south links Agadir with the Saharan provinces, which start at the coastal town of Tarfaya. The focal points of human life in the Sahara are a few large towns surrounded by banks of dunes stretching to infinity.

LOCATOR MAP

SIGHTS AT A GLANCE

Agadir pp286–7 ❶
Akka ❹
Guelmim ❾
Igherm to Tata ❸
Laayoune ⑫
Sidi Ifni ❼
Souss Massa
  National Park ❺
Tafraoute ❽
Tan Tan and
  Tan Tan Plage ❿
Tarfaya ⑪
Taroudannt ❷
Tiznit ❻

Sand dunes along the coast between Tan Tan Plage and Tarfaya

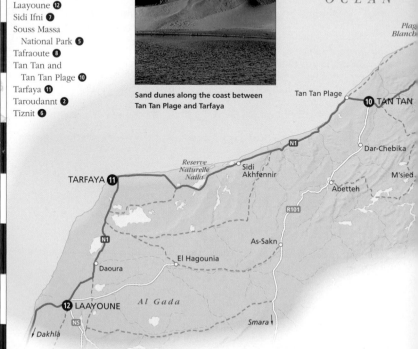

ATLANTIC OCEAN

Plag
Blanch

Tan Tan Plage

❿ TAN TAN

Dar-Chebika

N1

M'sied

Reserve
Naturelle
Naila

Sidi
Akhfennir

Abetteh

TARFAYA ⑪

R101

As-Sakn

N1

El Hagounia

Daoura

⑫ LAAYOUNE   *Al Gada*

N5

Smara

Dakhla

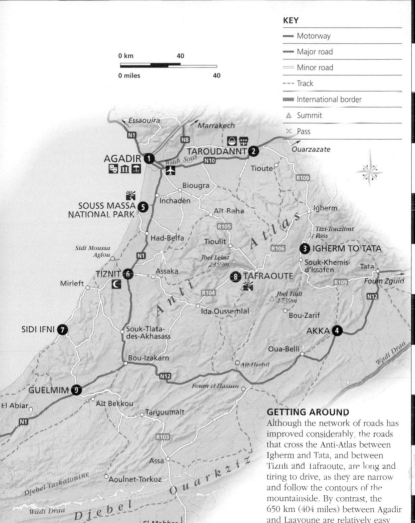

KEY

— Motorway

— Major road

═══ Minor road

--- Track

▬ International border

△ Summit

╳ Pass

0 km 40

0 miles 40

Essaouira N1

Marrakech

AGADIR **1**

TAROUDANNT **2** N10

Ouarzazate

Wadi Sous

Tioute

R109

Biougra

Inchaden

SOUSS MASSA NATIONAL PARK **5**

Aït Baha

Igherm

R105

A

n

t

i

A

t

l

a

s

Tizi-Touzlimt Pass

Had-Belfa

Tioulit

R106

IGHERM TO TATA **3**

Souk-Khemis-d'Issafen

Tata

Sidi Moussa Aglou

N1

Jbel Lekst 2359m

TIZNIT **6**

Assaka

TAFRAOUTE **8**

R109

Foum Zguid

Mirleft

R104

Jbel Tifilt 1739m

N12

Ida Oussemlal

Bou-Zarif

SIDI IFNI **7**

Souk-Tlata-des-Akhasass

AKKA **4**

Oua-Belli

Wadi Draa

Bou-Izakarn

Aït-Herbil

N12

GUELMIM **9**

Foum el-Hassun

El Abiar

Aït Bekkou

N1

Targoumalt

R103

Assa

Djebel Taskatounine

Aoulnet-Torkoz

O u a r k z i z

Wadi Draa

D j e b e l

El-Mahbas

GETTING AROUND

Although the network of roads has improved considerably, the roads that cross the Anti-Atlas between Igherm and Tata, and between Tiznit and Tafraoute, are long and tiring to drive, as they are narrow and follow the contours of the mountainside. By contrast, the 650 km (404 miles) between Agadir and Laayoune are relatively easy to cover, except when there are sandstorms. When travelling through the Saharan provinces it is extremely unwise to leave the road because landmines laid during the war between Morocco and the Polisario Front in the 1970s are still in place. The border with Mauritania can be crossed easily, as long as the required formalities are observed.

SEE ALSO

• **Where to Stay** pp319–21

• **Where to Eat** pp342–3

Tata, with many kasbahs and a palm grove

Agadir ❶

Agadir, the regional capital of the South beyond the Atlas, draws thousands of visitors a year. Its gentle climate – temperatures range from 7 °C to 20 °C (45 °F to 68 °F) in January, the coolest month – together with its sheltered beach and hotels make it Morocco's second tourist city after Marrakech. Having been completely rebuilt in the 1960s after the terrible earthquake that destroyed the city, Agadir has none of the charm of traditional Moroccan towns, although its wide-open spaces and its modernity appeal to many holiday-makers. The industrial quarter consists of oil storage tanks and cement works, as well as factories where fish is canned (Agadir is Morocco's foremost fishing port) and where fruit from the fertile Souss plain is processed.

Nouveau Talborj

Agadir's modern centre, the Nouveau Talborj, was built south of the old city, which was completely razed as the result of the earthquake of 1960.

The main streets of the city centre run parallel to the beach. Pedestrian areas, lined with restaurants, shops and crafts outlets are concentrated around Boulevard Hassan II and Avenue du Prince Moulay Abdallah.

There are some fine modern buildings, including the post office, the town hall and the stately law courts. The city's bright white buildings are interspersed by many gardens.

Traditional doorway

🏛 Musée Municipal du Patrimoine Amazighe

Avenue Hassan II, passage Ait Souss. *Tel* (0528) 82 16 32. 🕘 9:30am–5:30pm Mon–Sat. 🎫

This museum was opened on 29 February 2000, on the day of the commemoration of the reconstruction of Agadir, forty years after the violent earthquake that destroyed the city. The museum exhibits everyday objects derived from the peoples of the Souss plains and the pre-Saharan regions. Among the exhibits is a rich collection of magnificent Berber jewellery, superbly displayed alongside information on how the jewellery was made.

🎭 Open-Air Theatre

Boulevard 20 Août.
Concerts, shows and music festivals take place here throughout the year.

🌿 Vallée des Oiseaux

Avenue Hassan II. 🕘 9am–noon & 3–6pm Tue, pm–Sun.
This open space in the heart of the city, laid out on a narrow strip of greenery, contains aviaries with a multitude of exotic birds. A small zoo features mouflons (wild mountain sheep) and macaques. There is also a play area for children.

Polizzi Medina

Ben-Sergaou. 10 km (6 miles) south of Agadir, towards Inezgane. *Tel* (0528) 28 02 53. 🕘 9am–5:30pm daily. 🚫 Tue. 🎫
This medina was created by Coco Polizzi, an Italian architect, who used traditional Moroccan building methods. Houses, restaurants and craft workshops have been built in the medina.

Riding on the beach at Agadir

🌊 Beach

South of the city, the sheltered beach, in a bay with 9 km (6 miles) of fine sand, is Agadir's main attraction, offering some of the safest swimming off Morocco's Atlantic coast. However, although the city enjoys 300 day of sunshine a year, it is often shrouded in mist in the morning. Sailboards, jet-skis and water scooters can be hired on the beach, and rides, on horses or camels, are also on offer. Many cafés, hotels and restaurants line the beach.

🏯 Old Kasbah

At an altitude of 236 m (775 ft), the hilltop ruins of the kasbah, within restored ramparts, offer a stunning view of Agadir and the bay. The kasbah was built in 1540 by Mohammed ech-Cheikh, to keep the Portuguese fortress under surveillance. It was restored in 1752 by Moulay Abdallah and accommodated a garrison of renegade Christians and Turkish mercenaries.

White houses in Agadir, a city completely rebuilt in the 1960s

For hotels and restaurants in this region see pp319–21 and pp342–3

AGADIR'S HISTORY

The German cruiser *Berlin* off Agadir in 1911

The origins of Agadir are not fully known. In 1505, a Portuguese merchant built a fortress north of the present city. This was acquired by King Manuel I of Portugal and converted into a garrison. By then, Agadir had become a port of call on the sea routes to the Sudan and Guinea. A century of prosperity began in 1541, when the Portuguese were expelled by the Saadians. The Souss fell under the control of a Berber kingdom in the 17th century, but Moulay Ismaïl later reconquered the region. In 1760, Sidi Mohammed ben Abdallah sealed the city's fate when he closed its harbour and opened one in Essaouira. In 1911 Agadir was the object of a dispute between the French and the Germans relating to its strategic location. On 29 February 1960 an earthquake destroyed the city.

VISITORS' CHECKLIST

609,000. Agadir El-Massira, 22 km (13.5 miles) on the road to Taroudannt. from Casablanca, Essaouira, Marrakech & Tiznit. Immeuble Ignouan, Boulevard Mohammed V; (0528) 84 63 77. Tue–Sun.

The busy port at Agadir

Port

Located on the edge of the city, the port consists of a large complex with about 20 canning and freezing factories where the produce of the sea is processed. An auction takes place in the fish market here every afternoon. Agadir also exports citrus fruit, fresh vegetables, canned food and ore.

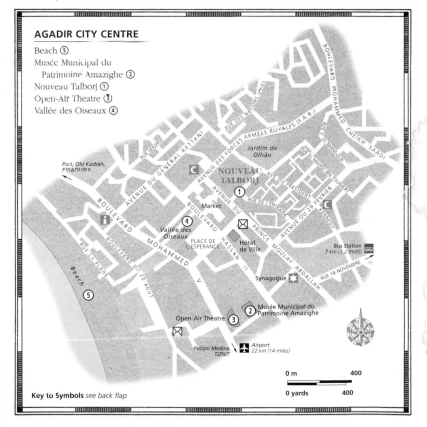

AGADIR CITY CENTRE

Beach ⑤
Musée Municipal du
   Patrimoine Amazighe ②
Nouveau Talborj ①
Open-Air Theatre ③
Vallée des Oiseaux ④

Port, Old Kasbah, ESSAOUIRA

Jardin de Olhão

NOUVEAU TALBORJ ①

Market

Vallée des Oiseaux ④

PLACE DE L'ESPERANCE

Hôtel de Ville

Bus Station
2 km (1.2 miles)

Synagogue

Musée Municipal du Patrimoine Amazighe ②

Open-Air Theatre ③

Polizzi Medina
TIZNIT

Airport
22 km (14 miles)

Beach ⑤

0 m		400
0 yards		400

Key to Symbols *see back flap*

The imposing ramparts of Taroudannt

Taroudannt ②

80 km (50 miles) east of Agadir.
🏃 36,000. 🚌 from Casablanca,
Agadir, Marrakech & Ouarzazate, or
grands taxis; Thu & Sun. ▲ Berber
souk daily. ◉ Moussem (Aug).

Enclosed within red-ochre
ramparts and encircled
by orchards, orange groves
and olive trees, Taroudannt
has all the appeal of an old
Moroccan fortified town. It
was occupied by the
Almoravids in 1056 and in
the 16th century became the
capital of the Saadians, who
used it as a base from which
to attack the Portuguese in
Agadir. Although the Saadians
eventually chose Marrakech
as their capital, they made
Taroudannt wealthy through
the riches of the Souss plain,
which included sugar cane,
cotton, rice and indigo.
    Under the Alaouites, the
town resisted royal control,

The daily Berber market in
Taroudannt

forming an alliance with
Ahmed ibn Mahrez, the dissident nephew of Moulay
Ismaïl. The latter regained
control of the region by
massacring the inhabitants.
    Taroudannt is a generally
peaceful town, except during
the annual olive harvest when
it is enlivened by itinerant
pickers. On its two main
squares, Place Assarag and
Place Talmoklate, horse-
drawn carriages can be hired
for a tour of the **ramparts**,
which are 7 km (4 miles)
long. Set with bastions and
pierced by five gates, they are
in a remarkably good state of
preservation, a part of them
dating from the 18th century.
    The **souks**, between the
two squares, are the town's
main attraction. The daily
Berber market sells spices,
vegetables, clothing, household goods, pottery and other
items. In the Arab souk the
emphasis is on handicrafts:
terracotta, wrought iron, brass
and copper, pottery, leather
goods, carpets and Berber
jewellery of a type once made
by Jews can be seen. Carvings
in chalky white stone are a
speciality of Taroudannt.
    Outside the ramparts is a
small tannery, which is open
to visitors. Its shop sells goatskin and camel-hide sandals,
lambskin rugs, soft leather
bags, belts and slippers.

Environs
The peaks of the western
High Atlas – particularly
Jbel Aoulime, at a height of
3,555 m (11,667 ft) – can be
reached via road 7020, north
of the town. About 37 km
(23 miles) southeast of

Taroudannt, the imposing
Tioute Kasbah dominates the
palm grove. This was the
location for the film Ali Baba
and the Forty Thieves, made
by Jacques Becker in 1954.
A restaurant adjacent to the
kasbah rather spoils the site.
On the banks of Wadi Souss,
which attracts migratory birds,
stands the older Freija kasbah,
now uninhabited.
    Between Taroudannt and
Ouarzazate, the road (N10)
passes through landscape of
wild beauty. Plains covered
with argan trees give way to
the volcanic massif of Jbel
Siroua, which bristles with
peaks and where soft geological folds alternate with
rocky plateaux.
    Taliouine, a town between
two mountain chains at an
altitude of 1,180 m (3,873 ft),
has a stately kasbah once
owned by the Glaoui (see p57).
Though dilapidated, it is still
inhabited. The town is the
centre of the world's biggest
saffron-growing area. In
Tazenakht, 85 km (53 miles)
east of Taliouine, beneath
Jbel Siroua, carpets with an
orange weft are woven by
the Ouaouzguite tribe.

Desert landscape in the Anti-Atlas

Igherm to Tata ③

Road N10 east from Taroudannt,
then road R109 to Tata.
🚌 Taroudannt, Tiznit, Agadir &
Bouizarkane. ▲ Souk Wed in
Igherm, Thu in Tata.

A relatively new road (built
in 1988), the N10 crosses the
Anti-Atlas, passing through
some remarkable landscapes.
Between Taroudannt and
Igherm, argan fields alternate
with dry-stone villages overlooking terraced plantations.

Saffron flowers, harvested for their stigmas

SAFFRON FROM TALIOUINE

Saffron (*Crocus sativus*) is a bulbed herbaceous plant that belongs to the iris family. It grows at altitudes of 1,200 to 2,000 m (4,000 to 6,600 ft), in slightly chalky soil. Almost 6 sq km (2.3 sq miles) of saffron fields around Taliouine are cultivated by families, each of which tends its own plot of land. The bulbs are planted in September at a density of 7,500 per 1,000 sq m (10,760 sq ft), and the mauve flowers appear at the end of October. Harvesting takes place before sunrise and goes on for 15 to 20 days. It is a delicate process, involving the separation of the red stigmas that contain the colorant from the plant. After drying, 100,000 flowers produce 1 kg (2.2 lb) of saffron, and just 1 gram (a tiny pinch) is enough to colour 7 litres (12 pints) of liquid. The precious powder is then poured into airtight boxes and stored away from daylight to preserve its flavour. Good-quality saffron is sold in the form of whole filaments. Saffron is used in food, as a dye for carpets and pottery, and for dyeing the hair and hands of brides. It is also a medicinal plant that is thought to aid digestion and calm toothache.

Igherm, 94 km (58 miles) southeast of Taroudannt, is a large mountain village at an altitude of 1,800 m (5,908 ft). It is the base of the Ida Oukensous tribe, renowned for the daggers and guns that they make. The houses here are built of pink stone, their windows outlined in blue. Women dressed in black and wearing coloured headbands fetch water in tall copper jars (*situle*) which they carry on their head.

Between Igherm and Tata the road crosses a rugged desert plain, with mountains of folded strata in hues of ochre, yellow and violet. The Tizi-Touzlimt Pass, at 1,692 m (5,553 ft), is followed by a succession of oases. In the Souk-Khemis-d'Issafen palm grove women dressed in indigo can be seen walking around the well-watered gardens, except when the Thursday souk is on. Some 30 *ksour* stand in the great **Tata Palm Grove**, where Berber and Arabic are spoken.

Crossing Wadi Tata, which irrigates the grove, the road leads to Agadir-Lehne, where a stone *koubba* stands below a spring. Some 4 km (2.5 miles) further on are the Messalite caves, which are inhabited sporadically by shepherds.

Akka ❹

62 km (39 miles) southwest of Tata on road N12. 🏘 6,500. 🚗 Souk Thu & Sun.

The Akka palm grove lies north of the village. A dozen *ksour* are interspersed among the date palms and the pomegranate, fig, peach, apricot and nut trees. On a hill is Tagadirt, a mellah, now in ruins, where the rabbi Mardoch was born in 1883. He discovered ancient rock engravings in the area and accompanied the French ascetic Charles de Foucauld, disguised as a Jew, on his peregrinations (*see p217*).

The troglodytic granary at Aït-Herbil, still in use

The Aït-Rahhal springs in the palm grove supply the oasis. A strange brick-built minaret dating from the Almohad period can also be seen here.

Environs

Many rock engravings can be seen at **Foum-el-Hassan**, 90 km (56 miles) southwest of Akka on the road to Bouizarkane (road N12), and at **Aït-Herbil**. To visit them, you need to hire a guide (details from Café-Hôtel Tamdoult in Akka). There are also many *igherm* (granaries), some dug into the cliff face.

The *koubba* at Agadir-Lehne, in the Tata Palm Grove

Greater flamingoes flying in the Souss Massa National Park

Souss Massa National Park ❺

65 km (40 miles) south of Agadir on road N1; 50 km (31 miles) north of Tiznit on road N1.

Created in 1991, the Souss Massa National Park extends along the banks of Wadi Massa, which, en route to the Atlantic, irrigates a large palm grove. This nature reserve, where river and sea water meet, where tides ebb and flow, and where winter temperatures are mild, attracts hundreds of migratory birds.

The reed beds on the banks of the *wadi* are inhabited by greater flamingoes from the Camargue, in southern France, and from Spain, as well as godwit, turnstone, snipe, dunlin, coots, grey heron and many other species. The primary purpose of creating the park was to preserve the bald ibis, a species threatened with extinction. Morocco is home to half the world's population of this curious bird, which has a pink featherless head.

Only certain areas of the park are open to the public. Visitors should approach the *wadi* from Sidi Rbat. The best time to see the birds is early in the morning, from March to April and October to November.

Tiznit ❻

91 km (57 miles) south of Agadir on road N1. 🕌 45,000. 🚌 from Agadir, Safi, Guelmim and Tafraoute, or grands taxis. 🚹 ONMT Agadir. 🏛 Souk Wed & Thu. 🕌 Moussem of Sidi Ahmed ou Moussa (Aug), 35 km (22 miles) east of Tiznit.

Located slightly inland from the coast, Tiznit is a small town where the proximity of both the Atlantic and the desert can be felt. In 1881, Sultan Moulay Hassan settled here in order to exert greater control over the dissident Berber tribes of the Souss.

The town came to fame in 1912, when El-Hiba, a populist rebel leader, was proclaimed sultan of Tiznit in the mosque. Opposed to the establishment of the French

Protectorate in Morocco, El-Hiba conquered the Souss by rallying the tribes of the Anti-Atlas and the Tuareg to his cause. He launched an attack on Marrakech, where he was repulsed by French troops.

It is possible to walk round the 5-km (3-mile) pink pisé ramparts that encircle the town. The *méchouar*, a rectangular parade ground that functioned as the pasha's reception courtyard, is lined with arcades beneath which are cafés and shops. The renowned craftsmen of Tiznit still work with silver here, as the Jews once did, producing chunky Berber jewellery, daggers and sabres with inlaid handles.

The vertical poles on the clay walls of the minaret of the Grand Mosque are put there to help the souls of the departed enter paradise.

Environs
Sidi Moussa Aglou, 15 km (9 miles) northwest of Tiznit, is a fine beach used by surfers. Caves in the cliffs are used by local fishermen.

Sidi Ifni ❼

75 km (47 miles) south of Tiznit. 🕌 20,000. 🚹 ONMT Agadir. 🚌 Tiznit or grands taxis. 🏛 Souk Sun. 🕌 Moussem (end of Jun).

From Tiznit, a scenic minor road leads to the coast, which it follows until Sidi Ifni. Formerly a Spanish coastal enclave, the town, on the crest of a rocky plateau over-looking the ocean, is buffeted by wind and is often shrouded

Women spreading washing out to dry on the banks of Wadi Massa

◁ Cube-like houses rendered with pink plaster in Tafraoute, in the Anti-Atlas in sea mist. The colonial style of some of the buildings – such as the former Spanish Consulate and the Hispano-Berber Art Deco church that is now the law courts – gives the town an unusual aspect.

Tafraoute ⑧

143 km (89 miles) southeast of Agadir. *Road N1 from Agadir then road R105; road R104 from Tiznit.* 🏠 *1,700.* 🚌 *Tiznit and Agadir, or grands taxis.* ℹ️ *ONMT Agadir.* 🛒 *Souk Tue & Wed. Mountain bikes can be hired in the town centre.*

At an altitude of 1,200 m (3,938 ft), Tafraoute stands in the heart of a stunning valley of the Anti-Atlas. It is surrounded by a cirque of granite whose colours at the end of the day change from ochre to pink. The palm groves here are lush and, for the brief period of their flowering – two weeks in February – the almond trees are covered with clouds of pink and white blossom.

The square dry-stone houses consist of a central courtyard and a tower. They are rendered with pastel pink plaster and their windows are outlined with white limewash.

Tafraoute is the territory of the Ameln, the best known of the six tribes of the Anti-Atlas. They are renowned for their

MONK SEALS

The largest colony of monk seals *(Monachus monachus)* in the Mediterranean area is found along the Atlantic coast, in the very south of Morocco. In 1995, 200 seals still existed here but half the colony was destroyed by disease in 1998, and it faces a very uncertain future. This brown seal can grow to a length of 3 m (10 ft) and weigh up to 300 kg (660 lb). During the 20th century it has disappeared from the Canary Islands archipelago, Madeira and most of the islands of the Mediterranean. Today, it is still to be found in the Black Sea and on the Bulgarian and Turkish coasts, and it may still survive in Sicily and Sardinia.

The monk seal, facing an uncertain future in Morocco

acumen as traders. As spice merchants, they have spread throughout Morocco and also abroad. Limited local resources have forced them to leave their homeland, so that their

The fortified village of Tioulit

villages are today inhabited only by children, elderly people and women shrouded in black. However, as soon as they can, the émigrés return to build comfortable houses.

Tafraoute is also a centre for the manufacture of round-toed slippers, in natural, red, yellow or embroidered leather.

Environs

Jean Vérame's **painted rocks** can be seen 3 km (2 miles) north of Tafraoute. The smooth, rounded rocks, painted by the Belgian artist in 1984, rise chaotically from a lunar landscape. Although their colours – red, purple and blue – have faded, the effect is still surreal.

About 4 km (2.5 miles) further north is the fertile **Ameln Valley**, carpeted with orchards and with olive and almond trees. It is dotted with 26 Berber villages perching on the mountain side, above which runs a precipitous mountain chain culminating in Jbel Lekst, at 2,359 m (7,743 ft). **Taghdichte**, the highest village, is the starting point for the ascent of Jbel Lekst.

North of Tafraoute, on the road to Agadir, is the *igherm* (communal granary) of Ida ou Gnidif, on the top of a hill. A little further on is the fortified village of **Tioulit**, perching on another outcrop and looks down into the valley.

About 3 km (2 miles) south of Tafraoute a cluster of huge, strangely shaped rocks known as Napoleon's Hat overlooks the village of Agard Oudad. A one-day detour from Tafraoute leads to the **Afella Ighir Oasis**. Laid out along the *wadi*, it is filled with tiny gardens, palm trees and almond trees clinging to the cliffs. Beyond the point where the road becomes a rough track, a four-wheel-drive vehicle is needed.

Houses in Tafraoute, covered in pink plaster

For hotels and restaurants in this region see pp319–21 and pp342–3

Angling from the cliff-top near Tan Tan Plage

Guelmim ❾

56 km (35 miles) south of Sidi Ifni.
🏠 38,000. 🛈 (0528) 87 29 11. 🚌
from Agadir, Marrakech, Laayoune and
Tan Tan, or grands taxis. 🐪 Camel
souk (Sat). 🎪 Moussem of Asrir (Jul).

Also known as Goulimine,
this small settlement of red
houses with blue shutters was
an important centre on the
caravan route from the 11th
to the 19th centuries. Today,
it is known chiefly for its
camel souk. The *moussem* of
Asrir, 6 km (4 miles) southeast,
is attended by the Sahraouis,
known as the "blue men"
because of their indigo clothing.

Environs
Fourteen kilometres (9 miles)
to the north are the **Abeino**
thermal springs with bathing
pools for men and women.
The vast **Plage Blanche** (White
Beach), 60 km (37 miles)
west of Guelmim, can be

A trader at the camel souk
in Guelmim

reached along tracks. The
beautiful **Aït Bekkou Oasis**,
17 km (11 miles) to the southeast, is the largest in the area.

Tan Tan and Tan Tan Plage ❿

125 km (78 miles) southwest of
Guelmim on road N1. 🏠 50,000.
✈ 🚌 Agadir, Tarfaya and Laayoune,
or grands taxis. 🎪 Moussem of
Sheikh Ma el-Ainin (May/Jun).

The province of Tan Tan
is sparsely populated by
pastoral nomads and fishermen. The road from Guelmim
is good but police checks are
frequent since the region
remains a military zone.

Tan Tan has a certain raffish
charm, with everything from
shops and mosques to the
petits taxis painted in blue or
mustard. In the medina, Saha-
ran-style bric-a-brac is for sale
and there is a colourful Sunday
souk. A *moussem* held in May
or June, honouring local resistance hero Sheikh Ma el-Ainin,
is the occasion of a huge camel
market. At night women dance
the *guedra* in tribal tents.

On the coast, 25 km
(15 miles) away, is Tan Tan
Plage where low-key tourism
development has begun.

Environs
Road R101 leads across the
desert to **Smara**, about 245 km
(152 miles) south of Tan Tan.
Today no more than a garrison
base, this legendary town put
up fierce resistance to the
expansion of French rule.

Tarfaya ⓫

235 km (146 miles) south of Tan Tan.
🚌 from Tan Tan or grands taxis.

The spectacularly scenic
route between Tan Tan and
Tarfaya follows the coastline,
where cliffs give way to
dunes of white sand.

Tarfaya, today an expanding
fishing port, was a stop on
the Service Aéropostale, the
French airmail service, in the
1920s and 1930s. There is a
statue of writer and airman
Saint-Exupéry who has left
vivid descriptions of flying
over this desolate region in
terrible sandstorms. It was
also the rallying point for the
Green March of 1975 *(see p58)*.

Boundless expanses of desert
near Laayoune

Laayoune ⓬

117 km (73 miles) south of Tarfaya.
🏠 100,000. ✈ from Agadir, Dakhla
and Tan Tan. 🚌 from Agadir, Dakhla
and Tan Tan. 🛈 Avenue de l'Islam;
(0528) 89 16 94.

A large oasis on Wadi Sagia
el-Hamra, Laayoune is today
the economic capital of the
Saharan provinces. Since
Spain relinquished the territory
in 1976 *(see p58)*, Morocco
has invested in making
Laayoune a modern town.

Dakhla, 540 km (335 km)
further south, stands on the
tip of an attractive peninsula. The bay is one of the
most beautiful places in the
country and an internationally renowned spot for kite
surfing. Dakhla is the last
town before the border with
Mauritania, 350 km (217
miles) away. The border can
be crossed easily.

The Nomad's Tent

The *khaïma*, or nomad's tent, seen on the desert plateaux of the High Atlas, outside the towns of Zagora and Guelmim, is the moveable home of shepherds who travel to provide their flocks with seasonal grazing. The sturdy tent is easy to set up and gives protection against the heat. The brown fabric is woven from goat or camel hair.

Detail of a carpet

It consists of *flijs*, strips 40 to 60 cm (16 to 24 in) wide, sewn together edge to edge. It rests on a ridgepole supported on two vertical wooden poles. The interior of the tent is divided into two. One side, with basic cooking equipment and a loom, is for the women. The other side, separated by a screen, is reserved for the men and for visitors.

Nomads *are rarely seen because they mostly frequent mountain or desert environments that are remote from civilization. However, for a few weeks of the year, some of them settle in an oasis. Their tents are very simply furnished, with little more than thick, heavy carpets and wooden chests where the women keep their most prized possessions. The hospitality of the nomads is legendary.*

The nomad's tent *is set up on level ground. In summer, the covering is laid over the poles in such a way as to allow air to circulate freely. In winter, the sides are drawn together and are insulated with long woollen blankets and carpets.*

Nomadic Berber women *card wool before spinning it into yarn. Using a loom unchanged since ancient times, they weave blankets and lengths of cloth.*

These nomads, *portrayed in a century-old photograph, lived in a way which hasn't changed much to this day. Nomads still travel from one source of water to another.*

Driving animals *to seasonal pastures occurs in Morocco's more arid regions. In summer, the nomads take their herds and flocks up to the high pastures of the Atlas, returning to the south in winter.*

TRAVELLERS'
NEEDS

WHERE TO STAY 298–321
WHERE TO EAT 322–343
SHOPPING IN MOROCCO 344–349
ENTERTAINMENT IN MOROCCO 350–353
SPORTS & OUTDOOR ACTIVITIES 354–357

WHERE TO STAY

In Morocco, choosing a hotel depends primarily on its location and on the services that you require during your stay. Hotels are graded according to an official system of classification that is now usually much more reliable than it once was, although at the cheaper end of the spectrum standards may be somewhat below European expectations. There are hotels in a wide range of price bands, so that visitors will have no difficulty in finding accommodation to suit their budget. Luxury

Hotel porter

hotels are becoming increasingly numerous, as are guesthouses, many of which are in *riads* (houses with patios). In the low season, prices are often negotiable, even in the smartest establishments. Beware of travelling without having made prior reservations, however, since at certain times of the year accommodation is almost impossible to find. For those with smaller budgets, youth hostels and guest rooms are attractive alternatives so long as visitors observe the ground rules.

Les Mérinides *(see p311)*, a hotel with a splendid view of Fès

CHOOSING A HOTEL

The location of your hotel, especially in large towns and cities, is an important criterion. It is usually best to stay somewhere near the old town, where the main tourist sites are often found. The disadvantage of such a location, however, is that the hotel is noisy and unlikely to offer parking. If you would like more space, especially a garden – and many gardens also have a swimming pool – it is best to choose a hotel on the edge of the old town or in a modern quarter.

Smaller towns rarely offer high-class accommodation, especially in the South. Here, your choice of hotel should be governed by your itinerary. In the South, most places of interest to tourists are not in the towns

themselves but along the roads between them, so that rather than planning your route according to the desirability of a hotel, it is best to choose where to stay in relation to the distance you intend to cover each day.

CLASSIFICATION OF HOTELS AND SERVICES

The Moroccan Ministry of Tourism has devised an official system of classification for hotels. Accordingly, hotels are graded on a scale of one to five stars, with two subcategories, A and B. In principle, each grade corresponds to certain standards of comfort, as well as criteria such as the size of the establishment.

Once bearing little relation to reality, the system by which stars are awarded has been overhauled. Although

some hotels may still be over-ambitiously graded, many have been downgraded to reflect more accurately the standard of accommodation that they offer.

As a general rule, four- and five-star hotels are well equipped, with satellite television, telephone, en-suite bathrooms and room service, as well as many other features such as a restaurant, swimming pool, sports centre and hammam. Two- and three-star hotels are comfortable and clean, with private bath or shower. The small one-star hotels, or hotels without classification, are often quite basic and may not be very clean. It is advisable to ask to see the room before you decide.

Although most ungraded hotels do not deserve to be listed, some are, in fact, very comfortable establishments. It is only reluctance on the part of their owners to do the necessary paperwork that prevents them from being listed.

Stylish decor in the Husa Casablanca Plaza *(see p305)*

◁ Multicoloured slippers laid out for sale

The Auberge Kasbah Derkaoua *(see p318)*, on the track to Merzouga

PRICES

By law, prices for accommodation must be shown in the reception area as well as in the rooms, and this requirement is widely fulfilled. Be aware, however, that advertised prices rarely include tax (ranging from 1 to 25 dirhams, according to the town and the hotel) and that they do not include breakfast.

The average price of a single room in a small one-star or unlisted hotel is 150 dirhams. A two- or three-star establishment will charge 250 to 400 dirhams, and a three star category-A hotel or a four star hotel 400 to 1,000 dirhams. The numerous five star hotels charge 1,200 dirhams, and some of them over 2,000 dirhams. There is no official upper limit.

Prices vary according to the season, and it is not unusual to see prices double around the holiday periods at the end of the year and in spring, and during the summer in the coastal resorts. Prices also vary according to the number of people renting the room. For example, for a child or a third adult sharing a room, a supplement will be charged, though usually with a reduction of 5 to 50 per cent.

The reliable **Kenzi** hotel chain, which has hotels all over Morocco, gives discounts when reservations are made in several of their establishments, and also in the low season. Information about hotels is available from the **Fédération Nationale de l'Industrie Hôtelière** in Casablanca.

NEGOTIATING A LOWER PRICE

Negotiating a lower price for a hotel room is quite common practice, and it bears results. At slack times, it is possible to obtain reductions of up to 30 per cent. However, it is a waste of time trying to negotiate at the peak of the high season, or in the very smart hotels, such as the La Mamounia in Marrakech.

RESERVATIONS

During the high seasons, and particularly over the spring and end-of-year holiday periods, the crowds of holiday-makers can be unexpectedly large. This is also true of coastal resorts during the summer. At such times, in small towns that have a limited number of hotels (particularly in the South) it can be quite impossible to find a room. This can also happen in towns with a much larger choice of hotels, such as Marrakech or Fès.

At these busy times, it is essential to make a reservation in advance. This can be done at a travel agency, through a tour operator covering Morocco or by contacting hotels directly. When making a direct booking, you will be asked to quote the number of your credit card so as to confirm the reservation. Doing this is usually quite safe, even though it is best to deal only with large establishments or with hotels belonging to a reputable chain.

One consequence of the European-style hotel management that has taken root in Morocco is the practice of overbooking. Put simply, the hotel accepts more reservations than it has rooms so as to compensate for any cancellations. Unfortunately, if you happen to be a victim of this practice, there is little that you can do. The best way to try to avoid this happening is to pay for your stay in full at the time of booking and check in at the hotel earlier rather than later in the day.

Rooftop of the Dar Attamani *(see p314)* offering fine views of the town

Swimming pool at the famous hotel La Mamounia *(see p316),* in a luxuriant garden

CHAIN AND LUXURY HOTELS

The Accor Group manages multiple international hotel brands such as **Sofitel**, **Novotel** and **Mercure**, which can be found in most major towns and cities throughout the country. Such leading international hotel chains as Hyatt and Le Méridien have several establishments in Morocco. The **Ibis** group manages several hotels belonging to the **Moussafir** chain.

There is a large number of luxury hotels in Morocco. Although many of them are modern, the country also boasts a few old legendary establishments, such as the charming La Mamounia in Marrakech *(see p316),* which, although it has lost some of its appeal as a result of renovation, still has a great atmosphere. The Sofitel Palais Jamaï in the imperial city of Fès *(see p311),* converted from a former palace, is not only an architectural marvel but has a unique location above the medina. The luxurious and elegant Hôtel El-Minzah in Tangier *(see p309)* looks like something from a film set and, although it is showing its age, is still one of Morocco's great hotels.

CAMPSITES

Campsites can be found in every large town, and they are very numerous on the Atlantic and Mediterranean coasts. As a general rule, standards of cleanliness in campsites leave much to be desired, and it is not safe to leave property unattended in tents. Staying in a campsite in Morocco is also something that best suits those who are not too fussy about hygiene and facilities.

Finding your own place to set up camp outside official sites is not officially unlawful, but it is definitely not recommended for reasons of personal safety and because the authorities do not like tourists camping anywhere they please.

GUESTHOUSES

In small seaside villages, where it is sometimes very difficult to find accommodation, many Moroccans offer rooms to let in their own houses. Comforts are often basic and, before accepting the room, it is wise to check the cleanliness of the bedclothes and that toilets and washing facilities are in working order.

Guesthouse accommodation can be a useful option when you are staying for a few days away from the large tourist coastal resorts.

Often, when travelling in the Atlas, visitors will be offered accommodation, rather than be left to camp in the open. In such cases, you may be offered space in a living room, or on the roof of a pisé house, which can be a magical experience. The owner of the house (often the village chief) will steadfastly refuse money, and will even invite you to share a meal. You can always offer a gift, or deal with the women of the house, who will often accept remuneration or a present for their children.

YOUTH HOSTELS

There are several youth hostels in Morocco, and these make it possible to stay in the country for a minimal cost. However, most youth hostels are not centrally located and are quite basic, although they are usually clean. If you do not have an international Youth Hostel Association membership card, you may be asked to pay a little extra. The easiest way to obtain a card is to join your country's youth hostel association, such as the **YHA** in Britain or the **HI-AYH** in the United States. Information in Morocco is available from the **Fédération Royale Marocaine des Auberges de Jeunesse** in Casablanca.

UNMARRIED COUPLES

It is as well to know that in Morocco strict rules apply to the accommodation of couples. A Muslim cannot sleep with a woman if the couple are not married. Some hoteliers scrupulously respect

The atmospheric interiors of Riad d'Or *(see p312)* in Meknès

this ruling. Allowances are normally made for Western couples, however, except by particularly strict hotel keepers.

DISABLED VISITORS

Apart from some modern hotels, few establishments in Morocco are equipped for disabled visitors. Nevertheless, Moroccans are very well disposed to anyone needing help, so that people with disabilities will be pleasantly surprised at the thoughtfulness and helpfulness that they encounter in Morocco.

RIADS

The literal translation of the Arabic word *riad* is "garden". Thus a *riad* should consist, theoretically, of a garden planted with trees. By extension, the word *riad* is applied to all old houses that have at least a patio or courtyard. These old-style Moroccan houses can be found in the medinas, and many have become available to visitors, especially in Marrakech, Fès and Essaouira.

These traditional residences each have their own particular architectural design

One of the many *riads* in Essaouira that are now guesthouses

and have usually been very well restored. Converted into guesthouse accommodation, they are very pleasant places to stay in, particularly because they are quiet and because of their often excellent location. By contrast to a large international hotel, staying in a *riad* is usually an experience that will transport you to another age.

Either individual rooms or the whole *riad* can be rented, and many also offer breakfast and an evening meal. No official grading applies to this type of accommodation, and standards, service and prices vary widely according to the individual *riad*.

While some *riads* are run by people who have only a vague idea of the hotel business, others are out of the ordinary. Into this category come Villa des Orangers (*see p317*) and La Maison Arabe, both in Marrakech (*see p316*). These *riads* will delight those who love old buildings and who expect a high standard of service.

Riads can be booked through **Riads au Maroc, Marrakech-Medina** and **Fès Medina Morocco** (US based). Of the agencies that handle the booking of *riads*, however, not all are reputable, some of them merely making the most of the popularity of this type of accommodation.

DIRECTORY

Fédération Nationale de l'Industrie Hôtelière
320 Boulevard Zerktouni,
20000 Casablanca.
Tel (0522) 26 73 13/14.
Fax (0522) 26 72 73.
www.fnih.ma

HOTEL CHAINS

Hôtels Ibis Moussafir
(Accor group)
Tel (00 33) 60 87 91 00.
(reservations, France).
www.accorhotels.com

Hôtel Mercure (Rabat)
Tel (0537) 72 22 26.
Fax (0537) 72 45 27.
www.mercure.com

Hôtel Novotel (Casablanca)
Tel (0522) 46 65 00.

Fax (0522) 46 65 01.
www.novotel.com

Hôtel Sofitel (Marrakech)
Tel (0524) 42 56 00.
www.sofitel.com

YOUTH HOSTEL ASSOCIATIONS

Australian Youth Hostel Association
Level 3, 10 Mallett Street,
Camperdown, NSW 2050.
Tel 02 9565 1699.
Fax 02 9565 1325.
www.yha.com.au

Canada Hostelling International/Canadian Hostelling Assoc.
Room 400, 205 Catherine St., Ottawa ON K2P 1C3.
Tel (1-800) 663 5777.
www.hostellingintl.ca

England & Wales Youth Hostel Association (YHA)
Trevelyan House,
Malock, Derbyshire
DE4 3YH. *Tel* 01727 845 047. www.yha.org.uk

Morocco Fédération Royale Marocaine des Auberges de Jeunesse
6 Place Ahmed el Bidaoui,
Casablanca. *Tel & Fax* (0522) 22 76 77.

New Zealand Youth Hostel Association
166 Moorhouse Ave,
Christchurch.
Tel (03) 379 9970.
www.yha.co.nz

USA Hostelling International-American Youth Hostels (HI-AYH)

733 15th St NW, Suite 840, PO Box 37613,
Washington, DC 20005
Tel (202) 783 6161.
www.hiayh.org

RIADS

Fès Medina Morocco
516 San Miguel
Canyon Rd, Royal Oaks,
California 95076.
Tel (831) 724 5835
Fax (904) 212 8814.
www.fesmedina.com

Marrakech-Medina
Tel (0524) 29 07 07.
www.marrakech-medina.com

Riads au Maroc
1 Rue Mahjoub-Rmiza,
Marrakech (Gueliz).
Tel (0524) 43 19 00.
www.riadomaroc.com

Choosing a Hotel

The hotels in this guide have been selected across a wide range of price categories for the excellence of their facilities, location or character. Hotels are listed under the region chapter headings. Entries are alphabetical within price category. For a listing of recommended restaurants, see pages 328–43.

RABAT

AGDAL Ibis Moussafir
Gare Oncf Agdal **Tel** *(0537) 77 49 19* **Rooms** *95*   **Road map** *C2*

Located in the quieter area of Agdal, on the outskirts of Rabat, the Ibis Moussafir hotel has a lot of character despite being modern in appearance. Its bright foyer is welcoming, while its restaurant and bar are inspired by Moroccan decor. Next door is the Rabat Agdal railway station. **www.ibishotels.com**

CITY CENTRE Riad Dar Soufa
7 Derb Souaf Legza, Avenue Mohamed V **Tel** *(0673) 19 45 37* **Rooms** *4*   **Road map** *C2*

The courtyard of this stylish yet simple *riad* is the perfect place to relax after a day of shopping in the medina. Dar Soufa offers spacious, clean and traditionally styled rooms, which are attractive and extremely good value. It has excellent service and has the added advantage of being centrally located. **http://riadrabatmedinadarsoufa.blogspot.com**

CITY CENTRE Art Riad
16 Rue Essam **Tel** *(0537) 20 20 28* **Rooms** *5*   **Road map** *C2*

Art Riad's cool lines and contemporary decor provides a wonderful alternative to the intricacy of traditional Moroccan interiors available elsewhere. The intimate and peaceful atmosphere shields guests from the bustling city and sets it apart from grander, larger establishments. Unwind on the sunny roof terrace or shaded courtyard. **www.artriad.com**

CITY CENTRE Dar Mayssane
13 Rue Faran, Khechen **Tel** *(0661) 06 66 66* **Rooms** *5*   **Road map** *C2*

This enchanting little *riad* is situated on the edge of the medina. It offers cosy, stylish rooms that have been tastefully decorated with great attention to detail, all at reasonable prices. The breakfast is served in beautiful surroundings. The hotel has friendly and welcoming staff. **www.rabat-riad.com**

CITY CENTRE Hôtel Balima
Avenue Mohammed V **Tel** *(0537) 70 77 55* **Rooms** *71*   **Road map** *C2*

Located opposite the parliament building, in one of the most interesting parts of Rabat, the Balima is a good option for a short break on a budget. Rooms are moderately priced, but it is worth seeing them before booking. The hotel decor is traditional Moroccan, and the restaurant/bar area is surrounded by palm trees. Parking is provided.

CITY CENTRE Hôtel Chellah
2 Rue d'Ifni **Tel** *(0537) 66 83 00* **Rooms** *120*   **Road map** *C2*

A delightful centrally located hotel decorated to echo the best of Moroccan design, the Chellah is popular with both holiday and business visitors. Rooms are well presented, with facilities that include satellite TV. The hotel offers a fitness suite and a roof-terrace bar among its amenities. **www.helnan.com**

CITY CENTRE Hôtel Majliss
6 Rue Zahla **Tel** *(0537) 73 37 26* **Rooms** *65*   **Road map** *C2*

With its central location, a nightclub, parking and conference facilities, Hôtel Majliss is popular with both business and leisure visitors. With traditional Moroccan decor and offering a restaurant with well-presented local and European specialities, it is a very comfortable and welcoming hotel. **www.majlisshotel.ma**

CITY CENTRE Hôtel Mercure Shéhérazade
21 Rue de Tunis **Tel** *(0537) 72 22 26* **Rooms** *78*   **Road map** *C2*

The Hôtel Mercure Shéhérazade is a small and beautifully presented venue with a decor inspired by Moroccan jewel colours and staff who greet guests with broad smiles, making it a welcoming place to stay. It is also close to several attractions, including the must-see Mausoleum of Mohammed V and the Hassan Tower. **www.accorhotels.com**

CITY CENTRE Riad El Batoul
7 Derb Jirari Rabat **Tel** *(0537) 72 72 50* **Rooms** *9*   **Road map** *C2*

Entering the Riad El Batoul – a small former Moorish palace located inside the medina – is a little like stepping back in time. You can laze on golden sofas drinking green tea or dine on local cuisine on a columnated terrace. Rooms are traditional in style with private bathrooms and lots of charm. **www.riadbatoul.com**

Key to Symbols *see back cover flap*

CITY CENTRE Riad El Maati

15 Rue sidi el Maâti **Tel** *(0673) 02 66 21* **Rooms** *6* **Road map** *C2*

This stunning and little-known *riad* is expertly run and owned by a French/Moroccan couple, eager to help guests get the best out of their stay. The rooms are beautifully decorated. Breakfast is served on the terrace, overlooking the capital's rooftops. Child friendly. **www.riadelmaati.com**

CITY CENTRE Riad Kalaa

3–5 Rue Zebdi **Tel** *(0537) 20 20 28* **Rooms** *11* **Road map** *C2*

A thoughtful renovation has helped this striking *riad* radiate elegance and old-world charm. The original structure, dating back to the early 1800s, has lost none of its beauty. The sumptuous bed linen and elegant fittings in the rooms add to the simple majesty of the building. **www.riadkalaa.com**

CITY CENTRE Riad Dar El Kebira

Rue des Consuls No.1, Impasse Belghazi, Ferrane Znaki **Tel** *(0537) 72 49 06* **Rooms** *10* **Road map** *C2*

Decorated in pure Moorish style, this hotel offers luxury on a grand scale. Renovated to a very high standard, these magnificent surroundings ooze a sense of privilege and grandeur that take you back to the courts of past eras. It has all the charms of a guesthouse combined with the trappings of a five-star hotel. **www.darelkebira.com**

CITY CENTRE Golden Tulip Farah

Place Sidi Makhlouf **Tel** *(0537) 23 74 00* **Rooms** *193* **Road map** *C2*

Located within a short walk from the seafront and overlooking the Atlantic Ocean, this hotel is close to many of the main attractions of Rabat. It is a lavish establishment with extremely comfortable rooms. Amenities include a health club, swimming pool, boutique and two restaurants. **www.goldentulipfarahrabat.com**

CITY CENTRE Hôtel Rabat

21 Avenue Chellah **Tel** *(0537) 70 00 71* **Rooms** *114* **Road map** *C2*

This modern hotel in a boat-shaped building is centrally located, close to the embassies, historical monuments and the medina. Rooms are decorated in Art Deco style and are well equipped, while the pool, fitness suite and spa with beauty therapies offer plenty of opportunity for relaxation. There are several dining options. **www.hotelrabat.com**

CITY CENTRE Hôtel Soundouss

10 Place Talha Agdal **Tel** *(0537) 27 88 88* **Rooms** *50* **Road map** *C2*

Located close to the airport and golf courses, and within easy walking distance of Rabat's main tourist attractions, the atmospheric Soundouss is ideal for the leisure traveller. Its rooms have amenities such as Wi-Fi Internet, while the hotel offers two restaurants and a piano bar. Parking is also available. **www.soundousshotel.ma**

CITY CENTRE La Tour Hassan

26 Rue Chellah BP 14 **Tel** *(0537) 23 90 00* **Rooms** *140* **Road map** *C2*

This is a charming hotel that oozes Moroccan style and yet has a distinctive European flavour. Its outside terraces overlooking its beautiful gardens and pool are pure elegance. Rooms are well presented and equipped, while the hotel has a number of restaurants from which to choose *(see p328)*. **www.palaces-traditions.ma**

CITY CENTRE Sofitel Diwan Rabat

Place de l'Unité Africaine 10005 **Tel** *(0537) 26 27 27* **Rooms** *94* **Road map** *C2*

Located in the city centre, near the Hassan Tower and the Mosque of Hassan II, the Sofitel Diwan is an elegant place to stay. Rooms are sumptuous, with many amenities, while its restaurant *(see p328)* serves fine French cuisine, and its spa offers Oriental treatments. Rabat's Dar Es-Salaam golf course is close by. **www.accorhotels.com**

SKHIRAT PLAGE Hôtel L'Amphitrite Palace

Skhirat Plage **Tel** *(0537) 62 10 00* **Rooms** *178* **Road map** *C2*

The luxurious and elegant L'Amphitrite Palace is located right next to the royal summer residence, overlooking Skhirat beach. Along with well-equipped, well-presented rooms and suites, it offers amenities such as a restaurant, a thalassotherapy and well-being centre, gardens and access to the beach. **www.lamphitrite-palace.com**

SOUISSI Sofitel Rabat Jardin des Roses

Aviation Souissi **Tel** *(0537) 67 56 56* **Rooms** *269* **Road map** *C2*

Set in lush gardens of palm trees and exotic plants, the former Hilton Rabat Hôtel is a top-quality home-from-home, popular with both business and holidaying travellers. It offers every amenity – from a gymnasium and spa, to restaurants serving Moroccan and international dishes – and well-equipped rooms. **www.sofitel.com**

NORTHERN ATLANTIC COAST

ASILAH Berbari

Medchar Ghanem, Cercle Tnine Sidi Yamani, Commune D'Assilah **Tel** *(0660) 29 54 54* **Rooms** *7* **Road map** *D1*

A short drive from Asilah's train station, this quirky, rural hotel with a zany decor offers a warm welcome. Come here for a retreat away from it all and to surround yourself with nature. It has great country views and from the porch you can watch donkeys and goats pass by. Storks also nest on the roof. **www.berbari.com**

ASILAH Hôtel Zelis

10 Avenue Mansour-Eddhabi **Tel** *(0539) 41 70 29* **Rooms** *55*   **Road map** *D1*

Located within easy reach of the Centre Hassan II des Rencontres Internationales, where cultural events are held during the summer months, the Hôtel Zelis offers high-quality, comfortable guest rooms, some with sea views, and lots of facilities, including a restaurant and pool.

ASILAH Dar Manara

23 Rue M'Jimma **Tel** *(0677) 39 82 67* **Rooms** *5*   **Raod map** *D1*

Dar Manara offers bright and well-presented rooms, a homely and tranquil atmosphere and extremely helpful and knowledgeable hosts, as well as excellent staff. A great option for those travelling on a budget but do not wish to sacrifice comfort and style. It is essential to book in advance. **www.asilah-darmanara.com**

ASILAH Hôtel El'Khaima

Corniche Asilah **Tel** *(0539) 41 74 28* **Rooms** *113*   **Road map** *D1*

The Hôtel El'Khaima is housed in a contemporary-looking building but as it is located in a town frequented by painters and writers, many of whom stay here as guests, it is usually lively and atmospheric. Its guest rooms are well presented, and it boasts a good range of facilities, including a pool, tennis courts and a nightclub.

KENITRA Hôtel d'Europe

63 Avenue Mohammed Diouri **Tel** *(0537) 37 14 50* **Rooms** *24*   **Road map** *C2*

The Hôtel d'Europe is a pleasant little hotel close to the centre of Kenitra, and although it doesn't offer a large number of facilities, it has helpful staff who make visitors feel welcome. Its guest rooms are clean and fresh, and its intimate restaurant offers some tasty Moroccan specialities.

KENITRA Hôtel Mamora

Avenue Hassan II **Tel** *(0537) 37 17 75* **Rooms** *69*   **Road map** *C2*

Housed in a renovated Art Deco-style building, the Mamora offers a good range of facilities for families, including a play area and a swimming pool surrounded by terraces and gardens. Guest rooms are finished to a high standard and have en-suite bathrooms. There is also a restaurant on site.

KENITRA Hôtel Jacaranda

Place Administrative **Tel** *(0537) 37 30 30* **Rooms** *85*   **Road map** *C2*

In a characterful building with a look inspired by colonial architecture, this hotel offers a pleasant and centrally located place to stay. The Jacaranda is within easy reach of both Kenitra's harbour and the Wadi Sebou river for relaxing strolls. It has terraces around its pool and a good restaurant.

LARACHE Hôtel España

2 Avenue Hassan II **Tel** *(0539) 91 31 95* **Rooms** *43*   **Road map** *D1*

Housed in a building that takes its inspiration from Andalusian and Arabian decor, and within easy distance from the medina in the Place de la Libération, the Hôtel España is ideal for short stays. Satellite TV, air conditioning and Wi-Fi is available in all rooms. It offers good value and a convenient town-centre location.

LARACHE La Maison Haute

6 Derb be Thami **Rooms** *7*   **Road map** *D1*

With good views and a warm welcome, this budget hotel occupies a Hispano-Moroccan house in the centre of this small town's medina. Rooms are brightly decorated with plenty of colour. As the name – the Tall House – suggests, there are plenty of stairs. The roof terrace has panoramic views of Larache. **http://lamaisonhaute.free.fr**

SALÉ Riad Marlinea

17 Derb Hrarta, Bab Lamrissa – Salé Medina **Tel** *(0537) 88 37 34* **Rooms** *4*   **Road map** *C2*

This pretty hotel is near all local sights and offers traditionally decorated rooms and ample communal seating areas. The Moroccan restaurant serves up classic dishes in an attractive setting. It can be difficult to find, so if you do have any trouble locating the hotel ask a local. **www.riad-marlinea.com**

SALÉ The Repose

17 Zankat Talaa, Salé Medina **Tel** *(0537) 88 29 58* **Rooms** *4*   **Road map** *C2*

The Repose is a unique guesthouse, packed with character and elegant decor. Located in the heart of Salé the riad's few rooms (all suites) are in high demand, so book ahead. Husband and wife owners live on-site, so guests benefit from their knowledge and their attention to details such as the interior and excellent cuisine. **www.therepose.com**

SALÉ Le Dawliz Hôtel

Avenue de Bouregreg **Tel** *(0537) 88 32 77* **Rooms** *45*   **Road map** *C2*

A popular holiday location for families, Le Dawliz Hôtel is set in the heart of a luxurious tourist complex, on the riverbank opposite Rabat. It offers almost every amenity, including a number of sports facilities, a swimming pool and a choice of themed restaurants. The accommodation is modern and to a high standard. **www.ledawliz.com**

SALÉ Hôtel Dar el Mouhit

12 Rue Moulay Goumri **Tel** *(0537) 84 48 04* **Rooms** *4*   **Road map** *C2*

Situated in the historic medina area of Salé, the Dar el Mouhit is housed in a traditional period property that exudes charm at every turn. Its restaurant serves pure Moroccan fare, along with fish, caught fresh daily. Rooms are large, with en-suite bathrooms, and are decorated with traditional tiles and drapes.

Key to Price Guide *see p302* **Key to Symbols** *see back cover flap*

CASABLANCA

BOUZNIKA Riad Des Plages

Plage Essanaoubar Nord **Tel** *(0659) 21 73 09* **Rooms** *6*

Road map *C2*

This attractive hotel is ideal for single travellers, or for those wishing to hire the entire building. Each bedroom is unique and decorated in traditional style. The *riad* has direct access to the beach and is close to several golf courses. The hotel has efficient and reliable staff. It is open from April to October. **www.riaddesplages.com**

CITY CENTRE Hôtel Guynemer

2 Rue Mohamed Belloul, Casa-Anfa **Tel** *(0522) 27 57 64* **Rooms** *29*

Road map *C2*

Centrally located in downtown Casablanca, this small, family-run hotel, is just about the only truly budget hotel in the city that really cares about its guests. It is bright and welcoming and the rooms are decorated with splashes of colour. Moroccan cuisine is served in the restaurant. Popular with travellers and hard to beat for the price.

CITY CENTRE Hôtel Suisse

Boulevard de la Corniche **Tel** *(0522) 36 02 02* **Rooms** *148*

Road map *C2*

A four-star hotel located right on the coast and yet close to the city centre, the Suisse is popular with business visitors as well as holidaymakers. Its facilities include an international restaurant, a courtyard bar and a swimming pool. There's also a nightclub for guests keen to dance the night away.

CITY CENTRE Ibis Moussafir

Angle Zaid Ouhmad Rue Sidi Belyout **Tel** *(0522) 46 65 60* **Rooms** *266*

Road map *C2*

A modern hotel, the Moussafir has guest rooms with features such as air conditioning, private bathroom and television, while the hotel itself features a restaurant serving a delicious à la carte menu. It is close to the great Mosque of Hassan II. **www.ibishotel.com**

CITY CENTRE Best Western Toubkal Hôtel

9 Rue Sidi Belyout **Tel** *(0522) 31 14 14* **Rooms** *68*

Road map *C2*

Part of the Best Western chain, the Toubkal is a popular hotel with both holiday and business travellers. It is set in the heart of the city and close to the main attractions. Guest rooms are finished to a high standard. A spa, squash and tennis courts, restaurants and even a nightclub are available on site. **www.hoteltoubkal.com**

CITY CENTRE Novotel Casablanca

Corner Rue Zaid Ouhmad & Rue Sidi Belyout **Tel** *(0522) 46 65 00* **Rooms** *281*

Road map *C2*

With modern, well-equipped rooms over 17 floors, this hotel offers great views of the port and Hassan II Mosque. Its central location means it is close to the Casa Port railway station and within walking distance of the old medina. Families are well catered for here with family rooms, a children's menu and play areas. **www.accorhotels.com**

CITY CENTRE Hôtel Royal Mansour Méridien

27 Avenue des FAR **Tel** *(0522) 31 30 11* **Rooms** *182*

Road map *C2*

You could be forgiven for never wanting to leave this splendid hotel, with its richly coloured air-conditioned guest rooms, complete with every amenity. The Royal Mansour Méridien has a choice of Moroccan and Mediterranean restaurants, a piano bar and a health complex. Close to the main city sights. **www.leroyalmansourmeridien.com**

CITY CENTRE Husa Casablanca Plaza

Rond Point Hassan II **Tel** *(0522) 48 80 00* **Rooms** *184*

Road map *C2*

This is a very swish establishment that is part of the prominent Spanish hotel chain Husa. The hotel has large rooms and an enviable location in the heart of the city. There are also facilities for business travellers, including a technology support desk. Prices are competitive. **www.husa.es/en/nuestros-hoteles**

CITY CENTRE Kenzi Tower Hôtel

Boulevard Zerktouni **Tel** *(0522) 97 80 00* **Rooms** *237*

Road map *C2*

Located on the 28th floor of one of the Twin Center skyscrapers, this hotel has incredible views and impeccable service. Kenzi Tower Hôtel offers all the facilities associated with a luxury hotel. Being away from the medina, it is a good option for those who wish to avoid the bustle of the city. Its lounge is famous for tea. **www.kenzi-hotels.com**

CITY CENTRE Palace d'Anfa

171 Boulevard d'Anfa **Tel** *(0522) 95 42 00* **Rooms** *139*

Road map *C2*

The Palace d'Anfa is a large but not overpowering five-star hotel close to the main attractions of Casablanca. Rooms are high end and include facilities such as a minibar and private bathroom, while the hotel offers a well-equipped fitness centre, swimming pool, spa and beauty parlour, as well as an elegant restaurant. **www.lepalacedanfa.ma**

CITY CENTRE Golden Tulip Farah Casablanca

160 Avenue des FAR **Tel** *(0522) 31 12 12* **Rooms** *294*

Road map *C2*

This hotel enjoys a city-centre location close to the main attractions of Casablanca. The old medina is within walking distance. Guest rooms and suites are well presented and feature facilities such as a private bathroom and air conditioning. The hotel has its own restaurants serving Moroccan and international cuisine.

CITY CENTRE Hôtel Hyatt Regency

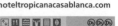

Place des Nations Unies **Tel** *(0522) 43 12 34* **Rooms** *255*   **Road map** *C2*

The Hyatt Regency is everything you would expect a luxury hotel to be. Guest rooms are lavish and offer high-speed Internet among many features, while the hotel offers squash courts, a hammam, a swimming pool, Moroccan- and Parisian-style eateries and a conference room. A babysitting service is also provided. **www.hyatt.com**

CITY CENTRE Hôtel and Spa Le Doge

9 rue du Docteur Veyre **Tel** *(0522) 46 78 00* **Rooms** *16*   **Road map** *C2*

One of this city's beautiful art deco buildings has been transformed into a luxury hotel, plus Spa Le Doge is of a standard rarely seen outside of Marrakech. Artful interiors and sumptuous fabrics have breathed new life into this wonderful 1930s building. It is very lavish, but worth every penny. **www.hotelledoge.com**

CITY CENTRE Sheraton Casablanca Hôtel & Towers

100 Avenue des FAR **Tel** *(0522) 43 94 94* **Rooms** *286*   **Road map** *C2*

The Sheraton Casablanca is a landmark building in the heart of the city. With all the main tourist attractions nearby, it makes an ideal and luxurious base from which to explore Casablanca. The hotel offers top-notch rooms, along with a restaurant serving an à la carte menu of Moroccan dishes. **www.sheraton.com**

CORNICHE Hôtel Tropicana

Boulevard de la Corniche **Tel** *(0522) 79 75 95* **Rooms** *62*   **Road map** *C2*

Lively and fun, the Tropicana has been designed as a family seaside-style hotel and has no fewer than five outdoor swimming pools and one indoor one. Other facilities include restaurants and a fitness centre. The hotel is located on the waterfront, near the Mosque of Hassan II; all rooms have sea views. **www.hoteltropicanacasablanca.com**

MOHAMMEDIA Amphitrite Beach Hôtel

Boulevard Moulay Youssef, La Corniche **Tel** *(0523) 30 68 00* **Rooms** *156*   **Road map** *C2*

Close to the beach, this luxury hotel offers an infinity pool, along with a spa, traditional cuisine, lush gardens, and spacious, comfortable rooms, some with ocean views. Located just outside Casablanca, near the airport, this is a useful overnight stop and suits travellers happy to lounge on the beach. **www.amphitritemohammedia.com**

NOUASSER Atlas Airport Hôtel

Aéroport Mohammed V **Tel** *(0522) 53 62 00* **Rooms** *198*   **Road map** *C2*

This large, modern hotel is located close to Casablanca's airport. It has gardens with palm-trees, a round swimming pool and a spa. It offers conference facilities, secretarial services and air conditioning throughout. The on-site restaurant serves a wide variety of cuisine. The staff are multilingual. **www.hotelsatlas.com**

SOUTHERN ATLANTIC COAST

DAR BOUAZZA Hôtel des Arts

1120 Jack Beach **Tel** *(0522) 96 54 50* **Rooms** *50*   **Road map** *C2*

A stylish hotel, Hôtel des Arts occupies a prime location in this pleasant beach resort and surfers' paradise. It has an excellent spa and pool overlooking the ocean, as well as a tapas bar and a good restaurant with an extensive wine menu. The beautifully landscaped gardens offer a relaxing place to unwind. **www.casablancahoteldesarts.com**

EL JADIDA Riad Soleil d'Orient

131 Derb El Hajjar **Tel** *(0661) 61 50 74* **Rooms** *6*   **Road map** *B2*

This simple yet comfortable hotel is situated in the heart of El-Jadida's medina and is a few minutes walk from the souk and the old Portuguese fort. The rooms are bright and clean and the gardens and roof terrace offer plenty of space for relaxing. Breakfast is generally served in the garden. **www.riadsoleildorient.net**

EL-JADIDA Pullman Mazagan Royal Golf & Spa

Route de Casablanca km 7 **Tel** *(0523) 35 41 41* **Rooms** *117*   **Road map** *B2*

Located amid the lawns of El-Jadida's respected 18-hole golf course, the Pullman Mazagan Royal Golf & Spa is popular with golfers and their families. Rooms are luxurious, and there are many amenities, including a piano bar and a spa complete with a hammam. It is just a few minutes' walk from the town's ancient ramparts. **www.accorhotels.com**

EL JADIDA Mazagan Beach Resort

Mazagan Beach Resort **Tel** *(0523) 38 80 00* **Rooms** *500*   **Road map** *B2*

One of the most extensive resorts on the entire Moroccan coast, Mazagan offers an 18-hole golf course, a casino, kids clubs, swimming pool, watersports, a nightclub, fitness centre and spa. Due to its extensive facilities guests rarely venture out of the complex to visit nearby El-Jadida or Casablanca. **www.mazaganbeachresort.com**

ESSAOUIRA Dar L'Oussia

4 Rue Mohamed Ben Messaoud, Bab Sbaa, Medina **Tel** *(0524) 78 37 56* **Rooms** *23*   **Road map** *B4*

With great views of the port and the ocean, this hotel is one of the most popular in town. This *riad* style building has just three floors and is light and airy. Breakfast is often served on the fabulous roof terrace. It has extensive spa facilities, tasteful furnishings and the vaulted restaurant serves excellent traditional food. **www.darloussia.com**

Key to Price Guide *see p302* **Key to Symbols** *see back cover flap*

ESSAOUIRA Riad Al-Madina

9 Rue El-Attarine **Tel** *(0524) 47 59 07* **Rooms** *54* **Road map** *B4*

This 19th-century Souiri house, situated within the medina, offers immense charm and a traditional Moroccan environment. Guest rooms are comfortable, and the hotel has an excellent restaurant, a garden terrace and a hammam. A conference room is also available. Largely caters to groups. **www.riadalmadina.com**

ESSAOUIRA Les Terrasses d'Essaouira

2 Rue Mohammed-Diouri **Tel** *(0524) 47 51 14* **Rooms** *15* **Road map** *B4*

Situated in the heart of the medina, this hotel is ideal for exploring the ancient town of Essaouira. It is also close to the seafront, and many rooms have sea views. There is an inspired contemporary Moroccan interior decor throughout, and facilities include a health suite. **www.les-terrasses-essaouira.com**

ESSAOUIRA Riad Baoussala

Baoussala, Douar el Ghazoua, BP423 **Tel** *(0666) 30 87 46* **Rooms** *6* **Road map** *B4*

Located 15 minutes from town, this delightful guesthouse has salmon coloured walls and crenellations. Within its gardens grow rambling roses, huge palms and scented jasmine, which creates a beautiful oasis of tranquility. The six bedrooms are artistically and tastefully decorated. **www.baoussala.com**

ESSAOUIRA Riad Madada Mogador

5 rue Youssef el fassi **Tel** *(0524) 47 55 12* **Rooms** *7* **Road map** *B4*

An attractive place to stay, Riad Madada Mogador is just a few minutes walk from the town's port, markets and beaches. Neutral colours and contemporary decor give the impression of a chic apartment rather than a hotel. The restaurant serves good French-Moroccan dishes and the breakfasts are highly recommended. **www.madada.com**

ESSAOUIRA Ryad Mogador

368 Route de Marrakech **Tel** *(0524) 78 35 55* **Rooms** *156* **Road map** *B4*

Located on the sea front and with an atmosphere and decor that are pure Moroccan, the Ryad Mogador makes a lovely place to stay. Its guest rooms and suites are luxurious, with all the facilities you would expect from a hotel of this class, and the restaurant and spa are exceptional. **www.ryadmogador.com**

ESSAOUIRA Villa Quieta

86 Boulevard Mohammed V **Tel** *(0524) 78 50 04* **Rooms** *13* **Road map** *B4*

The Villa Quieta offers the chance to holiday in a traditional Moroccan palace surrounded by lush gardens and next to the beach. Its en-suite guest rooms and lounges feature crafted wood furniture and Moroccan tiles as part of their decor, while meals are served in its grand salon or on the pleasant terrace. **www.villa-quieta.com**

ESSAOUIRA Villa De L'O

3 rue Mohamed Ben Messaoud **Tel** *(0524) 47 63 75* **Rooms** *12* **Road map** *B4*

The architecture of this 18th century *riad* is a blend of colonial and traditional styles. The interiors are ultra chic and mainly monochrome, giving it a fashionable boutique feel. Room prices are reasonable and services include babysitting, a deluxe spa and airport transfers. There is a golf course nearby. **www.villadelo.com**

ESSAOUIRA Sofitel Medina & Spa

Avenue Mohammed V **Tel** *(0524) 47 90 00* **Rooms** *119* **Road map** *B4*

White Moorish architecture and lush gardens combine to give this top-notch hotel its character. Inside, the atmosphere is one of tranquillity. Its spa offers numerous thalassotherapy treatments, while its restaurants *(see p333)* serve healthy international dishes such as seafood. **www.accorhotels.com**

IMOUZZER DES IDA OUATANANE Hôtel des Cascades

Imouzzer des Ida Outanane **Tel** *(0528) 82 60 16/23* **Rooms** *27* **Road map** *B4*

Reached on a single track 30-mile (48-km) mountain road, this rustic hotel has comfortable rooms, magnificent terraced gardens leading to paths in the countryside and a refreshing swimming pool. On clear evenings you can watch the sun set over the Atlantic. The owner organises treks into the surrounding uplands. **www.cascades-hotel.net**

OUALIDIA Hôtel Hippocampe

Route du Palais **Tel** *(0523) 36 61 08* **Rooms** *24* **Road map** *B3*

A pleasantly presented small hotel overlooking the lagoon at Oualidia, the Hôtel Hippocampe is popular with families and couples on a relaxing break. Its rooms comprise small bungalows dotted around well-maintained gardens, while local dishes are served in the restaurant or on a terrace. Half board is compulsory in high season.

OUALIDIA La Sultana Hôtel & Spa

Route du Palais **Tel** *(0524) 38 80 08* **Rooms** *11* **Road map** *B3*

Luxurious bed linen and marble floors help make this small but high-end hotel the best in town. The restaurant is popular with seafood lovers, especially because La Sultana operates its own oyster beds. Its beachside terrace is particularly appealing. This hotel is also spearheading Morocco's water recycling efforts. **www.lasultanaoualidia.com**

SAFI Riad du Pecheur

1 Rue De La Crête **Tel** *(0524) 61 02 91* **Rooms** *10* **Road map** *B3*

This is a small hotel, with brightly coloured rooms, set in luscious gardens. Riad du Pecheur is very well run and is excellent value for money. It is a good place to stop overnight if travelling along the coast and certainly the best establishment in Safi. The centre of town is within walking distance. **www.ryaddupecheur.com**

TANGIER

CITY CENTRE Dar Jameel

6 Rue Mohammed Bergach, Medina **Tel** *(0539) 33 46 80* **Rooms** *8*   **Road map** *D1*

The name of this small hotel – The House of Beauty – befits the decor, which is both intricate and delicate. The large terrace offers views of Spain, the medina and the Bay of Tangier. The hotel's five floors, built around a central courtyard, provide cool and comfortable accommodation all year round. **www.magicmaroc.com**

CITY CENTRE Hôtel Continental

36 Rue Dar Baroud **Tel** *(0539) 93 10 24* **Rooms** *53*   **Road map** *D1*

Shortly after opening its doors in 1888, this eccentric hotel welcomed Queen Victoria's son, Alfred, among its first guests. Today it is something of a Tangerine institution, commanding a key position overlooking the busy port and medina. The building is a sight in itself for those interested in this town's history. **www.continental-tanger.com**

CITY CENTRE Ibis

Lotissement Tanger Offshore Plazza **Tel** *(0539) 32 85 50* **Rooms** *196*   **Road map** *D1*

This is one of the more contemporary hotels in town. Similar in design to other hotels of the same chain, the Ibis hotel is reliable and provides good service, as well as clean, comfortable rooms and a small pool. There is Wi-Fi access in the lobby. It is situated close to the station. **www.ibishotel.com**

CITY CENTRE Maison Arabesque

73 Rue Naciria, Medina, Place Sakaya **Tel** *(0679) 46 68 76* **Rooms** *5*   **Road map** *D1*

Built in 1898, in the Spanish-Moorish style, this adorable guesthouse has since been restored and manages to effortlessly blend the old and new. Maison Arabesque makes best use of its light and space, offering guests many pleasant areas to lounge and relax in while sipping mint tea. The hotel also has a hammam. **www.maison-arabesque.com**

CITY CENTRE La Tangerina

19 Riad Sultan Kasbah **Tel** *(0539) 94 77 31* **Rooms** *10*   **Road map** *D1*

Relax on the roof terrace of this charming Colonial-style hotel, which has wonderful views over the medina and the Strait of Gibraltar. Centrally located, just next to the fabulous Cinema Rif, La Tangerina offers flawless service, great food and a multilingual staff. The rooms are arranged around a pretty central courtyard. **http://latangerina.com**

CITY CENTRE Dar Chams Tanger

2/4 Rue Jnane Kabtan, Porte Bab el Assa **Tel** *(0642) 27 96 37* **Rooms** *7*   **Road map** *D1*

This is an artistic and charming riad in the centre of town. Many rooms have traditional, painted wooden beds and cupboards. Dar Chams Tanger is a great favourite with those returning often to Tangier, so book in advance. The delightful owners will do all they can to help guests have a memorable stay. **www.darchamstanja.com**

CITY CENTRE Dar Mouchka

Fedan Chappo **Tel** *(0676) 38 46 33* **Rooms** *6*   **Road map** *D1*

Just a few minutes away from the town centre, this small hotel is perfect for those looking to escape the hustle of Tangier. The restaurant offers extremely good traditional food and is the perfect place to unwind. The attentive staff and the rambling grounds make this a good option for families. **www.darmouchka.com**

CITY CENTRE Hôtel El Oumnia Puerto

Avenue Beethoven **Tel** *(0539) 94 03 67* **Rooms** *90*   **Road map** *D1*

Located next to the marina and beach and just a short walk from the medina and the major sights of the city, the El Oumnia Puerto is an ideal base from which to explore Tangier. Its guest rooms are stylish and well equipped, and the bright restaurant specialises in tasty Moroccan dishes. **www.hoteleloumniapuerto.com**

CITY CENTRE Hôtel Intercontinental

Park Brooks, Blvd Sidi Mohd. Ben Abdellah **Tel** *(0539) 93 01 50* **Rooms** *115*   **Road map** *D1*

Considered one of the finer hotels in Tangier, although not the most expensive, the Intercontinental offers good value. It is, however, away from the main city centre, set quietly in the middle of a huge park. Rooms are well equipped, and the hotel has two good restaurants. **www.intercontinental-tanger.com**

CITY CENTRE Hôtel El-Minzah

85 Rue de la Liberté **Tel** *(0539) 93 58 85* **Rooms** *140*   **Road map** *D1*

The Hispano-Moorish architecture of this fashionable hotel makes it a landmark in Tangier. Inside, it is pure Moroccan luxury. The El-Minzah boasts rooms and suites designed to a high standard, many of which have views over the bay. Hôtel facilities include a wellness centre and a restaurant *(see p333).* **www.elminzah.com**

CITY CENTRE Husa Solazure

Avenue Mohammed VI **Tel** *(0539) 34 83 83* **Rooms** *348*   **Road map** *D1*

Occupying an excellent position on the waterfront, this hotel is an ideal choice for those looking for high standards of service. Husa Solazure is favoured by groups and business customers, but don't let that put you off. It also has a bar, nightclub and conference facilities. **www.husa.es**

CITY CENTRE Rif & Spa

152 Avenue Mohammed VI **Tel** *(0539) 34 93 00* **Rooms** *127*   **Road map** *D1*

This large modern hotel's distinct curved glass frontage has made it a local landmark. The rooms are spacious and comfortable. It has two restaurants serving international and Moroccan cuisine, a large lobby, cabaret and a bar. The outdoor pool, hammam, sauna and fitness rooms are popular.

CITY CENTRE Mövenpick Hôtel & Casino Malabata

22 Rue Malabata Bella Vista **Tel** *(0539) 32 93 00/50* **Rooms** *207*   **Road map** *D1*

Housing one of the largest casinos in Africa (boasting some 200 slot machines), the Mövenpick is not for the faint-hearted. Exuding pure luxury throughout, it is one of Tangier's foremost five-star hotels. Facilities range from informal and high-class restaurants to numerous leisure pursuits. **www.movenpick-hotels.com**

FURTHER AFIELD Villa Josephine

231 Route de la Vieille Montagne **Tel** *(0539) 33 45 35* **Rooms** *10*   **Road map** *D1*

Many regular visitors to Tangier stay at this charming landmark hotel. Villa Josephine has more of a French Riviera or country house feel than a *riad* or *dar*. It has timeless, romantic decor, stunning gardens, great service and the restaurant serves delicious food. **www.villajosephine-tanger.com**

MEDITERRANEAN COAST & THE RIF

AL-HOCEIMA Casa Paca

Playa de Sfiha **Tel** *(0539) 80 27 32* **Rooms** *5*   **Road map** *E1*

Seemingly set in the middle of nowhere, this welcoming guesthouse is located close to the beach. Casa Paca's rooms are simple yet stylish and offer magnificent ocean views. Guests are treated to good home-made food. Breakfast is served on the terrace overlooking the Mediterranean Sea.

AL-HOCEIMA Suites Hôtel Mohammed V

Place de la Marché Verte **Tel** *(0539) 98 22 33* **Rooms** *38*   **Road map** *E1*

The Suites Hôtel Mohammed V commands a good view of the bay, the island of Peñon de Alhucemas and the cliffs that form the town's backdrop from many of its suites, as well as from the attractive shrub-lined garden terrace. It is a small establishment, but a good base from which to explore the region.

CABO NEGRO Le Petit Mérou

Plage Cabo Negro **Tel** *(0661) 30 93 93* **Rooms** *23*   **Road map** *D1*

Le Petit Mérou is an attractive hotel in a classic Moroccan beach setting, perfect for a holiday or a short break. Quiet, unassuming and located close to the amenities at Cabo Negro, it offers pleasant rooms and a pretty garden terrace overlooking a pool. **www.lepetitmerou.com**

CAP SPARTEL Le Mirage

Rue Cap Spartel **Tel** *(0539) 33 33 32* **Rooms** *30*   **Road map** *D1*

With luxurious bungalows perched on the clifftop overlooking the waters where the Mediterranean Sea and the Atlantic Ocean meet, Le Mirage offers an especially memorable place to unwind. It features a richly decorated fine-dining restaurant *(see p334)* and piano bar, as well as a health suite. **www.lemirage-tanger.com**

CHEFCHAOUEN Dar Gabriel

Bab Souk **Tel** *(0539) 98 92 44* **Rooms** *7*   **Road map** *D1*

Pretty rooms, adorable bathrooms and just the right amount of traditional handicrafts make this small hotel one of the most memorable places to stay. The wood burners make this a possible retreat in winter, as well as summer, with great views of the pine and cedar clad Rif mountains all year round. **www.dargabriel.com**

CHEFCHAOUEN Casa Perleta

Avda Hassan II 68, Bab el Souk **Tel** *(0539) 98 89 79* **Rooms** *8*   **Road map** *D1*

Buried in the bustling medina of Chefchaouen, this quaint blue and white guesthouse has tiled floors and antique painted doors. Rooms are decorated with tranquil blends of white and natural shades. The terrace is perfect for breakfast. Not all rooms have air conditioning, so express a preference upon booking. **www.casaperleta.com**

OUJDA Ibis Moussafir Oujda

Boulevard Abdellah **Tel** *(0536) 68 82 02* **Rooms** *74*   **Road map** *F2*

Located in the city centre, close to the main attractions of Oujda, such as its *kissaria* arcade and the Rue el-Mazouzi, the ibis Moussafir is an attractive whitewashed hotel that has a lot of charm. Its rooms are well equipped, while the hotel offers a restaurant *(see p335)*, bar, pool and sports facilities. **www.ibishotel.com**

OUJDA Atlas Terminus and Spa

Boulevard Zerktouni, Place De La Gare **Tel** *(0536) 71 10 10* **Rooms** *82*   **Road map** *F2*

Atlas Terminus and Spa offers breathtaking views, a swimming pool, a children's pool, as well as a spa and poolside bar. The rooms are spacious and are fitted with all amenities. It is a good overnight stop for those wishing to find a place to base themselves for trekking. **www.hotelsatlas.com**

SAÏDIA Be Live Grand Saïdia

Parcela H7, Station Balnéaire **Tel** *(0536) 63 33 66* **Rooms** *488*

Road map *E1*

This huge resort, about an hour's drive from Melilla, can easily accommodate large groups and is also a good option for families. Tennis, aerobics and other activities are offered here. There is an 18-hole golf course nearby, as well as 14 km (9 miles) of white sandy beach. Closed from end October to early April. **www.belivehotels.com**

SAÏDIA Barceló Mediterránea Saïdia

Zone Turistica Saïdia **Tel** *(0536) 63 00 63* **Rooms** *420*

Road map *F1*

Set in lush gardens at the heart of a beachside resort, the Barceló is a medina-style hotel offering all-inclusive accommodation only. Guests can choose from three restaurants and a pool-side snack bar. Extensive facilities include six pools, a golf course and a wellness centre. Closed November to April. **www.barcelomediterraneasaidia.com**

TETOUAN Blanco Riad Hôtel and Restaurant

25 Rue Zawiya Kadiri **Tel** *(0539) 704 202* **Rooms** *7*

Road map *D1*

This beautiful, historic building once housed the Spanish consulate. Today, it is a lovely, well run boutique hotel, which mixes traditional tile-work with natural, earthy colours. There are also chandeliers and lanterns, which add to the ambience. The hotel has helpful staff, a spa, a fine restaurant and expert guides. **www.blancoriad.com**

TETOUAN Riad El Reducto

No. 38, Zawya Zanqat **Tel** *(0539) 96 81 20* **Rooms** *5*

Road map *D1*

The location of this budget hotel is unbeatable: close to the royal palace and deep in the heart of the medina. The intricately tiled rooms and heavily adorned communal areas are comfortable and clean. Staff and management are friendly and happy to help. **www.riadtetouan.com**

TETOUAN Barceló Marina Smir

Route de Sebta **Tel** *(0539) 97 12 34* **Rooms** *119*

Road map *D1*

A large, sprawling whitewashed hotel standing in beautifully kept gardens full of exotic plants, the Barceló Marina Smir is one of the finest hotels in the area. It lies next to the Marina Smir. Amenities, such as its French restaurants *(see p335)* and health-spa areas, are to a five-star standard. **www.barcelo.com**

FÈS

CITY CENTRE Hôtel Mounia

60 Boulevard Zerktouni **Tel** *(0535) 65 07 71* **Rooms** *93*

Road map *D2*

The Mounia has a choice of accommodation, from well-equipped double rooms to suites, all with private bathrooms. The lodgings – together with two restaurants, an English-style bar, beauty suite and nightclub, plus a terrace on which to take in the evening atmosphere – mean a stay here is excellent value. **www.hotelmouniafes.ma**

CITY CENTRE Hôtel Ibis Moussafir

Avenue des Almodhades **Tel** *(0535) 65 19 02* **Rooms** *125*

Road map *D2*

Good facilities – including air-conditioned rooms, a swimming pool, a garden and an international restaurant with à la carte menu, together with a location that puts the ancient medina of Fès within walking distance – ensure that this modern hotel remains a top choice for many visitors. **www.ibishotel.com**

CITY CENTRE Dar Bensouda

14 Zkak el Bghel, Quettanine **Tel** *(0524) 39 16 09* **Rooms** *11*

Road map *D2*

The rooms at this restored palace are surprisingly affordable and all have been individually decorated. There is a pool, two courtyards, and a roof terrace that has views of the medina and Atlas Mountains. Dar Bensouda offers a selection of interesting courses from cookery to calligraphy and tours of the surrounding areas. **www.riaddarbensouda.com**

CITY CENTRE Palais de Fès Dar TAZI

15 Rue Makhfia **Tel** *(0535) 76 15 90* **Rooms** *8*

Road map *D2*

Conveniently located for the centre of Fès and offering a beautiful place to stay, the Palais de Fès Dar TAZI is housed in an authentic Moroccan dwelling and is a popular choice with both businesspeople and travellers. Facilities include complimentary pick-up from the airport. **www.palaisdefes.com**

CENTRE VILLE Riad Numero 9

Derb el Masid **Tel** *(0535) 63 40 45* **Rooms** *3*

Road map *D2*

This charming *riad* has been restored to its original splendour. Furnished with Asian, French and English antiques the interiors are elegant and full of character. The Japanese-style dining area in the central courtyard is a pleasant place to have a meal. Closed in August. **www.riad9.com**

CITY CENTRE Riad Laaroussa

3 Derb Bechara, Talaa Sghira **Tel** *(0674) 18 76 39* **Rooms** *8*

Road map *D2*

Riad Laaroussa is a deluxe guesthouse set in a 17th-century palace in the centre of town. The interiors are traditional yet chic, with intricate mosaic work throughout. Relax by the blazing fireplace in the winter, or lounge in the courtyard under the cool shade of the orange trees in the summer. **www.riad-laaroussa.com**

Key to Price Guide *see p302* **Key to Symbols** *see back cover flap*

CITY CENTRE Riad Ibn Battouta

Avenue Allal El Fassi **Tel** *(0535) 63 71 91* **Rooms** *7* **Road map** *D2*

The Riad Ibn Battouta is a renovated atmospheric Maison in the heart of Fès, close to the Musée Dar el-Batha and the medina. It offers a series of terraces from which to enjoy the cityscape, along with a traditional hammam and an elegant restaurant. Its seven hi-spec suites are beautifully presented. **www.riadibnbattouta.com**

CITY CENTRE Royal Mirage

Avenue des Far **Tel** *(0535) 93 09 09* **Rooms** *271* **Road map** *D2*

"Sumptuous" is the word that springs to mind as you step inside the Royal Mirage. Its foyer reflects true Moroccan decor and introduces the high level of luxury that can be found throughout. The hotel's restaurants serve dishes from classic French to Moroccan, while guest rooms feature every comfort. **www.royalmiragehotels.com**

CITY CENTRE Zalagh Parc Palace

Lotissement Oued **Tel** *(0535) 94 99 49* **Rooms** *473* **Road map** *D2*

This is the largest hotel in Fès, with luxurious, individually designed rooms and suites. Its fifth-floor Moroccan restaurant offers panoramic views of the city, while leisure amenities include a beauty centre, racquet sports and bowling. This family-friendly hotel also offers children's play areas and babysitting services. **www.zalagh-palace.ma**

MEDINA Dar Sefarine

14 Derb Sbaa Louyate, Seffarine **Tel** *(0671) 11 35 28* **Rooms** *6* **Road map** *D2*

Nestled in the old medina and looking like it did in the middle ages, this palace has been restored many times. Local craftsmen have recreated and repaired the original interiors. As a result, the bedrooms are pristine with hand-painted detailing and tiled floors. Home-cooked meals are communal and served at a long table. **www.darseffarine.com**

MEDINA Hôtel Batha

Place L'Istiqlal, Rue de L'Unesco **Tel** *(0535) 74 10 77* **Rooms** *62* **Road map** *D2*

Located in the heart of the medina area of Fès and close to the city's main attractions, the Batha is a traditionally styled hotel set in gardens and full of charm – from the wall paintings in the restaurant and colourful rugs in the lounge, to the well-equipped guest rooms that overlook an inner courtyard.

MEDINA Dar El Ghalia

15 Ross Rhi Medina **Tel** *(0535) 63 41 67* **Rooms** *14* **Road map** *D2*

This 17th-century *riad*, nestling in a tiny street at the heart of Fès's medina, is a real gem. Step inside, and it's like going back to a bygone age. The Dar El Ghalia offers rooms and suites, each with an authentic Moroccan decor and private bathrooms. The hotel is noted for serving fine food

MEDINA Ryad Mabrouka

Talaa K'bira Derb el Miter **Tel** *(0535) 63 63 45* **Rooms** *8* **Road map** *D2*

Located in the medina of Fès, with views over its enchanting roofline from many of its rooms, the historic Ryad Mabrouka has an authentic Moroccan interior with columns, sculpted plasterwork, mosaics and an inner courtyard. Unusual for this type of property, it also offers a swimming pool. **www.ryadmabrouka.com**

MEDINA Hôtel Les Mérinides

Avenue Borj du Nord **Tel** *(0535) 64 52 26* **Rooms** *106* **Road map** *D2*

Les Mérinides is a modern purpose-designed hotel finished to such a standard as to give it immense character throughout. It overlooks the old town of Fès and the medina, and as such it is a good base for sightseeing. Facilities include a gourmet restaurant *(see p336)* and pool. **www.lesmerinides.com**

MEDINA Sofitel Palais Jamaï

Bab El Guissa **Tel** *(0535) 63 43 31* **Rooms** *133* **Road map** *D2*

Located right in the medina, in the heart of Fès, the five-star Sofitel Palais Jamaï is as good as it gets, in terms of both luxury and convenience. A former 19th-century palace built to an authentic Moorish style, it offers the lot: beautifully decorated rooms, fine-dining restaurants *(see p336)*, a spa and sports options. **www.sofitel.com**

VILLE NOUVELLE Dar Roumana

30 Derb El Amer, Zkak Roumana, Fès Medina **Tel** *(0535) 74 16 37* **Rooms** *5* **Road map** *D2*

In an already crowded hospitality market, American owner Jennifer Smith, has created something special. Her passion is reflected in the pride her staff takes in the discreet yet excellent service and in the beautifully decorated interiors. The spectacular Fasian Dar (house) is eco-friendly and has amazing mountain views. **www.darroumana.com**

VILLE NOUVELLE Riad Tizwa

5 Derb Guebbas, Douh Batha, Medina **Tel** *07973 115 471 (UK)* **Rooms** *9* **Road map** *D2*

Riad Tizwa has a vast roof terrace, and offers the option of renting the entire premises. Stained glass, tile work, lanterns and local pottery adorn the rooms, while the aromas of local perfumes fill the courtyard. This *riad* serves one of the best breakfasts in town. Wi-Fi is available throughout. **www.holidayfes.com**

VILLE NOUVELLE Hôtel Wassim

Avenue Hassan II and Rue de Liban **Tel** *(0535) 65 49 39* **Rooms** *104* **Road map** *D2*

Located where two main thoroughfares meet, and within a short distance of Fès's main tourist sights, the Hôtel Wassim is a modern, purpose-designed building finished to an exceptional standard. The welcoming rooms are nicely decorated, and there is a rooftop terrace where guests can unwind under the sun or the stars.

VILLE NOUVELLE Palais Shéhérazade & Spa

23, Arsat Bennis Douh Fès Medina **Tel** *(0535) 74 16 42* **Rooms** *24*　　　　　　**Road map** *D2*

Intensely romantic, this sumptuous palace has carved cedar ceilings, ornate columns with mosaic detail, and rooms worthy of royalty. Past guests include members of the Moroccan court, foreign ambassadors, actors, rock stars and the Queen of Jordan. One of the restaurants is located on the terrace and has panoramic views. **www.sheheraz.com**

VILLE NOUVELLE Hôtel Jnan Palace

Avenue Ahmed Chaouki **Tel** *(0535) 65 22 30* **Rooms** *195*　　　　　　**Road map** *D2*

This top-notch hotel oozes Moroccan charm. With luxurious facilities and an air of tranquillity, it stands in around 7 acres of parkland in the new area of Fès, amid trendy shops and bistros. Guest rooms are decorated and furnished to a high standard, and facilities include a gym and a spa. **www.sogatour.ma/jnanpalace.htm**

MEKNÈS & VOLUBILIS

MEKNÈS Hôtel Akouas

Rue Emir Abdelkader **Tel** *(0535) 51 59 67* **Rooms** *60*　　　　　　**Road map** *D2*

The Hôtel Akouas is housed in a somewhat unassuming building in one of Meknès's main thoroughfares, but the reception area and guest rooms are presented in a traditional manner and are full of character. The staff are helpful and will assist with organising excursions. **www.hotelakouas.com**

MEKNÈS Ibis Moussafir

Avenue des Far **Tel** *(0535) 40 41 41* **Rooms** *104*　　　　　　**Road map** *D2*

Popular with businesspeople and tourists alike, this hotel housed in a contemporary-style building is located close to the centre of Meknès. The town and most of its attractions are within walking distance. On-site facilities include a gym, international restaurants and quality rooms. **www.ibishotels.com**

MEKNÈS Riad Anne de Meknes

4 Derb Sidi M'Barek Biab Bardaine **Rooms** *5*　　　　　　**Road map** *D2*

Tucked slightly out of the way, this quiet and completely restored *riad* is named after its French Breton owner: Anne. The rooms are traditionally styled and the interiors are unfussy. The breakfast is served on the roof terrace, which has views of the city. Anne and husband Ali are at hand to offer help and advice. **www.riadannedemeknes.com**

MEKNÈS Riad La Maison D'A Coté

25 Derb Lakhouaja **Tel** *(0535) 53 51 01* **Rooms** *4*　　　　　　**Road map** *D2*

Absolute privacy is key at this intimate guesthouse with refreshingly serene rooms. Mature orange trees and a banana palm shade the central courtyard, which also features a fountain. The *riad* is expertly run, with staff happy to greet guests in the medina (5 minutes away). Not all rooms have air conditioning. **www.riadmaisondacote.com**

MEKNÈS Riad Mèknes

79 Ksar Chaacha-Dar Lakbira **Tel** *(0535) 53 05 42* **Rooms** *10*　　　　　　**Road map** *D2*

Riad Mèknes is a part of the palace of 17th-century ruler, Moulay Ismail. It has impressive facilities including an elaborate dining room, sun terraces, a plunge pool and excursions to surrounding areas. The generally regal rooms vary greatly in style, so it is advisable to request a particular room upon booking. **www.riadmeknes.com**

MEKNÈS Hôtel Menzah Dalia

Quarter Marjane **Tel** *(0535) 46 85 78* **Rooms** *143*　　　　　　**Road map** *D2*

The Menzah Dalia is one of the finest hotels – if not the finest – in Meknès. It is known for its high-quality restaurant that not only serves fine international and Moroccan dishes and wine, but also offers truly great views over the town and valley. On-site amenities include a pool and nightclub.

MEKNÈS Palais Didi

7 Dar Lakbira **Tel** *(0535) 55 85 90* **Rooms** *13*　　　　　　**Road map** *D2*

This is a great place for those interested in Moroccan history and art. Palais Didi has been fully renovated with rich colours and offers lounges and terraces with fine views of the old imperial city. Rooms are arranged around a central courtyard with a bubbling fountain. Not all rooms have air conditioning, so ask when booking. **www.palaisdidi.com**

MEKNÈS Riad D'Or

17 Rue Ain El Anboub and Lalla Aicha Adouia **Tel** *(0641) 07 86 25* **Rooms** *24*　　　　　　**Road map** *D2*

A large town house set in Mèknes medina, Riad D'Or has several patios, winding staircases, a plunge pool on the roof, impressive mosaic tiling, intricate carvings and great city views. Rooms are mosaicked and traditional in style. The bathrooms are decadent concoctions of ornate plasterwork and tile. **www.riaddor.com**

MEKNÈS Hôtel Zaki

Boulevard Al Massira **Tel** *(0535) 51 41 46* **Rooms** *169*　　　　　　**Road map** *D2*

This central, somewhat out-dated hotel, is popular with groups and tours. The restaurant has a full continental menu, useful for those tiring of traditional Moroccan food. The sizeable pool is popular, as is the nightclub and the bar holds oriental and karaoke nights. **www.hotelzaki.com**

Key to Price Guide *see p302* **Key to Symbols** *see back cover flap*

MOULAY IDRISS Dar Ines

57 Derb Amajout, Hay Tazga **Tel** *(0667) 15 67 95* **Rooms** *7*　　**Road map** *D2*

In a town in which good quality budget accommodation is scarce, Dar Ines is a great find. The attractive period building is set in the centre of town, yet there is very little street noise. Its interiors are bright, traditional and spotlessly clean and the food is excellent. The spa is available for a small fee and local tours can be arranged. **www.dar-ines.com**

MOULAY IDRISS Dar Zerhoune

42 Derb Zouak, Tazga **Tel** *(0535) 54 43 71* **Rooms** *5*　　**Road map** *D2*

Three years of intensive renovation and decoration went into the opening of this lovely guesthouse. Rooms are large and all have en suite bathrooms and Wi-Fi access. The terrace provides views of the Roman ruins. Bicycle hire and cooking classes are a few of the facilities on offer. Breakfast is included in the price. **www.buttonsinn.com**

MOULAY IDRISS Diyar Timnay

Rue L, 7 Ain Rjal, BP141 (next to the Grands Taxis rank) **Tel** *(0661) 10 43 18* **Rooms** *14*　　**Road map** *D2*

This cheery, small hotel has spacious rooms that are naturally well lit because of the large windows. Service is great, the decor is bright and clean and the prices are unbeatable. It is just a short walk through the olive grove to reach the Roman ruins. **www.diyar-timnay.com**

VOLUBILIS Volubilis Inn

Ruins of Volubilis **Tel** *(0535) 54 44 08* **Rooms** *54*　　**Road map** *D2*

Offering outstanding views of the Volubilis Valley and the ruins, this relatively small hotel is warm and welcoming and a great place to relax. It is within easy reach of nearby major towns, such as Fès and Meknès, and it is noted for its swimming pool with panoramic views and its Moroccan restaurant.

MIDDLE ATLAS

AFOURER Hôtel Le Tazarkount

Province d'Azilai **Tel** *(0523) 44 01 01* **Rooms** *135*　　**Road map** *D2*

Perfectly located between Marrakech and Fès, and a great base for exploring this region of Morocco, Le Tazarkount offers a high standard of accommodation, swimming pools, a restaurant and friendly staff. It is situated in a main thoroughfare, which is great for absorbing the local atmosphere. **www.tazarkount.com**

AZROU Hôtel du Panorama

Azrou **Tel** *(0535) 56 20 10* **Rooms** *42*　　**Road map** *D2*

Staying at the Hôtel du Panorama is a memorable experience, not least because it is housed in an Alpine chalet-style property on the site of an ancient inn. The hotel stands in a slightly elevated position overlooking Azrou, itself a town of immense charm. The decor is traditional Moroccan throughout.

BENI MELLAL Hotel Chems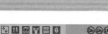

Route de Marrakech km 2 **Tel** *(0523) 48 34 60* **Rooms** *77*　　**Road map** *D3*

Located within easy walking distance of the town centre, and on a road to the Aïn Asserdoun springs, the Hôtel Chems enjoys a good position and is an ideal base from which to explore this region. Its amenities include pleasantly presented guest rooms, a swimming pool and tennis court, and a nightclub. **www.hotelchems.com**

BENI MELLAL Hôtel Ouzoud

Route de Marrakech km 3 **Tel** *(0523) 48 37 52* **Rooms** *58*　　**Road map** *D3*

While a tad nondescript from the outside, this hotel has a traditional Moroccan interior that comes as a pleasant surprise as you step inside. Amenities include a swimming pool, tennis courts and verdant gardens, while the attractive restaurant has a great atmosphere.

IFRANE Hôtel des Perce-Neige

Rue de Asphodèles Hay Riad **Tel** *(0535) 56 63 50/51* **Rooms** *27*　　**Road map** *D2*

This compact and welcoming hotel has a few frills for which it has become well known. Its restaurant *(see p337)*, for instance, serves some of the best Moroccan food in Ifrane, and as a result, it is frequented by locals as well as visitors. Guests can usually be found relaxing in or by the pool. **www.hotelperceneige.com**

IFRANE Michlifen Ifrane

Avenue Hassan II, Post Office Box 18 **Tel** *(0535) 86 40 00* **Rooms** *71*　　**Road map** *D2*

Unashamedly deluxe, this five-star hotel is fashioned on an ultra glamorous ski-lodge, albeit of enormous proportions. Michlifen Ifrane is a fairy-tale, "chalet" offering only the best in terms of accommodation, service, fine dining and style. The hotel also has a heliport. **www.michlifenifrane.com**

KHENIFRA Hôtel Atlas Zayan

Cité El Amal **Tel** *(0535) 58 60 20* **Rooms** *60*　　**Road map** *D3*

The Atlas Zayan, a relatively small hotel stands proudly in a wonderful open location with views out over unspoiled Khenifra. This mid-range hotel is air conditioned, and its amenities include a classic restaurant, a pool and a tennis court. It also offers access to a hiking trail.

KHOURIBGA Hôtel Golden Tulip Farah

Boulevard My Youssef **Tel** *(0523) 56 23 50* **Rooms** *76*   **Road map** *D3*

One of the most popular resort-style hotels in the Middle Atlas region, the Golden Tulip Farah is a modern, largely purpose-designed establishment and nestles in its own private gardens. It is a favourite of Moroccan families as well as visitors. It is air conditioned and has pleasantly presented en-suite guest rooms.

SEFROU Dar Attamani

414 Bastna **Tel** *(0645) 29 89 30* **Rooms** *5*   **Road map** *D2*

Located in the centre of Sefrou's medina, Dar Attamani is a simple but prettily painted guesthouse that has a charm of its own. The rooms are attractive and adorned with local handicrafts and ornaments. The restaurant serves up excellent traditional Moroccan dishes. Very reasonably priced. **www.darattamani.com**

SEFROU Dar Kamal Chaoui

60 Kaf Rhouni, Blalil **Tel** *(0535) 69 27 37* **Rooms** *4*   **Road map** *D2*

Situated deep in the Middle Atlas, a short distance from Sefrou, is Dar Kamal Chaoui. It is not hard to see why this chic yet budget guesthouse is popular. Rooms are clean, bright and tastefully decorated, while the terrace offers stunning views of the surrounding countryside. **www.kamalchaoui.com**

ZAOUIA AIT ISHAQ Hôtel Transatlas

Route National 08, Ait Ishaq Khenifra **Tel** *(0535) 39 90 30* **Rooms** *25*   **Road map** *D3*

A mid-range, whitewashed hotel that tends to dominate the small town of Zaouia ait Isshaq, the Transatlas is a well-known landmark and a hugely popular accommodation option. It has a particularly attractive restaurant that serves traditional Moroccan fare, such as *harira* soup with *kesra* bread, and local beverages.

MARRAKECH

GUÉLIZ Moroccan House

3 Rue Loubnane Gueliz **Tel** *(0524) 42 03 06* **Rooms** *50*   **Road map** *C3*

The Moroccan House is housed in a *riad*-style, pink-washed building with lots of charm. Close to the main sights, this five-storey hotel offers rooms with Moroccan textiles and modern amenities such as satellite television, along with a restaurant, spa and a terrace with panoramic city views. **www.moroccanhousehotels.com**

GUÉLIZ Bab Hôtel

Corner of Boulevard Mansour Eddahbi Rue Mohamed El Beqqal **Tel** *(0524) 43 52 50* **Rooms** *30*   **Road map** *C3*

Bab Hôtel's ultra modern and incredibly sleek decor is predominantly white with intense splashes of colour. Guest rooms are equipped with all amenities and have en suite bathrooms. The hotel offers several facilities including Wi-Fi, a pool, a solarium, bicycles and rental cars. **www.babhotelmarrakech.com**

GUÉLIZ Riad Magi

79 Derb Moulay Abdul Kader, Derb Dabachi, Medina **Tel** *(0677) 35 30 67* **Rooms** *6*   **Road map** *C3*

Delightfully unpretentious with its brightly painted rooms, Riad Magi offers fantastic value for money. It is ideally located, having both the souk and the main square practically on its doorstep. The friendly staff all have in-depth knowledge of the city. Breakfast is included in the price. **www.riad-magi.com**

GUÉLIZ Villa Hélène

89 Boulevard Moulay Rachid **Tel** *(0524) 43 16 81* **Rooms** *3*   **Road map** *C3*

One of Marrakech's hidden treasures, the colonial-style Villa Hélène, built in the 1930s, has just three rooms, all beautifully presented. They are set around the villa's own palm-fringed pool and are just minutes away from its own restaurant. Due to its small size and huge popularity, booking well in advance is essential.

HIVERNAGE Hivernage Hôtel & Spa

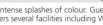

Avenue Echouhada **Tel** *(0524) 42 41 00* **Rooms** *85*   **Road map** *C3*

An imposing hotel at the junction of two main thoroughfares, the Hivernage is surprisingly quiet and relaxing. Attractive, air conditioned guest rooms have panoramic views of either the Bab Jdid ramparts or the Atlas Mountains. There is also a restaurant, La Table du Marché *(see p339)*. **www.hivernage-hotel.com**

HIVERNAGE Hôtel Es Saadi

Rue Brahim el Mazini **Tel** *(0524) 44 88 11* **Rooms** *150*   **Road map** *C3*

Probably best known for being located in one of the area's largest parks, the Es Saadi is something of a landmark building and full of character, both inside and out. It is minutes from the medina entrance, and as such it is especially convenient for sightseeing. Its facilities, which include a casino, exude pure luxury. **www.essaadi.com**

HIVERNAGE Riad Anayela

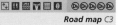

Derb Zerwal No 28 **Tel** *(0524) 38 69 69* **Rooms** *5*   **Road map** *C3*

This historic palace, built in the 18th century, has opulent but tasteful furnishings, huge rooms, calligraphy and beaten silver on the walls. The exquisite hand work was completed by over 100 craftsman. A driver is on call to ferry guests to and from the medina. **www.anayela.com**

Key to Price Guide *see p302* **Key to Symbols** *see back cover flap*

HIVERNAGE Sofitel Marrakech

Avenue Harroun Errachid **Tel** *(0524) 42 56 00* **Rooms** *360* **Road map** *C3*

A stay at the Sofitel Marrakech is sure to make a visit to this area unforgettable. From the antique furniture and the restaurants' crystal, to the lavish drapes of the guest rooms, the hotel oozes luxury from every corner and fully deserves its five-star status. It is located within an easy walk of the medina. **www.accor-hotels.com**

LA PALMERAIE Manzil La Tortue

Km 12 Route de Ouarzazate, Douar Gzoula, Commune Al Ouidane **Tel** *(0661) 95 55 17* **Rooms** *10* **Road map** *C3*

Set in former olive groves, this sprawling hotel is a welcome retreat from the city. Its has a pool with underwater speakers, putting greens and air-conditioned nomadic tents with bathrooms. Its restaurant offers excellent and innovative dishes, many made with organic produce from the gardens. **www.manzil-la-tortue.com**

LA PALMERAIE Hôtel Les Deux Tours

Douar Abiad **Tel** *(0524) 32 95 27* **Rooms** *36* **Road map** *C3*

With an authentic Moroccan interior decor inspired by local artisans, La Palmeraie's Hôtel Les Deux Tours offers visitors a truly memorable experience. It comprises six villas divided into guest rooms and has a swimming pool, hammam and a fine-dining restaurant. **www.les-deuxtours.com**

LA PALMERAIE Hôtel Octogone Terre

Wahat Sidi Brahim, Circuit de la Palmeraie **Tel** *(0524) 33 40 60* **Rooms** *26* **Road map** *C3*

A resort and spa-style luxury holiday complex, the Hôtel Octogone Terre is housed in one of Marrakesh's landmark buildings. Step through its entrance gates, and a traditional Moroccan palm tree-fringed desert-village atmosphere greets you. Guest rooms are beautifully presented, with many amenities. **www.octogonehotels.com**

LA PALMERAIE Amanjena

Route de Ouarzazate Km 12 **Tel** *(0524) 39 90 00* **Rooms** *32* **Road map** *C3*

This hotel is a must-see if only for its opulence. It is an unforgettable place to stay, even if for a single night, with king-sized beds and green marble in the bathrooms. Hollywood stars, such as Brad Pitt and Angelina Jolie have stayed here, and it was used as a set for much of *Sex and the City's* Moroccan episode. **www.amanjena.com**

LA PALMERAIE Dar Ayniwen

Tafrata, La Palmeraie **Tel** *(0524) 32 96 84* **Rooms** *14* **Road map** *C3*

Located in parklands on La Palmeraie complex, this pleasant, richly decorated guesthouse is quiet, relaxing and an ideal place to unwind. As one would expect from an establishment of this level, guest rooms are luxurious, as are the lounges and restaurant areas, while the service is discreet. **www.dar-ayniwen.com**

LA PALMERAIE Hôtel Jnane Tamsna

Douar Abiad **Tel** *(0524) 32 84 84* **Rooms** *24* **Road map** *C3*

The Jnane Tamsna is a warm, welcoming place, full of guests who come back time and again. Architecturally Moorish in style, it has many facilities, including beautifully presented guest rooms with luxury facilities, a restaurant and several sporting options, such as tennis and swimming. **www.jnanetamsna.com**

LA PALMERAIE Hôtel Palmeraie Golf Palace

Circuit de la Palmeraie **Tel** *(0524) 30 10 10* **Rooms** *314* **Road map** *C3*

Set in the heart of a palm tree-surrounded complex that features an 18-hole golf course, nine swimming pools, a spa, sports facilities and even an equestrian centre, the Palmeraie Golf Palace offers the chance of an unforgettable holiday. Guest rooms are finished to a luxurious standard, with every amenity included. **www.pgpmarrakech.com**

LA PALMERAIE Peacock Pavilions

Km 13, Route de Ouarzazate **Tel** *(0064) 41 46 53* **Rooms** *5* **Road map** *C3*

This refreshing boutique hotel is a delightful place to stay. The interiors have been tastefully decorated with hand-stencilled floors and ceilings, as well as pieces from all over the world, including West African masks. Amenities include a huge pool and an outdoor cinema, and cookery lessons are also offered. **www.peacockpavilions.com**

MEDINA Hôtel Gallia

30 Rue de la Recette **Tel** *(0524) 44 59 13* **Rooms** *17* **Road map** *C3*

An attractive hotel, the Gallia is housed in a landmark building standing at the foot of the 12th-century Koutoubia Mosque, in central Marrakesh. As such, it is ideally located for exploring the medina. Guest rooms are simple but nicely presented, as is its restaurant, where local specialities are served.

MEDINA Hôtel Tresor

77 Sidi Boulokat Riad Zitoun El Kadim **Tel** *(0524) 37 51 13* **Rooms** *14* **Road map** *C3*

This charming hotel, located just off the main square, has been decorated with items from the local collector's bazaar. The rooms are not large but are comfortable and clean. Breakfast is served on the roof terrace, which has a lovely view of the city. There is also a parlour with a fireplace. **www.hotel-du-tresor.com**

MEDINA Hôtel Les Almoravides

Arset Djebel Lakdar **Rooms** *167* **Road map** *C3*

Although Les Almoravides sounds rather grand, it is, in fact, a homely hotel, despite its size. Its interior design and architecture are traditional Moroccan. Guest rooms are spacious and with private bathrooms, while its location, near the Koutoubia Mosque, makes it popular for sightseeing.

MEDINA Riad 72

72 Arset Awsel, Bab Doukkala **Tel** *(0524) 38 76 29* **Rooms** *4*

Road map *C3*

This stylish Italian-owned *riad* is very Milan-meets-Marrakech, with palms and banana trees in the courtyard and its own hammam. The house is traditional, but the black-and-white colour scheme and sleek furniture are all imported. There is one dramatically large main suite and three smaller double rooms. **www.riad72.com**

MEDINA Riad El Ouarda

5 Derb That Sour Lakbir **Tel** *(0524) 38 57 14* **Rooms** *9*

Road map *C3*

A beautifully restored 17th-century *riad*, deep in the heart of the northern medina, well away from the crowds. Each room is differently styled. One suite has a stunning original painted ceiling. The roof terrace is one of the best in Marrakech, with views over Sidi Bel Abbès and the medina. **www.riadelouarda.com**

MEDINA Hôtel Dar Les Cigognes

108 Rue de Berrima **Tel** *(0524) 38 27 40* **Rooms** *11*

Road map *C3*

The Dar Les Cigognes is housed in an unassuming building in one of Marrakech's medina thoroughfares, but step inside and you'll see how the two former *riads* have been transformed into a boutique-style hotel of immense charm. The reception area and rooms are full of character. **www.lescigognes.com**

MEDINA Hôtel Les Jardins de la Medina

21 Rue Derb Chtouka **Tel** *(0524) 38 18 51* **Rooms** *36*

Road map *C3*

Situated in lush gardens behind high walls, in the heart of Marrakech's kasbah, Hôtel Les Jardins de la Medina certainly lives up to its name. It is an attractive hotel in traditional architectural style with large and pleasant guest rooms. The hotel restaurant serves Moroccan and international cuisine. **www.lesjardinsdelamedina.com**

MEDINA La Maison Arabe

1 Derb Assehbe **Tel** *(0524) 38 70 10* **Rooms** *26*

Road map *C3*

A compact, characterful hotel of luxury rooms and suites, La Maison Arabe began life as a noted restaurant in the 1940s and became a hotel in the mid-1990s. Located in the medina, near the Bab Doukkala Mosque, it also has a spa and pool and an outstanding restaurant. **www.lamaisonarabe.com**

MEDINA La Mamounia

Avenue Bab el-Jedid **Tel** *(0524) 38 86 00* **Rooms** *210*

Road map *C3*

Surrounded by ancient gardens and the city's ramparts, this world-famous 1920s Art Deco and Moorish hotel (completely renovated), lies within walking distance of the major tourist attractions. It offers four top-class restaurants *(see p339)*, five bars, a spa and leisure facilities. **www.mamounia.com**

MEDINA Le Méridien N'Fis

Avenue Mohammed VI **Tel** *(0524) 33 94 00* **Rooms** *277*

Road map *C3*

A spectacular hotel standing amid palm trees and sprawling Andalusian-style gardens and terraces, Le Méridien N'Fis is located close to the medina and is an ideal base for sightseeing. Guest rooms are spacious and luxurious, and the hotel also has top-quality restaurants and a spa. **www.lemeridiennfis.com**

MEDINA Riad Al Moussika

62 Derb Boutouil, Kennaria **Tel** *(0524) 38 90 67* **Rooms** *5*

Road map *C3*

A beautifully restored and maintained former grandee's home, all designed to exact specifications in traditional Moroccan style by its Italian owner. It is especially notable for its good food, including an enormous breakfast of eggs, pancakes, pastries and fruit. **www.riyad-al-moussika.com**

MEDINA Riad El Fenn

No. 2, Derb Moulay, Abdellah Ben Hussein, Bab El Ksour **Tel** *(0524) 44 12 10* **Rooms** *22*

Road map *C3*

Owned by the sister of British entrepreneur, Richard Branson, this high-end hotel is fast becoming the place for affluent artists and intellectuals. The hotel also plays an important role in the city's annual arts festival. It has a hip, boutiquey feel and well-trained staff. Poolside yoga and bespoke bouquets are also offered. **www.riadelfenn.com**

MEDINA Riad Hayati

27 Derb Bouderba, off rue Riad Zitoun El Jedid **Tel** *(44) 7770 431 194 (UK)* **Rooms** *3*

Road map *C3*

This elegant *riad* combines Moorish architecture with subtle tones of Arabia, Turkey and Persia, in the form of antique *kilims*, rich Ottoman tapestries and Damascene fountains, all memoirs from the years that its British owner spent in the Middle East. There is a columned courtyard edged with palms and lemon trees. **www.riadhayati.com**

MEDINA Riad Kaiss

65 Derb Jdid Zitoune Kedim **Tel** *(0524) 44 01 41* **Rooms** *8*

Road map *C3*

Situated in the medina, within walking distance of the famous Place Jemaa el-Fna, this beautiful period *riad* is tastefully decorated with traditional lanterns, candles and textiles. Guest rooms feature antique furniture, while meals are served in courtyard dining areas or on the rooftop terrace. **www.sanssoucicollection.com**

MEDINA The Royal Mansour

Rue Abou Abbas El Sebti **Tel** *(0529) 80 80 80* **Rooms** *53*

Road map *C3*

Master craftsmen were recruited from across the kingdom to create a cluster of breathtaking *riads*, complete with private swimming pools on their roofs. Each *riad* comes with its own butler. The hotel also has two restaurants – one Moroccan and the other French – with highly trained chefs. **www.royalmansour.com**

Key to Price Guide *see p302* **Key to Symbols** *see back cover flap*

MEDINA Villa des Orangers

6 Rue Sidi Mimoun **Tel** *(0524) 38 46 38* **Rooms** *27* **Road map** *C3*

The roof terrace at this luxurious, traditionally styled hotel offers wonderful views of the Koutoubia. Its stylish restaurant features Mediterranean cuisine, and there's the chance to relax at the on-site beauty centre with its traditional hammam or in the cigar cellar. **www.villadesorangers.com**

HIGH ATLAS

ASNI Kasbah Tamadot

Post Office Box 67 **Tel** *0208 600 0430 (UK)* **Rooms** *27* **Road map** *C4*

Entrepreneur Richard Branson's hotel is such a lure that some guests leave this mountain retreat after a week of pampering, without ever visiting Marrakech. It has several pools, tennis courts, a spa, formal and informal dining areas and a deluxe Berber tent. Children are allowed during UK school holidays. **www.kasbahtamadot.virgin.com**

IMLIL Hôtel Kasbah du Toubkal

Imlil **Tel** *(0524) 48 56 11* **Rooms** *14* **Road map** *C4*

Located 60 km (38 miles) from Marrakech, in a stunning setting at the foot of Jbel Toubkal, is this beautifully restored kasbah. Once the home of a feudal chief, traditional methods have been used to turn it into a welcoming and comfortable base for hill walking. Guided treks can be arranged. **www.kasbahdutoubkal.com**

OUIRGANE Au Sanglier Qui Fume

Km 61, 5 route Marrakech, Taroudant **Tel** *(0524) 48 57 07* **Rooms** *25* **Road map** *C4*

This rustic little mountain lodge will not disappoint those seeking a homely atmosphere. The owners and their staff are ever ready to help guests. Rooms are cosy and most have fireplaces. Amenities include bicycle hire for mountain biking, a swimming pool and a video lounge. **www.ausanglierquifume.com**

OUIRGANE Domaine Malika

Douar Marigha Commune de Ouirgane, Route d'Amizmiz, par Asni **Tel** *(0661) 49 35 41* **Rooms** *7* **Road map** *C4*

Domaine Malika became an overnight success and it is easy to see why. Its French owners have paid meticulous attention to detail, offering a stylish spa and pool, quirky modern interiors, and an excellent à la carte menu in the restaurant. Particularly romantic is the garden suite, which is tailored for honeymooners. **www.domaine-malika.com**

OUIRGANE Hôtel La Bergerie

Asni village **Tel** *(0524) 48 57 17* **Rooms** *18* **Road map** *C4*

The Hôtel La Bergerie is probably one of the area's best-kept secrets. Tucked down a tiny trail just before the entrance to Ouirgane, on the Marrakech road, this pretty little inn offers the chance to truly get away from it all. Facilities include a restaurant with views out over the countryside and a pool. Half board is compulsory. **www.labergerie-maroc.com**

OUIRGANE Hôtel La Roseraie

Route de Taroudannt Km 60, Ouirgane Valley **Tel** *(0524) 43 91 28* **Rooms** *45* **Road map** *C4*

In the heart of the Ouirgane Valley and surrounded by countryside, this well equipped hotel offers a relaxing experience. It has three swimming pools (one of which is indoors) and a characterful restaurant to keep guests entertained, while its accommodation takes the form of independent bungalows.**www.laroseraiehotel.com**

OUKAÏMEDEN Club Alpin Francais

Club Alpin Francais **Tel** *(0524) 31 90 36* **Rooms** *63* **Road map** *C4*

This mountain resort offers dormitory-style accommodation for those looking for fine walks, fresh air and snow. Although a budget option, it is spotlessly clean, has a fully equipped bar and serves excellent food. The Club Alpine Francais also coordinates the mountain refuges for this area. **www.caf-maroc.com**

OUKAÏMEDEN Hôtel L'Angour

Southern end of Oukaïmeden **Tel** *(0524) 31 90 05* **Rooms** *18* **Road map** *C4*

More commonly known as "Chez Juju", this small mountain inn was one of the first in Oukaïmeden. Sitting at the foot of the slopes, it makes a comfortable base from which to explore the surroundings. It has a warm, family atmosphere and is well known for its wholesome, traditional French cooking. **resachezjuju@gmail.com**

OURIKA VALLEY Kasbah Bab Ouirika

Post Office box 79, Tniine Ourika **Tel** *(0661) 63 42 34* **Rooms** *15* **Road map** *C4*

Overlooking a national park, this lofty kasbah was built using traditional Berber building techniques. The rooms all have stunning views of the Atlas Mountains. The extensive organic vegetable gardens in the area provide fresh produce for the restaurant's seasonally changing menu. The hotel also actively promotes eco-tourism. **www.kasbahbabourika.com**

OUZOUD FALLS Riad Cascades D'Ouzoud

Chemin des Moulin, Azilal **Tel** *(0523) 42 91 73* **Rooms** *9* **Road map** *C3*

This *riad* is built of red earth and its delightful rooms are set around an interior courtyard. Perched above the staggering falls, it offers panoramic views of the countryside and you might even catch a glimpse of the indigenous Barbary apes, which have been known to swing from the telephone poles. **www.ouzoud.com**

TISSELDAY Irocha

Village de Tisselday, Ouarzazate **Tel** *(0667) 73 70 02* **Rooms** *7*   **Road map** *C4*

This guesthouse is located in a small village high in the Atlas Mountains. The rooms are simply furnished and clean and the lounges provide the perfect setting for a relaxing evening. There is also a small pool, a hammam and telescopes are available for stargazing. Child friendly. **www.irocha.com**

OUARZAZATE & THE SOUTHERN OASES

AÏT BENHADDOU Hôtel Auberge Étoile Filante d'Or

Centre of Aït Benhaddou **Tel** *(0524) 89 03 22* **Rooms** *22*   **Road map** *C4*

This compact hotel is set in the heart of Aït Benhaddou with terraces overlooking its *ksar*. When it was built it was designed to blend in seamlessly with its surroundings, and it does just that. Guest rooms are equipped with basic amenities, while the hotel's small restaurant serves delicious local dishes.

AÏT BENHADDOU Hôtel de la Kasbah

Centre of Aït Behaddou **Tel** *(0524) 89 03 02* **Rooms** *83*   **Road map** *C4*

The Hôtel de la Kasbah is something of a legend in this High Atlas village. At one time a popular café, it grew to become one of the few hotels in the area. Located beside the road to the river, the hotel has a welcoming staff, and its guest rooms are comfortable. Its restaurant serves classic Moroccan dishes.

ERFOUD Hôtel Salam

Route de Rissani **Tel** *(0535) 57 64 26* **Rooms** *132*   **Road map** *E4*

Location is the key at this hotel, with the desert just on the doorstep. The rooms are modest but spacious and the buffet breakfast offers a good choice. The expansive communal areas, international and Moroccan food and the large number of rooms mean Hôtel Salam lends itself well to tour groups.

ERFOUD Kasbah Hôtel Chergui

Erfoud to Errachidia road, km 5, 5 Post Office Box BP-342 **Tel** *(0535) 57 85 04* **Rooms** *100*   **Road map** *E4*

Surrounded by sweeping views of sand and palm trees, this desert hotel has impressive facilities and is large enough to cater for groups. The rooms are spacious and clean with air conditioning and modern en-suite bathrooms, while the buffet-style dining offers a wide variety. The hotel has helpful and knowledgeable staff. **www.hotelchergui.com**

ERFOUD Hôtel Xaluca

205 Route d'Errachidia, Erfoud km 5 **Tel** *(0535) 57 84 50* **Rooms** *104*   **Road map** *E4*

This three-star hotel is ideal for a short business trip or a relaxing holiday, since it is within easy reach of the airport. It has all the necessary amenities – such as a characterful restaurant, impressive pools and attractive guest rooms with Turkish-style bathrooms that include fossil marble washbasins – for a memorable stay. **www.xaluca.com**

ERFOUD Palais Du Desert

Route de Jorf, BP 310 **Rooms** *4*   **Road map** *E4*

There are just four rooms at this magnificent kasbah in the oasis of Tizimi and they are all suites with outstanding facilities. The pool, restaurant, spa and fitness rooms are first-class and the bar serves cocktails and whiskies and also sells cigars. Palais Du Desert is plush and highly exclusive. **www.palaisdudesert.com**

MERZOUGA Auberge Kasbah Derkaoua

Route to Merzouga **Tel** *(0661) 34 36 77 I (0535) 57 71 40* **Rooms** *22*   **Road map** *D4*

A small and immensely attractive kasbah hotel in the heart of the desert, the Derkaoua is clearly a passion for its owners, and it is beautifully presented. There is a small restaurant full of character serving excellent local dishes, as well as a swimming pool. This is a real haven of peace. **www.aubergederkaoua.com**

OUARZAZATE Hôtel Ibis Moussafir

Boulevard Moulay Rachid **Tel** *(0524) 89 91 10* **Rooms** *104*   **Road map** *C4*

Morocco is awash with quality hotels, and the Ibis Moussafir is certainly among the best. The reception area is designed to capture the essence of Morocco, while the rooms, including some adapted for visitors with disabilities, offer every amenity. There is a pool on site, and a restaurant *(see p341)*. **www.accorhotels.com**

OUARZAZATE Hôtel La Gazelle

Avenue Mohammed V **Tel** *(0524) 88 21 51* **Rooms** *30*   **Road map** *C4*

Situated at the edge of the town, on the main thoroughfare through Ouarzazate, this attractive hotel is relatively small but makes a good base from which to explore the region. The rooms are comfortable and the popular restaurant *(see p341)* is cosy.

OUARZAZATE Hôtel Mercure

Boulevard Moulay Rachid **Tel** *(0524) 89 91 00* **Rooms** *68*   **Road map** *C4*

Conveniently situated for trips into the desert or the Dadès valley, the four-star Hôtel Mercure offers a central and comfortable place to stay. Guest rooms are attractive, have private bathrooms and are well-equipped, while the hotel has several on-site eateries and sports amenities. **www.accorhotels.com**

Key to Price Guide *see p302* **Key to Symbols** *see back cover flap*

OUARZAZATE Ryad Salam

Boulevard Mohammed V **Tel** *(0524) 88 37 84* **Rooms** *62*   **Road map** *C4*

Large rooms and a pleasant pool are on offer at this art deco hotel set in gardens. The restaurant serves a wide array of local and international dishes. The premises are split between two buildings, the hotel and a riad-style property. If possible, ask to see your room prior to check-in as these do vary.

OUARZAZATE Hôtel Karam Palace

Avenue Moulay Rachid **Tel** *(0524) 88 22 25* **Rooms** *147*   **Road map** *C4*

Combining comfort with a characterful decor that aims to capture Moroccan architecture and style, this modern hotel offers attractive fully equipped rooms, a good swimming pool and a restaurant serving international as well as Moroccan food. It stands in lush gardens close to the town centre.

OUARZAZATE Hôtel Kenzi Azgour

Avenue Moulay Rachid **Tel** *(0524) 88 65 01* **Rooms** *140*   **Road map** *C4*

A landmark building, the Kenzi Bélère is located in the older part of town. Well designed and adopting authentic Moroccan styling for its interior decor, it offers a range of amenities that include a good restaurant and nightclub, and well-equipped guest rooms, some with panoramic views.

OUARZAZATE Hôtel Sultana Royal Golf

Royal Golf-BP 448 **Tel** *(0524) 88 74 21* **Rooms** *12*   **Road map** *C4*

With beautifully landscaped gardens and fountains stretching out towards the dunes, this glamorous hotel offers a dazzling myriad of amenities. The bars are lavish and the restaurant is sleek, while the rooms are striking with bright and colourful textiles. **www.hotelsultanaroyalgolf.com**

OUARZAZATE Le Berbère Palace

Quartier Mansour Eddahbi **Tel** *(0524) 88 31 05* **Rooms** *222*   **Road map** *C4*

Situated in the heart of Ouarzazate, the luxurious Berbère Palace, with its Moroccan decor, is always popular with the most discerning holiday visitors. It offers its guests a superior standard of facilities with individual bungalows set among the gardens. **www.hotel-berberepalace.com**

OUARZAZATE Le Temple des Arts

173 and 174, Hay Al Wahda **Tel** *(0524) 88 88 31* **Rooms** *7*   **Road map** *C4*

End a tour of nearby Atlas film studios with a night in this temple dedicated to the moving image. Le Temple des Arts appeals to kids of all ages – it glimmers with brass, gold and film props and looks like a hotel one would expect to find in Las Vegas. **www.templedesarts-ouarzazate.com**

ZAGORA Dar Nekhla

Palmeraie d'Amezrou **Tel** *(0524) 846 472* **Rooms** *4*   **Road map** *D4*

Guests can sit in the gardens of this lovely family hotel, which is nestled in an oasis, and listen to the birds. The reasonably priced rooms are large and clean with attached showers. The staff will make sure that you have a very comfortable stay. **www.riadzagora.fr**

ZAGORA Villa Zagora

Piste du Djebel de Zagora **Tel** *(0524) 84 60 93* **Rooms** *6*   **Road map** *D4*

A charming, simple yet stylish hotel, Villa Zagora is in a fabulous setting at the gateway to the desert. Opt for a double room or share the Berber tent, which comes complete with beds and carpets. There is a beautiful pool, flower and fruit-filled gardens and excellent home-cooked food. **www.mavillaausahara.com**

ZAGORA Hôtel Riad Salam

Boulevard Mohammed V **Tel** *(0524) 84 74 00* **Rooms** *120*   **Road map** *D4*

The Riad Salam is one of the best hotels in Zagora, offering a good selection of amenities and lots of character. There's a pool around which most guests relax, along with a pretty garden terrace, a courtyard and two restaurants *(see p342)*. Its guest rooms are well equipped and boast breathtaking desert views. **www.mahdsalam.com**

SOUTHERN MOROCCO & WESTERN SAHARA

AGADIR Hôtel Sindibad

Place Lahcen ou brahim Tamri **Tel** *(0528) 82 34 77* **Rooms** *53*   **Road map** *B4*

Situated around 20 minutes from the beach, Hôtel Sindibad offers a swimming pool with loungers, a bar and a reasonable restaurant. Rooms are not luxurious, but are spacious and comfortable. For a menu more varied than the hôtel restaurant explore the surrounding area, which has many local cafés and bars.

AGADIR Hôtel Sud Bahia

Avenue des Administrations Publique **Tel** *(0528) 84 07 82* **Rooms** *246*   **Road map** *B4*

In a prime location with views of the beach and the Atlantic Ocean, this hotel offers good value and is a popular choice for tourists and businesspeople visiting the city. It has pleasant guest rooms with many amenities, a large swimming pool and a restaurant serving good international dishes.

AGADIR Hôtel Argana

Boulevard Mohammed B.P 93 **Tel** *(0528) 84 83 04* **Rooms** *236* **Road map** *B4*

This large hotel near the beach is a good, yet inexpensive option for some winter sun. The keyhole shaped swimming pool is popular, as are the surrounding sun loungers. Hôtel Argana also provides buffets and evening entertainment. Rooms are clean, no frills but attractive. **www.argana-hotel.com**

AGADIR Hôtel Ibis Moussafir

Avenue Abderrahim Bouabid **Tel** *(0528) 23 28 42* **Rooms** *104* **Road map** *B4*

Standing proudly on the corner of two main thoroughfares and close to the lively El Had market, the Ibis Moussafir is a city-centre hotel set away from the crowds in the more touristy beach areas. Its amenities are plentiful and include well-equipped rooms, a swimming pool and two restaurants. **www.accorhotels.com**

AGADIR Hôtel Tivoli

Secteur Balnéaire **Tel** *(0528) 84 76 40* **Rooms** *280* **Road map** *B4*

The Hôtel Tivoli is set right in the heart of Agadir, making it an ideal option for enjoying the beach or absorbing the atmosphere of the town centre. It is a large, modern, lavishly decorated four-star hotel with comfortable rooms and a restaurant. Its garden terrace is especially attractive.

AGADIR Hôtel Beach Club

Rue de Oued Souss **Tel** *(0528) 84 43 43* **Rooms** *450* **Road map** *B4*

The Beach Club is one of the best and most popular hotels in the tourist area of Agadir. Its rooms are beautifully presented, and most have views of the sea from a private balcony or terrace. The many facilities at this family-friendly hotel including a health and fitness suite, a business centre and several restaurants. **www.agadir-beach-club.net**

AGADIR Hôtel Best Western Odyssey Park

Boulevard Mohammed V **Tel** *(0528) 84 33 26* **Rooms** *140* **Road map** *B4*

If an intimate hotel with Moroccan-style decor is your preference, then the Odyssey Park could well fit the bill. Despite offering more than 100 guest rooms, it manages to retain a cosy, tranquil feel. It has its own fitness suite and pool, along with pleasant guest rooms and restaurants serving local dishes.

AGADIR Hôtel du Timoulay

Cité Founty F6 Baie des Palmiers, Bensergao **Tel** *(0528) 23 42 20* **Rooms** *58* **Road map** *B4*

A popular destination hotel near the beach, Hôtel du Timoulay has evening entertainment, a great pool and sun terrace and impressive buffets. The rooms vary in decor but are clean, comfortable and well maintained. A good option for families with children and those wanting to laze in the spa, pool or sun. **www.timoulayhotel.com**

AGADIR Hôtel Riu Tikida Beach

Chemin des Dunes **Tel** *(0528) 84 54 00* **Rooms** *233* **Road map** *B4*

Beautifully decorated and well maintained, this large hotel, set right on the edge of the beach in Agadir, offers attractive guest rooms in low-rise buildings and a range of amenities. Its swimming pools and bars are largely dotted around among lush, exotic gardens, as are the guest rooms themselves. **www.agadirtikida.com**

AGADIR Hôtel Kenzi Farah Europa

Boulevard 20 Août **Tel** *(0528) 82 12 12* **Rooms** *236* **Road map** *B4*

Located in the heart of Agadir's tourist area, this modern hotel offers ample facilities including a pool, tennis, spa, sauna, gym and conference rooms. The restaurant serves both traditional Moroccan dishes and continental foods with an Italian twist. The beach and a number of shops are within easy walking distance. **www.kenzi-hotels.com**

AGADIR Hôtel Palais des Roses

Secteur Touristique and Balnéaire, Cité Founty **Tel** *(0528) 84 94 00* **Rooms** *405* **Road map** *B4*

Situated along the Atlantic with its own private beach area, this hotel was built to impress. Communal areas such as the lobby, pool and restaurant have been tastefully decorated. The rooms, however, are a touch on the worn side for a hotel of this rank. A gym and conference rooms are among the facilities on offer. **www.palaisdesroses.com**

AGADIR Riad Villa Blanche

Baie des Palmiers, N°50 Cité Founty, Sonaba **Tel** *(0528) 21 13 13* **Rooms** *28* **Road map** *B4*

Glamorous yet refreshingly retained, Riad Villa Blanche has an old-world charm. Minutes from the beach, it offers extensive watersports and sea-water spa treatments, indoor and outdoor pools and attractive gardens. The rooms are decorated with Moroccan influences and are fitted with all amenities. **www.riadvillablanche.com**

AGADIR Sahara Hôtel

Boulevard Mohammed V **Tel** *(0528) 84 06 60* **Rooms** *236* **Road map** *B4*

This 1970s hotel, located between the beach and the city centre has undergone an extensive renovation, which has resulted in tasteful decor, four restaurants, a swimming pool, fitness rooms and central air conditioning. It is large enough to accommodate groups. **www.saharahotel.com**

AGADIR Atlantic Palace

Secteur Balnéaire & Touristique **Tel** *(0528) 82 41 46* **Rooms** *332* **Road map** *B4*

Located right in the centre of the tourist area, the large and luxurious Atlantic Palace is one of the best five-star hotels in Agadir. Every guest's need is catered for, from relaxing in a spa or dining on fine international and local cuisine, to swimming or engaging in sporting activities. **www.atlanticpalace-agadir.com**

Key to Price Guide *see p302* **Key to Symbols** *see back cover flap*

AGADIR Hôtel Beach Albatross

Boulevard Mohammed V **Tel** *(0528) 84 32 32* **Rooms** *183*   **Road map** *B4*

The Royal Mirage is a landmark building in the Bay of Agadir. It is beautifully presented, with lush gardens and whitewashed rooms that surround a lagoon-style swimming pool. It is situated right on the beachside and offers some superb leisure amenities for the entire family. **www.royalmiragehotels.com**

AGADIR Hôtel Sofitel Royal Bay Resort

Cité Founty Baie des Palmiers **Tel** *(0528) 82 00 88* **Rooms** *273*   **Road map** *B4*

Located alongside the beach of Agadir, in Palm Bay, the luxurious five-star Sofitel combines architecture that is pure Moroccan kasbah with contemporary amenities. It has an overall feel of tranquillity despite its size. Facilities include a large pool, four restaurants, numerous bars and guest rooms oozing quality. **www.sofitel.com**

GUELMIN Fort Bou-Jerif

Fort Bou-Jerif, Pierre Gerbens, Post Office Box 504 **Tel** *(0672) 13 00 17* **Rooms** *5*   **Road map** *A5*

This hotel occupies a fort constructed by the French in 1935 in the last town before the Sahara. It is popular with groups looking for comfort and a wide range of activities such as desert expeditions, paragliding, quad biking and camel safaris. In addition to the rooms there are plenty of comfortable tents. **www.fortboujerif.com**

SIDI IFNI Hôtel Bellevue

Place Hassan II **Tel** *(0528) 87 50 72* **Rooms** *38*   **Road map** *B5*

Situated in a clifftop location with an outstanding view of the Atlantic Ocean, the Bellevue lives up to its name. This hotel offers nicely presented rooms that are well maintained. It has an attractive terrace and a restaurant *(see p343)* that specialises in fish dishes.

TAFRAOUTE Hôtel des Amandiers

Centre of Tafraoute **Tel** *(0528) 80 00 08* **Rooms** *60*   **Road map** *B5*

The Hôtel des Amandiers is an attractive establishment that stands in a traditionally styled building on a hill in Tafraoute. Its central location makes it a good base for exploring the area. Its staff are welcoming and friendly, while rooms are simply equipped but clean, with great views of the surrounding countryside.

TAN TAN Hôtel Les Sables d'Or

Boulevard Hassan II **Tel** *(0528) 87 80 69* **Rooms** *32*   **Road map** *A5*

If a hotel with few frills close to the centre of town is needed, then Les Sables d'Or could fit the bill. Its modern rooms are surprisingly comfortable for a budget hotel, and they each have their own private bathroom, while the hotel itself offers an attractive little garden terrace.

TAROUDANNT Hôtel Palais Salam

Taroudannt Ramparts **Tel** *(0528) 85 25 01* **Rooms** *143*   **Road map** *B4*

One of the best things about pre-booking a stay at the Palais Salam is that you are almost guaranteed a room with a view of the ramparts. Built within the walls and offering maze-like accommodation wings, this hotel is a charming spot in the centre of town. Its pool, gardens and restaurant *(see p343)* are all lovely.

TAROUDANNT Ryad Dar El Hana

376 Jn Si Moussa **Tel** *(0662) 84 80 87* **Rooms** *4*   **Road map** *B4*

A fully renovated riad with carefully chosen furniture and attractive rooms, Dar El Hana provides wonderful views of palms, olive groves and the low Atlas mountains. Located in the heart of the walled city, it is only a minute's walk from the town's souks. Owner Sibyl de Deaufort is an excellent source of local information. **www.dar-el-hana.com**

TAROUDANNT Hôtel La Gazelle d'Or

Centre of Taroudannt **Tel** *(0528) 85 20 39* **Rooms** *30*   **Road map** *B4*

The sophisticated and legendary Gazelle d'Or is one of the region's most luxurious hotels. The rich and famous have been known to stay here and enjoy the tranquil garden setting. The hotel caters for its guests' every need. An on-site restaurant serves fine cuisine *(see p343)* prepared using own-grown organic products. **www.gazelledor.com**

TATA Dar Infiane

Maison d'Hôtes Dar Infiane, Douar Indfiane, BP 221, Tata **Tel** *(0661) 61 01 70* **Rooms** *10*   **Road map** *C5*

This beautiful 16th-century guesthouse, feels like a mountain home. The foot-and-a-half-thick walls are whitewashed, with splashes of colours coming from the painted woodwork and the carpets on the tiled floors. The oasis and mountain views are mesmerizing. **www.darinfiane.com**

TIZNIT Hôtel Tiznit

Rue Bir Inzaran **Tel** *(0528) 86 24 11* **Rooms** *36*   **Road map** *B5*

Popular with small tour groups, which is always a good sign, the Hôtel Tiznit is classic, clean and has a few good amenities, including an atmospheric restaurant serving international dishes and Moroccan specialities. A charming garden terrace and swimming pool provide outdoor areas for relaxation.

TIZNIT Kerdous Hôtel

Kerdous Pass **Tel** *(0528) 21 81 52* **Rooms** *35*   **Road map** *B5*

Moroccan hospitality and style are promised by the owners of this incredibly isolated kasbah-style hotel in the heart of the country, just a few kilometres inland from the coast. Offering good amenities at a competitive rate, the Kerdous has attractively presented rooms, two restaurants *(see p343)* and a pool.

WHERE TO EAT

In Morocco, cooking is an integral part of the art of living. Since this is also a country with a large number of restaurants, the choice of what and where to eat is boundless. Prices vary widely from one place to the next and from one town to the next, and tipping is still a well-entrenched custom. Although restaurant opening hours are similar to those of Western Europe, they may change during Ramadan.

Oysters, a speciality of Oualidia *(see p115)*

Religious strictures also mean that establishments serving alcohol are relatively rare and tightly regulated.

Restaurants span the full range, from the smartest, with international cuisine, to the more modest, which offer delicious Moroccan dishes. Finally, there are the little stalls that are found on every street corner or on the quay in harbours, which serve freshly cooked fish and other succulent treats.

Le Chalet de la Plage, a beach restaurant at Essaouira *(see p332)*

TYPES OF RESTAURANT

In large towns and cities in Morocco you will find every kind of restaurant. At one end of the scale are modest street stalls and small bistros; at the other are classic restaurants and prestigious gastronomic establishments. Athough, in this bracket, French and Italian establishments predominate, these restaurants enable you to sample specialities from all over the world. Fast-food outlets are also becoming ubiquitous, particularly in city centres.

In medium-sized towns, the choice is more limited, with relatively basic establishments offering mostly local specialities. In small seaside towns, fish restaurants are particularly numerous.

Restaurants serving typically Moroccan food are, in fact, comparatively rare. They can be roughly divided into two types: "tourist" restaurants, which cater for groups and

which sometimes put on shows such as fantasias *(see pp34–5)*, and higher-class restaurants, such as those in Fès or Marrakech. These are more like tables d'hôte in old traditional residences. The prices that they charge are higher (400 to 600 dirhams in the most renowned establishments), but you will enjoy a more refined cuisine and a more authentic atmosphere.

Given the pleasantly warm climate in Morocco, many restaurants like to serve their customers outdoors, setting out tables in a quiet and pleasantly shaded courtyard, in the corner of a garden or even on the pavement outside the restaurant.

MOROCCAN SPECIALITIES

Although Morocco is well provided with restaurants offering international specialities, it is essential to sample Moroccan cuisine *(see pp324–5)*, which is by far the best food that is served in the country.

A traditional Moroccan meal begins with a large number of starters, consisting of salad, or vegetables flavoured with different kinds of spices. Then follows the main course, often couscous or *tajine (see p325)*.

Tajine is a kind of stew made with fish, chicken, beef or lamb, and may include prunes or almonds. There is a great variety of *tajines*, which differ according to the region, and it is hardly an exaggeration to say

A restaurant and shop on the Tizi-n-Test Pass road

Food stalls on Place Jemaa el-Fna in Marrakech at nightfall

that there are almost as many variations as there are cooks. All, however, are prepared and served in a terracotta dish with a conical lid; this cooking vessel is called a *tajine*, hence the dish's name.

Moroccan desserts, especially milk *pastilla*, are mouth-watering. Meals are usually eaten with mint tea, although more and more restaurants now offer wine.

OPENING HOURS AND RESERVATIONS

In most restaurants, lunch is served between noon and 3pm and dinner between 7pm and 10:30pm. However, during the fast of Ramadan *(see p41)*, many restaurants, especially the less expensive ones, will not open at lunchtime.

In very fashionable restaurants, particularly those in the centre of the largest towns and cities, it is advisable for large parties to make a reservation, especially on Thursdays, Fridays and on Saturday evenings.

Reservation is absolutely essential for the tables d'hôte in Marrakech and Fès. Here it is often necessary to reserve several days in advance, since space can be limited, as can the number of sittings each evening.

PRICES AND TIPPING

Prices vary widely according to a restaurant's quality. They may range from 60 dirhams for a basic meal to about 300 dirhams for a meal with wine in a classic establishment, and between 400 and 600 dirhams in a high-class restaurant. Prices are higher

in large towns and cities and in places that attract many foreign visitors, such as Casablanca, Agadir and Marrakech. Prices given on menus usually include service and tax, so that unpleasant surprises are rare.

Tipping is a widely accepted custom in Morocco. It is customary to give 5 to 10 per cent of the bill. The tip should be in cash, and should be left on the table when you leave the restaurant. Do not add it to the total when you pay by cheque or bankers' card since the waiters will not receive it.

ALCOHOLIC DRINKS

Morocco is a Muslim country where stringent laws apply to the sale of alcohol. However, most restaurants from a certain level upwards have a license to serve alcohol, as do Moroccan restaurants with a largely Western clientele.

Unlicensed restaurants may sometimes serve wine discreetly. Visitors should not, however, insist on being

served alcohol in an unlicensed restaurant since not serving alcohol may be the manager's deliberate policy. During Ramadan, some restaurants that normally serve alcohol close or stop serving it.

DRESS

Moroccans usually dress quite smartly when they go out to eat. Restaurants never insist on a particular type of dress. The only exception is in a few very high-class establishments, where gentlemen will be expected to wear a tie, or where ties will be lent. It is best to avoid too relaxed a style of dress, and very revealing clothes, such as beachwear, are likely to be considered offensive.

STREET STALLS

Stalls selling cheap food are seen everywhere in Morocco. Typical dishes are soup, skewered meat or fish and sandwiches.

At dusk, Place Jemaa el-Fna in Marrakech *(see p234)* turns into a huge open-air restaurant. In coastal towns and villages, usually on the quays of harbours where fishing boats come in, trestle tables serving freshly cooked seafood are often set up.

Although the food served from stalls is usually fresh, it is best to single out those that are the most popular with Moroccans. This is the best indication of good quality.

Traditional dining room in a restaurant in Agadir

The Flavours of Morocco

From the indigenous, rural Berber people come the basics of Moroccan cuisine, such as couscous, but Moroccan food owes much to influences from neighbouring lands. In the 1600s the Arabs introduced bread, pulses and spices, notably chickpeas (garbanzos), cinnamon, ginger, saffron and tumeric, from their empire in the East. In the 11th century Bedouin tribes brought dates and milk from their wandering flocks. The Arabs returned from Andalusia with produce such as olives and lemons, and, later, tomatoes and peppers from the Americas.

Dried couscous

Meat and other products on sale at a market food stall in Morocco

MEAT

Lamb is the cornerstone of Moroccan cookery, and is found in the form of grills, *merguez* (thin, spicy red sausages) and brochettes (skewers); in *tagines* or a couscous; and roasted whole on a spit with aromatics as the traditional *m'choui*.

You will also find beef on the menu, usually served as kebabs, as well as rabbit, served as a couscous or *tagine*. Chicken and turkey are also readily available. Pigeon is more rarely on the menu these days, but is still a feature of *b'stilla*. This extravagant pie, a speciality of Fès, is made with tissue-thin *warkha* pastry. Offal, such as brains, heart, liver and tripe, are also popular.

FISH & SEAFOOD

Morocco has long coasts on the Atlantic and the Mediterranean, which provide a wide variety of seafood. Fish such as bream and bass are typically marinated in a garlicky, spicy mixture called *chermoula*, and are usually cooked whole. They may also be served stuffed, with an almond crust, as steaks or brochettes, or as fishcakes,

Some of the many spices used in traditional Moroccan dishes

Ginger · Saffron · Cloves · Ras el hanout · Cinnamon · Coriander seeds · Dried rose petals · Cumin

MOROCCAN DISHES AND SPECIALITIES

Preserved lemons and mint

A restaurant meal in Morocco will typically start with a full-flavoured soup, such as *harira*, a comforting soup of diced lamb, lentils and chickpeas with tomato, onion, coriander and parsley, or a selection of vibrant salads.

A *tagine* is a common main course, served with flat bread *(matlouh)*. The meat and vegetables are flavoured with saffron, garlic, coriander and cumin. Garnishes include olives, eggs, mint and preserved lemons. Another main course is couscous. Made with vegetables, chicken, lamb, *merguez*, rabbit, or even fish, it is usually served with a hot sauce made from *harissa* and tomato purée.

Harira, *a meal-like soup, is a dish traditionally served at sunset during Ramadan, in order to break the fast.*

and almonds. Other common fruits include peaches, figs, melons, bananas, plums, pomegranates and all types of citrus fruits. Lemons, preserved in brine, add piquancy to many dishes.

SPICES & FLAVOURINGS

Key Moroccan spices include aniseed, black pepper, cayenne, cardamom, cinnamon, coriander, cumin, ginger, paprika, parsley, saffron and turmeric. Three spice blends are important: *chermoula*, for marinades; *harissa*, a hot red pepper condiment; and *ras el hanout* ("top of the shop"), a blend of over 20 spices, used in *tagines*.

Food stall at dusk in the Place Jemaa el-Fna in Marrakech

known as *boulettes*, with a spicy tomato sauce. Prawns, squid, oysters and mussels are also available and good.

VEGETABLES

Morocco has many inventive and refreshing salad dishes. Often served as a starter, they include *mezgaldi*, which combines onions with saffron, ginger, cinnamon, sugar and celery. Aubergines (eggplants) are ubiquitous, served as a salad, fried or stuffed. Combinations of tomatoes, green peppers, hot red or sweet red peppers and red onions, all add colour and flavour to the table. Olives and their oil are abundant, and nutty argan oil is widely used. (Goats adore the outer pulp of the nut, and can be seen "grazing" in the branches of argan trees.)

FRUIT

Most Moroccan meals end with a dish of fruit, often a simple sliced-orange salad, sprinkled with cinnamon and orange-flower water, and sometimes chopped dates

Array of cakes and pastries in a patisserie in Fès

MOROCCAN PASTRIES

Briouats Triangular *warkha* pastries filled with almond and cinnamon paste.

Ghoriba Macaroons made with sugar, almonds, lemon zest, vanilla and cinnamon.

Kaab el ghzal Pastry crescents filled with sweet almond paste, dipped in orange-flower water and icing sugar.

M'hanncha "Coiled serpent" cake of pastry stuffed with almonds and decorated with icing sugar and cinnamon.

Sfenj Deep-fried doughnuts.

Shebbakia Deep-fried pastry ribbons, dipped in hot honey and coated in sesame seeds

B'stilla *is a rich pie of pigeon, eggs, almonds and raisins, flavoured with lemon, sugar, saffron and cinnamon.*

Tagine, *a slow-cooked stew, is named for the earthenware dish with a conical lid in which it is cooked.*

Couscous *is the Moroccan national dish – a semolina-based grain served with an accompanying stew.*

What to Drink in Morocco

Green mint tea is the national drink in Morocco. It is served several times a day at home, in the office, in shops and on café terraces. Moroccans are also very fond of coffee, which is usually served with milk but may sometimes be flavoured with cinnamon, orange-flower water or a few grains of pepper. Freshly squeezed orange juice is delicious, as are all fruit juices – cherry, grape and pomegranate being the most widely available choices. Although the Koran forbids the consumption of alcohol, fairly good-quality wines are produced in Morocco, and these can be bought in certain shops.

The tea ceremony, performed in front of guests

TEA

Known for 3,000 years in China, green tea, with long fine leaves, reached Morocco in 1854. It was introduced by the British, and immediately became popular in every Moroccan home. All over Morocco, from the sophisticated town house to the simple nomad's tent, green mint tea has become

Glass of mint tea

the thirst-quenching drink, which is made with varying amounts of sugar and mint, is a symbol of hospitality, and it is considered very ill-mannered to refuse it.

The tea ceremony is almost always performed in front of guests and according to immutable rules. Mint tea is always served in small, slender glasses decorated with a gold or coloured filigree pattern. The tea leaves are rinsed in the scalded teapot so as to remove their excessive bitterness. Whole mint leaves, complete with stems, are then added, together with large lumps of sugar, which prevent the leaves from rising to the surface. After being left for a few minutes to infuse, a little tea is poured into a glass and returned to the pot. This is repeated several times. The host finally tastes the tea, which will not be served to guests until it is deemed to be perfect.

Traditionally served mint tea

COFFEE

Although it is less widely drunk than tea, Moroccans are also fond of coffee, which they like to drink very strong. It is accceptable to ask for a little boiling water with which to dilute it. Unless you request otherwise, your coffee will automatically be served with milk. A black coffee is a *qahwa kahla*; a *noss noss* is half coffee and half milk; and *café cassé* consists of more coffee than milk.

Coffee with milk (*noss noss*)

Black coffee (*qahwa kahla*)

COLD DRINKS

Although lemonade and cola are sold on every street corner, freshly squeezed orange juice is the real Moroccan speciality. It is absolutely delicious, so long as it is served undiluted. The sweet, juicy and famously flavoursome Moroccan oranges can be seen laid out for sale everywhere, piled up in glossy pyramids on barrows and on market stalls. On Place Jemaa el-Fna in Marrakech *(see p234)*, they are almost a sideshow in themselves. Almond milk, banana milk, apple juice and pomegranate juice are also popular drinks.

Orange juice

Almond milk

BEER AND SPIRITS

All kinds of imported alcoholic drinks can be purchased in supermarkets. Flag Spéciale is a light ale brewed in Tangier and Casablanca. Stork is brewed in Casablanca. *Mahia* is a Moroccan fig distillation, 40 per cent proof. The sale of wine and other alcohol is forbidden to Muslims during Ramadan and after 7:30pm.

Casablanca beer

Flag Spéciale, from Tangier

MINERAL WATER

Although the tap water in towns is safe to drink, it tastes strongly of chlorine. Mineral water – such as Sidi Ali and Sidi Harazem, which are still, and Oulmès and San Pellegrino, which are sparkling – is much more palatable.

Sidi Ali mineral water

Sidi Harazem mineral water

Oulmès mineral water

MOROCCAN WINES

Wine has been produced in Morocco since Roman times, and local wine production was encouraged during the Protectorate. The country has three major wine-producing areas: around Oujda, in the northeast, in the Fès and Meknès area, and in the west, between Rabat and Casablanca.

The most popular wines include red and white Medaillon, red, white and rosé Siroua, and the higher-quality wines produced by the winemakers Celliers de Meknès: Merlot and Cabernet Sauvignon; Sémillant, a fruity, dry white wine, and two rosé wines – Gris de Guerouane and Gris de Boulaouane. Also produced are Aït Soual, Vieux-Papes, Oustalet, Valpierre, Chaud-Soleil and Spécial

Vineyard near Boulaouane

Coquillages, which is best drunk with fish and seafood. Note that the quality of Moroccan wines can differ widely from year to year and sometimes even from bottle to bottle.

Red Amazir

Red Cabernet

Red Siroua

Red Guerrouane

Red Oustalet

Rosé Guerrouane

Rosé Cabernet

Choosing a Restaurant

The restaurants in this guide have been selected across a wide range of price categories for their exceptional food, good value and interesting location. The restaurants are listed by region. Within each town or city, entries are listed by price category, from the least expensive to the most expensive.

PRICE CATEGORIES IN MOROCCAN DIRHAMS (DH)
For a three-course meal for one person, including tax and service (but without wine).
ⓓ Under 150 dirhams
ⓓⓓ 150–250 dirhams
ⓓⓓⓓ 250–350 dirhams
ⓓⓓⓓⓓ 350–450 dirhams
ⓓⓓⓓⓓⓓ Over 450 dirhams

RABAT

Agdal Le Puzzle
ⓓⓓ
79 Avenue Ibn Sina Agdal **Road map** C2

A bright and breezy little restaurant that combines French and Moroccan architecture and informal interior design, Le Puzzle is a popular eatery that specializes in Mediterranean cuisine. Chicken, kebabs, mezes-style meals, fish and stuffed vegetables, as well as a good selection of fruit, are all on the menu. There's live music daily.

Agdal Pizzeria Reggio
ⓓⓓ
Place Ibn Yassine **Tel** *(0537) 77 69 99* **Road map** C2

With a vast selection of freshly made pasta dishes, pizzas, salads and light snacks – all skillfully produced to authentic recipes and using fresh produce from Italy's various regions – Pizzeria Reggio is the ideal venue for either a quick lunchtime meal or a relaxed evening with friends. It is lively, informal and welcoming, and yet very chic.

AGDAL Fuji
ⓓⓓⓓ
2 Avenue de Michlifen **Tel** *(0537) 67 35 83* **Road map** C2

Situated in the heart of the capital, Fuji offers fine sushi, sashimi, bento boxes and teriyaki in minimalist yet comfortable surroundings. It is especially good as a lunch venue, although it is closed on Tuesdays and Wednesdays. The menu provides a welcome break from the city's meaty menus and vegetarians will find plenty of options here.

AGDAL L'Entrecôte
ⓓⓓⓓ
74 Charia Al-Amir-Fal-Ould-Oumeir **Tel** *(0537) 67 11 08* **Road map** C2

A beautifully presented restaurant decorated with *voile* fabric and traditional bistro-style pictures on the walls, L'Entrecôte specializes in classic French meat and fish dishes in rich sauces. Located close to the commercial centre in Rabat, it tends to attract trendy young diners and businesspeople, as well as visiting tourists.

CITY CENTRE L'Eperon
ⓓⓓ
8 Avenue d'Alger **Road map** C2

This traditional restaurant has earned itself a reputation for serving good French food at relatively low prices, making it popular with businesspeople at lunchtime and with locals and visitors in the evening. The menu offers a wide selection of meats, such as veal and beef, cooked slowly in herbs and spices. There is also a fine French wine list.

CITY CENTRE La Latium
ⓓⓓⓓ
16 Avenue Annakhil, Hay Riad **Tel** *(0537) 71 77 16* **Road map** C2

This authentic Italian restaurant with a cosy interior is a much-frequented venue in a vibrant area of town, with excellent home-made pastas, salads and wood-fired pizzas. Particularly popular are the traditional desserts such as ice cream and tiramisu. The menu and staff cater well for those dining with children.

CITY CENTRE La Brasserie
ⓓⓓⓓⓓ
Hotel Diwan Rabat, Place de L'Unité Africaine **Tel** *(0537) 26 27 27* **Road map** C2

This elegant restaurant is a slick operation. Run by the Sofitel group and located within the Sofitel Diwan *(see p303)*, near the Hassan Tower and the Hassan Mosque, La Brasserie offers a range of traditional French dishes. It is mostly frequented by tour groups and tourists staying at the hotel, although it is also open to non-residents.

CITY CENTRE Le Grand Comptoir
ⓓⓓⓓⓓ
279 Avenue Mohammed V **Tel** *(0537) 20 15 14* **Road map** C2

With its candelabras, sparkling gilt mirrors and a pianist playing background music, Le Grand Comptoir captures the atmosphere of a 1930s Parisian brasserie. The food is classic French with a menu that features steaks, grilled lobster and *crêpes suzettes* (pancakes). The bar stays open to 1am. There's live music on Thursday, Friday and Saturday.

CITY CENTRE Restaurants of La Tour Hassan
ⓓⓓⓓⓓ
La Tour Hassan, 26 Rue Chellah **Tel** *(0537) 23 90 00* **Road map** C2

One of several eateries located within the luxurious La Tour Hassan *(see p303)*, La Maison Arabe is richly decorated in a style designed to capture the essence of Moroccan living. La Brasserie offers a wide-ranging selection of international dishes. The à la carte menu offers everything from meat and fish in sauces to salads, all served with wine.

Key to Symbols *see back cover flap*

CITY CENTRE Le Ziryab

Off Rue des Consuls **Tel** *(0537) 73 36 36*   **Road map** *C2*

As you step through Le Ziryab's heavy door and walk down its dimly lit entrance hall and into its lavish dining area o be seated at elegantly dressed tables, you know you are in for a memorable experience. The menu revolves around Moroccan gastronomy, and large displays of fruit are a speciality. Open for dinner only.

KASBAH DES OUDAÏA Restaurant de la Plage

Kasbah des Oudaïa Plage **Tel** *(0537) 20 29 28*   **Road map** *C2*

This small and characterful eatery is something of an institution in the Kasbah des Oudaïa area. Its popularity is partly due to the fact that it is situated right on the beach and therefore has lovely views. Rabat's residents and tourists alike visit it time and again. The food, mainly fish and seafood, is renowned for its quality and freshness.

MEDINA Dinarjat

6 Rue Belgnaoui **Tel** *(0537) 70 42 39*   **Road map** *C2*

Located in the medina, close to Rabat's main tourist attractions, the Dinarjat is housed in a former 17th-century Maison-style residence and serves superlative Moroccan cuisine in lavish surroundings. In particular, the restaurant is well renowned for its excellent *tajine* – a typically Moroccan mix of meat, olives and fruit.

SOUSSI La Villa Mandarine

19 Rue Ouled Bousbaa **Tel** *(0537) 75 20 77*   **Road map** *C2*

Set in beautiful, fragrant gardens and orange groves in a residential area outside the city centre, this small hotel with a restaurant offers a haven of peace away from the bustling city. The decor is traditional Moroccan while the menu includes both Moroccan and international dishes. The dining room is closed on Sunday.

VILLE NOUVELLE Zerda

7 Rue Patrice Lumumba **Tel** *(0537) 73 09 12*   **Road map** *C2*

This restaurant is a quiet little gem located among the hustle and bustle of the city. With a richly decorated interior complete with family pictures on the walls, the family-run Zerda generally offers live music well into the evening. There are extremely good Moroccan and Jewish specialities included in the menu.

VILLE NOUVELLE Le Goéland

9 Rue Moulay Ali-Cherif **Tel** *(0537) 76 88 85*   **Road map** *C2*

The name Le Goéland suggests a restaurant oozing Parisian chic. Although this eatery serves dishes from all over Europe, the main inspiration behind the menu remains French. Fresh fish and seafood, along with classic French dishes, are its specialities. Diners can enjoy their meals in the pretty open air courtyard.

NORTHERN ATLANTIC COAST

ASILAH Miramar

Asilah Ramparts   **Road map** *D1*

If you adore freshly squeezed juice and seafood straight off the grill, then you will be impressed with the Miramar. Its menu is lengthy and refreshingly inexpensive, with both fish and international dishes such as chicken, steaks and burgers among the most popular items on offer. The Miramar is located below the ramparts.

ASILAH Sevilla

18 Avenue Iman al-Assili **Tel** *(0539) 41 85 05*   **Road map** *D1*

The Sevilla is a lively little restaurant that has a pleasant Moroccan decor with a hint of elegant French design. Its menu offers a wide range of inexpensive dishes. The emphasis is mainly on Moroccan fish cooked fresh, and the range of fish available changes daily, according to the catch. The Sevilla is popular with locals and tourists alike.

KENITRA Le Turbot Hôtel Ambassy

20 Avenue Hassan II **Tel** *(0537) 37 98 68*   **Road map** *C2*

Located in Hôtel Ambassy, which is in the centre of town, Le Turbot is a speciality seafood restaurant with colourful interiors. It offers a varied menu of local fish, shellfish and traditional meat recipes such as *mechoui* (slow baked lamb) and *pastilla* (a sweet yet savoury ground meat dish encased in filo pastry) and a well-stocked bar.

LARACHE Casa Bonita

1 Place de la Libération   **Road map** *D1*

Since it first opened, Casa Bonita has earned itself a reputation for being a friendly eatery where good, healthy food is served at prices that won't break the bank. Fresh fish cooked with herbs is a house speciality. Located close to the medina, it is a great stopping-off point when sightseeing around Larache.

LARACHE Estrella del Mar

68 Calle Mohammed Zerktouni **Tel** *(0539) 91 22 43*   **Road map** *D1*

The Estrella del Mar is housed in an attractive Andalusian- and Arabian-styled building and offers a wonderful choice of breakfast, lunch and evening dishes that take their inspiration from international cuisine. Grills, steaks and excellent fish dishes are followed by delicious desserts. The ground floor dining room is more casual than the upstairs one.

CASABLANCA

AIN DIAB La Scuderia da Flavio

Avenue de la Cote d'Emeraude **Tel** *(0522) 79 75 79* **Road map** *C2*

One of only a small number of restaurants in this exclusive area of Casablanca, La Scuderia offers traditional Italian cuisine in sleek, contemporary surroundings. Only the freshest ingredients and finest cured meats find their way into dishes served here.

ANFA Ryad Zitoun

31 Boulevard Rachidi **Tel** *(0522) 22 39 27* **Road map** *C2*

Situated within a beautiful period building, the Ryad Zitoun is in the heart of Anfa and therefore ideal for a stopover while exploring this luxurious residential area. Its menu features traditional Moroccan dishes such as meats with couscous and *tajine*, all washed down with excellent mint tea. Open Monday to Friday only.

ANFA L'Aéropostale

6 Rue Molière **Tel** *(0522) 36 02 52* **Road map** *C2*

Located at the crossing of Rue Molière and the Boulevard d'Anfa, this attractive restaurant is adorned with pictures on the walls and white linens on the tables. It is an informal yet elegant venue. Menu-wise, it offers classic French cuisine, with the emphasis on wholesome meat and fish recipes.

CITY CENTRE Au Petit Poucet Bar

86 Boulevard Mohammed V **Tel** *(0522) 27 54 20* **Road map** *C2*

The Au Petit Poucet Bar, which was established in the 1920s and is one of the landmark eateries of Casablanca, has no pretentions of grandeur; however, this restaurant does serve some exceptionally good meals almost round the clock. It specializes in good, informal French cuisine. It is open for breakfast until late.

CITY CENTRE Chez Paul

Villa Zevaco, Corner Boulevard d'Anfa et Boulevard Moulay Rachid **Tel** *(0522) 36 60 00* **Road map** *C2*

Considered the place to come to be seen, Paul's serves delicious light meals such as salads, pastas and sandwiches and also offers excellent afternoon tea and ice cream. Alcohol is served, except during religious holidays. Wi-Fi is available and there is even an onsite bakery.

CITY CENTRE L'Etoile Centrale

107 rue Allal ben Abdellah **Tel** *(0527) 01 86 25* **Road map** *C2*

Authentic home cooking is hard to come by outside the Moroccan home, but L'Etoile, located opposite the city's central food market, does much to rectify this. It offers flavoursome tagines and a fabulous couscous royale. Alcohol is not served but there is an ample selection of soft drinks.

CITY CENTRE La Bodéga de Casablanca

129 Rue Allal Ben Abdellah **Tel** *(0522) 54 18 42* **Road map** *C2*

This Spanish-style restaurant located near the central market is one of the liveliest in town. It's a place to eat well from the tapas menu, drink cocktails or wine, relax and have fun. The downstairs dancefloor is the scene of regular themed events, including salsa, reggae, rock and samba nights.

CITY CENTRE Al-Mounia

95 Rue du Prince Moulay Abdellah **Tel** *(0522) 22 26 69* **Road map** *C2*

The Al-Mounia caters for alfresco-dining enthusiasts with a beautifully planted garden and an outdoor courtyard area, although inside the restaurant is pleasant too, with a richly coloured Moroccan decor. Its menu is refined, and traditional dishes are served, including a good choice of vegetarian specialities.

CITY CENTRE La Brasserie Bavaroise

129 Rue Allal Ben Abdellah **Tel** *(0522) 31 17 60* **Road map** *C2*

Centrally located and within easy reach of many of Casablanca's main attractions, this beautifully presented restaurant offers a seemingly endless menu of Moroccan, French and international starters, mains and desserts. La Brasserie Bavaroise is particularly renowned for its meat and vegetarian dishes.

CITY CENTRE Taverne du Dauphin

115 Boulevard Houphouët Boigny **Tel** *(0522) 22 12 00* **Road map** *C2*

Packed into the various rooms of this delightful Casablanca fish restaurant are office workers, tourists, ex-pats and bon viveurs. They come for the great seafood, which is served by knowledgeable waiting staff. Excellent daily specials, full wine menu and a popular bar add to Dauphin's charms. The restaurant is closed on Sunday.

CITY CENTRE Café M Hôtel Hyatt Regency

Hôtel Hyatt Regency, Places des Nations Unies **Tel** *(0522) 43 12 78* **Road map** *C2*

This restaurant of the Hôtel Hyatt Regency *(see p306)* serves Parisian bistro-style meals to diners and boasts an excellent wine list. It is open to outside visitors as well as hotel guests, but reservations are advised. Drinks and meals can be enjoyed in the contemporary-styled dining room or on the terrace. Diners must be smartly dressed.

Key to Price Guide *see p328* **Key to Symbols** *see back cover flap*

CITY CENTRE Quai du Jazz

25 Rue Ahmed El Mokri

Road map C2

The Quai du Jazz is a high-class brasserie that is known for its gourmet French cuisine and fine wines. Classic French dishes on offer include *foie gras*, fish soup, steak with *gratin dauphinois* and to finish, *crème brûlée*. There's live jazz in the evening on Thursday and Friday. Closed from Saturday lunchtime and all day on Sunday.

CITY CENTRE La Table du Retro

22 Rue Abou Al Mahassin Arrouyani **Tel** *(0522) 94 05 55*

Road map C2

La Table du Retro is where local residents head when they have a celebration in the family or if they just want a special meal out. A restaurant with a particularly stylish décor and ambience, it serves classic French dishes prepared to a high standard. The food is complemented by a good wine list.

CITY CENTRE La Maison du Gourmet

159 Rue Taha Houcine **Tel** *(0522) 48 48 46*

Road map C2

With its combination of discretion and elegance, this gastronomic restaurant has become one of the business capital's top venues. If you can't decide what to order try the tasting menu, which gives a sample of many of the dishes prepared by the chef.There's an excellent list of wines to choose from as well.

CORNICHE Restaurant Le Poisson

15 Boulevard de la Corniche **Tel** *(0522) 79 80 70*

Road map C2

Le Poisson is one of the best-known restaurants in the Corniche area of Casablanca. It serves excellent fresh-fish dishes. Among the most popular on the menu are the fillet of sole with herbs, the lobster salad, and the sardines stuffed with garlic and herbs, all followed by pastries or classic French and Moroccan desserts.

CORNICHE Le Relais de Paris

Villa Blanca Urban Hotel, Boulevard de la Corniche **Tel** *(0522) 39 25 10*

Road map C2

In a good location, close to many of Casablanca's private beaches and the Royal Golf Course, Le Relais de Paris is a friendly, Parisian-style brasserie with a menu that features both French and international dishes. It is well known for its thinly sliced beef steak in a secret sauce. There's a heated terrace with great views of the Atlantic Ocean.

CORNICHE La Mer

Phare d'El-Hank, Boulevard de la Corniche **Tel** *(0522) 36 12 71*

Road map C2

Located next to the El-Hank lighthouse is this nautical-themed French restaurant. Offering a fine dining experience with crisp white linens and bone china, La Mer is well established and is known for its seafood and fish specialities. The terrace offers great views of the Atlantic Ocean.

CORNICHE Restaurant à Ma Bretagne

Boulevard de la Corniche **Tel** *(0522) 36 21 12*

Road map C2

Reservations are strongly advised if you wish to dine at this elegant and well-known restaurant in the Corniche district of Casablanca. Serving an à la carte menu of French-inspired meat and fish dishes, À Ma Bretagne also offers an interesting selection of vegetarian options. Its wine list is long and impressive.

CORNICHE Le Pilotis

Tahiti Beach Club, Boulevard de la Corniche **Tel** *(0522) 79 84 27*

Road map C2

This chic seaside restaurant in the Tahiti Beach Club offers sunsoaked Mediterranean cuisine including a wide selection of seafood, grilled fish and paella. Meals can be enjoyed in the elegant lounge area or on the beachside terrace with beautiful views of the ocean.

MOHAMMEDIA Restaurant du Port

1 Rue de Port **Tel** *(0523) 32 24 66*

Road map C2

Ask anyone where the Restaurant du Port is, and the chances are they will have been there, such is its reputation. Its interior design theme is that of a boat, making it a fun place to relax and enjoy a meal. As might be expected, fresh fish such as salmon, sardines and sea bream play a significant role on the menu.

PORT QUARTER Restaurant du Port

Port de Pêche **Tel** *(0522) 31 85 61*

Road map C2

Located close to the port in this lively area of Casablanca at the Port de Pêche, a few minutes' walk from the centre of town, this bustling restaurant specializes in fish and seafood. You'll understand why it's so popular with the locals once you've sampled the exquisite fresh fish.

PORT QUARTER La Sqala

Boulevard des Almohades **Tel** *(0522) 26 09 60*

Road map C2

Housed in an 18th-century saffron-stuccoed fort, overlooking the ocean, this traditionally Moroccan restaurant impresses by its calm beauty. Come here to lounge by the fountain in the beautiful gardens, while sipping mint tea and experiencing some of the best food in town. No alcohol served.

PORT QUARTER Rick's Café

248 Boulevard Sour Jdid, Place du Jardin Public **Tel** *(0522) 27 42 07*

Road map C2

This restaurant-bar is located in one of Casablanca's few *riads*, near the old medina. The menu is simple, bistro-style French with dishes such as fresh oysters and John Dory with peaches and peach-Port sauce. The surroundings are romantic and cool, even on hot summer days.

RACINE Restaurant Toscana
Rue Ibnou Yaasa El Ifrani **Tel** *(0522) 36 95 92*   **Road map** *C2*

With its colourful decor and music, often live, Restaurant Toscana is a fashionable eatery with the young and trendy of Casablanca, who mingle with tourists from around the world. The menu offers a wide range of classic Italian dishes complemented by wines, beers and non-alcoholic beverages.

SOUTHERN ATLANTIC COAST

DAR BOUAZZA Natti Natti
Dar Kouch, Dar Bouazza **Tel** *(0660) 72 03 70*   **Road map** *C2*

This delightful French deli offers hand-sliced cold meats and excellent French cheeses, accompanied by home-made chutneys and artfully prepared relishes and sweets. The deli has regular specials such as crêpes, pizzas and sushi and can prepare a picnic for guests to have on the beach, just 2 minutes away. Soft drinks and good coffee are available.

EL-JADIDA Ali Baba
Route RP8 **Tel** *(0523) 34 16 22*   **Road map** *B2*

A richly coloured decor and artifacts such as traditional lanterns combine to create a cosy feel at this restaurant. The family-run Ali Baba offers a good menu of fish and seafood, as well as an excellent selection of wines. The bar serves a variety of alcoholic drinks; a rarity in this small provincial town.

EL-JADIDA Restaurant of L'Hôtel de Provence
L'Hôtel de Provence, 42 Avenue Fquih Mohammed Errafii **Tel** *(0523) 34 23 47*   **Road map** *B2*

Located within L'Hôtel de Provence, this quietly elegant restaurant is considered one of the best in El-Jadida. Serving international dishes, and boasting a particularly good and varied vegetarian selection, it has a terrace where diners can choose to eat when the weather allows it. It also has a good wine list.

EL-JADIDA Restaurant of the Pullman Mazagan Royal Golf & Spa
Royal Golf Sofitel, Route de Casablanca **Tel** *(0523) 354141*   **Road map** *B2*

Lavishly presented and offering an exceptional à la carte menu with delicacies from around the world, this elegant restaurant is located within the luxurious Pullman Mazagan Royal Golf & Spa *(see p306)*. It is frequented by non-residents as well as the hotel's guests, and offers live entertainment most nights.

ESSAOUIRA Harbour
Essaouira Harbour   **Road map** *B4*

The combination of eating alfresco in the harbour area of Essaouira – watching boats out to sea and fishermen unload their catches – and enjoying the freshest of seafood makes eating here a truly memorable experience. The food is cooked and served from a series of small stalls that line the waterside.

ESSAOUIRA La Licorne
26 Rue Scala **Tel** *(0524) 47 36 26*   **Road map** *B4*

La Licorne offers traditional Moroccan dishes. Specialities include fish and seafood, along with a good selection of vegetarian dishes; the fare is complemented by a carefully selected wine list. Music and dance shows often take place here.

ESSAOUIRA Les Alizés
26 Rue de la Sqala **Tel** *(0524) 47 68 19*   **Road map** *B4*

Les Alizes is widely regarded as one of the best restaurants in Essaouira, and it certainly offers an elegant atmosphere with candlelit tables, not to mention good classic Moroccan dishes at low prices. The restaurant is housed in a lovely 19th-century Maison.

ESSAOUIRA Restaurant Taros
2 Rue de la Sqala **Tel** *(0524) 47 64 07*   **Road map** *B4*

This attractive café-cum-restaurant in the heart of Essaouira is full of character and atmosphere. This is partly down to the fact that its walls are lined with books on art, and that classical music plays in the background. Both art and music are passions of Taros's owners. The menu is Moroccan and European. Live music is played in the evening.

ESSAOUIRA Sylvestro
70 Rue Laalouj, Médina d'Essaouira **Tel** *(0524) 47 35 55*   **Road map** *B4*

A genuine Italian restaurant where the owner makes his own pizza and pasta (and amazing gnocchi), and imports all his hams and cheeses from Italy. The decor is not great but people keep coming back for the excellent locally caught seafood and large portions. Closed for lunch on Wednesday.

ESSAOUIRA Chalet de la Plage
Boulevard Mohammed V **Tel** *(0524) 47 59 72*   **Road map** *B4*

Sitting outside and dining at this smart beachside restaurant is especially memorable, not least because the views of the sea and the coastline are wonderfully relaxing. A variety of fish as well as lobster, shrimp, oysters and calamari appear on the menu along with a selection of salads, soups and meats.

ESSAOUIRA Elizir

1 Derb Agadir, Medina **Tel** *(0524) 47 21 03* **Road map** *B4*

Those lucky enough to secure a table at this tiny retro diner will delight in its quirky interior and outstanding food. The menu is deliberately brief, offering dishes such as pumpkin and saffron soup, and sirloin with balsamic sauce. Serves house wine only. Make sure you book in advance. Open evenings only.

ESSAOUIRA Restaurants of Sofitel Medina & Spa

Sofitel Medina & Spa, Avenue Mohammed V **Tel** *(0524) 47 90 00* **Road map** *B4*

There are two restaurants located in the Sofitel Medina & Spa *(see p307)*, and both have evocative views of its gardens and the sea. The Dar Dada, Arganier and Cote Plage serve top-notch international dishes. In addition to Moroccan delicacies, French classics and seafood are also on the menu, along with a good selection of wines.

ESSAOUIRA Heure Bleue Palais

2 Rue Ibn Batouta – Bab Marrakech **Tel** *(0524) 47 60 66* **Road map** *B4*

Perfectly capturing an authentic Moroccan ambience, the Heure Bleue Palais is housed in a Maison that has been lavishly decorated to a traditional style and stands in the heart of the medina. Its menu comprises good-quality Moroccan and European cuisine. The food is wonderfully prepared and presented.

OUALIDIA L'Araignée Gourmande

Oualidia Beach **Tel** *(0523) 36 64 47* **Road map** *D3*

Eating at the L'Araignée Gourmande, especially if you manage to secure a table on the attractive terrace that overlooks the beach and Oualidia's breathtaking lagoon, will be a wonderful and relaxing experience. Wholesome international dishes are served here, especially seafood, along with a range of vegetarian specialities.

OUALIDIA Ostrea II

Oualidia Oyster Farm **Tel** *(0523) 36 64 51* **Road map** *B3*

Ostrea II is located at the famous oyster farm that serves this and other establishments. It is right on the edge of the lagoon, and serves oysters in many ways, some more unusual than others. Other types of seafood also appear on the menu. The restaurant has friendly and helpful staff.

OUALIDIA La Sultana Restaurant

La Sultana Hôtel & Spa, Route du Palais **Tel** *(0523) 36 65 90* **Road map** *B3*

This attractive restaurant is within the sophisticated La Sultana Hôtel & Spa *(see p307)*. Quietly elegant, it offers outstanding views of the lagoon from its windows and garden terrace, making dining here a truly memorable experience. The menu largely comprises of light and healthy seafood and vegetarian dishes.

SAFI Restaurant Riad de Pecheur

1 Rue De La Crête **Tel** *(0524) 61 02 91* **Road map** *B3*

With practically one foot in the water, this excellent, primarily Moroccan restaurant offers top-notch seafood at very reasonable prices. Dine on local specialities, while seated on the flower-filled terrace, overlooking the bay of Safi. Spectacular views and a calm environment make this the perfect place to watch the setting sun.

TANGIER

CITY CENTRE Le Coeur de Tanger and Café de Paris

1 Rue Annoual **Tel** *(0539) 94 84 50 (Le Coeur de Tanger); (0539) 93 84 44 (Café de Paris)* **Road map** *D1*

The iconic Café de Paris, a longtime landmark of Tangier, does not serve meals these days but serves as a photographic opportunity for visitors to the city. Upstairs, Le Coeur de Tanger dining hall offers a classic à la carte Moroccan menu of meat, fish and vegetarian dishes. The beautiful building simply oozes character.

CITY CENTRE Le Nabab

4 Rue Al Kadiria **Tel** *(0661) 442 220* **Road map** *D1*

A classy restaurant nestled in the medina that serves fine Moroccan fare. Come here for a hearty meal – lamb with artichokes and aubergine purée is particularly recommended. Le Nabab has huge arches, candlelight and a fireplace, which is very welcome on cooler winter evenings.

CITY CENTRE El Korsan

Hôtel El-Minzah, 85 Rue de la Liberté **Tel** *(0539) 93 58 85* **Road map** *D1*

This stylish, lavishly decorated and refined restaurant is located in the beautiful Hispano-Moorish Hôtel El-Minzah *(see p308)*, a landmark building in Tangier. It offers a traditional à la carte menu in addition to light informal dishes from all the Moroccan regions, along with local wines and juices.

CITY CENTRE Riad Tanja

Riad Tanja, Rue du Portugal **Tel** *(0539) 33 35 38* **Road map** *D1*

Located close to the Bab el Baha and the Petit Socco, in the heart of Tangier, and housed in a historic *riad* complete with a courtyard garden, the Riad Tanja is a delightfully atmospheric eatery. It serves top-quality Moroccan dishes such as *tajine*, along with wines from several Moroccan regions.

CITY CENTRE San Remo

15 Rue Ahmed Chaouki **Tel** *(0539) 93 84 51*   **Road map** *D1*

This stylish Italian restaurant offers its patrons the opportunity to enjoy traditional specialities prepared with ingredients fresh from Italy. Try one of the many pasta dishes matched with a fine wine. Located within easy distance of Tangier's main attractions, the San Remo is a convenient venue for both lunch and evening dining.

CITY CENTRE Le Relais de Paris

Complexe Dawliz, 42 Rue de Hollande **Tel** *(0539) 33 18 19*   **Road map** *D1*

Diners come to Le Relais de Paris for the classic French dishes served in a friendly, Parisian brasserie-style setting with views of Tangier harbour. The menu includes daily specials prepared with produce from the local market. In the adjoining lounge bar, cocktails and nibbles can be enjoyed to the sound of live music.

CITY CENTRE Rif & Spa

Rif & Spa, 152 Avenue Mohammed VI **Tel** *(0539) 34 93 00*   **Road map** *D1*

The Rif & Spa is a health bar inside the hotel of the same name *(see p308)* in central Tangier, close to the medina. Frequented by health enthusiasts and holidaying visitors keen to eat wholesome foods, it features a menu that comprises healthy international dishes, salads and energy-giving juices. Its decor is contemporary.

CITY CENTRE La Fabrique

Résidence Salima I, 7 Rue d'Angleterre **Tel** *(0539) 37 40 57*   **Road map** *D1*

La Fabrique, with its New York loft-style interior, is sleek, self-conscious and very much a place to come to be seen. The food is good (specialities include terrine of figs and foie gras), and the swish leather armchairs on the ground floor offer an opportunity to indulge in comfortable surroundings after a very satisfying meal.

MEDITERRANEAN COAST & THE RIF

AL-HOCEIMA Café-Restaurant Paris

21 Avenue Mohammed V   **Road map** *E1*

The Café-Restaurant Paris is a pleasant eatery situated in the heart of Al-Hoceima, in one of the city's main thoroughfares and close to the Mediterranean coastline. It is on the upper floor of a period building, which may make it difficult for diners with mobility restrictions. Its menu is traditional Moroccan and French.

CAP SPARTEL Le Mirage

Le Mirage, Rue Cap Spartel **Tel** *(0539) 33 33 32*   **Road map** *D1*

Located on a clifftop, with outstanding views of both the Atlantic and Mediterranean seas, and set in the luxurious surroundings of Le Mirage hotel *(see p308)*, this restaurant is the ideal venue for a special meal. Serving an à la carte menu of French and international dishes, it specializes in fish and seafood with fine wines.

CHEFCHAOUEN Darcom

Old Mellah, behind the Great Mosque **Tel** *(0661) 70 55 70*   **Road map** *D1*

Situated next to the main square, this Moroccan speciality restaurant is well used to meeting the standards of discerning travellers. The *tagines* are good, the brochette even better and the staff are happy to assist diners. It is a good idea to have the set menu in order to try some new dishes.

CHEFCHAOUEN Zouar

Rue Tarik El Wahda **Tel** *(0539) 98 66 70*   **Road map** *D1*

For diners who crave Spanish tapas and paella, this welcoming little restaurant will fit the bill for lunchtime or evening dining. Run by a Spanish-Moroccan couple and traditionally Moorish in style, it is popular with locals as well as visitors. The produce is sourced locally as well as from Spain, and all the recipes are true to their origins.

CHEFCHAOUEN Casa Hassan

Rue Targui, 22 Chefchaouen **Tel** *(0539) 986 153*   **Road map** *D1*

This restaurant offers some of the best pastillas around, despite its low prices. These meat-filled, sweet or savoury pastries are tricky to get perfect, even for Moroccans. Mosaic tables, silken cushions and a log fire, that blazes on winter evenings, adds to the homely atmosphere. The open kitchen allows diners to see the chefs at work.

OUJDA Comme Chez Soi

Rue Sijilmassa **Tel** *(0536) 68 60 79*   **Road map** *F2*

This attractive restaurant with a welcoming feel is well located for the centre of town, not far from the medina. The Comme Chez Soi is open for lunch as well as late for evening meals, and serves a good choice of Moroccan and European dishes. It also serves alcohol, a rarity in Oujda.

OUJDA Le Dauphin

38 Rue Berkane **Tel** *(0536) 68 61 45*   **Road map** *F2*

Like many of the restaurants in Oujda, Le Dauphin serves some truly tasty and wholesome dishes, such as the chef's *tajine* – made with lamb, chicken or sometimes fish, with various herbs, spices and fruits. Locals can often be seen enjoying a meal in its cosy dining area, which is always an indication of good quality.

Key to Price Guide *see p328* **Key to Symbols** *see back cover flap*

OUJDA Restaurant of the Ibis Moussafir Oujda

Ibis Moussafir Oujda, Boulevard Abdellah Chefchaouni **Tel** *(0536) 68 82 02*   **Road map** F2

With an experienced team of chefs who excel in informal as well as more elaborate French and Moroccan specialities, the restaurant inside the Ibis Moussafir Oujda *(see p309)* is popular with visitors as well as guests of the hotel. Breakfast is served buffet-style from 4am onwards, along with lunches and evening meals.

TETOUAN La Restinga

21 Rue Mohammed V **Tel** *(0539) 96 35 76*   **Road map** D1

La Restinga is one of Tetouan's worst-kept secrets because anyone who is anyone can be found eating at its tables at one time or another. It is not a luxurious establishment, but its waiters are friendly, and the feel of the restaurant is warm and welcoming. Its reputation for serving good Moroccan food at inexpensive prices is well founded.

TETOUAN Barceló Marina Smir

Barceló Marina Smir, Route de Sebta **Tel** *(0539) 97 12 34*   **Road map** D1

This traditional restaurant has earned itself a reputation for serving a good à la carte menu, and although essentially serving the five-star Barceló Marina Smir hotel *(see p310)*, it welcomes visiting diners, too. Attractively furnished, the restaurant looks out over the hotel's gardens, which lie next to Marina Smir.

FÈS

CITY CENTRE Café Kortoba

Derb Boutouil   **Road map** D2

The wonderful Café Kortoba in the medina is located next to the country's second largest mosque. The Karaouiyine's domed and tiled rooftops and Almoravid-style minaret soar above, making this an excellent place to take a break for a mint tea, light snack, coffee or fresh juice.

CITY CENTRE Wong

Jnan Moulay Kamel **Tel** *(0535) 65 27 60*   **Road map** D2

Situated within an easy walk of the Musée Dar el-Batha and easy to find, the lavishly decorated Wong is a popular eatery with both locals and visitors alike. It offers Vietnamese cuisine, featuring an extensive menu of chicken, beef and fish specialities.

MEDINA Thami̇i̇i's

Bab Boujloud, at the top of Talaa Sghira, between the barbershop and Hammam Mernissi, Medina   **Road map** D2

Don't be deterred by the location of this hole-in-the-wall eatery – the street food here is excellent, as is evident from the crowds of people that head here every day. Expats and Moroccans vie for space at the simple tables to tuck into *kefta* (meatballs) and eggs and lamb with prunes.

MEDINA Café Clock

7 Derb El Magana, Talaa Kbira, Fes Medina **Tel** *(0535) 63 78 55*   **Road map** D2

Café Clock, home of the camel burger, also provides light takes on traditional dishes, delicious salads, and some of the best service in town. Offering cookery classes and food tours as well as breakfast, lunch and dinner, this stylish but fun establishment manages to get it all just right.

MEDINA Fès et Gestes

39 Arsat El Hamoumi, Ziat **Tel** *(0535) 63 85 32*   **Road map** D2

Set in the lush gardens of a restored Colonial house, is the art gallery and restaurant Fèz et Gestes. Choose from the tasty French/Moroccan seasonal menu and enjoy your meal in the relaxed surroundings – either on the shaded patio area or inside on cooler days. Wine is not served but call ahead to ask if you can bring your own.

MEDINA Le Chameau Bleu

1, Derb Tariana Talâa Kbira **Tel** *(0535) 63 89 91*   **Road map** D2

This is a Moroccan speciality restaurant that offers more than the basic five or six dishes and this wider variety makes Le Chameau Bleu a great place for families. Dine here on meat, pastries, pasta and fish. It can be hard to find, so ask at the tourist office for directions.

MEDINA Dar Roumana

Derb El Amer, Zkak Roumane **Tel** *(0535) 74 16 37*   **Road map** D2

Within the tiled walls of a beautiful traditional guesthouse, American owner Jennifer Smith and her team conjure up superb Moroccan-inspired Mediterranean food using only the best local ingredients. Make sure you book well in advance. Closed to non-guests on Sunday and Monday.

MEDINA El Firdaouss

10 Rue Gengfour **Tel** *(0535) 63 43 43*   **Road map** D2

No visit to Fès would be complete without a visit to one of its most enchanting restaurants, the El Firdaouss. This establishment has earned a reputation for serving authentic, wholesome Moroccan cuisine. Located in the medina area of Fès, it is the ideal place for a quick light snack or a more leisurely evening meal.

MEDINA Le Palais de Fès

15 Rue Makhfia **Tel** *(0535) 76 15 90* — **Road map** *D2*

All visitors to Fès should pay a visit to Le Palais de Fès, if only to gaze in wonder at its breathtaking view of the medina. Of course, its cuisine is remarkable, too, and a good and varied selection of Moroccan dishes is served on a pretty terrace. This spacious restaurant is a popular destination for tour groups.

MEDINA Al Jounaina at Jamaï Palais

Sofitel Fès Palais Jamaï, Bab Guissa **Tel** *(0535) 63 43 31* — **Road map** *D2*

This Moroccan restaurant, housed within the Sofitel Palais Jamaï (see p311), is quite possibly one of the most beautiful places to eat in town. Dine like royalty while listening to live traditional music during the evenings, or make the most of the lavish lunch buffet on the terrace earlier in the day. The salad bar alone offers a mountain of food.

MEDINA Palais de la Medina

8 Derb Chami **Tel** *(0535) 71 14 37* — **Road map** *D2*

One of the landmark buildings of the medina area of Fès, the Palais de la Medina is housed in a beautiful former Maison within the ancient walls. It is lavishly decorated with drapes and cushions, and it also has subtle lighting to create a cosy, evocative ambience. The food on offer is authentic Moroccan and delicious.

MEDINA Le Palais des Mérinides

36 Chrablyne **Tel** *(0535) 63 40 28* — **Road map** *D2*

Set in the heart of the medina, and overlooking the Royal Palace, Le Palais des Mérinides is housed in a handsome 14th-century palace. This attractive little eatery has an inner courtyard where it is a delight to sit, relax and enjoy the refined fare on offer. Its menu is comprehensive, with a good selection of traditional Moroccan dishes.

MEDINA La Maison Bleue

2 Place de Batha **Tel** *(0535) 74 18 43* — **Road map** *D2*

Located in a traditional townhouse built by a university professor in 1915, this guesthouse with a restaurant still retains some original furniture. Diners can begin with nibbles and cocktails in the courtyard and then sit on plump couches while eating Moroccan dishes such as *tajines* and *b'stilla*. Open for dinner only.

VILLE NOUVELLE Chez Vittorio

21 Rue Brahim Roudani **Tel** *(0535) 62 47 30* — **Road map** *D2*

Run by an Italian family, each member of which is clearly passionate about food, this restaurant in the heart of the city is known for its excellent fresh pasta dishes, pizzas, which come with a wide variety of toppings, and ice creams. You are always assured of a hearty meal and a warm welcome at Chez Vittorio's.

VILLE NOUVELLE L'Italien

Résidence Longchamp, Avenue Ibn Khattab, Champs de Courses **Tel** *(0535) 94 33 84* — **Road map** *D2*

Fresh, seasonal produce is on offer at this trendy pizzeria, making it a welcome addition to the Fès dining scene. Pizzas are authentic, prepared to order and cooked in wood-fired ovens, pastas come with a variety of sauces and salads are well-dressed. The loft-styled interior can get noisy later in the evenings.

VILLE NOUVELLE Les Trois Sources

Km 4, Route d'Immouzer, 30000 **Tel** *(0535) 606 532* — **Road map** *D2*

It's easy to see why this international restaurant, located in the Complexe Touristique, has such a dedicated following. The menu has excellent daily specials, reasonably priced wines and delicious fish. Although it is located outside of town, staff will come and pick you up if you call in advance. Live music on the weekends.

VILLE NOUVELLE The Majestic

Royal Tennis Club de Fès, Fès Country Club, Complexe Sportif El Merja **Tel** *(0535) 72 99 99* — **Road map** *D2*

Located on the edge of the new town, this deluxe restaurant offers to collect diners from their hotels (by prior arrangement). Once ensconced, guests are unlikely to be disappointed by the lavish array of Mediterranean dishes on offer: fish being the speciality here. Dress code is smart casual. Closed on Monday.

VILLE NOUVELLE Maison Blanche

12 Rue Ahmed Chaouki **Tel** *(0535) 62 27 27* — **Road map** *D2*

Sister restaurant of the famous Parisian eatery of the same name, this high-end establishment offers a Mediterranean menu, Moroccan and European wines, a full bar and a comprehensive cigar list. À la carte dining does not come cheap, but the set menus are both balanced and reasonably priced.

MEKNÈS & VOLUBILIS

MEKNÈS MEDINA Riad Meknès

79 Ksar Chaacha-Dar Lakbira **Tel** *(0535) 53 05 42* — **Road map** *D2*

The restaurant of the beautiful Riad Meknès, part of the palace of 17th century ruler Moulay Ismail, serves up mouth-watering Moroccan and Continental dishes, including roast spiced lamb and crisp salads. The restaurant also offers locally produced olive oil.

Key to Price Guide *see p328* **Key to Symbols** *see back cover flap*

MEKNÈS MEDINA Zitouna

44 Rue Jamaa Zitouna **Tel** *(0535) 53 02 81* **Road map** *D2*

Located close to the Grand Mosque and the souks, this restaurant can be a little difficult to find but well worth taking the time to do so. Zitouna is housed in a beautiful old building and has lots of character. Its menu comprises classic Moroccan dishes that are well presented. A set menu offers good value.

MEKNÈS VILLE NOUVELLE Annexe du Métropole
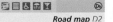

11 Rue Cherif Idrissi **Tel** *(0535) 51 35 11* **Road map** *D2*

Step inside the Annexe du Metropole building, and a space with a huge personality greets you. High ceilings combine with beautifully ornate walls to give a sense of space and elegance. Two menus offers good Moroccan dishes, while an outside dining area is perfect for eating alfresco.

MEKNÈS VILLE NOUVELLE Le Dauphin

5 Avenue Mohammed V **Tel** *(0535) 52 34 23* **Road map** *D2*

A traditional restaurant in one of Meknès's busiest thoroughfares, Le Dauphin is popular with lovers of fresh fish. Its menu offers a particularly wide selection of fish dishes, from lobster and sardines cooked traditionally with herbs to sole in a sauce. The restaurant is popular with touring groups and for private parties.

MEKNÈS VILLE NOUVELLE Gambrinus

Rue Omar Ibn Aïss **Tel** *(0535) 52 02 58* **Road map** *D2*

Intrepid diners need not be deterred by the somewhat faded interior of this popular budget eatery. Knowledgeable locals flock here for its tasty, cheap, wholesome food, such as *tagines*, couscous and brochettes, as well as good fruit salads and omelettes. It is situated next to the vibrant Marché Centrale.

MEKNÈS VILLE NOUVELLE Le Collier de la Colombe

67 Rue Driba **Tel** *(0535) 55 50 41* **Road map** *D2*

Panoramic views of the great Wadi Boutekrane Valley from the main dining hall and terraces ensure that Le Collier de la Colombe stands out from the rest. This restaurant is popular for family Sunday lunches and with holidaying visitors. Its menu is wide and focuses on traditional Moroccan and international cuisine.

MEKNÈS VILLE NOUVELLE Le Relais de Paris

46 Rue Oqba, Ibn Nafia **Tel** *(0619) 21 02 10* **Road map** *D2*

Offering a varied, yet faithfully French menu, and a terrace with fabulous views over Mont Zerhoun, Le Relais de Paris is a hugely popular high-end bistro. It is a welcome addition to the Meknès culinary scene, with its grilled meat specialities and lively lounge area.

MOULAY IDRISS Café Clock II at Scorpion House

54 Drouj El Hafa, Zerhoune **Tel** *(0535) 54 47 29* **Road map** *D2*

In the past, visitors tended to look at the shrine in Moulay Idriss, or the nearby roman ruins and continue on to eat elsewhere, however Café Clock II has changed all that. Sumptuous salads, marinated meats and barbequed chicken can all be enjoyed in the chic interior, peppered with private nooks and a view second to none.

VOLUBILIS La Corbeille Fleurie

Ruins of Volubilis **Road map** *D2*

The food at this restaurant is simple and straightforward, with *tajines*, sandwiches and light snacks being the most popular choices. La Corbeille Fleurie does a brisk trade thanks to its location, right at the entrance to the ruins of Volubilis. The views of the valley from its terraces are simply outstanding.

MIDDLE ATLAS

BENI MELLAL SAT Agadir

155 Boulevard el-Hansali **Road map** *D3*

This restaurant doesn't pretend to offer luxury decor and top notch food, but what the SAT Agadir does provide is good wholesome Moroccan cuisine at exceptionally low prices. As a consequence, it can usually be found full of diners, making a visit here a memorable, friendly experience. A great place for people-watching.

IFRANE La Paix

Avenue de la Marché Verte **Tel** *(0535) 56 66 75* **Road map** *D3*

La Paix is an atmospheric small restaurant that offers some good local dishes from a fairly limited menu. The theme is largely Moroccan, with the occasional European concession. Located central to the town, it is convenient for a light bite or an evening meal when staying in this popular Middle Atlas town.

IFRANE Restaurant of the Hôtel des Perce-Neige

Hôtel des Perce-Neige, Rue de Asphodèles Hay Riad **Tel** *(0535) 56 62 10* **Road map** *D2*

An attractive restaurant that, like the Hôtel des Perce-Neige itself *(see p313)*, has earned itself a good reputation for quality. Its lengthy menu of classic French dishes attracts locals and visitors to the town, as well as guests of the hotel. The restaurant is highly regarded in Ifrane.

IFRANE Michlifen Ifrane

Avenue Hassan 2, BP 18 **Tel** *(0535) 86 40 00*   **Road map** *D2*

Three restaurants and two bars, including one dedicated to cigars, are located within Michlifen Ifrane, a traditional Swiss chalet. This is the last word in mountain luxury and the quality of the food and attentiveness of the service lives up to Michlifen's shimmering stars.

KHENIFRA Restaurant de France

Quartier des Forces Armées Royales **Tel** *(0535) 58 61 14*   **Road map** *D3*

The Restaurant de France is a warm and welcoming restaurant that is part of a small hotel on the road linking Fès to Marrakech. Its terrace areas feature great views across the unspoilt town of Khenifra. It is here that most diners can be found enjoying the Moroccan and international dishes served.

OUZOUD Riad Cascades d'Ouzoud

Ouzoud **Tel** *(0523) 42 91 73 / (0662) 14 38 04*   **Road map** *D3*

Ouzoud is not replete with restaurants, but this *riad* has two restaurants, one in a traditional Moroccan-style lounge and the other on the panoramic roof terrace. Diners can relax and sample both local specialities and French cuisine, including dishes made with the freshest fruit and vegetables grown in local smallholdings.

OUZOUD Riad des Cascades

Cascades d'Ouzoud Tanant Azilal **Tel** *(0523) 42 91 73*   **Road map** *D2*

Overlooking Morocco's most impressive waterfalls, this delightful place serves an excellent lunch and supper. Here honest Moroccan staples are cooked to perfection. Walk off your meal by ambling down the path alongside the falls. You might even catch a glimpse of the indigenous Barbary apes.

MARRAKECH

GUELIZ Café du Livre

44 Rue Tarik Ben Ziad **Tel** *(0524) 43 21 49*   **Road map** *C3*

You don't have to love reading to come here to eat, although there is an impressive collection of Morocco-related books on sale. The salads, desserts and fresh juices are wonderful. This alternative venue is growing in popularity, perhaps because it has the atmosphere of a small private club. Closes at 10pm.

GUELIZ Café Les Negotiants

Corner of Avenue Mohammed V and Boulevard Mohammed Zertouni   **Road map** *C3*

A unique café to come to on the edge of Gueliz, which offers thick black coffee, snacks, the chance to have your shoes shined or to buy a fake Rolex from the street hawkers outside. Take the attention with good humour and you will have a memory of Marrakech you'll prize for years to come: all for the price of a cup of coffee.

GUÉLIZ Le Jardin des Arts

6 & 7 Rue Sakia el Hamra **Tel** *(0524) 44 66 34*   **Road map** *C3*

Le Jardin des Arts is housed within a characterful building in the northern part of Guéliz and is frequented by businesspeople as well as tourists and locals. Its decor is stylish, with bright colours, soft lighting and pictures on the walls. Its menu is international.

GUELIZ Ultimo Bacio

Angle rue Tarik Ibn Ziad & Moulay Ali **Tel** *(0661) 11 26 09*   **Road map** *C3*

The chic exterior of this establishment should not intimidate the casual diner. Ultimo Bacio is pasta heaven for those tired of traditional Moroccan meaty dishes. The interior is clean and predominantly white and gold, and the staff is attentive and helpful.

GUELIZ Bab Restaurant

Corner of Boulevard Mansour Eddahbi Rue Mohamed El Beqqal, Guéliz **Tel** *(0524) 43 52 50*   **Road map** *C3*

A fashion-conscious bar and restaurant that clamours to be noticed, Le Bab would hold its own in any major capital of the world. Splashes of colour, slick lines, great cocktails, good à la carte menu and the best possible place for people watching. Dress to impress.

GUÉLIZ El-Fassia

55 Boulevard Zerktouni **Tel** *(0524) 43 40 60*   **Road map** *C3*

This frill-free restaurant serving excellent food makes a convenient stopping-place if you are wandering around the Guéliz area. The all female staff manages to repeatedly wow Marrakech locals and visitors alike with no-nonsense, classic dishes, served in attractive surroundings. The alfresco dining area allows for fun people-watching sessions.

GUÉLIZ La Trattoria

179 Rue Mohammed el-Beqal **Tel** *(0524) 43 26 41*   **Road map** *C3*

La Trattoria is an Italian restaurant, and its owners pride themselves on their recipes being authentic. Located in a colonial-style Maison and beautifully decorated, this upmarket eatery is good for special occasions. The dessert trolley is especially tempting.

Key to Price Guide *see p328* **Key to Symbols** *see back cover flap*

HIVERNAGE Le Comptoir Paris-Marrakech

Avenue Echouada **Tel** *(0524) 43 77 02*   **Road map** *C3*

The Comptoir Paris-Marrakech, located in the upmarket area of Hivernage, is one of the most popular eateries-cum-bars in the area. Its menu is international with bistro-style dishes featured, while its decor is contemporary and its atmosphere cultural. Music from around the world plays in the background.

HIVERNAGE La Table du Marché

Hivernage Hôtel & Spa, Avenue Echouada **Tel** *(0524) 42 41 00*   **Road map** *C3*

With an impressive selection of freshly made sandwiches, pasta dishes, salads and light snacks, along with freshly squeezed juices and other beverages, La Table du Marché within the Hivernage Hôtel & Spa is the healthy option. Contemporary and luxurious in style, it is a good place to unwind.

LA PALMERAIE Restaurants at La Palmeraie Golf Palace

Hôtel Palmeraie Golf Palace, Circuit de la Palmeraie **Tel** *(0524) 30 10 10*   **Road map** *C3*

The Hôtel Palmeraie Golf Palace complex contains some of the most popular and luxurious eateries in the area. Views of the exclusive 18-hole golf course combine with a variety of international eateries with impressive à la carte menus, including Moroccan, Japanese and Italian. A visit here promises an elegant and refined dining experience.

MEDINA Place Jamaa el-Fna food stalls

Place Jamaa el-Fna   **Road map** *C3*

Every visitor to Marrakech should visit the food stalls in the medina at least once during their stay to enjoy the exciting experience of mingling with the locals. Small stalls open during the evening and cooking begins: mainly skewered meat and fish on grills, along with other Moroccan delicacies. Great aroma.

MEDINA Le Foundouk

55 Rue du Souk des Fassis **Tel** *(0524) 37 81 90*   **Road map** *C3*

Le Foundouk is housed in an interesting caravanserai-style building on two levels that allows for diners to look down on to an inner courtyard. The restaurant has a luxurious feel and yet is comfortable and a tad informal. Good Moroccan and Mediterranean dishes make for a tempting menu.

MEDINA Dar El-Yacout

79 Sidi Ahmed Soussi Bab Doukala **Tel** *(0524) 38 29 29/ (0524) 38 29 00*   **Road map** *C3*

One of the best, if not the best, luxury restaurants specializing in Moroccan cuisine in Marrakech, the Dar El-Yacout is housed in a restored palace in the heart of the medina, and offers the chance to enjoy a meal or a drink on its terrace and really appreciate the atmosphere of the city. Its extensive menu offers excellent quality.

MEDINA Dar Marjana

15 Derb Sidi Ali Tair Bab Doukkala **Tel** *(0524) 38 51 10*   **Road map** *C3*

Housed in a former palace within Marrakech's amazingly lively medina, and richly decorated with drapes and lanterns, the Dar Marjana will offer a memorable dining experience. It serves top-quality Moroccan cuisine with local wines; a show of traditional music and dance is also performed.

MEDINA Dar Moha

81 Rue Dar El Bacha **Tel** *(0524) 38 64 00*   **Road map** *C3*

Located in a beautiful *riad* building in the heart of the medina, the Dar Moha offers an elegant and lavishly decorated environment. It is open at lunchtime as well as in the evening, making it a bit of a rarity in the medina. The menu is modern Moroccan, with *tajines* cooked to original recipes.

MEDINA Gastro MK at Maison MK

4 Derb Sebaai, Quartier Ksour **Tel** *(0524) 37 61 73*   **Road map** *C3*

Some of the best food in Marrakech can be found at this establishment. An excellent union of tastes, colours and textures, an enviable wine menu and attentive and knowledgeable staff sets Gastro MK at Maison MK apart from the competition. It is wise to book well in advance. Closed on Wednesday.

MEDINA La Maison Arabe

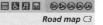

1, Derb Assehbé Bab Doukkala **Tel** *(0524) 38 70 10*   **Road map** *C3*

Highly romantic in style, this top-end restaurant prides itself on an unashamedly Moroccan menu. Dine here under an intricately hand-painted ceiling, surrounded by traditionally plastered tadelakht, tinkling fountains and shimmering candlelight. Dinner is eaten accompanied by Arab-Andalusian music played on lutes and guitars.

MEDINA La Mamounia

La Mamounia, Avenue Bab el-Jedid **Tel** *(0524) 44 40 44*   **Road map** *C3*

Diners at this prestigious hotel *(see p234)* set in magnificent gardens can choose between four restaurants, all offering meals of the highest standard. French, Italian and Moroccan restaurants (all requiring smart dress) are supplemented by the informal Pavillion de la Piscine, which offers Mediterranean cuisine by the pool.

MEDINA Le Tobsil

22 Derb Moulay Abdellah ben Hessaien Bab Ksour **Tel** *(0524) 44 40 52*   **Road map** *C3*

The reputation of this luxurious restaurant in the heart of the medina usually means that it is full to the brim with discerning diners, so making a reservation in advance is an absolute must. Its à la carte menu offers a range of refined Moroccan and French dishes, expertly cooked and presented by its experienced team.

PALMERAIE Flower Power Alternative Café

Pépinière Casa Botanica, Route de Sidi Abdellah Ghiat **Tel** *(0524) 48 40 87* **Road map** *C3*

This is a great location for families that will not break the bank. This eco-plant nursery serves the best eggs benedict in town, plus cinnamon toast, heavenly salad and zingy smoothies. There is also a delightful play area for youngsters and a petting zoo. Open during the day only and closed on Monday and Tuesday.

PALMERAIE Manzil La Tortue

Km 12 Route de Ouarzazate, Douar Gzoula, Commune Al Ouidane **Tel** *(0661) 95 55 17* **Road map** *C3*

The food here is excellent and offers diners the option to cook their food on a griddle at their table. Manzil La Tortue uses organic produce from its vegetable garden to create delicious international and Moroccan dishes. A fantastic wine list to suit all budgets is also available. Diners can eat indoors or on the terrace that surrounds the pool.

HIGH ATLAS

ASNI Kasbah Tamadot

Post Office Box 67, Asni 042150 **Road map** *C4*

Dine by the pool, on the terrace or in the restaurant at this mountain retreat *(see p317)*, owned by entrepreneur Richard Branson. For such a splendid place the menu is quite simple. Delicious sandwiches holding their own against richer dishes are all best washed down with one of many excellent local wines.

IMLIL Kasbah du Toubkal

Jbel Toubkal, 40000 **Tel** *(0524) 48 56 11* **Road map** *C4*

Perched on a crag above this tiny muleteer's village, this has to be one of the most striking places to eat in the whole of the Atlas region. The food is simple but tasty, including *tagines* and locally made bread. Kasbah du Toubkal is proud of its efforts to support the local community.

OUIRGANE Auberge de Sanglier Qui Fume

Km 61, 5 route Marrakech, Ouirgane **Tel** *(0524) 48 57 07* **Road map** *C4*

The restaurant at this mountain inn offers a varied menu. There are omelettes and salads, but they pale in comparison to the mix of fine French and traditional Moroccan cuisines on offer such as meaty *tajines*, couscous and lamb cooked on a spit. Meals can be enjoyed outdoors under the pergola or in the dining room.

OUIRGANE Domaine Malika

Douar Marigha, Route d'Amizmiz par Asni, Imlil **Tel** *(0661) 493 541* **Road map** *C4*

This restaurant takes vegetables from the garden, fruits from the orchards and meats from the local souk. Domaine Malika offers a colourful, aromatic and subtle menu, served on the poolside terrace on warm days or in the range-heated lounge in winter. Either way, the cedar scented Atlas air whets the appetite.

OUKAÏMEDEN L'Angour ("Chez Juju")

Signposted from the village **Tel** *(0524) 31 90 05* **Road map** *C4*

L'Angour is situated below the ski pistes in this popular winter-ski and summer-hiking resort. It resembles a French chalet, and features roaring fires and a pleasant decor. Its European menu is simple and straightforward, but dishes are freshly prepared, wholesome and quite delicious.

OURIKA VALLEY Le Maquis

Auberge Le Maquis, km 45 Aghbalou Ourika **Tel** *(0524) 48 45 31* **Road map** *C4*

Housed within the characterful Auberge Le Maquis, this restaurant serves Moroccan dishes such as *harira* and *tajines*, lemon chicken and couscous in pleasant surroundings. A children's menu is also available. An outside dining terrace overlooks the swimming pool.

OURIKA VALLEY Kasbah Bab Ourika

Tnine Ourika **Tel** *(0661) 63 42 34* **Road map** *C4*

Prepare to be amazed by the incredible mountainous landscape that surrounds this restaurant. Fresh, seasonal ingredients are procured from the surrounding villages daily in order to produce healthy Moroccan and French dishes. Meals can be enjoyed in the restaurant or in the gardens.

OURIKA VALLEY Nectarome

Lot Pinatel, Post Office Box142, Tniine **Tel** *(0524) 48 21 49* **Road map** *C4*

The plants at this botanical garden are not only pounded up to make blissful lotions and potions but are also served up as lunch. Snack on a fantastic salad or sip a herbal tea and perhaps have a relaxing or beautifying treatment later. These expansive gardens are equally suited to tours. Open for lunch only.

TIZI-N-TEST PASS ROAD La Belle Vue

Signposted from the pass **Road map** *C4*

Coming across the simple but welcoming establishment known as La Belle Vue as you explore the Tizi-n-Test Pass region is sure to be like a breath of fresh air, since there are very few alternatives for refreshment in this area. The menu is simple but wholesome, and the valley views from the terrace are remarkable.

Key to Price Guide *see p328* **Key to Symbols** *see back cover flap*

OUARZAZATE & THE SOUTHERN OASES

AÏT BENHADDOU Etoile Filante d'Or

Route Principale, Aït Ben Haddou **Tel** *(0661) 59 24 29*   **Road map** *C4*

Etoile Filante d'Or offers visitors to this UNESCO heritage site a warm welcome. The romantic terrace rewards evening visitors with spectacular views of the night sky, while the kitchen provides authentic Moroccan mains and desserts. Try the chicken *tagine*, which is especially good, as well as the grilled meats and pastillas.

BOULMALNE DU DADES Hôtel Xaluka Dades

Arfoud to Errachidia road km 5 **Tel** *(0524) 83 00 60*   **Road map** *D4*

Once you reach here after the numerous hairpin bends of the passes, or a night in the desert, you might think the overloaded buffet table is a mirage. Apart from mountains of delicious Moroccan and Continental food you will see waiters darting about in traditional dress and candles flickering by the pool.

ERFOUD Dunes

142 Avenue Moulay Ismaïl **Tel** *(0535) 57 67 93*   **Road map** *E4*

Located on the upper floor of a Moorish-inspired building complete with a terrace that overlooks the town, the Dunes is not the ideal eatery for visitors with mobility restrictions. However, its menu is wonderfully varied, with a good choice of Moroccan and international meat and fish dishes, and a selection of desserts.

ERFOUD Douira

Route de Rissani B.P. 188 **Tel** *(0535) 57 73 73*   **Road map** *E4*

With its palette of yellows, oranges and reds, the Douira manages to capture an authentic Moroccan vibe in terms of decor. The restaurant specializes in traditional local dishes prepared with fresh ingredients sourced in the Erfoud area. It is housed within the Hôtel El Ati, amid palm trees and gardens.

ERFOUD Restaurants of the Hôtel Bélère

Hôtel Bélère, Route de Rissani **Tel** *(0535) 57 81 90*   **Road map** *E4*

Four restaurants serving Italian, Asian, international and seafood dishes are housed within the Hôtel Bélère, one of the largest hotels in this relatively quiet desert town. Its team of chefs ensure that menus change regularly and that dishes are always freshly prepared and well presented. Bread is also baked on the premises.

ERFOUD Restaurant of the Hôtel Xaluca

Hôtel Xaluca, just before Erfoud **Tel** *(0535) 57 84 50*   **Road map** *E4*

Full to the brim with handsome local antiques and decorated in an authentic rustic Moroccan-style, complete with a massive fireplace, this air-conditioned restaurant in the Hôtel Xaluca *(see p310)* has lots of character. International and classic dishes are served daily, while special occasions are marked with traditional music and a feast.

OUARZAZATE Restaurant Er-Raha

11 Avenue al-Mouahidine   **Road map** *C4*

Since it opened a few years back, the Restaurant Er Raha has earned itself a reputation for being one of a few places in which to enjoy live music in Ourzazate. This means it is always busy with locals as well as tourists looking for an evening's entertainment. Food-wise, the menu is classic Moroccan and wholesome.

OUARZAZATE Restaurant de l'Hôtel La Gazelle

Hôtel La Gazelle, Avenue Mohammed V **Tel** *(0524) 88 21 51*   **Road map** *C4*

One of the first established in the town, this convivial and intimate little restaurant within the Hôtel La Gazelle is a popular venue with locals. Holiday companies use it, too. Classic Moroccan dishes of meat and fish *tajines* and salads are served, as well as international options.

OUARZAZATE Restaurant Chez Dimitri

22 Avenue Mohammed V **Tel** *(0524) 88 73 46*   **Road map** *C4*

Ask any local resident where Chez Dimitri is, and the chances are they would have dined there on several occasions. One of the first good restaurants to open in Ouarzazate and popular for family parties and celebrations, it serves international cuisine with a good choice of wines, alcoholic drinks and juices.

OUARZAZATE Restaurant of the Hôtel Ibis Moussafir

Hôtel Ibis Moussafir, Boulevard Moulay Rachid **Tel** *(0524) 89 91 10*   **Road map** *C4*

The restaurant of the Hôtel Ibis Moussafir, a quality establishment with an interior design concept that beautifully captures the distinctive Moroccan ambience, serves international cuisine to its guests and hotel visitors. A wine list is designed to blend harmoniously with the range of dishes offered.

RAMLIA Auberge Aghbalou Ramlia

Auberge Ramlia, Village Ramlia, Taouz Rissani   **Road map** *E4*

Those who make the trek to Auberge Aghbalou Ramlia will be rewarded with simple yet delicious food, which is served under a star-filled sky with mountains visible all around. Advance booking is recommended. The phone connection is unreliable and the roads can be tricky at night.

SKOURA Dar Ahlam
Douar Oulad Cheikh Ali, Casbah Madihi **Tel** *(0524) 85 22 39*
Road map *C4*

Eat like you have never thought possible before at this ultra deluxe haven in the middle of nowhere. A mouth-watering patisserie and fine wines are available to guests. Dine in the Sahara at a table laid with a crisp white tablecloth and not another person for miles around. Residents are given priority.

ZAGORA Restaurant of the Hôtel Ksar Tinsouline
Signposted from Zagora **Tel** *(0524) 84 72 52*
Road map *D4*

Located right in the heart of the countryside that surrounds Zagora, and signposted from the town towards the Wadi Draa, this restaurant is something of a hidden gem. Still relatively unknown, it serves good traditional Moroccan dishes such as *tajines* prepared to the team's own recipes, plus a good vegetarian selection.

ZAGORA Restaurant of the Hôtel Riad Salam
Hôtel Riad Salam, Boulevard Mohammed V **Tel** *(0524) 84 74 00*
Road map *D4*

An attractive restaurant, one of two, that looks out over the swimming pool, courtyards and gardens of the splendid Hôtel Riad Salam, this specializes in Moroccan cuisine along with international dishes. Displays of fruit and a good dessert trolley are notable features.

SOUTHERN MOROCCO & WESTERN SAHARA

AGADIR Harbour stalls
Agadir harbour
Road map *B4*

Numerous little stalls line the street alongside the harbour from which tempting aromas beg further investigation. Skewered meats and fish are among the freshly prepared dishes being cooked and eaten with relish by tourists and locals alike. This is a great place to enjoy the relaxed atmosphere of a balmy Moroccan evening.

AGADIR Jour et Nuit
Promenade de la Plage **Tel** *(0528) 84 06 10*
Road map *B4*

This air-conditioned restaurant located on the promenade beside the sea comes like a breath of fresh air when the sun is at its hottest, offering a welcoming place to spend a little time over a light lunch or to enjoy an evening meal. It serves a wide and varied selection of Moroccan cuisine.

AGADIR Jazz Restaurant
Boulevard du 20 Août **Tel** *(0528) 84 02 08*
Road map *B4*

The Jazz Restaurant lives up to its name, and has become a popular venue for a great evening listening to live jazz musicians. Situated conveniently in the Complexe Igoudar, a short walk from the seafront, it offers a wide range of European-style dishes, wines and alcoholic drinks.

AGADIR Jean Cocteau
Boulevard Mohammed V **Tel** *(0528) 82 11 11*
Road map *B4*

Located inside Casino Shem's, this restaurant is a lively atmospheric place to dine and is at the cutting edge of innovation when it comes to its menu. Dishes offered change almost on a daily basis. The theme is pure European, so everything from salads, tapas and mezes to burgers and steaks are offered.

AGADIR Via Veneto
Avenue Hassan II **Tel** *(0528) 84 14 67*
Road map *B4*

Vio Veneto is one of the top restaurants that locals head for when they have a celebration in the family or just want a special meal Italian-style. Located in the heart of Agadir, near the Vallée des Oiseaux, it offers authentic Italian dishes.

AGADIR Bamboo Thai
Immeuble Hasna, Avenue Hassan II, En Face Gendarmerie Royale **Tel** *(0528) 84 21 08*
Road map *B4*

This sumptuous Thai restaurant, located a stone's throw from the royal police station, is Agadir's premier Asian eatery. Romantic lighting, impeccable service and delicately presented dishes ensure that it remains an excellent place for a romantic evening or a business lunch to impress.

AGADIR Le Miramar
Boulevard Mohammed V **Tel** *(0528) 84 07 70*
Road map *B4*

The Italian and international-themed Miramar restaurant is especially welcoming and ideal for an elegant meal. Family-run, it offers a wide-ranging choice of Italian pasta dishes, pizzas with toppings created by the team, as well as seafood specialities and a good wine list. Many of the wines come straight from Italy.

AGADIR Mezzo Mezzo
19 Avenue Hassan II, Immeuble Hassania **Tel** *(0528) 84 88 19*
Road map *B4*

Mezzo Mezzo, with its modern interior and helpful staff, offers good wood-fired pizzas, suitably al dente pasta and a range of great salads. An excellent wine list and chilled bottled beers are also available. This restaurant is popular with holidaymakers as well as local families.

Key to Price Guide *see p328* **Key to Symbols** *see back cover flap*

AGADIR Mimi la Brochette

Promenade de la Plage **Tel** *(0528) 84 03 87* **Road map** *B4*

Situated along the promenade and looking out over the Atlantic Ocean, this attractive restaurant is frequented by tourists as well as local residents. It offers a pleasant way to spend a lunchtime or evening. Food-wise, it serves international cuisine, along with some classic Moroccan dishes and a range of vegetarian options.

AGADIR Les Blancs

Marina d'Agadir **Tel** *(0528) 82 83 68* **Road map** *B4*

Come here to marvel at the view, which stretches over Agadir's magnificent beach, and to select from a lengthy menu of Spanish dishes. With an incredible variety of paella and platters of grilled seafood, Les Blancs makes a great alternative to Moroccan dishes more widely available.

DAKHLA Hôtel Calipau Sahara

Km 5 Avenue El Walaa lagune **Tel** *(0661) 19 16 34*

Hôtel Calipau Sahara could be described as a luxurious paradise in the middle of nowhere. Given its location, on the water's edge, it is hardly surprising that its restaurant specializes in seafood, most notably oysters. In the evening, diners can sit out on the terrace and watch the sun go down.

SIDI IFNI Restaurant of the Hôtel Bellevue

Hôtel Bellevue, Place Hassan II **Tel** *(0528) 87 50 72* **Road map** *B5*

Specializing in fish and seafood dishes cooked in a Moroccan style with subtle herbs and sauces, this attractive restaurant is housed within the Hôtel Bellevue, easily the best hotel in the area. The clifftop location and views of the Atlantic Ocean from its dining area are breathtaking.

TAFRAOUTE L'Etoile d'Agadir

Place de la Marche Verte **Tel** *(0528) 80 02 68* **Road map** *B4*

Very popular with the inhabitants of Tafraoute, this cosy restaurant serves excellent almond *tajine*, couscous and other Moroccan specialities. With a warm ambience and Moroccan music played softly in the background, L'Etoile d'Agadir makes for an enjoyable local experience.

TAFRAOUTE Le Safran

Rue Principale **Tel** *(0528) 53 40 46* **Road map** *B5*

Perfectly capturing the theme of Moroccan desert living, this good restaurant serves meals in Berber tents. It is all rather fun and makes for a memorable experience. Tourists tend to be the main clientele of Le Safran. Food is wonderfully prepared and presented, and it is tailored to suit the desert environment.

TAROUDANNT Jnana Soussia

Route de Marrakech **Tel** *(0528) 85 49 80* **Road map** *B4*

For a truly Moroccan experience, try dining in Berber-style tents under the stars at the Jnana Soussia. A Moroccan restaurant just outside town, it tends to cater for holiday groups and is almost always lively, but individuals are welcomed, too and encouraged to join in with the music and dancing.

TAROUDANNT Restaurant of the Hôtel Saadien

Hôtel Saadien, Borj Oumansour **Tel** *(0528) 85 25 89* **Road map** *B4*

The Hôtel Saadien's restaurant is a cosy and intimate venue, renowned for its excellent and generous meals. The restaurant serves an à la carte menu of French and traditional Moroccan dishes, along with some classic desserts, and as such it attracts discerning diners. It has great views of the town.

TAROUDANNT Restaurant of the Palais Salam

Hôtel Palais Salam, Taroudannt Ramparts **Tel** *(0528) 85 25 01* **Road map** *B4*

Capturing the essence of Moroccan living beautifully, the richly decorated restaurant of the Hôtel Palais Salam is a great place to dine. Overlooking the walls and rooftops of the medina, its location is a definite asset. Extremely good international and Moroccan cuisine is served on tables elegantly dressed in linen.

TAROUDANNT Restaurant of the Hôtel La Gazelle d'Or

Hôtel La Gazelle d'Or, Centre of Taroudannt **Tel** *(0528) 85 20 39* **Road map** *B4*

If you are visiting Taroudannt, one of the best places to stay is the legendary Hôtel La Gazelle d'Or. This way, you can dine in its sophisticated international-themed restaurant. You would be following in the footsteps of the rich and famous. Organic produce is grown in the restaurant's own gardens and used in all food preparations.

TAROUDANNT Ryad Dar El Hana

376 Jn Si Moussa **Tel** *(0662) 84 80 87* **Road map** *B4*

Classic in style and timelessly charming, this fully restored *riad* does much to impress. It is tucked away in a quiet corner of the medina yet close to the centre of town. The talented chefs in the *riad's* restaurant produce excellent food amid outstanding surroundings and all the comforts one could wish for.

TIZNIT Restaurant of the Kerdous Hôtel

Kerdous Hôtel, Kerdous Pass, Tiznit **Tel** *(0528) 21 81 52* **Road map** *B5*

Eating at the Kerdous Hôtel's restaurant is a great way to meet and mix with local residents. Housed in a kasbah-style building in an outcrop in the middle of the desert landscape, it serves good wholesome international and Moroccan dishes. The restaurant's panoramic views are breathtaking.

SHOPPING IN MOROCCO

Every village in Morocco has its weekly souk. Lasting for a few hours, souks are busy, colourful places where agricultural produce and craft items brought by country people are sold alongside a range of other essential everyday items.

Ceramic box

Large towns have several souks. These take place in the medinas and are laid out according to the type of goods that they sell. Traders are friendly and always ready to please their customers. The rich and diverse range of Moroccan crafts can be found in the country's souks and markets, as well as at cooperative craft outlets and specialist shops, and are also offered for sale by the roadside along tourist routes.

Slipper merchant with a colourful range of footwear in Tafraoute

OPENING HOURS

Country souks take place only in the morning. Grocers' shops, local supermarkets and butchers' shops are open every weekday from 8am to 9pm, although they close for about two hours in the middle of the day. Some may also open on Sundays, when different opening hours apply. Friday is theoretically a day of rest for Muslims; however, business goes on as normal, although some larger shops close in the middle of the day. During Ramadan, grocers' shops open late in the morning, close for part of the day and then open from the evening until very late. Shops run by Jews close on Saturdays (the Sabbath). In large towns and cities, clothes shops and fabric shops open from 9am to noon and from 3pm to 7pm. They do not open on Sundays. The hypermarkets that have sprung up in all large towns are open from 9am to 9pm seven days a week.

METHODS OF PAYMENT

Credit cards are accepted only in large towns and cities and in modern shops. Some shopkeepers will add a percentage as tax onto the total automatically if you choose this form of payment. Also, credit card slips can be pre-dated or printed twice without your knowing. It is best, therefore, to carry sufficient amounts of cash before setting off on a shopping spree.

Dates for sale, Ziz Gorge

FOOD STORES

All towns are very well provided with grocers' shops. In villages, the grocer's is the only place, apart from the weekly souk, where people can buy provisions and essential items.

These shops are usually no bigger than a large cupboard. They are fitted with shelves from floor to ceiling, and offer all kinds of foods and household goods. It is wise to avoid buying perishable items such as yoghurt and milk, since there is no guarantee that they are fresh. In butchers' shops, what is on offer is neither labelled nor priced. Fruit and vegetable shops, dairies and bakers are found only in large towns. Although French bread was introduced during the Protectorate, Moroccans prefer *kesra*, a round loaf baked at home or in the local communal oven.

A few *charcuteries*, selling cooked meats, have appeared in Casablanca, Rabat and Marrakech but they are geared to an exclusively Western clientele, pork being forbidden to Muslims. By using a local supermarket, you can check the sell-by dates of fresh produce (when

Semi-precious stones laid out for sale at the roadside, Middle Atlas

they are marked, that is).
Imported foods can also
be bought in supermarkets.

Hypermarket chains
were set up in Morocco
several years ago. There
are supermarkets in all the
major towns.

MARKETS

All large towns have several
markets that supply fresh
fruit and vegetables to the
population every day of
the year. In every market
there is a fresh herb stall
and a spice and olive
stall. Household utensils,
basketry and craft items are
also on sale.

In the harbours along
the Atlantic coast, particularly
in the towns of Oualidia,
Safi, Essaouira and Agadir,
the fruits of the daily
catch – such as sole,
sardines, perch, shrimps,
squid and oysters – can
be eaten on the spot.

SOUKS

For foreign visitors, souks
are lively and authentic
expressions of rural life in
Morocco (see p201), offering
the opportunity to see a
fascinating and genuine
aspect of the country. Taking
place once a week, souks
are the focus of economic,
social and administrative life
in Morocco's rural areas.
Country people come from
miles around to stock up
on supplies or to exchange
agricultural produce (such as
fruit, vegetables, eggs, butter
and cereals) or craft items
(such as pottery and carpets)
for tea, oil, sugar and spices.
Also on offer are plastic
utensils and clothing made

A brassware and copperware shop in the Quartier Habbous, Casablanca

of synthetic fabrics, along
with chickens, sheep and
sometimes mules.

In the medinas of Rabat,
Fès, Marrakech and Tarou-
dannt, souks take place
almost daily. Their location
and layout are dictated by the
nature of what they offer.
More oriented towards tourists
than are the country souks,
they offer a huge range of
craft items from all over
Morocco. Fassi glazed pottery
is by no means identical to
that made in Salé or Safi, and
it differs from the Berber
pottery of the Rif or that
made in Tamegroute. Thuya
wood (see p122) is a
speciality of Essaouira;
Ouaouzguite carpets are
renowned in Tazenakht; and
El-Kelaa M'Goun is famous
for its daggers.

HOW TO BARGAIN

In Morocco, bargaining is
not so much a custom as a
duty. Every self-respecting
Moroccan uses this method,
even when buying vegetables
in the souk or renting a hotel
room. In craft shops, no
prices are marked and the
shopkeeper considers it quite
natural that potential clients
should bargain over
the price. When a
potential customer
shows an interest, the
shop-owner will quote
an initial price, which
often bears no relation
to the real price of the
object in question but
which tests the buyer's
willingness to make a
counter-offer.

In order to bargain
effectively, it is

important to know the value
of what you wish to buy or
at least to have a price in
mind beyond which you
will not go. By contrast, if
you refuse to raise your offer
sufficiently to allow the seller
to make a profit, he will not
pursue the transaction. The
real purpose of bargaining
is to obtain the desired
object while feigning indiffer-
ence. This is why bargaining
takes time and should be a
subtle game between buyer
and seller.

A bellows merchant in the souk
in Marrakech

FORGERIES

Souks in medinas and in
Morocco's major tourist
centres offer "authentic"
goods of dubious quality and
origin, and for very inflated
prices. You are advised to
be on your guard against
goods that, contrary to what
the seller may assure you,
are often no more than
skilfully concocted and
very convincing forgeries.

Vegetables for sale at the Tahar el-Alaoui
market in Casablanca

What to Buy in Morocco

Straw basket

Souks in Morocco present the visitor with a vast choice of jewellery, leather goods, wrought-iron work, brass and copper, pottery, carpets, basketry and fabrics. But the quantity, colours and sheer diversity of the items on offer can be bewildering and it can be difficult to distinguish quality pieces from inferior ones. Before deciding to buy, it is best to take some time to compare what is on offer in different shops. Country craft items offered for sale in markets are genuine and utilitarian, ranging from the baskets carried by donkeys and combs for carding wool to terracotta coolers for keeping milk or dried meat fresh.

Pouffe
Like other leather goods, this pouffe is made of good-quality goatskin or sheepskin, which, after tanning, is dyed and embroidered.

CERAMICS

The place of origin of ceramics can be identified by their colours and decoration. Pottery from Fès is the most refined, that from Salé is glazed in pale colours, and that from Safi features polychrome colours and Berber motifs. Potters also devise new designs, such as that on the vase shown on the left.

Vase

Vase from Safi

Ashtray
This is an example of Fès blue-glazed ware. The Fassi potting industry goes back to the 10th or 11th centuries.

Decorated *tajine* dish

Plate with a modern design

WOOD AND STONE CARVING

Fès, Tetouan and Azrou are renowned for their carved cedar. In Essaouira, craftsmen work with thuya wood *(see p122)*, making boxes in various shapes, statues, trays, frames and other pieces. In Taroudannt, objects are carved from soft stone, and in Erfoud trinkets and other small items are fashioned from marble.

Inlaid Wood
Boxes and other objects made of thuya are decoratively inlaid with yellow citron wood and ebony or cedar.

Duck carved in stone

Thuya Camel
Small pieces like this figure of a camel are easier to make than larger items, since thuya wood tends to split as it dries out.

METALWARE

Wrought iron, brown-hued copper, bright yellow brass (a mixture of copper and zinc) and nickel silver (a mixture of copper, zinc and nickel) are the main materials used in Moroccan metalware. The finest pieces are engraved or damascened (inlaid with contrasting metal).

Brass tray

Lantern

Teapot
A squat teapot with tapering lid, made of stainless steel or silver, is an essential piece of equipment for making mint tea.

TERRACOTTA

Berber pottery features a combination of simple, sturdy shapes, ochre and brown colours and geometric motifs.

Terracotta kasbah

Berber pottery

SILVER

Silver is the predominant material of Berber jewellery. The most common items are brooches, which Berber women wear in pairs, to secure their veils at each shoulder. The shape and decoration of brooches varies according to the region.

Hand of Fatima, a lucky charm

Anklet

Koumiya dagger

Silver and Coral Necklace
Berber women traditionally wear a lot of jewellery. Today, jewellery is made increasingly often of synthetic resin that mimics the colour of coral.

CLOTHING

Jellabas, loose-fitting hooded cloaks with long sleeves, and *gandouras*, tunics with short sleeves, can be purchased in souks. Burnouses, hooded woollen cloaks, are seen in rural areas. Embroidered silk belts, traditionally made in Fès, are highly sought-after but are increasingly difficult to find.

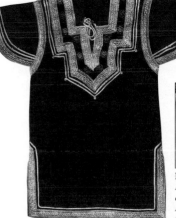

Embroidery
Each city has its own traditions and styles of embroidery. It adorns tablecloths, table napkins, cushions and other items, in a variety of stitches.

A child's *gandoura*

Babouches

Moroccan Carpets

Carpet knot

There are as many different types of carpets in Morocco as there are tribal traditions. Moroccan carpets can, however, be divided into two main groups: Berber carpets and city carpets. The former are either knotted or woven; they are pleasingly unrefined and each one is unique. Their wool, which the women weave into simple or complex patterns, their harmonious colours, their shape and size, and also their patterns, vary from one region to another. City carpets, influenced by Oriental traditions, are finer. Symbols of luxury, they grace the living rooms of wealthy houses.

The fringe, at one end of the carpet, is part of the warp.

BERBER CARPETS

Most of the carpets made in Tazenaght and Taliouine, in the High Atlas, are made by the Ouaouzguite tribe. These carpets are typically long, narrow and supple, and thus well suited to use in the interiors of kasbahs in the Atlas.

CARPET WEAVING

Carding wool

After the men have sheared the sheep in the spring, the women wash the wool and carefully pick over it. It is then carded, a process by which the strands are untangled by brushing with comb-like implements. Next, the wool is spun into yarn with a small spindle. Either in its natural colour or after it has been dyed, the wool is then ready to be woven. Berber women knot carpets on large, rudimentary looms consisting of two wooden vertical and two horizontal planks. The warp is set up by threading vertical strands vertically on the loom. These determine the length and thickness of the carpet. The weft (the horizontal threads) are threaded by hand between the strands of the warp, the weaver working row by row, pressing the weave together with an iron comb.

A weaver in Abachkou

Carpet from the High Atlas, *in which woven bands alternate with knotted bands. The well-ordered geometric motifs feature lozenges, triangles and broken lines.*

Carpet made by the Zaïane *of the Middle Atlas, featuring a combination of strict geometric and random motifs. These carpets are well suited to use in tents or for covering the beaten earth floors of houses.*

CITY CARPETS

Woven in Rabat, Salé and Casablanca, city carpets are perfectly symmetrical. They feature floral and geometric motifs and are edged with borders of differing widths.

A carpet seller in the Rue des Consuls in Rabat

BUYING A CARPET

Colour and pattern are the primary considerations when buying a carpet. Then come the material, the carpet's softness, the density of the weave or knotting, and condition. A good-quality carpet has clearly defined motifs and perfectly straight edges. The value of a carpet is based on the number of knots per row and the density of the warp and weft. Some carpets have up to 380,000 knots per square metre (11 sq ft) and official price bands per square metre apply. Carpets checked by the Ministry of Crafts are hallmarked with the date that they were checked, their provenance and their quality. An orange label indicates extra-superior quality; a blue label, superior quality; a yellow label, medium quality, and green label, ordinary quality. Once the carpet has been unrolled in front of you, you can start to bargain *(see p345)*.

Mediouna carpets, *made in Casablanca, feature shades of brick red or soft pink, and always have a lozenge-shaped or star-shaped central motif.*

Carpet shop in a crafts complex

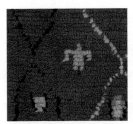
Haouz carpets, *made in Marrakech, are knotted. They are characterized by a background scattered with naive motifs.*

Middle Atlas carpets *have a woollen pile. The exact outlines of the pattern can be seen only on their smooth side.*

Dyes *are traditionally obtained from vegetable extracts but are now very often supplemented by synthetic dyes.*

ENTERTAINMENT IN MOROCCO

Most nightlife in Morocco takes place in the large towns and cities. International tourism and the desire for modernity on the part of the younger generation have both contributed to the development of centres of culture and entertainment. These are often the best places to meet young Moroccans. The number of fashionable

The Rialto, one of Casablanca's cinemas

bars and nightclubs is increasing, too, while Morocco's thriving cultural life ensures a wide variety of entertainment. Certain private art galleries showcase the country's artistic talent. The many feast days and *moussems* (pilgrimage festivals) provide opportunities to watch shows that are more authentically Moroccan than those aimed at tourists.

The Institut Français de Casablanca, a good source of cultural information

INFORMATION SOURCES

Scanning the entertainment section of various newspapers (entitled *"Spectacles"* in Francophone publications) is the best way of checking what's on, even though they give such information only very irregularly.

The main daily newspapers are *El-Bayane*, *Le Matin du Sahara*, *L'Opinion* and *Libération*. Weeklies include *Le Magazine* and *Tel Quel*. Monthly magazines, such as *Femmes du Maroc* and *Citadine*, or the fortnightly *Medina*, carry listings of cultural events. These publications are available from kiosks as well as in most tobacconists.

There are no good sources of entertainment information available in English.

CINEMAS

Taking up the threads of the movie culture that the country enjoyed in the 1950s, when Moroccans had the privilege of seeing early screenings of many American productions, Moroccan cinemas are enjoying a new lease of life as is, to a certain extent, the Moroccan film industry. Authentically restored auditoriums dating from the 1940s have reopened, particularly in Casablanca. The main cinemas in Rabat are the **Renaissance** and the **Salle du 7eme Art**. In Casablanca there are the **Rialto**, the **Lynx** and the **Megarama**; in Fès the **Empire** and the **Rex**; and, in Marrakech, the **Colisée** and the **Megarama**. In Tangier, the leading cinemas are **Le Paris** and the **Rif** with the **Cinémathèque de Tanger**.

But if you don't understand French or Arabic, this might not be your first choice of entertainment since almost all films are dubbed in French, or are in Arabic.

Daily local newspapers provide information on what is showing, or you can phone the cinemas themselves. The cultural institutes in various cities (*see p352*) are also good sources of information.

THEATRES

Morocco is not well endowed with theatres. They are found only in the cities, and productions are usually limited and irregular. Nevertheless, foreign theatrical companies perform in Morocco, and efforts are being made to launch the Moroccan theatre, which is still in its infancy.

Although theatre listings are usually given in the daily press, it is best to obtain information directly from the theatres or from cultural institutions.

Throne Day, a highly colourful and popular event

FEAST DAYS AND FESTIVALS

Prominent among the many feast days that punctuate the year *(see pp38–41)* are the *moussems*. These large popular gatherings usually focus on the tomb of a saint *(see pp198–9)*, and are spectacular shows with traditional dance performances.

Certain festivals, such as the Marrakech Folk Festival in June, draw dancers and musicians from all over Morocco, and the Gnaoua Music Festival in Essaouira, also in June, offers high-quality performances. Other festivals include the Sacred World Music Festival held in Fès in June and the Rabat Cultural Festival in July. Fantasias *(pp34–5)* are typically high-spirited Moroccan shows. They are performed most famously at the *moussem* of Moulay Abdallah, which takes place near El-Jadida in August.

The types of dances vary between the different Berber and rural tribes. Often performed are the *ahouach* of the High Atlas and Ouarzazate, and the *ahidou* of the Middle Atlas, in which men and women take part. The *guedra*, a dance from the Guelmim and Sahara, is performed by one woman within a circle of musicians.

A group performing at the Festival of Andalusian Music in Fès

SHOWS AND CONCERTS

Large hotels often organize Moroccan evenings giving visitors a chance to see authentic popular performances of music and dance.

Certain restaurants also put on performances of folk dance in the evenings. At **Chez Ali** in Marrakech, on certain evenings guests are served their meal in a tent while a fantasia is performed.

Those interested in hearing Moroccan music can choose between *raï*, which has roots in Bedouin music and whose star performer is Cheb Amrou; Gnaoua music, which Mustapha Baqbou has taken to many European jazz festivals; and the nostalgic chants of Andalusian music. Many such concerts are organized by various cultural institutes. Ask the local tourist office for information.

DIRECTORY

CINEMAS

AGADIR

Rialto
Avenue des F.A.R.
Tel (0528) 84 10 12.

CASABLANCA

Lynx
150 Avenue Mers Sultan.
Tel (0522) 22 02 29.

Megarama
Boulevard de la Corniche.
Tel 0890 10 20 20.

Rialto
35 Rue Med Qorri.

FÈS

Empire
60 Avenue Hassan II.
Tel (0535) 62 66 07.

Rex
Corner of Avenue
Mohammed Es-Slaoui
and Boulevard
Mohammed V.
Tel (0535) 62 24 96.

MARRAKECH

Colisée
Boulevard M. Zerktouni.
Tel (0524) 44 88 93.

Megarama
Jardins de L'Aguedal.
Tel 0890 10 20 20.

RABAT

Renaissance
266 Avenue Mohammed V.

Salle du 7eme Art
Avenue Allal Ben Abdellah.

TANGIER

Le Paris
11 Rue de Fès.
Tel (0539) 32 43 30.

Rif: Cinémathèque de Tanger
Place du 9 Avril 1947.
Tel (0539) 93 54 51.
www.cinematheque
detanger.com

THEATRES

AGADIR

Théâtre Municipal de Plein Air
Avenue Mohammed V.

CASABLANCA

Complexe Culturel Moulay Rachid
Avenue Akid Allam.
Tel (0522) 70 47 48.

Complex Culturel de Sidi-Belyout
28 Rue Léon l'Africain.
Tel (0661) 05 32 38.

RABAT

Théâtre Mohammed V
Charia al Mansour
Eddahbi.
Tel (0537) 70 73 00.

Salle Haj Mohammed Bahnini
1 Rue Gandhi.
Tel (0537) 20 94 94.

SHOWS

Chez Ali
After Pont de Tensift,
Marrakech.
Tel (0524) 30 77 30.

The Villa des Arts in Casablanca

CULTURAL CENTRES

Among the most dynamic cultural centres in Morocco are the **French Cultural Institutes**, which are found in major cities. These organize a wide-ranging programme, including exhibitions, film festivals highlighting the work of particular directors, as well as concerts and theatrical performances. The remarkably well laid-out **Institut Français de Marrakech** even has an amphitheatre for open-air performances. The Spanish **Instituto Cervantes** and the German **Goethe Institut** also contribute to the promotion of the artistic activity of the multiple cultures that coexist in Morocco.

These centres are good places to meet Moroccans who have an interest in Europe. Programmes in the form of a bimonthly pamphlet are available on the premises. The **British Council** in Rabat also organizes an interesting range of events.

ART GALLERIES

Since the Dane **Frederic Damgaard** *(see p124)*, opened an art gallery in Essaouira in 1988, the artistic world in Morocco has enjoyed a new dynamism. Galleries exhibit the work of painters from far and wide, including, for example, that of the well-known "free artists of Essaouira" *(see p125)*.

Galleries in Casablanca include the **Villa des Arts**, an extensive showcase of Moroccan artistic creativity

over the last 50 years, and in Marrakech the **Matisse Arts Gallery** and **Dar Bellarj**.

Painting by Mohammed Tabal, one of Essaouira's "free artists"

PIANO BARS

Places where traditional Moroccan music can be heard are relatively few. However, piano bars in large hotels and jazz clubs offer the opportunity of hearing European and North American bands.

The **Amstrong Jazz Bar** and the **Villa Fandango** in Casablanca, for example, are very fashionable. Marrakech has several modish venues such as the huge **Al Anbar**, whose restaurant contains several hundred tables and has live orchestras, and the **Montecristo**, which is more intimate and is located in one

of Gueliz's villas. In Essaouira, Fès, Ouarzazate, Rabat and Tangier, it is mostly in hotel bars that music can be heard. The best approach is to obtain information directly from the various bars and hotels themselves.

NIGHTCLUBS

Except in Casablanca, Rabat and Marrakech, most nightclubs in Morocco are located within hotels. In Rabat, one of the most fashionable discos is **L'Amnesia**. In Casablanca, nightclubs are concentrated around Aïn-Diab. They include **La Bodega** and the **Carré Rouge**. **Theatro at Hôtel Essaadi** in Marrakech has a good reputation, as does **Le Flamingo** in Agadir.

While discos and nightclubs are relatively empty on weekday nights, all are filled to capacity at weekends and during school holidays.

Some close at about 3am or 4am. Others stay open until dawn, particularly in Marrakech, Agadir and other large tourist centres.

CASINOS

Gambling is severely frowned on by Islam, so that there are very few casinos in Morocco. The casino in **La Mamounia**, the famous hotel in Marrakech *(see p314)*, is easily the most prestigious.

If you decide to spend the evening in a casino, dress smartly. A jacket is essential, and jeans, tracksuits and trainers are definitely not acceptable.

Nightclub in Agadir, with dancing beneath a replica of the Eiffel Tower

DIRECTORY

CULTURAL CENTRES

AGADIR

Institut Français d'Agadir
Rue Cheinguit,
Nouveau Talborjt.
Tel (0528) 84 20 01.

CASABLANCA

Dante Alighieri
4 Rue d'Aquitaine.
Tel (0522) 26 01 45.

Goethe Institut
11 Place du 16 Novembre.
Tel (0522) 20 77 35.

Instituto Cervantes
31 Rue d'Alger.
Tel (0522) 26 73 37.

Institut Français de Casablanca
121 Boulevard Zerktouni.
Tel (0522) 77 98 70.

FÈS

Institut Français de Fès
33 Rue Loukili.
Tel (0535) 62 39 21.

MARRAKECH

Institut Français de Marrakech
Route de Targa, Jbel Gueliz.
Tel (0524) 44 69 30.

RABAT

British Council
36 Rue de Tanger.
Tel (0537) 76 08 36.

Instituto Cervantes
5 Rue Madnine.
Tel (0537) 26 81 21.

Institut Français de Rabat
1 Rue Abou Inane.
Tel (0537) 68 96 50.

TANGIER

Instituto Cervantes
99 Ave Sidi Mohammed
Ben Abdellah.
Tel (0539) 93 20 01.

Institut Français de Tanger
2 Rue Hassan Ibn
Ouazzan
Tel (0539) 94 10 54.

ART GALLERIES

AGADIR

Artomania
El-Faïs Brahim estate
(next to the Ecole Pigier),
industrial quarter.

CASABLANCA

Almanar
Rue 204, No.19,
Boulevard de la Corniche.

Venise Cadre
25 Avenue Moulay Rachid.
Tel (0522) 36 60 76.

Villa des Arts
30 Boulevard Roudani.
Tel (0522) 29 50 87.

ESSAOUIRA

Galerie Frederic Damgaard
Avenue Oqba Ibn Nafiaa.
Tel (0524) 78 44 46.

MARRAKECH

Dar Bellarj
9 Toualate Zaouite
Lahdar.
Tel (0524) 44 45 55.

Matisse Arts Gallery
61 Rue de Yougoslavie.
Tel (0524) 44 83 26.

RABAT

Villa des Arts
10 Rue Beni Mellal
Hassan.
Tel (0537) 66 85 79.

TANGIER

Lawrence Arnott Art Gallery
68 Rue Amr Ibn Ass.

PIANO BARS

CASABLANCA

Amstrong Jazz Bar
16 Rue de la Mer Noire,
Boulevard de la Corniche.
Tel (0522) 79 77 59.

Villa Fandango
Rue de la Mer Egée,
Boulevard de la Corniche.
Tel (0522) 79 74 77.

FÈS

Le Birdy
Jnan Palace Hotel,
Avenue Ahmed Chaouki.
Tel (0535) 65 22 30.

Oasis Bar
Hotel Royal Mirage,
Avenue des F.A.R.
Tel (0535) 93 19 34 / 37.

MARRAKECH

Al Anbar
47 Rue Jbel Lakhadar.
Tel (0524) 37 77 83.

Le Churchill
La Mamounia Hotel,
Bab el-Jedid.
Tel (0524) 38 86 00.

Le Monecristo
20 Rue Ibn Aïcha.
Tel (0524) 43 90 31

OUARZAZATE

Le Piano-Bar
Hôtel Kenzi Azghor.
Tel (0524) 88 65 01.

Zagora Bar
Hôtel Karam Palace,
Tel (0524) 88 22 25.

RABAT

Amber Bar
Sofitel Rabat Jardin des
Roses, Souissi quarter.
Tel (0537) 67 56 56.

Barrio Latino
61 Rue Oulad Sbou,
Agdal.
Tel (0537) 68 33 50.

Le Puzzle
79 Avenue Ibn Sina,
Agdal.
Tel (0537) 67 00 30.

TANGIER

El Carabo
Chellah Beach Club.
Tel (0539) 32 50 68.

Le Caïd's
Hôtel El-Minzah,
85 Rue de la Liberté.
Tel (0539) 93 58 85.

Sable's Bar
Hôtel Tanjah-Flandria1,
Boulevard Med V.
Tel (0539) 93 30 00.

NIGHTCLUBS

AGADIR

Le Flamingo
Hôtel Beach Club.
Tel (0528) 84 43 43.

CASABLANCA

La Bodega
129–131 Rue Allal
Ben Abdellah.
Tel (0522) 54 18 42.

Carré Rouge
Avenue Assa.
Tel (0522) 39 25 10.

MARRAKECH

Theatro Hotel Essaadi
Avenue el Qadissa.
Tel (0524) 44 88 11.

RABAT

L'Amnesia
18 Rue Monastir.
Tel (0537) 73 52 03.

CASINO

CASABLANCA

Mazagan Beach Resort
El Jadida.
Tel (0523) 38 80 20/ 00.

MARRAKECH

La Mamounia
Bab el-Jedid.
Tel (0524) 38 86 00/ 35 61 09.

SPORTS & OUTDOOR ACTIVITIES

Morocco's mostly warm climate and great topographical diversity make it suitable for all sorts of sports and outdoor activities. The natural environment, often on a majestic scale, readily lends itself to horseback riding, trekking, birdwatching and, in winter, skiing. In areas suitably developed for the purpose, the Moroccan landscape is also a paradise for golfers.

The Atlantic coast is internationally renowned for surfing and sailboarding. Thalassotherapy (therapeutic treatment using sea water and marine products) has also developed, and thalassotherapy centres continue to burgeon in the major tourist centres.

The beach at Agadir, where horseback rides are available

HORSEBACK RIDING

Thanks to the impulse provided by King Hassan II, horseback riding has become very popular in Morocco. Many equestrian centres have been established, and an International Equestrian Week takes place every year in Dar es-Salam, near Rabat, where the **Fédération Royale Marocaine des Sports Equestres** is based.

Most horseback riding is organized by clubs and large hotels, mainly those in Agadir, Marrakech and Ouarzazate. All equestrian centres are staffed by instructors with state-approved qualifications.

SKIING

Although not primarily a winter sports destination, Morocco has several high-altitude resorts, including Ifrane *(see p212)*, near Fès, and Oukaïmeden *(see p248)*, 60 km (37 miles) from Marrakech. Oukaïmeden can be reached by *grand taxi* for a

one-way fare of about 400 dirhams. Although the resort is small, it is equipped with all the necessary facilities, including ski-lifts located near where ski equipment is hired. Hiring equipment for a day costs about 250 dirhams. Skiers can sleep in one of several gîtes. These elegant rest-houses are built in a combined European and traditional Moroccan style. There are not many areas of the country that are suitable for skiing, so this

remains a marginal activity in Morocco. Mountain resorts offer a diverse range of activities, however, including hang gliding, hiking and trekking *(see pp356–7)*. **Fédération Royale Marocaine de Ski et Montagne** can provide further information.

GOLF

Many overseas travel agents offer packaged golfing holidays. There are over 20 golf links in Morocco. Many are pleasant and popular. In addtion, there are the royal golf courses (which are open to the public) and numerous private courses, often forming part of hotel complexes, particularly in Agadir and Marrakech.

In April, the height of the holiday season, visitors are advised to book in advance so as to avoid a long wait. A handicap is theoretically required although in practice this is always overlooked. There are some excellent golf coaches in Morocco, and their services can be hired for much

Oukaïmeden *(see p248)*, renowned for its pistes

One of the many fine golf courses in Morocco

less than in Europe and the US. The low cost of tuition, combined with an often outstanding natural environment, are ideal conditions for an introduction to the sport. Further information can be obtained from the **Fédération Royale Marocaine de Golf**.

TENNIS

Almost all the large hotels have tennis courts. The major towns and cities are also well provided with tennis clubs. Most of them have beaten earth courts, of which the condition can vary. Around the courts it is not unusual to see young Moroccans, who readily offer their services as ball boys or tennis partners. Many are good players.

BIRD-WATCHING

Morocco offers many excellent opportunities for bird-watching, and many travellers, particularly Britons and Americans, tailor their visit around this interest.

The country has a small number of bird sanctuaries, the most important of them being at Souss Massa, south of Agadir *(see p292)*, and at Moulay Bousselham, north of Rabat *(see p90)*. The latter attracts large numbers of migratory birds, including some rare species.

Unfortunately, these areas are being threatened by the massive urban development that is spreading along the Moroccan coastline, despite the efforts of associations for the protection of birds.

OFF-ROAD DRIVING

Morocco is an excellent country for off-road activities, either in a four-wheel-drive vehicle or on a motorbike. The good network of tracks, even near large towns, means that the hinterland is always within easy reach.

It is, however, advisable to check your route thoroughly and preferable to travel in groups of two or more vehicles, since breaking down in a remote spot can be a real problem. Some areas, particularly in southern Morocco, near the border with Mauritania, are patrolled by the army and may be set with land mines. It is unwise to venture into this territory without the help of a reliable guide.

In Marrakech and Ouarzazate quad bikes and go-karts can be hired and **Wilderness Wheels** *(see p357)* organizes all-inclusive motorcycle excursions into the High Atlas mountains and the desert.

WATERSPORTS

For surfers, certain spots along Morocco's Atlantic coast are among the best in the world. Essaouira and its environs are the best-known locations, and these are Morocco's windsurfing and surfing centres, particularly in

Sailing, a popular sport off the Mediterranean coast

DIRECTORY

HORSEBACK RIDING

Fédération Royale Marocaine des Sports Equestres
Tel (0537) 75 44 24 (Rabat).

SKIING

Fédération Royale Marocaine de Ski et Montagne
Tel (0522) 47 49 79 (Casablanca).

GOLF

Fédération Royale Marocaine de Golf
Tel (0537) 75 59 60 (Rabat).

WATERSPORTS

Club Mistral
www.club-mistral.com (Essaouira).

Fédération Royale Marocaine de Jet Ski et Ski Nautique
Tel (0537) 70 43 15/20 (Rabat).

summer. Dakhla has also become very popular for kite-surfing. Most of these places are, however, suitable only for experienced surfers. Strong winds, currents and high waves are not safe for beginners.

The best surfing beaches are also on the Atlantic coast. In summer, the beaches between Agadir and Essaouira are overrun by surfers from all over the world. A particularly popular beach is La Madrague, near Taghazout, 20 km (12 miles) north of Agadir. There is also a surfing centre, **Club Mistral**, in Essaouira.

For less strenuous watersports, there are also some very fine beaches all along the Atlantic and Mediterranean coasts. Sailing boats and jet-skis can be hired on the latter.

Information on water-skiing, which is also available, can be obtained from the **Fédération Royale Marocaine de Jet Ski et Ski Nautique**.

Hiking and Trekking

Cotton sun hat

In the space of a few years, Morocco has become a paradise for hikers. The country's spectacular and varied landscape offers great scope for hikers and trekkers of all abilities. However, any hiking or trekking expedition requires preparation. It is essential to take proper equipment, and basic safety precautions must be observed. Options are many – whether to go on an organized or an independent trek, and whether or not to have porters: luggage carried by mule, camel or vehicle. The most important decision is the choice of route through Morocco's numerous and highly diverse geographical regions.

A hike in the South, with luggage carried by camels

Mountain biking, an increasingly popular activity in Morocco

BASIC SAFETY PRECAUTIONS

The first consideration is your physical condition. You must be able to withstand the sometimes arduous demands of a long trek. Do not venture even a little way off the beaten track without a reliable guide, or unless you are on a well-organized trek. Never set off alone, and if you are not part of an organized party, inform your next of kin or your country's embassy of your intended date of return so that emergency aid can be sent if necessary. The cost of mountain rescue in the more remote regions of Morocco is very high. Check your personal insurance to see whether it will cover you for this type of risk.

By far the best option is to let a specialist agency arrange your hike or trek. This may be a Western tour operator or one of the specialist agencies in Morocco. Using their infrastructure and logistics will give you peace of mind.

EQUIPMENT

The most important piece of equipment is a good pair of walking boots. Even though ordinary trainers may be quite adequate for a short walk on even ground, a strong pair of walking boots is essential for longer and more demanding walking over rough ground.

As for clothing, strong, lightweight fabrics are the best choice. Although it rarely rains in Morocco, it is prudent to pack a rainproof garment as well as a few warm clothes, since temperatures drop quickly at high altitudes. Finally, even for a short walk, always take enough water, and something to eat.

A first-aid kit is also necessary. The minimum that it should contain is treatment for minor cuts and blisters. More adequate first-aid equipment will also include anti-venom treatment, insect repellent, antihistamine for allergies, aspirins and sunblock cream.

For nights in a tent or in the open air, a good-quality body-hugging sleeping bag is recommended. Check carefully its insulating properties, but bear in mind that you will still need a light mattress to insulate you from cold or wet ground.

Finally, it is the small things that can be the most useful. Head lamps, for example, give you light while also leaving your hands free. Also remember to pack water-purifying tablets, so that you can drink from springs and refreshing mountain streams along the way.

TYPES OF HIKING

Some hikes are organized with the advantage of using animals to carry equipment. Hikes with mules take place in the Atlas, a region where this animal is particularly at home. Further south, camels are used to carry luggage and food supplies. Caravans of camels are a common sight here, particularly south of Zagora.

It is also possible to go on combined treks, alternating walking with mountain biking, or with canoeing or rafting. Vehicle-assisted treks allow greater distances to be

Participants in the Marathon des Sables

Four-wheel-drive vehicles, essential for negotiating rough tracks

covered. More luggage can also be carried, which means that camping can be much more comfortable.

POPULAR ROUTES

The main regions of Morocco that are most suitable for trekking and hiking are the Atlantic coast; the Middle Atlas, High Atlas and Atlantic slopes of the Atlas; Jbel Sirwa and Jbel Sarhro; the valleys of Wadi Draa, Wadi Dadès and Wadi Tafilalet; and the Saharan provinces of the South.

In the High Atlas, Jbel Toubkal, which reaches a height of 4,167 m (13,676 ft), is the highest point in North Africa (see p249). The mountain offers great scope for hikes. The summit can be reached in two days and climbing it does not require a high level of experience as a mountaineer. The only disadvantage is the fact that this is where most hikers come in the high season, so you will not be alone. The **Club Alpin Français** manages five refuges on Jbel Toubkal.

In the central High Atlas, the Aït Bouguemez valley (see pp254–7) offers a very fine itinerary. The route is not very demanding and passes through a striking variety of different landscapes. This expedition to the deep heart of Berber country takes five to six days, and the starting point is Demnate, four hours' drive from Marrakech.

On the other side of the Atlas, there are hikes that combine Jbel Sarhro, the foothills at the edge of the

Sahara, and the sublime Dadès gorge (see p273), one of the great attractions of the Moroccan South.

Many camel treks take place southwest of Zagora, their ultimate destination being Mhamid and Iriki, where the first dunes of the immense Sahara can be seen. Further east, towards Erfoud (see p280), the spectacular Merzouga dunes (see p281) offer many possibilities for hikes and camel rides through unforgettable scenery.

MARATHON DES SABLES

This long-distance race takes place in the Ouarzazate region every year. About 700 competitors from all over the world take part. The route covers 230 km (143 miles) and the race lasts seven days. Each competitor carries his or her own food and equipment. The Marathon des Sables is considered to be the most demanding race of its kind in the world.

Jbel Toubkal, to which large numbers of hikers are drawn

DIRECTORY

SPECIALIST TOUR OPERATORS

Backroads
801 Cedar Street, Berkeley, CA 94710-1800, USA.
Tel 1-800 228 8747.

Discover
Timbers, Oxted Road, Godstone, Surrey RH9 8AD, UK.
Tel 01883 744 392.
www.kasbahdutoubkal.com

Exodus
9 Weir Rd, London SW12 0LT, UK.
Tel 020 8675 5550.
www.exodus.co.uk

Morocco Travel International
5146 Leesburgh Pike, Alexandria, VA 22302, USA.
Tel 1-800 428 5550.

Overseas Adventure Travel
625 Mount Auburn St, Cambridge, MA 02138, USA.
Tel 1-800 221 0814.

Ramblers Holidays
Box 34, Welwyn Garden City, Herts, AL8 6PQ, UK.
Tel 01707 331 133.
www.ramblersholidays.co.uk

Sherpa Expeditions
131a Heston Road, Hounslow, Middlesex TW5 0RD, UK.
Tel 020 8577 2717.
www.sherpaexpeditions.com

AGENCIES IN MOROCCO

Atlas Sahara Trek
6 bis Rue HoudHoud, Majorelle Quarter, Marrakech.
Tel (0524) 31 39 01.

Club Alpin Français
BP 6178, Casablanca.
Tel (0522) 99 01 41.

Sport Travel
Third floor, 154 Boulevard Mohammed V, Gueliz, Marrakech.
Tel (0524) 43 63 69.
www.sporttravel-maroc.com

Wilderness Wheels
Tel (0524) 88 81 28 (Ouarzazate).
www.wildernesswheels.com

SURVIVAL
GUIDE

PRACTICAL INFORMATION 360–369
TRAVEL INFORMATION 370–377

PRACTICAL INFORMATION

Morocco, a country with a wide range of attractions, receives a large number of visitors. Much of its economic success is due to tourism. The country has a good tourism infrastructure and tourist offices, both at home and abroad. Moroccan hotels have undergone major restructuring and many regions have significantly increased their capacity to

Berber from the Sahara

accommodate visitors. The major museums and historic monuments have been reorganized so as to be seen to their best advantage by the maximum number of visitors. Customs formalities are minimal and while French is the most widely spoken foreign language, at least the bigger hotels and restaurants and all tourist offices have English-speaking staff.

Summer crowds on the beach at Casablanca

WHEN TO GO

Morocco is a relatively large country with a varied climate, ranging from the arid, desert conditions of the south to the Mediterranean climate of the north (see pp42–3).

The peak of the tourist season in the South, is in spring, from March to mid-May, and, to a lesser extent, in the early autumn, in September and October. At those times, visitors can enjoy many hours of sunshine and almost no rain.

Summer is the best time to visit the Mediterranean and Atlantic coasts. The South and the Centre, where the heat is then intense, are best avoided. Even when the winters are mild they are still very cold, and snowfall at high altitude, which can close passes, may interfere with your itinerary.

RESERVATIONS

Morocco is a fashionable tourist destination, and the publicity campaigns that are mounted to advertise its

attractions are effective in attracting large numbers of visitors. Some 6 million tourists visit Morocco each year.

Most months are busy and hotel reservations have become essential. It is best to arrange your visit several months in advance in so as to be able to use the most direct flights and the most convenient schedules, and particularly if you want to reserve a room in smaller hotels and guesthouses, which have more character and which get booked up quickly.

TOURIST INFORMATION

All the major tourist centres in Morocco have a branch of the Office National Marocain du Tourisme (ONMT), which often goes under the name "Délégation Générale du Tourisme". Smaller towns have a Syndicat d'Initiative (tourist bureau). These bureaux provide information on the

town's principal features of interest, and the addresses of hotels and restaurants. Official guides are also usually available. The Délégations Générales and Syndicats d'Initiative are open from 8:30am to noon and from 2:30 to 6:30pm. During Ramadan and in summer, in the busiest towns and cities they are open continuously from 9am to 5pm. Before leaving home, you may also wish to contact the Moroccan tourist office in your own country.

ENTRY CHARGES AND OPENING HOURS

Tourist brochure

An entry charge (usually about 10 to 20 dirhams) is made for museums and historic sites and buildings. When entry is free, it is customary to give the caretaker a tip equal to the average value of an entry ticket.

Opening hours can be irregular. Tourist sites are generally open from 9am to noon and from 3 to 6pm. However, these times may change during Ramadan and at times of the year when the heat is very intense. The opening of smaller sites sometimes depends on the goodwill of the caretaker.

PASSPORTS AND VISAS

Citizens of the European Union, Swiss nationals and citizens of the United States, Canada, Australia and New

◁ Horse-drawn carriages on Place el-Hedime in Meknès

Entrance to the Dar Si Saïd Museum in Marrakech

Zealand need a valid passport to visit Morocco. A passport, which should be valid for at least six months after the date of your arrival, allows you to stay in Morocco for three months. If this period is exceeded, the authorities react strictly and at the very least will escort you back to the frontier.

If you intend to stay in Morocco for more than three months, you will need to obtain a visa. Information on entry formalities is available from the Moroccan Consulate in your home country.

The border with Algeria is closed, but visas for Mauritania can be obtained quickly in Casablanca.

CUSTOMS

During your flight to Morocco, or when you arrive at the border, you will

be handed a customs declaration form which you should fill in and hand over at passport control. You are legally entitled to bring into the country 200 cigarettes, 75 cl of alcohol and small quantities of photographic material and video equipment.

Drugs, firearms and pornographic material are strictly prohibited. Permission must be obtained to bring in hunting weapons.

Importing a vehicle for a limited period is possible but the formalities are very lengthy. The vehicle should be registered in your exact first name and surname.

LANGUAGE

The official language is Arabic, which is spoken by almost all Moroccans. French, a vestige of the Protectorate, is also very widely used, at least in large towns. It is less current in country areas, except among older people. In the South, Berber is widely spoken, especially in rural and mountainous areas.

Because of the city's proximity to Spain, Spanish is widely understood in Tangier, and is spoken in the Spanish enclaves. German is most often heard in Agadir, which attracts large numbers of Germans. English is spoken only by those closely involved in the tourist industry, such as guides and certain staff in the larger hotels.

DIRECTORY

EMBASSIES IN MOROCCO

Canada
13 Bis, Rue Jaafar As-Sadik, Rabat.
Tel (0537) 68 74 00.

United Kingdom
Ave SAR Sidi Mohamed, Rabat.
Tel (0537) 63 33 33.

United States
2 Avenue Mohamed el-Fassi,
Rabat. **Tel** (0537) 76 22 65.

CONSULATES IN MOROCCO

United Kingdom
9 Rue Amérique du Sud, Tangier.
Tel (0539) 93 69 39.
British Commercial Consulate,
36 Rue de la Loire, Casablanca.
Tel (0522) 85 74 00.

United States
8 Boulevard Moulay Youssef,
Casablanca.
Tel (0522) 26 45 50.

Citizens of Australia and Eire may use the United Kingdom embassy and consulate. Citizens of New Zealand may use the Canadian embassy.

USEFUL WEBSITES

Adventures of Morocco
www.lexicorient.com/morocco
General information, maps, encyclopedia of Arabic words and useful links.

Conseil Régional du Tourisme
www.visitmarrakech.com

Office National Marocain du Tourisme
www.visitmorocco.com

Tourism in Morocco
www.tourism-in-Morocco.com
On tourist attractions and leisure activities.

US Consular Travel Advisory
travel.state.gov/morocco/html
Strictly practical matters, such as entry requirements for US citizens, personal safety, etc.

Trekkers following a high mountain trail in an arid region of Morocco

Etiquette

Moroccans are very friendly people. You will have many opportunities to talk to them, and may even be invited into their homes. However, Morocco is a Muslim country, and certain conventions must be observed to avoid inadvertently causing offence. It is especially important to dress appropriately, not to take photographs of Moroccans without their permission, and to avoid certain sensitive subjects in conversation. If you are invited into the home of a Moroccan family, it is as well to be aware of certain points of etiquette. Respecting a few simple rules will be appreciated by your naturally hospitable hosts.

Mint tea served to guests, one aspect of Moroccan hospitality

HOSPITALITY

Among Moroccans, hospitality is more than a tradition; it is an honour. After just a few minutes of conversation, traders in the souks and country people in the remotest regions of the Atlas may well invite you into their homes to drink a glass of tea or share a meal. It is difficult to decline these invitations, and a refusal may be interpreted as an offence.

When you enter a house, take your shoes off if shoes have already been left near the door; this is a sign of respect towards your host. It is often the men who will invite you in, although you are sure to see the women of the house as well, in which case avoid being over-familiar. Accepting an invitation from a trader in a souk puts you under no obligation to buy anything from him. Finally, even if you are invited in by Moroccans of very modest

means, never offer to pay for your meal. Offering a small gift is a far better and more acceptable way of thanking your hosts.

SHARING A MEAL

If you are invited to share a meal in the home of a Moroccan family, be prepared

Moroccans customarily eat with their right hand

to be plied with copious helpings of food. As with other invitations, it is difficult to refuse first, let alone second, helpings of food.

People usually eat with their fingers, with the additional aid of a piece of bread. If you cannot master the technique, you will be given eating implements. When eating, you should use your right hand since the left hand, used for personal hygiene, is traditionally considered to be impure.

A Moroccan meal invariably ends with mint tea. It is not unusual to drink three or four glasses of this very sweet infusion. Again, the offer is very hard to refuse.

PHOTOGRAPHY

You can take photographs almost anywhere in Morocco. In some museums, a supplementary fee is charged if you want to take photographs, and in others photography is forbidden.

Avoid taking pictures of military or official buildings since this may result in your film being confiscated and your being questioned at length about what you were trying to photograph.

Before turning the lens on anyone, always ask the person's permission, since Moroccans have an ingrained suspicion of any type of image. Bear in mind that anyone who agrees to your photographing them may ask you for a little money, especially in the major tourist spots.

MUSLIM CUSTOMS

Islam is a state religion, and the king of Morocco is the leader of the faithful. It is thus considered very bad form to criticize religion. It is also ill-mannered to disturb someone while they are at prayer, whether by speaking to them or by taking a photograph of them.

It is above all during Ramadan that certain rules must be obeyed. The fast of Ramadan is strictly observed in Morocco. Although non-Muslims may eat, drink and

The Grand Mosque in Casablanca, open to non-Muslims

smoke whenever they please, they should avoid doing so in public. Lastly, couples in the street must behave with decorum; they should not kiss in public, for example.

VISITING MOSQUES

All mosques, except the Grand Mosque in Casablanca and the old Tin Mal Mosque, are closed to non-Muslims. When visiting these mosques, remove your shoes and behave in a respectful manner, appropriate to the holy nature of the building.

Never insist on being admitted to a mosque and do not try to see inside it by peeping through the door. Acting like this is likely to be considered sacrilegious.

DRESS

Attitudes towards dress have changed significantly in Morocco, so that, in large towns and cities, it is far from unusual to see Moroccan women in Western-style dress. Even so, scanty clothing should not be worn when exploring traditional quarters of towns or venturing into the country. Very short skirts, shorts and clothes that leave the shoulders or chest bare are likely to cause deep offence to Moroccans. For women, wearing a headscarf may help avoid unwanted attention. Women going topless, on the beach or in the swimming pool, is severely frowned on. Nudity is strictly forbidden in Morocco, and nudists run the risk of being arrested.

THE MONARCHY

Since the accession of Mohammed VI, attitudes towards the monarchy are now much more relaxed. You may even hear Moroccans openly criticizing the king. Even so, the subject of the monarchy is surrounded by a great deal of taboo in Morocco. As a general rule, do not express too trenchant an opinion on the subject and never show disrespect towards the king's image,

which can be seen hanging in all shops and public places. Lastly, be aware that the Moroccans are very patriotic and that any discussion of their country can quickly become heated.

BARGAINING

You may bitterly disappoint a trader if you do not show a willingness to indulge in the ritual of bargaining, another Moroccan custom.

Bargaining revolves around the considerable difference between the price quoted by the buyer and that offered by the seller and the slow process by which both sides arrive at a mutually fair figure.

When bargaining, you should keep smiling since the whole process is treated as a game.

Moroccan women, customarily fully dressed, on the beach

SMOKING

Public places very rarely have no-smoking areas. However, smoking is now prohibited in most buses and modern cinemas.

Except in large towns and cities, where attitudes have changed, it may still be con-sidered shocking for women to smoke in public. Smoking *kif* (marijuana) is technically illegal, and it is best to avoid any contact with dealers.

Tourist negotiating the price of a camel ride

Health and Security

Mosquito repellent

Crime in Morocco is no worse than elsewhere and most visitors will experience no serious problems. The fact that the police have a high-profile presence contributes to this degree of personal safety. As in any other country, a few basic precautions should be taken so as to avoid the attentions of pickpockets. Visitors should also be aware that drug-taking, especially in the north of the country, is one of the prime threats to personal safety. The best policy is to have nothing whatsoever to do with drugs, however mild. While the standard of Morocco's public hospitals is uneven, private clinics are very expensive. It is advisable to take out health insurance in your own country before you leave.

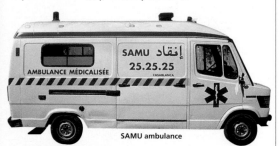

SAMU ambulance

VACCINATIONS AND MINOR HEALTH RISKS

No vaccinations are required for visitors entering Morocco, except for those coming from a country where yellow fever exists. However, vaccination against hepatitis A and B and typhoid is advised. Visiting certain regions of southern Morocco in summer carries a slight risk of exposure to malaria; anti-malaria pills are available locally.

However long you plan to stay in Morocco, and wherever you intend to go, take a first-aid kit with you. It should include gauze, bandages, antiseptic and syringes, particularly if you intend to spend any time in sparsely inhabited rural areas.

To prevent sunstroke, drink plenty of water, wear a hat and use a sunblock with a high UV-protection factor.

MEDICAL CARE

Although most public hospitals in Morocco have excellent specialist doctors,

they are underfunded and lacking in equipment. Standards of hygiene are also unsatisfactory.

If you have the option, choose a private clinic. Although these are expensive, standards of care are close to European ones. Your country's embassy or consulate will provide a list of approved doctors and hospitals.

EMERGENCIES

In the case of accidents that occur in the home or on the public highway, the fire brigade is the first to attend the scene. Its ambulances are usually run by the Moroccan Red Crescent and they are marked "ambulance".

In the case of medical emergencies that occur in the street, SAMU ambulances will take you to the nearest hospital. Tell the ambulance or taxi driver to which (private)

hospital or clinic you wish to go, otherwise you will be taken automatically to the nearest public hospital. In remote regions, the only way of reaching a hospital is to hire a taxi.

PHARMACIES

All pharmacies in Morocco are denoted by a sign in the form of a crescent. Duty pharmacies are open on Sundays, and their address is posted in the window of pharmacies that are closed. In large towns and cities, duty pharmacies stay open round the clock.

Pharmacies have helpful, knowledgeable staff who are able to give advice on minor health problems. Certain medicines that can only be obtained on prescription in Europe are available over the counter in Morocco.

FOOD AND WATER

Many visitors to Morocco suffer from stomach upsets, which are often caused by the change of diet. Avoid drinking tap water, especially in rural areas, and keep to bottled mineral water *(see p327)*. Make sure that the bottle is opened in front of you. Do not add ice to any drink and avoid diluted fruit juices.

On hikes and treks take water-purifying tablets to make spring water safe to drink. Alternatively, boil the water for 20 minutes. Be wary of salads and raw vegetables, and of unpeeled fruit and vegetables. They should be washed carefully. Food prepared at street stalls is another potential hazard. Although it is usually safe,

Pharmacy sign

A fire brigade vehicle

A pharmacy in Essaouira

as long as it is freshly cooked, people with delicate stomachs are advised to resist it.

Fortunately, Moroccans like their meat well cooked. This destroys such parasites as tapeworms, which are rampant in Morocco.

INSECTS

There are no particularly harmful insects in Morocco, but scorpions, snakes, cockroaches and spiders are common in the countryside. Check your clothes and shoes before dressing, particularly when camping in rural areas.

If you are bitten by a snake or stung by a scorpion, apply a suction pump to the wound. These devices are sold in pharmacies all over the country.

Mosquitoes can be particularly bad in desert oases. An effective mosquito repellent is essential, especially in summer.

SERIOUS ILLNESS

Being careful about what you eat should stop you contracting cholera. In case of serious diarrhoea that persists after taking ordinary medication, consult a doctor without delay.

Stray animals – especially dogs, which roam the streets of large towns during the night – may carry rabies. If you are bitten, it is essential to seek first aid immediately.

Although the authorities deny it, sexually transmitted diseases such as AIDS are spreading in Morocco. The use of condoms (which are available in all pharmacies) is strongly advised.

PERSONAL SAFETY

Violence is rare throughout Morocco, and it is safe to go anywhere with no great risk to personal safety. Serious theft and burglary are a widespread problem; this is because of the large number of caretakers who supplement the work of the police and act as an effective deterrent.

However, pickpockets with finely honed techniques are likely to patrol the souks, and unwary tourists are the most likely targets. If you are the victim of theft, report it

immediately at the nearest police station. If you intend to make an insurance claim, ask to be given a copy of the police record of the incident; this should be written in French rather than Arabic.

POLICE

Policemen are omnipresent both in towns and cities and on the roads in Morocco, and they have considerable powers. Uniformed police officers, traffic police on the roads and numerous plain-clothes officers are present everywhere.

The Moroccan police, who once had a reputation for corruption, have adopted a very courteous attitude in their dealings with tourists.

In the case of more serious problems, you should contact your country's consulate *(see p361)* as soon as possible. The consulate will give you advice and assistance in dealing with the finer details of the Moroccan legal system.

Entrance to the Hôpital Ibn Rochd in Casablanca

Banking and Currency

Logo of Banque
Centrale
Populaire

Moroccan currency cannot be obtained abroad. On your arrival in the country, you will find many exchange offices where you can easily obtain dirhams. With an international banker's card you will also be able to draw money from automatic cash dispensers, as well as over the counter in banks that do not have ATMs. In country areas it can sometimes be difficult to change foreign currency, and shopkeepers and traders are seldom able to give change for high-denomination banknotes. It is also useful to keep a collection of coins for small purchases.

A branch of the French bank Société Générale

BANKS

Morocco's main banks are Banque Marocaine du Commerce Extérieur (**BMCE**), Banque Marocaine du Commerce et de l'Industrie (**BMCI**), **Attijariwafa Bank** and **Crédit du Maroc**. Most of them either have agreements with certain large international banks, such as **Citibank** and the French bank **Société Générale**, or are their subsidiaries. There are branches throughout the country. Small towns usually have only one bank, and there are no banks at all in rural areas.

Banks are open continuously from 8am to about 4pm, Monday to Friday including Ramadan.

AUTOMATIC CASH DISPENSERS

In large towns, automatic cash dispensers (ATMs) are becoming increasingly easy to find. Most have instructions in several languages, and a notice or sticker lists those cards – Visa, Eurocard and MasterCard – that are accepted.

Some dispensers give cash only against accounts that are held in Morocco and may swallow your international card if you insert it by mistake. Cash dispensers give out dirhams, and there is often an upper limit to individual withdrawals. The machines do not always work properly, and it is advisable to withdraw money during bank opening hours so that you can retrieve your card immediately in the event of any problems arising.

Banks in Morocco charge commission for foreign cash withdrawals, usually between 4.50 and 7 dirhams, regardless of how much is withdrawn. Obtain information on charges from your bank and avoid making frequent withdrawals of small amounts. If the cash dispenser fails to work, most banks will issue cash over the counter to holders of a banker's card.

Automatic cash dispenser

DIRECTORY

MOROCCAN BANKS

Attijariwafa Bank
2 Bd My-Youssef,
Casablanca.
Tel (0522) 29 88 88 or
(0522) 22 41 69.

BMCE Bank
140 Avenue Hassan II,
Casablanca.
Tel (0522) 20 04 20.

BMCI
26 Place des Nations Unies,
Casablanca.
Tel (0522) 46 10 00.

Crédit du Maroc
48/58 Boulevard Mohammed V,
Casablanca.
Tel (0522) 47 70 00.

FOREIGN BANKS

Citibank
Lotissement Attaoufik,
Zenith Millenium, Immeuble 1,
Sidi Maarouf,
Casablanca.
Tel (0522) 48 96 00.

Société Générale
55 Boulevard Abdelmoumen,
Casablanca.
Tel (0522) 43 88 88.

BUREAUX DE CHANGE

Bureaux de change can be found in almost all banks, in hotels with a grading of three stars and upwards, and at airports. The exchange rate is uniform and variations in the commission charged are unusual. To avoid queueing, it is often best to change money at a hotel. While exchange offices in hotels and airports are open almost permanently, those attached to a bank have the same opening hours as the bank's.

When changing money, you will usually be asked to show your passport. All foreign currencies are accepted, but the euro and the dollar are the preferred currencies. Worn and torn banknotes are not accepted as a matter of policy. In the major tourist centres, money-changers may offer you their services in the street at a preferential rate, but it is best to decline the offer.

You can change back any dirhams that you have over at the end of your stay, although the exchange rate will be poor and, unlike dollars and euros, pounds sterling are not always available.

CREDIT CARDS

Most reasonably comfortable hotels (usually those with a rating of three stars and above), as well as mainstream restaurants in large towns, and certain stores (usually those in the most upmarket bracket) accept credit cards for payments.

TRAVELLER'S CHEQUES

The safest way of carrying money when travelling is still in the form of traveller's cheques (in sterling, euros or dollars). Traveller's cheques are accepted at almost all exchange offices and in most large hotels.

CURRENCY

The Moroccan unit of currency is the dirham (Dh in its abbreviated form), which is divided into 100 centimes. Banknotes are issued in the following denominations: 20, 50, 100 and 200 dirhams. Coins are issued in denominations of 5, 10, 20 and 50 centimes, and of 1, 2, 5 and 10 dirhams.

Notes and coins are inscribed in French and Arabic. In rural areas and in souks it is very difficult to obtain change for large-denomination notes. Always carry small change to cover ordinary purchases.

Both banknotes and coins bear the likeness of King Mohammed VI or of his father Hassan II. It is considered sacrilegious to tear or damage them. Any coin or banknote where the sovereign's portrait is defaced in any way may even be refused.

In some areas, especially in the countryside, prices are given in riales (or reales) instead of in centimes. One rial equals 5 centimes, but it is a purely conceptual unit: there are no rial coins.

Coins

Coins come in denominatons of 5, 10, 20 and 50 centimes and of 1, 2, 5 and 10 dirhams. While centime coins are not widely used, 1-dirham coins are handy, especially for paying someone to guard your car and for occasional tips.

10 dirhams   5 dirhams   2 dirhams

1 dirham   50 centimes   20 centimes   10 centimes   5 centimes

Banknotes

Banknotes are issued in denominations of 20 dirhams, 50 dirhams, 100 dirhams and 200 dirhams.

20-dirham note

50-dirham note

100-dirham note

200-dirham note

Communications

www 2m tv
**Logo of a
television channel**

Morocco's telephone network is run by national operators Maroc Télécom, Meditel and Wana. The network has developed significantly and provides an efficient service, despite occasional problems. The use of mobile telephones is widespread. Postal services are generally reliable, although deliveries can be subject to long delays. Moroccan television is fighting a losing battle against satellite channels and foreign programmes. Newspapers, many of which are in French, cover current affairs both in Morocco and on the international stage.

A *téléboutique*, where telephone calls can be made and faxes sent

Typical yellow postbox

PUBLIC TELEPHONES

Public phone boxes, which are relatively rare, are usually located outside post offices, markets and bus stations. Coin-operated telephones are still relatively common, and they take coins up to a denomination of 5 dirhams. Because of the number of coins needed, it is not practical to make international calls from a coin-operated telephone. Such calls are best made from a card-operated telephone. Phonecards are available at post offices and in tobacconists, which are indicated by a blue and white sign with three interlinked rings.

With some telephones, an illegal card rental system applies. The cardholder inserts the phonecard for you, noting the number of existing units on the card. You make the call, and then pay the cost (based on the difference between the number of units on the card before and after your call). Calls made by this method are more expensive but obviate the need to buy a whole card.

Moroccan phonecard

PUBLIC TELEPHONE CENTRES

The number of small public telephone centres, known as *téléboutiques*, has mushroomed in Morocco. These centres are run either by private operators or by one of the three national operators. They house plastic phone boxes or kiosks (which are usually a sandy colour) with card-operated, coin-operated or metered telephones. The cards that are sold here often only work in telephones in the centre from which the card was bought or in telephones owned by the relevant operator. Faxes can also usually be sent and received in these public telephone centres.

MOBILE PHONES

Almost everyone, it seems, has a mobile phone in Morocco. The three competing network operators – Méditel, Maroc Télécom and Wana – are locked in a fierce price war.

The network is excellent and mobile phones can be used in even the most remote regions of the country.

Most European network operators have arrangements with one or other of the two Moroccan network operators, so that visitors can use their mobile phones in Morocco (but bear in mind that calls will be expensive).

Mobile-phone users may also buy a prepaid SIM card from either of the Moroccan network operators. For a modest charge (no more than about 200 dirhams), you are provided with a Moroccan number through which national and international calls can be made at a more favourable rates.

USEFUL DIALLING CODES

- Telephone numbers consist of ten digits, and the country is divided into two zones (052 and 053).
  – Casablanca zone: 0522 + 6 digits
  – Rabat zone: 0537 + 6 digits
  – Marrakech zone: 0524 + 6 digits
  – Fès zone: 0535 + 6 digits.
- Always dial ten digits, whether calling from one zone to another or within a single zone.
- To call Morocco from abroad: dial 00 212 + nine digits (the ten-digit number minus the initial 0).
- To dial internationally: dial 00 + country code + telephone number.

An Internet café in a large town in Morocco

INTERNET CAFES

In large towns, it is increasingly common to find Internet cafés. Here, you can pick up and send e-mail and surf the Internet. Charges vary widely between different cybercafés, and are calculated according to the time spent on line.

POSTAL SERVICE

Morocco's postal service has a reputation for being very slow. This is often borne out by reality, especially in the case of international mail.

There are post offices in all sizeable towns. Here, you can buy stamps, send letters and parcels and cash, or send postal orders. Stamps are also

Moroccan postage stamps

available in tobacconists and at the reception desk of large hotels. Central post offices are open from 8.30am to 4pm. Sub-post offices close at lunchtime; precise times vary according to location.

Post offices also provide an express mail delivery service.

Newspaper vendor's display

However, if you have something urgent to send, it is better to use a private company such as **DHL Worldwide Express** or **Globex (Federal Express)**. It is also best to post letters at a central post office rather than use one of the yellow street postboxes as collections can be unreliable.

POSTE RESTANTE

Most post offices provide a poste restante service, and this system works well in Morocco. Mail should bear the first name and surname of the recipient, as well as the name of the town. You will need some form of identification when collecting mail from a poste restante. The service is free of charge.

NEWSPAPERS

Morocco has many daily newspapers in Arabic and in French. The major leading newspapers in French are *Le Matin du Sahara*, *L'Opinion*, *Libération* and *El-Bayane*. Several weekly magazines, such as *Maroc Hebdo*, *Tel Quel and Le Temps*, or the quarterly publications such as *Medina*, *Femmes du Maroc* and *Citadine* have given a new voice to the Moroccan press, which is usually quite conservative.

French newspapers like *Le Monde* and *Le Figaro* are printed in Casablanca at the same time as in France. English-language newspapers are available in Tangier, Agadir, Casablanca and Marrakech. Outside large towns you often find outdated daily newspapers on sale.

TELEVISION AND RADIO

Morocco has two television channels: Radio Télévision Marocaine (RTM), the public national channel that

DIRECTORY

DHL Worldwide Express
114 Lotissement La Colline, Sidi Maarouf, Casablanca.
Tel (0522) 97 20 20.

Globex (Federal Express)
La Colline Casablanca Business Centre, Sidi Maarouf.

Internet Cafés
Fès el-Jedid: Cyber Internet, 42 Rue des Etats Unis.
Marrakech: Cyber Behja, 27 Rue Bani Marine (in the medina); Cybercafé Hivernage, 106 bis Rue Yougoslavie (in Gueliz).
Rabat: Student Cyber, 83 Avenue Hassan II.
Tangier: Futurescope, 8 Rue Youssoufia.

Telegrams
Tel 140.

Telephone Information
Tel 160.

Medina, the quarterly magazine

broadcasts in Arabic and in French, and 2M, a privately run channel that also broadcasts in both languages, although programmes in French predominate.

Both the Moroccan television channels are, however, severely rivalled by the spread of satellite dishes, which provide access to a huge number of international channels. Most households, as well as upmarket hotels, have satellite dishes.

Broadcasts in English are obtainable only via satellite (mostly CNN and BBC). Around Tangier, it is also possible to tune in to broadcasts in English from Gibraltar.

After many years of state monopoly (by RTM and Médi 1), Moroccan radio has been liberalised and private stations such as Aswat and Radio Atlantic have been set up. It is also possible to tune into some European stations, including BBC World Service (on MHz 15,070) and Voice of America.

TRAVEL INFORMATION

The easiest way to reach Morocco is by air. The country is served by many regular flights from most major European cities and less frequent flights from North America. Internal flights link Morocco's major cities. During the high tourist season, many charter flights are also available. Getting to Morocco

Logo of Royal Air Maroc

by train or bus can be cheaper than travelling by air, but for most visitors the journey overland by these means is far too long to be practicable. It is also possible to reach Morocco by car and ship. Using your own car also saves the cost of hiring one on arrival in Morocco, which can be quite expensive.

A Royal Air Maroc aircraft taking off from Ouarzazate airport

ARRIVING BY AIR

Morocco has ten international airports. The busiest are those at Casablanca, Marrakech and Agadir. **Royal Air Maroc** (RAM), the national carrier, provides many links between Morocco and Europe, including departures from provincial cities, and a less frequent service between North America and Casablanca.

RAM provides flights from London Heathrow to Casablanca, Marrakech, Ouarzazate and Agadir, and from London Stansted to Marrakech. **EasyJet** serves Tangier, Marrakech and Agadir from London Gatwick. **Ryanair** flies to Marrakech from London Luton and to Fès from Frankfurt. **British Airways** operates flights to Marrakech from Gatwick. **BMI** serves Casablanca and Marrakech from Heathrow.

From North America, RAM flies three times a week from Montreal and New York JFK to Casablanca. From other North American cities, the best links are via London or Paris.

There are no direct flights to Morocco from Australia or New Zealand. Connections

can be made either via Singapore to Casablanca or via Dubai to Casablanca, or by flying to London.

During the high tourist season, many charter flights supplement scheduled services. Most charter flights serve Marrakech, Agadir and Ouarzazate. As part of the "Open Sky" agreement, low cost airlines can now fly to Marrakech. As well as Ryanair, these include EasyJet, Aigle Azur, Corsair and Jet4You.

Many tour operators offer economical package deals including flights and accommodation in hotels, villas or resorts. The deals may also include guided tours, desert trips, activity and sporting holidays, and trekking. Specialist tour operators offer all this and can provide tailor-made arrangements.

CASABLANCA AIRPORT

Mohammed V Airport in Casablanca is Morocco's main airport, both in terms of its size and of the

volume of traffic that it handles. Most international flights arrive in and depart from Casablanca, and many flights serving other cities in Morocco touch down here. Internal flights to smaller airports – at Agadir, Marrakech, Ouarzazate, Fès, Oujda and Essaouira – also depart from Mohammed V Airport. The airport is located about 30 km (19 miles) south of the city centre, and is served by efficient bus and train services.

MARRAKECH AIRPORT

Rebuilt and considerably enlarged, Marrakech-Ménara Airport is now able to handle a large volume of flights and passengers. Located not more than a few kilometres southwest of the city centre, it is very easy to reach by bus or taxi. Charter flights make up most of its traffic, although it also handles many scheduled flights.

AIRPORT LINKS

Mohammed V Airport, outside Casablanca, is served by bus and train links (there is one train service every hour). By contrast, the only way of reaching certain other airports is by taxi from the town centre. Only the *grands*

Ferry in the Straits of Gibraltar

taxis are permitted to wait for passengers at airports. The fact that they hold a monopoly allows them to charge relatively high fares, and they are unwilling to bargain. Airports are well provided with car-hire companies, and if you plan to travel around during your stay, you can hire a car upon arrival at the airport.

To reach an airport from a city centre, you can hire a *grand taxi*.

Sign for Casablanca's Mohammed V Airport

ARRIVING BY CAR AND FERRY

Several ferry companies provide various sea links between Spain and Morocco, including the Spanish Transmediterránea and the Moroccan Comarit. Their UK agent **Southern Ferries** has schedules and prices. The crossing from Algeciras, in Spain, to Tangier or Ceuta (the Spanish enclave in Morocco) takes about two hours but boarding can be very slow, especially in summer, when Moroccans working abroad return home.

Ferry tickets can be purchased in advance or at the time of travel. In either case, the time spent queuing is the same. The adult fare is about €40. Taking a car across costs between about €90 and €180 depending on its size. Most travellers take the ferry from Algeciras to Tangier, since services from here are more frequent,

but there are also ferry links to Tangier and to Melilla from Málaga and Almería; to Ceuta from Malaga; and to Tangier from Gibraltar.

In Spain, you need to collect an exit form before boarding. On leaving Morocco, you need to fill in an embarkation form and have this and your passport stamped before boarding the ferry.

ARRIVING BY TRAIN

Travelling by train means a long but scenic journey. From London, take the Eurostar to Paris, from where there is a daily TGV service to Algeciras, in Spain, changing at Irún, on the Spanish border. This is run by the French SNCF, but tickets (including Eurostar) can be bought at **European Rail Ltd** and **Rail Europe**. Holders of an InterRail card, which allows travel in 29 European countries (Spain, Portugal and Morocco are treated as a single zone), can break their journey anywhere they wish.

The fare from Paris to Algeciras is about 155 euros (£97). Avoid train services that go via Barcelona, as links between Catalonia and Algeciras are poor. It is better to use a service that goes via Madrid. From Algeciras, there are ferry services to Tangier and to Ceuta *(see Arriving by Car and Ferry, left)*.

DIRECTORY

AIRLINES

BMI
www.flybmi.com

British Airways
www.britishairways.com

EasyJet
www.easyjet.com

Royal Air Maroc (RAM)
www.royalairmaroc.com

Ryanair
www.ryanair.com

FERRY COMPANIES

Southern Ferries
179 Piccadilly, London W1V 9DB.
Tel (020) 7491 4968.

RAILWAYS

European Rail Ltd.
Tel (020) 7387 0444.
www.europeanrail.com

Rail Europe
179 Piccadilly, London W1V 9DB.
Tel (0870) 584 8848.
www.raileurope.com

TOUR OPERATORS

Best of Morocco
Seend Park, Wiltshire SN12 6NZ.
Tel (01380) 828 533.
www.morocco-travel.com

Cagodan Holidays
9–10 Portland Street,
Southampton SO14 7EB.
Tel (023) 8082 8304.
www.cadoganholidays.com

Morocco Made to Measure
69 Knightsbridge, London
SW1X 7RA. *Tel (020) 7235 0123.*
www.clmleisure.co.uk

The interior of Agadir's airport

Travelling by Car in Morocco

Caution, camels on road

The best way of travelling around Morocco, and of exploring the country's historic sites and natural environment in areas not served by local public transport, is by car. The imperfect road network is constantly being improved, and the number of metalled roads means that a four-wheel-drive vehicle is not essential, even in the South. A greater hazard is Moroccan driving standards. There are a number of car-hire companies in Morocco with varying standards of service. Satellite navigation is also available in Morocco for driving around major towns.

Traffic in town, where other cars are not the only obstacles

RULES OF THE ROAD

The Moroccan highway code is based on the one that is used in France, so you must usually give way to the right. At roundabouts, you should give way to cars already on the roundabout.

In general, Moroccan drivers obey traffic lights, perhaps because most junctions are patrolled by a gendarme or policeman.

The speed limits are 40 or 60 kmh (25 or 37 mph) in built-up areas, 100 kmh (60 mph) on the open road and 120 kmh (74 mph) on the motorway. In the approach to towns, drivers will sometimes see signs giving different speed limits; when in doubt, keep to 40 kmh (25 mph), since speed traps are common on these stretches of road. Fines for speeding and other traffic offences range from 300 to 600 dirhams.

ROAD SIGNS

The international system applies to road signs in Morocco, most of which have wording in Arabic and French. In large towns, direction signs are sparse, so that it is inadvisable to set out without a map or reliable instructions.

Road sign in French and Arabic

Signage on motorways and major roads is usually good. Lighting, however, is normally non-existent, except on the approaches to large towns.

TRAFFIC HAZARDS

Negotiating local traffic is difficult mainly because of the great variety of vehicles that use the roads. As a general rule, avoid driving at night, when carts and bicycles with no lights are a real hazard. In towns, the rules of the road are not meticulously observed at night. Be particularly careful about pedestrians crossing roads and even motorways.

Indicator lights are rarely used, and you will find that you must try to anticipate changes of direction of vehicles in your vicinity. Many major roads often have two carriageways, which can make overtaking hazardous. On mountain roads, taxis and buses are often driven somewhat dangerously. Sound your horn when driving into a blind bend.

ROADS AND TRACKS

Morocco's relatively dense road network is undergoing constant improvements. So as to reap the benefit of the latest new stretches of road, buy the most up-to-date road map.

The well-developed road network in northern Morocco is gradually being supplemented by motorways, which are very pleasant to use as they do not carry many trucks. The road network in southern Morocco is less dense and the few minor roads in the region are often in a bad state of repair.

In the South and in the Atlas mountains, metalled roads serve most places of interest to tourists, and they are complemented by a relatively good network of tracks. A four-wheel-drive vehicle is essential for journeys in these regions.

DRIVING IN TOWNS

Parking attendant wearing a badge

The volume of traffic in large towns and cities can be considerable, and the increasing number of vehicles on the roads leads to multiple jams and bottlenecks, which are aggravated by the flotilla of bicycles and mopeds that also impede traffic flow.

Although it is possible to drive into most medinas (the old areas of towns), their narrow streets and many dead ends can make circulation difficult. It is usually far more pleasurable to explore them on foot.

DRIVING IN THE COUNTRY

When driving on minor roads in rural areas, you should look out for animals, such as donkeys and flocks of sheep or goats. Wandering freely without human supervision, they may step into the road without warning.

The many trucks and buses that use the roads may slow your progress considerably, and overtaking, particularly in the mountains, is difficult. Passing on narrow roads is often hazardous. Slow down and hug the hard shoulder so as to reduce the risk of collision.

A "Stop" sign in Arabic

FUEL

Service stations are found at fairly frequent intervals along roads in Morocco, even in the most remote areas. Although four-star petrol (gas) and diesel are widely available, unleaded petrol is rarely sold outside large towns. Irregular deliveries to service stations in rural areas may mean that they run out of fuel. Wherever you are, you should fill up before starting a long journey.

Self-service is uncommon; you should wait for the attendant to arrive and then pay him in cash, including a tip.

PARKING

In large towns and cities, an attendant wearing a small brass badge is assigned to every pavement. He will help you to park, will watch your car in your absence and will help you manoeuvre out of your parking place.

Payment for this service varies according to how long the car is parked, and is at the driver's discretion; allow 1 to 2 dirhams for a short stay (even lasting no more than a

few minutes) and 5 dirhams for several hours' parking. If you want to park for a longer period (overnight, for example), it is advisable to come to an agreement with the attendant before leaving your vehicle. The advantage of this system is that car theft and break-ins are virtually non-existent. Parking meters are common in major cities.

CAR HIRE

Large towns and airports are well provided with car-hire companies, not all of which offer the same service. When hiring a car for an extended period, it is best to use an international car-hire company (such as **Hertz**, **Avis** or Europcar) or a Moroccan firm (such as Thrifty or First-Car) with an extensive network and reliable insurance and breakdown assistance. On payment of a supplement, the hire vehicle may be dropped off at a different place from where it was picked up. Check the terms of the agreement, especially clauses relating to insurance and cover in case of accident or theft. Also check the state of the vehicle and ask for any damage to be noted before you drive off.

Car hire in Morocco is quite expensive. Charges (excluding collision damage waiver) are about 600 dirhams per day for a Class A car (such as a Renault Logan) and 1,900 dirhams for

DIRECTORY

CAR-HIRE COMPANIES

Avis
www.avis.com

Agadir
Avenue Mohammed V.
Tel (0528) 82 14 14.

Casablanca
19 Avenue de l'Armée Royale.
Tel (0522) 31 24 24.

Marrakech
137 Avenue Mohammed V.
Tel (0524) 43 37 27 or 43 25 25.

Hertz
www.hertz.com

Agadir
Bungalow Marhaba,
Boulevard Mohammed V.
Tel (0528) 84 09 39.

Casablanca
25 Rue Al-Oraibi Jilali.
Tel (0522) 48 47 10/74.

Marrakech
154 Avenue Mohammed V.
Tel (0524) 43 99 84.

a four-wheel-drive vehicle. There is usually a wide range of cars to choose from.

IN CASE OF ACCIDENT

If you are involved in a road accident, you should wait for the police to arrive. They will usually arrive quickly and will arbitrate in case of any disagreement. Official statement forms similar to those used in Europe are available at tobacconists.

Driving in the desert, where a four-wheel-drive is essential

Getting Around in Towns

Bilingual street sign

The most important historic sites in Morocco's towns and cities are often located in the medinas, where, in a maze of narrow streets and frequent dead-ends, the only practical way of getting around is on foot. But because many hotels are located in the modern quarters of towns, visitors will frequently need to takes buses or taxis. Although buses are an inexpensive means of getting around in a town, visitors may be baffled by the way that they work and the routes that they follow. *Petits taxis* offer a greater degree of flexibility at relatively little cost. In some towns the services of a guide are virtually indispensable to save spending too much time working out a route, but others are much more straightforward to navigate.

BY BUS

All large towns in Morocco are served by a wide network of bus lines linking their various districts. It can, however, be difficult to find the bus that you need since the destination is often given only in Arabic. For visitors, the most useful routes are those running between the new town *(ville nouvelle)* and the medina. Bus fares are cheap (3 to 4 dirhams) and tickets are purchased on board from the driver. Be sure to carry some small change.

BY TRAM

The Rabat-Salé tramway began operating in 2011. The service links the towns of Rabat and Salé, which are separated by the Wadi Bou Regreg. The network has two lines with a total of 32 stations and is 19.5 km (12 m) long. Line 1 connects Hay Karima in Salé to the district of Agdal in Rabat while Line 2 serves the densely populated quarter known as L'Ocean in Rabat. It extends to the bus station in Salé passing through the Yacoub el Mansour locality and Bettana.

Tickets for the Rabat-Salé, tramway are available from the drivers for 6 dirhams. The service operates between 6am to 11pm daily. The tram stations have been designed to be accessible to disabled travellers, as well as for prams. In Casablanca, the first tramline is due to open in December 2012. It will link the town centre with outlying residential areas.

BY GRAND TAXI

The most frequent journeys made by *grands taxis*, many of which are Mercedes and which seat up to six passengers, are those between towns and cities *(see p377)*. They are also useful if you are a large party, are weighed down with luggage or want to explore the countryside beyond the town, although they won't leave until they are full.

Grands taxis are not fitted with meters, so the fare for your journey must be agreed according to mileage and the length of time that you hire it. The charge for hiring a *grand taxi* for a whole day will be about 500 dirhams.

Grands taxis often wait outside large hotels, and they should not be mistaken for *petits taxis*, which are cheaper and which are used for shorter runs.

BY PETIT TAXI

These vehicles are identifiable by their colour, which is different in every town, and by the words *"petit taxi"* on the roof. They are prohibited by law from going beyond built-up areas and can only be hired for short trips.

The use of meters is becoming more common. You should always ask for the meter to be switched on, and be prepared to round up the usually modest amount that is shown at the end of your journey. The usual fare for a short journey by *petit taxi* during the day is about 10–20 dirhams. At night a 50 per cent surcharge is added to the amount shown on the meter. Taxi fares are paid in cash, and it is important to have a good supply of small change as drivers are rarely able to give change for a 100- or 200-dirham banknote.

Petits taxis usually take up to three people (two in the back and one in front). They make frequent stops along the way to pick up other passengers going in the same direction. This should reduce the cost of the journey.

It is better to ask to be taken to a specific restaurant, hotel or historic building, rather than name the relevant street. Although most drivers have a good knowledge of the town in which they work, they navigate by landmarks rather than street names.

Local bus, a cheap but not always easy way of getting around in towns

The medina in Oujda, easily explored on foot

Taxi ranks are marked by white rectangular signs saying "taxi". You can also hail a taxi in the street by waving your hand. Because of the large number of taxis circulating in towns, it is unusual to wait for very long. There are no radio taxi firms, but some drivers have mobile phones and will give you their card.

If your journey entails driving along a track, the fare will automatically increase. In this case, the full amount should be agreed with the driver beforehand.

ON FOOT

Moroccan towns, and their medinas in particular, are typically very poorly signposted for pedestrians. A street map is therefore useful. You can also ask your way, in return for a few words of thanks in French or, if the person takes you there, a few dirhams. Town centres are easy to explore on foot and best appreciated at a relaxed pace, especially if you have time to enjoy the maze of narrow streets. Cars, mopeds and bicycles take little heed of pedestrians, and you should take special care when crossing the street.

Streets in towns throughout Morocco are very safe. There are, of course, insalubrious quarters, although these are rarely frequented by tourists. In tourist spots, an obvious

police presence together with large numbers of people (both Moroccans and visitors) is the best guarantee of safety. In small crowded streets where pickpockets may operate, take special care of personal possessions.

BY BICYCLE OR MOPED

In the major tourist centres, particularly Marrakech and Agadir, bicycles and mopeds can be hired. The level terrain in these two cities makes cycling here quite easy. Mopeds and bicycles are an ideal means of getting around the old quarters, where the streets are narrow. However, a degree of caution is called for, since car drivers show little consideration to other road-users.

Bicycle attendants, who can be found where there is a concentration of parked cycles and mopeds, are worth using. Charges range from 1 to 2 dirhams for a few hours to 10 dirhams for a night. Lock your bicycle or moped even if an attendant is guarding it.

BY CARRIAGE

Horse-drawn carriages are found mainly in Marrakech. Hiring one costs more than

ارقـوف
الحافـلات
ARRET DE BUS

8
38
67 بوركـون
شارع الزبراوي

Bus stop in a town

a *petit taxi*, but they can be a fun way of getting around towns. In Marrakech, the largest carriage "rank" is at the foot of the Koutoubia Mosque.

GUIDES

The bogus guides who were once so ubiquitous in tourist spots have become more discreet since measures were taken to clamp down on anyone without an official card acting as a guide.

Even if you have a street map, you will find some towns very confusing to explore. The services of a guide may be necessary on your first day in a certain town or city, particularly in the largest medinas, like that of Fès.

Official guides are identifiable by the cards that they carry, almost always pinned to their clothing. These cards are issued by the Ministry of Tourism and bear an identity photograph of the holder. Official guides can be requested at tourist information offices, and also by hotels (in which case make sure they carry the card). They also often wait near hotels and major historic buildings. Specify which buildings and other features you wish to see, and whether or not you wish to be taken into shops. The fees are fixed by the government, but always agree the fee with the guide beforehand.

A horse-drawn carriage, a popular form of transport in Marrakech

Travelling Around in Morocco

Sign indicating a train station

The Moroccan rail network (ONCF) links the towns and cities of northern Morocco, the southernmost town with a rail link being Marrakech. Trains are clean and reliable, and journey times depend on the number of stops along the route. The rail network is complemented by long-distance bus services, which are run either by public or by private companies, and which are cheaper than the train. Whatever your chosen means of transport, you should check beforehand the various timetables and any stops that may seriously lengthen your journey. *Grands taxis (see p374)* are a swift means of travelling from one town to another, but their fares are not fixed and bargaining is a matter of course. The best way to travel between principal cities is often on a domestic flight.

Grand entrance of the train station in Marrakech

Train drawing into the station at Mohammedia, near Casablanca

THE RAIL NETWORK

Run by the Office National des Chemins de Fer (**ONCF**), the Moroccan rail network, while very good, is not very extensive. It covers just 1,700 km (1,056 miles) and serves mainly the northern part of the country, linking Tangier, Oujda, Rabat, Casablanca, Fès, Marrakech and El-Jadida. Plans to extend the railways southwards, particularly to Agadir, are under way. The Atlas, however, is an insuperable barrier.

Services are frequent, since trains are the preferred means of transport for ordinary

people. A separate rail network is used for transporting phosphates, of which Morocco is the world's largest producer.

Casablanca and Rabat have several railway stations, located in different districts but served by the same line.

TRAINS

With a few exceptions, Moroccan trains are relatively modern. Those known as Trains Navettes Rapides, or TNR (express shuttles), and referred to as "Aouita" after a famous Moroccan Olympic runner, link Casablanca and Rabat in 50 minutes, Mohammed V Airport and Casablanca in 40 minutes, and Rabat and Kenitra in 30 minutes. The service is frequent at peak times.

Trains known as Trains Rapides Climatisés (air-conditioned express trains) cover the longer distances between Casablanca, Fès, Oujda, Tangier and Marrakech, and are identified by names such as Koutoubia and Hassan. They are air-conditioned and soundproofed and have proper toilets. On the most heavily used route (from Casablanca to Marrakech, Fès and Tangier), there is a service at least every two hours, and it is possible to make the round trip from Casablanca to Tangier and back again in a single day.

For long journeys, the compartments on night trains can be converted into couchettes. Second class, which is air-conditioned, is very comfortable. The toilets are located at the end of the coach and are reasonably clean. On-board catering services are rather basic. Vendors walk up and down the coaches offering cakes, confectionery, drinks and sometimes sandwiches.

TRAIN TICKETS AND FARES

The cheapest way to buy a train ticket is at a railway station. Passengers must have a ticket valid for the relevant class of seat and type of train. If you reserve a couchette or a bed in a sleeper, you must be able to show the ticket for the relevant supplement.

You can purchase a ticket without booking a seat six days in advance, a combined

A grand taxi, used for longer journeys

train and bus ticket one month in advance, and a ticket with a bed booked on a sleeper two months in advance. You can break your journey so long as you collect a form *(bulletin d'arrêt)* at the station where you alighted. This form makes your ticket valid for an extra five days.

If you have to board a train without having bought a ticket at the station ticket office, ask for a boarding ticket *(ticket d'accès)*, which is issued free of charge at the entrance to the platform, or tell the inspector before you board the train. A ticket bought on the train is always more expensive than one bought from a station ticket office before boarding.

The train is a relatively inexpensive means of getting around. A second-class ticket on an express train from Casablanca to Marrakech or Fès costs about 125 dirhams, and from Marrakech to Tangier about 250 dirhams. There are various concessions for families, young people and groups, and season tickets are also available, although these are economical only for regular travel on a particular route.

COACHES

Many coach (bus) companies operate in Morocco. The best known is **CTM**, the national company that runs services between towns in Morocco and also abroad. Two private companies, **SATCOMA SATAS** and **Supratours**, also cover long-distance routes. Coaches are comfortable and air-conditioned, and are very convenient, especially in the South. They depart from bus stations, which are usually well signposted. A combined train and Supratours coach will take you from Casablanca to Dakhla in the far south.

It is advisable to buy your ticket, and thus reserve a seat, at least 24 hours in advance since coaches are often fully booked at time of departure. Luggage is checked in ahead of departure and is carried in the hold. Make sure that yours has been loaded.

Many small local coach companies also operate in Morocco, although the comfort of their buses is often minimal and journey times painfully long.

GRANDS TAXIS

This is the most flexible way of travelling from one town to another. *Grands taxis* are mostly found at bus stations, parked according to their destination.

Grands taxis are not fitted with meters, and fares must be agreed by bargaining. The main factors involved are the length of the journey and how many people are to be carried. If the taxi is full (with seven or perhaps eight people), each person's fare will be only slightly higher than for the same journey made by bus.

If you do not wish to share the taxi, expect to pay the equivalent that the driver would receive for a fully loaded car. This allows you the option of a tailor-made route. Any stops along the way, to visit places of interest, should be agreed beforehand, since they will lengthen the journey time and add to the fare.

DOMESTIC FLIGHTS

The most economical way of making longer journeys between Morocco's largest cities is often on one of the internal flights provided by **Royal Air Maroc**, especially

to Agadir or Ouarzazate, neither of which has a rail link. The one-way fare to either place is about 700 dirhams, although prices may vary according to the time of year. **Air Arabia** also operates internal flights.

An air-conditioned CTM coach parked near a fuel station

Index

Page numbers in **bold**
type refer to main entries

A

Abachkou 256
Abbar Ksar (Rissani) 281
Abbassid caliphate 46
Abd el-Krim Khattabi 56
Abd el-Malik, Sultan 92
Abd el-Moumen, Sultan 50
  Grand Mosque (Taza)
  210
  Koutoubia Mosque
  (Marrakech) 223, 236,
  237
  Rabat 65, 69
  Tin Mal 252
Abdel Krim 147
Abderrahman III, Caliph
  47
Abeino 294
Abou el-Hassan, Black
  Sultan 51, 238
  Ben Youssef Medersa
  (Marrakech) 230
  Chellah Necropolis 80,
  81
  Ech Cherabliyine
  Mosque (Fès) 167
  El-Mesabahiya Medersa
  (Fès) 175
  Grand Mosque (Salé) 86
Abou Fares Abdelaziz,
  Sultan 76
Abou Faris, Sultan 226
Abou Inan, Sultan 51, 80,
  81, 181
  Bou Inania Medersa
  (Fès) 172
  Dar el-Magana (Fès) 167
  Karaouiyine Library (Fès)
  175
  necropolis (Fès el-Jedid)
  180
Abou Saïd Othman, Sultan
  Chellah Necropolis 80
  Dar el-Makhzen (Fès el-
  Jedid) 180
  El-Attarine Medersa (Fès)
  171
Abou Tacoub Youssef,
  Caliph, Fès 167
Abou Thabit, Caliph 80

Abou Yacoub, Caliph 80
Abou Yacoub Youssef,
  Caliph 50, 51, 231
  Chellah Necropolis 80
Abou Yahia, Caliph 50, 51
Abou Youssef, Caliph
  80–81
Abraham ben Diouanne,
  Rabbi, tomb of 152
Abubacer (Ibn Tufayl) 231
Accidents, road 373
Achoura 41
Acropolis (Lixus) 91
Adeyel 167
Adventures of Morocco
  361
Aéropostale 294
Afella Ighir Oasis 293
Afourer, hotels 312
Africa, map 15
Africanus, Leo 182
  Chellah Necropolis 80
  Fès 167
  Karaouiyine Library (Fès)
  175
Agadir 13, 62, 109, **286–7**
  art galleries 353
  car hire 373
  cinemas 351
  climate 42
  cultural centre 353
  festivals 39
  fish market 119
  hotels 319–21
  map 287
  nightclubs 353
  restaurants 342–3
  thuya wood 122
Agadir-Lehne 289
Agdz 268
Agouti **256**
Aguedal Gardens
  (Marrakech) 13, **242**
Aguelmane Azigza **216**
Aguelmane Sidi Ali **216**
Ahel Sefrou tribe 211
Ahmed el-Mansour, Sultan
  52, 92, 231
  Chrob ou Chouf
  Fountain (Marrakech) 226
  Fès 166
  Marrakech 223
  Mhamid 269

Ahmed el-Mansour, Sultan
  (cont.)
  Palais el-Badi
  (Marrakech) 235
  Saadian Tombs
  (Marrakech) 25, 238–9
Ahmed el-Tijani, tomb of
  167
Ahmed ibn Mahrez 288
Aïcha Gazelles' Trophy 38
Aïd el-Kebir 41
Aïd es-Seghir 41
AIDS 365
Aïn Asserdoun springs 220
Aïn Leuh 212
Air Arabia 371, 376, 377
Air travel
  domestic flights 377
  international flights
  370–71
Aïssaoua brotherhood 188,
  189, **198**
Les Aïssaouas (Clairin)
  198–9
Aït Abou 272
Aït Arbi Kasbah 273
Aït Atta tribe 257, 258, 265
Aït-Attab, festivals 38
Aït Bekkou oasis 294
Aït Benhaddou 2–3, 253,
  265, 270–71, 275
  hotels 318
  restaurants 341
Aït Bou Oulli valley **256**
Aït Bouguemez valley 13,
  247, **254–7**
  map 254–5
Aït Boujane Ksar 274
Aït Haddidou tribe 258,
  259
Aït Haddou Ameur 258
Aït-Herbil 289
Aït Mhamed 254
Aït Mouted Kasbah 273
Aït Ziri **257**
Akka **289**
Akrar d'El-Kelaa 154
Al-Hoceima 143, **153**, 155
  festivals 39
  hotels 309
  restaurants 334
Al-Hoceima Bay 155
Al Idrissi 51

Al Qods Committee 59
Alaouite dynasty 45, 52, **53**
  architecture 25
  Fès 163, 166
  Marrakech 223
  Ouarzazate and the
    Southern Oases 261
  Rabat 70, 76
  royal cities 193
  Taroudannt 288
Alarcos, Battle of (1165)
  50, 65
Alcohol
  beer and spirits 327
  in restaurants 323
  wines 327
Alfonso III, King of Castile
  68
Alfonso VI, King of Castile
  47
Alfonso VIII, King of
  Castile 50, 65
Algeciras, Treaty of (1906)
  129
Ali (artist) 124
Ali ben Youssef, Sultan 47
  Marrakech 223, 231
Ali, Caliph 52, 200
Allegiance Day 41
Almohad dynasty 33, **50–51**
  Aguedal Gardens
    (Marrakech) 242
  architecture 24
  Azemmour 113
  Bab Oudaïa (Rabat) 70
  En-Nejjarine Mosque
    (Meknès) 188
  Fès 163, 166
  Kasbah Boulaouane
    112
  Kasbah Mosque
    (Marrakech) 238
  Ksar el-Kebir 92
  Ksar es-Seghir 147
  Marrakech 223, 227
  Mehdya 87
  Menara (Marrakech)
    242
  Moulay Abdallah 115
  Rabat 65, 70, 76–7
  royal cities 193
  Taza 210
  Tin Mal 252

Almond trees
  Almond Blossom Festival
    (Tafraoute) 41
  The Rif 155
  Zegzel Gorge tour
    161
Almoravid dynasty **46–7**,
  50
  Aguedal Gardens
    (Marrakech) 242
  architecture 24
  Fès 163
  Grand Mosque (Meknès)
    188
  Koubba Ba'Adiyn
    (Marrakech) 231
  Ksar el-Kebir 92
  Marrakech 223, 227
  Ouarzazate and the
    Southern Oases 261
  Taroudannt 288
Amarlouch, Rachid 124
Amateur Theatre Festival
  (Casablanca) 38
Amazraou 268–9
Ambulances 364
Ameln tribe 293
Ameln valley 293
Amerhidil Kasbah (Skoura)
  272
American Legation
  (Tangier) **134**
Amizmiz 252
Ampelusium, Cape 146
Ancien Palais de Mendoub
  (Tangier) 128, **139**
Al-Andalus 47, **48–9**, 50
Andalusian Garden (Rabat)
  68
Andalusian Mosque (Fès)
  175
Andalusian Quarter (Fès)
  175
Andalusian Wall (Rabat)
  76
Anemiter 253
Anfa (Casablanca) **107**
Anglican Church of St
  Andrew (Tangier) **138**
Anne Marie de Bourbon
  55
Anoual, Battle of (1921)
  143

Anti-Atlas 283, 288–9, 293
Aouli Gorge 278
Aouraba 46
Apple Festival (Imouzzer
  de Kandar) 39
Apple Festival (Midelt) 40
Arabic phrasebook 408
Arab.net 361
Arabs
  calligraphy **170**
  language 18, 361, 408
  Ouarzazate and the
    Southern Oases 261
Archaeology
  Musée Archéologique
    (Larache) 90
  Musée Archéologique
    (Rabat) 10, **78–9**
  Musée Archéologique
    (Tetouan) 148
  see also Prehistoric sites
Architecture
  Andalusian 48–9
  Architectural heritage of
    Moulay Ismaïl **55**
  Architecture of the 1920s
    and 1930s **101**
  kasbahs **266–7**
  medinas **26–7**
  minarets 48–9
  Morocco's architectural
    heritage **275**
  ramparts of Marrakech
    227
  urban architecture of
    Morocco **24–5**
Aremd, Jbel Toubkal
  Massif tour 249
Argan trees **127**
Aristocratic Quarter
  (Volubilis) 205
Aristotle 231
Art
  Arabic calligraphy
    170
  art galleries **352**, 353
  Artists and Writers in
    Tangier **135**
  Painters of Essaouira
    125
  Roman 93
  see also Museums and
    galleries

Artomania (Agadir) 353
Asayag residential block
  (Casablanca) 99
Asfalou Ksar 274
Asfiha (Al-Hoceima) 153
Asilah 10, 83, 85, **91**
  festivals 39
  hotels 303–4
  restaurants 329
Asjen 152
Asmi **252**
Assif el-Had, Imouzzer des
  Ida Outanane tour 127
Atlantic Coast
  Northern **83–93**
  Sea Fishing in Morocco
  119
  Southern **109–27**
Atlas Film Studios
  (Ouarzazate) 264
Atlas Mountains
  High Atlas **245–59**
  Middle Atlas **207–21**
Atlas Sahara Trek
  (Marrakech) 357
Attijariwafa Bank
  (Casablanca) 366
Au Petit Poucet
  (Casablanca) 17, 330
Audience Given by
  Moulay Ismaïl (Denis)
  54–5
Augustus, Emperor 45, 93
Aurelius, Marcus 205
Automatic cash dispensers
  (ATMs) 366
Autumn in Morocco 40
Avenue des Forces Armées
  Royales (Casablanca) **98**
Avenue Pasteur (Tangier)
  139
Averroës (Ibn Rushd) 48,
  50, **231**
  Karaouiyine Library (Fès)
  175
  Karaouiyine Mosque
  (Fès) 176
Avis 373
Ayuntamiento (Ceuta)
  147
Azemmour 110, **113**
Azrou 12, 207, **212**
  hotels 312

B

Ba Ahmed, Grand Vizier 53
  Palais Bahia (Marrakech)
  234, 235
Bab Agnaou (Marrakech)
  227, **239**
Bab Berrima (Meknès) 188
Bab Boujat (Fès el-Jedid)
  180
Bab Boujeloud (Fès) **166**
Bab Dekaken (Fès el-
  Jedid) 180
Bab Doukkala Mosque
  (Marrakech) **231**
Bab el-Berdaïne (Meknès)
  55, 188
Bab el-Chorfa (Fès) 26
Bab el-Ftouh (Fès) **175**
Bab el-Had (Rabat) 76
Bab el-Jedid (Casablanca)
  100
Bab el-Jedid (Meknès)
  188, 193
Bab el-Khemis
  (Marrakech) 227
Bab el-Khemis (Meknès)
  188
Bab el-Makhzen (Meknès)
  193
Bab el-Marsa (Casablanca)
  100
Bab el-Mrisa (Salé) 86
Bab el-Seba (Fès el-Jedid)
  183
Bab el-Semarine (Fès el-
  Jedid) 181
Bab el-Siba (Meknès) 188
Bab er-Rouah (Rabat) **80**
Bab Mansour el-Aleuj
  (Meknès) 12, **189**
Bab Marrakech
  (Casablanca) 100
Bab Oudaïa (Rabat) 68, **70**
Bab Taghzout (Marrakech)
  226
Backroads 357
Badajoz, Battle of (1086)
  47
Baha Kasbah (Nekob) 265
Balcon d'Ito 212
Banasa 78, **92**, 93
Banker's cards 366

Banknotes 367
Banks **366–7**
Bargaining 345, 363
Bars, piano **352**, 353
Basilica (Volubilis) 203, 205
Basri, Driss 19, 20, 59, 112
Bassin de l'Aguedal
  (Meknès) **193**
Bastion Sisi Makhlouf
  (Rabat) 76
Battle of the Three Kings
  (1578) 52, 92
Beaches
  Agadir 286
  Asfiha (Al-Hoceima)
  153
  Essaouira 123
  Haouzia (Azemmour)
  113
  Oualidia 115
  Plage des Amiraux 141
  Plage Blanche
  (Guelmim) 294
  Plage Quemado (Al-
  Hoceima) 153
  Saïda 160
  Sidi Bouzid 115
  Sidi Kaouki 124
  Sidi Moussa Aglou 292
  Tangier **140–41**
Beat generation 129, 135
The Beatles 140
Becker, Jacques 288
Beckett, Samuel 141
Beer 327
Bel, Alfred 168
Belamine, Fouad 138
Ben Arafa 57
Ben Barka, Mehdi 58
Ben Morro Kasbah
  (Skoura) 272
Ben Youssef Medersa
  (Marrakech) **230**
Beni Bou Ayach 153
Beni Enzar 158
Beni Mellal **220**
  festivals 38
  hotels 313
  restaurants 337
Beni Meskin tribe 220
Beni M'Gild tribe 190, 212,
  216
Beni Saad tribe 52

Beni-Snassen Mountain
Road, Zegzel Gorge tour
161
Beni-Snassen Mountains,
Zegzel Gorge tour 160
Berbers **32–3**
Berbers (cont.)
Berbers of the High Atlas
13, **259**
carpets 348–9
Chiadma Region 118
dress and jewellery 36
High Atlas 245
history 45, 46
language and culture
18–19
Ouarzazate and the
Southern Oases 261
Tamanar 126
Bergé, Pierre 243
Bergman, Ingrid 98
Bert Flint Museum
(Marrakech) 235
Bertolucci, Bernardo 141,
264
Bertuchi, Mariano 147
Bessonneau residential
block (Casablanca) 99
Best of Morocco 371
Bhalil 211
Bicycles 375
Bigoudine, Imouzzer des
Ida Outanane tour 127
Bin el-Ouidane Dam
220–21
Birds
bird-watching 355
Dayet Srji 281
Îles Purpuraires 124
Lakes tour 213
Moulay Bousselham 10,
90
Moulouya Estuary 11,
159
Sidi Bouhaba Lagoon 87
Souss Massa National
Park 13, **292**
Tamri 127
Vallée des Oiseaux 265
Black Guard 54
BMCE Bank (Casablanca)
366
BMCI (Casablanca) 366

Boabdil 49
Boats
ferries 371
sailing 355
Bofill, Ricardo 106
Bogart, Humphrey 98
Borj en Naam (Tangier)
133
Bou Inania Medersa (Fès)
12, 24, 162, **172–3**
Bou Inania Medersa
(Meknès) **189**
Bou Thrarar 273
Bouabid, Abder Rahim 58
Bouhouda, festivals 39
Boujad **220**
Boulaouane 108, 112
Boulaouane wine **113**
Boulevard Houphouët
Boigny (Casablanca) 98
Boulevard Mohammed V
(Casablanca) 10, **98–9**
Boumalne du Dadès **273**
Bowles, Jane 139
Bowles, Paul 129, 135
American Legation
(Tangier) 134
Café Hafa (Tangier) 140
Café de Paris (Tangier)
139
Hôtel el-Minzah
(Tangier) 139
Boyer, M. 98, 99
Braque, Georges 132
Brass 29
Bravo, Claudio 134, 135
Brayer 134
Bride, H. 99
British Council (Rabat)
352, 353
Bureaux de change 366–7
Burroughs, William 135
Bay of Tangier 141
Café Hafa (Tangier) 140
Buses 374
Byzantine Empire 45

C
Cabo Negro, hotels 308
Cadet, A. 106
Cadi Ayad 226
Cadogan Holidays 371
Café Hafa (Tangier) **140**

Café Maure (Rabat) 68
Café de Paris (Tangier) 11,
139, 333
Caligula, Emperor 45, 78
Calligraphy, Arabic **170**
Camel treks 13, 356, 357
Campsites 300
Canadian Embassy (Rabat)
361
Canadian Hostelling
Association 301
Candle Festival (Salé) 38
Cannabis **159**
Cap Beddouza 115
Cap Malabata 141, **146**
Cap Sim 123
Cap Spartel 140, **146**
hotels 309
restaurants 334
Cap des Trois Fourches
159
Capitol (Volubilis) 203, 205
Capote, Truman 135
Caracalla, Emperor 93
Banasa 92
Volubilis 205
Carpets 29, **348–9**
Dar Si Said Museum
(Marrakech) 241
Musée Dar Jamaï
(Meknès) 190
Carriages
Dar Si Saïd Museum
(Marrakech) 240
horse-drawn 375
Cars
Aïcha Gazelles' Trophy
38
Classic Car Rally 38
driving in Morocco
372–3
ferries 371
hiring 373
off-road driving 355
see also Tours by car
Carthaginians 45
Mehdya 87
Tangier 129
Casablanca 10–11, 62,
95–107
airport 370–71
Architecture of the 1920s
and 1930s **101**

Casablanca (cont.)
art galleries 353
car hire 373
cinemas 351
climate 43
cultural centres 353
festivals 38, 40
Hassan II Mosque **102–5**
hospitals and clinics 365
hotels 305–6
map 96–7
nightclubs 353
piano bars 353
restaurants 330–32
theatres 351
Casablanca Conference
(1943) 107
Casablanca Twin Center
(Casablanca) **106**
Cascades d'Ouzoud 12,
206, **221**
Cascades de Ras el-Oued
210
Cascades des Vierges
(Ifrane) 212
Casinos **352**, 353
Castel 113
La Cathédrale (Aït
Bouguemez valley) 257
Cathedrals
Cathédrale Saint-Pierre
(Rabat) 77
Ceuta 147
Catholic Cemetery
(Larache) 90
Cato the Younger 205
Caves
Chiker Caves 211
Gouffre du Friouato **211**
Grotte du Chameau 160
Grotte de Tghasrout 160
Grottes d'Hercule **146**
Imouzzer du Kandar 211
Kef el-Moumen Caves
(Sefrou) 211
Win t'mdoum Caves 126
Central Market
(Casablanca) 98, 99
Centre Hassan II des
Rencontres
Internationales (Asilah)
91
Ceramics 29

Colline des Potiers (Safi)
118
Dar Si Saïd Museum
(Marrakech) 241
Musée Dar el-Batha (Fès)
168
Ceramics (cont.)
Musée Dar Jamaï
(Meknès) 190
Musée National de la
Céramique (Safi) 118
What to Buy in Morocco
346, 347
Cercle Militaire
(Casablanca) 99
Ceuta 11, 51, 143, **147**
Chams el-Doha 81
Chaouia 112
Chefchaouen 11, 142, 144,
150–51
festivals 40
hotels 309
map 151
restaurants 334
Chellah Necropolis (Rabat)
10, **80–81**
Cherada tribe 201
Cherry Festival (Sefrou) 39
Chez Ali (Marrakech) 351
Chez Bennis (Casablanca)
106
Chiadma Region **118**
Chigaga dunes 269
Chiker 210
Chiker Caves 211
Cholera 365
Choukri, Mohammed 135
Christian Prison (Meknès)
192
Christianity 45
Chrob ou Chouf Fountain
(Marrakech) **226**
Churches
Anglican Church of St
Andrew (Tangier) **138**
Church of the
Immaculate Conception
(Tangier) 134
Église Notre-Dame
(Essaouira) 123
Église Notre-Dame-de
Lourdes (Casablanca)
100

Churches (cont.)
Église du Sacré-Coeur
(Casablanca) 100
Nuestra Señora de Africa
(Ceuta) 147
Portuguese Chapel (Safi)
118
Purísima Concepción
(Melilla), La 158
Churchill, Winston
Casablanca Conference
107
Hôtel el-Minzah
(Tangier) 139
La Mamounia Hotel
(Marrakech) 234
Cinema **350**, 351
Atlas Film Studios
(Ouarzazate) 264
Cirque de Jaffar 278
Citerne Portugaise
(Portuguese Cistern) (El-
Jadida) 111, **114**, **115**
Citibank (Casablanca) 366
Cities, royal **193**
City Walls
Rabat 68, **70**
see also Ramparts
Clairin, Georges 135
Les Aïssaouas 198–9
Classic Car Rally 38
Claudius, Emperor 45, 93,
202
Cleopatra Selene 78
Climate **42–3**, 360
Clinics 365
Clocktower (Casablanca)
98
Clothing
Berber 32–3
Dar Si Saïd Museum
(Marrakech) 241
etiquette 363
hiking and trekking 356
Moroccan dress and
jewellery **36–7**
Musée Dar Jamaï
(Meknès) 191
in restaurants 323
What to Buy in Morocco
347
Club Alpin Français
(Casablanca) 357

Club Mistral (Essaouira) 355
Coach travel 377
Coffee 326
Cogné 99
Coins 367
Colline du Charf (Tangier) **141**
Colline des Potiers (Safi) 118
Commodius, Emperor 93
Communications **368–9**
Complexe Culturel Moulay Rachid (Casablanca) 351
Complexe Culturel du Sidi-Belyout (Casablanca) 351
Concerts 351
Consernor 119
Consulat de France (Casablanca) 99
Consulates 361
Copper 29
Córdoba 47, 50, 77
Corniche d'Aïn Diab (Casablanca) **107**
Cornut, Théodore 120, 121
Cortège of Venus (Volubilis) 205
Cotta, Ruins of 146
Cotton Festival (Beni Mellal) 38
Country souks **201**
Crafts **28–9**
  Crafts Festival (Ouarzazate) 38
  Musée Dar el-Batha (Fès) 168–9
Credit cards **367**
  in shops 344
Crédit du Maroc (Casablanca) 366
Crime 364, 365
CTM 377
Cultural centres **352**, 353
Currency **367**
Curtiz, Michael 98
Customs, Muslim 362–3
Customs and excise 361
Cycling 375

D

Dadès Gorge 263, **273**
Dadès valley 261, 262, 273
Dakhla 294
  restaurants 343

Damgaard, Frederic 124, 352
Danan Synagogue (Fès el-Jedid) 182–3
Daniel 211
Dante Alighieri (Casablanca) 353
Dar Bellarj (Marrakech) 353
Dar Bouazza
  hotels 306
  restaurants 332
Dar Caïd Ouriki 247
Dar el-Bahr (Safi) 118
Dar el-Batha (Fès) 168
Dar el-Glaoui (Marrakech) 231
Dar el-Kebira Quarter (Meknès) **192**
Dar el-Ma (Meknès) 55, **193**
Dar el-Magana (Fès) 167
Dar el-Makhzen (Fès el-Jedid) 180
Dar el-Makhzen (Marrakech) **239**
Dar el-Makhzen (Meknès) 12, **192–3**
Dar el-Makhzen (Rabat) 64, **80**
Dar el-Makhzen (Tangier) 11, **132–3**
Dar Si Saïd Museum (Marrakech) 13, **240–41**
Dar Soltane Mahdounia (Diabet) 123
Darius Boyer House (Casablanca) 101
Dates
  Date Festival (Erfoud) 40
  Tafilalt Palm Grove 280
Day of the Green March 41
Dayet Aoua, Lakes tour 213
Dayet Hachlaf, Lakes tour 213
Dayet Ifrah, Lakes tour 213
Dayet Srji 281
Decumanus Maximus (Volubilis) 205
Degas, Edgar 133
Dehodencq, Alfred
  Jewish Feast Day in Tetouan 149
  King Boabdil's Farewell 49

Delacroix, Eugène **135**, 216
  The Sultan Moulay Abderrahman Leaving Meknès 44
Denis, M.P., *Audience Given by Moulay Ismaïl* 54–5
DHL Worldwide Express 369
Diabet 123
Dialling codes 368
Diarrhoea 365
Diesel 373
Disabled visitors 301
Discos 352, 353
Discover 357
Dlimi 59
Doctors 364
Dongen, Kees van 135
Doors
  Dar Si Saïd Museum (Marrakech) 240
  Musée Dar el-Batha (Fès) 169
Draa valley 260, 261, 262, **268**
Dress *see* Clothing
Driving *see* Cars
Drugs
  kif (cannabis) **159**
  personal safety 364
Dunes
  Chigaga dunes 269
  Erg Chebbi dunes 281
  Nesrate dunes 269
  Tinfou dunes 269
Dyers' Souk (Marrakech) 228

E

Eastern Oases **276–7**
Ech Cherabliyine Mosque (Fès) 167
Écochard, Michel 77
Economy 18, 20–21
Ed-Dlala Kissaria (Meknès) 188
Education 18
Église Notre-Dame (Essaouira) 123
Église Notre-Dame-de-Lourdes (Casablanca) 100

Église du Sacré-Coeur (Casablanca) 100
El-Atika Mosque (Rabat) 69
El-Attarine Medersa (Fès) 11, **171**
El-Attarine Souk (Fès) 167
El-Cherratine Medersa (Fès) **171**
El-Fassi, Allal 57, 58
El-Glaoui 57
  Dar el-Glaoui (Marrakech) 231
  Telouet 253
El-Had 254, 257
El-Hank Lighthouse (Casablanca) 107
El-Hart-n-Igouramene 274
El-Hiba 292
El-Jadida 11, 109, 111, **114–15**
  festivals 39
  hotels 306
  restaurants 332
El-Jazouli 168, 198
El-Jebha **152**
El-Kaïm 52
El-Kebab 217
El-Kelaa M'Gouna **272–3**
  festivals 38
El-Ksiba 217
El-Mansour Eddahbi Dam 264
El-Mdint 253
El-Mesabahiya Medersa (Fès) 175
El-Mjadlia Souk (Marrakech) 226
El-Mutawakkil, Sultan 92
El-Oualid, Sultan 115
El-Sahrij Medersa (Fès) **175**, 178–9
El-Seffarine Medersa (Fès) 175
Elatrach, Abdallah 125
Embassies 361
Embroidery **191**
  Musée Dar el-Batha (Fès) 169
  Musée Dar Jamaï (Meknès) 191
  What to Buy in Morocco 347
Emergencies 364, 365

En-Nejjarine Mosque (Meknès) 188
Entertainment **350–53**
  art galleries **352**, 353
  casinos **352**, 353
  cinemas **350**, 351
  cultural centres **352**, 353
  feast days and festivals 351
  information sources 350
  nightclubs **352**, 353
  piano bars **352**, 353
  shows and concerts 351
  theatres **350**, 351
Entry charges 360
Equipment, hiking and trekking 356
Er-Rachidia **279**
Erfoud **280**
  festivals 40
  hotels 318
  restaurants 341
Erg Chebbi dunes 13, **281**
Ernst, Max 132
Essaouira 11, 62, 109, 111, 116–17, **120–25**
  art galleries 353
  festivals 39
  hotels 306–7
  map 121
  Painters of Essaouira **125**
  piano bars 353
  restaurants 332–3
  sardine fishing 119
  thuya wood 122
Etiquette **362–3**
Ettalbi, Fatima 124
European Rail Ltd 371
Events **38–41**
Excelsior Hotel (Casablanca) 98
Exodus 357

F

Fatima bint Mohammed el-Fihri 176
Fauna *see* Wildlife
Feast days 351
Fédération Nationale de l'Industrie Hôtelière 301
Fédération Royale Marocaine des Auberges de Jeunesse 301

Fédération Royale Marocaine de Golf 355
Fédération Royale Marocaine de Jet Ski et de Ski Nautique 355
Fédération Royale Marocaine de Ski et Montagne 355
Fédération Royale Marocaine des Sports Equestres 355
Ferries 371
Fès 12, 63, **163–83**
  Bou Inania Medersa **172–3**
  cinemas 351
  climate 43
  cultural centres 353
  festivals 38, 40
  hotels 310–12
  Karouiyine Mosque **176–7**
  map 164–5
  Musée Dar el-Batha **168–9**
  piano bars 353
  restaurants 335–6
  Tanneries of Fès **174**
Fès, Treaty of (1912) 56
Fès el-Bali 163, 164
Fès el-Jedid 163, 164, **180–83**
  map 181
Fès Medina Morocco 301
Festival of Fantasia (Meknès) 40
Festivals **38–41**, 351
  Holy Men and Mystics 198–9
  religious festivals 31, **41**
Fig Festival (Bouhouda) 39
Figuig **161**
Film **350**, 351
  Atlas Film Studios (Ouarzazate) 264
  Finnt Oasis 264
Fire brigade 364, 365
Fishing, Sea fishing in Morocco **119**
Flint, Bert 235
  Bert Flint Museum (Marrakech) 235
Flynn, Errol 139

Folk Music Festival
   (Al-Hoceima) 39
Fondation Lorin (Tangier)
   134
Fondouk (Chefchaouen)
   150
Fondouk Chejra (Tangier)
   11, **138**
Fondouk el-Nejjarine (Fés)
   12, **167**
Food and drink
   Flavours of Morocco
   324–5
   Olives and olive oil **217**
   safety 364–5
   sharing a meal 362
   shopping 344–5
   What to drink in
   Morocco **326–7**
   see also Restaurants
Forbes, Malcolm 139
Foreign Legion
   Ouarzazate 264
   Source Bleue de Meski
   279
   Tunnel de Foum-Zabel
   278–9
Forest of Mamora **87**, 88–9
Forêt de Cèdres 212
Forgeries 345
Former Mellah (Essaouira)
   123
Fortresses **266–7**
Forum (Volubilis) 205
Foucauld, Charles de 217,
   289
Foucault, Michel 141
Foum el-Anser 220
Foum el-Hassan 289
Foum-Rjam 269
Franco, General Francisco
   56
François, Marcel 86
French phrasebook 407
French Protectorate **56–7**
   architecture 25
   Casablanca 95, 99, 106
   El-Jadida 114
   Er-Rachidia 279
   Erfoud 280
   Fès 163
   Kenitra 87
   Rabat 77

French Protectorate (cont.)
   Zagora 268
   see also Foreign Legion
Friday prayers 31
Fuel 373
Funerary architecture,
   Musée Dar el-Batha (Fès)
   169

G

Galerie Damgaard
   (Essaouira) 124, 353
Galerie Delacroix
   (Tangier) 138, 139
Galleries see Museums and
   galleries
Gardens see Parks and
   gardens
Genet, Jean 135
   Café de Paris (Tangier)
   139
   Hôtel el-Minzah
   (Tangier) 139
   tomb of 90
Genseric, King of the
   Vandals 45
Geography **51**
Gibraltar 147
Gibraltar, Straits of
   129
Glaoui family
   Aït Mouted Kasbah
   (Dadès Gorge) 273
   Amerhidil Kasbah
   (Skoura) 272
   Taliouine 288
   Tamdaght 265
   Taourirt Kasbah 264
Glaoui residential block
   (Casablanca) 98, 99
Globex (Federal Express)
   369
Glossary 405–6
Gnaoua 132
Gnaoua Festival
   (Essaouira) 39
Go-Kart 24-Hour Race
   (Marrakech) 41
Goethe Institüt
   (Casablanca) 353
Golf 354–5
Gordian III, Emperor 205
Gorge of Wadi Laou 154

Gouffre du Friouato **211**
Goulimine see Guelmim
Goulmima **275**
Goundafa tribe 252
Gran Teatro Cervantes
   (Tangier) 139
Granada 49, 50, 51
Grand Mosque
   (Chefchaouen) 150
Grand Mosque (Fés el-
   Jedid) 180
Grand Mosque (Meknès)
   12, **188**
Grand Mosque (Salé) 86
Grand Mosque (Tangier)
   133
Grand Mosque (Taza)
   210
Grand Rue de Fès el-Jedid
   (Fès el-Jedid) 180–81
Grand Socco (Place du 9
   Avril 1947) (Tangier) 11,
   138
Grands taxis 374, 377
Great Mosque (Rabat) 76
Great Synagogue (Tangier)
   139
Green March (1975) 58,
   283, 294
Gris de Boulaouane **113**
Grotte du Chameau,
   Zegzel tour 160
Grotte de Tghasrout 160
Grottes d'Hercule **146**
Guéliz (Marrakech) **242–3**
Guelmin (Goulimine) 13,
   294
   festivals 39
   hotels 321
   moussem 199
Guesthouses 300
Guides 375

H

Ha Dra 118
Habs Qara (Meknès)
   192
Hadj Tenim 54
Hafsid dynasty 50
Haha 126
Hanno 45
Haouzia 113
Haras de Meknès **193**

Haratines, Ouarzazate and the Southern Oases 261
Harley-Davidson Raid 38
Harris, Walter
  grave of 138
  Villas Harris (Cap Malabata) 146
Hassan, Fatima 138
Hassan I *see* Moulay el-Hassan, Sultan
Hassan II, King 19–20, 57, 58–9
  Al-Akhawaya University (Ifrane) 212
  death of 17, 19, 59
  Green March 283
  Mausoleum of Mohammed V (Rabat) 74
Hassan II Mosque (Casablanca) 10–11, 94, **102–5**
Hassan Tower (Rabat) 49, **76–7**
Hassan-Addakhil dam 279
Hayworth, Rita 139
Health **364–5**
Hendrix, Jimi 123, 127
Henna 32
Henna Souk (Fès) 167
Henry the Navigator, Prince 51
Hercules 90, 146
Heri es-Souani (Meknès) **193**
Hertz 373
High Atlas 13, 63, **245–59**
  Aït Bouguemez valley **254–7**
  Berbers of the High Atlas **259**
  hotels 317–18
  Jbel Toubkal Massif tour 249
  map 246–7
  restaurants 340
Higueruela, Battle of 49
Hiking **356–7**
Hippies 135
Hiring cars 373
History **45–59**
Holidays, public 41
Holy Men and Mystics **198–9**

Honey Festival (Imouzzer des Ida Outanane) 39
Hornacheros 70
Horses **34–5**
  Haras de Meknès **193**
  Horse Festival (Tissa) 40
  horse-drawn carriages 375
  riding **354**, 355
Hospitality 362
Hospitals 364, 365
Hostels 301
Hôtel Continental (Tangier) 133
Hôtel el-Minzah (Tangier) 138–9
Hotels **298–321**
  Casablanca 305–6
  chain and luxury hotels **300**, 301
  choosing a hotel 298
  classification of hotels and services 298
  disabled visitors 301
  Fès 310–12
  guesthouses 300
  High Atlas 317–18
  Marrakech 314–17
  Mediterranean Coast and the Rif 309–10
  Meknès and Volubilis 312–13
  Middle Atlas 313–14
  negotiating a lower price 299
  Northern Atlantic Coast 303–4
  Ouarzazate and the Southern Oases 318–19
  prices 299
  Rabat 302–3
  reservations 299
  riads 301
  Southern Atlantic Coast 306–7
  Southern Morocco and Western Sahara 319–21
  Tangier 308–9
  unmarried couples 300–301
Hôtels Ibis Moussafir 301
Hôtels Kenzi (Marrakech) 301
Hôtels Kenzi (Paris) 301

House of the Athlete (Volubilis) 205
House of the Columns (Volubilis) 202
House of Dionysus and the Four Seasons (Volubilis) 184
House of the Dog (Volubilis) 205
House of the Ephebe (Volubilis) 205
House of Orpheus (Volubilis) 204
Hyatt Regency Hotel (Casablanca) 98

I

Ibn Battuta 51
Ibn el-Khatib 176
Ibn Khaldoun 50, **181**
  Karaouiyine Library (Fès) 175
  Karaouiyine Mosque (Fès) 176
Ibn Toumart 50, 252
Ibn Tufayl 50, 175
Idriss I, Sultan 46, 211
  Fès 163
  tomb of 200
  Volubilis 202
Idriss II, Sultan 46
  Bhalil 211
  Fès 163
  Zaouia of Moulay Idriss II (Fès) **171**
Idrissid dynasty 24, **46**
Idrissid *shorfa* 150, 152
Ifni, Lake, Jbel Toubkal Massif tour 249
Ifrane 12, 207, **212**
  climate 43
  hotels 313
  restaurants 337–8
Igdaoun Kasbah 268
Igherm **288–9**
Igherm-n-Ougdal 253
Ijoukak 252
Île de Mogador 124
Îles Purpuraires 124
Illness
  minor health risks 364
  serious illness 365
Im Zouren 153

Imelghas **257**
Imessouane 109
Imi Irhzer, Imouzzer des
  Ida Outanane tour 127
Imi n Ifri 221
Imilchil **258**, 259
  festivals 40
Imlil
  hotels 317
  Jbel Toubkal Massif tour
  249
Imouzzer des Ida
  Outanane 11, **126–7**
  festivals 39
  tour by car **126–7**
Imouzzer du Kandar 12,
  207, 209, **211**
  festivals 39
Imperial City (Meknès) 192
Independence Day 41
Insects 365
Institut Français d'Agadir
  353
Institut Français de
  Casablanca 353
Institut Français de Fès
  353
Institut Français de
  Marrakech 353
Institut Français de Rabat
  353
Institut Français de Tangier
  353
Instituto Cervantes
  (Casablanca) 353
Instituto Cervantes (Rabat)
  353
Instituto Cervantes
  (Tangier) 353
International Cultural
  Festival (Asilah) 39
International Festival of
  Sacred Music (Fès) 38
International Music
  Festival (Ouarzazate) 40
Internet 361
Internet cafés 369
Irrigation 276–7
Iskattafène **257**
Islam
  Arabic calligraphy 170
  customs 362–3
  festivals 31, **41**

Islam (cont.)
  history of Morocco 46
  Islamic faith in Morocco
  30–31
  Regraga Berbers 118
  see also Medersas;
  Mosques
Isly, Battle of (1844) 53
Istiqlal Party 57, 58
Izourar, Lake 254, 255, 257

J
Jardins Exotiques (Sidi
  Bouknadel) 86
Jazz
  Jazz Festival (Tangier)
  40
  Oudaïa Jazz Festival 39
Jbel Alam 154
Jbel Angour 248
Jbel Aoulime 288
Jbel Attar 248
Jbel Ayachi 246, 278
Jbel Bou Iblane 208
Jbel Bou Naceur 208
Jbel Fourhal, Zegzel Gorge
  tour 161
Jbel Ghat 256
Jbel Lekst 293
Jbel M'Goun 246
Jbel Oukaïmeden 248
Jbel Sarhro **265**
Jbel Tassemit 220
Jbel Tazzeka National Park
  12, 207, **210**
Jbel Tidirhin 143, 152
Jbel Toubkal Massif 13,
  246
  tour by car **249**
Jbel Yagour 248
Jbel Zagora 269
Jebala 154
Jebala tribe 151
Jewellery
  Dar Si Saïd Museum
  (Marrakech) 240–41
  Moroccan dress and
  jewellery **36–7**
  Musée Dar Jamaï
  (Meknès) 191
*Jewish Feast Day in
  Tetouan* (Dehodencq)
  149

Jews
  Danan Synagogue (Fès
  el-Jedid) **182–3**
  El-Jadida 114
  Essaouira 123
  Judaism in Morocco **49**
  Mellah (Fès el-Jedid)
  180, **182**
  Mellah (Marrakech) **235**
  Musée du Judaïsme
  Marocain (Casablanca)
  106
  Ouezzane 152
  Sefrou 211
  Tetouan 148, **149**
John the Baptist, St 39, 161
John Paul II, Pope 59
Juba II, King of
  Mauretania 45, 93, 203
  Essaouira 120
  Îles Purpuraires 124
  Musée Archéologique
  (Rabat) 78
Judaism **49**
  see also Jews
Julia Domna 205

K
Kacimi, Mohammed 138
Kaftans 37
Kalah Iris 153, 155
Karaouiyine Library (Fès)
  175
Karaouiyine Mosque (Fès)
  12, 24, **176–7**
Kasbah Mosque
  (Marrakech) **238**
Kasbah Mosque (Tangier)
  11, **132**
Kasbahs **266–7**
  Chefchaouen 150
  Kasba Tadla **217**
  Kasbah Boulaouane 11,
  112–13
  Kasbah Cherarda (Fès el-
  Jedid) 183
  Kasbah Hadrach
  (Meknès) 193
  Kasbah Hamidouch **118**
  Morocco's architectural
  heritage 275
  Oudaïa Kasbah (Rabat)
  68–9

Kasbahs (cont.)
Tangier 11, **132**
Kean, Emily 138
Kef el-Moumen Caves
(Sefrou) 211
Kenitra 84, **87**
hotels 304
restaurants 329
Ketama **152**
Khemisset **201**
Khenifra **216–17**
hotels 313
restaurants 338
Khouribga, hotels 313
Kif (Cannabis) **159**
King Boabdil's Farewell
(Dehodencq) 49
Kissarias, Marrakech 229
Koran 30–31
Arabic calligraphy 170
Koranic Library
(Tamegroute) 269
Koubba Ba'Adiyn
(Marrakech) 24, 47, **231**
Koubba el-Khayatine
(Meknès) **192**
Koubba of Sidi bou Ali
Serghine 211
Koubba of Sidi Othman
(Boujad) 220
Koutoubia Mosque
(Marrakech) 13, 24, 46,
48, **236–7**
Ksar el-Kebir **92**
Ksar es-Seghir **147**
beach 141
Ksour in the oases 13, **279**

L

La Palmeraie (Marrakech)
13, 232–3, **243**
hotels 315
restaurants 339
Laayoune **294**
Labour Day 41
Laforgue, A. 99
Lakes tour **213**
Lalla Aouda Mosque
(Meknès) **192**
Lalla el-Azhar Mosque (Fès
el-Jedid) 181
Lalla Messaouda, tomb of
239

Lalla Mina Gardens (Fès
el-Jedid) 180
Lalla Rekia 211
Lamali, Boujmaa 118
Landscape and wildlife of
Morocco **22–3**
Language 361
Arabic phrasebook 408
Berber 18–19
French phrasebook 407
Laprade, A. 99, 100
Larache **90**
hotels 304
restaurants 329
Las Navas de Tolosa,
Battle of (1212) 50, 65
Lawrence Arnott Art
Gallery (Tangier) 353
Lean, David 264
Leatherwork 28
Musée Dar el-Batha (Fès)
168
Tanneries of Fès **174**
Lepiney Hut, Jbel Toubkal
Massif tour 249
Librairie des Colonnes
(Tangier) 139
Le Lido (Casablanca) 107
Lighthouses
Cap Spartel 146
El-Hank Lighthouse
(Casablanca) 107
Punto Almina 147
Sidi Boubeker 113
Lions of the Atlas **216**
Literature, Artists and
Writers in Tangier 135
Lixus 10, **90–91**, 93
Loire, G. 100
Louis XIV, King of France
54, 55, 194
Louis XV, King of France 120
Lyautey, Marshal Hubert
56, 57, 243
Casablanca 95
Palais Bahia (Marrakech)
235
Rabat 65, 77
statue of 99

M

Macaques (Barbary apes) 23
McBey, James 134

McBey, Margarite 134
McLean, Sir Harry, grave
of 138
Magdaz 250–51
Maghrebi Union Treaty
(1988) 59
Mahakma du Pacha
(Casablanca) 106
Mahd Salam Hotels 301
Maïmoune, Ali 124, **125**
Majorelle, Jacques 99, 135,
243
Majorelle, Louis 243
Majorelle Garden
(Marrakech) 13, **243**
Makina (Fés el-Jedid) 183
Malabata, Cap *see* Cap
Malabata
La Mamounia Hotel
(Marrakech) **234**, 352,
353
Manifesto of
Independence (1944) 57
Manifesto of
Independence Day 41
Manuel I, King of Portugal
287
Manuscripts, Arabic
calligraphy 170
Maps
Africa 15
Agadir 287
Aït Bouguemez valley
254–5
Beaches around Tangier
140–41
Casablanca 96–7
Chefchaouen 151
Climate of Morocco 42–3
Essaouira 121
Fès 164–5
Fès el-Jedid 181
High Atlas 246–7
Imouzzer des Ida
Outanane tour 126–7
Jbel Toubkal Massif tour
249
Lakes tour 213
Marrakech 224–5
Marrakech: souks 228–9
Mediterranean Coast and
the Rif 144–5
Meknès 186–7

Maps (cont.)
Meknès and Volubilis 185
Middle Atlas 208–9
Morocco 14–15, 62–3
Morocco: road map see Back endpaper
Northern Atlantic Coast 84–5
Ouarzazate and the Southern Oases 262–3
Rabat 66–7
Rabat: Oudaïa Kasbah 68–9
The Rif 154–5
Southern Atlantic Coast 110–11
Southern Morocco and Western Sahara 284–5
Tangier 130–31
Zegzel Gorge tour 160–61
Marabout of Sidi Abderrahman (Casablanca) 107
Marabout of Sidi M'Barek 272
Marabouts, Aït Bouguemez valley 257
Marathon des Sables 38, 357
Marchisio, Antoine 234
Mardoch, Rabbi 289
Mariam el-Fihri 175
Markets, see also Souks
Marrakech 12–13, 63, **223–43**
airport 370
art galleries 353
car hire 373
casino 352, 353
cinemas 351
climate 43
cultural centres 353
Dar Si Saïd Museum **240–41**
festivals 39, 40, 41
hospitals and clinics 365
hotels 314–17
Koutoubia Mosque **236–7**
map 224–5
nightclubs 353

Marrakech (cont.)
piano bars 353
ramparts **227**
restaurants 338–40
souks **228–9**
Marrakech-Medina 301
Marrast, J. 99
Marriage Fair (Imilchil) 40, 258, 259
Masmouda 33
Matisse Arts Gallery (Marrakech) 352, 353
Matisse, Henri 129
Odalisque à la Culotte Grise 135
Mauretania 45
Roman towns **93**
Mausoleum of Mohammed V (Rabat) 10, 25, 65, **72–5**
Mausoleum of Moulay Ali Cherif (Rissani) 280, 281
Mausoleum of Moulay Ismaïl (Meknès) 11, 25, 55, **194–5**
Mausoleum of Sidi Bou Ghaleb (Fès) 175
Mausoleum of Sidi Mohammed ben Aïssa (Meknès) 198
Mazagan 114
Méchouars (Fès el-Jedid) 183
Méchouars (Marrakech) **239**
Medersas **173**
Ben Youssef Medersa (Marrakech) **230**
Bou Inania Medersa (Fès) 12, **172–3**
Bou Inania Medersa (Meknès) **189**
El-Attarine Medersa (Fès) 11, **171**
El-Cherratine Medersa (Fès) **171**
El-Mesabahiya Medersa (Fès) 175
El-Sahrij Medersa (Fès) **175**, 178–9
El-Seffarine Medersa (Fès) 175
Medical care 364

Medinas **26–7**
Chefchaouen 150–51
El-Jadida 114
Essaouira 121
Old Medina (Casablanca) 11, **100**
Quartier Habous (New Medina, Casablanca) 11, **106**
Safi 118
Tetouan 148–9
Mediterranean Coast and the Rif 11, **143–61**
Chefchaouen **150–51**
hotels 309–10
map 144–5
restaurants 334–5
sea fishing in Morocco **119**
Tetouan **148–9**
The Rif **154–5**
Zegzel Gorge tour **160–61**
Mehdya **86–7**
Meknassa tribe 210
Meknès 12, **185–201**
architecture 55
festivals 40
hotels 312–13
maps 185, 186–7
Mausoleum of Moulay Ismaïl 55, **194–5**
Musée Dar Jamaï **190–91**
restaurants 336–7
Melilla 11, 143, **158–9**
Mellah (Fès el-Jedid) 180, **182**
Mellah (Marrakech) **235**
Menara (Marrakech) 13, **242**
Merinid dynasty 33, 50, **51**
Andalusian Mosque (Fès) 175
architecture 24
Bou Inania Medersa (Fès) 172
Bou Inania Medersa (Meknès) 189
Chellah Necropolis (Rabat) 80–81
Fès 163, 180, 182
Ksar es-Seghir 147
royal cities 193

Merinid dynasty (cont.)
  Salé 86
  Taza 210
  Tin Mal 252
  tombs (Fès) **166**
Merzouga 13, **281**
  hotels 318
Metalwork
  Musée Dar Jamaï
  (Meknès) 191
  What to Buy in Morocco
  347
M'Goun 219, 272
Mhamid **269**
Middle Atlas 12, **207–21**
  hotels 313–14
  Lakes tour **213**
  lions **216**
  map 208–9
  Mountains of Morocco
  218–19
  olives and olive oil **217**
  restaurants 337–8
Midelt **278**
  festivals 40
Minarets 48–9
Mineral water 327
Mischliffen **212**
Mobile phones 368
Mogodor see Essaouira
Mohammed, Prophet 52,
  150
  Arabic calligraphy 170
  Islamic festivals 31
  Regrara Berbers 118
  Sunna 30
Mohammed II, Sultan see
  Sidi Mohammed ben
  Abdallah
Mohammed IV,
  Sultan 53
Mohammed V, King 56–8
  Casablanca Conference
  107
  Grand Mosque (Tangier)
  133
  Grand Socco (Place du 9
  Avril 1947, Tangier) 138
  Hassan Tower (Rabat) 77
  Mausoleum of
  Mohammed V (Rabat)
  25, **72–5**
  Oualidia 115

Mohammed V Airport
  (Casablanca) 370–71
Mohammed VI, King 17,
  20, 21, 59, 363
  Islamic faith 30
  King Mohammed VI's
  Birthday 41
  Tangier 129
  Throne Day 39, 41
Mohammed Belarbi el-
  Jamaï 190
Mohammed ben Abdallah,
  Sultan
  Aguedal Gardens
  (Marrakech) 242
  En-Nejjarine Mosque
  (Meknès) 188
Mohammed ben Ali Rbati
  134
Mohammed Bou Nasri
  269
Mohammed ech-Cheikh
  52, 286
Mohammed el-Nasser 50,
  175
Mohammedia **107**
  hotels 306
  restaurants 331
Moharem 41
Monarchy, etiquette 363
Money **366–7**
Monk seals **293**
Monte Hacho 147
Moors 148
Mopeds 375
Morand, Paul 135
Moretti Milone
  (Casablanca) 98
Moriscos 52
  Rabat 71, 76
Moroccan Festival
  (Suréda) 8–9
Moroccan Links 361
Morocco Made to Measure
  371
Morocco Travel
  International 357
Morrice, James Wilson 135
Mosques (general)
  minarets 48–9
  The Role of the Mosque
  177
  visiting 363

Mosques (individual)
  Andalusian Mosque (Fès)
  175
  Ech Cherabliyine
  Mosque (Fès) 167
  El-Atika Mosque (Rabat)
  69
  En-Nejjarine Mosque
  (Meknès) 188
  Grand Mosque
  (Chefchaouen) 150
  Grand Mosque (Fés el-
  Jedid) 180
  Grand Mosque (Meknès)
  12, **188**
  Grand Mosque (Salé) 86
  Grand Mosque (Tangier)
  133
  Grand Mosque (Taza)
  210
  Great Mosque (Rabat) 76
  Hassan II Mosque
  (Casablanca) 10–11, 94,
  102–5
  Hassan Tower (Rabat)
  76–7
  Karaouiyine Mosque
  (Fès) 12, 24, **176–7**
  Kasbah Mosque
  (Marrakech) **238**
  Kasbah Mosque
  (Tangier) 11, **132**
  Koutoubia Mosque
  (Marrakech) 13, 24, 46,
  48, **236–7**
  Lalla Aouda Mosque
  (Meknès) **192**
  Lalla el-Azhar Mosque
  (Fès el-Jedid) 181
  Mosque of Moulay
  Abdallah (Fés el-Jedid)
  180
  Mosque of Sidi Bou Abib
  (Tangier) 138
  Mouassine Mosque
  (Marrakech) **231**
  Sliman Mosque (Rabat) 66
  Tin Mal **252–3**
Motorbikes
  Harley-Davidson Raid 38
  off-road driving 355, 357
Mouassine Mosque
  (Marrakech) **231**

Moulay Abdallah **115**
  moussem 199
Moulay Abdallah (holy
  man) 115
Moulay Abdallah, Sultan
  (Alaouite) 53
  Bab Mansour el-Aleuj
    (Meknès) 189
  Old Kasbah (Agadir) 286
Moulay Abdallah, Sultan
  (Saadian)
  Ben Youssef Medersa
    (Marrakech) 230
  Mellah (Marrakech) 235
  Mouassine Mosque
    (Marrakech) 231
Moulay Abdallah Cherif
  152
Moulay Abdallah Quarter
  (Fès el-Jedid) 180
Moulay Abdel Aziz, Sultan
  53, 56, 91, 234, 240
Moulay Abderrahman,
  Sultan 53
  Aguedal Gardens
    (Marrakech) 242
  Mausoleum of Moulay
    Ismaïl (Meknès) 194
  Menara (Marrakech) 242
Moulay Abdessalam ben
  Mchich, tomb of 154
Moulay Ahmed al-Dahbi
  194
Moulay Ali ben Rachid 150
Moulay Ali Cherif,
  mausoleum of (Rissani)
  280, 281
Moulay Bouchaïb 113
Moulay Bousselham 10,
  85, **90**
  festivals 40
Moulay Bouzerktoun 123
Moulay Brahim 252
Moulay el-Hassan, Sultan
  53, 190, 281
  Anglican Church of St
    Andrew (Tangier) 138
  Bab el-Makhzen
    (Meknès) 193
  Dar el-Batha (Fès) 168
  Îles Purpuraires 124
  Makina (Fès) 166, 183
  Tiznit 292

Moulay Hafidh, Sultan 53,
  56
  Quartier du Marshan
    (Tangier) 140
Moulay Idriss **200**
  restaurants 337
Moulay Idriss II, *moussem*
  of 199
Moulay Ismaïl, Sultan 52,
  53, **54–5**
  Agadir 287
  Architectural Heritage of
    Moulay Ismaïl **55**
  Asilah 91
  Bab el-Berdaïne
    (Meknès) 188
  Bab Mansour el-Aleuj
    (Meknès) 189
  Bassin de l'Aguedal
    (Meknès) 193
  Beni Mellal 220
  Dar el-Kebira Quarter
    (Meknès) 192
  Dar el-Ma (Meknès) 193
  Fès 163, 171
  Grand Mosque (Tangier)
    133
  Kasba Tadla 217
  Kasbah (Chefchaouen)
    150
  Kasbah (Tangier) 132
  Kasbah Boulaouane 112
  Kasbah Hamidouch 118
  Kasbah Ismaïla (Settat)
    112
  Khenifra 216
  Lalla Aouda Mosque
    (Meknès) 192
  Larache 90
  Mausoleum of Moulay
    Ismaïl (Meknès) 12, 25,
    55, **194–5**
  Mehdya 87
  Meknès 185
  Moulay Idriss 200
  Musée des Oudaïa
    (Rabat) 70
  Palais el-Badi
    (Marrakech) 235
  Rabat 68
  Regraga 226
  Saadian Tombs
    (Marrakech) 238

Moulay Ismaïl, Sultan (cont.)
  Tangier 129
  Taroudannt 288
  Taza 210
  Zaouia of Sidi bel Abbès
    (Marrakech) 226
Moulay Mehdi Hassan,
  Sultan 230
Moulay Mohammed 52
Moulay Rachid, Sultan 52,
  53, 281
  El-Cherratine Medersa
    (Fès) 171
  Er-Rachidia 279
  Kasbah Cherarda (Fès
    el-Jedid) 183
  Rabat 70
Moulay Sherif 52
Moulay Sliman 53
  American Legation
    (Tangier) 134
  Andalusian Wall (Rabat)
    76
  Grand Mosque (Tangier)
    133
Moulay Yazid 53, 182
Moulay Youssef, Sultan 56
Mouloud 41
Moulouya Estuary 11, **159**
Mount Tidirhine 155
Mountain biking 356
Mountain Crests Road 154
Mountains of Morocco
  218–19
Moussa ibn Nosaïr 46
Moussems (festivals) 33
  Dar Zhira (Tangier) 40
  Dar Zhiroun (Rabat) 39
  Mohammed Bou Nasri
    (Tamegroute) 40
  Moulay Abdallah
    Amghar (El-Jadida) 39
  Moulay Abdallah ben
    Brahim (Ouezzane) 38–9
  Moulay Abdessalam ben
    Mchich (Tetouan) 39
  Moulay Aissa ben Driss
    (Aït-Attab) 38
  Moulay Bousselham 39
  Moulay Idriss II (Fès) 40
  Moulay Idriss Zerhoun 40
  Regraga 38
  Setti Fatma 39

Moussems (festivals) (cont.)
Sidi Ahmed ben Mansour
(Moulay Bousselham)
40
Sidi Ahmed (Tiznit) 39
Sidi Alla el-Hadj
(Chefchaouen) 40
Sidi Daoud (Ouarzazate)
39
Sidi el-Ghazi (Guelmim)
39
Sidi Lahcen ben Ahmed
(Sefrou) 39
Sidi Mohammed Laghdal
(Tan Tan) 39
Sidi Mohammed Ma al-
Aïnin (Tan Tan) 39
Sidi Yahya ben Younes
(Oujda) 39
Mouyal, Elie 106
Mrissa, beach 141
Msemrir 262
M'Soura Stone Circle 10,
91
Museums and galleries
entry charges and
opening hours 360
Bert Flint Museum
(Marrakech) 235
Dar Si Saïd Museum
(Marrakech) 13, **240–41**
Fondation Lorin
(Tangier) 134
Galerie Damgaard
(Essaouira) 124
Galerie d'Art
Contemporain
Mohammed Drissi
(Tangier) **138**
Galerie Delacroix
(Tangier) 138, 139
Musée Archéologique
(Rabat) 10, **78–9**
Musée Archéologique
(Tangier) **132–3**
Musée Archéologique
(Tetouan) 148
Musée des Armes (Fès)
166
Musée d'Art
Contemporain 132
Musée d'Art Morocain
(Tetouan) 149

Museums and galleries (cont.)
Musée du Bois (Fès)
167
Musée Dar Belghazi 86
Musée Dar el-Batha (Fès)
12, **168–9**
Musée Dar Jamaï
(Meknès) 12, **190–91**
Musée Ethnographique
(Oujda) 161
Musée Ethnographique
(Tetouan) 150
Musée du Judaïsme
Marocain (Casablanca)
106
Musée de Marrakech
230
Musée de la Monnaie
77
Musée Municipal
(Melilla) 158–9
Musée Municipal du
Patrimonie Amazighe
(Agadir) 282, 286
Musée National de la
Céramique (Safi) 118
Musée des Oudaïa
(Rabat) 68, **70–71**
Musée Sidi-Mohammed-
ben-Abdallah (Essaouira)
124
Museo de la Legión
(Ceuta) 147
Museo Municipal (Ceuta)
147
Villa des Arts
(Casablanca) 100, 352,
353
Music
International Festival of
Sacred Music (Fès) 38
International Music
Festival (Ouarzazate) 40
Jazz Festival (Tangier)
40
Music Festival (Tangier)
39
Oudaïa Jazz Festival 39
shows and concerts 351
Muslim Quarters (Fès el-
Jedid) 180–81
Muslims *see* Islam
Mystics **198**

N
Nador **158**
Napoleon's Hat
(Tafraoute) 293
Nasrid dynasty 48, 49
National Folklore Festival
(Marrakech) 39
National parks
Jbel Tazzeka 12, 207, **210**
Souss Massa **292**
Nekkor Valley 156–7
Nekob 265
Neltner Hut, Jbel Toubkal
Massif tour 249
Nesrate dunes 269
Newspapers 369
Nightclubs **352**, 353
Nixon, Richard 234
Nomad's tent **295**
Northern Atlantic Coast 10,
83–93
hotels 303–4
map 84–5
restaurants 329
Roman Towns in
Morocco **93**
Nouveau Talborj (Agadir)
286
Nuestra Señora de Africa
(Ceuta) 147
Numidia 45

O
Oases
ksour in the oases **279**
Southern and Eastern
Oases **276–7**
*Odalisque à la Culotte
Grise* (Matisse) 135
Off-road driving 355
Oil press (Volubilis) 204–5
Old Kasbah (Agadir) 286
Old Medina (Casablanca)
11, **100**
Olive Tree Festival
(Rhafsaï) 41
Olives and olive oil **217**
Omnium Nord Africain
(Casablanca) 98
ONCF 377
Open-Air Theatre (Agadir)
286

Opening hours **360**
restaurants 323
shops and souks 344
Ottoman empire 52
Oualidia 11, **115**
hotels 307
oysters 109, 115
restaurants 333
Ouaouzguite tribe 288
Ouarzazate 13, **264**
festivals 38, 39, 40
hotels 318–19
piano bars 353
restaurants 341
Ouarzazate and the
Southern Oases 13,
261–81
hotels 318–19
map 262–3
restaurants 341–2
Southern and Eastern
Oases **276–7**
Oudaïa Jazz Festival 39
Oudaïa Kasbah (Rabat) 10,
68–9
Oudaïa Signal Station
(Rabat) 69
Ouezzane **152**
festivals 38–9
Oufkir, General 59
Ouirgane 252
hotels 317
restaurants 340
Oujda **160–61**
festivals 39
hotels 309
restaurants 334–5
Oukaïmeden 13, **248**
hotels 317
restaurants 340
Oukensous tribe 289
Oulad Abdelhalim Ksar
(Rissani) 281
Oulad Driss 261
Oulad Jabeur Fouaga,
Zegzel Gorge tour 161
Oum el-Izz 80
Oum er-Rbia 207
sources of **216**
Ourika valley 247, **248**
hotels 317
restaurants 340
Outdoor activities **354–7**

Ouzoud
restaurants 338
Overseas Adventure Travel
357
Oysters, Oualidia 109, 115

P

Painted rocks, Tafraoute 293
Painters of Essaouira **125**
Palaces
Ancien Palais de Mendoub
(Tangier) 128, **139**
Dar el-Batha (Fès) 168
Dar el-Glaoui
(Marrakech) 231
Dar el-Kebira Quarter
(Meknès) **192**
Dar el-Makhzen (Fès el-
Jedid) 180
Dar el-Makhzen
(Marrakech) **239**
Dar el-Makhzen
(Meknès) 12, **192–3**
Dar el-Makhzen (Rabat)
64, **80**
Dar el-Makhzen
(Tangier) 11, **132–3**
Dar Si Saïd Museum
(Marrakech) 240
Musée des Oudaïa
(Rabat) **70–71**
Palais Bahia (Marrakech)
13, **234–5**
Palais el-Badi
(Marrakech) 25, **235**
Palais el-Mansour
(Meknès) 188
Royal Palace
(Casablanca) 106
Palais de Justice
(Casablanca) 99
Palais Ibn Séoud
(Casablanca) 107
Parking 373
Parks and gardens
Aguedal Gardens
(Marrakech) 13, **242**
Andalusian Garden
(Rabat) 68
Jardins Exotiques (Sid
Bouknadel) 86
Lalla Mina Gardens (Fès
el-Jedid) 180

Parks and gardens (cont.)
Majorelle Garden
(Marrakech) 13, **243**
La Mamounia Hotel
(Marrakech) 234
Menara (Marrakech) 13,
242
Parc de la Ligue Arabe
(Casablanca) 95, **100**
Vallée des Oiseaux
(Agadir) 286
Passage du Glaoui
(Casablanca) 99
Passage Sumica
(Casablanca) 99
Passports 360–61
Pedestrians 375
Peñon de Alhucemas
153
Peñon de Velez de la
Gomera 152–3
Pepys, Samuel 132
Personal safety 365
Pertuzio brothers 106
Pétain, Philippe 56
Petit Socco (Tangier) **133**
Petit taxis 374–5
Petrol 373
Peyriguère, Father Albert
217
Pharmacies 364
Philip II, King of Spain 52
Philip III, King of Spain 65
Phoenicians 45
Asilah 91
Essaouira 120
Île de Mogador 124
Lixus 90
Tangier 129
Phonecards 368
Photography 362
Piano bars **352**, 353
Picasso, Pablo 132
Pickpockets 364, 365
Pilgrimages 199
Pinseau, Michel 102
Place du 9 Avril 1947 *see*
Grand Socco (Tangier)
Place el-Hedime (Meknès)
189, 358–9
Place el-Seffarine (Fès) **175**
Place de Faro (Tangier) 11,
139

Place de France (Tangier)
11, **139**
Place Jemaa el-Fna
(Marrakech) 13, **234**
Place Mohammed V
(Casablanca) **99**
Place des Nations Unies
(Casablanca) 10, **98**
Place Souk el-Ghezel
(Rabat) **71**
Place Uta el-Hammam
(Chefchaouen) 150
Plage des Amiraux 141
Plage Blanche (Guelmim)
294
Plage Quemado (Al-
Hoceima) 153
Plateau des Lacs 258
Plaza de Africa (Ceuta)
147
Police 365
Polisario Front 58, 59
Politics 19–20, 58–9
Polizzi, Coco 286
Polizzi Medina (Agadir)
286
Port de Jorf Lasfar 115
Porte de la Marine
(Essaouira) 120
Ports
Agadir 287
Casablanca **100**
Essaouira 120–21
Portuguese 51, 52, 143
Agadir 287
Azemmour 113
Casablanca 95
El-Jadida 114
Essaouira 120
Kasbah Boulaouane 112
Ksar es-Seghir 147
Mehdya 87
Safi 118
Tangier 129, 132
Portuguese Chapel (Safi)
118
Portuguese Cistern (El-
Jadida) 111, **114, 115**
Post Office (Casablanca)
25, 99, 101
Postal service 369
Poste restante 369
Pottery *see* Ceramics

Prayers, Friday 31
Préfecture (Casablanca) 99
Prehistoric sites
Akka 289
Foum-Rjam 269
M'Soura Stone Circle 10,
91
Oukaïmeden 248
Primo de Rivera, José 148
Prost, Henri
Gueliz (Marrakech) 242
La Mamounia Hotel
(Marrakech) 234
Ville Nouvelle (Rabat) 77
Ptolemy, King of
Mauretania 45, 78, 93
Public holidays 41
Purísima Concepción, La
(Melilla) 158

Q

Quarters, medinas 27
Quartier Al-Andalus
(Chefchaouen) 151
Quartier Habous (New
Medina, Casablanca) 11,
106
Quartier du Marshan
(Tangier) **140–41**

R

Rabat 10, 63, **65–81**
art galleries 353
cinemas 351
cultural centres 353
festivals 39
hospitals and clinics 365
hotels 302–3
map 66–7
Mausoleum of
Mohammed V 65, **72–5**
Musée Archéologique
78–9
nightclubs 353
Oudaïa Kasbah: Street-
by-Street 68–9
piano bars 353
restaurants 328–9
Rabia, Abdelkebir 138
Rabies 365
Radio 369
Rahba Kedima
(Marrakech) 229

Rail Europe 371
Railways 371, **376–7**
Rainfall 42–3
Raissouli 91
Ramadan 31, 41
Ramblers Holidays 357
Ramparts
El-Jadida 114
Essaouira 120
Marrakech **227**
Meknès **188**
Rabat 68, **70**
Tangier **133**
Taroudannt 288
Ras el-Aïn 220
Ras el-Ma and the Mills
(Chefchaouen) 151
Regraga Berbers 38, 118
Religion
Holy Men and Mystics
198–9
moussems 33
see also Festivals; Islam
Renaissance Café
(Marrakech) 243
"Republic of Bou Regreg"
65
Reservations 360
La Réserve (Casablanca)
107
Restaurants **322–43**
alcoholic drinks 323
Casablanca 330–32
dress 323
Fès 335–6
Flavours of Morocco
324–5
High Atlas 340
Marrakech 338–40
Mediterranean Coast and
the Rif 334–5
Meknès and Volubilis
336–7
Middle Atlas 337–8
Moroccan specialities
322–3
North Atlantic Coast 329
opening hours and
reservations 323
Ouarzazate and the
Southern Oases 341–2
prices and tipping
323

Restaurants (cont.)
Rabat 328–9
Southern Atlantic Coast
332–3
Southern Morocco and
Western Sahara 342–3
Tangier 333–4
types of restaurants
322
see also Food and drink
Rhafsaï, festivals 41
Rharb 87
Riads 301
Riads au Maroc 301
Rialto (Casablanca) 99
Riding, horseback 354
The Rif 11, 63, 143, 145,
154–5
see also Mediterranean
Coast and the Rif
Rissani **280–81**
Rissani Souk 281
Road signs 372
Roads 372
Rock engravings
Akka 289
Draa valley 268
Oukaïmeden 248
Rock formations, Lakes
tour 213
Rock generation 135
Rolling Stones 140
Romans
Banasa 92
history 45
Îles Purpuraires 124
Lixus 90–91
Rabat 65
Roman Towns in
Morocco **93**
Sala Colonia 81
Tangier 129, 134
Thamusida 87
Volubilis **202–5**
Roosevelt, Franklin D. 57,
107
Rose Festival (El-Kelaa
M'Gouna) 38, 272, 273
Royal Air Maroc (RAM)
370, 371, 377
Royal cities **193**
Royal Palace (Casablanca)
106

Rue Boukhessissat (Fès
el-Jedid) 182
Rue des Consuls (Rabat) **71**
Rue Es-Siaghine (Tangier)
134
Rue Hadj Daoui (Rabat) **71**
Rue de la Liberté (Tangier)
138–9
Rue des Mérinides (Fès
el-Jedid) 182
Rue du Prince Moulay
Abdallah (Casablanca) 99
Rue Souïka (Rabat) **76**
Rue Souk es-Sebat (Rabat)
76
Rue Talaa Kebira (Fès)
166–7
Rue des Teinturiers (Fès)
175
Ruins of Cotta 146
Rules of the road 372

S

Saadian dynasty **52**
Ageudal Gardens
(Marrakech) 242
architecture 25
Marrakech 223, 227
Ouarzazate and the
Southern Oases 261
Saadian Tombs
(Marrakech) 25, **238–9**
Taroudannt 288
Sacred snakes **189**
Safety **364–5**
hiking and trekking 356
Saffron from Taliouine **289**
Safi 109, **118**
hotels 307
restaurants 333
Sahara *see* Southern
Morocco and Western
Sahara
Sahraoui Festival (Agadir)
39
Sahraouis tribe 294
Saïd Ahansal 257
Saïdia **160**
Sailing 355
Saint-Exupéry, Antoine de
294
Saint-Laurent, Yves
243

Saint-Olon, François Pidou
de 55
Sala 93
Sala Colonia 81
Sala-Chellah
Musée Arcéologique
(Rabat) 78
see also Chellah Necropolis
Salé **86**
festivals 38
hotels 304
Salle Haj Mohammed
Bahnini (Rabat) 351
SAMU Casablanca 365
Sanhaja 33
Sanjurjo, General 153
Sardine fishing 119
SATCOMA SATAS 377
Scorpions 365
Scorsese, Martin 264
Sea fishing in Morocco **119**
Seals, monk **293**
Seamen's Cemetery (Salé)
86
Sebastião I, King of
Portugal 52, 92
Sebou Gorge 211
Security **364–5**
Sefrou **211**
festivals 39
hotels 314
Seguibat tribe 220
Settat **112**
Sctti Fatma 248
Seville 48, 50
Sexually transmitted
diseases 365
Sharing a meal 362
Sherpa Expeditions 357
Shi'ite Muslims 46
Ships, travelling to
Morocco 371
Shopping **344–9**
food stores 344–5
forgeries 345
how to bargain 345, 363
markets 345
methods of payment 344
Moroccan carpets **348–9**
opening hours 344
souks 345
What to Buy in Morocco
346–7

Shorfa dynasties 52
Shows 351
Si Moussa, Grand Vizier 234
Si Saïd ben Moussa 240
Sidi Abdallah ben Hassoun
86
Sidi Ahmed Ou Mghanni
198, 258
Sidi Ali Lake 208
Sidi Allal el-Kairouani,
tomb of 100
Sidi bel Abbès, Zaouia of
(Marrakech) 223, **226**
Sidi Belyout 98
Sidi ben Achir 86
Sidi ben Slimane
el-Jazouli, Zaouia of
(Marrakech) **226**
Sidi Bou Ghaleb,
Mausoleum of (Fès) 175
Sidi Boubeker lighthouse
113
Sidi Bouknadel **86**
Sidi Bourhaba Lagoon 87
Sidi Bouzid 115
Sidi Chamharouch, Jbel
Toubkal Massif tour 249
Sidi Ifni **292–3**
hotels 321
restaurants 343
Sidi Kacem **201**
Sidi Kaouki 123, 124
Sidi Khankroucht, beach
141
Sidi Lahcen Lyoussi 211
Sidi Mancar, tomb of 112
Sidi Mohammed ben
Abdallah (Mohammed
II), Sultan 25, 53
Agadir 287
Bab el-Ftouh (Fès) 175
Boujad 220
Casablanca 95
Dar el-Makhzen (Fès
el-Jedid) 180
Dar el-Makhzen
(Marrakech) 239
Dar Soltane Mahdounia
(Essaouira) 123
El-Jadida 114
Essaouira 120, 123
Great Mosque (Rabat)
77

Sidi Mohammed ben
Abdallah (Mohammed
II), Sultan (cont.)
Old Medina (Casablanca)
100
Oudaïa Signal Station
(Rabat) 69
Zaouia of Sidi bel Abbès
(Marrakech) 226
Zaouia of Sidi ben
Slimane el-Jazouli 226
Sidi Mohammed ben
Abderrahman 226, 234
Sidi Mohammed ben Aïssa
188, 189, 198
Sidi Mohammed ech-
Cherki 220
Sidi Moussa 86, 254,
256
Sidi Moussa Aglou 292
Sidi Oqba ibn Nafi 46
Sidi Yahia 161
Sidi Yahia ben Younes,
tomb of 161
Sijilmassa 280–81
Silver, What to Buy in
Morocco 347
Sinoir 243
Skiing **354**, 355
Skoura 13, **272**
Sliman Mosque (Rabat)
66
Slipper Souk (Fès) 167
Smara 294
Smoking 363
Snakes 365
sacred snakes **189**
Société Générale
(Casablanca) 366
Society 18, 58–9
SOS Médecins Marrakech
365
SOS Médecins Rabat 365
Souks 26, 345
country souks **201**
Fès 12, **167**
Marrakech **228–9**
Meknès **188**
Souk el-Arba du Rharb
92
Taroudannt 288
Source Bleue de Meski
279

Sources of the Oum
er-Riba **216**
Souss Massa National Park
13, **292**
Souss plain 283
Southern Atlantic Coast 11,
109–27
El-Jadida **114–15**
Essaouira **120–25**
hotels 306–7
Imouzzer des Ida
Outanane tour **126–7**
map 110–11
restaurants 332–3
sea fishing in Morocco
119
Working with thuya **122**
Southern Ferries 371
Southern Morocco and
Western Sahara 13, 62,
283–95
Agadir **286–7**
hotels 319–21
map 284–5
restaurants 342–3
Southern oases **276–7**
see also Ouarzazate and
the Southern Oases
Spain and Spanish settlers
Al-Hoceima 153
Ceuta 147
Larache 90
Mehdya 87
Melilla 158–9
Morocco and Al-Andalus
47, **48–9**
Rif 143
Sidi Ifni 292–3
Tangier 129
Tetouan 148
Spartel, Cap *see* Cap
Spartel
Spiders 365
Sports and outdoor
activities **354–7**
Sport Travel (Marrakech)
357
Spring in Morocco 38–9
Sqala du Port (Essaouira)
120
Sqala de la Ville
(Essaouira) 120
St-Gobain 75

Stein, Gertrude 135
Stomach upsets 364–5
Stone carving 346
Stone Circle, M'Soura 91
Street stalls, food 323
Studs, horse breeding 34
Sufism 154, 198
The Sultan Moulay Abderrahman Leaving Meknès (Delacroix) 44
Summer in Morocco 39
Sunni Islam 30, 46, 47
Sunshine 42–3
Supratours 377
Suréda, André, *Moroccan Festival* 8–9
Surfing 355
  Essaouira 123
  Oualidia 115
  Sidi Kaouki 124
  Sidi Moussa Aglou 292
  see also Windsurfing
Sylvester II, Pope 176
Synagogues, Danan Synagogue (Fès el-Jedid) 182–3

T

Tabal, Mohammed 124, 125
Tabant 254
Tacheddirt, Jbel Toubkal Massif tour 249
Tafelney 123, 126
Tafilalt Palm Grove 280
Tafilalt valley 52, 262
Tafraoute 13, 290–91, 293
  festivals 41
  hotels 321
  restaurants 343
Taghazoute 127
Taghdichte 293
Taïbia brotherhood 152
Talassemtane 154
Taliouine 288
  saffron 289
Tallal, Chraibia 138
Tamanar 126
Tamaroute, Imouzzer des Ida Outanane tour 127
Tamdaght 265
Tamegroute 263, 269
  festivals 40

Tamnalt Kasbahs 273
Tamnougalt 268
Tamri 126–7
Tamtattouchte 274–5
Tan Tan 294
  festivals 39
  hotels 321
Tan Tan Plage 294
Tangier 11, 129–41
  art galleries 353
  Artists and Writers in Tangier 135
  beaches 140–41
  cinemas 351
  climate 43
  cultural centres 353
  festivals 39, 40
  hotels 308–9
  map 130–31
  Piano bars 353
  restaurants 333–4
Tangier, Bay of 140, 141
Tanneries of Fès 174
Tanners' Quarter (Fès) 11, 175
Taourirt Kasbah 264–5
Tarfaya 57, 294
Tarhzirte Gorge 220
Tariq ibn Ziyad 46, 48
Taroudannt 13, 288
  hotels 321
  restaurants 343
Tata 285, 288–9
  hotels 321
Tata palm grove 289
Taxis
  airport 370–71
  grands taxis 374, 377
  petits taxis 374–5
Taylor, Elizabeth 139
Taza 12, 210
Tazenakht 288
Tea 326
Telegrams 369
Telephones 368, 369
Television 369
Telouet 245, 253
Temperatures 42–3
Tennis 355
Tents, nomad's 295
Terracotta, What to Buy in Morocco 347

Tetouan 11, 148–9
  festivals 39
  hotels 310
  Jewish community 148, 149
  restaurants 335
Tetouani Fondouk (Fès) 175
Thamusida 10, 78, 82, 87
Theatre 350, 351
Théâtre Mohammed V (Rabat) 351
Théâtre Municipal de Plein Air (Agadir) 351
Theft 364, 365
Throne Day 39, 41
Thuya wood 122
Tickets, trains 376–7
Tiffoultoute Kasbah 264
Tiles
  Bou Inania Medersa (Fès) 172
  Musée Dar el-Batha (Fès) 169
  see also Zellij tilework
Timiderte Kasbah 268
Timit 257
Tin Mal 252–3
Tinerhir 274, 277
Tinfou dunes 269
Tioulit 293
Tioute Kasbah 288
Tipping, in restaurants 323
Tirhboula 217
Tiselit, Lake 258
Tissa, festivals 40
Tizi-Beni-Selmane Pass 269
Tizi-n-Aït Imger 253
Tizi-n-Talrhemt Pass 278
Tizi-n'Tazazert Pass 265
Tizi-n-Test Pass 219
Tizi-n-Test Pass Road 252
  restaurants 340
Tizi-n-Tichka Pass Road 253
Tizi-n-Tinififft Pass 268
Tizi-Touzlimt Pass 289
Tiznit 292
  festivals 39
  hotels 321
  restaurants 343
Tnine-de-l'Ourika 248

Todra Gorge 13, **274**
Tombs
  holy men 199
  Merinid tombs (Fès) **166**
  Saadian tombs
    (Marrakech) **238**
Torres de Alcalá **152–3**
Toundout 272
Tour operators 371
  hiking and trekking
    357
Tourism in Morocco
  website 361
Tourist information 360
Tournon, Paul 100
Tours by car
  Imouzzer des Ida
    Outanane **126–7**
  Jbel Toubkal Massif **249**
  Lakes tour **213**
  Zegzel Gorge **160–61**
Towns
  driving in 372–3
  getting around 374–5
Traffic hazards 372
Trains **376–7**
  arriving by 371
Travel **370–77**
  air **370–71**, 377
  bus 374
  car **372–3**
  Casablanca 97
  coach 377
  Fès 165
  High Atlas 247
  Marrakech 225
  Mediterranean Coast and
    the Rif 145
  Meknès 187
  Middle Atlas 209
  Northern Atlantic Coast
    85
  Ouarzazate and the
    Southern Oases 262
  Rabat 67
  Southern Atlantic Coast
    110
  Southern Morocco and
    Western Sahara 285
  Tangier 131
  taxis 374–5, 377
  trains 371, **376–7**
Traveller's cheques 367

Trees
  argan **127**
  Mountains of Morocco
    218–19
  working with thuya **122**
Trekking **356–7**
Tribes, Berber 33
Triumphal Arch (Volubilis)
  202, **205**
Troglodyte dwellings,
  Imouzzer du Kandar 211
Trois Fourches, Cap des
  see Cap des Trois
  Fourches
Tunnel de Foum-Zabel
  278–9

U

Umayyad caliphs 46, 47, 48
UNESCO World Heritage
  Sites
  Aït Benhaddou **265**, 275
  Fès 12, 163, 167
  Lixus 90–91
  Medina (Tetouan) 148
  Place Jemaa el-Fna
    (Marrakech) 234
  Tin Mal 253
Union Nationale des
  Forces Populaires (USFP)
  58
United Kingdom Consulate
  (Tangier) 361
United Kingdom Embassy
  (Rabat) 361
United Nations 57, 58
United States Consulate
  (Casablanca) 361
United States Embassy
  (Rabat) 361
Unmarried couples in
  hotels 300–301
Urban architecture of
  Morocco **24–5**
US Consular Travel
  Advisory website 361
Usine de Marmar (Erfoud)
  280

V

Vaccinations 364
Vallée des Oiseaux
  (Agadir) 286

Vallée des Oiseaux (Jbel
  Sarhro) 265
Vallée des Roches, Lakes
  tour 213
Vallée des Roses 273
Vandals 45
Venise Cadre (Casablanca)
  353
Vérame, Jean 293
Vernet, Horace 53
Villa des Arts (Casablanca)
  100, 352, 353
Villa des Arts (Rabat) 353
Villa Harris (Cap Malabata)
  146
Villa Majorelle (Marrakech)
  222
Ville Nouvelle (Marrakech)
  242–3
Ville Nouvelle (Rabat) **77**
  restaurants 329
Ville Nouvelle (Tetouan)
  148
Vineyards, Boulaouane
  wine **113**
Visas 360–61
Visigoths 46
Vo Toan 74
Volubilis 12, 63, 93, 196–7,
  202–5
  Festival of (Meknés) 40
  hotels 313
  Musée Archéologique
    (Rabat) 78, 79
  restaurants 337
  see also Meknès and
    Volubilis

W

Wadi Aggaï Falls (Sefrou)
  211
Wadi Aliane, beach 141
Wadi Kiss 160
Wadi Laou, Gorge of 154
Wadi Massa 292
Wadi Oum er-Rbia 110,
  112
Wadi Ourika 248
Wadi Souss 283
Wadi Zegzel Gorge 160
Walking
  in towns 375
  see also Hiking; Trekking

Walls *see* Ramparts
Water
  mineral water 327
  safety 364
  Southern and Eastern
    oases 276–7
Water-skiing 355
Waterfalls
  Cascades d'Ouzoud 12,
    206, **221**
  Cascades de Ras el Oued
    210
  Cascades des Vierges
    (Ifrane) 212
  Foum el-Anser 220
  Sources of the Oum er
    Rbia **216**
  Tamaroute 127
  Wadi Aggaï Falls (Sefrou)
    211
Watersports 355
Wattasid dynasty 51, 226
Weather **42–3**, 360
Weaving
  carpets 348
  Chefchaouen 150–51
  Musée Dar el Batha (Fès)
    169
Websites 361
Welles, Orson
  Citerne Portugaise
    (El-Jadida) 115
  Essaouira 120
  La Mamounia Hotel
    (Marrakech) 234
Western Sahara 58
Wheelchair access *see*
  Disabled travellers
Wilderness Wheels
  (Ouarzazate) 355, 357
Wildlife **22–3**
  bird-watching 355
  Dayet Srji 281
  Îles Purpuraires 124
  Lakes tour 213
  lions of the Atlas **216**
  macaques (Barbary apes)
    23
  monk seals **293**
  Moulay Bousselham 10, **90**
  Moulay Estuary 11, **159**
  Mountains of Morocco 219
  oases 277

Wildlife (cont.)
  Sidi Bourhaba Lagoon 87
  Souss Massa National
    Park 13, **292**
  Tamri 127
  Vallée des Oiseaux 265
Wilhelm II, Kaiser 56, 129
Williams, Tennessee 135,
    139
Win t'mdoum Caves,
  Imouzzer des Ida
  Outanane tour 126
Windsurfing 355
  Essaouira 123
  see also Surfing
Wines
  Boulaouane wine **113**
  What to Drink in
    Morocco 327
Winter in Morocco 41
Women
  Berber women 32–3
  dress codes 363
  status of 19
Woodwork 28
  Dar Si Saïd Museum
    (Marrakech) 241
  Musée Dar el-Batha (Fès)
    168–9
  Musée Dar Jamaï
    (Meknès) 190
  thuya **122**
  What to Buy in Morocco
    346
World Bank 21
World War II 57, 107
Writers, Artists and Writers
  in Tangier **135**
Writing, Arabic calligraphy
  170

Y

Yacoub el-Mansour, Sultan
  50, 231
  Bab Agnaou (Marrakech)
    239
  Bab el-Mrisa (Salé) 86
  Bab Oudaïa (Rabat) 68, 70
  Bab Zaer (Rabat) 80
  Hassan Tower (Rabat)
    76–7
  Kasbah Mosque
    (Marrakech) 238

Yacoub el-Mansour, Sultan
  (cont.)
  Koutoubia Mosque 236
  Rabat 65
  Skoura 272
Yahia ibn Ibrahim 46
Year's Day 41
Youssef ben Tachfine,
  Sultan 47, 243
Youssoufi, Abderrahmane
  20, 59
Youth Day 41
Youth hostels **300**, 301

Z

Zad Pass 216
Zagora **268–9**
  hotels 319
  restaurants 342
Zaïane tribe 216
Zaouïa Ahansal 255, **257**
Zaouïa aït Ishaq, hotels 313
Zaouïa Oulemsi 254, **257**
Zaouïas
  Aït Bouguemez valley
    257
  el-Tijaniya (Fès) 167
  Moulay Idriss II (Fès) **171**
  Sidi bel Abbès
    (Marrakech) 223, **226**
  Sidi ben Slimane el-
    Jazouli (Marrakech) **226**
Zegzel Gorge **160–61**
Zellij tilework
  Bou Inania Medersa
    (Fès) 24, 172
  Musée Dar el-Batha (Fès)
    169
Zemmour tribe 36, 190, 201
Zenaga 161
Zenet tribes 33, 280
Zerhoun Massif **200–201**
Ziz Gorge **278–9**
Ziz valley 261
  ksour in the oases 279
Zouzaf 124

Acknowledgments

Dorling Kindersley and Hachette Livre would like to thank the following people whose contributions and assistance have made the preparation of this guide possible. Special thanks are extended to the staff of the Institut du Monde Arabe in Paris.

Publishing Manager
Jane Ewart.

Managing Editor
Anna Streiffert.

Publisher
Douglas Amrine.

Cartography
Dave Pugh.

Senior DTP Designer
Jason Little.

Consultant
Christine Osborne.

Translator & Editor, UK Edition
Lucilla Watson.

Design, DTP & Editorial Assistance
Shruti Bahl, Younès Cherkaoui Jaouad, Karen Faye D'Souza, Caroline Elliker, Mariana Evmolpidou, Emily Hatchwell, Jacky Jackson, Jude Ledger, Carly Madden, Nicola Malone, Alison McGill, Rebecca Milner, Jane Oliver-Jedrzejak, Rada Radojicic, Ellen Root, Sands Publishing Solutions, Dawn Schwartz, Safiya Shah, Leah Tether, Ian Thomas, Conrad van Dyk, Karen Villabona.

Proofreader
Stewart J. Wild.

Indexer
Helen Peters.

Main Contributors
Rachida Alaoui
Rachida Alaoui was born in Morocco. She lives and works in Paris. After studying the history of art in France, she specialized in Moroccan fashion, and in Arab fashion in particular.

Jean Brignon
A history teacher, Jean Brignon has taught Muslim history for 12 years at the University of Rabat. He was the general editor of *Histoire du Maroc*, published by Hatier, and has written many academic works. He is president of Rives Sud, the cultural tours organizer and leads cultural and other thematic tours in Morocco

Nathalie Campodonico
A literary translator, Nathalie Campodonico has lived in Casablanca for about ten years. She is a contributor to various periodicals.

Fabien Cazenave
After having lived in Morocco for many years, Fabien Cazenave now heads the Arabic world division of the specialist travel agency Voyageurs dans le Monde Arabe. He thus has an extensive knowledge of Morocco and its facilities for foreign visitors.

Gaëtan du Chatenet
An entomologist, ornithologist, corresponding member of the Musée National d'Histoire Naturelle in Paris, draughtsman and painter, Gaëtan du Chatenet is the author of many works published by Delachaux et Niestlé and Gallimard.

Alain Chenal
A specialist in international relations and in the Arab world, Alain Chenal teaches law and political science at the Université de Paris X-Nanterre. He is also Director of the Institut du Monde Arabe in Paris.

Emmanuelle Honorin
An ethnologist and freelance journalist who contributes to *Géo* and *Le Monde de la Musique*, Emmanuelle Honorin has special knowledge of Morocco, a country on which she has written extensively.

Maati Kabbal
Maati Kabbal teaches philosophy at the Faculty of Humanities in Marrakech. He is also a translator and journalist, and head of cultural activities at the Institut du Monde Arabe.

Mohamed Métalsi
Specializing in town planning and music, Mohamed Métalsi is director of cultural affairs at the Institut du Monde Arabe in Paris. He is the author of many articles and of a book on the imperial cities of Morocco (published by Terrail).

Marie-Pascale Rauzier
The historian and journalist Marie-Pascale Rauzier lived in Morocco for nine years, during which time she explored the Atlas and the Moroccan desert. Besides writing on Morocco, she contributed to the launch of Morocco's first large-circulation weekly publication. She is also the author of three books and a CD-Rom on Morocco.

Additional Contributors
Sophie Berger, Carole French, Delphine Pont, Sonia Rocton, Sarah Thurin, Sébastien Tomasi, Richard Williams.

Photography
Ian O'Leary, Cécile Tréal, Jean-Michel Ruiz.

Studio Photography
Anne Chopin, Cécile Tréal, Jean-Michel Ruiz.

Picture Research
Marie-Christine Petit, Ellen Root.

Cartography
Fabrice Le Goff.

Additional Cartography
Quadrature Créations.

Illustrations
François Brosse
Architectural drawings, Street-by Street maps and drawings on pp68–9, 74–5, 102–3, 114, 172–3, 176–7, 194–5, 202–3, 204, 236–7, 266–7 and 276–7.

Gaëtan du Chatenet
Drawing on pp218–19.

Éric Geoffroy
Illustrations on "Exploring" and "At a Glance" maps, on small town and city maps and tour maps on pp62–3, 84–5, 110–11, 121, 126–7, 144–5, 151, 160–61, 181, 208–9, 213, 246–7, 249, 262–3, 284–5 and 287.

Emmanuel Guillon
Architectural drawings on pp24–5, 26–7, 48–9 and 101.

Special Assistance
Taoufiq Agoumy, Babette and François Aillot, A. Akoudad (tourist officer, Ifrane), Jamal Atbir (Hôtel des Cascades, Imouzzer), Amina Bouabid (Office National Marocain du Tourisme, Paris), Ahmed Derouch (tourist officer, Beni Mellal), Soraya Eyles, Kadiri Fakir (Ministère des Affaires Culturelles, Rabat), M. Hassani, Hôtel Tombouctou (Tinerhir), Ali Lemnaouar (Boumalne du Dadès), Sisi Mohamed (Hôtel Asmaa, Zagora), M. Mokthari (Fujifilm Maroc), Natasha, Georges Philippe (Académie d'Architecture de Paris), Joël Poitevin (Météo France), Marie-José Taube (Ministère des Affaires étrangères, Paris), Mohammed Temsamani, Abdelaziz Touri (Ministère des Affaires Culturelles, Rabat), Adolfo de Velasco, Eric Vo Toan (architect of Mausoleum of Mohammed V), Oulya Zwitten.

Photography Permissions
Franciscan sisters' weaving workshop (Midelt), Askaoum inn (Taliouine), Kahina inn (Imessouane), André Azoulay (royal chamber), Banque d'État du Maroc, M. Belghazi (Musée Belghazi), M. Bennani, Pierre Berger (Villa

Majorelle Gardens), M. Binbin (library of the Palais Royal), M. Bruno (rose-distillation factory, El-Kelaa M'Gouna), Amastou campsite (Tazarine), CTM, Frederic Damgaard (Galerie Damgaard, Essaouira), 2M Télévision, Fibule du Draa (Zagora), M. Gérard and Françoise (Ksar Sania, Merzouga), Mahmoud Guinea, M. Hamid (royal stud at Bouznika), Hôtel Salam (Taroudannt), M. Jeannot (Chalet de la Plage restaurant, Essaouira), M. Lahcen, M. Larossi (Ministère de la Communication in Rabat), Marrakech Médina, M'Barek Bougue-moun (Kasba Dadès), M. Michel (Derkaoua kasbah-inn, Merzouga), Ministère d'Affaires Etrangères in Rabat, Ministère des Eaux et Forêts in Rabat, Ministère des Habbous, M. Ibrahimi (Office National de Pêche), Ministère de l'Intérieur in Rabat, M. Laforêt (Les Sablons royal stud), Ministère des Postes et Télécommunications in Rabat, Ministère de Santé in Rabat, Ministère de Tourisme in Rabat, Ministère des Transports in Rabat, M. Lahcen, Office National des Aéroports au Maroc, Office National des Chemins de Fer in Morocco, Office National d'Exploitation des Ports in Morocco, M. Oulhaj (Mosque of Hassan II), M. Painclou (oyster farm No. 7, Oualidia), Liliane Phan (Gallimard), Madame Michel Pinseau and her children, Coco Polizzi (medina of Agadir), Radio Télévision Marocaine, M. Ribi (Sous Massa Nature Reserve), Royal Air Maroc, M. Saf (Ministère de l'Information in Rabat), Commandant Skali (Mausoleum of Mohammed V), M. Tarik (Hôtel Anezi, Agadir), M. Tazi (Palais de Fès restaurant, Fès), Daudouin de Witte (Élan-Sud), a society for the protection of the architectural heritage of the Atlas and the Moroccan South).

Picture Credits
The page number (in bold) is followed, where necessary, by a letter referring to the position of the photograph on the relevant page; a-above; b-below/bottom; c-centre; f-far; l-left; r-right; t top.

8–9: Réunion des Musées Nationaux/ Arnaudet, *Fête Marocaine*, André Suréda (1872–1930). Musée des Arts d'Afrique et d'Océanie, Paris. **9m**: Photothèque Hachette, *Le Tour du Monde* (1879).

10cl, tc: Hemispheres Images/John Frumm; **10b**: Hemispheres Images/Stefano Torrione. **11tl**: Alamy Images/Alfonso Pérez; **11c**: Corbis/Kurt-Michael Westermann; **11br**: Hemispheres Images/René Mattes.

12bl, crb: Hemispheres Images/Paule Seux;

12tl: Hemispheres Images/Emilio Suetone.
13tc: Hemispheres Images/Stéphane Frances;
13br: Hemispheres Images/Bertrand Gardel.

14a: Explorer/ CNES/Spot Image.

20a: Corbis Sygma/J. Langevin.

22al: Jacana/J.-L. Dubois. **22bl**: Jacana/
PHR/D. Nigel. **22bc**: Jacana/PHR/
Mc. T. Hugh. **22bcl**: Jacana/C. Pissavini.
22br: Jacana/M. Willemeit. **22bcr**: Jacana/
J.-L. Dubois. **23cbl**: Jacana/J.-L. Dubois.
23cr: Jacana/Th. Dressler. **23bl**: Jacana/P.
Jaunet. **23bc**: Jacana/C. Nardin. **23br**:
Jacana/A. Brosset.

30ar: Corbis Sygma/M. Attar. **30-31c**:
A.K.G./J.-L. Nou. **30bl**: Arthephot/Oronoz/
J.-C. Varga. Musée des Arts d'Afrique et
d'Océanie, Paris. **30br**: Réunion des Musées
Nationaux/Arnaudet. Musée des Arts d'Afrique
et d'Océanie, Paris.

36-37c: Paris Musées/K. Maucotel. Musée des
Oudaïas, Rabat. **44**: J.-L. Josse; *Mulay Abd
Ar-Rahman, Sultan du Maroc, Sortant de son
Palais de Meknès* (1845). Musée des Augustins,
Toulouse.

45br: G. Dagli Orti. Musée Leone, Vercelli
(Italy).

46al: Philippe Maillard. **47b**: Réunion des
Musées Nationaux/Arnaudet. Musée des
Arts d'Afrique et d'Océanie, Paris.

48al: J.-L. Charmet. **48ar**: G. Dagli Orti.
Bibliothèque Marciana, Venice. **48cl**:
Arthephot/Oronoz. Biblioteca Apostolica,
Vatican. **48bl**: G. Dagli Orti, *The Triumph of
St Thomas Aquinas* Gozzoli (v.1420/2-1497).
Musée du Louvre, Paris. **49ar**: Réunion des
Musées Nationaux/J. G. Berizzi, Th. Le Mage.
Musée des Arts d'Afrique et d'Océanie, Paris.
49cr: Rapho/R. S. Michaud. Escorial, Madrid.
49br: Réunion des Musées Nationaux/G. Blot,
King Boabdil's Farewell to Granada, Alfred
Dehodencq (1822–82). Musée d'Orsay, Paris.

50cr: Réunion des Musées Nationaux/Arnaudet.
Musée des Arts d'Afrique et d'Océanie, Paris.
50b: Arthephot/Oronoz, monastery of Las
Huelgas, Burgos. **50bl**: Arthephot/Oronoz.
Diputación Foral, Pamplona. **51ar**: Bibliothèque
Nationale, Paris. Eldressi's map. **51bm**:
G. Dagli Orti. Azulero Portimao (Portugal).
51br: Photothèque Hachette. Army

Museum, Lisbon.
52br: Roger-Viollet. **52a**: Philippe Maillard.
Musée Numismatique de la Banque du Maroc,
Marrakech. **52c**: Arthephot/Oronoz. Descalzas
Reales, Madrid. **53a**: J.-L. Charmet. Archives of
the Ministry of Foreign Affairs. **53b**: J.-L. Josse,
Battle of Isly (1844), E. Vernet, known as Horace
(1789–1867). Musée du Château, Versailles.
53br: Photothèque Hachette/ Meurisse.

54-5c: Réunion des Musées Nationaux/
G. Blot; *Audience Given in Meknès by the
Moroccan Sultan Moulay Ismaïl to François
Pidou, Chevalier de Saint-Olon, Ambassador
of Louis XIV, on 11 June 1693*, Martin Pierre
Denis (1663–1742). Château de Versailles
and Château du Trianon. **54ar**: Photothèque
Hachette. Bibliothèque Nationale, Paris.
54cl: J.-L. Josse; *The Moroccan Ambassador
Mohammed Temin, at the Commedia dell' Arte
in Paris* (1682), Antoine Coypel (1661–1722).
Musée du Château, Versailles. **54b**: Réunion
des Musées Nationaux/F. Raux; *The Moroccan
Emperor's Ambassadors*. Château de Versailles
and Château du Trianon. **55a**: Bridgeman Art
Library/Giraudon; *Portrait of Anne Marie of
Bourbon, Mademoiselle de Blois* (1666–1739).
Coll. Lobkowicz, Nelahozeves Castle (Czech
Republic).

56a: Roger-Viollet/coll. Viollet.
56c: Photothèque Hachette. **56bl**:
Photothèque Hachette. **56br**: Photothèque
Hachette/Meurisse. **57b**: Roger-Viollet.

58a: Magnum/B. Barbey. **58bm**: Roger-
Viollet/coll. Viollet. **58bl**: Corbis Sygma/
M. Attar. **59al**: Corbis Sygma/A. Nogues.
59mr: Corbis Sygma/J. Langevin. **59bl**: Corbis
Sygma/P. Robert.

65b: Hemispheres Images/Stéphane Frances.

93mal: Réunion des Musées Nationaux/
Popovitch. Musée du Louvre, Paris.
93ma: Réunion des Musées Nationaux/
H. Lewandowski. Musée du Louvre, Paris.

113ar: Anne Chopin. **113b**: Réunion des
Musées Nationaux. Musée des Arts d'Afrique
et d'Océanie, Paris.

122br: Horizon Features/A. Lehalle.

129b: Gamma.

135a: Photothèque Hachette; Seated *Arab*,
Eugène Delacroix (1798–1863). Musée du
Louvre, Paris. **135ma**: Réunion des Musées

Nationaux/C. Jean. *Odalisque à la Culotte Grise* Henri Matisse (1869–1954). Musée de l'Orangerie, Paris © Succession Matisse/DACS, London 2011. **135mb**: Magnum/D. Stock. **135bl**: G. Rondeau. **135br**: © Flammarion. *Hécate et ses Chiens* Paul Morand, Gallimard coll. Folio, 1974 (cover illustration by H.P.G. Berthier).

136–7: Hémisphères/C. Heeb.

149br: Réunion des Musées Nationaux/ J.G. Berizzi; *Jewish Festival in Tetouan* (c.1848), Alfred Dehodencq (1822–82). Musée du Judaïsme, Paris.

168b: Arthephot/Oronoz. Musée Dar Batha, Fès.

170b: Philippe Maillard.

181ml: © Actes Sud/rights reserved

189br: Gamma/Hadjih.

191bl: Réunion des Musées Nationaux. Musée des Arts d'Afrique et d'Océanie, Paris. **191bl**: Réunion des Musées Nationaux. Musée des Arts d'Afrique et d'Océanie, Paris.

198c: ACR Editions; *Les Aïssaouas*, Georges Clairin (1843–1919) private collection.

213ar: Jacana/S. Cordier.

216br: Réunion des Musées Nationaux/ R.G. Ojeda; *Reclining Lion with Prey*, Eugène Delacroix (1798–1863). Musée Bonnat, Bayonne.

218al: Jacana/S. Cordier. **219bml**: Jacana/ M. Bahr. **219bmr**: Jacana/S. Cordier. **219br**: Jacana/J. and P. Wegner.

231ar: G. Dagli Orti; Islamic Museum, Cairo, pharaonic village.

276al: Jacana/Yoff. **277bl**: Jacana/J.-L. Dubois. **277bm**: Jacana/PHIR/S. J. Collins. **277br**: Jacana/Frédéric.

287al: Photothèque Hachette. *L'Illustration* (11 September 1911).

293ar: Jacana/J. Trotignon.

295bl: Photothèque Hachette.

298br: HUSA Casablanca Plaza.

299br: Dar Attamani.

300br: Riad d'Or.

324cla: Alamy Images/Danita Delimont collection/John and Lisa Merrill. **325tl**: Alamy Images/Kevin Foy; **325c**: PunchStock/ PhotoAlto/Jean-Blaise Hall.

349bl: Réunion des Musées Nationaux/ Arnaudet. Musée des Arts d'Afrique et d'Océanie, Paris.

376tr: Alamy Images/Rob Crandall.

377br: Alamy Images/Peter Erik Forsberg.

Jacket
Front - GETTY IMAGES: Martin Child.
Back - ALAMY IMAGES: Hemis/Bertrand Rieger clb; DK IMAGES: cla, Cecile Treal and Jean-Michel Ruiz tl, bl.
Spine - GETTY IMAGES: Martin Child t.

All other images © Dorling Kindersley. For further information see: www.dkimages.com

Further Reading

History and Society
David Hart, *Tribe and Society in Rural Morocco*, Frank Cass, UK and US. Essays on Moroccan tribes and the Berbers.

Donna Lee Bowen and Evelyn A. Early (eds), *Everyday Life in the Muslim Middle East*, Indiana University Press, US. Focusing on Morocco.

Peter Mansfield, *The Arabs*, Penguin, UK and US. General history, with a section on Morocco.

Gavin Maxwell, *Lords of the Atlas, The Rise and Fall of the House of Glaoui 1893–1956*, Cassell, UK.

Susan Raven, *Rome in Africa*, Routledge, US and UK. North Africa in Roman times.

Barnaby Rogerson, *A Traveller's History of North Africa*, Windrush, UK; Interlink, US. Readable general history, from the Roman period to the present day.

Natural and Urban Landscapes
Ann and Yan Arthus-Bertrand, *Morocco Seen from the Air*, Vendome Press, UK and US, 1994. A fascinating literal overview.

Jean-Marc Tingaud and Tahar Ben Jelloun, *Medinas: Morocco's Hidden Cities*, Thames & Hudson, UK and US. An intimate glimpse into the palaces of the imperial cities.

Hugues Demeude, Jacques Bravo and Xavier Richer, *Morocco*, Taschen, Germany. Lavish photographic survey.

Art and Architecture
Titus Burkhardt, *Art of Islam, Language and Meaning*.

Lisl and Landt Dennis, *Living in Morocco*, Thames & Hudson, UK. Lavishly illustrated portrait of the domestic environment.

James F. Jereb, *Arts and Crafts of Morocco*, Thames & Hudson, UK; Chronicle Books, US. Well-illustrated survey, including a guide to major museums in Morocco.

A. Khatabi and M. Sigilmassa, *The Splendours of Islamic Calligraphy*, Thames & Hudson, UK.

Richard Parker, *A Practical Guide to Islamic Monuments in Morocco*, Baraka Press, US.

Flora and Fauna
T. Haltenorth and H. Diller, Heinzel, BA, *Field Guide to the Mammals of Africa*, Collins, UK.

Fitter and Parslow, *The Birds of Britain and Europe with North Africa and the Middle East*, Collins, UK.

Cooking
Robert Carrier, *Taste of Morocco*, Arrow, London.

Anissa Helou, *Café Morocco*, Conran Octopus, UK and US.

Paula Wolfert, *Couscous and Other Good Foods from Morocco*, HarperCollins, US.

Travel, Biography and Fiction
Paul Bowles, *The Sheltering Sky*, Penguin, UK; Ecco Press, US. *Let It Come Down*, Penguin, UK; Black Sparrow Press, US. *Collected Stories of Paul Bowles 1939–76*, Black Sparrow Press, US. *Midnight Mass*, Peter Owen, UK; Black Sparrow Press, US. On the theme of Westerners in a foreign land, from the best-known writer on Morocco. *Their Heads are Green*, Peter Owen, UK. Travel essays. *Without Stopping*, Peter Owen, UK; Ecco Press, US. Bowles' autobiography.

William Burroughs, *Naked Lunch*, Flamingo, UK; Grove Press, US. Revolutionary novel of sexuality and drug addiction, set in Tangier.

Anthony Burgess, *Earthly Powers*, Penguin, UK; Carroll & Graf, US. *The Complete Enderby*, Carroll & Graf, US. Tangier in the 1950s.

Elias Canetti, *The Voices of Marrakesh*, Marion Boyars, UK. Marrakech near the end of the Protectorate.

Esther Freud, *Hideous Kinky*, Penguin UK, WW Norton, US. An English hippy in Marrakech.

Walter Harris, *Morocco That Was*, Eland Books, UK. Observations by *The Times* correspondent, 1890s–1933.

Richard Hughes, *In the Lap of Atlas*, Chatto, UK. Moroccan tales.

Amin Malouf, *Leo the African*, Abacus, UK; *Leo Africanus*, New Amsterdam, US. Historical novel about the 15th-century geographer.

Moroccan Writing in English
Tahar Ben Jalloun, *The Sand Child*, Hamish Hamilton UK, Johns Hopkins UP, US. Novel of childhood in southern Morocco.

Mohammed Choukri, *For Bread Alone*, I.B. Tauris, UK. Volume I of the Rif-born Choukri's autobiography.

Five Eyes, Black Sparrow Press, US. Stories by five Moroccan writers.

Driss Chraibi, *Heirs to the Past*, Heinemann, UK and US. Semi-autobiographical novel set in post-colonial times.

Glossary

adrar: mountain.

agadir: collective granary in the western Atlas.

agdal: large garden, orchard.

aguelmane: permanent natural lake

ahidou: collective dance performed by the Berber tribes of the Middle Atlas and eastern High Atlas.

ahwach: collective dance performed by villagers of the western High Atlas and the Anti-Atlas.

aïd: festival.

aït: "son of", referring to a tribe or the region occupied by this tribe.

Ammeln: Berber tribe of the Anti-Atlas whose language is Chleuh (qv).

assif: river or watercourse.

bab: city gate.

baraka: divine blessing, which is passed down from parent to child. *Baraka* is also obtained by making a pilgrimage to a holy shrine.

hendir: drum consisting of a goatskin stretched over a frame.

bled: countryside, village.

borj: bastion or tower set at the corners of the defensive walls of fortified houses.

burnous: voluminous woollen hooded cloak worn by men.

cadi: religious judge, once having the power to impose *sharia* law.

caid: chief of a defined territory, subordinate to the governor of a province.

caliph: title held by a Muslim chief, designating Mohammed's successor.

chergui: hot, dry southeasterly wind.

Chikhate: female dancer from the Middle Atlas.

Chleuh: Berber tribe of the Atlas and Anti-Atlas. Also the language spoken by the tribes of these regions.

dahir: decree having the force of law in Morocco.

dar: house.

dayet: natural lake formed by underground water.

diffa: feast-day meal.

dirham: Moroccan unit of currency.

douar: hamlet.

emir: personal title meaning "he who commands".

erg: expanse of sand or ridge of dunes.

Fassi: inhabitant of Fès.

fiqh: Islamic legal code.

fondouk: in the past, hostelry for travelling merchants, their beasts of burden and their merchandise.

gebs: plaster that can be decoratively carved. Also known as stucco.

gurbi: house of semi-nomadic people, built with mud and branches.

Gnaoua: religious brotherhood of popular belief originating in black Africa. Followers consider themselves to be the spiritual descendants of Bilal, an Ethiopian slave, whom the Prophet Mohammed set free before making him his muezzin (qv).

guedra: dance characteristic of the Goulimine region of Morocco, performed by kneeling women. Also the large drum that is played to accompany the dancers.

Hadith: collection of legends relating to the life, words and deeds of the Prophet Mohammed.

Hadj: pilgrimage to Mecca.

haik: long woman's wrap made from a single piece of fabric, worn draped around the body.

hamada: stony, arid plateau in the Sahara.

hammam: Turkish bath.

hanbel: carpet or blanket woven by Berbers.

Hegira: starting point of the Muslim era, on 16 July 622.

henna: shrub grown for its leaves, which, among other things, are used in the manufacture of cosmetics.

igherm: communal fortified granary typical of the central High Atlas.

imam: Islamic leader of congregational prayer.

jbel: mountain.

jellaba: wide-sleeved, hooded garment worn by both men and women.

jemaa: village assembly of the heads of families in Berber tribes.

kaftan: long woman's garment secured at the front and decorated with passementerie and embroidery.

kasbah: fortified house with a single crenellated tower, or four crenellated towers, one at each corner of the walls.

khoubz: bread (usually a circular loaf).

khaima: tent made of woven goat-hair or camel-hair, used by the nomads of the Sahara and the semi-nomadic people of the Atlas.

Glossary

adrar: mountain.

agadir: collective granary in the western Atlas.

agdal: large garden, orchard.

aguelmane: permanent natural lake.

ahidou: collective dance performed by the Berber tribes of the Middle Atlas and eastern High Atlas.

ahwach: collective dance performed by villagers of the western High Atlas and the Anti-Atlas.

aïd: festival.

aït: "son of", referring to a tribe or the region occupied by this tribe.

Ammeln: Berber tribe of the Anti-Atlas whose language is Chleuh (qv).

assif: river or watercourse.

bab: city gate.

baraka: divine blessing, which is passed down from parent to child. *Baraka* is also obtained by making a pilgrimage to a holy shrine.

bendir: drum consisting of a goatskin stretched over a frame.

bled: countryside, village.

borj: bastion or tower set at the corners of the defensive walls of fortified houses.

burnous: voluminous woollen hooded cloak worn by men.

cadi: religious judge, once having the power to impose *sharia* law.

caid: chief of a defined territory, subordinate to the governor of a province.

caliph: title held by a Muslim chief, designating Mohammed's successor.

chergui: hot, dry southeasterly wind.

Chikhate: female dancer from the Middle Atlas.

Chleuh: Berber tribe of the Atlas and Anti-Atlas. Also the language spoken by the tribes of these regions.

dahir: decree having the force of law in Morocco.

dar: house.

dayet: natural lake formed by underground water.

diffa: feast-day meal.

dirham: Moroccan unit of currency.

douar: hamlet.

emir: personal title meaning "he who commands".

erg: expanse of sand or ridge of dunes.

Fassi: inhabitant of Fès.

fiqh: Islamic legal code.

fondouk: in the past, hostelry for travelling merchants, their beasts of burden and their merchandise.

gebs: plaster that can be decoratively carved. Also known as stucco.

gurbi: house of semi nomadic people, built with mud and branches.

Gnaoua: religious brotherhood of popular belief originating in black Africa. Followers consider themselves to be the spiritual descendants of Bilal, an Ethiopian slave, whom the Prophet Mohammed set free before making him his muezzin (qv).

guedra: dance characteristic of the Goulimine region of Morocco, performed by kneeling women. Also the large drum that is played to accompany the dancers.

Hadith: collection of legends relating to the life, words and deeds of the Prophet Mohammed.

Hadj: pilgrimage to Mecca.

haik: long woman's wrap made from a single piece of fabric, worn draped around the body.

hamada: stony, arid plateau in the Sahara.

hammam: Turkish bath.

hanbel: carpet or blanket woven by Berbers.

Hegira: starting point of the Muslim era, on 16 July 622.

henna: shrub grown for its leaves, which, among other things, are used in the manufacture of cosmetics.

igherm: communal fortified granary typical of the central High Atlas.

imam: Islamic leader of congregational prayer.

jbel: mountain.

jellaba: wide-sleeved, hooded garment worn by both men and women.

jemaa: village assembly of the heads of families in Berber tribes.

kaftan: long woman's garment secured at the front and decorated with passementerie and embroidery.

kasbah: fortified house with a single crenellated tower, or four crenellated towers, one at each corner of the walls.

khoubz: bread (usually a circular loaf).

khaima: tent made of woven goat-hair or camel-hair, used by the nomads of the Sahara and the semi-nomadic people of the Atlas.

khettara: underground channels for the provision of water, along whose course wells are sunk. Synonymous with foggara.

koubba: cube-like building crowned by a dome and housing the tomb of a venerated individual.

ksar (pl. *ksour*)**:** fortified village surrounded by solid walls set with towers at the angles.

Lalla: title of respect given to women.

maalem: master-craftsman.

makhzen: central power, royal authority.

marabout: prestigious head of a religious brotherhood. By extension, the term also refers to the tomb of such a holy man.

mashrabiyya: wooden latticework panel used as a screen in front of balconies and in the windows of mosques and houses, to hide those within from view.

méchouar: parade ground at the entrance to a royal palace.

medersa: Koranic school with resident students.

medina: traditional Arab town enclosed by ramparts; from Medina, the city where the Prophet Mohammed found refuge from persecution.

mellah: Jewish quarter of a medina.

menzah: pavilion in a palace garden.

mihrab: niche in a mosque, indicating the direction of Mecca.

minaret: tower of a mosque from the top of which the muezzin (qv), or an electric recording, calls the faithful to prayer.

minbar: pulpit in a mosque, from which the imam (qv) leads Friday prayers.

moqqade: head of a village or of a religious brotherhood.

Mouloud: birthday of the Prophet Mohammed.

moussem: important annual festival involving a pilgrimage to the tomb of a saint, a commercial fair and popular entertainment.

muezzin: religious official who calls the faithful to prayer.

muqarna: decorative elements in the form of stalactites, made of stucco or wood and suspended from the ceiling.

nisrani: "Nazarene"– a Christian, or European.

pisé: mixture of sun-baked earth, grit and sometimes straw used as a building material in rural areas.

qibla: direction of Mecca, indicated in mosques by a wall in the centre of which is the mihrab (qv).

Ramadan: ninth month of the Muslim (lunar) year, during which Muslims are required to fast from sunrise to sunset.

reg: stony desert.

riad: traditional residence organized around a court-yard planted with trees and flowers.

ribat: fortified monastery from where Muslim warrior monks set out to spread the Islamic faith.

seguia: irrigation canal for crops.

serdal: brightly coloured scarf worn by Berber women, decorated with coins.

seroual: loose, calf-length trousers fastened at the waist and the knees, worn under the *jellaba* (qv).

shamir: long, wide-sleeved man's shirt worn under another garment.

sharia: religious law based on the teachings of the Koran.

sheikh: chief of a tribal subdivision or the leader of a religious brotherhood.

sherif (pl. shorfa)**:** descendant of the Prophet Mohammed.

shorfa: *see sherif.*

souk: market, laid out according to the various goods and services that the stallholders offer.

sura: verse of the Koran.

tighremt: Berber word for a kasbah (qv). A fortified patriarchal house several storeys high with towers at the corners.

tizi: mountain pass.

wadi: river bed that is dry or semidry except in rainy season; river; river valley. Anglicized form of *oued*.

zakat: obligatory almsgiving. One of the five pillars of Islam.

zaouia: seat of a religious brotherhood that gives religious instruction, the shrine where a *marabout* (qv) is buried.

zellij: geometric tilework, typically arranged in intricate, colourful patterns.

Nationaux/C. Jean. *Odalisque à la Culotte Grise* Henri Matisse (1869–1954). Musée de l'Orangerie, Paris © Succession Matisse/DACS, London 2011. **135mb**: Magnum/D. Stock. **135bl**: G. Rondeau. **135br**: © Flammarion. *Hécate et ses Chiens* Paul Morand, Gallimard coll. Folio, 1974 (cover illustration by H.P.G. Berthier).

136–7: Hémisphères/C. Heeb.

149br: Réunion des Musées Nationaux/ J.G. Berizzi; *Jewish Festival in Tetouan* (c.1848), Alfred Dehodencq (1822–82). Musée du Judaïsme, Paris.

168b: Arthephot/Oronoz. Musée Dar Batha, Fès.

170b: Philippe Maillard.

181ml: © Actes Sud/rights reserved.

189br: Gamma/Hadjih.

191bl: Réunion des Musées Nationaux. Musée des Arts d'Afrique et d'Océanie, Paris. **191bl**: Réunion des Musées Nationaux. Musée des Arts d'Afrique et d'Océanie, Paris.

198c: ACR Éditions; *Les Aïssaouas,* Georges Clairin (1843–1919) private collection.

213ar: Jacana/S. Cordier.

216br: Réunion des Musées Nationaux/ R.G. Ojeda; *Reclining Lion with Prey,* Eugène Delacroix (1798–1863). Musée Bonnat, Bayonne

218al: Jacana/S. Cordier. **219bml**: Jacana/ M. Bahr. **219bmr**: Jacana/S. Cordier. **219br**: Jacana/J. and P. Wegner.

231ar: G. Dagli Orti; Islamic Museum, Cairo, pharaonic village.

276al: Jacana/Yoff. **277bl**: Jacana/J.-L. Dubois. **277bm**: Jacana/PHR/S. J. Collins. **277br**. Jacana/Frédéric.

287al: Photothèque Hachette. *L'Illustration* (11 September 1911).

293ar: Jacana/J. Trotignon.

295bl: Photothèque Hachette.

298br: HUSA Casablanca Plaza.

299br: Dar Attamani.

300br: Riad d'Or.

324cla: Alamy Images/Danita Delimont collection/John and Lisa Merrill. **325tl**: Alamy Images/Kevin Foy; **325c**: PunchStock/ PhotoAlto/Jean-Blaise Hall.

349bl: Réunion des Musées Nationaux/ Arnaudet. Musée des Arts d'Afrique et d'Océanie, Paris.

376tr: Alamy Images/Rob Crandall.

377br: Alamy Images/Peter Erik Forsberg.

Jacket
Front - GETTY IMAGES: Martin Child.
Back - ALAMY IMAGES: Hemis/Bertrand Rieger clb; DK IMAGES: cla, Cecile Treal and Jean-Michel Ruiz tl, bl.
Spine - GETTY IMAGES: Martin Child t.

All other images © Dorling Kindersley. For further information see: www.dkimages.com

SPECIAL EDITIONS OF DK TRAVEL GUIDES

DK Travel Guides can be purchased in bulk quantities at discounted prices for use in promotions or as premiums. We are also able to offer special editions and personalized jackets, corporate imprints, and excerpts from all of our books, tailored specifically to meet your own needs.

To find out more, please contact:
(in the United States) **SpecialSales@dk.com**
(in the UK) **travelspecialsales@uk.dk.com**
(in Canada) DK Special Sales at **general@tourmaline.ca**
(in Australia) **business.development@pearson.com.au**

Further Reading

History and Society

David Hart, *Tribe and Society in Rural Morocco*, Frank Cass, UK and US. Essays on Moroccan tribes and the Berbers.

Donna Lee Bowen and Evelyn A. Early (eds), *Everyday Life in the Muslim Middle East*, Indiana University Press, US. Focusing on Morocco.

Peter Mansfield, *The Arabs*, Penguin, UK and US. General history, with a section on Morocco.

Gavin Maxwell, *Lords of the Atlas, The Rise and Fall of the House of Glaoui 1893–1956*, Cassell, UK.

Susan Raven, *Rome in Africa*, Routledge, US and UK. North Africa in Roman times.

Barnaby Rogerson, *A Traveller's History of North Africa*, Windrush, UK; Interlink, US. Readable general history, from the Roman period to the present day.

Natural and Urban Landscapes

Ann and Yan Arthus-Bertrand, *Morocco Seen from the Air,* Vendome Press, UK and US, 1994. A fascinating literal overview.

Jean-Marc Tingaud and Tahar Ben Jelloun, *Medinas: Morocco's Hidden Cities*, Thames & Hudson, UK and US. An intimate glimpse into the palaces of the imperial cities.

Hugues Demeude, Jacques Bravo and Xavier Richer, *Morocco*, Taschen, Germany. Lavish photographic survey.

Art and Architecture

Titus Burkhardt, *Art of Islam, Language and Meaning*.

Lisl and Landt Dennis, *Living in Morocco*, Thames & Hudson, UK. Lavishly illustrated portrait of the domestic environment.

James F. Jereb, *Arts and Crafts of Morocco*, Thames & Hudson, UK; Chronicle Books, US. Well-illustrated survey, including a guide to major museums in Morocco.

A. Khatabi and M. Sigilmassa, *The Splendours of Islamic Calligraphy*, Thames & Hudson, UK.

Richard Parker, *A Practical Guide to Islamic Monuments in Morocco*, Baraka Press, US.

Flora and Fauna

T. Haltenorth and H. Diller, Heinzel, BA, *Field Guide to the Mammals of Africa,* Collins, UK.

Fitter and Parslow, *The Birds of Britain and Europe with North Africa and the Middle East*, Collins, UK.

Cooking

Robert Carrier, *Taste of Morocco*, Arrow, London.

Anissa Helou, *Café Morocco*, Conran Octopus, UK and US.

Paula Wolfert, *Couscous and Other Good Foods from Morocco*, HarperCollins, US.

Travel, Biography and Fiction

Paul Bowles, *The Sheltering Sky*, Penguin, UK; Ecco Press, US. *Let It Come Down*, Penguin, UK; Black Sparrow Press, US. *Collected Stories of Paul Bowles 1939–76*, Black Sparrow Press, US. *Midnight Mass*, Peter Owen, UK; Black Sparrow Press, US. On the theme of Westerners in a foreign land, from the best-known writer on Morocco. *Their Heads are Green,* Peter Owen, UK. Travel essays. *Without Stopping*, Peter Owen, UK; Ecco Press, US. Bowles' autobiography.

William Burroughs, *Naked Lunch*, Flamingo, UK; Grove Press, US. Revolutionary novel of sexuality and drug addiction, set in Tangier.

Anthony Burgess, *Earthly Powers*, Penguin, UK; Carroll & Graf, US. *The Complete Enderby*, Carroll & Graf, US. Tangier in the 1950s.

Elias Canetti, *The Voices of Marrakesh*, Marion Boyars, UK. Marrakech near the end of the Protectorate.

Esther Freud, *Hideous Kinky*, Penguin UK, WW Norton, US. An English hippy in Marrakech.

Walter Harris, *Morocco That Was*, Eland Books, UK. Observations by *The Times* correspondent, 1890s–1933.

Richard Hughes, *In the Lap of Atlas*, Chatto, UK. Moroccan tales.

Amin Malouf, *Leo the African*, Abacus, UK; *Leo Africanus*, New Amsterdam, US. Historical novel about the 15th-century geographer.

Moroccan Writing in English

Tahar Ben Jalloun, *The Sand Child*, Hamish Hamilton UK, Johns Hopkins UP, US. Novel of childhood in southern Morocco.

Mohammed Choukri, *For Bread Alone*, I.B. Tauris, UK. Volume I of the Rif-born Choukri's autobiography.

Five Eyes, Black Sparrow Press, US. Stories by five Moroccan writers.

Driss Chraibi, *Heirs to the Past*, Heinemann, UK and US. Semi-autobiographical novel set in post-colonial times.

French Phrase Book

In Emergency

Help!	Au secours!	oh se**koor**
Stop!	Arrêtez!	aret-**ay**
Call a doctor!	Appelez un médecin!	apuh-**lay** uñ medsañ
Call an ambulance!	Appelez une ambulance!	apuh-**lay** oon oñboo-**loñs**
Call the police!	Appelez la police!	apuh-**lay** lah poh-**lees**
Call the fire department!	Appelez les pompiers!	apuh-**lay** leh poñ-peeyay
Where is the nearest hospital?	Où est l'hôpital le plus proche?	oo ay l'opeetal luh ploo **prosh**

Communication Essentials

Yes	Oui	wee
No	Non	noñ
Please	S'il vous plaît	seel voo **play**
Thank you	Merci	mer-**see**
Excuse me	Excusez-moi	exkoo-**zay** mwah
Hello	Bonjour	boñzhoor
Goodbye	Au revoir	oh ruh-**vwar**
Good night	Bonsoir	boñ-**swàr**
Morning	Le matin	matañ
Afternoon	L'après-midi	l'apreh-**meedee**
Evening	Le soir	swar
Yesterday	Hier	eeyehr
Today	Aujourd'hui	oh-zhoor **dwee**
Tomorrow	Demain	dulmañ
Here	Ici	ee-**see**
There	Là	lah
What?	Quel, quelle?	kel, kel
When?	Quand?	koñ
Why?	Pourquoi?	poor-**kwah**
Where?	Où?	oo

Useful Phrases

How are you?	Comment allez-vous?	kom-moñ talay **voo**
Very well, thank you.	Très bien, merci.	treh byañ, mer-**see**
Pleased to meet you.	Enchanté de faire votre connaissance.	oñshoñ-**tay** duh fehr votr kon-ay-**sans**
See you soon.	A bientôt.	byañ-**toh**
Where is/are...?	Où est/sont...?	oo ay/soñ
How far is it to...?	Combien de kilomètres d'ici à...?	kom **byañ** duh keelo-metr d'ec-**see** ah
Which way to...?	Quelle est la direction pour...?	kel ay lah **deer**-ek-syoñ poor
Do you speak English?	Parlez-vous anglais?	par-**lay** voo oñg-**lay**
I don't understand.	Je ne comprends pas.	zhuh nuh kom-**proñ** pah
Could you speak slowly please?	Pouvez-vous parler moins vite s'il vous plaît?	poo-**vay** voo par-**lay** mwañ veet seel voo play
I'm sorry.	Excusez-moi.	exkoo-**zay** mwah

Useful Words

big	grand	groñ
small	petit	puh-**tee**
hot	chaud	show
cold	froid	frwah
good	bon	boñ
bad	mauvais	moh-**veh**
enough	assez	assay
open	ouvert	oo-**ver**
closed	fermé	fer-**meh**
left	gauche	gohsh
right	droite	drwaht
straight ahead	tout droit	too drwah
near	près	preh
far	loin	lwañ
early	de bonne heure	duh bon **urr**
late	en retard	oñ ruh-**tar**
entrance	l'entrée	l'on-**tray**
exit	la sortie	sor-**tee**
toilet	les toilettes, les WC	twah-let, vay-see
free, no charge	gratuit	grah-**twee**
Monday	lundi	luñ-**dee**
Tuesday	mardi	mar-**dee**
Wednesday	mercredi	mehrkruh-**dee**
Thursday	jeudi	zhuh-**dee**
Friday	vendredi	voñdruh-**dee**
Saturday	samedi	sam-**dee**
Sunday	dimanche	dee-**moñsh**

Making a Telephone Call

I'd like to place a long-distance call.	Je voudrais télé-phoner a l'etranger.	zhuh voo-dreh fehr uñ añter-oorbañ
I'll try again later.	Je rappelerai plus tard.	zhuh rapel-eray ploo tar
Hold on.	Ne quittez pas, s'il vous plaît.	nuh kee-**tay** pah seel voo play
Could you speak up a little please?	Pouvez-vous parler un peu plus fort?	poo-**vay** voo par-**lay** uñ puh ploo for
local call	la communication locale	komoonikah-**syoñ** low-kal

Shopping

How much does this cost?	C'est combien s'il vous plaît?	say kom-**byañ** seel voo play
I would like ...	je voudrais...	zhuh voo-**dray**
Do you have?	Est-ce que vous avez?	es-kuh voo zavay
I'm just looking.	Je regarde seulement.	zhuh ruh**gar** suhlmoñ
Do you take credit cards?	Est-ce que vous acceptez les cartes de crédit?	es-kuh voo zaksept-**ay** leh kart duh kreh-**dee**
This one.	Celui-ci.	suhl-wee-**see**
That one.	Celui-là.	suhl-wee-**lah**
expensive	cher	shehr
cheap	pas cher, bon marché	pah shehr, boñ mar-**shay**
size, clothes	la taille	tye

Sightseeing

art gallery	la galerie d'art	galer-**ree** dart
bus station	la gare routière	gahr roo-tee-**yehr**
garden	le jardin	zhar-**dañ**
mosque	la mosquée	mos-**qay**
museum	le musée	moo-**zay**
tourist information office	les renseignements touristiques, le syndicat d'initiative	roñsayn-**moñ** too rees-**teek**, sandee-ka d'eenee-syateev
train station	la gare	gahr

Staying in a Hotel

Do you have a vacant room?	Est-ce que vous avez une chambre?	es-kuh voo-zavay oon shambr
double room with double bed	la chambre à deux personnes, avec un grand lit	shambr ah duh pehr-**son** avek un gronñ lee
twin room	la chambre à deux lits	shambr ah duh lee
single room	la chambre à une personne	shambr ah oon pehr **son**
room with a bath, shower	la chambre avec salle de bains, une douche	shambr avek sal duh bañ, oon doosh
I have a reservation.	J'ai fait une réservation.	zhay fay oon rayzehrva-**syoñ**

Eating Out

Have you got a table?	Avez-vous une table de libre?	avay-**voo** oon tahbl duh leebr
I want to reserve a table.	Je voudrais réserver une table.	zhuh voo-**dray** rayzehr-**vay** oon tahbl
The check please.	L'addition s'il vous plaît.	l'adee-**syoñ** seel voo play
I am a vegetarian.	Je suis végétarien.	zhuh swee vezhay-**tehryañ**
menu	le menu, la carte	men-**oo**, karte
breakfast	le petit déjeuner	puh-**tee** deh-**zhuh**-nay
lunch	le déjeuner	deh-**zhuh**-nay
dinner	le dîner	dee-**nay**

Numbers

1	un, une	uñ, oon
2	deux	duh
3	trois	trwah
4	quatre	katr
5	cinq	sañk
6	six	sees
7	sept	set
8	huit	weet
9	neuf	nerf
10	dix	dees

Moroccan Arabic Phrase Book

Moroccan Arabic is unique to Morocco and is not understood by other Arabic speakers. Moroccans speak faster and abbreviate words. Pronunciation is gentler due to the influence of French.

In Emergency

Help!	aawenooni
Stop!	owkof!
Can you call a doctor?	momkin **kellem** el ta**beeb**?
Call an ambulance!	aaye**to aala** el isaaf
Can you call the police?	**mom**kin **kellem** el po**lees**?
Call the fire department!	aaye**to aala** el matafie
Where is the nearest hospital?	fin **kayn** akrab mos**tash**fa

Communication Essentials

Yes	na-am
No	laa
Please	min **fad**lak
Thank you	se'hha / **shuk**ran
Excuse me	is**mah**lee
Hello / Peace be upon you	selaam
Goodbye	ma'eel sa**laa**ma
Good evening	ma**saal** kheer
Good morning	es**be'h** elk**heer**
Yesterday	el **baar**eh
Today	el yoom
Tomorrow	**gha**dan
Here	**hi**na
There	hinak
What?	shnoo?
When?	**im**ta?
Why?	a**lash**?
Where?	fayn?

Useful Phrases

How are you?	wash**raak**?
I'm fine.	laa**bas**
Pleased to meet you.	metshar-fin
Where is/are…?	fayn…?
Which way to…?	ina te**rik**… ?
Do you speak English?	tatkalam englee**ze**-ya?
I don't understand.	ana mafhim**taksh**
I'm sorry.	esme**'h**lee

Useful Words

big	k**beer**
small	s**geer**
hot	so**khoon**
cold	**baa**red
good	m**lee'**ha
bad	mashem**lee**'ha
open	maf**too'**h
closed	magh**look**
left	li**seer**
right	li**meen**
straight ahead	**nee**shan
near	qu**ray**ab
far	ba**eed**
entrance	do**khool**
exit	khrooj
toilet	towa**lett**
tonight	fel**leel**
day	ne**haar**
hour	sa'aa
week	se**maa**na
Monday	el et**neen**
Tuesday	el t**laa**ta
Wednesday	el **arbe**'aa
Thursday	el kha**mees**
Friday	el **jom**o'aa
Saturday	el **sa**bet
Sunday	el a'**had**

Shopping

How much is it?	kam else'**er**?
I would like…	ana 'hab**bayt** …
Do you have?	andak…?
This one	haazi
expensive	**ghaal**ya
cheap	rek**hee**sa

Sightseeing

art gallery	gali**ree** daar
bus station	**stas**yon do boos
garden	el**jo**nayna
mosque	mas**jid**
museum	**moo**zi
tourist office	mek**tab** so**yaa**'h
train station	ma**hat**tat el tren
beach	bhar
guide	geed
map	kaart
park	baark
ticket	te**kee**

Staying in a Hotel

Do you have a room?	**en**ta 'an**dak ghor**fa?
double room,	**ghor**fa le shakh**sayn**
with double bed	joj bioot
single room	**ghor**fa le shakhs **waa**'hid
with bathroom / shower	ma'al 'ham-**maam** / doosh
I have a reservation.	ana me**reser**ve hna

Eating Out/Food

Have you got a table for…?	**en**ta 'an**dak **tow**la le…?
I want to reserve a table.	b**rit** re**serve** wahd tabla
The check please.	te'e**teeni** elfa**too**ra min **fad**lak?
I am a vegetarian.	ana na**bati** wa la a**kulu** lehoum **wa**la hout
breakfast	if**tar**
lunch	reda
dinner	**aa**sha
steamed pot of vegetables with meat, etc.	ta**jeen**
hand-made couscous	kus**kus**
pastry filled with vegetables and meat, etc.	elbas**teela**
soup	'h**ree**ra
meatballs with herbs	**kef**ta
fish	el'**hoot**
chicken	djaaj
meat	l'hem
vegetables	le**goom**/**kho**dra
water	**maa**'a

Numbers

1	**waa**'hid
2	zooj
3	t**laa**ta
4	ara**ba**'aa
5	**kham**sa
6	**set**-ta
7	**seb**a'a
8	t**maan**ya
9	**tes**'aa
10	'**ash**ra
20	esh**reen**
50	kham**seen**
100	**me**ya